Family Law

PRACTICE AND PROCEDURE

FOURTH EDITION

VOLUME II: SUPPLEMENTARY MATERIALS

JoAnn Kurtz, LLB

emond • Toronto, Canada • 2015

Copyright © 2015 Emond Montgomery Publications Limited.

NOTICE & DISCLAIMER: All rights reserved. No part of this publication may be reproduced in any form by any means without the written consent of Emond Montgomery Publications. Emond Montgomery Publications and all persons involved in the creation of this publication disclaim any warranty as to the accuracy of this publication and shall not be responsible for any action taken in reliance on the publication, or for any errors or omissions contained in the publication. Nothing in this publication constitutes legal or other professional advice. If such advice is required, the services of the appropriate professional should be obtained.

Emond Montgomery Publications Limited
60 Shaftesbury Avenue
Toronto ON M4T 1A3
http://www.emond.ca/highered

Printed in Canada.
Reprinted November 2017.

We acknowledge the financial support of the Government of Canada. Canadä

Publisher: Mike Thompson
Director, editorial & production: Jim Lyons
Production & copy editor: Cindy Fujimoto
Proofreader: Patricia Drake
Typesetter: Shani Sohn
Text & cover designer: Tara Wells
Indexer: Paula Pike
Cover image: Kamil Sarna / Getty Images

Library and Archives Canada Cataloguing in Publication

Kurtz, JoAnn, 1951-, author
Family law : practice and procedure / JoAnn Kurtz.—Fourth edition.

Includes index. Includes text of Divorce Act (for Canada) and related Ontario family law legislation.

ISBN 978-1-55239-560-8 (pbk.)

1. Domestic relations—Ontario—Textbooks. I. Title.

KEO213.K87 2014   346.71301'5   C2014-902149-6
KF505.ZB3K87 2014

Contents

Child and Family Services Act

RSO 1990, c. C.11
Current to December 31, 2011

Paramount purpose and other purposes

Paramount purpose

1. (1) The paramount purpose of this Act is to promote the best interests, protection and well being of children.

Other purposes

(2) The additional purposes of this Act, so long as they are consistent with the best interests, protection and well being of children, are:

1. To recognize that while parents may need help in caring for their children, that help should give support to the autonomy and integrity of the family unit and, wherever possible, be provided on the basis of mutual consent.
2. To recognize that the least disruptive course of action that is available and is appropriate in a particular case to help a child should be considered.
3. To recognize that children's services should be provided in a manner that,
   i. respects a child's need for continuity of care and for stable relationships within a family and cultural environment
   ii. takes into account physical, cultural, emotional, spiritual, mental and developmental needs and differences among children,
   iii. provides early assessment, planning and decision-making to achieve permanent plans for children in accordance with their best interests, and
   iv. includes the participation of a child, his or her parents and relatives and the members of the child's extended family and community, where appropriate.
4. To recognize that, wherever possible, services to children and their families should be provided in a manner that respects cultural, religious and regional differences.
5. To recognize that Indian and native people should be entitled to provide, wherever possible, their own child and family services, and that all services to Indian and native children and families should be provided in a manner that recognizes their culture, heritage and traditions and the concept of the extended family.

Note: Despite the proclamation of the Statutes of Ontario, 1999, chapter 2, section 1, section 1 of this Act, as it read before March 31, 2000, continues to apply with respect to any proceeding under Part III, including a status review proceeding, that was commenced before March 31, 2000. See: 1999, c. 2, ss. 37(5), 38.

Duties of service providers

French language services

2. (1) Service providers shall, where appropriate, make services to children and their families available in the French language.

Duties of service providers

(2) Service providers shall ensure,

(a) that children and their parents have an opportunity where appropriate to be heard and represented when decisions affecting their interests are made and to be heard when they have concerns about the services they are receiving; and

(b) that decisions affecting the interests and rights of children and their parents are made according to clear, consistent criteria and are subject to procedural safeguards.

Interpretation

Definitions

3. (1) In this Act,

"agency" means a corporation;

"approved agency" means an agency that is approved under subsection 8(1) of Part I (Flexible Services);

"approved service" means a service provided,

(a) under subsection 7(1) of Part I or with the support of a grant or contribution made under subsection 7(2) of that Part,

(b) by an approved agency, or

(c) under the authority of a licence;

"band" has the same meaning as in the *Indian Act* (Canada);

"Board" means the Child and Family Services Review Board continued under Part IX (Licensing);

"child" means a person under the age of eighteen years;

"child development service" means a service for a child with a developmental disability or physical disability, for the family of a child with a developmental disability or physical disability, or for the child and the family;

Note: On a day to be named by proclamation of the Lieutenant Governor, subsection (1) is amended by the Statutes of Ontario, 2008, chapter 21, section 1 by adding the following definition:

"child pornography" means,

(a) a photographic, film, video or other visual representation, whether or not it was made by electronic or mechanical means,

(i) that shows a child engaged in, or depicted as engaged in, explicit sexual activity, or

(ii) the dominant characteristic of which is the depiction, for a sexual purpose, of a sexual organ of a child or the anal region of a child,

(b) any written material or visual representation that advocates or counsels sexual activity with a child that would be an offence under the *Criminal Code* (Canada),

(c) any written material whose dominant characteristic is the description, for a sexual purpose, of sexual activity with a child that would be an offence under the *Criminal Code* (Canada), or

(d) any audio recording that has as its dominant characteristic, the description, presentation or representation, for a sexual purpose, of sexual activity with a child that would be an offence under the *Criminal Code* (Canada);

See: 2008, c. 21, ss. 1, 6.

"child treatment service" means a service for a child with a mental or psychiatric disorder, for the family of a child with a mental or psychiatric disorder, or for the child and the family;

"child welfare service" means,

(a) a residential or non-residential service, including a prevention service,

(b) a service provided under Part III (Child Protection),

(c) a service provided under Part VII (Adoption), or

(d) individual or family counselling;

"community support service" means a support service or prevention service provided in the community for children and their families;

"court" means the Ontario Court of Justice or the Family Court of the Superior Court of Justice;

"developmental disability" means a condition of mental impairment present or occurring in a person's formative years that is associated with limitations in adaptive behaviour;

"Director" means a Director appointed under subsection 5(1) of Part I (Flexible Services);

"extended family" means persons to whom a child is related by blood, through a spousal relationship or through adoption and, in the case of a child who is an Indian or native person, includes any member of the child's band or native community;

"federal Act" means the *Youth Criminal Justice Act* (Canada);

"foster care" means the provision of residential care to a child, by and in the home of a person who,

(a) receives compensation for caring for the child, except under the *Ontario Works Act, 1997* or the *Ontario Disability Support Program Act, 1997,* and

(b) is not the child's parent or a person with whom the child has been placed for adoption under Part VII,

and "foster home" and "foster parent" have corresponding meanings;

"Indian" has the same meaning as in the *Indian Act* (Canada);

"licence" means a licence issued under Part IX (Licensing), and "licensed" and "licensee" have corresponding meanings;

"local director" means a local director appointed under section 16 of Part I (Flexible Services);

"Minister" means the Minister of Children and Youth Services or such other member of the Executive Council as may be designated under the *Executive Council Act* to administer this Act;

"native community" means a community designated by the Minister under section 209 of Part X (Indian and Native Child and Family Services);

"native person" means a person who is a member of a native community but is not a member of a band, and "native child" has a corresponding meaning;

"order" includes a refusal to make an order;

"place of open custody" means a place or facility designated as a place of open custody under subsection 24.1(1) of the *Young Offenders Act* (Canada), whether in accordance with section 88 of the federal Act or otherwise;

"place of open temporary detention" means a place of temporary detention in which the Minister has established an open detention program;

"place of secure custody" means a place or facility designated for the secure containment or restraint of young persons under subsection 24.1(1) of the *Young Offenders Act* (Canada), whether in accordance with section 88 of the federal Act or otherwise;

"place of secure temporary detention" means a place of temporary detention in which the Minister has established a secure detention program;

"place of temporary detention" means a place or facility designated as a place of temporary detention under the *Young Offenders Act* (Canada) or under the federal Act;

"program supervisor" means a program supervisor appointed under subsection 5(2) of Part I (Flexible Services);

"provincial director" means

(a) a person, the group or class of persons or the body appointed or designated by the Lieutenant Governor in Council or his or her delegate to perform any of the duties or functions of a provincial director under the *Young Offenders Act* (Canada) or under the federal Act, or

(b) a person as appointed under clause 90(1)(a);

"regulations" means the regulations made under this Act;

"relative" means, with respect to a child, a person who is the child's grandparent, great-uncle, great-aunt, uncle or aunt, whether by blood, through a spousal relationship or through adoption;

"residential service" means boarding, lodging and associated supervisory, sheltered or group care provided for a child away from the home of the child's parent, other than boarding, lodging or associated care for a child who has been placed in the lawful care and custody of a relative or member of the child's extended family or community, and "residential care" and "residential placement" have corresponding meanings;

"service" means,

(a) a child development service,

(b) a child treatment service,

(c) a child welfare service,

(d) a community support service, or

(e) a youth justice service;

"service provider" means,

(a) the Minister,

(b) an approved agency,

(c) a society,

(d) a licensee, or

(e) a person who provides an approved service or provides a service purchased by the Minister or an approved agency,

but does not include a foster parent;

"society" means an approved agency designated as a children's aid society under subsection 15(2) of Part I (Flexible Services);

"Tribunal" means the Licence Appeal Tribunal;

"young person" means a person who is or, in the absence of evidence to the contrary, appears to be 12 years of age or older but less than 18 years old and, if the context requires, includes any person who is charged under the federal Act with having committed an offence while he or she was a young person or who is found guilty of an offence under the federal Act;

"youth justice service" means a service provided under Part IV (Youth Justice) or under a program established under that Part.

Idem: "parent"

(2) In this Act, a reference to a child's parent shall be deemed to be a reference to,

(a) both parents, where both have custody of the child;

(b) one parent, where that parent has lawful custody of the child or the other parent is unavailable or unable to act as the context requires; or

(c) another individual, where that individual has lawful custody of the child,

except where this Act provides otherwise.

Child's community

(3) For the purposes of this Act, the following persons are members of a child's community:

1. A person who has ethnic, cultural or religious ties in common with the child or with a parent, sibling or relative of the child.
2. A person who has a beneficial and meaningful relationship with the child or with a parent, sibling or relative of the child.

Consents and Participation in Agreements

Consents and agreements

4. (1) In this section,

"capacity" means the capacity to understand and appreciate the nature of a consent or agreement and the consequences of giving, withholding or revoking the consent or making, not making or terminating the agreement;

"nearest relative," when used in reference to a person who is less than 16 years old, means the person with lawful custody of him or her, and when used in reference to a person who is 16 years old or more, means the person who would be authorized to give or refuse consent to a treatment on his or her behalf under the *Health Care Consent Act, 1996* if he or she were incapable with respect to the treatment under that Act.

Elements of valid consent or agreement, etc.

(2) A person's consent or revocation of a consent or participation in or termination of an agreement under this Act is valid if, at the time the consent is given or revoked or the agreement is made or terminated, the person,

(a) has capacity;

(b) is reasonably informed as to the nature and consequences of the consent or agreement, and of alternatives to it;

(c) gives or revokes the consent or executes the agreement or notice of termination voluntarily, without coercion or undue influence; and

(d) has had a reasonable opportunity to obtain independent advice.

Where person lacks capacity

(3) A person's nearest relative may give or revoke a consent or participate in or terminate an agreement on the per-

son's behalf if it has been determined on the basis of an assessment, not more than one year before the nearest relative acts on the person's behalf, that the person does not have capacity.

Exception

(4) Subsection (3) does not apply to a consent under section 137 (consents to adoption) of Part VII (Adoption) or to a parent's consent referred to in clause 37(2)(l) (child in need of protection) of Part III (Child Protection).

Consent, etc., of minor

(5) A person's consent or revocation of a consent or participation in or termination of an agreement under this Act is not invalid by reason only that the person is less than eighteen years old.

PART I FLEXIBLE SERVICES

Directors and Program Supervisors

Directors and program supervisors

Appointment of Director

5. (1) The Minister may appoint any person as a Director to perform any or all of the duties and functions and exercise any or all of the powers of a Director under this Act and the regulations.

Appointment of program supervisor

(2) The Minister may appoint any person as a program supervisor to perform any or all of the duties and functions and exercise any or all of the powers of a program supervisor under this Act and the regulations.

Limitations, etc., on appointments

(3) The Minister may set out in an appointment made under this section any conditions or limitations to which it is subject.

Remuneration and expenses

(4) The remuneration and expenses of a person appointed under this section who is not a public servant employed under Part III of the *Public Service of Ontario Act, 2006* shall be fixed by the Minister and shall be paid out of legislative appropriations.

Reports and information

(5) A service provider shall,

(a) make the prescribed reports and furnish the prescribed information to the Minister, in the prescribed form and at the prescribed intervals; and

(b) make a report to the Minister whenever the Minister requests it, in the form and containing the information specified by the Minister.

Powers of program supervisor

6. (1) For the purpose of ensuring compliance with this Act and the regulations a program supervisor may, at all reasonable times, upon producing proper identification, enter premises where an approved service is provided, inspect the facilities, the service provided, the books of account and the records relating to the service, and make copies of those books and records or remove them from the premises to copy them as may be reasonably required.

Offence

(2) No person shall hinder, obstruct or attempt to hinder or obstruct a program supervisor in the performance of the program supervisor's duties or knowingly give false information about an approved service to a program supervisor.

Idem

(3) No service provider or person in charge of premises where an approved service is provided shall refuse to give a program supervisor access to the books and records referred to in subsection (1) or refuse to give a program supervisor information about the approved service that the program supervisor reasonably requires.

Regulations re exercise of power of entry

(4) A program supervisor shall exercise the power of entry set out in subsection (1) in accordance with the regulations.

Approvals and Funding

Provision of services directly or by purchase

7. (1) The Minister may,

(a) provide services and establish, operate and maintain facilities for the provision of services; and

(b) make agreements with persons, municipalities and agencies for the provision of services,

and may make payments for those services and facilities out of legislative appropriations.

Grants and contributions for services, consultation, etc.

(2) The Minister may make grants and contributions, out of legislative appropriations, to any person, organization or municipality for consultation, research and evaluation with respect to services and for the provision of services.

Approval of agencies

8. (1) Where the Minister is satisfied that an agency is, with financial assistance under this Part and the regulations, financially capable of establishing, maintaining and operating a service and that its affairs are carried on under competent management in good faith, the Minister may approve the agency to provide that service.

Funding for establishment of services

(2) Where the Minister intends to approve an agency to provide a service under subsection (1), the Minister may enter into an agreement with the agency for the establishment of the service.

Financial assistance, etc.

(3) Where the Minister approves an agency to provide a service under subsection (1), the Minister may give the agen-

cy financial and other assistance, in accordance with the regulations.

Effective date

(4) The Minister's approval under subsection (1) shall be deemed to have retroactive effect if the Minister so specifies.

Approval of premises for provision of services

9. (1) Where the Minister is satisfied that premises are suitable for providing a service, the Minister may approve all or any part of the premises for the provision of the service by an approved agency and may give the agency financial and other assistance in accordance with the regulations, for the maintenance and operation of the premises and the provision of the service.

Approval may relate to all or part of building, etc.

(2) The Minister's approval under subsection (1) may specify a building, a group of buildings, part of a building or a location in a building as the approved premises.

Effective date

(3) The Minister's approval of premises under subsection (1) shall be deemed to have retroactive effect if the Minister so specifies, but it shall not be deemed to take effect on a day before the Minister's approval of the agency concerned becomes effective under section 8.

Terms and conditions and services to adults

Terms and conditions

10. (1) The Minister may impose terms and conditions on an approval given under subsection 8(1) or 9(1) and, upon reasonable written notice to the approved agency, may vary, remove or amend the terms and conditions or impose new terms and conditions.

Duty of Director

(2) A Director shall review any objections from an approved agency which has received notice under subsection (1).

Transfer of assets

(3) An approved agency shall not transfer or assign any of its assets acquired with financial assistance from the Province of Ontario, except in accordance with the regulations.

Services to persons over eighteen

(4) The Minister may,

(a) provide services under clause 7(1)(a);

(b) make agreements for the provision of services under clause 7(1)(b);

(c) make grants and contributions for the provision of services under subsection 7(2);

(d) approve agencies for the provision of services under subsection 8(1);

(e) approve premises for the provision of services under subsection 9(1),

to persons who are not children, and to their families, as if those persons were children.

Co-ordinating or advisory groups

11. The Minister may make agreements with persons, organizations or municipalities for the establishment, support and operation of co-ordinating or advisory groups or committees, may make payments for the purpose out of legislative appropriations and may give other assistance for the purpose.

Security for payment of funds

12. The Minister may, as a condition of making a payment under this Part or the regulations, require the recipient of the funds to secure them by way of mortgage, lien, registration of agreement or in such other manner as the Minister determines.

Approved agency

13. (1) An approved agency shall file a certified copy of its by-laws and of any amendment to them with the Minister forthwith after they are made.

Idem

(2) The by-laws of an approved agency shall contain the prescribed provisions.

Band or native community representatives

(3) An approved agency that provides services to Indian or native children and families shall have the prescribed number of band or native community representatives on its board of directors, appointed in the prescribed manner and for the prescribed terms.

Employee may not sit on board

(4) An employee of an approved agency shall not be a member of the agency's board of directors.

Placements must comply with Act and regulations

14. No approved agency shall place a child in a residential placement except in accordance with this Act and the regulations.

Children's Aid Societies

Children's Aid Society

15. (1) In this section,

"prescribed" means prescribed in a regulation made by the Minister under subsection 214(4) of Part XI (Regulations).

Designation of children's aid society

(2) The Minister may designate an approved agency as a children's aid society for a specified territorial jurisdiction and for any or all of the functions set out in subsection (3), may impose terms and conditions on a designation and may vary, remove or amend the terms and conditions or impose new terms and conditions at any time, and may at any time amend a designation to provide that the society is no longer designated for a particular function set out in subsection (3) or to alter the society's territorial jurisdiction.

Functions of society

(3) The functions of a children's aid society are to,

(a) investigate allegations or evidence that children who are under the age of sixteen years or are in the society's care or under its supervision may be in need of protection;

(b) protect, where necessary, children who are under the age of sixteen years or are in the society's care or under its supervision;

(c) provide guidance, counselling and other services to families for protecting children or for the prevention of circumstances requiring the protection of children;

(d) provide care for children assigned or committed to its care under this Act;

(e) supervise children assigned to its supervision under this Act;

(f) place children for adoption under Part VII; and

(g) perform any other duties given to it by this or any other Act.

Prescribed standards, etc.

(4) A society shall,

(a) provide the prescribed standard of services in its performance of its functions; and

(b) follow the prescribed procedures and practices.

(5) Repealed.

Protection from personal liability

(6) No action shall be instituted against an officer or employee of a society for an act done in good faith in the execution or intended execution of the person's duty or for an alleged neglect or default in the execution in good faith of the person's duty.

Appointment of local director

16. Every society shall appoint a local director with the prescribed qualifications, powers and duties.

Duties of Director with respect to societies

17. (1) A Director,

(a) shall advise and supervise societies;

(b) shall inspect or direct and supervise the inspection of the operation and records of societies;

(c) shall exercise the powers and duties of a society in any area in which no society is functioning;

(d) shall inspect or direct and supervise the inspection of places in which children in the care of societies are placed; and

(e) shall ensure that societies provide the standard of services and follow the procedures and practices required by subsection 15(4).

Designation of places of safety

18. For the purposes of Part III, a Director or local director may designate a place as a place of safety and may designate a class of places as places of safety.

Financial provisions

19. (1) Repealed.

Payments by Minister

(2) The Minister shall pay to every society out of legislative appropriations an amount determined in accordance with the regulations.

(3) Repealed.

How society's estimates determined

(4) A society's estimated expenditures shall be determined and shall be approved by the Minister in accordance with the regulations.

(5) Repealed.

Manner of payment

(6) An amount payable to a society under subsection (2), including advances on expenditures before they are incurred, shall be paid at the times and in the manner determined by the Minister.

Local board

20. (1) Repealed.

Society deemed to be a local board

(2) A society shall be deemed to be a local board of each municipality in which it has jurisdiction for the purposes of the *Ontario Municipal Employees Retirement System Act, 2006* and the *Municipal Conflict of Interest Act*.

Directives to societies

20.1 A Director may issue directives to one or more societies, including directives respecting their provision of services under this Act.

Resolution of issues by prescribed method of alternative dispute resolution

20.2 (1) If a child is or may be in need of protection under this Act, a society shall consider whether a prescribed method of alternative dispute resolution could assist in resolving any issue related to the child or a plan for the child's care.

Where child is Indian or native person

(2) If the issue referred to in subsection (1) relates to a child who is an Indian or native person, the society shall consult with the child's band or native community to determine whether an alternative dispute resolution process established by that band or native community or another prescribed process will assist in resolving the issue.

Children's Lawyer

(3) If a society or a person, including a child, who is receiving child welfare services proposes that a prescribed method of alternative dispute resolution be undertaken to assist in resolving an issue relating to a child or a plan for the child's care, the Children's Lawyer may provide legal representation to the child if in the opinion of the Children's Lawyer such legal representation is appropriate.

Notice to band, native community

(4) If a society makes or receives a proposal that a prescribed method of alternative dispute resolution be undertaken under subsection (3) in a matter involving a child who is an Indian or native person, the society shall give the child's band or native community notice of the proposal.

Agreements with other Governments

Minister may make agreements with other governments

21. The Minister may, with the approval of the Lieutenant Governor in Council, make agreements on behalf of the Government of Ontario with the Crown in right of Canada and with the Crown in right of any other province of Canada respecting services under this Act or the care or protection of children.

Revocation and Take-Over Powers

Powers of Minister

22. (1) Where the Minister believes on reasonable grounds that,

(a) an approved agency is not providing services in accordance with this Act or the regulations or in accordance with any term or condition imposed on the approval under subsection 8(1) or 9(1) or, in the case of a society, on the designation under subsection 15(2);

(b) a director, officer or employee of an approved agency has contravened or knowingly permitted any person under his or her control and direction to contravene any provision of this Act or the regulations or any term or condition imposed on the approval under subsection 8(1) or 9(1) or, in the case of a society, on the designation under subsection 15(2);

(c) approval of the agency under subsection 8(1) or of the premises under subsection 9(1) would be refused if it were being applied for in the first instance; or

(d) in the case of a society, the society,

(i) is not able to or fails to perform any or all of its functions under section 15,

(ii) fails to perform any or all of its functions in any part of its territorial jurisdiction, or

(iii) fails to follow a directive issued under section 20.1,

the Minister may,

(e) revoke or suspend the approval; or

(f) in the case of a society,

(i) revoke or suspend the designation under subsection 15(2),

(ii) remove any or all of the members of the board of directors and appoint others in their place, or

(iii) operate and manage the society in the place of the board of directors.

Notice of proposal

(2) Where the Minister proposes to act under clause (1)(e) or (f), the Minister shall serve notice of the proposal and written reasons for it on the approved agency, unless the agency has requested that the Minister so act or has consented to the Minister's proposal.

Request for hearing

(3) A notice under subsection (2) shall inform the agency that it is entitled to a hearing under this section if the agency mails or delivers to the Minister, within sixty days after the notice under subsection (2) is served, a written request for a hearing.

Where agency does not request hearing

(4) Where the agency does not require a hearing under subsection (3), the Minister may carry out the proposal stated in the Minister's notice under subsection (2) without a hearing.

Hearing

(5) Where the agency requires a hearing under subsection (3),

(a) if the Minister proposes to act under clause (1)(e) only, the Minister; and

(b) in all other cases, the Lieutenant Governor in Council,

shall appoint one or more persons not employed by the Ministry to hear the matter and recommend whether the Minister should carry out the proposal.

Procedure

(6) Sections 17, 18, 19 and 20 of the *Statutory Powers Procedure Act* do not apply to a hearing under this section.

Report to Minister

(7) The person or persons appointed under subsection (5) shall hold a hearing and make a report to the Minister setting out,

(a) recommendations as to the carrying out of the proposal; and

(b) the findings of fact, any information or knowledge used in making the recommendations and any conclusions of law arrived at that are relevant to the recommendations,

and shall provide a copy of the report to the agency.

Minister's decision

(8) After considering a report made under this section, the Minister may carry out the proposal and shall give notice of the Minister's decision to the agency with reasons.

Provisional suspension

(9) Despite subsection (2), the Minister, by notice to the agency and without a hearing, may provisionally exercise any of the powers set out in clauses (1)(e) and (f) where it is necessary to do so, in the Minister's opinion, to avert an immediate threat to the public interest or to a person's health, safety or

welfare and the Minister so states in the notice, with reasons, and thereafter the Minister shall cause a hearing to be held and subsections (3) to (8) apply with necessary modifications.

Minister's order to cease activity

23. (1) Where the Minister is of the opinion, upon reasonable grounds, that an activity carried on, or the manner of carrying on an activity, in the course of the provision of an approved service is causing or is likely to cause harm to a person's health, safety or welfare, the Minister may by order require the service provider to suspend or cease the activity and may take such other action as the Minister deems to be in the best interests of the persons receiving the approved service.

Notice of proposal

(2) Where the Minister proposes to make an order requiring the suspension or cessation of an activity under subsection (1), the Minister shall serve notice of the proposal and written reasons for it on the service provider, and subsections 22(3) to (8), except clause (5)(b), apply with necessary modifications.

Where order may be made immediately

(3) Despite subsection (2), the Minister, by notice to the service provider and without a hearing, may require that the service provider immediately suspend or cease the activity where the continuation of the activity is, in the Minister's opinion, an immediate threat to the public interest or to a person's health, safety or welfare and the Minister so states in the notice, with reasons, and thereafter the Minister shall cause a hearing to be held and subsections 22(3) to (8), except clause (5)(b), apply with necessary modifications.

Minister has powers of board

24. (1) Where the Minister operates and manages a society under subclause 22(1)(f)(iii), the Minister has all the powers of its board of directors.

Idem

(2) Without restricting the generality of subsection (1), where the Minister operates and manages a society under subclause 22(1)(f)(iii), the Minister may,

(a) carry on the society's business;

(b) enter into contracts on the society's behalf;

(c) arrange for bank accounts to be opened in the society's name, and authorize persons to sign cheques and other documents on the society's behalf;

(d) appoint or dismiss employees of the society; and

(e) make by-laws.

Occupation and operation of premises

(3) Without restricting the generality of subsection (1), where the Minister operates and manages a society under subclause 22(1)(f)(iii), the Minister may,

(a) despite sections 25 and 41 of the *Expropriations Act*, immediately occupy and operate, or arrange for the occupation and operation by a person or organization designated by the Minister, of any premises occupied or used by the society for the provision of approved services; or

(b) apply without notice to the Superior Court of Justice for an order directing the sheriff to assist the Minister as may be necessary in occupying the premises.

Maximum period

(4) The Minister shall not occupy and operate premises under subsection (3) for a period exceeding one year without the society's consent, but the Lieutenant Governor in Council may extend the period from time to time.

Offences

Offence

25. A person who knowingly,

(a) fails to furnish a report required by the Minister under subsection 5(5);

(b) contravenes subsection 6(2) or (3) (obstructing program supervisor, etc.); or

(c) furnishes false information in an application under this Part or in a report or return required under this Part or the regulations,

and a director, officer or employee of a corporation who authorizes, permits or concurs in such a contravention or furnishing by the corporation, is guilty of an offence and is liable upon conviction to a fine of not more than $2,000.

PART II VOLUNTARY ACCESS TO SERVICES

Definitions

26. In this Part,

"advisory committee" means a Residential Placement Advisory Committee established under subsection 34(2);

"institution" means,

(a) a children's residence, other than a maternity home, operated by the Minister or under the authority of a licence issued under Part IX (Licensing) with the capacity of providing residential services to ten or more children at a time, or

(b) premises designated by a Director under subsection 34(5);

"record," when used in reference to a person, has the same meaning as in Part VIII (Confidentiality of and Access to Records);

"special need" means a need that is related to or caused by a developmental disability or a behavioural, emotional, physical, mental or other disability.

Consents

Consent to service

Consent to service: person over sixteen

27. (1) A service provider may provide a service to a person who is sixteen years of age or older only with the person's consent, except where the court orders under this Act that the service be provided to the person.

Consent to residential service: child under sixteen

(2) A service provider may provide a residential service to a child who is less than sixteen years of age only with the consent of the child's parent or, where the child is in a society's lawful custody, the society's consent, except where this Act provides otherwise.

Exception

(3) Subsections (1) and (2) do not apply where a service is provided to a child under Part IV (Youth Justice).

Discharge from residential placement

(4) A child who is placed in a residential placement with the consent referred to in subsection (2) may only be discharged from the placement,

(a) with the consent that would be required for a new residential placement; or

(b) where the placement is made under the authority of an agreement made under subsection 29(1) (temporary care agreements) or subsection 30(1) or (2) (special needs agreements), in accordance with section 33 (termination by notice).

Transfer to another placement

(5) A child who is placed in a residential placement with the consent referred to in subsection (2) shall not be transferred from one placement to another unless the consent that would be required for a new residential placement is given.

Child's wishes

(6) Before a child is placed in or discharged from a residential placement or transferred from one residential placement to another with the consent referred to in subsection (2), the service provider shall take the child's wishes into account, if they can be reasonably ascertained.

Counselling service: child twelve or older

28. A service provider may provide a counselling service to a child who is twelve years of age or older with the child's consent, and no other person's consent is required, but if the child is less than sixteen years of age the service provider shall discuss with the child at the earliest appropriate opportunity the desirability of involving the child's parent.

Temporary Care Agreements

Temporary care agreement

29. (1) A person who is temporarily unable to care adequately for a child in his or her custody, and the society having jurisdiction where the person resides, may make a written agreement for the society's care and custody of the child.

Child's age

(2) No temporary care agreement shall be made in respect of a child,

(a) who is sixteen years of age or older; or

(b) who is twelve years of age or older, unless the child is a party to the agreement.

Exception: developmental disability

(3) Clause (2)(b) does not apply where it has been determined on the basis of an assessment, not more than one year before the agreement is made, that the child does not have capacity to participate in the agreement because of a developmental disability.

Duty of society

(4) A society shall not make a temporary care agreement unless the society,

(a) has determined that an appropriate residential placement that is likely to benefit the child is available; and

(b) is satisfied that no less disruptive course of action, such as care in the child's own home, is appropriate for the child in the circumstances.

Term of agreement limited

(5) No temporary care agreement shall be made for a term exceeding six months, but the parties to a temporary care agreement may, with a Director's written approval, agree to extend it for a further period or periods if the total term of the agreement, as extended, does not exceed an aggregate of twelve months.

Time limit

(6) No temporary care agreement shall be made or extended so as to result in a child being in a society's care and custody, for a period exceeding,

(a) 12 months, if the child is less than 6 years of age on the day the agreement is entered into or extended; or

(b) 24 months, if the child is 6 years of age or older on the day the agreement is entered into or extended.

Note: For the purposes of subsection (6), as re-enacted by the Statutes of Ontario, 1999, chapter 2, subsection 8(2), no period that a child was in a society's care and custody before March 31, 2000 shall be counted. See: 1999, c. 2, s. 37(1).

Note: Despite the proclamation of the Statutes of Ontario, 1999, chapter 2, subsection 8(2), subsection (6) of this section, as it read before March 31, 2000, shall continue to apply with respect to a child who is in the care and custody of a society on March 31, 2000 so long as that child continues to be in the care and custody of a society. See: 1999, c. 2, ss. 37(2), 38.

Same

(6.1) In calculating the period referred to in subsection (6), time during which a child has been in a society's care and custody,

(a) as a society ward under paragraph 2 of subsection 57(1);

(b) under a temporary care agreement under subsection 29(1); or

(c) under a temporary order made under clause 51(2)(d),

shall be counted.

Previous periods to be counted

(6.2) The period referred to in subsection (6) shall include any previous periods that the child was in a society's care and custody as described in subsection (6.1) other than periods that precede a continuous period of five or more years that the child was not in a society's care and custody.

Note: For the purposes of subsections (6.1) and (6.2), as enacted by the Statutes of Ontario, 1999, chapter 2, subsection 8(2), no period that a child was in a society's care and custody before March 31, 2000 shall be counted. See: 1999, c. 2, s. 37(1).

Authority to consent to medical treatment may be transferred

(7) A temporary care agreement may provide that the society is entitled to consent to medical treatment for the child where a parent's consent would otherwise be required.

Contents of temporary care agreement

(8) A temporary care agreement shall include:

1. A statement by all the parties to the agreement that the child's care and custody are transferred to the society.
2. A statement by all the parties to the agreement that the child's placement is voluntary.
3. A statement, by the person referred to in subsection (1), that he or she is temporarily unable to care for the child adequately and has discussed with the society alternatives to residential placement of the child.
4. An undertaking by the person referred to in subsection (1) to maintain contact with the child and be involved in the child's care.
5. If it is not possible for the person referred to in subsection (1) to maintain contact with the child and be involved in the child's care, the person's designation of another named person who is willing to do so.
6. The name of the individual who is the primary contact between the society and the person referred to in subsection (1).
7. Such other provisions as are prescribed.

Designation by advisory committee

(9) Where the person referred to in subsection (1) does not give an undertaking under paragraph 4 or designate another person under paragraph 5 of subsection (8), an advisory committee that has jurisdiction may, in consultation with the society, name a suitable person who is willing to maintain contact with the child and be involved in the child's care.

Variation of agreement

(10) The parties to a temporary care agreement may vary the agreement from time to time in a manner that is consistent with this Part and the regulations made under it.

Special Needs Agreements

Special needs agreements

Special needs agreement with society

30. (1) A person who is unable to provide the services required by a child in his or her custody because the child has a special need, and a society having jurisdiction where the person resides, may with a Director's written approval make a written agreement for,

(a) the society's provision of services to meet the child's special need; and

(b) the society's supervision or care and custody of the child.

Special needs agreement with Minister

(2) A person who is unable to provide the services required by a child in his or her custody because the child has a special need, and the Minister, may make a written agreement for,

(a) the Minister's provision of services to meet the child's special need; and

(b) the Minister's supervision or care and custody of the child.

Term to be specified

(3) A special needs agreement shall only be made for a specific period, but may be extended, with a Director's written approval in the case of an agreement with a society, for a further period or periods.

S. 29(7-10) apply

(4) Where a special needs agreement provides for a child's residential placement, subsections 29(7), (8), (9) and (10) (authority to consent to medical treatment, contents of agreement, variation) apply with necessary modifications, and subsection 29(4) (duty of society) applies to the society or the Minister, as the case may be, with necessary modifications.

Sixteen and seventeen year olds

Society agreements with sixteen and seventeen year olds

31. (1) A child who is sixteen years of age or older and is not in the care of his or her parent and has a special need, and the society having jurisdiction where the child resides, may with a Director's written approval make a written agreement for the society's provision of services to meet the child's special need.

Idem: special needs agreement with Minister

(2) A child who is sixteen years of age or older and is not in the care of his or her parent and has a special need, and the Minister, may make a written agreement for the Minister's provision of services to meet the person's special need.

Contents of agreements

(3) An agreement made under subsection (1) or (2) shall contain the prescribed provisions.

S. 29(10) applies

(4) Subsection 29(10) (variation) applies to an agreement made under subsection (1) or (2).

Expiry and Termination of Agreements

Agreement expires at eighteen

32. No agreement made under section 29, 30 or 31 shall continue beyond the eighteenth birthday of the person who is its subject.

Notice of termination of agreement

33. (1) A party to an agreement made under section 29, 30 or 31 may terminate the agreement at any time by giving every other party written notice that the party wishes to terminate the agreement.

When notice takes effect

(2) Where notice is given under subsection (1), the agreement terminates on the expiry of five days, or such longer period not exceeding twenty-one days as the agreement specifies, after the day on which every other party has actually received the notice.

Return of child, etc., by society

(3) Where notice of a wish to terminate an agreement for care and custody made under subsection 29(1) or 30(1) is given by or to a society under subsection (1), the society shall as soon as possible, and in any event before the agreement terminates under subsection (2),

(a) cause the child to be returned to the person who made the agreement, or to a person who has obtained an order for the child's custody since the agreement was made; or

(b) where the society is of the opinion that the child would be in need of protection within the meaning of subsection 37(2) of Part III (Child Protection) if returned to the person referred to in clause (a), bring the child before the court under that Part to determine whether the child would be in need of protection in that case, and thereafter Part III applies to the child, with necessary modifications.

Idem: Minister

(4) Where notice of a wish to terminate an agreement for care and custody made under subsection 30(2) is given by or to the Minister under subsection (1), subsection (3) applies to the Minister, with necessary modifications.

Idem: expiry of agreement

(5) Where a temporary care agreement expires or is about to expire under subsection 29(6), and where a temporary care agreement or a special needs agreement that provides for care and custody expires or is about to expire according to its own terms and is not extended, the society or the Minister, as the case may be, shall before the agreement expires or as soon as practicable thereafter, but in any event within twenty-one days after the agreement expires,

(a) cause the child to be returned to the person who made the agreement, or to a person who has obtained an order for the child's custody since the agreement was made; or

(b) where the society or the Minister, as the case may be, is of the opinion that the child would be in need of protection within the meaning of subsection 37(2) of Part III (Child Protection) if returned to the person referred to in clause (a), bring the child before the court under that Part to determine whether the child would be in need of protection in that case, and thereafter Part III applies to the child, with necessary modifications.

Review by Residential Placement Advisory Committee

Residential placement review

34. (1) In this section,

"residential placement" does not include,

(a) a placement made under the *Youth Criminal Justice Act* (Canada) or under Part IV (Youth Justice),

(b) commitment to a secure treatment program under Part VI (Extraordinary Measures), or

(c) a placement with a person who is neither a service provider nor a foster parent.

Residential placement advisory committees

(2) The Minister may establish residential placement advisory committees each consisting of,

(a) persons engaged in providing services;

(b) other persons who have demonstrated an informed concern for the welfare of children;

(c) one representative of the Ministry; and

(d) if the Minister wishes, another person or persons, including a representative of a band or native community, whom the Minister considers appropriate,

and shall specify the territorial jurisdiction of each advisory committee.

Payments, etc., to members

(3) The Minister may pay allowances and reasonable travelling expenses to any or all of the members of an advisory committee, and may authorize an advisory committee to hire support staff.

Duties of committee

(4) An advisory committee has a duty to advise, inform and assist parents, children and service providers with respect to the availability and appropriateness of residential services and alternatives to residential services, to conduct reviews under this section, and to name persons for the purpose of subsection 29(9) (contact with child under temporary care agreement), and has such further duties as are prescribed.

Designation by Director

(5) A Director may designate a building, group of buildings or part of a building in which residential services can be provided to ten or more children at a time as an institution for the purposes of this section.

Mandatory review by committee

(6) An advisory committee shall review,

(a) every residential placement in an institution of a child who resides within the advisory committee's jurisdiction, if the placement is intended to last or actually lasts ninety days or more,

(i) as soon as possible, but in any event within forty-five days of the day on which the child is placed in the institution,

(ii) unless the placement is reviewed under subclause (i), within twelve months of the establishment of the committee or within such longer period as the Minister allows, and

(iii) while the placement continues, at least once during each nine month period succeeding the review under subclause (i) or (ii);

(b) every residential placement of a child twelve years of age or older who objects to the placement and resides within the advisory committee's jurisdiction,

(i) within the week immediately following the day that is fourteen days after the child is placed, and

(ii) while the placement continues, at least once during each nine month period succeeding the review under subclause (i); and

(c) an existing or proposed residential placement of a child that the Minister refers to the advisory committee, within thirty days of the referral.

Discretionary review

(7) An advisory committee may at any time review or re-review, on a person's request or on its own initiative, an existing or proposed residential placement of a child who resides within the advisory committee's jurisdiction.

Review to be informal, etc.

(8) An advisory committee shall conduct a review under this section in an informal manner, in the absence of the public, and in the course of the review may,

(a) interview the child, members of the child's family and any representatives of the child and family;

(b) interview persons engaged in providing services and other persons who may have an interest in the matter or may have information that would assist the advisory committee;

(c) examine documents and reports that are presented to the committee; and

(d) examine records of the child and of members of the child's family, as defined in Part VIII (Confidentiality of and Access to Records), that are disclosed to the committee in accordance with that Part.

Service providers to assist advisory committee

(9) At an advisory committee's request, a service provider shall assist and co-operate with the advisory committee in its conduct of a review.

What committee shall consider

(10) In conducting a review, an advisory committee shall,

(a) determine whether the child has a special need;

(b) consider what programs are available for the child in the residential placement or proposed residential placement, and whether a program available to the child is likely to benefit the child;

(c) consider whether the residential placement or proposed residential placement is appropriate for the child in the circumstances;

(d) if it considers that a less restrictive alternative to the placement would be more appropriate for the child in the circumstances, specify that alternative;

(e) consider the importance of continuity in the child's care and the possible effect on the child of disruption of that continuity; and

(f) where the child is an Indian or native person, consider the importance, in recognition of the uniqueness of Indian and native culture, heritage and traditions, of preserving the child's cultural identity.

Recommendations

35. (1) An advisory committee that conducts a review shall advise,

(a) the service provider;

(b) any representative of the child;

(c) the child's parent or, where the child is in a society's lawful custody, the society;

(d) the child, where it is reasonable to expect him or her to understand; and

(e) where the child is an Indian or native person, a representative chosen by the child's band or native community,

of its recommendations as soon as the review has been completed, and shall advise the child of his or her rights under section 36 if the child is twelve years of age or older.

Report of review to Minister

(2) An advisory committee that conducts a review shall, within thirty days of completing the review, make a report of its findings and recommendations to the Minister.

Recommendation for less restrictive service

(3) Where an advisory committee considers that the provision of a less restrictive service to a child would be more appropriate for the child than the residential placement, the advisory committee shall recommend in its report under subsection (2) that the less restrictive service be provided to the child.

Additional reports at Minister's request

(4) An advisory committee shall make a report of its activities to the Minister whenever the Minister requests it, in addition to making the reports required by subsection (2).

Review by Child and Family Services Review Board

36. (1) A child who is twelve years of age or older and is in a residential placement to which he or she objects may, if the placement has been reviewed by an advisory committee under section 34 and,

(a) the child is dissatisfied with the advisory committee's recommendation; or

(b) the advisory committee's recommendation is not followed,

apply to the Board for a determination of where he or she should remain or be placed.

Duty of Board

(2) The Board shall conduct a review with respect to an application made under subsection (1) and may do so by holding a hearing.

Idem

(3) The Board shall advise the child whether it intends to hold a hearing or not within ten days of receiving the child's application.

Parties

(4) The parties to a hearing under this section are,

(a) the child;

(b) the child's parent or, where the child is in a society's lawful custody, the society;

(c) where the child is an Indian or native person, a representative chosen by the child's band or native community; and

(d) any other persons that the Board specifies.

Time for determination

(5) The Board shall complete its review and make a determination within thirty days of receiving a child's application, unless,

(a) the Board holds a hearing with respect to the application; and

(b) the parties consent to a longer period for the Board's determination.

Board's recommendation

(6) After conducting a review under subsection (2), the Board may,

(a) order that the child be transferred to another residential placement, if the Board is satisfied that the other residential placement is available;

(b) order that the child be discharged from the residential placement; or

(c) confirm the existing placement.

PART III CHILD PROTECTION

Interpretation

37. (1) In this Part,

"child" does not include a child as defined in subsection 3(1) who is actually or apparently sixteen years of age or older, unless the child is the subject of an order under this Part;

"child protection worker" means a Director, a local director or a person authorized by a Director or local director for the purposes of section 40 (commencing child protection proceedings);

"parent," when used in reference to a child, means each of,

(a) the child's mother,

(b) an individual described in one of paragraphs 1 to 6 of subsection 8(1) of the *Children's Law Reform Act*, unless it is proved on a balance of probabilities that he is not the child's natural father,

(c) the individual having lawful custody of the child,

(d) an individual who, during the twelve months before intervention under this Part, has demonstrated a settled intention to treat the child as a child of his or her family, or has acknowledged parentage of the child and provided for the child's support,

(e) an individual who, under a written agreement or a court order, is required to provide for the child, has custody of the child or has a right of access to the child, and

(f) an individual who has acknowledged parentage of the child in writing under section 12 of the *Children's Law Reform Act*,

but does not include a foster parent;

"place of safety" means a foster home, a hospital, a person's home that satisfies the requirements of subsection (5) or a place or one of a class of places designated as a place of safety by a Director or local director under section 18, but does not include,

(a) a place of secure custody as defined in Part IV (Youth Justice), or

(b) a place of secure temporary detention as defined in Part IV.

Child in need of protection

(2) A child is in need of protection where,

(a) the child has suffered physical harm, inflicted by the person having charge of the child or caused by or resulting from that person's,

(i) failure to adequately care for, provide for, supervise or protect the child, or

(ii) pattern of neglect in caring for, providing for, supervising or protecting the child;

(b) there is a risk that the child is likely to suffer physical harm inflicted by the person having charge of the child or caused by or resulting from that person's,

(i) failure to adequately care for, provide for, supervise or protect the child, or

(ii) pattern of neglect in caring for, providing for, supervising or protecting the child;

(c) the child has been sexually molested or sexually exploited, by the person having charge of the child or by another person where the person having charge of the child knows or should know of the possibility of sexual molestation or sexual exploitation and fails to protect the child;

Note: On a day to be named by proclamation of the Lieutenant Governor, clause (c) is repealed by the Statutes of Ontario, 2008, chapter 21, section 2 and the following substituted:

(c) the child has been sexually molested or sexually exploited, including by child pornography, by the person having charge of the child or by another person where the person having charge of the child knows or should know of the possibility of sexual molestation or sexual exploitation and fails to protect the child;

See: 2008, c. 21, ss. 2, 6.

(d) there is a risk that the child is likely to be sexually molested or sexually exploited as described in clause (c);

(e) the child requires medical treatment to cure, prevent or alleviate physical harm or suffering and the child's parent or the person having charge of the child does not provide, or refuses or is unavailable or unable to consent to, the treatment;

(f) the child has suffered emotional harm, demonstrated by serious,

(i) anxiety,

(ii) depression,

(iii) withdrawal,

(iv) self-destructive or aggressive behaviour, or

(v) delayed development,

and there are reasonable grounds to believe that the emotional harm suffered by the child results from the actions, failure to act or pattern of neglect on the part of the child's parent or the person having charge of the child;

(f.1) the child has suffered emotional harm of the kind described in subclause (f)(i), (ii), (iii), (iv) or (v) and the child's parent or the person having charge of the child does not provide, or refuses or is unavailable or unable to consent to, services or treatment to remedy or alleviate the harm;

(g) there is a risk that the child is likely to suffer emotional harm of the kind described in subclause (f)(i), (ii), (iii), (iv) or (v) resulting from the actions, failure to act or pattern of neglect on the part of the child's parent or the person having charge of the child;

(g.1) there is a risk that the child is likely to suffer emotional harm of the kind described in subclause (f)(i), (ii), (iii), (iv) or (v) and that the child's parent or the person having charge of the child does not provide, or refuses or is unavailable or unable to consent to, services or treatment to prevent the harm;

(h) the child suffers from a mental, emotional or developmental condition that, if not remedied, could seriously impair the child's development and the child's parent or the person having charge of the child does not provide, or refuses or is unavailable or unable to consent to, treatment to remedy or alleviate the condition;

(i) the child has been abandoned, the child's parent has died or is unavailable to exercise his or her custodial rights over the child and has not made adequate provision for the child's care and custody, or the child is in a residential placement and the parent refuses or is unable or unwilling to resume the child's care and custody;

(j) the child is less than twelve years old and has killed or seriously injured another person or caused serious damage to another person's property, services or treatment are necessary to prevent a recurrence and the child's parent or the person having charge of the child does not provide, or refuses or is unavailable or unable to consent to, those services or treatment;

(k) the child is less than twelve years old and has on more than one occasion injured another person or caused loss or damage to another person's property, with the encouragement of the person having charge of the child or because of that person's failure or inability to supervise the child adequately; or

(l) the child's parent is unable to care for the child and the child is brought before the court with the parent's consent and, where the child is twelve years of age or older, with the child's consent, to be dealt with under this Part.

Best interests of child

(3) Where a person is directed in this Part to make an order or determination in the best interests of a child, the per-

son shall take into consideration those of the following circumstances of the case that he or she considers relevant:

1. The child's physical, mental and emotional needs, and the appropriate care or treatment to meet those needs.
2. The child's physical, mental and emotional level of development.
3. The child's cultural background.
4. The religious faith, if any, in which the child is being raised.
5. The importance for the child's development of a positive relationship with a parent and a secure place as a member of a family.
6. The child's relationships and emotional ties to a parent, sibling, relative, other member of the child's extended family or member of the child's community.
7. The importance of continuity in the child's care and the possible effect on the child of disruption of that continuity.
8. The merits of a plan for the child's care proposed by a society, including a proposal that the child be placed for adoption or adopted, compared with the merits of the child remaining with or returning to a parent.
9. The child's views and wishes, if they can be reasonably ascertained.
10. The effects on the child of delay in the disposition of the case.
11. The risk that the child may suffer harm through being removed from, kept away from, returned to or allowed to remain in the care of a parent.
12. The degree of risk, if any, that justified the finding that the child is in need of protection.
13. Any other relevant circumstance.

Where child an Indian or native person

(4) Where a person is directed in this Part to make an order or determination in the best interests of a child and the child is an Indian or native person, the person shall take into consideration the importance, in recognition of the uniqueness of Indian and native culture, heritage and traditions, of preserving the child's cultural identity.

Place of safety

(5) For the purposes of the definition of "place of safety" in subsection (1), a person's home is a place of safety for a child if,

(a) the person is a relative of the child or a member of the child's extended family or community; and

(b) a society or, in the case of a child who is an Indian or native person, an Indian or native child and family service authority designated under section 211 of Part X has conducted an assessment of the person's home in accordance with the prescribed procedures and is satisfied that the person is willing and able to provide a safe home environment for the child.

Note: Despite the proclamation of the Statutes of Ontario, 1999, chapter 2, section 9, section 37 of this Act, as it read before March 31, 2000, continues to apply with respect to any proceeding under Part III, including a status review proceeding, that was commenced before March 31, 2000. See: 1999, c. 2, ss. 37(5), 38.

Legal Representation

Legal representation of child

38. (1) A child may have legal representation at any stage in a proceeding under this Part.

Court to consider issue

(2) Where a child does not have legal representation in a proceeding under this Part, the court,

(a) shall, as soon as practicable after the commencement of the proceeding; and

(b) may, at any later stage in the proceeding,

determine whether legal representation is desirable to protect the child's interests.

Direction for legal representation

(3) Where the court determines that legal representation is desirable to protect a child's interests, the court shall direct that legal representation be provided for the child.

Criteria

(4) Where,

(a) the court is of the opinion that there is a difference of views between the child and a parent or a society, and the society proposes that the child be removed from a person's care or be made a society or Crown ward under paragraph 2 or 3 of subsection 57(1);

(b) the child is in the society's care and,

(i) no parent appears before the court, or

(ii) it is alleged that the child is in need of protection within the meaning of clause 37(2)(a), (c), (f), (f.1) or (h); or

(c) the child is not permitted to be present at the hearing,

legal representation shall be deemed to be desirable to protect the child's interests, unless the court is satisfied, taking into account the child's views and wishes if they can be reasonably ascertained, that the child's interests are otherwise adequately protected.

Where parent a minor

(5) Where a child's parent is less than eighteen years of age, the Children's Lawyer shall represent the parent in a proceeding under this Part unless the court orders otherwise.

Note: Despite the proclamation of the Statutes of Ontario, 1999, chapter 2, section 10, section 38 of this Act, as it read before March 31, 2000, continues to apply with respect to any proceeding under Part III, including a status review proceeding, that was commenced before March 31, 2000. See: 1999, c. 2, ss. 37(5), 38.

Parties and Notice

Parties

39. (1) The following are parties to a proceeding under this Part:

1. The applicant.
2. The society having jurisdiction in the matter.
3. The child's parent.
4. Where the child is an Indian or a native person, a representative chosen by the child's band or native community.

Director to be added

(2) At any stage in a proceeding under this Part, the court shall add a Director as a party on his or her motion.

Right to participate

(3) Any person, including a foster parent, who has cared for the child continuously during the six months immediately before the hearing,

(a) is entitled to the same notice of the proceeding as a party;

(b) may be present at the hearing;

(c) may be represented by a solicitor; and

(d) may make submissions to the court,

but shall take no further part in the hearing without leave of the court.

Child twelve or older

(4) A child twelve years of age or more who is the subject of a proceeding under this Part is entitled to receive notice of the proceeding and to be present at the hearing, unless the court is satisfied that being present at the hearing would cause the child emotional harm and orders that the child not receive notice of the proceeding and not be permitted to be present at the hearing.

Child under twelve

(5) A child less than twelve years of age who is the subject of a proceeding under this Part is not entitled to receive notice of the proceeding or to be present at the hearing unless the court is satisfied that the child,

(a) is capable of understanding the hearing; and

(b) will not suffer emotional harm by being present at the hearing,

and orders that the child receive notice of the proceeding and be permitted to be present at the hearing.

Child's participation

(6) A child who is the applicant under subsection 64(4) (status review), receives notice of a proceeding under this Part or has legal representation in a proceeding is entitled to participate in the proceeding and to appeal under section 69 as if he or she were a party.

Dispensing with notice

(7) Where the court is satisfied that the time required for notice to a person might endanger the child's health or safety, the court may dispense with notice to that person.

Commencing Child Protection Proceedings

Warrants, orders, apprehension, etc.

Application

40. (1) A society may apply to the court to determine whether a child is in need of protection.

Warrant to apprehend child

(2) A justice of the peace may issue a warrant authorizing a child protection worker to bring a child to a place of safety if the justice of the peace is satisfied on the basis of a child protection worker's sworn information that there are reasonable and probable grounds to believe that,

(a) the child is in need of protection; and

(b) a less restrictive course of action is not available or will not protect the child adequately.

Idem

(3) A justice of the peace shall not refuse to issue a warrant under subsection (2) by reason only that the child protection worker may bring the child to a place of safety under subsection (7).

Order to produce or apprehend child

(4) Where the court is satisfied, on a person's application upon notice to a society, that there are reasonable and probable grounds to believe that,

(a) a child is in need of protection, the matter has been reported to the society, the society has not made an application under subsection (1), and no child protection worker has sought a warrant under subsection (2) or apprehended the child under subsection (7); and

(b) the child cannot be protected adequately otherwise than by being brought before the court,

the court may order,

(c) that the person having charge of the child produce him or her before the court at the time and place named in the order for a hearing under subsection 47(1) to determine whether he or she is in need of protection; or

(d) where the court is satisfied that an order under clause (c) would not protect the child adequately, that a child protection worker employed by the society bring the child to a place of safety.

Child's name, location not required

(5) It is not necessary, in an application under subsection (1), a warrant under subsection (2) or an order made under subsection (4), to describe the child by name or to specify the premises where the child is located.

Authority to enter, etc.

(6) A child protection worker authorized to bring a child to a place of safety by a warrant issued under subsection (2) or an order made under clause (4)(d) may at any time enter any premises specified in the warrant or order, by force if necessary, and may search for and remove the child.

Apprehension without warrant

(7) A child protection worker who believes on reasonable and probable grounds that,

(a) a child is in need of protection; and

(b) there would be a substantial risk to the child's health or safety during the time necessary to bring the matter on for a hearing under subsection 47(1) or obtain a warrant under subsection (2),

may without a warrant bring the child to a place of safety.

Police assistance

(8) A child protection worker acting under this section may call for the assistance of a peace officer.

Consent to examine child

(9) A child protection worker acting under subsection (7) or under a warrant issued under subsection (2) or an order made under clause (4)(d) may authorize the child's medical examination where a parent's consent would otherwise be required.

Place of open temporary detention

(10) Where a child protection worker who brings a child to a place of safety under this section believes on reasonable and probable grounds that no less restrictive course of action is feasible, the child may be detained in a place of safety that is a place of open temporary detention as defined in Part IV (Youth Justice).

Right of entry, etc.

(11) A child protection worker who believes on reasonable and probable grounds that a child referred to in subsection (7) is on any premises may without a warrant enter the premises, by force, if necessary, and search for and remove the child.

Regulations re power of entry

(12) A child protection worker authorized to enter premises under subsection (6) or (11) shall exercise the power of entry in accordance with the regulations.

Peace officer has powers of child protection worker

(13) Subsections (2), (6), (7), (10), (11) and (12) apply to a peace officer as if the peace officer were a child protection worker.

Protection from personal liability

(14) No action shall be instituted against a peace officer or child protection worker for any act done in good faith in the execution or intended execution of that person's duty under this section or for an alleged neglect or default in the execution in good faith of that duty.

Special Cases of Apprehension of Children

Apprehension of children in care

Warrant to apprehend child in care

41. (1) A justice of the peace may issue a warrant authorizing a peace officer or child protection worker to bring a child to a place of safety if the justice of the peace is satisfied on the basis of a peace officer's or child protection worker's sworn information that,

(a) the child is actually or apparently under the age of sixteen years and has left or been removed from a society's lawful care and custody without its consent; and

(b) there are reasonable and probable grounds to believe that there is no course of action available other than bringing the child to a place of safety that would adequately protect the child.

Idem

(2) A justice of the peace shall not refuse to issue a warrant to a person under subsection (1) by reason only that the person may bring the child to a place of safety under subsection (4).

No need to specify premises

(3) It is not necessary in a warrant under subsection (1) to specify the premises where the child is located.

Apprehension of child in care without warrant

(4) A peace officer or child protection worker who believes on reasonable and probable grounds that,

(a) a child is actually or apparently under the age of sixteen years and has left or been removed from a society's lawful care and custody without its consent; and

(b) there would be a substantial risk to the child's health or safety during the time necessary to obtain a warrant under subsection (1),

may without a warrant bring the child to a place of safety.

Apprehension of child absent from place of open temporary detention

(5) Where a child is detained under this Part in a place of safety that has been designated as a place of open temporary detention as defined in Part IV (Youth Justice) and leaves the place without the consent of,

(a) the society having care, custody and control of the child; or

(b) the person in charge of the place of safety,

a peace officer, the person in charge of the place of safety or that person's delegate may apprehend the child without a warrant.

Idem

(6) A person who apprehends a child under subsection (5) shall,

(a) take the child to a place of safety to be detained until the child can be returned to the place of safety the child left; or

(b) return the child or arrange for the child to be returned to the place of safety the child left.

Apprehension of child under twelve

42. (1) A peace officer who believes on reasonable and probable grounds that a child actually or apparently under twelve years of age has committed an act in respect of which a person twelve years of age or older could be found guilty of an offence may apprehend the child without a warrant and on doing so,

(a) shall return the child to the child's parent or other person having charge of the child as soon as practicable; or

(b) where it is not possible to return the child to the parent or other person within a reasonable time, shall take the child to a place of safety to be detained there until the child can be returned to the parent or other person.

Notice to parent, etc.

(2) The person in charge of a place of safety in which a child is detained under subsection (1) shall make reasonable efforts to notify the child's parent or other person having charge of the child of the child's detention so that the child may be returned to the parent or other person.

Where child not returned to parent, etc., within twelve hours

(3) Where a child detained in a place of safety under subsection (1) cannot be returned to the child's parent or other person having charge of the child within twelve hours of being taken to the place of safety, the child shall be dealt with as if the child had been taken to a place of safety under subsection 40(7) and not apprehended under subsection (1).

Runaways

43. (1) In this section,

"parent" includes,

(a) an approved agency that has custody of the child,

(b) a person who has care and control of the child.

Warrant to apprehend runaway child

(2) A justice of the peace may issue a warrant authorizing a peace officer or child protection worker to apprehend a child if the justice of the peace is satisfied on the basis of the sworn information of a parent of the child that,

(a) the child is under the age of sixteen years;

(b) the child has withdrawn from the parent's care and control without the parent's consent; and

(c) the parent believes on reasonable and probable grounds that the child's health or safety may be at risk if the child is not apprehended.

Idem

(3) A person who apprehends a child under subsection (2) shall return the child to the child's parent as soon as practicable and where it is not possible to return the child to the parent within a reasonable time, take the child to a place of safety.

Notice to parent, etc.

(4) The person in charge of a place of safety to which a child is taken under subsection (3) shall make reasonable efforts to notify the child's parent that the child is in the place of safety so that the child may be returned to the parent.

Where child not returned to parent within twelve hours

(5) Where a child taken to a place of safety under subsection (3) cannot be returned to the child's parent within twelve hours of being taken to the place of safety, the child shall be dealt with as if the child had been taken to a place of safety under subsection 40(2) and not apprehended under subsection (2).

Where custody enforcement proceedings more appropriate

(6) A justice of the peace shall not issue a warrant under subsection (2) where a child has withdrawn from the care and control of one parent with the consent of another parent under circumstances where a proceeding under section 36 of the Children's Law Reform Act would be more appropriate.

No need to specify premises

(7) It is not necessary in a warrant under subsection (2) to specify the premises where the child is located.

Child protection proceedings

(8) Where a peace officer or child protection worker believes on reasonable and probable grounds that a child apprehended under this section is in need of protection and there may be a substantial risk to the health or safety of the child if the child were returned to the parent,

(a) the peace officer or child protection worker may take the child to a place of safety under subsection 40(7); or

(b) where the child has been taken to a place of safety under subsection (5), the child shall be dealt with as if the child had been taken there under subsection 40(7).

Power of Entry and Other Provisions for Special Cases of Apprehension

Authority to enter, etc.

44. (1) A person authorized to bring a child to a place of safety by a warrant issued under subsection 41(1) or 43(2) may at any time enter any premises specified in the warrant, by force, if necessary, and may search for and remove the child.

Right of entry, etc.

(2) A person authorized under subsection 41(4) or (5) or 42(1) who believes on reasonable and probable grounds that a child referred to in the relevant subsection is on any premises may without a warrant enter the premises, by force, if necessary, and search for and remove the child.

Regulations re power of entry

(3) A person authorized to enter premises under this section shall exercise the power of entry in accordance with the regulations.

Police assistance

(4) A child protection worker acting under section 41 or 43 may call for the assistance of a peace officer.

Consent to examine child

(5) A child protection worker who deals with a child under subsection 42(3) or 43(5) as if the child had been taken to a place of safety may authorize the child's medical examination where a parent's consent would otherwise be required.

Place of open temporary detention

(6) Where a person who brings a child to a place of safety under section 41 or 42 believes on reasonable and probable grounds that no less restrictive course of action is feasible, the child may be detained in a place of safety that is a place of open temporary detention as defined in Part IV (Youth Justice).

Protection from personal liability

(7) No action shall be instituted against a peace officer or child protection worker for any act done in good faith in the execution or intended execution of that person's duty under this section or section 41, 42 or 43 or for an alleged neglect or default in the execution in good faith of that duty.

Hearings and Orders

Rules re hearings

45. (1) In this section,

"media" means the press, radio and television media.

Application

(2) This section applies to hearings held under this Part, except hearings under section 76 (child abuse register).

Hearings separate from criminal proceedings

(3) A hearing shall be held separately from hearings in criminal proceedings.

Hearings private unless court orders otherwise

(4) A hearing shall be held in the absence of the public, subject to subsection (5), unless the court, after considering,

(a) the wishes and interests of the parties; and

(b) whether the presence of the public would cause emotional harm to a child who is a witness at or a participant in the hearing or is the subject of the proceeding,

orders that the hearing be held in public.

Media representatives

(5) Media representatives chosen in accordance with subsection (6) may be present at a hearing that is held in the absence of the public, unless the court makes an order excluding them under subsection (7).

Idem

(6) The media representatives who may be present at a hearing that is held in the absence of the public shall be chosen as follows:

1. The media representatives in attendance shall choose not more than two persons from among themselves.
2. Where the media representatives in attendance are unable to agree on a choice of persons, the court may choose not more than two media representatives who may be present at the hearing.
3. The court may permit additional media representatives to be present at the hearing.

Order excluding media representatives or prohibiting publication

(7) The court may make an order,

(a) excluding a particular media representative from all or part of a hearing;

(b) excluding all media representatives from all or a part of a hearing; or

(c) prohibiting the publication of a report of the hearing or a specified part of the hearing,

where the court is of the opinion that the presence of the media representative or representatives or the publication of the report, as the case may be, would cause emotional harm to a child who is a witness at or a participant in the hearing or is the subject of the proceeding.

Prohibition: identifying child

(8) No person shall publish or make public information that has the effect of identifying a child who is a witness at or a participant in a hearing or the subject of a proceeding, or the child's parent or foster parent or a member of the child's family.

Idem: order re adult

(9) The court may make an order prohibiting the publication of information that has the effect of identifying a person charged with an offence under this Part.

Transcript

(10) No person except a party or a party's solicitor shall be given a copy of a transcript of the hearing, unless the court orders otherwise.

Time of detention limited

46. (1) As soon as practicable, but in any event within five days after a child is brought to a place of safety under section 40 or subsection 79(6) or a homemaker remains or is placed on premises under subsection 78(2),

(a) the matter shall be brought before a court for a hearing under subsection 47(1) (child protection hearing);

(b) the child shall be returned to the person who last had charge of the child or, where there is an order for the child's custody that is enforceable in Ontario, to the person entitled to custody under the order; or

(c) a temporary care agreement shall be made under subsection 29(1) of Part II (Voluntary Access to Services).

Idem: place of open temporary detention

(2) Within twenty-four hours after a child is brought to a place of safety that is a place of open temporary detention, or as soon thereafter as is practicable, the matter shall be brought before a court for a hearing and the court shall,

(a) where it is satisfied that no less restrictive course of action is feasible, order that the child remain in the place of open temporary detention for a period or periods not exceeding an aggregate of thirty days and then be returned to the care and custody of the society;

(b) order that the child be discharged from the place of open temporary detention and returned to the care and custody of the society; or

(c) make an order under subsection 51(2) (temporary care and custody).

Child protection hearing

47. (1) Where an application is made under subsection 40(1) or a matter is brought before the court to determine whether the child is in need of protection, the court shall hold a hearing to determine the issue and make an order under section 57.

Child's name, age, etc.

(2) As soon as practicable, and in any event before determining whether a child is in need of protection, the court shall determine,

(a) the child's name and age;

(b) the religious faith, if any, in which the child is being raised;

(c) whether the child is an Indian or a native person and, if so, the child's band or native community; and

(d) where the child was brought to a place of safety before the hearing, the location of the place from which the child was removed.

Where sixteenth birthday intervenes

(3) Despite anything else in this Part, where the child was under the age of sixteen years when the proceeding was commenced or when the child was apprehended, the court may hear and determine the matter and make an order under this Part as if the child were still under the age of sixteen years.

Territorial jurisdiction

48. (1) In this section,

"territorial jurisdiction" means a society's territorial jurisdiction under subsection 15(2).

Place of hearing

(2) A hearing under this Part with respect to a child shall be held in the territorial jurisdiction in which the child ordinarily resides, except that,

(a) where the child is brought to a place of safety before the hearing, the hearing shall be held in the territorial jurisdiction in which the place from which the child was removed is located;

(b) where the child is in a society's care under an order for society wardship under section 57 or an order for Crown wardship under section 57 or 65.2, the hearing shall be held in the society's territorial jurisdiction; and

(c) where the child is the subject of an order for society supervision under section 57 or 65.2, the hearing may be held in the society's territorial jurisdiction or in the territorial jurisdiction in which the parent or other person with whom the child is placed resides.

Transfer of proceeding

(3) Where the court is satisfied at any stage of a proceeding under this Part that there is a preponderance of convenience in favour of conducting it in another territorial jurisdiction, the court may order that the proceeding be transferred to that other territorial jurisdiction and be continued as if it had been commenced there.

Orders affecting society

(4) The court shall not make an order placing a child in the care or under the supervision of a society unless the place where the court sits is within the society's territorial jurisdiction.

Power of court

49. The court may, on its own initiative, summon a person to attend before it, testify and produce any document or thing, and may enforce obedience to the summons as if it had been made in a proceeding under the *Family Law Act*.

Evidence

Past conduct toward children

50. (1) Despite anything in the *Evidence Act*, in any proceeding under this Part,

(a) the court may consider the past conduct of a person toward any child if that person is caring for or has access to or may care for or have access to a child who is the subject of the proceeding; and

(b) any oral or written statement or report that the court considers relevant to the proceeding, including a transcript, exhibit or finding or the reasons for a decision in an earlier civil or criminal proceeding, is admissible into evidence.

Evidence re disposition not admissible before finding

(2) In a hearing under subsection 47(1), evidence relating only to the disposition of the matter shall not be admitted be-

fore the court has determined that the child is in need of protection.

Note: Despite the proclamation of the Statutes of Ontario, 1999, chapter 2, section 12, section 50 of this Act, as it read before March 31, 2000, continues to apply with respect to any proceeding under Part III, including a status review proceeding, that was commenced before March 31, 2000. See: 1999, c. 2, ss. 37(5), 38.

Adjournments

51. (1) The court shall not adjourn a hearing for more than thirty days,

(a) unless all the parties present and the person who will be caring for the child during the adjournment consent; or

(b) if the court is aware that a party who is not present at the hearing objects to the longer adjournment.

Custody during adjournment

(2) Where a hearing is adjourned, the court shall make a temporary order for care and custody providing that the child,

(a) remain in or be returned to the care and custody of the person who had charge of the child immediately before intervention under this Part;

(b) remain in or be returned to the care and custody of the person referred to in clause (a), subject to the society's supervision and on such reasonable terms and conditions as the court considers appropriate;

(c) be placed in the care and custody of a person other than the person referred to in clause (a), with the consent of that other person, subject to the society's supervision and on such reasonable terms and conditions as the court considers appropriate; or

(d) remain or be placed in the care and custody of the society, but not be placed in,

(i) a place of secure custody as defined in Part IV (Youth Justice), or

(ii) a place of open temporary detention as defined in that Part that has not been designated as a place of safety.

Criteria

(3) The court shall not make an order under clause (2)(c) or (d) unless the court is satisfied that there are reasonable grounds to believe that there is a risk that the child is likely to suffer harm and that the child cannot be protected adequately by an order under clause (2)(a) or (b).

Placement with relative, etc.

(3.1) Before making a temporary order for care and custody under clause (2)(d), the court shall consider whether it is in the child's best interests to make an order under clause (2)(c) to place the child in the care and custody of a person who is a relative of the child or a member of the child's extended family or community.

Terms and conditions in order

(3.2) A temporary order for care and custody of a child under clause (2)(b) or (c) may impose,

(a) reasonable terms and conditions relating to the child's care and supervision;

(b) reasonable terms and conditions on the child's parent, the person who will have care and custody of the child under the order, the child and any other person, other than a foster parent, who is putting forward a plan or who would participate in a plan for care and custody of or access to the child; and

(c) reasonable terms and conditions on the society that will supervise the placement, but shall not require the society to provide financial assistance or to purchase any goods or services.

Application of s. 62

(4) Where the court makes an order under clause (2)(d), section 62 (parental consents) applies with necessary modifications.

Access

(5) An order made under clause (2)(c) or (d) may contain provisions regarding any person's right of access to the child on such terms and conditions as the court considers appropriate.

Power to vary

(6) The court may at any time vary or terminate an order made under subsection (2).

Evidence on adjournments

(7) For the purpose of this section, the court may admit and act on evidence that the court considers credible and trustworthy in the circumstances.

Note: Despite the proclamation of the Statutes of Ontario, 1999, chapter 2, section 13, section 51 of this Act, as it read before March 31, 2000, continues to apply with respect to any proceeding under Part III, including a status review proceeding, that was commenced before March 31, 2000. See: 1999, c. 2, ss. 37(5), 38.

Use of prescribed methods of alternative dispute resolution

51.1 At any time during a proceeding under this Part, the court may, in the best interests of the child and with the consent of the parties, adjourn the proceeding to permit the parties to attempt through a prescribed method of alternative dispute resolution to resolve any dispute between them with respect to any matter that is relevant to the proceeding.

Delay: court to fix date

52. Where an application is made under subsection 40(1) or a matter is brought before the court to determine whether a child is in need of protection and the determination has not been made within three months after the commencement of the proceeding, the court,

(a) shall by order fix a date for the hearing of the application, and the date may be the earliest date that is compatible with the just disposition of the application; and

(b) may give such directions and make such orders with respect to the proceeding as are just.

Reasons, etc.

53. (1) Where the court makes an order under this Part, the court shall give,

(a) a statement of any terms or conditions imposed on the order;

(b) a statement of every plan for the child's care proposed to the court;

(c) a statement of the plan for the child's care that the court is applying in its decision; and

(d) reasons for its decision, including,

(i) a brief statement of the evidence on which the court bases its decision, and

(ii) where the order has the effect of removing or keeping the child from the care of the person who had charge of the child immediately before intervention under this Part, a statement of the reasons why the child cannot be adequately protected while in the person's care.

Idem

(2) Clause (1)(b) does not require the court to identify a person with whom or a place where it is proposed that a child be placed for care and supervision.

Assessments

Order for assessment

54. (1) In the course of a proceeding under this Part, the court may order that one or more of the following persons undergo an assessment within a specified time by a person appointed in accordance with subsections (1.1) and (1.2):

1. The child.
2. A parent of the child.
3. Any other person, other than a foster parent, who is putting forward or would participate in a plan for the care and custody of or access to the child.

Assessor selected by parties

(1.1) An order under subsection (1) shall specify a time within which the parties to the proceeding may select a person to perform the assessment and submit the name of the selected person to the court.

Appointment by court

(1.2) The court shall appoint the person selected by the parties to perform the assessment if the court is satisfied that the person meets the following criteria:

1. The person is qualified to perform medical, emotional, developmental, psychological, educational or social assessments.
2. The person has consented to perform the assessment.

Same

(1.3) If the court is of the opinion that the person selected by the parties under subsection (1.1) does not meet the criteria set out in subsection (1.2), the court shall select and appoint another person who does meet the criteria.

Regulations

(1.4) An order under subsection (1) and the assessment required by that order shall comply with such requirements as may be prescribed.

Report

(2) The person performing an assessment under subsection (1) shall make a written report of the assessment to the court within the time specified in the order, which shall not be more than thirty days unless the court is of the opinion that a longer assessment period is necessary.

Copies of report

(3) At least seven days before the court considers the report at a hearing, the court or, where the assessment was requested by a party, that party, shall provide a copy of the report to,

(a) the person assessed, subject to subsections (4) and (5);

(b) the child's solicitor or agent of record;

(c) a parent appearing at the hearing, or the parent's solicitor of record;

(d) the society caring for or supervising the child;

(e) a Director, where he or she requests a copy;

(f) where the child is an Indian or a native person, a representative chosen by the child's band or native community; and

(g) any other person who, in the opinion of the court, should receive a copy of the report for the purposes of the case.

Child under twelve

(4) Where the person assessed is a child less than twelve years of age, the child shall not receive a copy of the report unless the court considers it desirable that the child receive a copy of the report.

Child twelve or older

(5) Where the person assessed is a child twelve years of age or more, the child shall receive a copy of the report, except that where the court is satisfied that disclosure of all or

part of the report to the child would cause the child emotional harm, the court may withhold all or part of the report from the child.

Conflict

(5.1) Subsections (4) and (5) prevail despite anything in the *Personal Health Information Protection Act, 2004*.

Assessment is evidence

(6) The report of an assessment ordered under subsection (1) is evidence and is part of the court record of the proceeding.

Inference from refusal

(7) The court may draw any inference it considers reasonable from a person's refusal to undergo an assessment ordered under subsection (1).

Report inadmissible

(8) The report of an assessment ordered under subsection (1) is not admissible into evidence in any other proceeding except,

(a) a proceeding under this Part, including an appeal under section 69;

(b) a proceeding referred to in section 81;

(b.1) a proceeding under Part VII respecting an application to make, vary or terminate an openness order; or

(c) a proceeding under the *Coroners Act*,

without the consent of the person or persons assessed.

Note: Despite the proclamation of the Statutes of Ontario, 1999, chapter 2, section 14, section 54 of this Act, as it read before March 31, 2000, continues to apply with respect to any proceeding under Part III, including a status review proceeding, that was commenced before March 31, 2000. See: 1999, c. 2, ss. 37(5), 38.

Consent order: special requirements

55. Where a child is brought before the court on consent as described in clause 37(2)(l), the court shall, before making an order under section 57 or 57.1 that would remove the child from the parent's care and custody,

(a) ask whether,

(i) the society has offered the parent and child services that would enable the child to remain with the parent, and

(ii) the parent and, where the child is twelve years of age or older, the child has consulted independent legal counsel in connection with the consent; and

(b) be satisfied that,

(i) the parent and, where the child is twelve years of age or older, the child understands the nature and consequences of the consent,

(ii) every consent is voluntary, and

(iii) the parent and, where the child is twelve years of age or older, the child consents to the order being sought.

Society's plan for child

56. The court shall, before making an order under section 57, 57.1, 65 or 65.2, obtain and consider a plan for the child's care prepared in writing by the society and including,

(a) a description of the services to be provided to remedy the condition or situation on the basis of which the child was found to be in need of protection;

(b) a statement of the criteria by which the society will determine when its wardship or supervision is no longer required;

(c) an estimate of the time required to achieve the purpose of the society's intervention;

(d) where the society proposes to remove or has removed the child from a person's care,

(i) an explanation of why the child cannot be adequately protected while in the person's care, and a description of any past efforts to do so, and

(ii) a statement of what efforts, if any, are planned to maintain the child's contact with the person;

(e) where the society proposes to remove or has removed the child from a person's care permanently, a description of the arrangements made or being made for the child's long-term stable placement; and

(f) a description of the arrangements made or being made to recognize the importance of the child's culture and to preserve the child's heritage, traditions and cultural identity.

Order where child in need of protection

57. (1) Where the court finds that a child is in need of protection and is satisfied that intervention through a court order is necessary to protect the child in the future, the court shall make one of the following orders or an order under section 57.1, in the child's best interests:

Supervision order

1. That the child be placed in the care and custody of a parent or another person, subject to the supervision of the society, for a specified period of at least three months and not more than 12 months.

Society wardship

2. That the child be made a ward of the society and be placed in its care and custody for a specified period not exceeding twelve months.

Crown wardship

3. That the child be made a ward of the Crown, until the wardship is terminated under section 65 or expires under subsection 71(1), and be placed in the care of the society.

Consecutive orders of society wardship and supervision

4. That the child be made a ward of the society under paragraph 2 for a specified period and then be returned to a parent or another person under paragraph 1, for a period or periods not exceeding an aggregate of twelve months.

Court to inquire

(2) In determining which order to make under subsection (1) or section 57.1, the court shall ask the parties what efforts the society or another agency or person has made to assist the child before intervention under this Part.

Less disruptive alternatives preferred

(3) The court shall not make an order removing the child from the care of the person who had charge of him or her immediately before intervention under this Part unless the court is satisfied that alternatives that are less disruptive to the child, including non-residential services and the assistance referred to in subsection (2), would be inadequate to protect the child.

Community placement to be considered

(4) Where the court decides that it is necessary to remove the child from the care of the person who had charge of him or her immediately before intervention under this Part, the court shall, before making an order for society or Crown wardship under paragraph 2 or 3 of subsection (1), consider whether it is possible to place the child with a relative, neighbour or other member of the child's community or extended family under paragraph 1 of subsection (1) with the consent of the relative or other person.

Idem: where child an Indian or a native person

(5) Where the child referred to in subsection (4) is an Indian or a native person, unless there is a substantial reason for placing the child elsewhere, the court shall place the child with,

(a) a member of the child's extended family;

(b) a member of the child's band or native community; or

(c) another Indian or native family.

(6) Repealed.

Idem

(7) When the court has dispensed with notice to a person under subsection 39(7), the court shall not make an order for Crown wardship under paragraph 3 of subsection (1), or an order for society wardship under paragraph 2 of subsection (1) for a period exceeding thirty days, until a further hearing under subsection 47(1) has been held upon notice to that person.

Terms and conditions of supervision order

(8) If the court makes a supervision order under paragraph 1 of subsection (1), the court may impose,

(a) reasonable terms and conditions relating to the child's care and supervision;

(b) reasonable terms and conditions on,

(i) the child's parent,

(ii) the person who will have care and custody of the child under the order,

(iii) the child, and

(iv) any other person, other than a foster parent, who is putting forward or would participate in a plan for the care and custody of or access to the child; and

(c) reasonable terms and conditions on the society that will supervise the placement, but shall not require the society to provide financial assistance or purchase any goods or services.

Where no court order necessary

(9) Where the court finds that a child is in need of protection but is not satisfied that a court order is necessary to protect the child in the future, the court shall order that the child remain with or be returned to the person who had charge of the child immediately before intervention under this Part.

Note: Despite the proclamation of the Statutes of Ontario, 1999, chapter 2, section 15, section 57 of this Act, as it read before March 31, 2000, continues to apply with respect to any proceeding under Part III, including a status review proceeding, that was commenced before March 31, 2000. See: 1999, c. 2, ss. 37(5), 38.

Custody order

57.1 (1) Subject to subsection (6), if a court finds that an order under this section instead of an order under subsection 57(1) would be in a child's best interests, the court may make an order granting custody of the child to one or more persons, other than a foster parent of the child, with the consent of the person or persons.

Deemed to be order under *Children's Law Reform Act*

(2) An order made under subsection (1) and any access order under section 58 that is made at the same time as the order under subsection (1) shall be deemed to be made under section 28 of the *Children's Law Reform Act* and the court,

(a) may make any order under subsection (1) that the court may make under section 28 of that Act; and

(b) may give any directions that it may give under section 34 of that Act.

Restraining Order

(3) When making an order under subsection (1), the court may, without a separate application under section 35 of the *Children's Law Reform Act*.

Same

(4) An order under subsection (3) is deemed to be a final order made under section 35 of the *Children's Law Reform Act*, and shall be treated for all purposes as if it had been made under that section.

Appeal under s. 69

(5) Despite subsections (2) and (4), an order under subsection (1) or (3) and any access order under section 58 that is made at the same time as an order under subsection (1) are orders under this Part for the purposes of appealing from the orders under section 69.

Conflict of laws

(6) No order shall be made under this section if,

(a) an order granting custody of the child has been made under the *Divorce Act* (Canada); or

(b) in the case of an order that would be made by the Ontario Court of Justice, the order would conflict with an order made by a superior court.

Application of s. 57(3)

(7) Subsection 57(3) applies for the purposes of this section.

Effect of custody proceedings

57.2 If, under this Part, a proceeding is commenced or an order for the care, custody or supervision of a child is made, any proceeding respecting custody of or access to the same child under the *Children's Law Reform Act* is stayed except by leave of the court in the proceeding under that Act.

Access

Access order

58. (1) The court may, in the child's best interests,

(a) when making an order under this Part; or

(b) upon an application under subsection (2),

make, vary or terminate an order respecting a person's access to the child or the child's access to a person, and may impose such terms and conditions on the order as the court considers appropriate.

Who may apply

(2) Where a child is in a society's care and custody or supervision,

(a) the child;

(b) any other person, including, where the child is an Indian or a native person, a representative chosen by the child's band or native community; or

(c) the society,

may apply to the court at any time for an order under subsection (1).

Notice

(3) An applicant referred to in clause (2)(b) shall give notice of the application to the society.

Idem

(4) A society making or receiving an application under subsection (2) shall give notice of the application to,

(a) the child, subject to subsections 39(4) and (5) (notice to child);

(b) the child's parent;

(c) the person caring for the child at the time of the application; and

(d) where the child is an Indian or a native person, a representative chosen by the child's band or native community.

Child over sixteen

(5) No order respecting access to a person sixteen years of age or more shall be made under subsection (1) without the person's consent.

Six-month period

(6) No application shall be made under subsection (2) by a person other than a society within six months of,

(a) the making of an order under section 57;

(b) the disposition of a previous application by the same person under subsection (2);

(c) the disposition of an application under section 64 or 65.1; or

(d) the final disposition or abandonment of an appeal from an order referred to in clause (a), (b) or (c),

whichever is later.

No application where child placed for adoption

(7) No person or society shall make an application under subsection (2) where the child,

(a) is a Crown ward;

(b) has been placed in a person's home by the society or by a Director for the purpose of adoption under Part VII (Adoption); and

(c) still resides in that person's home.

Access: where child removed from person in charge

59. (1) Where an order is made under paragraph 1 or 2 of subsection 57(1) removing a child from the person who had charge of the child immediately before intervention under this Part, the court shall make an order for access by the person unless the court is satisfied that continued contact with him or her would not be in the child's best interests.

Access after custody order under s. 57.1

(1.1) If a custody order is made under section 57.1 removing a child from the person who had charge of the child immediately before intervention under this Part, the court shall make an order for access by the person unless the court is satisfied that continued contact will not be in the child's best interests.

Access after supervision order or custody order under s. 65.2(1)

(1.2) If an order is made for supervision under clause 65.2(1)(a) or for custody under clause 65.2(1)(b), the court shall make an order for access by every person who had access before the application for the order was made under section 65.1, unless the court is satisfied that continued contact will not be in the child's best interests.

Termination of access to Crown ward

(2) Where the court makes an order that a child be made a ward of the Crown, any order for access made under this Part with respect to the child is terminated.

Access: Crown ward

(2.1) A court shall not make or vary an access order made under section 58 with respect to a Crown ward unless the court is satisfied that,

(a) the relationship between the person and the child is beneficial and meaningful to the child; and

(b) the ordered access will not impair the child's future opportunities for adoption.

Termination of access: Crown ward

(3) The court shall terminate an access order with respect to a Crown ward if,

(a) the order is no longer in the best interests of the child; or

(b) the court is no longer satisfied that the requirements set out in clauses (2.1)(a) and (b) are satisfied.

Society may permit contact or communication

(4) If a society believes that contact or communication between a person and a Crown ward is in the best interests of the Crown ward and no openness order under Part VII or access order is in effect with respect to the person and the Crown ward, the society may permit contact or communication between the person and the Crown ward.

Note: Despite the proclamation of the Statutes of Ontario, 1999, chapter 2, section 16, section 59 of this Act, as it read before March 31, 2000, continues to apply with respect to any proceeding under Part III, including a status review proceeding, that was commenced before March 31, 2000. See: 1999, c. 2, ss. 37(5), 38.

Review of access order made concurrently with custody order

59.1 No order for access under section 58 is subject to review under this Act if it is made at the same time as a custody order under section 57.1, but it may be the subject of an application under section 21 of the *Children's Law Reform Act* and the provisions of that Act apply as if the order had been made under that Act.

Restriction on access order

59.2 If a society has applied to a court for an order under this Act respecting access to a child by a parent of the child and the court makes the order, the court shall specify in the order the supervision to which the access is subject if, at the time of making the order, the parent has been charged with or convicted of an offence under the *Criminal Code* (Canada) involving an act of violence against the child or the other parent of the child, unless the court considers it appropriate not to make the access subject to such supervision.

Payment Orders

Order for payment by parent

60. (1) Where the court places a child in the care of,

(a) a society; or

(b) a person other than the child's parent, subject to a society's supervision,

the court may order a parent or a parent's estate to pay the society a specified amount at specified intervals for each day the child is in the society's care or supervision.

Criteria

(2) In making an order under subsection (1), the court shall consider those of the following circumstances of the case that the court considers relevant:

1. The assets and means of the child and of the parent or the parent's estate.
2. The child's capacity to provide for his or her own support.
3. The capacity of the parent or the parent's estate to provide support.
4. The child's and the parent's age and physical and mental health.
5. The child's mental, emotional and physical needs.
6. Any legal obligation of the parent or the parent's estate to provide support for another person.
7. The child's aptitude for and reasonable prospects of obtaining an education.
8. Any legal right of the child to support from another source, other than out of public money.

Order ends at eighteen

(3) No order made under subsection (1) shall extend beyond the day on which the child attains the age of eighteen years.

Power to vary

(4) The court may vary, suspend or terminate an order made under subsection (1) where the court is satisfied that the circumstances of the child or parent have changed.

Collection by municipality

(5) The council of a municipality may enter into an agreement with the board of directors of a society providing for the collection by the municipality, on the society's behalf, of the amounts ordered to be paid by a parent under subsection (1).

Enforcement

(6) An order made against a parent under subsection (1) may be enforced as if it were an order for support made under Part III of the *Family Law Act*.

Society and Crown Wardship

Placement of wards

61. (1) This section applies where a child is made a society ward under paragraph 2 of subsection 57(1) or a Crown ward under paragraph 3 of subsection 57(1) or under subsection 65.2(1).

Placement

(2) The society having care of a child shall choose a residential placement for the child that,

(a) represents the least restrictive alternative for the child;

(b) where possible, respects the religious faith, if any, in which the child is being raised;

(c) where possible, respects the child's linguistic and cultural heritage;

(d) where the child is an Indian or a native person, is with a member of the child's extended family, a member of the child's band or native community or another Indian or native family, if possible; and

(e) takes into account the child's wishes, if they can be reasonably ascertained, and the wishes of any parent who is entitled to access to the child.

Education

(3) The society having care of a child shall ensure that the child receives an education that corresponds to his or her aptitudes and abilities.

Placement outside or removal from Ontario

(4) The society having care of a child shall not place the child outside Ontario or permit a person to remove the child from Ontario permanently unless a Director is satisfied that extraordinary circumstances justify the placement or removal.

Rights of child, parent and foster parent

(5) The society having care of a child shall ensure that,

(a) the child is afforded all the rights referred to in Part V (Rights of Children); and

(b) the wishes of any parent who is entitled to access to the child and, where the child is a Crown ward, of any foster parent with whom the child has lived continuously for two years are taken into account in the society's major decisions concerning the child.

Change of placement

(6) The society having care of a child may remove the child from a foster home or other residential placement where, in the opinion of a Director or local director, it is in the child's best interests to do so.

Notice of proposed removal

(7) If a child is a Crown ward and has lived continuously with a foster parent for two years and a society proposes to remove the child from the foster parent under subsection (6), the society shall,

(a) give the foster parent at least 10 days notice in writing of the proposed removal and of the foster parent's right to apply for a review under subsection (7.1); and

(b) if the child is an Indian or native person,

(i) give at least 10 days notice in writing of the proposed removal to a representative chosen by the child's band or native community, and

(ii) after the notice is given, consult with representatives chosen by the band or community relating to the plan for the care of the child.

Application for review

(7.1) A foster parent who receives a notice under clause (7)(a) may, within 10 days after receiving the notice, apply to the Board in accordance with the regulations for a review of the proposed removal.

Board hearing

(8) Where a foster parent requests a review under section 68 within ten days of receiving a notice under subsection (7), the society shall not remove the child until the review and any further review by a Director have been completed and unless the society's board of directors or the Director, as the case may be, recommend that the child be removed.

Where child is Indian or native person

(8.1) Upon receipt of an application for review of a proposed removal of a child who is an Indian or native person, the Board shall give a representative chosen by the child's band or native community notice of receipt of the application and of the date of the hearing.

Practices and procedures

(8.2) The *Statutory Powers Procedure Act* applies to a hearing under this section and the Board shall comply with such additional practices and procedures as may be prescribed.

Composition of Board

(8.3) At a hearing under this section, the Board shall be composed of members with the prescribed qualifications and prescribed experience.

Parties

(8.4) The following persons are parties to a hearing under this section:

1. The applicant.
2. The society.
3. If the child is an Indian or a native person, a representative chosen by the child's band or native community.
4. Any person that the Board adds under subsection (8.5).

Additional parties

(8.5) The Board may add a person as a party to a review if, in the Board's opinion, it is necessary to do so in order to decide all the issues in the review.

Board decision

(8.6) The Board shall, in accordance with its determination of which action is in the best interests of the child, confirm the proposal to remove the child or direct the society not to carry out the proposed removal, and shall give written reasons for its decision.

No removal before decision

(8.7) Subject to subsection (9), the society shall not carry out the proposed removal of the child unless,

(a) the time for applying for a review of the proposed removal under subsection (7.1) has expired and an application is not made; or

(b) if an application for a review of the proposed removal is made under subsection (7.1), the Board has confirmed the proposed removal under subsection (8.6).

Where child at risk

(9) A society may remove the child from the foster home before the expiry of the time for applying for a review under subsection (7.1) or at any time after the application for a review is made if, in the opinion of a local director, there would be a risk that the child is likely to suffer harm during the time necessary for a review by the Board.

Review of certain placements

(10) Sections 34, 35 and 36 (review by Residential Placement Advisory Committee, further review by Children's Services Review Board) of Part II (Voluntary Access to Services) apply to a residential placement made by a society.

Transitional

(11) This section as it read on the day before this subsection came into force continues to apply in respect of proposed removals and requests for review under section 68 if the notice of the proposed removal of the child was given by the society on or before that day.

Society wards — medical treatment and marriage

Society ward: consent to medical treatment

62. (1) Where a child is made a society ward under paragraph 2 of subsection 57(1), the society may consent to and authorize medical treatment for the child where a parent's consent would otherwise be required, unless the court orders that the parent shall retain any right that he or she may have to give or refuse consent to medical treatment for the child.

Idem

(2) The court shall not make an order under subsection (1) where failure to consent to necessary medical treatment was a ground for finding that the child was in need of protection.

Court order

(3) Where a parent referred to in an order made under subsection (1) refuses or is unavailable or unable to consent to medical treatment for the child and the court is satisfied that the treatment would be in the child's best interests, the court may authorize the society to consent to the treatment.

Consent to child's marriage

(4) Where a child is made a society ward under paragraph 2 of subsection 57(1), the child's parent retains any right that he or she may have under the *Marriage Act*to give or refuse consent to the child's marriage.

Custodianship of wards

Crown custodian of Crown wards

63. (1) Where a child is made a Crown ward under paragraph 3 of subsection 57(1) or under subsection 65.2(1), the Crown has the rights and responsibilities of a parent for the purpose of the child's care, custody and control and has the right to give or refuse consent to medical treatment for the child where a parent's consent would otherwise be required, and the Crown's powers, duties and obligations in respect of the child, except those assigned to a Director by this Act or the regulations, shall be exercised and performed by the society caring for the child.

Society custodian of society wards

(2) Where a child is made a society ward under paragraph 2 of subsection 57(1), the society has the rights and responsibilities of a parent for the purpose of the child's care, custody and control.

Society's obligation to a Crown ward

63.1 Where a child is made a Crown ward, the society shall make all reasonable efforts to assist the child to develop a positive, secure and enduring relationship within a family through one of the following:

1. An adoption.
2. A custody order under subsection 65.2(1).
3. In the case of a child who is an Indian or native person, a plan for customary care as defined in Part X.

Review

Status review

64. (1) This section applies where a child is the subject of an order under subsection 57(1) for society supervision or society wardship.

Society to seek status review

(2) The society having care, custody or supervision of a child,

(a) may apply to the court at any time for a review of the child's status;

(b) shall apply to the court for a review of the child's status before the order expires, unless the expiry is by reason of subsection 71(1); and

(c) shall apply to the court for a review of the child's status within five days after removing the child, if the society has removed the child from the care of a person with whom the child was placed under an order for society supervision.

Application of cl. (2)(a) and (c)

(3) If a child is the subject of an order for society supervision, clauses (2)(a) and (c) also apply to the society that has jurisdiction in the county or district in which the parent or other person with whom the child is placed resides.

Others may seek status review

(4) An application for review of a child's status may be made on notice to the society by,

(a) the child, if the child is at least 12 years of age;

(b) a parent of the child;

(c) the person with whom the child was placed under an order for society supervision; or

(d) a representative chosen by the child's band or native community, if the child is an Indian or native person.

Notice

(5) A society making an application under subsection (2) or receiving notice of an application under subsection (4) shall give notice of the application to,

(a) the child, except as otherwise provided under subsection 39(4) or (5);

(b) the child's parent;

(c) the person with whom the child was placed under an order for society supervision;

(d) any foster parent who has cared for the child continuously during the six months immediately before the application; and

(e) a representative chosen by the child's band or native community, if the child is an Indian or native person.

Six-month period

(6) No application shall be made under subsection (4) within six months after the latest of,

(a) the day the original order was made under subsection 57(1);

(b) the day the last application by a person under subsection (4) was disposed of; or

(c) the day any appeal from an order referred to in clause (a) or the disposition referred to in clause (b) was finally disposed of or abandoned.

Exception

(7) Subsection (6) does not apply if the court is satisfied that a major element of the plan for the child's care that the court applied in its decision is not being carried out.

Interim care and custody

(8) If an application is made under this section, the child shall remain in the care and custody of the person or society having charge of the child, until the application is disposed of, unless the court is satisfied that the child's best interests require a change in the child's care and custody.

Court may vary, etc.

65. (1) Where an application for review of a child's status is made under section 64, the court may, in the child's best interests,

(a) vary or terminate the original order made under subsection 57(1), including a term or condition or a provision for access that is part of the order;

(b) order that the original order terminate on a specified future date;

(c) make a further order or orders under section 57; or

(d) make an order under section 57.1.

(2) Repealed.

(3) Repealed.

Note: Despite the proclamation of the Statutes of Ontario, 1999, chapter 2, section 19, subsection (3) of this section, as it read before March 31, 2000, continues to apply with respect to any proceeding under Part III, including a status review proceeding, that was commenced before March 31, 2000. See: 1999, c. 2, ss. 37(5), 38.

Status review, Crown ward and former Crown wards

65.1 (1) This section applies where a child is a Crown ward or is the subject of an order for society supervision under clause 65.2(1)(a) or a custody order under clause 65.2(1)(b).

Society to seek status review

(2) The society that has or had care, custody or supervision of the child,

(a) may apply to the court at any time, subject to subsection (9), for a review of the child's status;

(b) shall apply to the court for a review of the child's status before the order expires if the order is for society supervision, unless the expiry is by reason of subsection 71(1); and

(c) shall apply to the court for a review of the child's status within five days after removing the child, if the society has removed the child,

(i) from the care of a person with whom the child was placed under an order for society supervision described in clause 65.2(1)(a), or

(ii) from the custody of a person who had custody of the child under a custody order described in clause 65.2(1)(b).

Application of cl. (2)(a) and (c)

(3) Clauses (2)(a) and (c) also apply to the society that has jurisdiction in the county or district,

(a) in which the parent or other person with whom the child is placed resides, if the child is the subject of an order for society supervision under clause 65.2(1)(a); or

(b) in which the person who has custody resides, if the child is the subject of a custody order under clause 65.2(1)(b).

Others may seek status review

(4) An application for review of a child's status under this section may be made on notice to the society by,

(a) the child, if the child is at least 12 years of age;

(b) a parent of the child;

(c) the person with whom the child was placed under an order for society supervision described in 65.2(1)(a);

(d) the person to whom custody of the child was granted, if the child is subject to an order for custody described in clause 65.2(1)(b);

(e) a foster parent, if the child has lived continuously with the foster parent for at least two years immediately before the application; or

(f) a representative chosen by the child's band or native community, if the child is an Indian or native person.

When leave to apply required

(5) Despite clause (4)(b), a parent of a child shall not make an application under subsection (4) without leave of the court if the child has, immediately before the application, received continuous care for at least two years from the same foster parent or from the same person under a custody order.

Notice

(6) A society making an application under subsection (2) or receiving notice of an application under subsection (4) shall give notice of the application to,

(a) the child, except as otherwise provided under subsection 39(4) or (5);

(b) the child's parent, if the child is under 16 years of age;

(c) the person with whom the child was placed, if the child is subject to an order for society supervision described in clause 65.2(1)(a);

(d) the person to whom custody of the child was granted, if the child is subject to an order for custody described in clause 65.2(1)(b);

(e) any foster parent who has cared for the child continuously during the six months immediately before the application; and

(f) a representative chosen by the child's band or native community, if the child is an Indian or native person.

Six-month period

(7) No application shall be made under subsection (4) within six months after the latest of,

(a) the day the order was made under subsection 57(1) or 65.2(1), whichever is applicable;

(b) the day the last application by a person under subsection (4) was disposed of; or

(c) the day any appeal from an order referred to in clause (a) or a disposition referred to in clause (b) was finally disposed of or abandoned.

Exception

(8) Subsection (7) does not apply if,

(a) the child is the subject of,

(i) an order for society supervision described in clause 65.2(1)(a),

(ii) an order for custody described in clause 65.2(1)(b), or

(iii) an order for Crown wardship under subsection 57(1) or clause 65.2(1)(c) and an order for access under section 58; and

(b) the court is satisfied that a major element of the plan for the child's care that the court applied in its decision is not being carried out.

No review if child placed for adoption

(9) No person or society shall make an application under this section with respect to a Crown ward who has been placed in a person's home by the society or by a Director for the purposes of adoption under Part VII, if the Crown ward still resides in the person's home.

Interim care and custody

(10) If an application is made under this section, the child shall remain in the care and custody of the person or society having charge of the child until the application is disposed of, unless the court is satisfied that the child's best interests require a change in the child's care and custody.

Court order

65.2 (1) If an application for review of a child's status is made under section 65.1, the court may, in the child's best interests,

(a) order that the child be placed in the care and custody of a parent or another person, subject to the supervision of the society, for a specified period of at least three months and not more than 12 months;

(b) order that custody be granted to one or more persons, including a foster parent, with the consent of the person or persons;

(c) order that the child be made a ward of the Crown until wardship is terminated under this section or expires under subsection 71(1); or

(d) terminate or vary any order made under section 57 or this section.

Variation, etc.

(2) When making an order under subsection (1), the court may, subject to section 59, vary or terminate an order for access or make a further order under section 58.

Same

(3) Any previous order for Crown wardship is terminated if an order described in clause (1)(a) or (b) is made in respect of a child.

Terms and conditions of supervision order

(4) If the court makes a supervision order described in clause (1)(a), the court may impose,

(a) reasonable terms and conditions relating to the child's care and supervision;

(b) reasonable terms and conditions on the child's parent, the person who will have care and custody of the child under the order, the child and any other person, other than a foster parent, who is putting forward a plan or who would participate in a plan for care and custody of or access to the child; and

(c) reasonable terms and conditions on the society that will supervise the placement, but shall not require the society to provide financial assistance or purchase any goods or services.

Access

(5) Section 59 applies with necessary modifications if the court makes an order described in clause (1)(a), (b) or (c).

Custody proceeding

(6) Where an order is made under this section or a proceeding is commenced under this Part, any proceeding respecting custody of or access to the same child under the Children's Law Reform Act is stayed except by leave of the court in the proceeding under that Act.

Rights and responsibilities

(7) A person to whom custody of a child is granted by an order under this section has the rights and responsibilities of a parent in respect of the child and must exercise those rights and responsibilities in the best interests of the child.

Director's annual review of Crown wards

66. (1) A Director or a person authorized by a Director shall, at least once during each calendar year, review the status of every child,

(a) who is a Crown ward;

(b) who was a Crown ward throughout the immediately preceding twenty-four months; and

(c) whose status has not been reviewed under this section or under section 65.2 during that time.

Idem

(2) After a review under subsection (1), the Director may direct the society to make an application for review of the child's status under subsection 65(1) or give any other direction that, in the Director's opinion, is in the child's best interests.

Investigation by judge

67. (1) The Minister may appoint a judge of the Court of Ontario to investigate a matter relating to a child in a society's care or the proper administration of this Part, and a judge who is appointed shall conduct the investigation and make a written report to the Minister.

Application of *Public Inquiries Act, 2009*

(2) Section 33 of the *Public Inquiries Act, 2009* applies to an investigation by a judge under subsection (1).

Complaint to society

68. (1) A person may make a complaint to a society relating to a service sought or received by that person from the society in accordance with the regulations.

Complaint review procedure

(2) Where a society receives a complaint under subsection (1), it shall deal with the complaint in accordance with the complaint review procedure established by regulation, subject to subsection 68.1(2).

Available to public

(3) A society shall make information relating to the complaint review procedure available to any person upon request.

Society's decision

(4) Subject to subsection (5), the decision of a society made upon completion of the complaint review procedure is final.

Application for review by Board

(5) If a complaint relates to one of the following matters, the complainant may apply to the Board in accordance with the regulations for a review of the decision made by the society upon completion of the complaint review procedure:

1. An alleged inaccuracy in the society's files or records regarding the complainant.
2. A matter described in subsection 68.1(4).
3. Any other prescribed matter.

Review by Board

(6) Upon receipt of an application under subsection (5), the Board shall give the society notice of the application and conduct a review of the society's decision.

Composition of Board

(7) The Board shall be composed of members with the prescribed qualifications and prescribed experience.

Hearing optional

(8) The Board may hold a hearing and, if a hearing is held, the Board shall comply with the prescribed practices and procedures.

Non-application

(9) The *Statutory Powers Procedure Act* does not apply to a hearing under this section.

Board decision

(10) Upon completing its review of a decision by a society in relation to a complaint, the Board may,

(a) in the case of a review of a matter described in paragraph 1 of subsection (5), order that a notice of disagreement be added to the complainant's file;

(b) in the case of a matter described in subsection 68.1(4), make any order described in subsection 68.1(7), as appropriate;

(c) redirect the matter to the society for further review;

(d) confirm the society's decision; or

(e) make such other order as may be prescribed.

Notice of disagreement

(11) A notice of disagreement referred to in clause (10)(a) shall be in the prescribed form if the regulations so provide.

No review if matter within purview of court

(12) A society shall not conduct a review of a complaint under this section if the subject of the complaint,

(a) is an issue that has been decided by the court or is before the court; or

(b) is subject to another decision-making process under this Act or the *Labour Relations Act, 1995.*

Transitional

(13) This section as it read immediately before the day this subsection came into force continues to apply in respect of complaints made to a society before that day and of any reviews requested of the Director before that day.

Complaint to Board

68.1 (1) If a complaint in respect of a service sought or received from a society relates to a matter described in subsection (4), the person who sought or received the service may,

(a) decide not to make the complaint to the society under section 68 and make the complaint directly to the Board under this section; or

(b) where the person first makes the complaint to the society under section 68, submit the complaint to the Board before the society's complaint review procedure is completed.

Notice to society

(2) If a person submits a complaint to the Board under clause (1)(b) after having brought the complaint to the society under section 68, the Board shall give the society notice of that fact and the society may terminate or stay its review, as it considers appropriate.

Complaint to Board

(3) A complaint to the Board under this section shall be made in accordance with the regulations.

Matters for Board review

(4) The following matters may be reviewed by the Board under this section:

1. Allegations that the society has refused to proceed with a complaint made by the complainant under subsection 68(1) as required under subsection 68(2).
2. Allegations that the society has failed to respond to the complainant's complaint within the timeframe required by regulation.
3. Allegations that the society has failed to comply with the complaint review procedure or with any other procedural requirements under this Act relating to the review of complaints.
4. Allegations that the society has failed to comply with clause 2(2)(a).
5. Allegations that the society has failed to provide the complainant with reasons for a decision that affects the complainant's interests.
6. Such other matters as may be prescribed.

Review by Board

(5) Upon receipt of a complaint under this section, the Board shall conduct a review of the matter.

Application

(6) Subsections 68(7), (8) and (9) apply with necessary modification to a review of a complaint made under this section.

Board decision

(7) After reviewing the complaint, the Board may,

(a) order the society to proceed with the complaint made by the complainant in accordance with the complaint review procedure established by regulation;

(b) order the society to provide a response to the complainant within a period specified by the Board;

(c) order the society to comply with the complaint review procedure established by regulation or with any other requirements under this Act;

(d) order the society to provide written reasons for a decision to a complainant;

(e) dismiss the complaint; or

(f) make such other order as may be prescribed.

No review if matter within purview of court

(8) The Board shall not conduct a review of a complaint under this section if the subject of the complaint,

(a) is an issue that has been decided by the court or is before the court; or

(b) is subject to another decision-making process under this Act or the *Labour Relations Act, 1995.*

Appeals

Appeal

69. (1) An appeal from a court's order under this Part may be made to the Superior Court of Justice by,

(a) the child, if the child is entitled to participate in the proceeding under subsection 39(6) (child's participation);

(b) any parent of the child;

(c) the person who had charge of the child immediately before intervention under this Part;

(d) a Director or local director; or

(e) where the child is an Indian or a native person, a representative chosen by the child's band or native community.

Exception

(2) Subsection (1) does not apply to an order for an assessment under section 54.

Care and custody pending appeal

(3) Where a decision regarding the care and custody of a child is appealed under subsection (1), execution of the decision shall be stayed for the ten days immediately following service of the notice of appeal on the court that made the decision, and where the child is in the society's custody at the time the decision is made, the child shall remain in the care and custody of the society until,

(a) the ten-day period of the stay has expired; or

(b) an order is made under subsection (4),

whichever is earlier.

Temporary order

(4) The Superior Court of Justice may, in the child's best interests, make a temporary order for the child's care and custody pending final disposition of the appeal, except an order placing the child in a place of secure custody as defined in Part IV (Youth Justice) or a place of secure temporary detention as defined in that Part that has not been designated as a place of safety, and the court may, on any party's motion before the final disposition of the appeal, vary or terminate the order or make a further order.

No extension where child placed for adoption

(5) No extension of the time for an appeal shall be granted where the child has been placed for adoption under Part VII (Adoption).

Further evidence

(6) The court may receive further evidence relating to events after the appealed decision.

Place of hearing

(7) An appeal under this section shall be heard in the county or district in which the order appealed from was made.

S. 45 applies

(8) Section 45 (hearings private, etc.) applies with necessary modifications to an appeal under this section.

Expiry of Orders

Time limit

70. (1) Subject to subsections (3) and (4), the court shall not make an order for society wardship under this Part that results in a child being a society ward for a period exceeding,

(a) 12 months, if the child is less than 6 years of age on the day the court makes an order for society wardship; or

(b) 24 months, if the child is 6 years of age or older on the day the court makes an order for society wardship.

Note: For the purposes of subsection (1), as re-enacted by the Statutes of Ontario, 1999, chapter 2, subsection 21(1), no period that a child was in a society's care and custody before March 31, 2000 shall be counted. See: 1999, c. 2, s. 37(3).

Note: Despite the proclamation of the Statutes of Ontario, 1999, chapter 2, subsection 21(1), subsection (1) of this section, as it read before March 31, 2000, shall continue to apply with respect to a child who is in the care and custody of a society on March 31, 2000 so long as that child continues to be in the care and custody of a society. See: 1999, c. 2, ss. 37(4), 38.

Same

(2) In calculating the period referred to in subsection (1), time during which a child has been in a society's care and custody under,

(a) an agreement made under subsection 29(1) or 30(1) (temporary care or special needs agreement); or

(b) a temporary order made under clause 51(2)(d),

shall be counted.

Note: For the purposes of subsection (2), as re-enacted by the Statutes of Ontario, 1999, chapter 2, subsection 21(1), no period that a child was in a society's care and custody before March 31, 2000 shall be counted. See: 1999, c. 2, s. 37(3).

Note: Despite the proclamation of the Statutes of Ontario, 1999, chapter 2, subsection 21(1), subsection (2) of this section, as it read before March 31, 2000, shall continue to apply with respect to a child who is in the care and custody of a society on March 31, 2000 so long as that child continues to be in the care and custody of a society. See: 1999, c. 2, ss. 37(4), 38.

Previous periods to be counted

(2.1) The period referred to in subsection (1) shall include any previous periods that the child was in a society's care and custody as a society ward or as described in subsection (2) other than periods that precede a continuous period of five or more years that the child was not in a society's care and custody.

Note: For the purposes of subsection (2.1), as enacted by the Statutes of Ontario, 1999, chapter 2, subsection 21(1), no period that a child was in a society's care and custody before March 31, 2000 shall be counted. See: 1999, c. 2, s. 37(3).

Idem

(3) Where the period referred to in subsection (1) or (4) expires and,

(a) an appeal of an order made under subsection 57(1) has been commenced and is not yet finally disposed of; or

(b) the court has adjourned a hearing under section 65 (status review),

the period shall be deemed to be extended until the appeal has been finally disposed of and any new hearing ordered on appeal has been completed or an order has been made under section 65, as the case may be.

Note: Despite the proclamation of the Statutes of Ontario, 1999, chapter 2, subsection 21(2), subsection (3) of this section, as it read before March 31, 2000, shall continue to apply with respect to a child who is in the care and custody of a society on March 31, 2000 so long as that child continues to be in the care and custody of a society. See: 1999, c. 2, ss. 37(4), 38.

Six-month extension

(4) Subject to paragraphs 2 and 4 of subsection 57(1), the court may by order extend the period permitted under subsection (1) by a period not to exceed six months if it is in the child's best interests to do so.

Expiry of orders

71. (1) An order under this Part expires when the child who is the subject of the order,

(a) attains the age of eighteen years; or

(b) marries,

whichever comes first.

(2) Repealed.

Extended care

71.1 (1) A society may provide care and maintenance to a person in accordance with the regulations if,

(a) a custody order under subsection 65.2(1) or an order for Crown wardship was made in relation to that person as a child; and

(b) the order expires under section 71.

Same, Indian and native person

(2) A society or agency may provide care and maintenance in accordance with the regulations to a person who is an Indian or native person who is 18 years of age or more if,

(a) immediately before the person's 18th birthday, he or she was being cared for under customary care as defined in section 208; and

(b) the person who was caring for the child was receiving a subsidy from the society or agency under section 212.

Same, prescribed support services

(3) A society or agency may provide care and maintenance in accordance with the regulations to a person who is 18 years of age or more if, when the person was 16 or 17 years of age, he or she was eligible for support services prescribed by the regulations, whether or not he or she was receiving such support services.

Resuming receipt

(4) Subject to the terms and conditions in this section, a person who chooses to stop receiving care and maintenance under this section may choose to resume receiving it.

Same

(5) Subsection (4) applies where the person has chosen to stop receiving care and maintenance on one occasion or, at the discretion of the society or agency providing the care and maintenance, on more than one occasion.

Duty to Report

Duty to report child in need of protection

72. (1) Despite the provisions of any other Act, if a person, including a person who performs professional or official duties with respect to children, has reasonable grounds to suspect one of the following, the person shall forthwith report the suspicion and the information on which it is based to a society:

1. The child has suffered physical harm, inflicted by the person having charge of the child or caused by or resulting from that person's,
   i. failure to adequately care for, provide for, supervise or protect the child, or
   ii. pattern of neglect in caring for, providing for, supervising or protecting the child.
2. There is a risk that the child is likely to suffer physical harm inflicted by the person having charge of the child or caused by or resulting from that person's,
   i. failure to adequately care for, provide for, supervise or protect the child, or
   ii. pattern of neglect in caring for, providing for, supervising or protecting the child.
3. The child has been sexually molested or sexually exploited, by the person having charge of the child or by another person where the person having charge of the child knows or should know of the possibility of sexual molestation or sexual exploitation and fails to protect the child.

Note: On a day to be named by proclamation of the Lieutenant Governor, paragraph 3 is repealed by the Statutes of Ontario, 2008, chapter 21, subsection 3(1) and the following substituted:

3. The child has been sexually molested or sexually exploited, including by child pornography, by the person having charge of the child or by another person where the person having charge of the

child knows or should know of the possibility of sexual molestation or sexual exploitation and fails to protect the child.

See: 2008, c. 21, ss. 3(1), 6.

4. There is a risk that the child is likely to be sexually molested or sexually exploited as described in paragraph 3.
5. The child requires medical treatment to cure, prevent or alleviate physical harm or suffering and the child's parent or the person having charge of the child does not provide, or refuses or is unavailable or unable to consent to, the treatment.
6. The child has suffered emotional harm, demonstrated by serious,
   i. anxiety,
   ii. depression,
   iii. withdrawal,
   iv. self-destructive or aggressive behaviour, or
   v. delayed development,

   and there are reasonable grounds to believe that the emotional harm suffered by the child results from the actions, failure to act or pattern of neglect on the part of the child's parent or the person having charge of the child.
7. The child has suffered emotional harm of the kind described in subparagraph i, ii, iii, iv or v of paragraph 6 and the child's parent or the person having charge of the child does not provide, or refuses or is unavailable or unable to consent to, services or treatment to remedy or alleviate the harm.
8. There is a risk that the child is likely to suffer emotional harm of the kind described in subparagraph i, ii, iii, iv or v of paragraph 6 resulting from the actions, failure to act or pattern of neglect on the part of the child's parent or the person having charge of the child.
9. There is a risk that the child is likely to suffer emotional harm of the kind described in subparagraph i, ii, iii, iv or v of paragraph 6 and that the child's parent or the person having charge of the child does not provide, or refuses or is unavailable or unable to consent to, services or treatment to prevent the harm.
10. The child suffers from a mental, emotional or developmental condition that, if not remedied, could seriously impair the child's development and the child's parent or the person having charge of the child does not provide, or refuses or is unavailable or unable to consent to, treatment to remedy or alleviate the condition.
11. The child has been abandoned, the child's parent has died or is unavailable to exercise his or her custodial rights over the child and has not made adequate provision for the child's care and custody, or the child is in a residential placement and the parent refuses or is unable or unwilling to resume the child's care and custody.
12. The child is less than 12 years old and has killed or seriously injured another person or caused serious damage to another person's property, services or treatment are necessary to prevent a recurrence and the child's parent or the person having charge of the child does not provide, or refuses or is unavailable or unable to consent to, those services or treatment.
13. The child is less than 12 years old and has on more than one occasion injured another person or caused loss or damage to another person's property, with the encouragement of the person having charge of the child or because of that person's failure or inability to supervise the child adequately.

Note: On a day to be named by proclamation of the Lieutenant Governor, section 72 is amended by the Statutes of Ontario, 2008, chapter 21, subsection 3(2) by adding the following subsections:

Reporting child pornography

(1.1) In addition to the duty to report under subsection (1), any person who reasonably believes that a representation or material is, or might be, child pornography shall promptly report the information to an organization, agency or person designated by a regulation made under clause 216(c.3).

Seeking out child pornography not required or authorized

(1.2) Nothing in this section requires or authorizes a person to seek out child pornography.

Protection of informant

(1.3) No action lies against a person for providing information in good faith in compliance with subsection (1.1).

Identity of informant

(1.4) Except as required or permitted in the course of a judicial proceeding, in the context of the provision of child welfare services, otherwise by law or with the written consent of an informant, no person shall disclose,

(a) the identity of an informant under subsection (1) or (1.1),

(i) to the family of the child reported to be in need of protection, or

(ii) to the person who is believed to have caused the child to be in need of protection; or

(b) the identity of an informant under subsection (1.1) to the person who possessed or accessed the representation or material that is or might be child pornography.

Retaliation against informant prohibited

(1.5) No person shall dismiss, suspend, demote, discipline, harass, interfere with or otherwise disadvantage an informant under this section.

See: 2008, c. 21, ss. 3(2), 6.

Ongoing duty to report

(2) A person who has additional reasonable grounds to suspect one of the matters set out in subsection (1) shall make a further report under subsection (1) even if he or she has made previous reports with respect to the same child.

Note: On a day to be named by proclamation of the Lieutenant Governor, subsection (2) is repealed by the Statutes of Ontario, 2008, chapter 21, subsection 3(3) and the following substituted:

Ongoing duty to report

(2) A person who has additional reasonable grounds to suspect one of the matters set out in subsection (1) or to believe that a representation or material is, or might be, child pornography under subsection (1.1) shall make a further report under subsection (1) or (1.1) even if he or she has made previous reports with respect to the same child.

See: 2008, c. 21, ss. 3(3), 6.

Person must report directly

(3) A person who has a duty to report a matter under subsection (1) or (2) shall make the report directly to the society and shall not rely on any other person to report on his or her behalf.

Note: On a day to be named by proclamation of the Lieutenant Governor, subsection (3) is repealed by the Statutes of Ontario, 2008, chapter 21, subsection 3(3) and the following substituted:

Person to report directly

(3) A person who has a duty to report under subsection (1) or (2) shall make the report directly to the society, a person who has a duty to report under subsection (1.1) shall make the report directly to any organization, agency or person designated by regulation to receive such reports, and such persons shall not rely on any other person to report on their behalf.

See: 2008, c. 21, ss. 3(3), 6.

Offence

(4) A person referred to in subsection (5) is guilty of an offence if,

(a) he or she contravenes subsection (1) or (2) by not reporting a suspicion; and

(b) the information on which it was based was obtained in the course of his or her professional or official duties.

Note: On a day to be named by proclamation of the Lieutenant Governor, section 72 is amended by the Statutes of Ontario, 2008, chapter 21, subsection 3(4) by adding the following subsections:

Same

(4.1) A person is guilty of an offence if the person fails to report information as required under subsection (1.1).

Same

(4.2) A person is guilty of an offence if the person,

(a) discloses the identity of an informant in contravention of subsection (1.4); or

(b) dismisses, suspends, demotes, disciplines, harasses, interferes with or otherwise disadvantages an informant in contravention of subsection (1.5).

See: 2008, c. 21, ss. 3(4), 6.

Same

(5) Subsection (4) applies to every person who performs professional or official duties with respect to children including,

(a) a health care professional, including a physician, nurse, dentist, pharmacist and psychologist;

(b) a teacher, person appointed to a position designated by a board of education as requiring an early childhood educator, school principal, social worker, family counsellor, operator or employee of a day nursery and youth and recreation worker;

(b.1) a religious official, including a priest, a rabbi and a member of the clergy;

(b.2) a mediator and an arbitrator;

(c) a peace officer and a coroner;

(d) a solicitor; and

(e) a service provider and an employee of a service provider.

Same

(6) In clause (5)(b),

"youth and recreation worker" does not include a volunteer.

Same

(6.1) A director, officer or employee of a corporation who authorizes, permits or concurs in a contravention of an offence under subsection (4) by an employee of the corporation is guilty of an offence.

Note: On a day to be named by proclamation of the Lieutenant Governor, subsection (6.1) is repealed by the Statutes of Ontario, 2008, chapter 21, subsection 3(5) and the following substituted:

Same

(6.1) A director, officer or employee of a corporation who authorizes, permits or concurs in a contravention of an offence under subsection (4) or (4.1) by an employee of the corporation is guilty of an offence.

See: 2008, c. 21, ss. 3(5), 6.

Same

(6.2) A person convicted of an offence under subsection (4) or (6.1) is liable to a fine of not more than $1,000.

Note: On a day to be named by proclamation of the Lieutenant Governor, subsection (6.2) is repealed by the Statutes of Ontario, 2008, chapter 21, subsection 3(6) and the following substituted:

Penalty

(6.2) A person convicted of an offence under subsection (4), (4.1), (4.2) or (6.1) is liable to a fine of not more than $50,000 or to imprisonment for a term of not more than two years, or to both.

See: 2008, c. 21, ss. 3(6), 6.

Section overrides privilege

(7) This section applies although the information reported may be confidential or privileged, and no action for making the report shall be instituted against a person who acts in accordance with this section unless the person acts maliciously or without reasonable grounds for the suspicion.

Exception: solicitor client privilege

(8) Nothing in this section abrogates any privilege that may exist between a solicitor and his or her client.

Conflict

(9) This section prevails despite anything in the *Personal Health Information Protection Act, 2004*.

Note: On a day to be named by proclamation of the Lieutenant Governor, the Act is amended by the Statutes of Ontario, 2008, chapter 21, section 4 by adding the following section:

Action by organization receiving report of child pornography

72.0.1 (1) An organization, agency or person that obtains information on child pornography under subsection 72(1.1) shall review the report and, if it reasonably believes that the representation or material is or might be child pornography, it shall report the matter to a society or a law enforcement agency, or to both as necessary.

Annual report

(2) The organization, agency or person shall prepare and submit to the Minister an annual report with respect to its activities and actions relating to information it obtains on child pornography, and the Minister shall submit the report to the Lieutenant Governor in Council and then table the report in the Assembly if it is in session or, if not, at the next session.

See: 2008, c. 21, ss. 4, 6.

Duty of society

72.1 (1) A society that obtains information that a child in its care and custody is or may be suffering or may have suffered abuse shall forthwith report the information to a Director.

Definition

(2) In this section and sections 73 and 75,

"to suffer abuse," when used in reference to a child, means to be in need of protection within the meaning of clause 37(2)(a), (c), (e), (f), (f.1) or (h).

Duty to report child's death

72.2 A person or society that obtains information that a child has died shall report the information to a coroner if,

(a) a court made an order under this Act denying access to the child by a parent of the child or making the access subject to supervision;

(b) on the application of a society, a court varied the order to grant the access or to make it no longer subject to supervision; and

(c) the child subsequently died as a result of a criminal act committed by a parent or family member who had custody or charge of the child at the time of the act.

Review Teams

Review team

73. (1) In this section,

"review team" means a team established by a society under subsection (2).

Same

(2) Every society shall establish a review team that includes,

(a) persons who are professionally qualified to perform medical, psychological, developmental, educational or social assessments; and

(b) at least one legally qualified medical practitioner.

Chair

(3) The members of a review team shall choose a chair from among themselves.

Duty of team

(4) Whenever a society refers the case of a child who may be suffering or may have suffered abuse to its review team, the

review team or a panel of at least three of its members, designated by the chair, shall,

(a) review the case; and

(b) recommend to the society how the child may be protected.

Disclosure to team permitted

(5) Despite the provisions of any other Act, a person may disclose to a review team or to any of its members information reasonably required for a review under subsection (4).

Subsection overrides privilege

(6) Subsection (5) applies although the information disclosed may be confidential or privileged and no action for disclosing the information shall be instituted against a person who acts in accordance with subsection (5), unless the person acts maliciously or without reasonable grounds.

Where child not to be returned without review or hearing

(7) Where a society with a review team has information that a child placed in its care under subsection 51(2) (temporary care and custody) or subsection 57(1) (order where child in need of protection) may have suffered abuse, the society shall not return the child to the care of the person who had charge of the child at the time of the possible abuse unless,

(a) the society has,

(i) referred the case to its review team, and

(ii) obtained and considered the review team's recommendations; or

(b) the court has terminated the order placing the child in the society's care.

Court-Ordered Access to Records

Record

74. (1) In this section and sections 74.1 and 74.2,

"record" means recorded information, regardless of physical form or characteristics;

"record of personal health information" has the same meaning as in the *Mental Health Act*.

Motion or application, production of record

(2) A Director or a society may at any time make a motion or an application for an order under subsection (3) or (3.1) for the production of a record or part of a record.

Order

(3) Where the court is satisfied that a record or part of a record that is the subject of a motion referred to in subsection (2) contains information that may be relevant to a proceeding under this Part and that the person in possession or control of the record has refused to permit a Director or the society to inspect it, the court may order that the person in possession or control of the record produce it or a specified part of it for inspection and copying by the Director, by the society or by the court.

Same

(3.1) Where the court is satisfied that a record or part of a record that is the subject of an application referred to in subsection (2) may be relevant to assessing compliance with one of the following and that the person in possession or control of the record has refused to permit a Director or the society to inspect it, the court may order that the person in possession or control of the record produce it or a specified part of it for inspection and copying by the Director, by the society or by the court:

1. An order under clause 51(2)(b) or (c) that is subject to supervision.
2. An order under clause 51(2)(c) or (d) with respect to access.
3. A supervision order under section 57.
4. An access order under section 58.
5. An order with respect to access or supervision on an application under section 64 or 65.1.

5.1 A custody order under section 65.2.

6. A restraining order under section 80.

Court may examine record

(4) In considering whether to make an order under subsection (3) or (3.1), the court may examine the record.

Information confidential

(5) No person who obtains information by means of an order made under subsection (3) or (3.1) shall disclose the information except,

(a) as specified in the order; and

(b) in testimony in a proceeding under this Part.

Conflict

(5.1) Subsection (5) prevails despite anything in the *Personal Health Information Protection Act, 2004*.

Application: solicitor client privilege excepted

(6) Subject to subsection (7), this section applies despite any other Act, but nothing in this section abrogates any privilege that may exist between a solicitor and his or her client.

Matters to be considered by court

(7) Where a motion or an application under subsection (2) concerns a record of personal health information, subsection 35(6) (attending physician's statement, hearing) of the *Mental Health Act* applies and the court shall give equal consideration to,

(a) the matters to be considered under subsection 35(7) of that Act; and

(b) the need to protect the child.

Same

(8) Where a motion or an application under subsection (2) concerns a record that is a record of a mental disorder within the meaning of section 183, that section applies and the court shall give equal consideration to,

(a) the matters to be considered under subsection 183(6); and

(b) the need to protect the child.

Warrant for access to record

74.1 (1) The court or a justice of the peace may issue a warrant for access to a record or a specified part of it if the court or justice of the peace is satisfied on the basis of information on oath from a Director or a person designated by a society that there are reasonable grounds to believe that the record or part of the record is relevant to investigate an allegation that a child is or may be in need of protection.

Authority conferred by warrant

(2) The warrant authorizes the Director or the person designated by the society to,

(a) inspect the record specified in the warrant during normal business hours or during the hours specified in the warrant;

(b) make copies from the record in any manner that does not damage the record; and

(c) remove the record for the purpose of making copies.

Return of record

(3) A person who removes a record under clause (2)(c) shall promptly return it after copying it.

Admissibility of copies

(4) A copy of a record that is the subject of a warrant under this section and that is certified as being a true copy of the original by the person who made the copy is admissible in evidence to the same extent as and has the same evidentiary value as the record.

Duration of warrant

(5) The warrant is valid for seven days.

Execution

(6) The Director or the person designated by the society may call on a peace officer for assistance in executing the warrant.

Solicitor-client privilege

(7) This section applies despite any other Act, but nothing in this section abrogates any privilege that may exist between a solicitor and his or her client.

Matters to be considered

(8) If a warrant issued under this section concerns a record of personal health information and the warrant is challenged under subsection 35(6) (attending physician's statement, hearing) of the *Mental Health Act*, equal consideration shall be given to,

(a) the matters set out in subsection 35(7) of that Act; and

(b) the need to protect the child.

Same

(9) If a warrant issued under this section concerns a record of a mental disorder within the meaning of section 183 and the warrant is challenged under section 183, equal consideration shall be given to,

(a) the matters set out in subsection 183(6); and

(b) the need to protect the child.

Telewarrant

74.2 (1) Where a Director or a person designated by a society believes that there are reasonable grounds for the issuance of a warrant under section 74.1 and that it would be impracticable to appear personally before the court or a justice of the peace to make application for a warrant in accordance with section 74.1, the Director or person designated by the society may submit an information on oath by telephone or other means of telecommunication to a justice designated for the purpose by the Chief Justice of the Ontario Court of Justice.

Same

(2) The information shall,

(a) include a statement of the grounds to believe that the record or part of the record is relevant to investigate an allegation that a child is or may be in need of protection; and

(b) set out the circumstances that make it impracticable for the Director or person designated by the society to appear personally before a court or justice of the peace.

Warrant to be issued

(3) The justice may issue a warrant for access to the record or the specified part of it if the justice is satisfied that the application discloses,

(a) reasonable grounds to believe that the record or the part of a record is relevant to investigate an allegation that a child is or may be in need of protection; and

(b) reasonable grounds to dispense with personal appearance for the purpose of an application under section 74.1.

Validity of warrant

(4) A warrant issued under this section is not subject to challenge by reason only that there were not reasonable grounds to dispense with personal appearance for the purpose of an application under section 74.1.

Application of provisions

(5) Subsections 74.1(2) to (9) apply with necessary modifications with respect to a warrant issued under this section.

Definition

(6) In this section,

"justice" means justice of the peace, a judge of the Ontario Court of Justice or a judge of the Family Court of the Superior Court of Justice.

Child Abuse Register

Register

75. (1) In this section and in section 76,

"Director" means the person appointed under subsection (2);

"register" means the register maintained under subsection (5);

"registered person" means a person identified in the register, but does not include,

(a) a person who reports to a society under subsection 72(2) or (3) and is not the subject of the report, or

(b) the child who is the subject of a report.

Director

(2) The Minister may appoint an employee of the Ministry as Director for the purposes of this section.

Duty of society

(3) A society that receives a report under section 72 that a child, including a child in the society's care, is or may be suffering or may have suffered abuse shall forthwith verify the reported information, or ensure that the information is verified by another society, in the manner determined by the Director, and if the information is verified, the society that verified it shall forthwith report it to the Director in the prescribed form.

Protection from liability

(4) No action or other proceeding for damages shall be instituted against an officer or employee of a society, acting in good faith, for an act done in the execution or intended execution of the duty imposed on the society by subsection (3) or for an alleged neglect or default of that duty.

Child abuse register

(5) The Director shall maintain a register in the manner prescribed by the regulations for the purpose of recording information reported to the Director under subsection (3), but the register shall not contain information that has the effect of identifying a person who reports to a society under subsection 72(2) or (3) and is not the subject of the report.

Register confidential

(6) Despite any other Act, no person shall inspect, remove, alter or permit the inspection, removal or alteration of information maintained in the register, or disclose or permit the disclosure of information that the person obtained from the register, except as this section authorizes.

Coroner's inquest, etc.

(7) A person who is,

(a) a coroner, or a legally qualified medical practitioner or peace officer authorized in writing by a coroner, acting in connection with an investigation or inquest under the *Coroners Act*; or

(b) the Children's Lawyer or the Children's Lawyer's authorized agent,

may inspect, remove and disclose information in the register in accordance with his or her authority.

Minister or Director may permit access to register

(8) The Minister or the Director may permit,

(a) a person who is employed by,

(i) the Ministry,

(ii) a society, or

(iii) a recognized child protection agency outside Ontario; or

(b) a person who is providing or proposes to provide counselling or treatment to a registered person,

to inspect and remove information in the register and to disclose the information to a person referred to in subsection (7) or to another person referred to in this subsection, subject to such terms and conditions as the Director may impose.

Director may disclose information

(9) The Minister or the Director may disclose information in the register to a person referred to in subsection (7) or (8).

Research

(10) A person who is engaged in research may, with the Director's written approval, inspect and use the information in the register, but shall not,

(a) use or communicate the information for any purpose except research, academic pursuits or the compilation of statistical data; or

(b) communicate any information that may have the effect of identifying a person named in the register.

Registered person

(11) A child, a registered person or the child's or registered person's solicitor or agent may inspect only the information in the register that refers to the child or registered person.

Physician

(12) A legally qualified medical practitioner may, with the Director's written approval, inspect the information in the register that is specified by the Director.

Amendment of register

(13) The Director or an employee of the Ministry acting under the Director's authority,

(a) shall remove a name from or otherwise amend the register where the regulations require the removal or amendment; and

(b) may amend the register to correct an error.

Register inadmissible: exceptions

(14) The register shall not be admitted into evidence in a proceeding except,

(a) to prove compliance or non-compliance with this section;

(b) in a hearing or appeal under section 76;

(c) in a proceeding under the *Coroners Act*; or

(d) in a proceeding referred to in section 81 (recovery on child's behalf).

Hearing re registered person

76. (1) In this section,

"hearing" means a hearing held under clause (4)(b).

Notice to registered person

(2) Where an entry is made in the register, the Director shall forthwith give written notice to each registered person referred to in the entry indicating that,

(a) the person is identified in the register;

(b) the person or the person's solicitor or agent is entitled to inspect the information in the register that refers to or identifies the person; and

(c) the person is entitled to request that the Director remove the person's name from or otherwise amend the register.

Request to amend register

(3) A registered person who receives notice under subsection (2) may request that the Director remove the person's name from or otherwise amend the register.

Director's response

(4) On receiving a request under subsection (3), the Director may,

(a) grant the request; or

(b) hold a hearing, on ten days written notice to the parties, to determine whether to grant or refuse the request.

Delegation

(5) The Director may authorize another person to hold a hearing and exercise the Director's powers and duties under subsection (8).

Procedure

(6) The *Statutory Powers Procedure Act* applies to a hearing and a hearing shall be conducted in accordance with the prescribed practices and procedures.

Hearing

(7) The parties to a hearing are,

(a) the registered person;

(b) the society that verified the information referring to or identifying the registered person; and

(c) any other person specified by the Director.

Director's decision

(8) Where the Director determines, after holding a hearing, that the information in the register with respect to a registered person is in error or should not be in the register, the Director shall remove the registered person's name from or otherwise amend the register, and may order that the society's records be amended to reflect the Director's decision.

Appeal to Divisional Court

(9) A party to a hearing may appeal the Director's decision to the Divisional Court.

Hearing private

(10) A hearing or appeal under this section shall be held in the absence of the public and no media representative shall be permitted to attend.

Publication

(11) No person shall publish or make public information that has the effect of identifying a witness at or a participant in a hearing, or a party to a hearing other than a society.

Record inadmissible: exception

(12) The record of a hearing or appeal under this section shall not be admitted into evidence in any other proceeding except a proceeding under clause 85(1)(d) (confidentiality of register) or clause 85(1)(e) (amendment of society's records).

Powers of Director

Director's power to transfer

77. (1) A Director may direct, in the best interests of a child in the care or supervision of a society, that the child,

(a) be transferred to the care or supervision of another society; or

(b) be transferred from one placement to another placement designated by the Director.

Criteria

(2) In determining whether to direct a transfer under clause (1)(b), the Director shall take into account,

(a) the length of time the child has spent in the existing placement;

(b) the views of the foster parents; and

(c) the views and preferences of the child, where they are reasonably ascertainable.

Homemakers

Homemaker

78. (1) In this section,

"homemaker" means a person who is approved by a Director or local director for the purposes of this section.

Homemaker may remain on premises

(2) Where it appears to a person entering premises under section 40 or 44 that,

(a) a child who in the person's opinion is unable to care for himself or herself has been left on the premises without competent care or supervision; and

(b) no person having charge of the child is available or able to consent to the placement of a homemaker on the premises,

the person may, instead of taking the child to a place of safety,

(c) remain on the premises; or

(d) arrange with a society for the placement of a homemaker on the premises.

Homemaker's authority

(3) A homemaker who remains or is placed on premises under subsection (2) may enter and live there, carry on normal housekeeping activities that are reasonably necessary for the care of any child on the premises and exercise reasonable control and discipline over any such child.

Protection from personal liability

(4) No action shall be instituted against a homemaker who remains or is placed on premises under subsection (2) for,

(a) entering and living on the premises;

(b) anything done or omitted in connection with normal housekeeping activities on the premises;

(c) providing goods and services reasonably necessary for the care of any child on the premises; or

(d) the exercise of reasonable control and discipline over any child on the premises,

so long as the homemaker acts in good faith with reasonable care in the circumstances.

Notice to person having charge of child

(5) Where a homemaker remains or is placed on premises under subsection (2), the society shall forthwith notify or make reasonable efforts to notify the person last having charge of the child that a homemaker has been placed on the premises.

Court order, etc.

(6) Where a child with whom a homemaker has been placed under subsection (2),

(a) is found not to be in need of protection, the homemaker shall leave the premises; or

(b) is found to be in need of protection, the court may authorize the homemaker to remain on the premises until,

(i) a specified day not more than thirty days from the date of the order, or

(ii) a person who is entitled to custody of the child returns to care for the child,

whichever is sooner.

Extension

(7) Where no person returns to care for the child before the day specified in an order under clause (6)(b), the court may,

(a) extend the order; or

(b) hold a further hearing under section 47 and make an order under section 57.

Offences, Restraining Orders, Recovery on Child's Behalf

Abuse, failure to provide for reasonable care, etc.

Definition

79. (1) In this section,

"abuse" means a state or condition of being physically harmed, sexually molested or sexually exploited.

Child abuse

(2) No person having charge of a child shall,

(a) inflict abuse on the child; or

(b) by failing to care and provide for or supervise and protect the child adequately,

(i) permit the child to suffer abuse, or

(ii) permit the child to suffer from a mental, emotional or developmental condition that, if not remedied, could seriously impair the child's development.

Leaving child unattended

(3) No person having charge of a child less than sixteen years of age shall leave the child without making provision for his or her supervision and care that is reasonable in the circumstances.

Reverse onus

(4) Where a person is charged with contravening subsection (3) and the child is less than ten years of age, the onus of establishing that the person made provision for the child's supervision and care that was reasonable in the circumstances rests with the person.

Allowing child to loiter, etc.

(5) No parent of a child less than sixteen years of age shall permit the child to,

(a) loiter in a public place between the hours of midnight and 6 a.m.; or

(b) be in a place of public entertainment between the hours of midnight and 6 a.m., unless the parent accompanies the child or authorizes a specified individual eighteen years of age or older to accompany the child.

Police may take child home or to place of safety

(6) Where a child who is actually or apparently less than sixteen years of age is in a place to which the public has access between the hours of midnight and 6 a.m. and is not accompanied by a person described in clause (5)(b), a peace officer may apprehend the child without a warrant and proceed as if the child had been apprehended under subsection 42(1).

Child protection hearing

(7) The court may, in connection with a case arising under subsection (2), (3) or (5), proceed under this Part as if an application had been made under subsection 40(1) (child protection proceeding) in respect of the child.

Restraining order

80. (1) Instead of making an order under subsection 57(1) or section 65.2 or in addition to making a temporary order under subsection 51(2) or an order under subsection 57(1) or section 65.2, the court may make one or more of the following orders in the child's best interests:

1. An order restraining or prohibiting a person's access to or contact with the child, and may include in the or-

der such directions as the court considers appropriate for implementing the order and protecting the child.

2. An order restraining or prohibiting a person's contact with the person who has lawful custody of the child following a temporary order under subsection 51(2) or an order under subsection 57(1) or clause 65.2(1)(a) or (b).

Idem: notice

(2) An order shall not be made under subsection (1) unless notice of the proceeding has been served personally on the person to be named in the order.

Duration of the order

(3) An order made under subsection (1) shall continue in force for such period as the court considers in the best interests of the child and,

(a) if the order is made in addition to a temporary order under subsection 51(2) or an order made under subsection 57(1) or clause 65.2(1)(a), (b) or (c), the order may provide that it continues in force, unless it is varied, extended or terminated by the court, as long as the temporary order under subsection 51(2) or the order under subsection 57(1) or clause 65.2(1)(a), (b) or (c), as the case may be, remains in force; or

(b) if the order is made instead of an order under subsection 57(1) or clause 65.2(1)(a), (b) or (c) or if the order is made in addition to an order under clause 65.2(1)(d), the order may provide that it continues in force until it is varied or terminated by the court.

Extension, variation and termination

(4) An application for the extension, variation or termination of an order made under subsection (1) may be made by,

(a) the person who is the subject of the order;
(b) the child;
(c) the person having charge of the child;
(d) a society;
(e) a Director; or
(f) where the child is an Indian or a native person, a representative chosen by the child's band or native community.

Idem

(5) Where an application is made under subsection (4), the court may, in the child's best interests,

(a) extend the order for such period as the court considers to be in the best interests of the child, in the case of an order described in clause (3)(a); or
(b) vary or terminate the order.

Child in society's care not to be returned while order in force

(6) Where a society has care of a child and an order made under subsection (1) prohibiting a person's access to the child is in force, the society shall not return the child to the care of,

(a) the person named in the order; or
(b) a person who may permit that person to have access to the child.

Recovery because of abuse

81. (1) In this section,

"to suffer abuse," when used in reference to a child, means to be in need of protection within the meaning of clause 37(2)(a), (c), (e), (f), (f.1) or (h).

Recovery on child's behalf

(2) When the Children's Lawyer is of the opinion that a child has a cause of action or other claim because the child has suffered abuse, the Children's Lawyer may, if he or she considers it to be in the child's best interests, institute and conduct proceedings on the child's behalf for the recovery of damages or other compensation.

Idem: society

(3) Where a child is in a society's care and custody, subsection (2) also applies to the society with necessary modifications.

Prohibition

82. No person shall place a child in the care and custody of a society, and no society shall take a child into its care and custody, except,

(a) in accordance with this Part; or
(b) under an agreement made under subsection 29(1) or 30(1) (temporary care or special needs agreement) of Part II (Voluntary Access to Services).

Offence

83. If a child is the subject of an order for society wardship under subsection 57(1) or an order for society supervision or Crown wardship under that subsection or subsection 65.2(1), no person shall,

(a) induce or attempt to induce the child to leave the care of the person with whom the child is placed by the court or by the society, as the case may be;
(b) detain or harbour the child after the person or society referred to in clause (a) requires that the child be returned;
(c) interfere with the child or remove or attempt to remove the child from any place; or
(d) for the purpose of interfering with the child, visit or communicate with the person referred to in clause (a).

Offence

84. No person shall,

(a) knowingly give false information in an application under this Part; or
(b) obstruct, interfere with or attempt to obstruct or interfere with a child protection worker or a peace officer who is acting under section 40, 41, 42, 43 or 44.

Offences

85. (1) A person who contravenes,

(a) an order for access made under subsection 58(1);

(b) Repealed.

(c) subsection 74(5) (disclosure of information obtained by court order);

(d) subsection 75(6) or (10) (confidentiality of child abuse register);

(e) an order made under subsection 76(8) (amendment of society's records);

(f) subsection 79(3) or (5) (leaving child unattended, etc.);

(g) a restraining order made under subsection 80(1);

(h) section 82(unauthorized placement);

(i) any provision of section 83 (interference with child, etc.); or

(j) clause 84(a) or (b),

and a director, officer or employee of a corporation who authorizes, permits or concurs in such a contravention by the corporation is guilty of an offence and on conviction is liable to a fine of not more than $1,000 or to imprisonment for a term of not more than one year, or to both.

Idem

(2) A person who contravenes subsection 79(2) (child abuse), and a director, officer or employee of a corporation who authorizes, permits or concurs in such a contravention by the corporation is guilty of an offence and on conviction is liable to a fine of not more than $2,000 or to imprisonment for a term of not more than two years, or to both.

Idem

(3) A person who contravenes subsection 45(8) or 76(11) (publication of identifying information) or an order prohibiting publication made under clause 45(7)(c) or subsection 45(9), and a director, officer or employee of a corporation who authorizes, permits or concurs in such a contravention by the corporation, is guilty of an offence and on conviction is liable to a fine of not more than $10,000 or to imprisonment for a term of not more than three years, or to both.

Child's Religious Faith

How child's religious faith determined

86. (1) For the purposes of this section, a child shall be deemed to have the religious faith agreed upon by the child's parent, but where there is no agreement or the court cannot readily determine what the religious faith agreed upon is or whether any religious faith is agreed upon, the court may decide what the child's religious faith is, if any, on the basis of the child's circumstances.

Child's wishes to be consulted

(2) The court shall consider the child's views and wishes, if they can be reasonably ascertained, in determining what the child's religious faith is, if any.

Religious faith of child

(3) A Protestant child shall not be committed under this Part to the care of a Roman Catholic society or institution and a Roman Catholic child shall not be committed under this Part to a Protestant society or institution, and a Protestant child shall not be placed in a foster home with a Roman Catholic family and a Roman Catholic child shall not be placed in a foster home with a Protestant family, and, where a child committed under this Part is other than Protestant or Roman Catholic, the child shall be placed where practicable with a family of his or her own religious faith, if any.

Where only one society

(4) Subsection (3) does not apply to the commitment of a child to the care of a society in a municipality in which there is only one society.

Director's discretion re foster placement

(5) Where a society,

(a) is unable to place a child in a suitable foster home within a reasonable time because of the operation of subsection (3); and

(b) would be able to place the child in a suitable foster home but for the operation of subsection (3),

the society may apply to a Director who may order that subsection (3) does not apply to the child in respect of the placement.

Injunctions

Injunction

87. (1) The Superior Court of Justice may grant an injunction to restrain a person from contravening section 83, on the society's application.

Variation, etc.

(2) The court may vary or terminate an order made under subsection (1), on any person's application.

PART IV YOUTH JUSTICE

Definitions

88. In this Part,

"bailiff" means a bailiff appointed under clause 90(1)(c);

"Board" means the Custody Review Board established under subsection 96(1);

"probation officer" means,

(a) a person appointed or designated by the Lieutenant Governor in Council or his or her delegate to perform any of the duties or functions of a youth worker under the *Young Offenders Act* (Canada) or under the federal Act, or

(b) a probation officer appointed under clause 90(1)(b);

"services and programs" means services and programs provided pursuant to the *Young Offenders Act* (Canada), the federal Act or the *Provincial Offences Act* and other related services and programs.

Programs and Officers

Services and programs

89. (1) The Minister may,

(a) establish, operate and maintain services and programs; and

(b) make agreements with persons for the provision of services and programs,

for or on behalf of young persons for the purposes of the *Young Offenders Act* (Canada), the federal Act and the *Provincial Offences Act*, and may make payments for those services and programs out of legislative appropriations.

Secure and open temporary detention programs

(2) The Minister may establish,

(a) secure temporary detention programs, in which restrictions are continuously imposed on the liberty of young persons by physical barriers, close staff supervision or limited access to the community; and

(b) open temporary detention programs, in which restrictions that are less stringent than in a secure temporary detention program are imposed on the liberty of young persons,

in places of temporary detention.

Secure custody programs

(3) The Minister may establish secure custody programs in places of secure custody.

Open custody programs

(4) The Minister may establish open custody programs in places of open custody.

Where locking up permitted

(5) A place of secure custody and a place of secure temporary detention may be locked for the detention of young persons.

Appointments by Minister

90. (1) The Minister may appoint any person or class of persons as,

(a) a provincial director, to perform any or all of the duties and functions of a provincial director,

(i) under the federal Act,

(ii) under the *Young Offenders Act* (Canada), and

(iii) under this Act and the regulations;

(b) a probation officer, to perform any or all of the duties and functions,

(i) of a youth worker under the federal Act and under the *Young Offenders Act* (Canada),

(ii) of a probation officer for the purpose of dealing with young persons under the *Provincial Offences Act*, and

(iii) of a probation officer under this Act and the regulations; and

(c) a bailiff, to perform any or all of the duties and functions of a bailiff under the regulations.

Limitations, etc., on appointments

(2) The Minister may set out in an appointment made under subsection (1) any conditions or limitations to which it is subject.

Probation officer and bailiff have powers of peace officer

(3) While performing their duties and functions, a probation officer appointed under clause (1)(b) and a bailiff appointed under clause (1)(c) have the powers of a peace officer.

Designation of peace officers

(3.1) The Minister may designate in writing,

(a) a person who is an employee in the Ministry or is employed in a place of open custody, of secure custody or of temporary detention to be a peace officer while performing the person's duties and functions; or

(b) a class of persons, from among the persons described in clause (a), to be peace officers while performing their duties and functions,

and may set out in the designation any conditions or limitations to which it is subject.

Remuneration and expenses

(4) The remuneration and expenses of a person appointed under subsection (1) who is not a public servant employed under Part III of the *Public Service of Ontario Act, 2006* shall be fixed by the Minister and shall be paid out of legislative appropriations.

91. Repealed.

Reports and information

92. A person in charge of a service or program provided under subsection 89(1), a person in charge of a place of temporary detention, open custody or secure custody, a bailiff and a probation officer,

(a) shall make the prescribed reports and furnish the prescribed information to the Minister, in the prescribed form and at the prescribed intervals; and

(b) shall make a report to the Minister whenever the Minister requests it, in the form and containing the information specified by the Minister.

Temporary Detention

Open and secure detention

Open detention unless provincial director determines otherwise

93. (1) A young person who is detained under the federal Act or the *Young Offenders Act* (Canada) in a place of temporary detention shall be detained in a place of open temporary detention unless a provincial director determines under subsection (2) that the young person is to be detained in a place of secure temporary detention.

Where secure detention available

(2) A provincial director may detain a young person in a place of secure temporary detention if the provincial director is satisfied that it is necessary on one of the following grounds:

1. The young person is charged with an offence for which an adult would be liable to imprisonment for five years or more and,
   i. the offence includes causing or attempting to cause serious bodily harm to another person,
   ii. the young person has, at any time, failed to appear in court when required to do so under the federal Act or the *Young Offenders Act* (Canada) or escaped or attempted to escape from lawful detention, or
   iii. the young person has, within the 12 months immediately preceding the offence on which the current charge is based, been convicted of an offence for which an adult would be liable to imprisonment for five years or more.
2. The young person is detained in a place of temporary detention and leaves or attempts to leave without the consent of the person in charge or is charged with having escaped or attempting to escape from lawful custody or being unlawfully at large under the *Criminal Code* (Canada).
3. The provincial director is satisfied, having regard to all the circumstances, including any substantial likelihood the young person will commit a criminal offence or interfere with the administration of justice if placed in a place of open temporary detention, that it is necessary to detain the young person in a place of secure temporary detention,
   i. to ensure the young person's attendance at court,
   ii. for the protection and safety of the public, or
   iii. for the safety or security within a place of temporary detention.

Idem

(3) Despite subsection (1), a young person who is apprehended because he or she has left or has not returned to a place of secure custody may be detained in a place of secure temporary detention until he or she is returned to the first-named place of custody.

Idem

(4) Despite subsection (1), a young person who is detained under the federal Act or under the *Young Offenders Act* (Canada) in a place of temporary detention may be detained in a place of secure temporary detention for a period not exceeding twenty-four hours while a provincial director makes a determination in respect of the young person under subsection (2).

Review by youth justice court

(5) A young person who is being detained in a place of secure temporary detention and who is brought before a youth justice court for a review of an order for detention made under the federal Act or the *Criminal Code* (Canada) may request that the youth justice court review the level of his or her detention.

Same

(6) The youth justice court conducting a review of an order for detention may confirm the provincial director's decision under subsection (2) or may direct that the young person be transferred to a place of open temporary detention.

Application for return to secure temporary detention

(7) A provincial director may apply to a youth justice court for a review of an order directing that a young person be transferred to a place of open temporary detention under subsection (6) on the basis that,

(a) the provincial director is satisfied that because of a material change in the circumstances; or

(b) on any other grounds that the provincial director considers appropriate,

it is necessary that the young person be returned to a place of secure temporary detention.

Same

(8) The youth justice court conducting a review of an order transferring a young person to a place of open temporary detention may confirm the court's decision under subsection (6) or may direct that the young person be transferred to a place of secure temporary detention.

Custody

Detention under *Provincial Offences Act*

Pre-trial detention

94. (1) Where a young person is ordered to be detained in custody under subsection 150(4) (order for detention) or 151(2) (further orders) of the *Provincial Offences Act*, the young person shall be detained in a place of temporary detention.

Open custody for provincial offences

(2) Where a young person is sentenced to a term of imprisonment under the *Provincial Offences Act*,

(a) the term of imprisonment shall be served in a place of open custody, subject to subsections (3) and (4);

(b) section 91 of the federal Act applies with necessary modifications; and

(c) sections 28 (remission) and 28.1 (determinations of remission) and Part III (Ontario Parole and Earned Release Board) of the *Ministry of Correctional Services Act* apply with necessary modifications.

Transfer to place of secure custody

(3) Where a young person is placed in open custody under clause (2)(a), the provincial director may transfer the young person to a place of secure custody if, in the opinion of the provincial director, the transfer is necessary for the safety of the young person or the safety of others in the place of open custody.

Concurrent terms

(4) Where a young person is committed to secure custody under the *Young Offenders Act* (Canada) or under the federal Act and is sentenced concurrently to a term of imprisonment under the *Provincial Offences Act*, the term of imprisonment under the *Provincial Offences Act* shall be served in the same place as the disposition under the *Young Offenders Act* (Canada) or the sentence under the federal Act.

Young persons in open custody

95. Where a young person is sentenced to a term of imprisonment for breach of probation under clause 75(d) of the *Provincial Offences Act*, to be served in open custody as set out in section 103 of that Act,

(a) the young person shall be held in a place of open custody specified by a provincial director; and

(b) the provisions of section 91 (reintegration leave) of the federal Act apply with necessary modifications.

Custody Review Board

Custody Review Board

96. (1) The Custody Review Board is continued under the name Custody Review Board in English and Commission de révision des placements sous garde in French and shall have the powers and duties given to it by this Part and the regulations.

Chair and vice-chairs

(2) The Board shall be composed of the prescribed number of members who shall be appointed by the Lieutenant Governor in Council.

Members

(3) The Lieutenant Governor in Council may appoint a member of the Board as chair and may appoint one or more other members as vice-chairs.

(4) Repealed.

Quorum

(5) The prescribed number of members of the Board are a quorum.

Remuneration

(6) The chair and vice-chairs and the other members of the Board shall be paid the remuneration determined by the Lieutenant Governor in Council and are entitled to their reasonable and necessary travelling and living expenses while attending meetings or otherwise engaged in the work of the Board.

Duties of Board

(7) The Board shall conduct reviews under section 97 and perform such other duties as are assigned to it by the regulations.

Application to Board

97. (1) A young person may apply to the Board for a review of,

(a) Repealed.

(b) the particular place where the young person is held or to which the young person has been transferred;

(c) a provincial director's refusal to authorize the young person's temporary release under section 35 of the federal Act; or

(d) the young person's transfer from a place of open custody to a place of secure custody under subsection 24.2(9) of the federal Act,

within thirty days of the decision, placement or transfer, as the case may be.

Duty of Board

(2) The Board shall conduct a review with respect to an application made under subsection (1) and may do so by holding a hearing.

Idem

(3) The Board shall advise the young person whether it intends to hold a hearing or not within ten days of receiving the young person's application.

Procedure

(4) The *Statutory Powers Procedure Act* does not apply to a hearing held under subsection (2).

Idem

(5) The Board shall complete its review and make a determination within thirty days of receiving a young person's application, unless,

(a) the Board holds a hearing with respect to the application; and

(b) the young person and the provincial director whose decision is being reviewed consent to a longer period for the Board's determination.

Board's recommendations

(6) After conducting a review under subsection (2), the Board may,

(a) recommend to the provincial director,

(i) where the Board is of the opinion that the place where the young person is held or to which he or she has been transferred is not appropriate to meet the young person's needs, that the young person be transferred to another place,

(ii) that the young person's temporary release be authorized under section 35 of the *Young Offenders Act*

(Canada) or the young person's reintegration leave be authorized under section 91 of the federal Act, or

(iii) where the young person has been transferred as described in clause (1)(d), that the young person be returned to a place of open custody; or

(b) confirm the decision, placement or transfer.

Apprehension of Young Persons who are Absent from Custody without Permission

Apprehension

Apprehension of young person absent from place of temporary detention

98. (1) A peace officer, the person in charge of a place of temporary detention or that person's delegate, who believes on reasonable and probable grounds that a young person detained under the *Young Offenders Act* (Canada) or the federal Act or the *Provincial Offences Act* in a place of temporary detention has left the place without the consent of the person in charge and fails or refuses to return there may apprehend the young person with or without a warrant and take the young person or arrange for the young person to be taken to a place of temporary detention.

Idem: place of open custody

(2) A peace officer, the person in charge of a place of open custody or that person's delegate, who believes on reasonable and probable grounds that a young person held in a place of open custody as described in section 95,

(a) has left the place without the consent of the person in charge and fails or refuses to return there; or

(b) fails or refuses to return to the place of open custody upon completion of a period of reintegration leave under clause 95(b),

may apprehend the young person with or without a warrant and take the young person or arrange for the young person to be taken to a place of open custody or a place of temporary detention.

Young person to be returned within forty-eight hours

(3) A young person who is apprehended under this section shall be returned to the place from which he or she is absent within forty-eight hours after being apprehended unless the provincial director detains the young person in secure temporary detention under paragraph 2 of subsection 93(2).

Warrant to apprehend young person

(4) A justice of the peace who is satisfied on the basis of a sworn information that there are reasonable and probable grounds to believe that a young person held in a place of temporary detention or open custody,

(a) has left the place without the consent of the person in charge and fails or refuses to return there; or

(b) fails or refuses to return to a place of open custody upon completion of a period of reintegration leave under clause 95(b),

may issue a warrant authorizing a peace officer, the person in charge of the place of temporary detention or open custody or that person's delegate to apprehend the young person.

Authority to enter, etc.

(5) Where a person authorized to apprehend a young person under subsection (1) or (2) believes on reasonable and probable grounds that a young person referred to in the relevant subsection is on any premises, the person may with or without a warrant enter the premises, by force, if necessary, and search for and remove the young person.

Regulations re exercise of power of entry

(6) A person authorized to enter premises under subsection (5) shall exercise the power of entry in accordance with the regulations.

Inspections and Investigations

Inspections and investigations

98.1 (1) The Minister may designate any person to conduct such inspections or investigations as the Minister may require in connection with the administration of this Part.

Dismissal for cause for obstruction, etc., of inspection

(2) Any person employed in the Ministry who obstructs an inspection or investigation or withholds, destroys, conceals or refuses to furnish any information or thing required for purposes of an inspection or investigation may be dismissed for cause from employment.

PART V RIGHTS OF CHILDREN

Definition

99. In this Part,

"child in care" means a child or young person who is receiving residential services from a service provider and includes,

(a) a child who is in the care of a foster parent, and

(b) a young person who is,

(i) detained in a place of temporary detention under the federal Act,

(ii) committed to a place of secure or open custody designated under subsection 24.1(1) of the *Young Offenders Act* (Canada), whether in accordance with section 88 of the federal Act or otherwise, or

(iii) held in a place of open custody under section 95 of Part IV (Youth Justice).

Locking Up

Locking up restricted

100. (1) No service provider shall detain a child or permit a child to be detained in locked premises in the course of the provision of a service to the child, except as Part IV (Youth Justice) and Part VI (Extraordinary Measures) authorize.

Application of subs. (1)

(2) Subsection (1) does not prohibit the routine locking of premises for security at night.

Corporal Punishment

No corporal punishment

101. No service provider or foster parent shall inflict corporal punishment on a child or permit corporal punishment to be inflicted on a child in the course of the provision of a service to the child.

102. Repealed.

Rights of Children in Care

Rights of communication, etc.

103. (1) A child in care has a right,

(a) to speak in private with, visit and receive visits from members of his or her family regularly, subject to subsection (2);

(b) to speak in private with and receive visits from,

(i) the child's solicitor,

(ii) another person representing the child, including the Provincial Advocate for Children and Youth,

(iii) the Ombudsman appointed under the *Ombudsman Act* and members of the Ombudsman's staff, and

(iv) a member of the Legislative Assembly of Ontario or of the Parliament of Canada; and

(c) to send and receive written communications that are not read, examined or censored by another person, subject to subsections (3) and (4).

When child a Crown ward

(2) A child in care who is a Crown ward is not entitled as of right to speak with, visit or receive visits from a member of his or her family, except under an order for access made under Part III or an openness order or openness agreement made under Part VII.

Opening, etc., of written communication to child

(3) Subject to subsection (4), written communications to a child in care,

(a) may be opened by the service provider or a member of the service provider's staff in the child's presence and may be inspected for articles prohibited by the service provider;

(b) subject to clause (c), may be examined or read by the service provider or a member of the service provider's staff in the child's presence, where the service provider believes on reasonable grounds that the contents of the written communication may cause the child physical or emotional harm;

(c) shall not be examined or read by the service provider or a member of the service provider's staff if it is to or from the child's solicitor; and

(d) shall not be censored or withheld from the child, except that articles prohibited by the service provider may be removed from the written communication and withheld from the child.

Opening, etc., of young person's written communications

(4) Written communications to and from a young person who is detained in a place of temporary detention or held in a place of secure custody or of open custody,

(a) may be opened by the service provider or a member of the service provider's staff in the young person's presence and may be inspected for articles prohibited by the service provider;

(b) may be examined or read by the service provider or a member of the service provider's staff and may be withheld from the recipient in whole or in part where the service provider or the member of their staff believes on reasonable grounds that the contents of the written communications may,

(i) be prejudicial to the best interests of the young person, the public safety or the safety or security of the place of detention or custody, or

(ii) contain communications that are prohibited under the federal act or by court order;

(c) shall not be examined or read under clause (b) if it is to or from the young person's solicitor; and

(d) shall not be opened and inspected under clause (a) or examined or read under clause (b) if it is to or from a person described in subclause (1)(b)(ii), (iii) or (iv).

Definition

(5) In this section,

"written communications" includes mail and electronic communication in any form.

Limitations on rights

Conditions and limitations on visitors

103.1 (1) A service provider may impose such conditions and limitations upon persons who are visiting a young person in a place of temporary detention, of open custody or of secure custody as are necessary to ensure the safety of staff or young persons in the facility.

Suspending visits in emergencies

(2) Where a service provider has reasonable grounds to believe there are emergency circumstances within a facility that is a place of temporary detention, of open custody or of secure custody or within the community that may pose a risk to staff or young persons in the facility, the service provider may suspend visits until there are reasonable grounds to believe the emergency has been resolved and there is no longer a risk to staff or young persons in the facility.

Limited exception

(3) Despite subsection (2), the service provider may not suspend visits from,

(a) the Provincial Advocate for Children and Youth and members of his or her staff;

(b) the Ombudsman appointed under the *Ombudsman Act* and members of the Ombudsman's staff; or

(c) a member of the Legislative Assembly of Ontario or of the Parliament of Canada,

unless the provincial director determines that suspension is necessary to ensure public safety or the safety of staff or young persons in the facility.

Personal liberties

104. A child in care has a right,

(a) to have reasonable privacy and possession of his or her own personal property; and

(b) to receive the religious instruction and participate in the religious activities of his or her choice, subject to section 106.

Plan of care

105. (1) A child in care has a right to a plan of care designed to meet the child's particular needs, which shall be prepared within thirty days of the child's admission to the residential placement.

Rights to care

(2) A child in care has a right,

(a) to participate in the development of the child's individual plan of care and in any changes made to it;

(b) to receive meals that are well-balanced, of good quality and appropriate for the child;

(c) to be provided with clothing that is of good quality and appropriate for the child, given the child's size and activities and prevailing weather conditions;

(d) to receive medical and dental care, subject to section 106, at regular intervals and whenever required, in a community setting whenever possible;

(e) to receive an education that corresponds to the child's aptitudes and abilities, in a community setting whenever possible; and

(f) to participate in recreational and athletic activities that are appropriate for the child's aptitudes and interests, in a community setting whenever possible.

Parental consent, etc.

106. Subject to subsection 51(4) and sections 62 and 63 (temporary order, society and Crown wards) of Part III (Child Protection), the parent of a child in care retains any right that he or she may have,

(a) to direct the child's education and religious upbringing; and

(b) to give or refuse consent to medical treatment for the child.

Right to be heard

107. A child in care has a right to be consulted and to express his or her views, to the extent that is practical given the child's level of understanding, whenever significant decisions concerning the child are made, including decisions with respect to medical treatment, education or training or work programs and religion and decisions with respect to the child's discharge from the placement or transfer to another residential placement.

Right to be informed

108. A child in care has a right to be informed, in a language suitable for the child's level of understanding, of,

(a) the child's rights under this Part;

(b) the internal complaints procedure established under subsection 109(1) and the further review available under section 110;

(c) the existence of the office of the Provincial Advocate for Children and Youth;

(d) the review procedures available for children twelve years of age or older under sections 34, 35 and 36 of Part II (Voluntary Access to Services);

(e) the review procedures available under section 97 of Part IV (Youth Justice), in the case of a young person described in clause (b) of the definition of "child in care" in section 99;

(f) the child's responsibilities while in the placement; and

(g) the rules governing day-to-day operation of the residential service, including disciplinary procedures,

upon admission to the residential placement, to the extent that is practical given the child's level of understanding.

Complaint and Review Procedures

Internal complaints procedure

109. (1) A service provider who provides residential services to children or places children in residential placements shall establish a written procedure, in accordance with the regulations, for hearing and dealing with complaints regarding alleged violations of the rights under this Part of children in care.

Idem

(2) A service provider shall conduct a review or ensure that a review is conducted, in accordance with the procedure established under subsection (1), on the complaint of,

(a) a child in care;

(b) the child's parent; or

(c) another person representing the child,

and shall seek to resolve the complaint.

Further review

110. (1) Where a person referred to in subsection 109(2) who makes a complaint and is not satisfied with the result of the review conducted under that subsection requests in writing that the Minister appoint a person to conduct a further review of the complaint, the Minister shall appoint a person who is not employed by the service provider to do so.

Idem

(2) A person appointed under subsection (1) shall review the complaint in accordance with the regulations and may, but is not required to, do so by holding a hearing.

Procedure

(3) The *Statutory Powers Procedure Act* does not apply to a hearing held under subsection (2).

Powers of appointed person

(4) A person appointed under subsection (1) has, for the purposes of the review, all the powers of a program supervisor appointed under subsection 5(2) of Part I (Flexible Services).

Review and report within thirty days

(5) A person appointed under subsection (1) shall, within thirty days after the day of the appointment, complete the review, set out in a report his or her findings and recommendations, including the reasons for not holding a hearing if none was held, and provide copies of the report to,

(a) the person who made the complaint;
(b) the service provider; and
(c) the Minister.

Minister to advise persons affected of any decision

111. (1) Where the Minister decides to take any action with respect to a complaint after receiving a report under subsection 110(5), the Minister shall advise the person who made the complaint and the service provider of the decision.

Remedies preserved

(2) The Minister's decision referred to in subsection (1) does not affect any other remedy that may be available.

PART VI EXTRAORDINARY MEASURES

Definitions

112. In this Part,

"administrator" means the person in charge of a secure treatment program;

"intrusive procedure" means,

(a) a mechanical means of controlling behaviour,
(b) an aversive stimulation technique, or
(c) any other procedure that is prescribed as an intrusive procedure;

"mental disorder" means a substantial disorder of emotional processes, thought or cognition which grossly impairs a person's capacity to make reasoned judgments;

"psychotropic drug" means a drug or combination of drugs prescribed as a psychotropic drug;

"review team" means an interdisciplinary review team established under subsection 129(1);

"secure isolation room" means a locked room approved under subsection 126(1) for use for the secure isolation of children;

"secure treatment program" means a program established or approved by the Minister under subsection 113(1).

Secure Treatment Programs

Minister may establish or approve programs

113. (1) The Minister may,

(a) establish, operate and maintain; or
(b) approve,

programs for the treatment of children with mental disorders, in which continuous restrictions are imposed on the liberty of the children.

Terms and conditions

(2) The Minister may impose terms and conditions on an approval given under subsection (1) and may vary or amend the terms and conditions or impose new terms and conditions at any time.

Admission of children

(3) No child shall be admitted to a secure treatment program except by a court order under section 117 (commitment to secure treatment program) or under section 124 (emergency admission).

Locking up permitted

(4) The premises of a secure treatment program may be locked for the detention of children.

Commitment to Secure Treatment

Application for order for child's commitment

114. (1) Any one of the following persons may, with the administrator's written consent, apply to the court for an order for the child's commitment to a secure treatment program:

1. Where the child is less than sixteen years of age,
   i. the child's parent,
   ii. a person other than an administrator who is caring for the child, if the child's parent consents to the application, or
   iii. a society that has custody of the child under an order made under Part III (Child Protection).
2. Where the child is sixteen years of age or more,
   i. the child,
   ii. the child's parent, if the child consents to the application,
   iii. a society that has custody of the child under an order made under Part III (Child Protection), if the child consents to the application, or
   iv. a physician.

Time for hearing

(2) Where an application is made under subsection (1), the court shall deal with the matter within ten days of the making of an order under subsection (6) (legal representation) or, where no such order is made, within ten days of the making of the application.

Adjournments

(3) The court may adjourn the hearing of an application but shall not adjourn it for more than thirty days unless the applicant and the child consent to the longer adjournment.

Interim order

(4) Where a hearing is adjourned, the court may make a temporary order for the child's commitment to a secure treatment program if the court is satisfied that the child meets the criteria for commitment set out in clauses 117(1)(a) to (f) and, where the child is less than twelve years old, the Minister consents to the child's admission.

Evidence on adjournments

(5) For the purpose of subsection (4), the court may admit and act on evidence that the court considers credible and trustworthy in the circumstances.

Legal representation of child

(6) Where an application is made under subsection (1) in respect of a child who does not have legal representation, the court shall, as soon as practicable and in any event before the hearing of the application, direct that legal representation be provided for the child.

Hearing private

(7) A hearing under this section shall be held in the absence of the public and no media representative shall be permitted to attend.

Child entitled to be present

(8) The child who is the subject of an application under subsection (1) is entitled to be present at the hearing unless,

(a) the court is satisfied that being present at the hearing would cause the child emotional harm; or

(b) the child, after obtaining legal advice, consents in writing to the holding of the hearing in his or her absence.

Court may require child's presence

(9) The court may require a child who has consented to the holding of the hearing in his or her absence under clause (8)(b) to be present at all or part of the hearing.

Oral evidence

115. (1) Where an application is made under subsection 114(1), the court shall deal with the matter by holding a hearing and shall hear oral evidence unless the child, after obtaining legal advice, consents in writing to the making of an order under subsection 117(1) without the hearing of oral evidence, and the consent is filed with the court.

Court may hear oral evidence despite consent

(2) The court may hear oral evidence although the child has given a consent under subsection (1).

Time limitation

(3) A child's consent under subsection (1) is not effective for more than the period referred to in subsection 118(1) (period of commitment).

Assessment

116. (1) The court may, at any time after an application is made under subsection 114(1), order that the child attend within a specified time for an assessment before a specified person who is qualified, in the court's opinion, to perform an assessment to assist the court to determine whether the child should be committed to a secure treatment program and has consented to perform the assessment.

Report

(2) The person performing an assessment under subsection (1) shall make a written report of the assessment to the court within the time specified in the order, which shall not be more than thirty days unless the court is of the opinion that a longer assessment period is necessary.

Who may not perform assessment

(3) The court shall not order an assessment to be performed by a person who provides services in the secure treatment program to which the application relates.

Copies of report

(4) The court shall provide a copy of the report to,

(a) the applicant;

(b) the child, subject to subsection (6);

(c) the child's solicitor;

(d) a parent appearing at the hearing;

(e) a society that has custody of the child under an order made under Part III (Child Protection);

(f) the administrator of the secure treatment program; and

(g) where the child is an Indian or a native person, a representative chosen by the child's band or native community.

Idem

(5) The court may cause a copy of the report to be given to a parent who does not attend the hearing but is, in the court's opinion, actively interested in the proceedings.

Court may withhold report from child

(6) The court may withhold all or part of the report from the child where the court is satisfied that disclosure of all or part of the report to the child would cause the child emotional harm.

Commitment to secure treatment: criteria

117. (1) The court may order that a child be committed to a secure treatment program only where the court is satisfied that,

(a) the child has a mental disorder;

(b) the child has, as a result of the mental disorder, within the forty-five days immediately preceding,

(i) the application under subsection 114(1),

(ii) the child's detention or custody under the *Young Offenders Act* (Canada), under the *Youth Criminal Jus-*

tice Act (Canada) or under the *Provincial Offences Act*, or

(iii) the child's admission to a psychiatric facility under the *Mental Health Act* as an involuntary patient,

caused or attempted to cause serious bodily harm to himself, herself or another person;

(c) the child has,

(i) within the twelve months immediately preceding the application, but on another occasion than that referred to in clause (b), caused, attempted to cause or by words or conduct made a substantial threat to cause serious bodily harm to himself, herself or another person, or

(ii) in committing the act or attempt referred to in clause (b), caused or attempted to cause a person's death;

(d) the secure treatment program would be effective to prevent the child from causing or attempting to cause serious bodily harm to himself, herself or another person;

(e) treatment appropriate for the child's mental disorder is available at the place of secure treatment to which the application relates; and

(f) no less restrictive method of providing treatment appropriate for the child's mental disorder is appropriate in the circumstances.

Where child under twelve

(2) Where the child is less than twelve years old, the court shall not make an order under subsection (1) unless the Minister consents to the child's commitment.

Additional requirement where applicant is physician

(3) Where the applicant is a physician, the court shall not make an order under subsection (1) unless the court is satisfied that the applicant believes the criteria set out in that subsection are met.

Period of commitment

118. (1) The court shall specify in an order under subsection 117(1) the period not exceeding 180 days for which the child shall be committed to the secure treatment program.

Where society is applicant

(2) Where a child is committed to a secure treatment program on a society's application and the period specified in the court's order is greater than sixty days, the child shall be released on a day sixty days after the child's admission to the secure treatment program unless before that day,

(a) the child's parent consents to the child's commitment for a longer period; or

(b) the child is made a Crown or society ward under Part III (Child Protection),

but in no case shall the child be committed to the secure treatment program for longer than the period specified under subsection (1).

How time calculated

(3) In the calculation of a child's period of commitment, time spent in the secure treatment program before an order has been made under section 117 (commitment) or pending an application under section 120 (extension) shall be counted.

Where order expires after eighteenth birthday

(4) A person who is the subject of an order made under subsection 117(1) or 120(5) may be kept in the secure treatment program after attaining the age of eighteen years, until the order expires.

Reasons, plans, etc.

119. (1) Where the court makes an order under subsection 117(1) or 120(5), the court shall give,

(a) reasons for its decision;

(b) a statement of the plan, if any, for the child's care on release from the secure treatment program; and

(c) a statement of the less restrictive alternatives considered by the court, and the reasons for rejecting them.

Plan for care on release

(2) Where no plan for the child's care on release from the secure treatment program is available at the time of the order, the administrator shall, within ninety days of the date of the order, prepare such a plan and file it with the court.

Extension of Period of Commitment

Extension

120. (1) Where a child is the subject of an order made under subsection 117(1) (commitment) or subsection (5),

(a) a person referred to in subsection 114(1), with the administrator's written consent; or

(b) the administrator, with a parent's written consent or, where the child is in a society's lawful custody, the society's consent,

may, before the expiry of the period of commitment, apply for an order extending the child's commitment to the secure treatment program.

Idem

(2) Where a person is kept in the secure treatment program under subsection 118(4) after attaining the age of eighteen years,

(a) the person, with the written consent of the administrator;

(b) the person's parent, with the written consent of the person and the administrator;

(c) a physician, with the written consent of the administrator and the person; or

(d) the administrator, with the written consent of the person,

may, before the expiry of the period of commitment, apply for one further order extending the person's commitment to the secure treatment program.

Child may be kept in program while application pending

(3) Where an application is made under subsection (1) or (2), the child may be kept in the secure treatment program until the application is disposed of.

Ss. 114(3), (6-9), 115, 116 apply

(4) Subsections 114(3), (6), (7), (8) and (9) (hearing) and sections 115 (child's waiver) and 116 (assessment) apply with necessary modifications to an application made under subsection (1) or (2).

Criteria for extension

(5) The court may make an order extending a child's commitment to a secure treatment program only where the court is satisfied that,

(a) the child has a mental disorder;

(b) the secure treatment program would be effective to prevent the child from causing or attempting to cause serious bodily harm to himself, herself or another person;

(c) no less restrictive method of providing treatment appropriate for the child's mental disorder is appropriate in the circumstances;

(d) the child is receiving the treatment proposed at the time of the original order under subsection 117(1), or other appropriate treatment; and

(e) there is an appropriate plan for the child's care on release from the secure treatment program.

Period of extension

(6) The court shall specify in an order under subsection (5) the period not exceeding 180 days for which the child shall be committed to the secure treatment program.

Release by Administrator

Release

Unconditional release by administrator

121. (1) The administrator may release a child from a secure treatment program unconditionally where the administrator,

(a) has given the person with lawful custody of the child reasonable notice of the intention to release him or her; and

(b) is satisfied that,

(i) the child no longer requires the secure treatment program, and

(ii) there is an appropriate plan for the child's care on release from the secure treatment program.

Conditional release

(2) The administrator may release a child from a secure treatment program temporarily for medical or compassionate reasons, or for a trial placement in an open setting, for such period and on such terms and conditions as the administrator determines.

Administrator may release despite court order

(3) Subsections (1) and (2) apply despite an order made under subsection 117(1) (commitment) or 120(5) (extension).

Review of Commitment

Review of commitment

122. (1) Any one of the following persons may apply to the court for an order terminating an order made under subsection 117(1) (commitment) or 120(5) (extension):

1. The child, where the child is twelve years of age or more.
2. The child's parent.
3. The society having care, custody or supervision of the child.

Ss. 114(3), (6-9), 115, 116 apply

(2) Subsections 114(3), (6), (7), (8) and (9) (hearing) and sections 115 (child's waiver) and 116 (assessment) apply with necessary modifications to an application made under subsection (1).

Termination of order

(3) The court shall make an order terminating a child's commitment unless the court is satisfied that,

(a) the child has a mental disorder;

(b) the secure treatment program would continue to be effective to prevent the child from causing or attempting to cause serious bodily harm to himself, herself or another person;

(c) no less restrictive method of providing treatment appropriate for the child's mental disorder is appropriate in the circumstances; and

(d) the child is receiving the treatment proposed at the time of the most recent order under subsection 117(1) or 120(5), or other appropriate treatment.

Idem

(4) In making an order under subsection (3), the court shall consider whether there is an appropriate plan for the child's care on release from the secure treatment program.

Ss. 120(3-6), 121, 122 apply

123. Subsections 120(3), (4), (5) and (6) and sections 121 and 122 apply with necessary modifications to a person who is eighteen years of age or older and committed to a secure treatment program as if the person were a child.

Emergency Admission

Emergency admission

124. (1) Any one of the following persons may apply to the administrator for the emergency admission of a child to a secure treatment program:

1. Where the child is less than sixteen years of age,
   i. the child's parent,
   ii. a person who is caring for the child with a parent's consent,

iii. a child protection worker who has apprehended the child under section 40 of Part III (Child Protection), or
iv. a society that has custody of the child under an order made under Part III.
2. Where the child is sixteen years of age or more,
i. the child,
ii. the child's parent, if the child consents to the application,
iii. a society that has custody of the child under an order made under Part III (Child Protection), if the child consents to the application, or
iv. a physician.

Criteria for admission

(2) The administrator may admit a child to the secure treatment program on an application under subsection (1) for a period not to exceed thirty days where the administrator believes on reasonable grounds that,

(a) the child has a mental disorder;

(b) the child has, as a result of the mental disorder, caused, attempted to cause or by words or conduct made a substantial threat to cause serious bodily harm to himself, herself or another person;

(c) the secure treatment program would be effective to prevent the child from causing or attempting to cause serious bodily harm to himself, herself or another person;

(d) treatment appropriate for the child's mental disorder is available at the place of secure treatment to which the application relates; and

(e) no less restrictive method of providing treatment appropriate for the child's mental disorder is appropriate in the circumstances.

Admission on consent

(3) The administrator may admit the child under subsection (2) although the criterion set out in clause (2)(b) is not met, where,

(a) the other criteria set out in subsection (2) are met;

(b) the child, after obtaining legal advice, consents to his or her admission; and

(c) if the child is less than sixteen years of age, the child's parent or, where the child is in a society's lawful custody, the society consents to the child's admission.

Where child under twelve

(4) Where the child is less than twelve years old, the administrator shall not admit the child under subsection (2) unless the Minister consents to the child's admission.

Additional requirement where applicant is physician

(5) Where the applicant is a physician, the administrator shall not admit the child under subsection (2) unless the administrator is satisfied that the applicant believes the criteria set out in that subsection are met.

Notices required

(6) The administrator shall ensure that within twenty-four hours after a child is admitted to a secure treatment program under subsection (2),

(a) the child is given written notice of his or her right to a review under subsection (9); and

(b) the Provincial Advocate for Children and Youth and the Children's Lawyer are given notice of the admission.

Mandatory advice

(7) The Provincial Advocate for Children and Youth shall ensure that forthwith after the notice is received a person who is not employed by the secure treatment facility explains to the child his or her right to a review in language suitable for the child's level of understanding.

Children's Lawyer to ensure child represented

(8) The Children's Lawyer shall represent the child at the earliest possible opportunity and in any event within five days after receiving a notice under subsection (6) unless the Children's Lawyer is satisfied that another person will provide legal representation for the child within that time.

Application for review

(9) Where a child is admitted to a secure treatment program under this section, any person, including the child, may apply to the Board for an order releasing the child from the secure treatment program.

Child may be kept in program while application pending

(10) Where an application is made under subsection (9), the child may be kept in the secure treatment program until the application is disposed of.

Procedure

(11) Subsections 114(7), (8) and (9) (hearing) and section 115 (waive oral evidence) apply with necessary modifications to an application made under subsection (9).

Time for review

(12) Where an application is made under subsection (9), the Board shall dispose of the matter within five days of the making of the application.

Order

(13) The Board shall make an order releasing the child from the secure treatment program unless the Board is satisfied that the child meets the criteria for emergency admission set out in clauses 124(2)(a) to (e).

Police Assistance

Powers of peace officers, period of commitment

Police may take child for secure treatment

125. (1) A peace officer may take a child to a place where there is a secure treatment program,

(a) for emergency admission, at the request of an applicant referred to in subsection 124(1); or

(b) where an order for the child's commitment to the secure treatment program has been made under section 117.

Apprehension of child who leaves

(2) Where a child who has been admitted to a secure treatment program leaves the facility in which the secure treatment program is located without the consent of the administrator, a peace officer may apprehend the child with or without a warrant and return the child to the facility.

Period of commitment

(3) Where a child is returned to a facility under subsection (2), the time that the child was absent from the facility shall not be taken into account in calculating the period of commitment.

Secure Isolation

Director's approval

126. (1) A Director may approve a locked room that complies with the prescribed standards and is located in premises where an approved service or a service purchased by an approved agency is provided, for use for the secure isolation of children or young persons, on such terms and conditions as the Director determines.

Withdrawal of approval

(2) Where a Director is of the opinion that a secure isolation room is unnecessary or is being used in a manner that contravenes this Part or the regulations, the Director may withdraw the approval given under subsection (1) and shall give the affected service provider notice of the decision, with reasons.

Secure isolation

127. (1) No service provider or foster parent shall isolate in a locked place a child or young person who is in his or her care or permit the child or young person to be isolated in a locked place, except in accordance with this section and the regulations.

Secure treatment, secure custody and secure temporary detention

(2) Subsection (1) does not prohibit the routine locking at night of rooms in the premises of secure treatment programs or in places of secure custody and places of secure temporary detention under Part IV (Youth Justice).

Criteria for use of secure isolation

(3) A child or young person may be placed in a secure isolation room where,

(a) in the service provider's opinion,

(i) the child's or young person's conduct indicates that he or she is likely, in the immediate future, to cause serious property damage or to cause another person serious bodily harm, and

(ii) no less restrictive method of restraining the child or young person is practicable; and

(b) where the child is less than 12 years of age, a Director gives permission for the child to be placed in a secure isolation room because of exceptional circumstances.

One-hour limit

(4) A child or young person who is placed in a secure isolation room shall be released within one hour unless the person in charge of the premises approves the child's or young person's longer isolation in writing and records the reasons for not restraining the child or young person by a less restrictive method.

Continuous observation of child

(5) Subject to subsection (9), the service provider shall ensure that a child or young person who is placed in a secure isolation room is continuously observed by a responsible person.

Review

(6) Where a child or young person is kept in a secure isolation room for more than one hour, the person in charge of the premises shall review the child's or young person's isolation at prescribed intervals.

Release

(7) A child or young person who is placed in a secure isolation room shall be released as soon as the person in charge is satisfied that the child or young person is not likely to cause serious property damage or serious bodily harm in the immediate future.

Maximum periods

(8) Subject to subsection (9), in no event shall a child or young person be kept in a secure isolation room for a period or periods that exceed an aggregate of eight hours in a given 24-hour period or an aggregate of 24 hours in a given week.

Exception

(9) A service provider is not required to comply with subsections (5) and (8) with respect to a young person who is aged 16 years or older and who is held in a place of secure custody or of secure temporary detention, but a service provider shall comply with the prescribed standards and procedures in respect of such young persons who are held in such places.

Review of use of secure isolation

128. (1) A person in charge of premises containing a secure isolation room shall review,

(a) the need for the secure isolation room; and

(b) the prescribed matters,

every three months or, in the case of secure custody or secure temporary detention, every six months from the date on which the secure isolation room is approved under subsection 126(1), shall make a written report of each review to a Director and shall make such additional reports as are prescribed.

(2) Repealed.

Review Teams

Review team

129. (1) A service provider who is approved under subsection 130(1) shall establish an interdisciplinary review team with the duty of reviewing and approving or refusing the proposed use of intrusive procedures.

Idem

(2) A review team shall consist of,

(a) persons employed by the service provider; and

(b) one person who is not employed by the service provider and is approved by the Minister,

and may also include a legally qualified medical practitioner.

Panel

(3) Any three members of a review team may review and approve or refuse the proposed use of an intrusive procedure.

Report to service provider

(4) A review team shall make a report to the service provider concerning every review conducted under subsection (3) and subsection 133(1) (review of certain recommended procedures).

Report to Minister

(5) A review team shall make reports of its activities to the Minister at the prescribed intervals.

130, 131. Repealed.

Psychotropic Drugs

Consents required for use of psychotropic drug

132. (1) A service provider shall not administer or permit the administration of a psychotropic drug to a child in the service provider's care without,

(a) if the child is sixteen years of age or more, the child's consent; or

(b) if the child is less than sixteen years of age, the consent of the child's parent or, where the child is in a society's lawful custody, the society's consent.

Idem

(2) A consent referred to in subsection (1) shall identify the psychotropic drug clearly and shall specify,

(a) what condition the psychotropic drug is intended to alleviate;

(b) the range of intended dosages;

(c) the risks and possible side effects associated with the psychotropic drug, and how they vary with different dosages; and

(d) the frequency with which and the period of time during which the psychotropic drug is to be administered.

Child's views and preferences

(3) A service provider shall not administer or permit the administration of a psychotropic drug to a child in the service provider's care who is less than sixteen years of age or lacks capacity within the meaning of section 4 without first considering the child's views and preferences, where they can be reasonably ascertained, except under subsection (4).

(4), (5) Repealed.

(6) Spent.

Additional Duty of Review Teams

Review of certain recommended procedures

133. (1) Where it is recommended that a child in the care of or regularly receiving services from a service provider who has established a review team undergo,

(a) non-therapeutic medical or chemical experimentation;

(b) psychosurgery;

(c) non-therapeutic sterilization; or

(d) electro-convulsive therapy,

three members of the review team shall review the matter and advise the child's parent or, where the child is in a society's lawful custody, the society, and the service provider of the review team's opinion as to the appropriateness of the recommendation.

Panel to include medical practitioner

(2) One of the members of the review team acting under subsection (1) shall be a legally qualified medical practitioner.

Prohibition

(3) No procedure referred to in subsection (1) shall be carried out in premises where an approved service or a service purchased by an approved agency is provided.

Professional Advisory Board

Professional Advisory Board

134. (1) The Minister may establish a Professional Advisory Board, composed of physicians and other professionals who,

(a) have special knowledge in the use of intrusive procedures and psychotropic drugs;

(b) have demonstrated an informed concern for the welfare and interests of children; and

(c) are not employed by the Ministry.

Chair

(2) The Minister shall appoint one of the members of the Professional Advisory Board as its chair.

Duties of Board

(3) The Professional Advisory Board shall, at the Minister's request,

(a) advise the Minister on,

(i) prescribing procedures as intrusive procedures, and

(ii) making, amending, suspending and revoking approvals under section 130;

(b) investigate and review the use of intrusive procedures and psychotropic drugs and make recommendations to the Minister; and

(c) review the practices and procedures of service providers with respect to,

(i) secure isolation,

(ii) intrusive procedures, and

(iii) psychotropic drugs,

and make recommendations to the Minister.

Request for review

135. Any person may request that the Minister refer the matter of the use of secure isolation or an intrusive procedure in respect of a child, or the administration of a psychotropic drug to a child, to the Professional Advisory Board for investigation and review.

PART VII ADOPTION

Interpretation

136. (1) In this Part,

"birth parent" means a person who satisfies the prescribed criteria;

"birth relative" means,

(a) in respect of a child who has not been adopted, a relative of the child, and

(b) in respect of a child who has been adopted, a person who would have been a relative of the child if the child had not been adopted;

"birth sibling" means, in respect of a person, a child of the same birth parent as the person, and includes a child adopted by the birth parent and a person whom the birth parent has demonstrated a settled intention to treat as a child of his or her family;

"licensee" means the holder of a licence issued under Part IX (Licensing) to place children for adoption;

"openness agreement" means an agreement referred to in section 153.6;

"openness order" means an order made by a court in accordance with this Act for the purposes of facilitating communication or maintaining a relationship between the child and,

(a) a birth parent, birth sibling or birth relative of the child,

(b) a person with whom the child has a significant relationship or emotional tie, including a foster parent of the child or a member of the child's extended family or community, or

(c) if the child is an Indian or native person, a member of the child's band or native community who may not have had a significant relationship or emotional tie with the child in the past but will help the child recognize the importance of his or her Indian or native culture and preserve his or her heritage, traditions and cultural identity;

"spouse" has the same meaning as in Parts I and II of the *Human Rights Code*.

Best interests of child

(2) Where a person is directed in this Part to make an order or determination in the best interests of a child, the person shall take into consideration those of the following circumstances of the case that he or she considers relevant:

1. The child's physical, mental and emotional needs, and the appropriate care or treatment to meet those needs.
2. The child's physical, mental and emotional level of development.
3. The child's cultural background.
4. The religious faith, if any, in which the child is being raised.
5. The importance for the child's development of a positive relationship with a parent and a secure place as a member of a family.
6. The child's relationships by blood or through an adoption order.
7. The importance of continuity in the child's care and the possible effect on the child of disruption of that continuity.
8. The child's views and wishes, if they can be reasonably ascertained.
9. The effects on the child of delay in the disposition of the case.
10. Any other relevant circumstance.

Where child an Indian or native person

(3) Where a person is directed in this Part to make an order or determination in the best interests of a child and the child is an Indian or native person, the person shall take into consideration the importance, in recognition of the uniqueness of Indian and native culture, heritage and traditions, of preserving the child's cultural identity.

Consent to Adoption

Consents

137. (1) In this section,

"parent," when used in reference to a child, means each of,

(a) the child's mother,

(b) an individual described in one of paragraphs 1 to 6 of subsection 8(1) of the *Children's Law Reform Act*, unless it is proved on a balance of probabilities that he is not the child's natural father,

(c) the individual having lawful custody of the child,

(d) an individual who, during the twelve months before the child is placed for adoption under this Part, has demonstrated a settled intention to treat the child as a child of his or her family, or has acknowledged parentage of the child and provided for the child's support,

(e) an individual who, under a written agreement or a court order, is required to provide for the child, has custody of the child or has a right of access to the child, and

(f) an individual who has acknowledged parentage of the child in writing under section 12 of the *Children's Law Reform Act*,

but does not include a licensee or a foster parent.

Consent of parent, etc.

(2) An order for the adoption of a child who is less than sixteen years of age, or is sixteen years of age or more but has not withdrawn from parental control, shall not be made without,

(a) the written consent of every parent; or

(b) where the child has been made a Crown ward under Part III (Child Protection), the written consent of a Director.

Idem

(3) A consent under clause (2)(a) shall not be given before the child is seven days old.

Idem

(4) Where a child is being placed for adoption by a society or licensee, a consent under clause (2)(a) shall not be given until,

(a) the society or licensee has advised the parent of his or her right,

(i) to withdraw the consent under subsection (8), and

(ii) to be informed, on his or her request, whether an adoption order has been made in respect of the child;

(a.1) the society or licensee has advised the parent of such other matters as may be prescribed; and

(b) the society or licensee has given the parent an opportunity to seek counselling and independent legal advice with respect to the consent.

Custody of child

(5) Where,

(a) a child is being placed for adoption by a society or licensee;

(b) every consent required under subsection (2) has been given and has not been withdrawn under subsection (8); and

(c) the twenty-one day period referred to in subsection (8) has expired,

the rights and responsibilities of the child's parents with respect to the child's custody, care and control are transferred to the society or licensee, until the consent is withdrawn under subsection 139(1) (late withdrawal with leave of court) or an order is made for the child's adoption under section 146.

Consent of person to be adopted

(6) An order for the adoption of a person who is seven years of age or more shall not be made without the person's written consent.

Idem

(7) A consent under subsection (6) shall not be given until the person has had an opportunity to obtain counselling and independent legal advice with respect to the consent.

Withdrawal of consent

(8) A person who gives a consent under subsection (2) or (6) may withdraw it in writing within twenty-one days after the consent is given and where that person had custody of the child immediately before giving the consent, the child shall be returned to him or her as soon as the consent is withdrawn.

Dispensing with person's consent

(9) The court may dispense with a person's consent required under subsection (6) where the court is satisfied that,

(a) obtaining the consent would cause the person emotional harm; or

(b) the person is not able to consent because of a developmental disability.

Consent of applicant's spouse

(10) An adoption order shall not be made on the application of a person who is a spouse without the written consent of the other spouse.

Consents by minors: role of Children's Lawyer

(11) Where a person who gives a consent under clause (2)(a) is less than eighteen years of age, the consent is not valid unless the Children's Lawyer is satisfied that the consent is fully informed and reflects the person's true wishes.

Affidavits of execution

(12) An affidavit of execution in the prescribed form shall be attached to a consent and a withdrawal of a consent under this section.

Form of foreign consents

(13) A consent required under this section that is given outside Ontario and whose form does not comply with the requirements of subsection (12) and the regulations is not invalid for that reason alone, if its form complies with the laws of the jurisdiction where it is given.

Dispensing with consent

138. The court may dispense with a consent required under section 137 for the adoption of a child, except the consent of the child or of a Director, where the court is satisfied that,

(a) it is in the child's best interests to do so; and

(b) the person whose consent is required has received notice of the proposed adoption and of the application to dispense with consent, or a reasonable effort to give the notice has been made.

Late withdrawal of consent

139. (1) The court may permit a person who gave a consent to the adoption of a child under section 137 to withdraw the consent after the twenty-one day period referred to in subsection 137(8) where the court is satisfied that it is in the child's best interests to do so, and where that person had custody of the child immediately before giving the consent, the child shall be returned to him or her as soon as the consent is withdrawn.

Exception: child placed for adoption

(2) Subsection (1) does not apply where the child has been placed with a person for adoption and remains in that person's care.

Placement for Adoption

140. Repealed.

Only societies and licensees may place children, etc.

141. (1) No person except a society or licensee shall,

(a) place a child with another person for adoption; or

(b) take, send or attempt to take or send a child who is a resident of Ontario out of Ontario to be placed for adoption.

Only societies, etc., may bring children into Ontario

(2) No person except a society or a licensee whose licence contains a term permitting the licensee to act under this subsection shall bring a child who is not a resident of Ontario into Ontario to be placed for adoption.

Licensee to notify Director of placement

(3) No licensee except a licensee exempted under subsection (5) shall,

(a) place a child with another person for adoption; or

(b) take, send or attempt to take or send a child who is a resident of Ontario out of Ontario to be placed for adoption,

without first notifying a Director of the proposed placement.

Director's approval required

(4) No person shall receive a child for adoption, except from a society or from a licensee exempted under subsection (5), without first receiving a Director's approval of the placement under clause 142(2)(a).

Designation of licensee

(5) A Director may designate a licensee that is an agency as exempt from the requirements of subsections (3) and (4).

Placements to be registered

(6) A society or licensee who places a child with another person for adoption shall register the placement in the prescribed manner within thirty days of placing the child.

Idem: Director

(7) A Director who becomes aware of any placement for adoption of a child that has not been registered under subsection (6) shall forthwith register the placement in the prescribed manner.

Exception: family adoptions

(8) Subsections (1), (2), (3), (4), (6) and (7) do not apply to,

(a) the placement for adoption of a child with the child's relative, the child's parent or a spouse of the child's parent; or

(b) the taking or sending of a child out of Ontario for adoption by the child's relative, the child's parent or a spouse of the child's parent.

Limitation on placement by society

141.1 A society shall not place a Crown ward for adoption until,

(a) the time for commencing an appeal of the order for Crown wardship under subsection 57(1) or 65.2(1) has expired; or

(b) any appeal of the order for Crown wardship has been finally disposed of or abandoned.

Adoption planning

141.1.1 (1) Nothing in this Act prohibits a society from planning for the adoption of a Crown ward in respect of whom there is an access order in effect under Part III (Child Protection).

Openness

(2) Where a society begins planning for the adoption of a child who is a Crown ward, the society shall consider the benefits of an openness order or openness agreement in respect of the child.

Where child an Indian or native person

141.2 (1) If a society intends to begin planning for the adoption of a child who is an Indian or native person, the society shall give written notice of its intention to a representative chosen by the child's band or native community.

Care plan proposed by band or native community

(2) Where a representative chosen by a band or native community receives notice that a society intends to begin planning for the adoption of a child who is an Indian or native person, the band or native community may, within 60 days of receiving the notice,

(a) prepare its own plan for the care of the child; and

(b) submit its plan to the society.

Condition for placement

(3) A society shall not place a child who is an Indian or native person with another person for adoption until,

(a) at least 60 days after notice is given to a representative chosen by the band or native community have elapsed; or

(b) if a band or native community has submitted a plan for the care of the child, the society has considered the plan.

Adoption homestudy

142. (1) A licensee who notifies a Director of a proposed placement under subsection 141(3) shall at the same time provide the Director with a report of an adoption homestudy of the person with whom placement is proposed, prepared by a person who, in the opinion of the Director or a local director, is qualified to make an adoption homestudy.

Director's approval

(2) A Director who receives a report under subsection (1) shall consider it and, as soon as possible,

(a) approve the proposed placement; or

(b) refuse to approve the placement and give notice of the refusal to the licensee and the person with whom placement is proposed.

Right to hearing

(3) Where a Director gives notice under clause (2)(b), the licensee and the person with whom placement is proposed are entitled to a hearing before the Board.

Application of other sections

(3.1) Sections 197, 199, 201 and 202 of Part IX (Licensing) apply to the hearing with necessary modifications and for that purpose references to the Tribunal shall be deemed to be references to the Board.

Extension of time

(3.2) If the Board is satisfied that there are reasonable grounds for the licensee or the person with whom placement is proposed to apply for an extension of the time fixed for requiring the hearing and for the Board to grant relief, it may,

(a) extend the time either before or after the expiration of the time; and

(b) give the directions that it considers proper as a result of extending the time.

Recording of evidence

(3.3) The evidence taken before the Board at the hearing shall be recorded.

Placement outside Canada

(4) A Director shall not approve the proposed placement of a child outside Canada unless the Director is satisfied that a prescribed special circumstance justifies the placement.

Terms and conditions

(5) A Director may approve a proposed placement under clause (2)(a) subject to any terms and conditions that the Director considers appropriate, including supervision of the placement by,

(a) a specified society, licensee or person; or

(b) in the case of a placement outside Ontario, a specified child protection agency recognized in the jurisdiction of the placement.

Right to hearing

(6) Where a Director imposes a term or condition on an approval under subsection (5), the licensee and the person with whom placement is proposed are entitled to a hearing before the Board.

Application of other sections

(7) Sections 198, 199, 201 and 202 of Part IX (Licensing) apply to the hearing with necessary modifications and for that purpose references to the Tribunal shall be deemed to be references to the Board.

Access orders terminate

143. (1) When a child is placed for adoption by a society or licensee, every order respecting access to the child is terminated, including an access order made under Part III (Child Protection) in respect of a Crown ward.

No interference, etc., with child in placement

(2) Where a child has been placed for adoption by a society or licensee and no adoption order has been made, no person shall,

(a) interfere with the child; or

(b) for the purpose of interfering with the child, visit or communicate with the child or with the person with whom the child has been placed.

Decision to Refuse to Place Child or to Remove Child after Placement

Decision of society or licensee

144. (1) This section applies if,

(a) a society decides to refuse an application to adopt a particular child made by a foster parent, or other person; or

(b) a society or licensee decides to remove a child who has been placed with a person for adoption.

Notice of decision

(2) The society or licensee who makes a decision referred to in subsection (1) shall,

(a) give at least 10 days notice in writing of the decision to the person who applied to adopt the child or with whom the child had been placed for adoption;

(b) include in the notice under clause (a) notice of the person's right to apply for a review of the decision under subsection (3); and

(c) if the child is an Indian or native person,

(i) give at least 10 days notice in writing of the decision to a representative chosen by the child's band or native community, and

(ii) after the notice is given, consult with the band or community representatives relating to the planning for the care of the child.

Application for review

(3) A person who receives notice of a decision under subsection (2) may, within 10 days after receiving the notice, apply to the Board in accordance with the regulations for a review of the decision subject to subsection (4).

Where no review

(4) If a society receives an application to adopt a child and, at the time of the application, the child had been placed for adoption with another person, the applicant is not entitled to a review of the society's decision to refuse the application.

Board hearing

(5) Upon receipt of an application under subsection (3) for a review of a decision, the Board shall hold a hearing under this section.

Where child is Indian or native person

(6) Upon receipt of an application for review of a decision relating to a child who is an Indian or native person, the Board shall give a representative chosen by the child's band or native community notice of the application and of the date of the hearing.

Practices and procedures

(7) The *Statutory Powers Procedure Act* applies to a hearing under this section and the Board shall comply with such additional practices and procedures as may be prescribed.

Composition of Board

(8) At a hearing under subsection (5), the Board shall be composed of members with the prescribed qualifications and prescribed experience.

Parties

(9) The following persons are parties to a hearing under this section:

1. The applicant.
2. The society.
3. If the child is an Indian or a native person, a representative chosen by the child's band or native community.
4. Any person that the Board adds under subsection (10).

Additional parties

(10) The Board may add a person as a party to a review if, in the Board's opinion, it is necessary to do so in order to decide all the issues in the review.

Board decision

(11) The Board shall, in accordance with its determination of which action is in the best interests of the child, confirm or rescind the decision under review and shall give written reasons for its decision.

Subsequent placement

(12) After a society or licensee has made a decision referred to in subsection (1) in relation to a child, the society shall not place the child for adoption with a person other than the person who has a right to apply for a review under subsection (3) unless,

(a) the time for applying for a review of the decision under subsection (3) has expired and an application is not made; or

(b) if an application for a review of the decision is made under subsection (3), the Board has confirmed the decision.

No removal before Board decision

(13) Subject to subsection (14), if a society or licensee has decided to remove a child from the care of a person with whom the child was placed for adoption, the society or licensee, as the case may be, shall not carry out the proposed removal of the child unless,

(a) the time for applying for a review of the decision under subsection (3) has expired and an application is not made; or

(b) if an application for a review of the decision is made under subsection (3), the Board has confirmed the decision.

Where child at risk

(14) A society or licensee may carry out a decision to remove a child from the care of a person with whom the child was placed for adoption before the expiry of the time for applying for a review under subsection (3) or at any time after the application for a review is made if, in the opinion of a Director or local director, there would be a risk that the child is likely to suffer harm during the time necessary for a review by the Board.

Transitional

(15) This section as it read immediately before the day this subsection came into force continues to apply where a request to adopt a child or a decision to remove a child was made before that day.

Notice to Director

145. (1) Where a child has been placed for adoption under this Part, no order for the child's adoption has been made and,

(a) the person with whom the child is placed asks the society or licensee that placed the child to remove the child; or

(b) the society or licensee proposes to remove the child from the person with whom the child was placed,

the society or licensee shall notify a Director.

Idem

(2) Where no order for a child's adoption has been made and a year has expired since,

(a) the earlier of the child's placement for adoption or the giving of the most recent consent under clause 137(2)(a); or

(b) the most recent review under subsection (3),

whichever is later, the society or licensee shall notify a Director, unless the child is a Crown ward.

Director to review

(3) A Director who receives a notice under subsection (1) or (2) shall conduct a review in accordance with the regulations.

(4) Repealed.

Openness Orders

No access order in effect

Application for openness order

145.1 (1) If a child who is a Crown ward is the subject of a plan for adoption, and no access order is in effect under Part III, the society having care and custody of the child may apply to the court for an openness order in respect of the child at any time before an order for adoption of the child is made under section 146.

Notice of application

(2) A society making an application under this section shall give notice of the application to,

(a) the child, except as otherwise provided under subsection 39(4) or (5);

(b) every person who will be permitted to communicate with or have a relationship with the child if the order is made;

(c) any person with whom the society has placed or plans to place the child for adoption; and

(d) any society that will supervise or participate in the arrangement under the openness order.

Openness order

(3) The court may make an openness order under this section in respect of a child if the court is satisfied that,

(a) the openness order is in the best interests of the child;

(b) the openness order will permit the continuation of a relationship with a person that is beneficial and meaningful to the child; and

(c) the following entities and persons have consented to the order:

(i) the society,

(ii) the person who will be permitted to communicate with or have a relationship with the child if the order is made,

(iii) the person with whom the society has placed or plans to place the child for adoption, and

(iv) the child if he or she is 12 years of age or older.

Termination of openness order if Crown wardship terminates

(4) Any openness order made under this section in respect of a child terminates if the child ceases to be a Crown ward by reason of an order made under subsection 65.2(1).

Access order in effect

Notice of intent to place for adoption

145.1.1 (1) This section applies where,

(a) a society intends to place a child who is a Crown ward for adoption; and

(b) an order under Part III (Child Protection) has been made respecting a person's access to the child or the child's access to another person.

Notice

(2) In the circumstances described in subsection (1), the society shall give notice to the following persons:

1. The person who has been granted an access order.
2. The person with respect to whom an access order has been granted.

Right to apply for openness order

(3) The society shall include in the notice the following information:

1. Notice that the society intends to place the child for adoption.
2. Notice that the access order terminates upon placement for adoption.
3. In the case of notice to a person described in paragraph 1 of subsection (2), the fact that the person has a right to apply for an openness order within 30 days after notice is received.
4. In the case of notice to a person described in paragraph 2 of subsection (2), the fact that the person described in paragraph 1 of subsection (2) has the right to apply for an openness order within 30 days after notice is received.

Method of giving notice

(4) Notice may be given by any of the following methods:

1. Leaving a copy,

i. with the person,

ii. if the person appears to be mentally incapable in respect of an issue in the notice, with the person and with the guardian of the person's property or, if none, with the Public Guardian and Trustee, or

iii. if the person is a child, with the child and with the child's lawyer, if any.

2. Leaving a copy with a lawyer who accepts the notice in writing on a copy of the document.

Alternate method

(5) On application without notice by a society, the court may order that notice under subsection (2) be given by another method chosen by the court if the society,

(a) provides detailed evidence showing,

(i) what steps have been taken to locate the person to whom the notice is to be given, and

(ii) if the person has been located, what steps have been taken to give the notice to the person; and

(b) shows that the method of giving notice could reasonably be expected to bring the notice to the person's attention.

Notice not required

(6) On application without notice by a society, the court may order that the society is not required to give notice under subsection (2) if,

(a) reasonable efforts to locate the person to whom the notice is to be given have not been or would not be successful; and

(b) there is no method of giving notice that could reasonably be expected to bring the notice to the person's attention.

Access order in effect

Application for openness order

145.1.2 (1) A person described in paragraph 1 of subsection 145.1.1(2) may, within 30 days after notice is received, apply to the court for an openness order.

Notice of application

(2) A person making an application for an openness order under this section shall give notice of the application to,

(a) the society having care and custody of the child;

(b) the child, except as otherwise provided under subsection 39(4) or (5); and

(c) if the child is bringing the application, the person who will be permitted to communicate with or have a relationship with the child if the order is made.

Condition on placement

(3) A society shall not place a child for adoption before the time for applying for an openness order under subsection (1) has expired unless every person who is entitled to do so has made an application for an openness order under this section.

Information before placement

(4) Where an application for an openness order under this section has been made, a society shall, before placing the child for adoption, advise the person with whom it plans to place the child of the following:

1. The fact that such an application has been made.
2. The relationship of the applicant to the child.
3. The details of the openness arrangement requested.

Outcome of application

(5) Where an application for an openness order under this section has been made, a society shall advise the person with whom the society has placed or plans to place the child for adoption or, after an adoption order is made, the adoptive parent of the outcome of the application.

Openness order

(6) The court may make an openness order under this section in respect of a child if it is satisfied that,

(a) the openness order is in the best interests of the child;

(b) the openness order will permit the continuation of a relationship with a person that is beneficial and meaningful to the child; and

(c) the child has consented to the order, if he or she is 12 years of age or older.

Same

(7) In deciding whether to make an openness order under this section, the court shall consider the ability of the person with whom the society has placed or plans to place the child for adoption or, after the adoption order is made, the adoptive parent to comply with the arrangement under the openness order.

Consent of society required

(8) The court shall not, under this section, direct a society to supervise or participate in the arrangement under an openness order without the consent of the society.

Termination of openness order if Crown wardship terminates

(9) Any openness order made under this section in respect of a child terminates if the child ceases to be a Crown ward by reason of an order made under subsection 65.2(1).

Temporary orders

(10) The court may make such temporary order relating to openness under this section as the court considers to be in the child's best interests.

Application to vary or terminate openness order

145.2 (1) A society or a person with whom a child has been placed for adoption may apply to the court for an order to vary or terminate an openness order made under section 145.1 or 145.1.2.

Time for making application

(2) An application under this section shall not be made after an order for the adoption of the child is made under section 146.

Notice of application

(3) A society or person making an application under this section shall give notice of the application to,

(a) the child, except as otherwise provided under subsection 39(4) or (5);

(b) every person who is permitted to communicate with or have a relationship with the child under the openness order;

(c) any person with whom the society has placed or plans to place the child for adoption, if the application under this section is made by the society; and

(d) any society that supervises or participates in the arrangement under the openness order that is the subject of the application.

Order to vary openness order

(4) The court shall not make an order to vary an openness order under this section unless the court is satisfied that,

(a) a material change in circumstances has occurred;

(b) the proposed order is in the child's best interests; and

(c) the proposed order would continue a relationship that is beneficial and meaningful to the child.

Order to terminate openness order

(5) The court shall not terminate an openness order under this section unless the court is satisfied that,

(a) a material change in circumstances has occurred;

(b) termination of the order is in the child's best interests; and

(c) the relationship that is the subject of the order is no longer beneficial and meaningful to the child.

Consent of society required

(6) The court shall not, under this section, direct a society to supervise or participate in the arrangement under an openness order without the consent of the society.

Alternative dispute resolution

(7) At any time during a proceeding under this section, the court may, in the best interests of the child and with the consent of the parties, adjourn the proceedings to permit the parties to attempt through a prescribed method of alternative dispute resolution to resolve any dispute between them with respect to any matter that is relevant to the proceeding.

Temporary orders

(8) The court may make such temporary order relating to openness under this section as the court considers to be in the child's best interests.

Adoption Orders

Orders for adoption

Adoption of child

146. (1) The court may make an order for the adoption of a child who is less than sixteen years of age, or is sixteen years of age or more but has not withdrawn from parental control, and,

(a) has been placed for adoption by a society or licensee; or

(b) has been placed for adoption by a person other than a society or licensee and has resided with the applicant for at least two years,

in the child's best interests, on the application of the person with whom the child is placed.

Family adoption

(2) The court may make an order for the adoption of a child, in the child's best interests, on the application of,

(a) a relative of the child;

(b) the child's parent; or

(c) the spouse of the child's parent.

Adoption of adult, etc.

(3) The court may make an order for the adoption of,

(a) a person eighteen years of age or more; or

(b) a child who is sixteen years of age or more and has withdrawn from parental control,

on another person's application.

Who may apply

(4) An application under this section may only be made,

(a) by one individual; or

(b) jointly, by two individuals who are spouses of one another.

(c) Repealed.

Residency requirement

(5) The court shall not make an order under this section for the adoption of, or on the application of, a person who is not a resident of Ontario.

Where applicant a minor

147. The court shall not make an order under section 146 on the application of a person who is less than eighteen years of age unless the court is satisfied that special circumstances justify making the order.

Where order not to be made

148. Where the court has made an order,

(a) dispensing with a consent under section 138; or

(b) refusing to permit the late withdrawal of a consent under subsection 139(1),

the court shall not make an order under section 146 until,

(c) the time for commencing an appeal of the order has expired; or

(d) any appeal of the order has been finally disposed of or abandoned,

whichever is later.

Director's statement

149. (1) Where an application is made for an order for the adoption of a child under subsection 146(1), a Director shall, before the hearing, file a written statement with the court indicating,

(a) that the child has resided with the applicant for at least six months or, in the case of an application under clause 146(1)(b), for at least two years and, in the Director's opinion, it would be in the child's best interests to make the order;

(b) in the case of an application under clause 146(1)(a), that for specified reasons it would be in the child's best interests, in the Director's opinion, to make the order although the child has resided with the applicant for less than six months; or

(c) that the child has resided with the applicant for at least six months or, in the case of an application under clause 146(1)(b), for at least two years and, in the Director's opinion, it would not be in the child's best interests to make the order,

and referring to any additional circumstances that the Director wishes to bring to the court's attention.

Local director may make statement

(2) Where a child was placed by a society and has resided with the applicant for at least six months, the statement under subsection (1) may be made and filed by the local director.

Amendment of statement, etc.

(3) The Director or local director, as the case may be, may amend the statement referred to in subsection (1) at any time and may attend at the hearing and make submissions.

Where recommendation negative

(4) Where the statement under subsection (1) indicates that, in the Director's or local director's opinion, it would not be in the child's best interests to make the order, a copy of the statement shall be filed with the court and served on the applicant at least thirty days before the hearing.

Report of child's adjustment

(5) The statement under subsection (1) shall be based on a report of the child's adjustment in the applicant's home, prepared by,

(a) the society that placed the child or has jurisdiction where the child is placed; or

(b) a person approved by the Director or local director.

Family adoptions: court may require statement

(6) Where an application is made for an order for the adoption of a child under subsection 146(2), the court may order that subsections (1), (3), (4) and (5) shall apply to the application.

Place of hearing

150. (1) An application for an adoption order shall be heard and dealt with in the county or district in which,

(a) the applicant; or

(b) the person to be adopted,

resides at the time the application is filed.

Transfer of proceeding

(2) Where the court is satisfied at any stage of an application for an adoption order that there is a preponderance of convenience in favour of conducting it in another county or district, the court may order that it be transferred to that other county or district and be continued as if it had been commenced there.

Rules re applications

Hearing in private

151. (1) An application for an adoption order shall be heard and dealt with in the absence of the public.

Court files private

(2) No person shall have access to the court file concerning an application for an adoption order, except,

(a) the court and authorized court employees;

(b) the parties and the persons representing them under the authority of the *Law Society Act*; and

(c) a Director and a local director.

Stale applications

(3) Where an application for an adoption order is not heard within twelve months of the day on which the applicant signed it,

(a) the court shall not hear the application unless the court is satisfied that it is just to do so; and

(b) the applicant may make another application.

No right to notice

(4) No person,

(a) who has given a consent under clause 137(2)(a) and has not withdrawn it;

(b) whose consent has been dispensed with under section 138; or

(c) who is a parent of a Crown ward who is placed for adoption,

is entitled to receive notice of an application under section 146.

Power of court

152. (1) The court may, on its own initiative, summon a person to attend before it, testify and produce any document or thing, and may enforce obedience to the summons as if it had been made in a proceeding under the *Family Law Act*.

Duty of court

(2) The court shall not make an order for the adoption of a child under subsection 146(1) or (2) unless the court is satisfied that,

(a) every person who has given a consent under section 137 understands the nature and effect of the adoption order; and

(b) every applicant understands and appreciates the special role of an adoptive parent.

Participation of child

(3) Where an application is made for an order for the adoption of a child under subsection 146(1) or (2), the court shall,

(a) inquire into the child's capacity to understand and appreciate the nature of the application; and

(b) consider the child's views and wishes, if they can be reasonably ascertained,

and where it is practical to do so shall hear the child.

Participation of adult, etc.

(4) Where an application is made for an order for the adoption of a person under subsection 146(3), the court shall consider the person's views and wishes and, on request, hear the person.

Change of name

153. (1) Where the court makes an order under section 146, the court may, at the request of the applicant or applicants and, where the person adopted is twelve years of age or more, with the person's written consent,

(a) change the person's surname to a surname that the person could have been given if he or she had been born to the applicant or applicants; and

(b) change the person's given name.

When child's consent not required

(2) A child's consent to a change of name under subsection (1) is not required where the child's consent was dispensed with under subsection 137(9).

Varying or terminating openness orders after adoption

153.1 (1) Any of the following persons may apply to the court to vary or terminate an openness order made under section 145.1 or 145.1.2 after an order for adoption has been made under section 146:

1. An adoptive parent.
2. A person who is permitted to communicate or have a relationship with a child under the order.
3. Any society that supervises or participates in the arrangement under the openness order that is the subject of the application.

Leave

(2) Despite paragraph 2 of subsection (1), a person who is permitted to communicate or have a relationship with a child under an openness order shall not make an application under subsection (1) without leave of the court.

Jurisdiction

(3) An application under subsection (1) shall be made in the county or district,

(a) in which the child resides, if the child resides in Ontario; or

(b) in which the adoption order for the child was made if the child does not reside in Ontario, unless the court is satisfied that the preponderance of convenience favours having the matter dealt with by the court in another county or district.

Notice

(4) A person making an application under subsection (1) shall give notice of the application to every other person who could have made an application under that subsection with respect to the order.

Child 12 or older

(5) A child 12 years of age or more who is the subject of an application under this section is entitled to receive notice of the application and to be present at the hearing, unless the court is satisfied that being present at the hearing would cause the child emotional harm and orders that the child not receive notice of the application and not be permitted to be present at the hearing.

Child under 12

(6) A child less than 12 years of age who is the subject of an application under this section is not entitled to receive notice of the application or to be present at the hearing unless,

(a) the court is satisfied that the child is capable of understanding the hearing and will not suffer emotional harm by being present at the hearing; and

(b) the court orders that the child receive notice of the application and be permitted to be present at the hearing.

Order to vary openness order

(7) The court shall not make an order to vary an openness order under this section unless the court is satisfied that,

(a) a material change in circumstances has occurred;

(b) the proposed order is in the child's best interests; and

(c) the proposed order would continue a relationship that is beneficial and meaningful to the child.

Order to terminate openness order

(8) The court shall not terminate an openness order under this section unless the court is satisfied that,

(a) a material change in circumstances has occurred;

(b) termination of the order is in the child's best interests; and

(c) the relationship that is the subject of the order is no longer beneficial and meaningful to the child.

Consent of society required

(9) The court shall not, under this section, direct a society to supervise or participate in the arrangement under an openness order without the consent of the society.

Alternative dispute resolution

(10) At any time during a proceeding under this section, the court may, in the best interests of the child and with the

consent of the parties, adjourn the proceedings to permit the parties to attempt through a prescribed method of alternative dispute resolution to resolve any dispute between them with respect to a matter relevant to the proceeding.

Appeal of order to vary or terminate openness order

153.2 (1) An appeal from a court's order under section 145.2 or 153.1 may be made to the Superior Court of Justice by,

(a) the child if the child had legal representation in a proceeding under section 145.2 or 153.1; or

(b) any person who was entitled to notice of the application to vary or terminate the openness order that is the subject of the appeal.

Temporary order

(2) Pending final disposition of the appeal, the Superior Court of Justice may on any party's motion make a temporary order in the child's best interests that varies or suspends an openness order.

No time extension

(3) No extension of the time for an appeal shall be granted.

Further evidence

(4) The court may receive further evidence relating to events after the appealed decision.

Place of hearing

(5) An appeal under this section shall be heard in the county or district in which the order appealed from was made.

Application of s. 151

153.3 Subsections 151(1) and (2) apply with necessary modifications to proceedings under sections 145.1, 145.1.2, 145.2, 153.1 and 153.2.

Child may participate

153.4 A child who receives notice of a proceeding under section 145.1, 145.1.2, 145.2, 153.1 or 153.2 is entitled to participate in the proceeding as if he or she were a party.

Legal representation of child

153.5 (1) A child may have legal representation at any stage in a proceeding under section 145.1, 145.1.2, 145.2 or 153.1, and subsection 38(2) applies with necessary modifications to such a proceeding.

Children's Lawyer

(2) Where the court determines that legal representation is desirable, the court may, with the consent of the Children's Lawyer, authorize the Children's Lawyer to represent the child.

Openness Agreements

Who may enter into openness agreement

153.6 (1) For the purposes of facilitating communication or maintaining relationships, an openness agreement may be made by an adoptive parent of a child or by a person with whom a society or licensee has placed or plans to place a child for adoption and any of the following persons:

1. A birth parent, birth relative or birth sibling of the child.
2. A foster parent of the child or another person who cared for the child or in whose custody the child was placed at any time.
3. A member of the child's extended family or community with whom the child has a significant relationship or emotional tie.
4. An adoptive parent of a birth sibling of the child or a person with whom a society or licensee has placed or plans to place a birth sibling of the child for adoption.
5. If the child is an Indian or native person, a member of the child's band or native community who may not have had a significant relationship or emotional tie with the child in the past but will help the child recognize the importance of his or her Indian or native culture and preserve his or her heritage, traditions and cultural identity.

When agreement may be made

(2) An openness agreement may be made at any time before or after an adoption order is made.

Agreement may include dispute resolution process

(3) An openness agreement may include a process to resolve disputes arising under the agreement or with respect to matters associated with it.

Views and wishes of child

(4) Where the views and wishes of the child can be reasonably ascertained, they shall be considered before an openness agreement is made.

Interim Orders

Interim order

154. (1) Where an application is made for an order for the adoption of a child under subsection 146(1) or (2), the court, after considering the statement made under subsection 149(1), may postpone the determination of the matter and make an interim order in the child's best interests placing the child in the applicant's care and custody for a specified period not exceeding one year.

Terms and conditions

(2) The court may make an order under subsection (1) subject to any terms and conditions that the court considers appropriate respecting,

(a) the child's maintenance and education;

(b) supervision of the child; and

(c) any other matter the court considers advisable in the child's best interests.

Not an adoption order

(3) An order under subsection (1) is not an adoption order.

Consents required

(4) Sections 137 and 138 (consents to adoption) apply to an order under subsection (1) with necessary modifications.

Departure from Ontario

(5) Where an applicant takes up residence outside Ontario after obtaining an order under subsection (1), the court may nevertheless make an adoption order under subsection 146(1) or (2) where the statement made under subsection 149(1) indicates that, in the Director's or local director's opinion, it would be in the child's best interests to make the order.

Successive adoption orders

155. An adoption order under subsection 146(1) or (2) or an interim custody order under subsection 154(1) may be made in respect of a person who is the subject of an earlier adoption order.

Appeals

Appeals

Appeal: adoption order

156. (1) An appeal from a court's order under section 146 may be made to the Superior Court of Justice by,

(a) the applicant for the adoption order; and
(b) the Director or local director who made the statement under subsection 149(1).

Idem: dispensing with consent

(2) An appeal from a court's order under section 138 dispensing with a consent may be made to the Superior Court of Justice by,

(a) the persons referred to in subsection (1); and
(b) the person whose consent was dispensed with.

Idem: late withdrawal of consent

(3) An appeal from a court's order under subsection 139(1) permitting the late withdrawal of a consent may be made to the Superior Court of Justice by,

(a) the persons referred to in subsection (1); and
(b) the person who gave the consent.

No extension of time for appeal

(4) No extension of the time for an appeal shall be granted.

Place of hearing

(5) An appeal under this section shall be heard in the county or district in which the order appealed from was made.

Hearing in private

(6) An appeal under this section shall be heard in the absence of the public.

Effect of Adoption Order

Order final

157. An adoption order under section 146 is final and irrevocable, subject only to section 156 (appeals), and shall not be questioned or reviewed in any court by way of injunction, declaratory judgment, *certiorari*, *mandamus*, prohibition, *habeascorpus*or application for judicial review.

Validity of adoption order not affected by openness order or agreement

(2) Compliance or non-compliance with the terms of an openness order or openness agreement relating to a child does not affect the validity of an order made under section 146 for the adoption of the child.

Status of adopted child

158. (1) In this section,

"adopted child" means a person who was adopted in Ontario.

Same

(2) For all purposes of law, as of the date of the making of an adoption order,

(a) the adopted child becomes the child of the adoptive parent and the adoptive parent becomes the parent of the adopted child; and
(b) the adopted child ceases to be the child of the person who was his or her parent before the adoption order was made and that person ceases to be the parent of the adopted child, except where the person is the spouse of the adoptive parent.

How relationships determined

(3) The relationship to one another of all persons, including the adopted child, the adoptive parent, the kindred of the adoptive parent, the parent before the adoption order was made and the kindred of that former parent shall for all purposes be determined in accordance with subsection (2).

Reference in will or other document

(4) In any will or other document made at any time before or after the 1st day of November, 1985, and whether the maker of the will or document is alive on that day or not, a reference to a person or group or class of persons described in terms of relationship by blood or marriage to another person shall be deemed to refer to or include, as the case may be, a person who comes within the description as a result of an adoption, unless the contrary is expressed.

Application of section

(5) This section applies and shall be deemed always to have applied with respect to any adoption made under any Act heretofore in force, but not so as to affect,

(a) any interest in property or right of the adopted child that has indefeasibly vested before the date of the making of an adoption order; and
(b) any interest in property or right that has indefeasibly vested before the 1st day of November, 1985.

Exception

(6) Subsections (2) and (3) do not apply for the purposes of the laws relating to incest and the prohibited degrees of marriage to remove a person from a relationship that would have existed but for those subsections.

Effect of foreign adoption

159. An adoption effected according to the law of another jurisdiction, before or after the 1st day of November, 1985, has the same effect in Ontario as an adoption under this Part.

No order for access by birth parent, etc.

160. (1) Where an order for the adoption of a child has been made under this Part, no court shall make an order under this Part for access to the child by,

(a) a birth parent; or
(b) a member of a birth parent's family.

Definition

(2) In this section,

"birth parent" has the same meaning as in section 166.

Records, Confidentiality and Disclosure

Parent to be informed on request

161. At the request of a person whose consent to an adoption was required under clause 137(2)(a) or a predecessor of that provision and was given or was dispensed with, any society or the licensee that placed the child for adoption shall inform the person whether an order has been made for the child's adoption.

Court papers

162. (1) In this section,

"court" includes the Superior Court of Justice.

Requirement to seal documents

(2) Subject to subsections (3) and 162.2(2), the documents used on an application for an adoption order under this Part or a predecessor of this Part shall be sealed up together with a certified copy of the original order and filed in the court office by the appropriate court officer, and shall not be opened for inspection except by court order.

Transmission of order

(3) Within thirty days after an adoption order is made under this Part, the proper officer of the court shall cause a sufficient number of certified copies of it to be made, under the seal of the proper certifying authority, and shall transmit,

(a) the original order to the adoptive parent;
(b) Repealed.
(c) one certified copy to the Registrar General under the *Vital Statistics Act*, or, if the adopted child was born outside Ontario, two certified copies;
(d) if the adopted child is an Indian, one certified copy to the Registrar under the *Indian Act* (Canada);
(e) one certified copy to such other persons as may be prescribed.

Other court files

(4) Unless the court orders otherwise, only the court may examine identifying information that comes from the records of any of the following persons that is contained in any court file respecting the judicial review of a decision made by any of them:

1. A designated custodian under section 162.1.
2. A person who, by virtue of a regulation made under clause 220(1)(c.5), reviews or hears appeals of decisions concerning the disclosure of information under section 162.2 or 162.3.
3. A person referred to in subsection 162.2(1) or 162.3(1).

Same

(5) No person shall, without the court's permission, disclose identifying information described in subsection (4) that the person obtained from the court file.

Definition

(6) In subsections (4) and (5),

"identifying information" means information whose disclosure, alone or in combination with other information, will in the circumstances reveal the identity of the person to whom it relates.

Designation of custodians of information

162.1 (1) The Lieutenant Governor in Council may, by regulation, designate one or more persons to act as custodians of information that relates to adoptions and may impose such conditions and restrictions with respect to the designation as the Lieutenant Governor in Council considers appropriate.

Powers and duties

(2) A designated custodian may exercise such powers and shall perform such duties as may be prescribed with respect to the information provided to the custodian under this Act.

Same, disclosure of information

(3) A designated custodian may exercise such other powers and shall perform such other duties as may be prescribed for a purpose relating to the disclosure of information that relates to adoptions, including performing searches upon request for such persons, and in such circumstances, as may be prescribed.

(4) Repealed.

Agreements

(5) The Minister may enter into agreements with designated custodians concerning their powers and duties under this section and the agreements may provide for payments to be made to the designated custodians.

Disclosure to designated custodian

162.2 (1) The Minister, the Registrar General under the *Vital Statistics Act*, a society, a licensee and such other persons as may be prescribed shall give a designated custodian under section 162.1 such information that relates to adoptions as may be prescribed in such circumstances as may be prescribed.

Same, adoption orders

(2) A court shall give a designated custodian a certified copy of an adoption order made under this Part together with

such other documents as may be prescribed in such circumstances as may be prescribed.

Disclosure to others

By the Minister

162.3 (1) The Minister shall give such information that relates to adoptions as may be prescribed to such persons as may be prescribed in such circumstances as may be prescribed.

By a society

(2) A society shall give such information that relates to adoptions as may be prescribed to such persons as may be prescribed in such circumstances as may be prescribed.

By a licensee

(3) A licensee shall give such information that relates to adoptions as may be prescribed to such persons as may be prescribed in such circumstances as may be prescribed.

By a custodian

(4) A designated custodian under section 162.1 shall give such information that relates to adoptions as may be prescribed to such persons as may be prescribed in such circumstances as may be prescribed.

Scope of application

162.4 Sections 162.2 and 162.3 apply with respect to information that relates to an adoption regardless of when the adoption order was made.

163. (1) Repealed.

(2) Repealed.
(3) Repealed.
(4) Repealed.

164. Repealed.

Confidentiality of Adoption Records

Confidentiality of adoption information

165. (1) Despite any other Act, after an adoption order is made, no person shall inspect, remove, alter or disclose information that relates to the adoption and is kept by the Ministry, a society, a licensee or a designated custodian under section 162.1 and no person shall permit it to be inspected, removed, altered or disclosed unless the inspection, removal, alteration or disclosure is,

(a) necessary for the maintenance or updating of the information by the Ministry, society, licensee or designated custodian or their staff; or
(b) authorized under this Act.

Application

(2) This section applies regardless of when the adoption order was made.

(3), (4) Repealed.

Privacy

(5) The *Freedom of Information and Protection of Privacy Act*does not apply to information that relates to an adoption.

166. Repealed.
167. Repealed.
168. Repealed.
168.1. Repealed.
169. Repealed.
170. Repealed.
171. Repealed.
172. Repealed.
173. Repealed.
174. Repealed.

Offences

No payments for adoption

175. No person, whether before or after a child's birth, shall give, receive or agree to give or receive a payment or reward of any kind in connection with,

(a) the child's adoption or placement for adoption;
(b) a consent under section 137 to the child's adoption; or
(c) negotiations or arrangements with a view to the child's adoption,

except for,

(d) the prescribed expenses of a licensee, or such greater expenses as are approved by a Director;
(e) proper legal fees and disbursements; and
(f) a subsidy paid by an approved agency or by the Minister to an adoptive parent or to a person with whom a child is placed for adoption.

Offence

176. (1) A person who contravenes subsection 141(1), (2) or (3) (placement for adoption) and a director, officer or employee of a corporation who authorizes, permits or concurs in such a contravention by the corporation is guilty of an offence, whether an order is subsequently made for the child's adoption or not, and on conviction is liable to a fine of not more than $2,000 or to imprisonment for a term of not more than two years, or to both.

Idem

(2) A person who contravenes subsection 141(4) (receiving child) is guilty of an offence and on conviction is liable to a fine of not more than $2,000 or to imprisonment for a term of not more than two years, or to both.

Idem

(3) A person who contravenes subsection 143(2) (interference with child) is guilty of an offence and on conviction is liable to a fine of not more than $1,000 or to imprisonment for a term of not more than one year, or to both.

Idem

(4) A person who contravenes section 175 and a director, officer or employee of a corporation who authorizes, permits or concurs in such a contravention by the corporation is guilty of an offence and on conviction is liable to a fine of not more than $25,000 or to imprisonment for a term of not more than three years, or to both.

Limitation period

(5) A proceeding under subsection (1), (2) or (4) shall not be commenced after the expiration of two years after the date on which the offence was, or is alleged to have been, committed.

Note: On a day to be named by proclamation of the Lieutenant Governor, the Act is amended by the Statutes of Ontario, 2005, chapter 25, section 30 by adding the following section:

Unauthorized disclosure of information by designated custodian

176.1 (1) No designated custodian under section 162.1 shall disclose any information provided to the custodian under section 162.2 unless the disclosure is made in accordance with the regulations.

Offence

(2) A person who contravenes subsection (1) is guilty of an offence.

Same

(3) A director, officer or employee of a corporation who authorizes, permits or concurs in a contravention of subsection (1) by the corporation is guilty of an offence.

See: 2005, c. 25, ss. 30, 36(2).

Injunction

Injunction

177. (1) The Superior Court of Justice may grant an injunction to restrain a person from contravening subsection 143(2), on the society's or licensee's application.

Variation, etc.

(2) The Court may vary or terminate an order made under subsection (1), on any person's application.

PART VIII CONFIDENTIALITY OF AND ACCESS TO RECORDS

178. Repealed.

Exceptions

179. (1), (2) Repealed.

Exception re adoption-related information

(2.1) This Part does not apply to information given to a designated custodian under section 162.2 or to another person under section 162.3.

(3) Spent.

Disclosure of Records

180.-182. Repealed.

Disclosure of records of mental disorders

183. (1) In this section,

"record of a mental disorder" means a record or a part of a record made about a person concerning a substantial disorder of emotional processes, thought or cognition of the person which grossly impairs the person's capacity to make reasoned judgments.

Disclosure pursuant to summons

(2) A service provider shall disclose, transmit or permit the examination of a record of a mental disorder pursuant to a summons, order, direction, notice or similar requirement in respect of a matter in issue or that may be in issue in a court of competent jurisdiction or under any Act unless a physician states in writing that he or she believes that to do so,

(a) is likely to result in harm to the treatment or recovery of the person to whom the record relates; or

(b) is likely to result in,

(i) injury to the mental condition of another person, or

(ii) bodily harm to another person.

Hearing to be held

(3) The court before which a matter described in subsection (2) is in issue on motion or, where a disclosure, transmittal or examination is not required by a court, the Divisional Court on motion shall determine whether the record referred to in the physician's statement should be disclosed, transmitted or examined.

Idem

(4) A motion under subsection (3) shall be on notice to the physician and shall be held in the absence of the public.

Consideration of court

(5) In a motion under subsection (3), the court shall consider whether or not the disclosure, transmittal or examination of the record referred to in the physician's statement is likely to have a result described in clause (2)(a) or (b) and for the purpose the court may examine the record.

Order of court

(6) The court shall not order that the record referred to in the physician's statement be disclosed, transmitted or examined if the court is satisfied that a result described in clause (2)(a) or (b) is likely unless satisfied that to do so is essential in the interests of justice.

Conflict

(6.1) Subsections (2) to (6) prevail despite anything in the *Personal Health Information Protection Act, 2004*.

Return of record to service provider

(7) Where a record of a mental disorder is required under this section, the clerk of the court or body in which it is ad-

mitted in evidence or, if not so admitted, the person to whom the record is transmitted shall return the record to the service provider forthwith after the determination of the matter in issue in respect of which the record was required.

184-191. Repealed.

PART IX LICENSING

Definitions

192. In this Part,

"children's residence" means,

(a) a parent model residence where five or more children not of common parentage, or

(b) a staff model residence where three or more children not of common parentage,

live and receive residential care, and includes a foster home or other home or institution that is supervised or operated by a society or a place of temporary detention or a place of secure or of open custody, but does not include,

(c) a house licensed under the *Private Hospitals Act*,

(d) a day nursery as defined in the *Day Nurseries Act*,

(e) a recreational camp under the *Health Protection and Promotion Act*,

(f) a home for special care under the *Homes for Special Care Act*,

(g) a school or private school as defined in the *Education Act*,

(h) a hostel intended for short term accommodation,

(i) a hospital that receives financial aid from the Government of Ontario, or

(j) a group home or similar facility that receives financial assistance from the Minister of Correctional Services but receives no financial assistance from the Minister under this Act;

"non-profit agency" means a corporation without share capital that has objects of a charitable nature and,

(a) to which Part III of the *Corporations Act* applies, or

Note: On a day to be named by proclamation of the Lieutenant Governor, clause (a) is amended by striking out "Part III of the *Corporations Act*" and substituting "the *Not-for-Profit Corporations Act, 2010* or a predecessor of that Act". See: 2010, c. 15, ss. 217, 249.

(b) that is incorporated by or under a general or special Act of the Parliament of Canada;

"parent model residence" means a building, group of buildings or part of a building where not more than two adult persons live and provide care for children on a continuous basis;

"staff model residence" means a building, group of buildings or part of a building where adult persons are employed to provide care for children on the basis of scheduled periods of duty.

Where Licence Required

Licences

Licence required to operate children's residence, etc.

193. (1) No person shall,

(a) establish, operate or maintain a children's residence; or

(b) provide, directly or indirectly, residential care for three or more children not of common parentage in places that are not children's residences,

except under the authority of a licence issued by a Director under this Part.

Idem: placement for adoption

(2) No person other than a society shall place a child for adoption, except under the authority of a licence issued by a Director under this Part.

Issuing licence

(3) Subject to section 195, a person who applies for a licence in accordance with this Part and the regulations and pays the prescribed fee is entitled to be issued a licence by a Director, subject to any terms and conditions imposed by the Director.

Idem

(4) Despite subsection (3),

(a) a licence shall not be issued to a partnership or association of persons; and

(b) a licence to place a child for adoption shall only be issued to an individual or a non-profit agency.

Renewal of licence

(5) Subject to section 196, a licensee who applies for renewal of the licence in accordance with this Part and the regulations and pays the prescribed fee is entitled to have the licence renewed by a Director, subject to any terms and conditions imposed by the Director.

Provisional licence or renewal

(6) Where an applicant for a licence or renewal of a licence does not meet all the requirements for the issuing or renewal of the licence and requires time to meet them, a Director may, subject to such terms and conditions as the Director may prescribe, issue a provisional licence for the period that the Director considers necessary to give the applicant time to meet the requirements.

Not transferable

(7) A licence is not transferable.

Placements must be in accord with Act and regulations

(8) No licensee shall place a child in a residential placement except in accordance with this Act and the regulations.

Licences, terms and conditions

193.1 During the course of a licence, a Director may impose terms and conditions on the licence or amend the terms and conditions on the licence.

Powers of Program Supervisor

Powers of program supervisor

194. (1) For the purpose of ensuring compliance with this Act and the regulations a program supervisor may, at all reasonable times, upon producing proper identification, enter,

(a) the premises of a licensee;
(b) a children's residence; or
(c) a place where a child receives residential care,

and may inspect the facilities, the services provided, the books of account and the records relating to the services, and make copies of those books and records or remove them from the premises to copy them as may be reasonably required.

Offence

(2) No person shall hinder, obstruct or attempt to hinder or obstruct a program supervisor in the performance of the program supervisor's duties or knowingly give false information about the premises or services to a program supervisor.

Idem

(3) No licensee or person in charge of premises referred to in clause (1)(a), (b) or (c) shall refuse to give a program supervisor access to the books and records referred to in subsection (1) or refuse to give a program supervisor information about the premises or services that the program supervisor reasonably requires.

Regulations re exercise of power of entry

(4) A program supervisor shall exercise the power of entry set out in subsection (1) in accordance with the regulations.

Refusal and Revocation

Grounds for refusal

195. A Director may refuse to issue a licence where, in the Director's opinion,

(a) the applicant or an employee of the applicant, or, where the applicant is a corporation, an officer or director of the corporation is not competent to carry on the activity for which the licence is required in a responsible manner in accordance with this Act and the regulations;

(b) the past conduct of the applicant or an employee of the applicant or, where the applicant is a corporation, of an officer or director of the corporation, affords reasonable grounds for belief that the activity for which the licence is required will not be carried on in a responsible manner in accordance with this Act and the regulations; or

(c) the premises in which the applicant proposes to establish, operate and maintain a children's residence or to provide residential care, as the case may be, do not comply with the requirements of this Part and the regulations.

Refusal to renew; revocation

196. A Director may refuse to renew or may revoke a licence where, in the Director's opinion,

(a) the licensee or an employee of the licensee, or where the licensee is a corporation, an officer or director of the corporation has contravened or has knowingly permitted a person under his or her control or direction or associated with him or her to contravene,

(i) this Act or the regulations,
(ii) another Act, or the regulations made under another Act, that applies to the activity for which the licence is required, or
(iii) a term or condition of the licence;

(b) the premises where the children's residence is located or the residential care is provided do not comply with the requirements of this Part and the regulations;

(c) the activity for which the licence is required is carried on in a manner that is prejudicial to the children's health, safety or welfare;

(d) a person has made a false statement in the application for the licence or for its renewal, or in a report or document required to be furnished by this Act or the regulations, or by another Act or the regulations made under another Act that applies to the activity for which the licence is required; or

(e) a change has occurred in the employees, officers or directors of the applicant that would, if the applicant were applying for the licence in the first instance, afford grounds under clause 195(b) for refusing to issue the licence.

Hearing by Tribunal

Hearings arising out of s. 195 or 196

Notice of proposal

197. (1) Where a Director proposes to refuse to issue a licence under section 195 or to refuse to renew or to revoke a licence under section 196, the Director shall cause notice of the proposal, together with written reasons, to be served on the applicant or licensee, who may require a hearing.

Request for hearing

(2) A notice under subsection (1) shall inform the applicant or licensee that the applicant or licensee is entitled to a hearing by the Tribunal if he, she or it mails or delivers to the Director and to the Tribunal, within ten days after the notice under subsection (1) is served, a written request for a hearing.

Note: Despite the amendment made by the Statutes of Ontario, 1999, chapter 12, Schedule G, subsection 16(4), members of the Child and Family Services Review Board immediately before April 1, 2000 shall be members of the Licence Appeal Tribunal for the purpose of performing the duties of the Tribunal with respect to proceedings before the Board that were commenced before April 1, 2000. See: 1999, c. 12, Sched. G, s. 16(5).

Powers of Director where no hearing required

(3) Where an applicant or licensee does not require a hearing under subsection (2), the Director may carry out the proposal.

Powers of Tribunal where hearing required

(4) Where an applicant or licensee requires a hearing under subsection (2), the Tribunal shall appoint a time for and hold a hearing and may, on hearing the matter,

(a) order the Director to carry out the proposal; or

(b) order the Director to take such other action as the Tribunal considers appropriate, in accordance with this Part and the regulations,

and the Tribunal may substitute its opinion for that of the Director.

Note: Despite the amendment made by the Statutes of Ontario, 1999, chapter 12, Schedule G, subsection 16(4), members of the Child and Family Services Review Board immediately before April 1, 2000 shall be members of the Licence Appeal Tribunal for the purpose of performing the duties of the Tribunal with respect to proceedings before the Board that were commenced before April 1, 2000. See: 1999, c. 12, Sched. G, s. 16(5).

Review of terms of licence by Tribunal

198. (1) A licensee who is dissatisfied with the terms and conditions prescribed by a Director under subsection 193(3), (5) or (6) or section 193.1 is entitled to a hearing by the Tribunal if the licensee mails or delivers to the Director and to the Tribunal, within fifteen days after receiving the licence, a written request for a hearing.

Note: Despite the amendment made by the Statutes of Ontario, 1999, chapter 12, Schedule G, subsection 16(4), members of the Child and Family Services Review Board immediately before April 1, 2000 shall be members of the Licence Appeal Tribunal for the purpose of performing the duties of the Tribunal with respect to proceedings before the Board that were commenced before April 1, 2000. See: 1999, c. 12, Sched. G, s. 16(5).

Powers of Tribunal

(2) Where a licensee requires a hearing under subsection (1), the Tribunal shall appoint a time for and hold a hearing and may, on hearing the matter,

(a) confirm any or all of the terms and conditions;

(b) strike out any or all of the terms and conditions; or

(c) impose such other terms and conditions as the Tribunal considers appropriate.

Note: Despite the amendment made by the Statutes of Ontario, 1999, chapter 12, Schedule G, subsection 16(4), members of the Child and Family Services Review Board immediately before April 1, 2000 shall be members of the Licence Appeal Tribunal for the purpose of performing the duties of the Tribunal with respect to proceedings before the Board that were commenced before April 1, 2000. See: 1999, c. 12, Sched. G, s. 16(5).

Receipt of licence

(3) For the purposes of subsection (1), a licensee shall be deemed to receive the licence on the tenth day after the day of its mailing, unless the licensee establishes that he, she or it did not receive it or did not, through absence, accident, illness or another cause beyond the licensee's control, acting in good faith, receive the licence until a later date.

Continuation of licence

199. (1) Repealed.

Continuation of licence pending renewal

(2) Subject to section 200, where a licensee has applied for renewal of the licence and paid the prescribed fee within the prescribed time or, if no time is prescribed, before the licence expires, the licence shall be deemed to continue,

(a) until the renewal is granted; or

(b) where the licensee is served with notice that the Director proposes to refuse to grant the renewal, until the time for requiring a hearing has expired and, where a hearing is required, until the Tribunal has made its decision.

Provisional suspension of licence

200. (1) A Director may, by causing notice to be served on a licensee, provisionally and without a hearing suspend the licence where, in the Director's opinion, the manner in which the children's residence is operated, residential care is provided or children are placed for adoption, as the case may be, is an immediate threat to the health, safety or welfare of the children.

Contents of notice

(2) A notice served under subsection (1) shall contain a statement of the grounds for suspending the licence.

When suspension takes effect

(3) A provisional suspension takes effect on the date that the licensee receives the notice.

S. 197(2-4) apply

(4) Where a notice is served under subsection (1), subsections 197(2), (3) and (4) apply with necessary modifications.

Rules re proceedings

Parties

201. (1) The Director, the applicant or licensee who requires the hearing and any other persons that the Tribunal specifies are parties to a proceeding under this Part.

Members with prior involvement

(2) A member of the Tribunal who has taken part before a hearing in any investigation or consideration of its subject matter, including a review under section 188 of Part VIII (Confidentiality of and Access to Records) that relates to the applicant or licensee, shall not take part in the hearing.

Discussion of subject matter of hearing

(3) A member of the Tribunal who takes part in a hearing shall not communicate with any person, except another member, a solicitor who is not the solicitor of any party, or an employee of the Tribunal, about the subject matter of the hearing, unless all parties are notified and given an opportunity to participate.

When Tribunal seeks independent legal advice

(4) The Tribunal may seek independent legal advice about the subject matter of a hearing and, if it does so, shall disclose the nature of the advice to the parties to enable them to respond.

Examination of documentary evidence

(5) A party to a proceeding under this Part shall be given an opportunity, before the hearing, to examine any written or documentary evidence that will be produced and any report whose contents will be given in evidence at the hearing.

(6) Repealed.

Only members at hearing to participate in decision, etc.

(7) No member of the Tribunal shall participate in a decision of the Tribunal under this Part unless he or she was present throughout the hearing and heard the evidence and argument of the parties and, unless the parties consent, the Tribunal shall not make a decision under this Part unless all the members who were present at the hearing participate in the decision.

Final decision of Tribunal within ninety days

(8) Despite section 21 of the *Statutory Powers Procedure Act*, the Tribunal shall make a final decision and notify the parties of it within ninety days from the day the Tribunal receives the applicant's or licensee's request for a hearing under subsection 197(2) or 198(1).

Appeal

Appeal

202. (1) An appeal lies to the Divisional Court from the Tribunal's decision under this Part.

Record to be filed in the court-

(2) Where notice of an appeal is served under this section, the Tribunal shall forthwith file with the court the record of the proceeding in which the decision appealed from was made.

Minister entitled to be heard

(3) The Minister is entitled to be heard, by counsel or otherwise, on the argument of an appeal under this section.

Delivery of Licence and Records

Records and licence, removal of children

Records and licence to be handed over to Minister

203. (1) A licensee whose licence is revoked or who ceases to carry on the activity for which the licence is required shall deliver up to the Minister the licence and all the records in the licensee's possession or control that relate to the children to whom services were being provided.

Removal of children

(2) Where a licence to operate a children's residence or to provide residential care is suspended or revoked, the parent of every child in the children's residence or other place where residential care is provided shall arrange for the child's removal from the residence or other place as soon as is practicable, having regard to the child's best interests, and the Minister may assist in finding an alternative placement for the child.

Occupation by Minister

Order for Minister's occupation

204. (1) The Minister may, where a Director's proposal to revoke or not to renew a licence under subsection 197(1) or notice of provisional suspension under subsection 198(1) has been served on a licensee who operates a children's residence or provides residential care and the matter has not yet been finally disposed of, apply without notice to the Superior Court of Justice for an order,

(a) authorizing the Minister to occupy and operate the children's residence or the premises where the residential care is provided, pending the outcome of the proceeding until alternative accommodation may be found for the children who are being cared for; and

(b) directing the sheriff to assist the Minister as may be necessary in occupying the premises.

Where court may make order

(2) The court may make an order referred to subsection (1) where it is satisfied that the health, safety or welfare of the children being cared for require it.

Interim management

(3) Where an order has been made under subsection (2), the Minister may, despite sections 25 and 39 of the *Expropriations Act*, immediately occupy and operate or arrange for the occupation and operation of the premises for a period not exceeding six months.

Injunctions

Injunction

205. (1) A Director may apply to the Superior Court of Justice for an order enjoining any person from,

(a) contravening subsection 193(1) (licence requirement); or

(b) carrying on an activity for which a licence is required while the licence is provisionally suspended under section 200.

Idem

(2) Any person may apply to the court for an order varying or discharging an order made under subsection (1).

Offences

Offence

206. (1) Every person who,

(a) contravenes subsection 193(1);

(b) contravenes a term or condition of a licence relating to the maximum number of children to be cared for in a children's residence or other place where residential care is provided under the authority of a licence;

(c) causes a child to be cared for in a children's residence operated by a person who is not licensed under this Part, or in another place where residential care is provided by a person who is required to be but is not licensed to provide residential care under this Part; or

(d) is a child's parent or a person under a legal duty to provide for the child and permits the child to be cared for in a children's residence or other place referred to in clause (c),

and every director, officer or employee of a corporation who authorizes, permits or concurs in such an act by the corporation is guilty of an offence and on conviction is liable to a fine of not more than $1,000 for each day on which the offence continues or to imprisonment for a term of not more than one year, or to both.

Idem

(2) Every person who,

(a) knowingly contravenes subsection 194(2) or (3) (obstructing program supervisor, etc.);

(b) knowingly furnishes false information in an application under this Part or in a statement, report or return required to be furnished under this Part or the regulations; or

(c) fails to comply with an order or direction made by a court under this Part,

and every director, officer or employee of a corporation who authorizes, permits or concurs in such a contravention, furnishing or failure by the corporation is guilty of an offence and on conviction is liable to a fine of not more than $2,000.

Child and Family Services Review Board

Child and Family Services Review Board

207. (1) The Child and Family Services Review Board is continued under the name Child and Family Services Review Board in English and Commission de révision des services à l'enfance et à la famille in French.

Idem

(2) The Board is composed of the prescribed number of members appointed by the Lieutenant Governor in Council and has the powers and duties given to it by this Act and the regulations.

Chair and vice-chairs

(3) The Lieutenant Governor in Council may appoint a member of the Board as chair and may appoint one or more other members as vice-chairs.

(4) Repealed.

Quorum

(5) The prescribed number of members of the Board are a quorum.

Remuneration

(6) The chair and vice-chairs and the other members of the Board shall be paid the remuneration determined by the Lieutenant Governor in Council and are entitled to their reasonable and necessary travelling and living expenses while attending meetings or otherwise engaged in the work of the Board.

PART X INDIAN AND NATIVE CHILD AND FAMILY SERVICES

Definition

208. In this Part,

"customary care" means the care and supervision of an Indian or native child by a person who is not the child's parent, according to the custom of the child's band or native community.

Designation of native communities

209. The Minister may designate a community, with the consent of its representatives, as a native community for the purposes of this Act.

Agreements with bands and native communities

210. The Minister may make agreements with bands and native communities, and any other parties whom the bands or native communities choose to involve, for the provision of services.

Designation of child and family service authority

211. (1) A band or native community may designate a body as an Indian or native child and family service authority.

Agreements, etc.

(2) Where a band or native community has designated an Indian or native child and family service authority, the Minister,

(a) shall, at the band's or native community's request, enter into negotiations for the provision of services by the child and family service authority;

(b) may enter into agreements with the child and family service authority and, if the band or native community agrees, any other person, for the provision of services; and

(c) may designate the child and family service authority, with its consent and if it is an approved agency, as a society under subsection 15(2) of Part I (Flexible Services).

Subsidy for customary care

212. Where a band or native community declares that an Indian or native child is being cared for under customary care, a society or agency may grant a subsidy to the person caring for the child.

Consultation with bands and native communities

213. A society or agency that provides services or exercises powers under this Act with respect to Indian or native children shall regularly consult with their bands or native communities about the provision of the services or the exercise of the powers and about matters affecting the children, including,

(a) the apprehension of children and the placement of children in residential care;

(b) the placement of homemakers and the provision of other family support services;

(c) the preparation of plans for the care of children;

(d) status reviews under Part III (Child Protection);

(e) temporary care and special needs agreements under Part II (Voluntary Access to Services);

(f) adoption placements;

(g) the establishment of emergency houses; and

(h) any other matter that is prescribed.

Consultation in specified cases

213.1 A society or agency that proposes to provide a prescribed service to a child who is an Indian or native person or to exercise a prescribed power under this Act in relation to such a child shall consult with a representative chosen by the child's band or native community in accordance with the regulations.

PART XI REGULATIONS

Regulations: Part I (Flexible Services)

214. (1) The Lieutenant Governor in Council may make regulations for the purposes of Part I,

1. prescribing additional powers and duties of Directors and program supervisors;
2. prescribing reports to be made and information to be furnished under subsection 5(5), their form and the intervals at which they are to be made or furnished;
3. governing the exercise of the power of entry set out in subsection 6(1);
4. governing the management and operation of approved agencies or any class of them;
5. governing the provision of approved services or any class of them;
6. exempting designated approved agencies or approved services or any class of them from any provision of this Act or the regulations for a specified period or periods;

6.1 respecting the composition of boards of approved agencies or classes of approved agencies, requiring board members to undertake training programs and prescribing those programs;

7. governing the accommodation, facilities and equipment to be provided,
   i. in buildings in which approved services are provided, and
   ii. in the course of the provision of approved services;
8. further defining "service," "child development service," "child treatment service," "child welfare service," "community support service" and "youth justice service";
9. defining "prevention service";
10. governing the establishment, management, operation, location, construction, alteration and renovation of buildings, or any class of them, in which approved services are provided;
11. prescribing procedures and conditions of eligibility for the admission of children and other persons to and their discharge from places where approved services are provided;
12. prescribing the qualifications, powers and duties of persons employed in providing approved services or any class of approved services;

12.1 prescribing classes of persons employed or to be employed in providing approved services or any class of approved services who must undertake training, prescribing that training and prescribing the circumstances under which that training must be undertaken;

13. governing the residential placement of children and prescribing procedures for placements, discharge, assessments and case management;
14. requiring and prescribing medical and other related or ancillary services for the care and treatment of children and other persons in places where services or any class of them are provided;
15. governing applications by agencies for approval under subsections 8(1) and 9(1) and establishing criteria for approval;
16. governing applications by approved agencies for payments under this Part, prescribing the method, time, manner, terms and conditions of payments and providing for the suspension and withholding of payments and for the making of deductions from payments;
17. prescribing the manner of computing the amount of financial assistance for the purposes of sections 8 and 9, prescribing classes of payments for the purposes of those sections and determining the amounts of payments;
18. governing the transfer and assignment of the assets of approved agencies acquired with financial assistance from the Province of Ontario, or of any class of such assets, for the purposes of subsection 10(3), and prescribing classes of such assets;
19. requiring approved agencies to provide the prescribed information to the prescribed persons, and prescribing the information and the persons;

20. prescribing the accounts and records to be kept by approved agencies, the claims, returns and reports to be made and budgets to be submitted to the Minister and the methods, time and manner in which they shall be made or submitted;
21. requiring service providers, or any class of service providers, to keep records, and prescribing the form and content of those records;
22. providing for the recovery, by an approved agency or by the Minister, from the person or persons in whose charge a child is or has been or from the estate of that person or persons of amounts paid by the agency for the child's care and maintenance, and prescribing the circumstances and the manner in which such a recovery may be made;
23. providing for the recovery of payments made to approved agencies under this Part and the regulations;
24. prescribing provisions to be included in the by-laws of approved agencies, or any class of them, for the purpose of subsection 13(2);
25. prescribing the number of band or native community representatives on the boards of directors of agencies or any class of them, the manner of their appointment and their terms, for the purpose of subsection 13(3);
26. prescribing forms and providing for their use;
27. prescribing fees or classes of fees that may be charged for services and the terms and conditions under which a fee may be charged;
28. Repealed.
29. providing for an executive committee of the board of directors of a society, its composition, quorum, powers and duties;
30. prescribing a system for determining,
    i. the amounts of payments under subsection 19(2) (payments by Minister), and
    ii. a society's estimated expenditures;
31. Repealed.
32. governing the construction, alteration, renovation, extension, furnishing and equipping of homes operated or supervised by societies, other than children's residences as defined in Part IX (Licensing), where residential care is provided to children.

Same

(2) A regulation made under paragraph 6.1, 12.1, 18, 24 or 25 of subsection (1) (boards of approved agencies, training of persons providing approved services, transfer of assets, prescribed provisions in agency by-laws, band or native community representatives) may be general or specific in its application.

Same

(3) A regulation made under paragraph 17 or 30 of subsection (1) (financial assistance for the purposes of sections 8 and 9, amounts of payments to societies) is, if it so provides, effective with reference to a period before it is filed.

Idem

(4) The Minister shall prescribe,

(a) standards of services; and

(b) procedures and practices to be followed by societies,

for the purposes of subsection 15(4).

Standards of service, etc.

(5) In regulations made under subsection (4), the Minister,

(a) may exempt one or more societies from anything that is prescribed under that subsection;

(b) may prescribe standards of services that only apply to one or more societies provided for in the regulations;

(c) may prescribe procedures and practices that are only required to be followed by one or more societies provided for in the regulations.

Regulations: Part II (Voluntary Access to Services)

215. The Lieutenant Governor in Council may make regulations for the purposes of Part II,

(a) defining "counselling";

(b) prescribing provisions to be contained in agreements made under section 29 (temporary care agreements) and sections 30 and 31 (special needs agreements);

(c) requiring that residential placements with or by service providers be made in accordance with written agreements, and prescribing their form and contents;

(d) prescribing practices, procedures and further duties for advisory committees;

(e) further defining "special need" and "developmental disability."

Regulations: Part III (Child Protection)

216. (1) The Lieutenant Governor in Council may make regulations for the purposes of Part III,

(a) governing the exercise of the powers of entry set out in subsections 40(6) and (11) and section 44;

(a.1) respecting the procedures to be followed by a society for the purposes of subsection 37(5);

(b) assigning to a Director any powers, duties or obligations of the Crown with respect to Crown wards;

(b.1) governing when an assessment may be ordered under section 54, the scope of an assessment, and the form of an assessment report;

(b.2) respecting applications for a review by the Board under subsection 61(7.1);

(b.3) prescribing additional practices and procedures for the purposes of subsection 61(8.2);

(b.4) prescribing the qualifications or experience a member of the Board is required to have in order to conduct reviews under subsection 61(8), 68(6) or 68.1(5);

(b.5) respecting the making of complaints to a society under subsection 68(1) or to the Board under subsection 68.1(1);

(b.6) governing the complaint review procedure that societies are required to follow when dealing with a complaint under subsection 68(1);

(b.7) prescribing matters for the purposes of paragraph 3 of subsection 68(5) and paragraph 6 of subsection 68.1(4);

(b.8) prescribing additional orders that may be made by the Board for the purposes of clauses 68(10)(e) and 68.1(7)(f);

(b.9) prescribing practices and procedures for the purposes of hearings conducted by the Board under subsection 68(8) or during a review of a complaint under section 68.1;

(c) Repealed.

(c.1) respecting the format of warrants under sections 74.1 and 74.2 and the procedures to be followed in applying for, issuing, receiving and filing warrants of different formats;

(c.2) prescribing manners of applying for a warrant under section 74.2, including a manner other than submitting an information on oath, setting out the circumstances under which those manners may be used and providing for any additional requirements that must be met if those manners are used;

Note: On a day to be named by proclamation of the Lieutenant Governor, section 216 is amended by the Statutes of Ontario, 2008, chapter 21, section 5 by adding the following clause:

(c.3) designating one or more organizations, agencies or persons for the purpose of receiving reports of child pornography under subsection 72(1.1);

See: 2008, c. 21, ss. 5, 6.

(d) prescribing the form in which reports are to be made under subsection 75(3);

(e) respecting the manner in which the register referred to in subsection 75(5) is to be kept;

(f) requiring the removal of a name from the register referred to in subsection 75(5), or the amendment of the register, under specified circumstances, and specifying those circumstances;

(g) prescribing practices and procedures for hearings held under clause 76(4)(b) (amendment of register);

(h) prescribing forms and providing for their use.

Same

(2) The Minister may make regulations,

(a) prescribing the care and maintenance that may be provided to persons under section 71.1, and the terms and conditions on which the care and maintenance may be provided;

(b) prescribing support services for the purposes of subsection 71.1(3).

Regulations: Part IV (Youth Justice)

217. (1) The Lieutenant Governor in Council may make regulations for the purposes of Part IV,

(a) governing the establishment, operation, maintenance, management and use of places of temporary detention, open custody and secure custody and other services and programs provided under subsection 89(1);

(b) governing the establishment and operation of and the accommodation, equipment and services to be provided in any premises or class of premises established, operated, maintained or designated for the purposes of the federal Act or for providing services or programs under subsection 89(1);

(c) prescribing additional duties and functions of,

(i) probation officers, and

(ii) provincial directors;

(d) prescribing the duties and functions of bailiffs;

(e) prescribing the qualifications of probation officers;

(f) prescribing additional duties and functions of persons in charge of places of temporary detention, open custody and secure custody;

(g) prescribing reports to be made and information to be furnished under section 92, their form and the intervals at which they are to be made or furnished;

(h) governing the conduct, discipline, rights and privileges of young persons in places of temporary detention, open custody or secure custody or any class of them or in a service or program provided under subsection 89(1);

(i) prescribing procedures for the admission of young persons to and their discharge from places of temporary detention, open custody or secure custody or any class of them or premises in which a service or program is provided under subsection 89(1);

(j) prescribing classes of payment by way of provincial aid for the establishment, operation or maintenance of places of temporary detention, open custody or secure custody, the methods of determining the payments, the manner and time of making them, the terms and conditions of such payments and the circumstances under which such payments may be suspended or withheld or deductions may be made from them;

(k) prescribing the number of members of the Board and the number of members that is a quorum;

(l) prescribing additional powers, duties and procedures of the Board;

(m) governing the exercise of the power of entry given under subsection 98(5);

(n) respecting any matter considered necessary or advisable to carry out effectively the intent and purpose of Part IV.

Idem

(2) A regulation made under clause (1)(j) (classes of payment by way of provincial aid) is, if it so provides, effective with reference to a period before it is filed.

Regulations: Part V (Rights of Children)

218. The Lieutenant Governor in Council may make regulations for the purposes of Part V,

(a) governing internal complaints procedures to be established under section 109;

(b) establishing procedures for reviews under section 110;

(c) Repealed.

Regulations: Part VI (Extraordinary Measures)

219. The Lieutenant Governor in Council may make regulations for the purposes of Part VI,

(a) prescribing procedures for the admission of persons to and their discharge from secure treatment programs;

(b) prescribing standards for secure treatment programs;

(c) prescribing standards for secure isolation rooms;

(d) prescribing procedures to be followed when a child is placed in or released from a secure isolation room;

(e) prescribing the frequency of reviews under subsection 127(6);

(e.1) governing standards and procedures with which a service provider must comply under subsection 127(9);

(f) prescribing matters to be reviewed and prescribing additional reports under section 128;

(g) prescribing procedures as intrusive procedures;

(h) prescribing the intervals at which reports are to be made by review teams under subsection 129(5);

(i) prescribing drugs, combinations of drugs or classes of drugs as psychotropic drugs;

(j) prescribing forms and requiring their use.

Regulations: Part VII (Adoption)

220. (1) The Lieutenant Governor in Council may make regulations for the purposes of Part VII,

(a) prescribing the form of an affidavit of execution for the purposes of subsection 137(12);

(a.1) prescribing matters for the purposes of clause 137(4)(a.1);

(a.2) prescribing criteria for the purposes of the definition of "birth parent" in subsection 136(1);

Note: Clause 220(1)(a.2) was enacted as clause 220(1)(a.1) in source law, Statutes of Ontario, 2006, chapter 5, section 46. The clause is renumbered in this consolidation to distinguish it from existing clause 220(1)(a.1), enacted by Statutes of Ontario 2005, chapter 25, subsection 32(1).

(b) prescribing the manner in which placements are to be registered under subsection 141(6);

(b.1) governing applications for review under subsection 144(3);

(b.2) prescribing additional practices and procedures for the purposes of subsection 144(7);

(b.3) prescribing the qualifications or experience a member of the Board is required to have in order to conduct reviews under subsection 144(8);

(b.4) governing procedures to be followed by a Director in making a review under subsection 145(3), what types of decisions and directions the Director is authorized to make after conducting a review, and any consequences following as a result of a decision or direction;

(c) prescribing special circumstances for the purposes of subsection 142(4) (placement outside Canada);

(c.1) prescribing persons for the purposes of clause 162(3)(e);

(c.2) prescribing the powers and duties of a designated custodian under section 162.1 and governing the fees that the designated custodian may charge in connection with the exercise of its powers and the performance of its duties;

(c.3) governing the disclosure of information under section 162.2 to a designated custodian;

(c.4) governing the disclosure of information under section 162.3 by the Minister, a society, a licensee or a designated custodian;

(c.5) establishing and governing a mechanism for the review or appeal of a decision made by the Minister, a society, a licensee or a designated custodian concerning the disclosure of information under section 162.2 or 162.3;

(c.6) governing the fees that a society, licensee or designated custodian may charge for the disclosure of information under section 162.2 or 162.3;

(c.7) defining "openness" for the purposes of,

(i) openness orders under Part VII,

(ii) openness agreements under section 153.6;

(c.8) governing openness orders under Part VII;

Note: Clauses 220(1)(c.7) and (c.8) were enacted as clauses 220(1)(c.1) and (c.2) in source law, Statutes of Ontario, 2006, chapter 5, section 46. The clauses are renumbered in this consolidation to distinguish them from existing clauses 220(1)(c.1) and (c.2), enacted by Statutes of Ontario 2005, chapter 25, subsection 32(2).

(d) prescribing forms and providing for their use;
(e) Repealed.
(f) Repealed.
(f.1) Repealed.
(g) Repealed.
(h) Repealed.
(i) Repealed.
(j) prescribing expenses that may be charged under clause 175(d), classes of such expenses and the terms and conditions under which such expenses or classes of expenses may be charged.

Classes

(2) A regulation under clauses (1)(c.2) to (c.6) may establish different standards and requirements with respect to different classes of persons.

Transitional matters

(3) The Lieutenant Governor in Council may make regulations providing for transitional matters which, in the opinion of the Lieutenant Governor in Council, are necessary or desirable in connection with the enactment of sections 162.1 to 162.4 by the *Adoption Information Disclosure Act, 2005* and the amendment or repeal, as the case may be, of sections 162 to 174 by that Act.

Regulations: Part VIII (Confidentiality of and Access to Records)

221. The Lieutenant Governor in Council may make regulations for the purposes of Part VIII,

(a) prescribing the manner in which a Director's approval is to be obtained under subsection 182(2) (disclosure for research);
(b) prescribing review procedures for the Board under subsection 188(3);
(c) prescribing provisions for the purposes of subsection 191(2) (service providers' codes of procedure);
(d) prescribing retention, storage and destruction schedules for the purposes of subsection 191(3).

Regulations: Part IX (Licensing)

222. The Lieutenant Governor in Council may make regulations for the purposes of Part IX,

(a) governing the establishment, management, operation and use of children's residences, and other premises where residential care is provided under the authority of a licence;
(b) defining "common parentage" for the purposes of the definition of "children's residence" in section 192 and clause 193(1)(b);
(c) governing the issuing, renewal and expiry of licences and prescribing fees payable by an applicant for a licence or its renewal;
(d) governing the exercise of the power of entry set out in subsection 194(1);
(e) governing the establishment of and the accommodation, facilities, equipment and services to be provided in,

(i) children's residences, and
(ii) other premises where residential care is provided under the authority of a licence,

or any class of them;

(f) exempting from any or all provisions of Part IX or the regulations, either indefinitely or for any time that may be provided for in the regulations,

(i) a children's residence or a prescribed class of children's residences,
(ii) premises or a prescribed class of premises where residential care is provided under the authority of a licence,
(iii) a person or class of persons who place children for adoption,
(iv) a person or class of persons who provide residential care under the authority of a licence;

(g) prescribing the accounts and records to be kept by licensees;
(h) prescribing the qualifications, powers and duties of persons supervising children in,

(i) children's residences, or
(ii) other premises where residential care is provided under the authority of a licence,

or any class of them;

(i) governing procedures for the admission to and discharge of children from,

(i) children's residences, or
(ii) other premises where residential care is provided under the authority of a licence,

or any class of them;

(j) requiring the operators of children's residences or persons who provide residential care or place children for adoption under the authority of a licence to provide the prescribed information and to make the prescribed returns and reports, and prescribing the information, returns and reports;
(k) prescribing the number of members of the Board and the number of members that is a quorum;
(l) prescribing additional powers, duties and procedures of the Board;
(m) governing the placement of children for adoption;
(n) prescribing rules and standards governing the placement of children by licensees for adoption;
(o) providing for the inspection of the records of persons licensed to place children for adoption;
(p) governing the qualifications of persons or classes of persons employed by persons licensed to place children for adoption;

(q) requiring persons licensed to place children for adoption to be bonded or to submit letters of credit in the prescribed form and terms and with the prescribed collateral security, prescribing the form, terms and collateral security and providing for the forfeiture of bonds and letters of credit and the disposition of the proceeds;

(r) prescribing forms and providing for their use.

Regulations: Part X (Indian and Native Child and Family Services)

223. The Lieutenant Governor in Council may make regulations for the purposes of Part X,

(a) exempting an Indian or native child and family service authority, a band or native community or specified persons or classes of persons, including persons caring for children under customary care, from any provision of this Act or the regulations;

(b) prescribing matters requiring consultation between societies or agencies and bands or native communities for the purposes of clause 213(h).

(c) governing consultations with bands and native communities under sections 213 and 213.1 and prescribing the procedures and practices to be followed by societies and agencies and the duties of societies and agencies during the consultations;

(d) prescribing services and powers for the purposes of section 213.1.

Regulations: methods of dispute resolution

223.1 (1) The Lieutenant Governor in Council may make regulations,

(a) prescribing methods of alternative dispute resolution for the purposes of this Act, defining methods of alternative dispute resolution, and governing procedures for and the use of prescribed methods of alternative dispute resolution;

(b) respecting qualifications of persons providing a prescribed alternative dispute resolution service;

(c) respecting the confidentiality of and access to records and information related to alternative dispute resolution.

Same

(2) A regulation made under subsection (1) may prescribe different methods of alternative dispute resolution, different definitions of methods of alternative dispute resolution and different procedures for prescribed methods of alternative dispute resolution for the purposes of different provisions of this Act.

Regulations: transitional

223.2 The Lieutenant Governor in Council may make regulations governing transitional issues that may arise due to the enactment of the *Child and Family Services Statute Law Amendment Act, 2006* and facilitating the implementation of provisions that are enacted or re-enacted by that Act, and without restricting the generality of the preceding, may make regulations,

(a) respecting alternative dispute resolution and legal representation for children for the purposes of section 20.2 if a form of alternative dispute resolution commenced before that section came into force;

(b) respecting circumstances in which subsections 51(3.1) and (3.2) do not apply in respect of the placement of a child;

(c) respecting types of terms and conditions that may be imposed for the purposes of sections 51, 57 and 65.2 and persons or classes of persons subject to terms and conditions under those sections;

(d) respecting assessments for the purposes of section 54 that were made or commenced before this section came into force;

(e) respecting orders that may be made under section 57, 57.1 or 65.2;

(f) respecting circumstances in which sections 57.2 and 59.1 will not apply;

(g) respecting circumstances in which section 59 as it read before subsection 59(2.1) came into force will apply;

(h) respecting applications under sections 64 and 65.1;

(i) respecting the provision of care and maintenance under subsection 71(2);

(j) respecting reviews by a Director under section 145.

PART XII MISCELLANEOUS

Review of Act

224. (1) The Minister shall periodically conduct a review of this Act or those provisions of it specified by the Minister.

Beginning of review

(2) The Minister shall inform the public when a review under this section begins and what provisions of this Act are included in the review.

Written report

(3) The Minister shall prepare a written report respecting the review and shall make that report available to the public.

Period for review

(4) The first review shall be completed and the report made available to the public within five years after the day this section comes into force.

Same

(5) Each subsequent review shall be completed and the report made available to the public within five years after the day the report on the previous review has been made available to the public.

Review re disclosure of adoption information

225. The Lieutenant Governor in Council shall ensure that a review of the operation of sections 161 to 165 and section 176.1 is conducted within five years after section 4 of the

Access to Adoption Records Act (Vital Statistics Statute Law Amendment), 2008 comes into force.

Review re: aboriginal issues

226. Every review of this Act shall include a review of provisions imposing obligations on societies when providing services to a person who is an Indian or native person or in respect of children who are Indian or native persons, with a view to ensuring compliance by societies with those provisions.

Children's Law Reform Act

RSO 1990, c. C.12
Current to June 20, 2012

PART I EQUAL STATUS OF CHILDREN

Rule of parentage

1. (1) Subject to subsection (2), for all purposes of the law of Ontario a person is the child of his or her natural parents and his or her status as their child is independent of whether the child is born within or outside marriage.

Exception for adopted children

(2) Where an adoption order has been made, section 158 or 159 of the *Child and Family Services Act* applies and the child is the child of the adopting parents as if they were the natural parents.

Kindred relationships

(3) The parent and child relationships as determined under subsections (1) and (2) shall be followed in the determination of other kindred relationships flowing therefrom.

Common law distinction of legitimacy abolished

(4) Any distinction at common law between the status of children born in wedlock and born out of wedlock is abolished and the relationship of parent and child and kindred relationships flowing therefrom shall be determined for the purposes of the common law in accordance with this section.

Rule of construction

2. (1) For the purposes of construing any instrument, Act or regulation, unless the contrary intention appears, a reference to a person or group or class of persons described in terms of relationship by blood or marriage to another person shall be construed to refer to or include a person who comes within the description by reason of the relationship of parent and child as determined under section 1.

Application

(2) Subsection (1) applies to,

(a) any Act of the Legislature or any regulation, order or by-law made under an Act of the Legislature enacted or made before, on or after the 31st day of March, 1978; and

(b) any instrument made on or after the 31st day of March, 1978.

PART II ESTABLISHMENT OF PARENTAGE

Court under ss. 4 to 7

3. The court having jurisdiction for the purposes of sections 4 to 7 is,

(a) the Family Court, in the areas where it has jurisdiction under subsection 21.1(4) of the *Courts of Justice Act*;

(b) the Superior Court of Justice, in the rest of Ontario.

Paternity and maternity declarations

4. (1) Any person having an interest may apply to a court for a declaration that a male person is recognized in law to be the father of a child or that a female person is the mother of a child.

Declaration of paternity recognized at law

(2) Where the court finds that a presumption of paternity exists under section 8 and unless it is established, on the balance of probabilities, that the presumed father is not the father of the child, the court shall make a declaratory order confirming that the paternity is recognized in law.

Declaration of maternity

(3) Where the court finds on the balance of probabilities that the relationship of mother and child has been established, the court may make a declaratory order to that effect.

Idem

(4) Subject to sections 6 and 7, an order made under this section shall be recognized for all purposes.

Application for declaration of paternity where no presumption

5. (1) Where there is no person recognized in law under section 8 to be the father of a child, any person may apply to the court for a declaration that a male person is his or her father, or any male person may apply to the court for a declaration that a person is his child.

Limitation

(2) An application shall not be made under subsection (1) unless both the persons whose relationship is sought to be established are living.

Declaratory order

(3) Where the court finds on the balance of probabilities that the relationship of father and child has been established, the court may make a declaratory order to that effect and, subject to sections 6 and 7, the order shall be recognized for all purposes.

Reopening on new evidence

6. Where a declaration has been made under section 4 or 5 and evidence becomes available that was not available at the previous hearing, the court may, upon application, discharge or vary the order and make such other orders or directions as are ancillary thereto.

Corresponding change of surname

6.1 (1) Any person declared under section 4, 5 or 6, as the case may be, to be the mother or father of a child may apply to the court for an order that the child's surname be changed to any surname that the child could have been given at birth under subsection 10(3), (4) or (5) of the *Vital Statistics Act*.

Same

(2) An application under subsection (1) to change a child's surname may be made at the same time that an application for a declaration under section 4, 5 or 6 is made.

Best interests of the child

(3) An order under subsection (1) changing a child's surname may only be made if it is in the best interests of the child.

Appeal

7. An appeal lies from an order under section 4, 5 or 6.1 or a decision under section 6 in accordance with the rules of the court.

Presumption of paternity

8. (1) Unless the contrary is proven on a balance of probabilities, there is a presumption that a male person is, and he shall be recognized in law to be, the father of a child in any one of the following circumstances:

1. The person is married to the mother of the child at the time of the birth of the child.
2. The person was married to the mother of the child by a marriage that was terminated by death or judgment of nullity within 300 days before the birth of the child or by divorce where the decree *nisi* was granted within 300 days before the birth of the child.
3. The person marries the mother of the child after the birth of the child and acknowledges that he is the natural father.
4. The person was cohabiting with the mother of the child in a relationship of some permanence at the time of the birth of the child or the child is born within 300 days after they ceased to cohabit.
5. The person has certified the child's birth, as the child's father, under the *Vital Statistics Act* or a similar Act in another jurisdiction in Canada.
6. The person has been found or recognized in his lifetime by a court of competent jurisdiction in Canada to be the father of the child.

Where marriage void

(2) For the purpose of subsection (1), where a man and woman go through a form of marriage with each other, in good faith, that is void and cohabit, they shall be deemed to be married during the time they cohabit and the marriage shall be deemed to be terminated when they cease to cohabit.

Conflicting presumptions

(3) Where circumstances exist that give rise to a presumption or presumptions of paternity by more than one father under subsection (1), no presumption shall be made as to paternity and no person is recognized in law to be the father.

Admissibility in evidence of acknowledgment against interest

9. A written acknowledgment of parentage that is admitted in evidence in any civil proceeding against the interest of the person making the acknowledgment is proof, in the absence of evidence to the contrary, of the fact.

Leave for blood tests and DNA tests

10. (1) On the application of a party in a civil proceeding in which the court is called on to determine a child's parentage, the court may give the party leave to obtain blood tests or DNA tests of the persons who are named in the order granting leave and to submit the results in evidence.

Conditions

(2) The court may impose conditions, as it thinks proper, on an order under subsection (1).

Consent to procedure

(3) The *Health Care Consent Act*, 1996 applies to the blood test or DNA test as if it were treatment under that Act.

Inference from refusal

(4) If a person named in an order under subsection (1) refuses to submit to the blood test or DNA test, the court may draw such inferences as it thinks appropriate.

Exception

(5) Subsection (4) does not apply if the refusal is the decision of a substitute decision-maker as defined in section 9 of the *Health Care Consent Act*, 1996.

11. Repealed.

Statutory declaration of parentage

12. (1) A person may file in the office of the Registrar General a statutory declaration, in the form provided by the Ministry of the Attorney General, affirming that he or she is the father or mother, as the case may be, of a child.

Note: On a day to be named by proclamation of the Lieutenant Governor, subsection (1) is amended by striking out "in the office of the Registrar General" and substituting in each case "with the Registrar General." See: 2012, c. 8, Sch. 7, ss. 1, 2.

Idem

(2) Two persons may file in the office of the Registrar General a statutory declaration, in the form provided by the Ministry of the Attorney General, jointly affirming that they are the father and mother of a child.

Note: On a day to be named by proclamation of the Lieutenant Governor, subsection (2) is amended by striking out "in the office of the Registrar General" and substituting in each case "with the Registrar General." See: 2012, c. 8, Sch. 7, ss. 1, 2.

Copies of statutory declarations under *Vital Statistics Act*

13. Upon application and upon payment of the fee prescribed under the *Vital Statistics Act*, any person who has an interest, furnishes substantially accurate particulars and satisfies the Registrar General as to the reason for requiring it may obtain from the Registrar General a certified copy of a statutory declaration filed under section 12.

Filing of court decisions respecting parentage

14. (1) Every registrar or clerk of a court in Ontario shall furnish the Registrar General with a statement in the form provided by the Ministry of the Attorney General respecting each order or judgment of the court that confirms or makes a finding of parentage.

Inspection by public

(2) Upon application and upon payment of the fee prescribed under the *Vital Statistics Act*, any person may inspect a statement respecting an order or judgment filed under subsection (1) and obtain a certified copy thereof from the Registrar General.

Certified copies as evidence

15. A certificate certifying a copy of a document to be a true copy, obtained under section 12, 13 or 14, purporting to be signed by the Registrar General or Deputy Registrar General or on which the signature of either is lithographed, printed or stamped is, without proof of the office or signature of the Registrar General or Deputy Registrar General, receivable in evidence as proof, in the absence of evidence to the contrary, of the filing and contents of the document for all purposes in any action or proceeding.

Duties of Registrar General

16. Nothing in this Act shall be construed to require the Registrar General to amend a registration showing parentage other than in recognition of an order made under section 4, 5 or 6.

17. Repealed.

PART III CUSTODY, ACCESS AND GUARDIANSHIP

Interpretation

Definitions, Part III

18. (1) In this Part,

"court" means the Ontario Court of Justice, the Family Court or the Superior Court of Justice;

"extra-provincial order" means an order, or that part of an order, of an extra-provincial tribunal that grants to a person custody of or access to a child;

"extra-provincial tribunal" means a court or tribunal outside Ontario that has jurisdiction to grant to a person custody of or access to a child;

"separation agreement" means an agreement that is a valid separation agreement under Part IV of the *Family Law Act*.

Child

(2) A reference in this Part to a child is a reference to the child while a minor.

Purposes, Part III

19. The purposes of this Part are,

(a) to ensure that applications to the courts in respect of custody of, incidents of custody of, access to and guardianship for children will be determined on the basis of the best interests of the children;

(b) to recognize that the concurrent exercise of jurisdiction by judicial tribunals of more than one province, territory or state in respect of the custody of the same child ought to be avoided, and to make provision so that the courts of Ontario will, unless there are exceptional circumstances, refrain from exercising or decline jurisdiction in cases where it is more appropriate for the matter to be determined by a tribunal having jurisdiction in another place with which the child has a closer connection;

(c) to discourage the abduction of children as an alternative to the determination of custody rights by due process; and

(d) to provide for the more effective enforcement of custody and access orders and for the recognition and enforcement of custody and access orders made outside Ontario.

Custody and Access

Father and mother entitled to custody

20. (1) Except as otherwise provided in this Part, the father and the mother of a child are equally entitled to custody of the child.

Rights and responsibilities

(2) A person entitled to custody of a child has the rights and responsibilities of a parent in respect of the person of the child and must exercise those rights and responsibilities in the best interests of the child.

Authority to act

(3) Where more than one person is entitled to custody of a child, any one of them may exercise the rights and accept the responsibilities of a parent on behalf of them in respect of the child.

Where parents separate

(4) Where the parents of a child live separate and apart and the child lives with one of them with the consent, implied consent or acquiescence of the other of them, the right of the other to exercise the entitlement of custody and the incidents of custody, but not the entitlement to access, is suspended until a separation agreement or order otherwise provides.

Access

(5) The entitlement to access to a child includes the right to visit with and be visited by the child and the same right as a parent to make inquiries and to be given information as to the health, education and welfare of the child.

Marriage of child

(6) The entitlement to custody of or access to a child terminates on the marriage of the child.

Entitlement subject to agreement or order

(7) Any entitlement to custody or access or incidents of custody under this section is subject to alteration by an order of the court or by separation agreement.

Application for custody or access

21. (1) A parent of a child or any other person may apply to a court for an order respecting custody of or access to the child or determining any aspect of the incidents of custody of the child.

Affidavit

(2) An application under subsection (1) for custody of or access to a child shall be accompanied by an affidavit, in the form prescribed for the purpose by the rules of court, of the person applying for custody or access, containing,

(a) the person's proposed plan for the child's care and upbringing;

(b) information respecting the person's current or previous involvement in any family proceedings, including proceedings under Part III of the *Child and Family Services Act* (child protection), or in any criminal proceedings; and

(c) any other information known to the person that is relevant to the factors to be considered by the court under subsections 24(2), (3) and (4) in determining the best interests of the child.

Police records checks, non-parents

21.1 (1) Every person who applies under section 21 for custody of a child and who is not a parent of the child shall file with the court the results of a recent police records check respecting the person in accordance with the rules of court.

Admissibility

(2) The results obtained by the court under subsection (1) and any information, statement or document derived from the information contained in the results are admissible in evidence in the application, if the court considers it to be relevant.

Use of evidence

(3) Subject to subsection 24(3), evidence that is determined by the court to be admissible under subsection (2) shall be considered in determining the best interests of the child under section 24.

Regulations

(4) The Lieutenant Governor in Council may make regulations defining "police records check" for the purposes of subsection (1).

CAS records search, non-parents

Definition

21.2. (1) In this section,

"society" means an approved agency designated as a children's aid society under the *Child and Family Services Act*.

Request for report

(2) Every person who applies under section 21 for custody of a child and who is not a parent of the child shall submit a request, in the form provided by the Ministry of the Attorney General, to every society or other body or person prescribed by the regulations, for a report as to,

(a) whether a society has records relating to the person applying for custody; and

(b) if there are records and the records indicate that one or more files relating to the person have been opened, the date on which each file was opened and, if the file was closed, the date on which the file was closed.

Request to be filed

(3) A copy of each request made under subsection (2) shall be filed with the court.

Report required

(4) Within 30 days of receiving a request under subsection (2), a society or other body or person shall provide the court in which the application was filed with a report, in the form provided by the Ministry of the Attorney General, containing the information required under that subsection, and shall provide a copy of the report to the requesting party.

Duty of clerk

(5) Subject to subsection (6), if the report indicates that there are records relating to the requesting party, the clerk of the court shall, 20 days after all of the reports that were requested by the party have been received by the court,

(a) give a copy of the report to every other party and to counsel, if any, representing the child; and

(b) file the report in the court file.

Exception

(6) The court may, on motion by the requesting party, order,

(a) that the time period referred to in subsection (5) be lengthened; or

(b) that all or part of the report be sealed in the court file and not disclosed if,

(i) the court determines that some or all of the information contained in the report is not relevant to the application, or

(ii) the party withdraws the application.

Admissibility

(7) A report that is filed under subsection (5) and any information, statement or document derived from the information contained in the report is admissible in evidence in the application, if the court considers it to be relevant.

Use of evidence

(8) Subject to subsection 24(3), evidence that is determined by the court to be admissible under subsection (7) shall be considered in determining the best interests of the child under section 24.

Interpretation

(9) Nothing done under this section constitutes publication of information or making information public for the purposes of subsection 45(8) of the *Child and Family Services Act* or an order under clause 70(1)(b).

Regulations

(10) The Lieutenant Governor in Council may make regulations for the purposes of subsection (2),

(a) specifying one or more societies or other bodies or persons to whom a request must be submitted;

(b) governing the manner and scope of the search required to be undertaken in response to a request;

(c) specifying classes of files that shall be excluded from the report.

Other proceedings

Application by non-parent

21.3. (1) Where an application for custody of a child is made by a person who is not a parent of the child, the clerk of the court shall provide to the court and to the parties information in writing respecting any current or previous family proceedings involving the child or any person who is a party to the application and who is not a parent of the child.

Same

(2) Where an application for custody of a child is made by a person who is not a parent of the child, the court may require the clerk of the court to provide to the court and to the parties information in writing respecting any current or previous criminal proceedings involving any person who is a party to the application and who is not a parent of the child.

Same

(3) Written information provided under subsection (1) or (2) shall also be provided to counsel, if any, representing the child who is the subject of the application.

Admissibility

(4) Written information that is provided to the court under subsection (1) or (2) and any information, statement or document derived from that information is admissible in evidence in the application, if the court considers it to be relevant.

Use of evidence

(5) Subject to subsection 24(3), evidence that is determined by the court to be admissible under subsection (4) shall be considered in determining the best interests of the child under section 24.

Interpretation

(6) Nothing done under this section constitutes publication of information or making information public for the purposes of subsection 45(8) of the *Child and Family Services Act* or an order under clause 70(1)(b).

Regulations

(7) The Attorney General may make regulations for the purposes of this section,

(a) defining "family proceeding" and "criminal proceeding";

(b) prescribing the scope, content and form of the written information that shall or may be provided under this section;

(c) providing for a process for removing from the written information provided under subsection (1) or (2) information respecting a proceeding that does not involve the child who is the subject of the application or a person who is a party and is not a parent of the child, as the case may be.

Jurisdiction

22. (1) A court shall only exercise its jurisdiction to make an order for custody of or access to a child where,

(a) the child is habitually resident in Ontario at the commencement of the application for the order;

(b) although the child is not habitually resident in Ontario, the court is satisfied,

(i) that the child is physically present in Ontario at the commencement of the application for the order,

(ii) that substantial evidence concerning the best interests of the child is available in Ontario,

(iii) that no application for custody of or access to the child is pending before an extra-provincial tribunal in another place where the child is habitually resident,

(iv) that no extra-provincial order in respect of custody of or access to the child has been recognized by a court in Ontario,

(v) that the child has a real and substantial connection with Ontario, and

(vi) that, on the balance of convenience, it is appropriate for jurisdiction to be exercised in Ontario.

Habitual residence

(2) A child is habitually resident in the place where he or she resided,

(a) with both parents;

(b) where the parents are living separate and apart, with one parent under a separation agreement or with the consent, implied consent or acquiescence of the other or under a court order; or

(c) with a person other than a parent on a permanent basis for a significant period of time,

whichever last occurred.

Abduction

(3) The removal or withholding of a child without the consent of the person having custody of the child does not alter the habitual residence of the child unless there has been acquiescence or undue delay in commencing due process by the person from whom the child is removed or withheld.

Serious harm to child

23. Despite sections 22 and 41, a court may exercise its jurisdiction to make or to vary an order in respect of the custody of or access to a child where,

(a) the child is physically present in Ontario; and

(b) the court is satisfied that the child would, on the balance of probabilities, suffer serious harm if,

(i) the child remains in the custody of the person legally entitled to custody of the child,

(ii) the child is returned to the custody of the person legally entitled to custody of the child, or

(iii) the child is removed from Ontario.

Merits of application for custody or access

24. (1) The merits of an application under this Part in respect of custody of or access to a child shall be determined on the basis of the best interests of the child, in accordance with subsections (2), (3) and (4).

Best interests of child

(2) The court shall consider all the child's needs and circumstances, including,

(a) the love, affection and emotional ties between the child and,

(i) each person entitled to or claiming custody of or access to the child,

(ii) other members of the child's family who reside with the child, and

(iii) persons involved in the child's care and upbringing;

(b) the child's views and preferences, if they can reasonably be ascertained;

(c) the length of time the child has lived in a stable home environment;

(d) the ability and willingness of each person applying for custody of the child to provide the child with guidance and education, the necessaries of life and any special needs of the child;

(e) the plan proposed by each person applying for custody of or access to the child for the child's care and upbringing;

(f) the permanence and stability of the family unit with which it is proposed that the child will live;

(g) the ability of each person applying for custody of or access to the child to act as a parent; and

(h) the relationship by blood or through an adoption order between the child and each person who is a party to the application.

Past conduct

(3) A person's past conduct shall be considered only,

(a) in accordance with subsection (4); or

(b) if the court is satisfied that the conduct is otherwise relevant to the person's ability to act as a parent.

Violence and abuse

(4) In assessing a person's ability to act as a parent, the court shall consider whether the person has at any time committed violence or abuse against,

(a) his or her spouse;

(b) a parent of the child to whom the application relates;

(c) a member of the person's household; or

(d) any child.

Same

(5) For the purposes of subsection (4), anything done in self-defence or to protect another person shall not be considered violence or abuse.

Declining jurisdiction

25. A court having jurisdiction under this Part in respect of custody or access may decline to exercise its jurisdiction where it is of the opinion that it is more appropriate for jurisdiction to be exercised outside Ontario.

Delay

26. (1) Where an application under this Part in respect of custody of or access to a child has not been heard within six months after the commencement of the proceedings, the clerk of the court shall list the application for the court and give notice to the parties of the date and time when and the place where the court will fix a date for the hearing of the application.

Exception

(1.1) Subsection (1) does not apply to an application under this Part that relates to the custody of or access to a child if the child is the subject of an application or order under Part III of the *Child and Family Services Act*, unless the application under this Part relates to,

(a) an order in respect of the child that was made under subsection 57.1(1) of the *Child and Family Services Act*;

(b) an order referred to in subsection 57.1(3) of the *Child and Family Services Act* that was made at the same time as an order under subsection 57.1(1) of that Act; or

(c) an access order in respect of the child under section 58 of the *Child and Family Services Act* that was made at the same time as an order under subsection 57.1(1) of that Act.

Directions

(2) At a hearing of a matter listed by the clerk in accordance with subsection (1), the court by order may fix a date for the hearing of the application and may give such directions in respect of the proceedings and make such order in respect of the costs of the proceedings as the court considers appropriate.

Early date

(3) Where the court fixes a date under subsection (2), the court shall fix the earliest date that, in the opinion of the court, is compatible with a just disposition of the application.

Effect of divorce proceedings

27. Where an action for divorce is commenced under the *Divorce Act* (Canada), any application under this Part in respect of custody of or access to a child that has not been determined is stayed except by leave of the court.

Custody and Access—Orders

Powers of court

28. (1) The court to which an application is made under section 21,

(a) by order may grant the custody of or access to the child to one or more persons;

(b) by order may determine any aspect of the incidents of the right to custody or access; and

(c) may make such additional order as the court considers necessary and proper in the circumstances, including an order,

(i) limiting the duration, frequency, manner or location of contact or communication between any of the parties, or between a party and the child,

(ii) prohibiting a party or other person from engaging in specified conduct in the presence of the child or at any time when the person is responsible for the care of the child,

(iii) prohibiting a party from changing the child's residence, school or day care facility without the consent of another party or an order of the court,

(iv) prohibiting a party from removing the child from Ontario without the consent of another party or an order of the court,

(v) requiring the delivery, to the court or to a person or body specified by the court, of the child's passport, the child's health card within the meaning of the *Health Insurance Act* or any other document relating to the child that the court may specify,

(vi) requiring a party to give information or to consent to the release of information respecting the health, education and welfare of the child to another party or other person specified by the court, or

(vii) requiring a party to facilitate communication by the child with another party or other person specified by the court in a manner that is appropriate for the child.

Exception

(2) If an application is made under section 21 with respect to a child who is the subject of an order made under section 57.1 of the *Child and Family Services Act*, the court shall treat the application as if it were an application to vary an order made under this section.

Same

(3) If an order for access to a child was made under Part III of the *Child and Family Services Act* at the same time as an order for custody of the child was made under section 57.1 of that Act, the court shall treat an application under section 21 relating to access to the child as if it were an application to vary an order made under this section.

Order varying an order

29. (1) A court shall not make an order under this Part that varies an order in respect of custody or access made by a court in Ontario unless there has been a material change in circumstances that affects or is likely to affect the best interests of the child.

Custody and Access—Assistance to Court

Assessment of needs of child

30. (1) The court before which an application is brought in respect of custody of or access to a child, by order, may appoint a person who has technical or professional skill to assess and report to the court on the needs of the child and the ability and willingness of the parties or any of them to satisfy the needs of the child.

When order may be made

(2) An order may be made under subsection (1) on or before the hearing of the application in respect of custody of or access to the child and with or without a request by a party to the application.

Agreement by parties

(3) The court shall, if possible, appoint a person agreed upon by the parties, but if the parties do not agree the court shall choose and appoint the person.

Consent to act

(4) The court shall not appoint a person under subsection (1) unless the person has consented to make the assessment and to report to the court within the period of time specified by the court.

Attendance for assessment

(5) In an order under subsection (1), the court may require the parties, the child and any other person who has been given notice of the proposed order, or any of them, to attend for assessment by the person appointed by the order.

Refusal to attend

(6) Where a person ordered under this section to attend for assessment refuses to attend or to undergo the assessment, the court may draw such inferences in respect of the ability and willingness of any person to satisfy the needs of the child as the court considers appropriate.

Report

(7) The person appointed under subsection (1) shall file his or her report with the clerk of the court.

Copies of report

(8) The clerk of the court shall give a copy of the report to each of the parties and to counsel, if any, representing the child.

Admissibility of report

(9) The report mentioned in subsection (7) is admissible in evidence in the application.

Assessor may be witness

(10) Any of the parties, and counsel, if any, representing the child, may require the person appointed under subsection (1) to attend as a witness at the hearing of the application.

Directions

(11) Upon motion, the court by order may give such directions in respect of the assessment as the court considers appropriate.

Fees and expenses

(12) The court shall require the parties to pay the fees and expenses of the person appointed under subsection (1).

Idem, proportions or amounts

(13) The court shall specify in the order the proportions or amounts of the fees and expenses that the court requires each party to pay.

Idem, serious financial hardship

(14) The court may relieve a party from responsibility for payment of any of the fees and expenses of the person appointed under subsection (1) where the court is satisfied that payment would cause serious financial hardship to the party.

Other expert evidence

(15) The appointment of a person under subsection (1) does not prevent the parties or counsel representing the child from submitting other expert evidence as to the needs of the child and the ability and willingness of the parties or any of them to satisfy the needs of the child.

Mediation

31. (1) Upon an application for custody of or access to a child, the court, at the request of the parties, by order may appoint a person selected by the parties to mediate any matter specified in the order.

Consent to act

(2) The court shall not appoint a person under subsection (1) unless the person,

(a) has consented to act as mediator; and

(b) has agreed to file a report with the court within the period of time specified by the court.

Duty of mediator

(3) It is the duty of a mediator to confer with the parties and endeavour to obtain an agreement in respect of the matter.

Form of report

(4) Before entering into mediation on the matter, the parties shall decide whether,

(a) the mediator is to file a full report on the mediation, including anything that the mediator considers relevant to the matter in mediation; or

(b) the mediator is to file a report that either sets out the agreement reached by the parties or states only that the parties did not reach agreement on the matter.

Filing of report

(5) The mediator shall file his or her report with the clerk of the court in the form decided upon by the parties under subsection (4).

Copies of report

(6) The clerk of the court shall give a copy of the report to each of the parties and to counsel, if any, representing the child.

Admissions made in the course of mediation

(7) Where the parties have decided that the mediator's report is to be in the form described in clause (4)(b), evidence of anything said or of any admission or communication made in the course of the mediation is not admissible in any proceeding except with the consent of all parties to the proceeding in which the order was made under subsection (1).

Fees and expenses

(8) The court shall require the parties to pay the fees and expenses of the mediator.

Idem, proportions or amounts

(9) The court shall specify in the order the proportions or amounts of the fees and expenses that the court requires each party to pay.

Idem, serious financial hardship

(10) The court may relieve a party from responsibility for payment of any of the fees and expenses of the mediator where the court is satisfied that payment would cause serious financial hardship to the party.

Further evidence from outside Ontario

32. (1) Where a court is of the opinion that it is necessary to receive further evidence from a place outside Ontario before making a decision, the court may send to the Attorney General, Minister of Justice or similar officer of the place outside Ontario such supporting material as may be necessary together with a request,

(a) that the Attorney General, Minister of Justice or similar officer take such action as may be necessary in order to require a named person to attend before the proper tribunal in that place and produce or give evidence in respect of the subject-matter of the application; and

(b) that the Attorney General, Minister of Justice or similar officer or the tribunal send to the court a certified copy of the evidence produced or given before the tribunal.

Cost of obtaining evidence

(2) A court that acts under subsection (1) may assess the cost of so acting against one or more of the parties to the application or may deal with such cost as costs in the cause.

Request from outside Ontario for further evidence

33. (1) Where the Attorney General receives from an extra-provincial tribunal a request similar to that referred to in section 32 and such supporting material as may be necessary, it is the duty of the Attorney General to refer the request and the material to the proper court.

Obtaining evidence

(2) A court to which a request is referred by the Attorney General under subsection (1) shall require the person named in the request to attend before the court and produce or give evidence in accordance with the request.

Custody and Access—Enforcement

Supervision of custody or access

34. (1) Where an order is made for custody of or access to a child, a court may give such directions as it considers appropriate for the supervision of the custody or access by a person, a children's aid society or other body.

Consent to act

(2) A court shall not direct a person, a children's aid society or other body to supervise custody or access as mentioned in subsection (1) unless the person, society or body has consented to act as supervisor.

Restraining order

35. (1) On application, the court may make an interim or final restraining order against any person if the applicant has reasonable grounds to fear for his or her own safety or for the safety of any child in his or her lawful custody.

Provisions of order

(2) A restraining order made under subsection (1) shall be in the form prescribed by the rules of court and may contain one or more of the following provisions, as the court considers appropriate:

1. Restraining the respondent, in whole or in part, from directly or indirectly contacting or communicating with the applicant or any child in the applicant's lawful custody.
2. Restraining the respondent from coming within a specified distance of one or more locations.
3. Specifying one or more exceptions to the provisions described in paragraphs 1 and 2.
4. Any other provision that the court considers appropriate.

Transition

(3) This section, as it read immediately before the day section 15 of the *Family Statute Law Amendment Act, 2009* came into force, continues to apply to,

(a) any prosecution or other proceeding begun under this section before that day; and

(b) any order made under this section that was in force immediately before that day.

Order where child unlawfully withheld

36. (1) Where a court is satisfied upon application by a person in whose favour an order has been made for custody of or access to a child that there are reasonable and probable grounds for believing that any person is unlawfully withholding the child from the applicant, the court by order may authorize the applicant or someone on his or her behalf to apprehend the child for the purpose of giving effect to the rights of the applicant to custody or access, as the case may be.

Order to locate and take child

(2) Where a court is satisfied upon application that there are reasonable and probable grounds for believing,

(a) that any person is unlawfully withholding a child from a person entitled to custody of or access to the child;

(b) that a person who is prohibited by court order or separation agreement from removing a child from Ontario proposes to remove the child or have the child removed from Ontario; or

(c) that a person who is entitled to access to a child proposes to remove the child or to have the child removed from Ontario and that the child is not likely to return,

the court by order may direct a police force, having jurisdiction in any area where it appears to the court that the child may be, to locate, apprehend and deliver the child to the person named in the order.

Application without notice

(3) An order may be made under subsection (2) upon an application without notice where the court is satisfied that it is necessary that action be taken without delay.

Duty to act

(4) The police force directed to act by an order under subsection (2) shall do all things reasonably able to be done to locate, apprehend and deliver the child in accordance with the order.

Entry and search

(5) For the purpose of locating and apprehending a child in accordance with an order under subsection (2), a member of a police force may enter and search any place where he or she has reasonable and probable grounds for believing that the child may be with such assistance and such force as are reasonable in the circumstances.

Time

(6) An entry or a search referred to in subsection (5) shall be made only between 6 a.m. and 9 p.m. standard time unless the court, in the order, authorizes entry and search at another time.

Expiration of order

(7) An order made under subsection (2) shall name a date on which it expires, which shall be a date not later than six months after it is made unless the court is satisfied that a longer period of time is necessary in the circumstances.

When application may be made

(8) An application under subsection (1) or (2) may be made in an application for custody or access or at any other time.

Court orders, removal and return of children

To prevent unlawful removal of child

37. (1) Where a court, upon application, is satisfied upon reasonable and probable grounds that a person prohibited by court order or separation agreement from removing a child from Ontario proposes to remove the child from Ontario, the court in order to prevent the removal of the child from Ontario may make an order under subsection (3).

To ensure return of child

(2) Where a court, upon application, is satisfied upon reasonable and probable grounds that a person entitled to access to a child proposes to remove the child from Ontario and is not likely to return the child to Ontario, the court in order to secure the prompt, safe return of the child to Ontario may make an order under subsection (3).

Order by court

(3) An order mentioned in subsection (1) or (2) may require a person to do any one or more of the following:

1. Transfer specific property to a named trustee to be held subject to the terms and conditions specified in the order.
2. Where payments have been ordered for the support of the child, make the payments to a specified trustee subject to the terms and conditions specified in the order.
3. Post a bond, with or without sureties, payable to the applicant in such amount as the court considers appropriate.
4. Deliver the person's passport, the child's passport and any other travel documents of either of them that the court may specify to the court or to an individual or body specified by the court.

Idem, Ontario Court of Justice

(4) The Ontario Court of Justice shall not make an order under paragraph 1 of subsection (3).

Terms and conditions

(5) In an order under paragraph 1 of subsection (3), the court may specify terms and conditions for the return or the disposition of the property as the court considers appropriate.

Safekeeping

(6) A court or an individual or body specified by the court in an order under paragraph 4 of subsection (3) shall hold a passport or travel document delivered in accordance with the order in safekeeping in accordance with any directions set out in the order.

Directions

(7) In an order under subsection (3), a court may give such directions in respect of the safekeeping of the property, payments, passports or travel documents as the court considers appropriate.

Contempt of orders of Ontario Court of Justice

38. (1) In addition to its powers in respect of contempt, the Ontario Court of Justice may punish by fine or imprisonment, or both, any wilful contempt of or resistance to its process or orders in respect of custody of or access to a child, but the fine shall not in any case exceed $5,000 nor shall the imprisonment exceed ninety days.

Conditions of imprisonment

(2) An order for imprisonment under subsection (1) may be made conditional upon default in the performance of a condition set out in the order and may provide for the imprisonment to be served intermittently.

Information as to address

39. (1) Where, upon application to a court, it appears to the court that,

(a) for the purpose of bringing an application in respect of custody or access under this Part; or

(b) for the purpose of the enforcement of an order for custody or access,

the proposed applicant or person in whose favour the order is made has need to learn or confirm the whereabouts of the proposed respondent or person against whom the order referred to in clause (b) is made, the court may order any person or public body to provide the court with such particulars of the address of the proposed respondent or person against whom the order referred to in clause (b) is made as are contained in the records in the custody of the person or body, and the person or body shall give the court such particulars as are contained in the records and the court may then give the particulars to such person or persons as the court considers appropriate.

Exception

(2) A court shall not make an order on an application under subsection (1) where it appears to the court that the purpose of the application is to enable the applicant to identify or to obtain particulars as to the identity of a person who has custody of a child, rather than to learn or confirm the whereabouts of the proposed respondent or the enforcement of an order for custody or access.

Compliance with order

(3) The giving of information in accordance with an order under subsection (1) shall be deemed for all purposes not to be a contravention of any Act or regulation or any common law rule of confidentiality.

Section binds Crown

(4) This section binds the Crown in right of Ontario.

Custody and Access—Extra-provincial Matters

Interim powers of court

40. Upon application, a court,

(a) that is satisfied that a child has been wrongfully removed to or is being wrongfully retained in Ontario; or

(b) that may not exercise jurisdiction under section 22 or that has declined jurisdiction under section 25 or 42,

may do any one or more of the following:

1. Make such interim order in respect of the custody or access as the court considers is in the best interests of the child.
2. Stay the application subject to,
   - i. the condition that a party to the application promptly commence a similar proceeding before an extra-provincial tribunal, or
   - ii. such other conditions as the court considers appropriate.
3. Order a party to return the child to such place as the court considers appropriate and, in the discretion of the court, order payment of the cost of the reasonable travel and other expenses of the child and any parties to or witnesses at the hearing of the application.

Enforcement of extra-provincial orders

41. (1) Upon application by any person in whose favour an order for the custody of or access to a child has been made by an extra-provincial tribunal, a court shall recognize the order unless the court is satisfied,

(a) that the respondent was not given reasonable notice of the commencement of the proceeding in which the order was made;

(b) that the respondent was not given an opportunity to be heard by the extra-provincial tribunal before the order was made;

(c) that the law of the place in which the order was made did not require the extra-provincial tribunal to have regard for the best interests of the child;

(d) that the order of the extra-provincial tribunal is contrary to public policy in Ontario; or

(e) that, in accordance with section 22, the extra-provincial tribunal would not have jurisdiction if it were a court in Ontario.

Effect of recognition of order

(2) An order made by an extra-provincial tribunal that is recognized by a court shall be deemed to be an order of the court and enforceable as such.

Conflicting orders

(3) A court presented with conflicting orders made by extra-provincial tribunals for the custody of or access to a child that, but for the conflict, would be recognized and enforced by the court under subsection (1) shall recognize and enforce the order that appears to the court to be most in accord with the best interests of the child.

Further orders

(4) A court that has recognized an extra-provincial order may make such further orders under this Part as the court considers necessary to give effect to the order.

Superseding order, material change in circumstances

42. (1) Upon application, a court by order may supersede an extra-provincial order in respect of custody of or access to a child where the court is satisfied that there has been a material change in circumstances that affects or is likely to affect the best interests of the child and,

(a) the child is habitually resident in Ontario at the commencement of the application for the order; or

(b) although the child is not habitually resident in Ontario, the court is satisfied,

(i) that the child is physically present in Ontario at the commencement of the application for the order,

(ii) that the child no longer has a real and substantial connection with the place where the extra-provincial order was made,

(iii) that substantial evidence concerning the best interests of the child is available in Ontario,

(iv) that the child has a real and substantial connection with Ontario, and

(v) that, on the balance of convenience, it is appropriate for jurisdiction to be exercised in Ontario.

Declining jurisdiction

(2) A court may decline to exercise its jurisdiction under this section where it is of the opinion that it is more appropriate for jurisdiction to be exercised outside Ontario.

Superseding order, serious harm

43. Upon application, a court by order may supersede an extra-provincial order in respect of custody of or access to a child if the court is satisfied that the child would, on the balance of probability, suffer serious harm if,

(a) the child remains in the custody of the person legally entitled to custody of the child;

(b) the child is returned to the custody of the person entitled to custody of the child; or

(c) the child is removed from Ontario.

True copy of extra-provincial order

44. A copy of an extra-provincial order certified as a true copy by a judge, other presiding officer or registrar of the tribunal that made the order or by a person charged with keeping the orders of the tribunal is proof, in the absence of evidence to the contrary, of the making of the order, the content of the order and the appointment and signature of the judge, presiding officer, registrar or other person.

Court may take notice of foreign law

45. For the purposes of an application under this Part, a court may take notice, without requiring formal proof, of the law of a jurisdiction outside Ontario and of a decision of an extra-provincial tribunal.

Convention on Civil Aspects of International Child Abduction

Definition

46. (1) In this section,

"convention" means the Convention on the Civil Aspects of International Child Abduction, set out in the Schedule to this section.

Convention in force

(2) On, from and after the 1st day of December, 1983, except as provided in subsection (3), the convention is in force in Ontario and the provisions thereof are law in Ontario.

Crown, legal costs under convention

(3) The Crown is not bound to assume any costs resulting under the convention from the participation of legal counsel or advisers or from court proceedings except in accordance with the *Legal Aid Services Act*, 1998.

Central Authority

(4) The Ministry of the Attorney General shall be the Central Authority for Ontario for the purpose of the convention.

Application to court

(5) An application may be made to a court in pursuance of a right or an obligation under the convention.

Request to ratify convention

(6) The Attorney General shall request the Government of Canada to submit a declaration to the Ministry of Foreign Affairs of the Kingdom of the Netherlands, declaring that the convention extends to Ontario.

Regulations

(7) The Lieutenant Governor in Council may make such regulations as the Lieutenant Governor in Council considers necessary to carry out the intent and purpose of this section.

Conflict

(8) Where there is a conflict between this section and any other enactment, this section prevails.

SCHEDULE

Convention on the Civil Aspects of International Child Abduction

The States signatory to the present Convention,

Firmly convinced that the interests of children are of paramount importance in matters relating to their custody,

Desiring to protect children internationally from the harmful effects of their wrongful removal or retention and to establish procedures to ensure their prompt return to the State of their habitual residence, as well as to secure protection for rights of access,

Have resolved to conclude a Convention to this effect and have agreed upon the following provisions:

Chapter I—Scope of the Convention

Article 1

The objects of the present Convention are:

(a) to secure the prompt return of children wrongfully removed to or retained in any Contracting State; and

(b) to ensure that rights of custody and of access under the law of one Contracting State are effectively respected in the other Contracting States.

Article 2

Contracting States shall take all appropriate measures to secure within their territories the implementation of the objects of the Convention. For this purpose they shall use the most expeditious procedures available.

Article 3

The removal or the retention of a child is to be considered wrongful where:

(a) it is in breach of rights of custody attributed to a person, an institution or any other body, either jointly or alone, under the law of the State in which the child was habitually resident immediately before the removal or retention; and

(b) at the time of removal or retention those rights were actually exercised, either jointly or alone, or would have been so exercised but for the removal or retention.

The rights of custody mentioned in sub-paragraph (a) above, may arise in particular by operation of law or by reason of a judicial or administrative decision, or by reason of an agreement having legal effect under the law of that State.

Article 4

The Convention shall apply to any child who was habitually resident in a Contracting State immediately before any breach of custody or access rights. The Convention shall cease to apply when the child attains the age of 16 years.

Article 5

For the purposes of this Convention:

(a) "rights of custody" shall include rights relating to the care of the person of the child and, in particular, the right to determine the child's place of residence;

(b) "rights of access" shall include the right to take a child for a limited period of time to a place other than the child's habitual residence.

Chapter II—Central Authorities

Article 6

A Contracting State shall designate a Central Authority to discharge the duties which are imposed by the Convention upon such authorities.

Federal States, States with more than one system of law or States having autonomous territorial organizations shall be free to appoint more than one Central Authority and to specify the territorial extent of their powers. Where a State has appointed more than one Central Authority, it shall designate the Central Authority to which applications may be addressed for transmission to the appropriate Central Authority within that State.

Article 7

Central Authorities shall co-operate with each other and promote co-operation amongst the competent authorities in their respective States to secure the prompt return of children and to achieve the other objects of this Convention.

In particular, either directly or through any intermediary, they shall take all appropriate measures:

(a) to discover the whereabouts of a child who has been wrongfully removed or retained;

(b) to prevent further harm to the child or prejudice to interested parties by taking or causing to be taken provisional measures;

(c) to secure the voluntary return of the child or to bring about an amicable resolution of the issues;

(d) to exchange, where desirable, information relating to the social background of the child;

(e) to provide information of a general character as to the law of their State in connection with the application of the Convention;

(f) to initiate or facilitate the institution of judicial or administrative proceedings with a view to obtaining the return of the child and, in a proper case, to make arrangements for organizing or securing the effective exercise of rights of access;

(g) where the circumstances so require, to provide or facilitate the provision of legal aid and advice, including the participation of legal counsel and advisers;

(h) to provide such administrative arrangements as may be necessary and appropriate to secure the safe return of the child;

(i) to keep each other informed with respect to the operation of this Convention and, as far as possible, to eliminate any obstacles to its application.

Chapter III—Return of Children

Article 8

Any person, institution or other body claiming that a child has been removed or retained in breach of custody rights may apply either to the Central Authority of the child's habitual residence or to the Central Authority of any other Contracting State for assistance in securing the return of the child.

The application shall contain:

(a) information concerning the identity of the applicant, of the child and of the person alleged to have removed or retained the child;

(b) where available, the date of birth of the child;

(c) the grounds on which the applicant's claim for return of the child is based;

(d) all available information relating to the whereabouts of the child and the identity of the person with whom the child is presumed to be.

The application may be accompanied or supplemented by:

(e) an authenticated copy of any relevant decision or agreement;

(f) a certificate or an affidavit emanating from a Central Authority, or other competent authority of the State of the child's habitual residence, or from a qualified person, concerning the relevant law of that State;

(g) any other relevant document.

Article 9

If the Central Authority which receives an application referred to in Article 8 has reason to believe that the child is in another Contracting State, it shall directly and without delay transmit the application to the Central Authority of that Contracting State and inform the requesting Central Authority, or the applicant, as the case may be.

Article 10

The Central Authority of the State where the child is shall take or cause to be taken all appropriate measures in order to obtain the voluntary return of the child.

Article 11

The judicial or administrative authorities of Contracting States shall act expeditiously in proceedings for the return of children.

If the judicial or administrative authority concerned has not reached a decision within six weeks from the date of commencement of the proceedings, the applicant or the Central Authority of the requested State, on its own initiative or if asked by the Central Authority of the requesting State, shall have the right to request a statement of the reasons for the delay. If a reply is received by the Central Authority of the requested State, that Authority shall transmit the reply to the Central Authority of the requesting State, or to the applicant, as the case may be.

Article 12

Where a child has been wrongfully removed or retained in terms of Article 3 and, at the date of commencement of the proceedings before the judicial or administrative authority of the Contracting State where the child is, a period of less than one year has elapsed from the date of the wrongful removal or retention, the authority concerned shall order the return of the child forthwith.

The judicial or administrative authority, even where the proceedings have been commenced after the expiration of the period of one year referred to in the preceding paragraph, shall also order the return of the child, unless it is demonstrated that the child is now settled in its new environment.

Where the judicial or administrative authority in the requested State has reason to believe that the child has been taken to another State, it may stay the proceedings or dismiss the application for the return of the child.

Article 13

Despite the provisions of the preceding Article, the judicial or administrative authority of the requested State is not bound to order the return of the child if the person, institution or other body which opposes its return establishes that:

(a) the person, institution or other body having the care of the person of the child was not actually exercising the custody rights at the time of removal or retention, or had consented to or subsequently acquiesced in the removal or retention; or

(b) there is a grave risk that his or her return would expose the child to physical or psychological harm or otherwise place the child in an intolerable situation.

The judicial or administrative authority may also refuse to order the return of the child if it finds that the child objects to being returned and has attained an age and degree of maturity at which it is appropriate to take account of its views.

In considering the circumstances referred to in this Article, the judicial and administrative authorities shall take into account the information relating to the social background of the child provided by the Central Authority or other competent authority of the child's habitual residence.

Article 14

In ascertaining whether there has been a wrongful removal or retention within the meaning of Article 3, the judicial or administrative authorities of the requested State may take notice directly of the law of, and of judicial or administrative decisions, formally recognized or not in the State of the habitual residence of the child, without recourse to the specific procedures for the proof of that law or for the recognition of foreign decisions which would otherwise be applicable.

Article 15

The judicial or administrative authorities of a Contracting State may, prior to the making of an order for the return of the child, request that the applicant obtain from the authorities of the State of the habitual residence of the child a decision or other determination that the removal or retention was wrongful within the meaning of Article 3 of the Convention, where such a decision or determination may be obtained in that State. The Central Authorities of the Contracting States shall so far as practicable assist applicants to obtain such a decision or determination.

Article 16

After receiving notice of a wrongful removal or retention of a child in the sense of Article 3, the judicial or administrative authorities of the Contracting State to which the child has been removed or in which it has been retained shall not decide on the merits of rights of custody until it has been determined that the child is not to be returned under this Convention or unless an application under this Convention is not lodged within a reasonable time following receipt of the notice.

Article 17

The sole fact that a decision relating to custody has been given in or is entitled to recognition in the requested State shall not be a ground for refusing to return a child under this Convention, but the judicial or administrative authorities of the requested State may take account of the reasons for that decision in applying this Convention.

Article 18

The provisions of this Chapter do not limit the power of a judicial or administrative authority to order the return of the child at any time.

Article 19

A decision under this Convention concerning the return of the child shall not be taken to be a determination on the merits of any custody issue.

Article 20

The return of the child under the provisions of Article 12 may be refused if this would not be permitted by the fundamental principles of the requested State relating to the protection of human rights and fundamental freedoms.

Chapter IV—Rights of Access

Article 21

An application to make arrangements for organizing or securing the effective exercise of rights of access may be presented to the Central Authorities of the Contracting States in the same way as an application for the return of a child.

The Central Authorities are bound by the obligations of co-operation which are set forth in Article 7 to promote the peaceful enjoyment of access rights and the fulfilment of any conditions to which the exercise of those rights may be subject. The Central Authorities shall take steps to remove, as far as possible, all obstacles to the exercise of such rights.

The Central Authorities, either directly or through intermediaries, may initiate or assist in the institution of proceedings with a view to organizing or protecting these rights and securing respect for the conditions to which the exercise of these rights may be subject.

Chapter V—General Provisions

Article 22

No security, bond or deposit, however described, shall be required to guarantee the payment of costs and expenses in the judicial or administrative proceedings falling within the scope of this Convention.

Article 23

No legalization or similar formality may be required in the context of this Convention.

Article 24

Any application, communication or other document sent to the Central Authority of the requested State shall be in the original language, and shall be accompanied by a translation into the official language or one of the official languages of the requested State or, where that is not feasible, a translation into French or English.

However, a Contracting State may, by making a reservation in accordance with Article 42, object to the use of either French or English, but not both, in any application, communication or other document sent to its Central Authority.

Article 25

Nationals of the Contracting States and persons who are habitually resident within those States shall be entitled in matters concerned with the application of this Convention to legal aid and advice in any other Contracting State on the same conditions as if they themselves were nationals of and habitually resident in that State.

Article 26

Each Central Authority shall bear its own costs in applying this Convention.

Central Authorities and other public services of Contracting States shall not impose any charges in relation to applications submitted under this Convention. In particular, they may not require any payment from the applicant towards the costs and expenses of the proceedings or, where applicable, those arising from the participation of legal counsel or advisers. However, they may require the payment of the expenses incurred or to be incurred in implementing the return of the child.

However, a Contracting State may, by making a reservation in accordance with Article 42, declare that it shall not be bound to assume any costs referred to in the preceding paragraph resulting from the participation of legal counsel or advisers or from court proceedings, except insofar as those costs may be covered by its system of legal aid and advice.

Upon ordering the return of a child or issuing an order concerning rights of access under this Convention, the judicial or administrative authorities may, where appropriate, direct the person who removed or retained the child, or who prevented the exercise of rights of access, to pay necessary expenses incurred by or on behalf of the applicant, including travel expenses, any costs incurred or payments made for locating the child, the costs of legal representation of the applicant, and those of returning the child.

Article 27

When it is manifest that the requirements of this Convention are not fulfilled or that the application is otherwise not well founded, a Central Authority is not bound to accept the application. In that case, the Central Authority shall forthwith inform the applicant or the Central Authority through which the application was submitted, as the case may be, of its reasons.

Article 28

A Central Authority may require that the application be accompanied by a written authorization empowering it to act on behalf of the applicant, or to designate a representative so to act.

Article 29

This Convention shall not preclude any person, institution or body who claims that there has been a breach of custody or access rights within the meaning of Article 3 or 21 from applying directly to the judicial or administrative authorities of a Contracting State, whether or not under the provisions of this Convention.

Article 30

Any application submitted to the Central Authorities or directly to the judicial or administrative authorities of a Contracting State in accordance with the terms of this Convention, together with documents and any other information appended thereto or provided by a Central Authority, shall be admissible in the courts or administrative authorities of the Contracting States.

Article 31

In relation to a State which in matters of custody of children has two or more systems of law applicable in different territorial units:

(a) any reference to habitual residence in that State shall be construed as referring to habitual residence in a territorial unit of that State;

(b) any reference to the law of the State of habitual residence shall be construed as referring to the law of the territorial unit in that State where the child habitually resides.

Article 32

In relation to a State which in matters of custody of children has two or more systems of law applicable to different categories of persons, any reference to the law of that State shall be construed as referring to the legal system specified by the law of that State.

Article 33

A State within which different territorial units have their own rules of law in respect of custody of children shall not be bound to apply this Convention where a State with a unified system of law would not be bound to do so.

Article 34

This Convention shall take priority in matters within its scope over the Convention of 5 October 1961 concerning the powers of authorities and the law applicable in respect of the protection of minors, as between Parties to both Conventions. Otherwise the present Convention shall not restrict the application of an international instrument in force between the State of origin and the State addressed or other law of the State addressed for the purposes of obtaining the return of a child who has been wrongfully removed or retained or of organizing access rights.

Article 35

This Convention shall apply as between Contracting States only to wrongful removals or retentions occurring after its entry into force in those States.

Where a declaration has been made under Article 39 or 40, the reference in the preceding paragraph to a Contracting State shall be taken to refer to the territorial unit or units in relation to which this Convention applies.

Article 36

Nothing in this Convention shall prevent two or more Contracting States, in order to limit the restrictions to which the return of the child may be subject, from agreeing among themselves to derogate from any provisions of this Convention which may imply such a restriction.

Chapter VI—Final Clauses

Article 37

The Convention shall be open for signature by the States which were Members of the Hague Conference on Private International Law at the time of its Fourteenth Session.

It shall be ratified, accepted or approved and the instruments of ratification, acceptance or approval shall be deposited with the Ministry of Foreign Affairs of the Kingdom of the Netherlands.

Article 38

Any other State may accede to the Convention.

The instrument of accession shall be deposited with the Ministry of Foreign Affairs of the Kingdom of the Netherlands.

The Convention shall enter into force for a State acceding to it on the first day of the third calendar month after the deposit of its instrument of accession.

The accession will have effect only as regards the relations between the acceding State and such Contracting States as will have declared their acceptance of the accession. Such a declaration will also have to be made by any Member State ratifying, accepting or approving the Convention after an accession. Such declaration shall be deposited at the Ministry of Foreign Affairs of the Kingdom of the Netherlands; this Ministry shall forward, through diplomatic channels, a certified copy to each of the Contracting States.

The Convention will enter into force as between the acceding State and the State that has declared its acceptance of the accession on the first day of the third calendar month after the deposit of the declaration of acceptance.

Article 39

Any State may, at the time of signature, ratification, acceptance, approval or accession, declare that the Convention shall extend to all the territories for the international relations of which it is responsible, or to one or more of them. Such a declaration shall take effect at the time the Convention enters into force for that State.

Such declaration, as well as any subsequent extension, shall be notified to the Ministry of Foreign Affairs of the Kingdom of the Netherlands.

Article 40

If a Contracting State has two or more territorial units in which different systems of law are applicable in relation to matters dealt with in this Convention, it may at the time of signature, ratification, acceptance, approval or accession declare that this Convention shall extend to all its territorial units or only to one or more of them and may modify this declaration by submitting another declaration at any time.

Any such declaration shall be notified to the Ministry of Foreign Affairs of the Kingdom of the Netherlands and shall state expressly the territorial units to which the Convention applies.

Article 41

Where a Contracting State has a system of government under which executive, judicial and legislative powers are distributed between central and other authorities within that State, its signature or ratification, acceptance or approval of, or accession to this Convention, or its making of any declaration in terms of Article 40 shall carry no implication as to the internal distribution of powers within that State.

Article 42

Any State may, not later than the time of ratification, acceptance, approval or accession, or at the time of making a declaration in terms of Article 39 or 40, make one or both of the reservations provided for in Article 24 and Article 26, third paragraph. No other reservation shall be permitted.

Any State may at any time withdraw a reservation it has made. The withdrawal shall be notified to the Ministry of Foreign Affairs of the Kingdom of the Netherlands.

The reservation shall cease to have effect on the first day of the third calendar month after the notification referred to in the preceding paragraph.

Article 43

The Convention shall enter into force on the first day of the third calendar month after the deposit of the third instrument of ratification, acceptance, approval or accession referred to in Articles 37 and 38.

Thereafter the Convention shall enter into force:

1. for each State ratifying, accepting, approving or acceding to it subsequently, on the first day of the third calendar month after the deposit of its instrument of ratification, acceptance, approval or accession;
2. for any territory or territorial unit to which the Convention has been extended in conformity with Article 39 or 40, on the first day of the third calendar month after the notification referred to in that Article.

Article 44

The Convention shall remain in force for five years from the date of its entry into force in accordance with the first paragraph of Article 43 even for States which subsequently have ratified, accepted, approved it or acceded to it. If there has been no denunciation, it shall be renewed tacitly every five years.

Any denunciation shall be notified to the Ministry of Foreign Affairs of the Kingdom of the Netherlands at least six months before the expiry of the five year period. It may be limited to certain of the territories or territorial units to which the Convention applies.

The denunciation shall have effect only as regards the State which has notified it. The Convention shall remain in force for the other Contracting States.

Article 45

The Ministry of Foreign Affairs of the Kingdom of the Netherlands shall notify the States Members of the Conference, and the States which have acceded in accordance with Article 38, of the following:

1. the signatures and ratifications, acceptances and approvals referred to in Article 37;
2. the accessions referred to in Article 38;
3. the date on which the Convention enters into force in accordance with Article 43;
4. the extensions referred to in Article 39;
5. the declarations referred to in Articles 38 and 40;
6. the reservations referred to in Article 24 and Article 26, third paragraph, and the withdrawals referred to in Article 42;
7. the denunciations referred to in Article 44.

Done at The Hague, on the 25th day of October, 1980.

Guardianship

Appointment of guardian

47. (1) Upon application by a child's parent or by any other person, on notice to the Children's Lawyer, a court may appoint a guardian of the child's property.

Responsibility of guardian

(2) A guardian of the property of a child has charge of and is responsible for the care and management of the property of the child.

Parents and joint guardians

Parents as guardians

48. (1) As between themselves and subject to any court order or any agreement between them, the parents of a child are equally entitled to be appointed by a court as guardians of the property of the child.

Parent and other person

(2) As between a parent of a child and a person who is not a parent of the child, the parent has a preferential entitlement to be appointed by a court as a guardian of the property of the child.

More than one guardian

(3) A court may appoint more than one guardian of the property of a child.

Guardians jointly responsible

(4) Where more than one guardian is appointed of the property of a child, the guardians are jointly responsible for the care and management of the property of the child.

Criteria

49. In deciding an application for the appointment of a guardian of the property of a child, the court shall consider all the circumstances, including,

(a) the ability of the applicant to manage the property of the child;

(b) the merits of the plan proposed by the applicant for the care and management of the property of the child; and

(c) the views and preferences of the child, where such views and preferences can reasonably be ascertained.

Effect of appointment

50. The appointment of a guardian by a court under this Part has effect in all parts of Ontario.

Payment of debt due to child if no guardian

51. (1) If no guardian of a child's property has been appointed, a person who is under a duty to pay money or deliver personal property to the child discharges that duty, to the extent of the amount paid or the value of the personal property delivered, subject to subsection (1.1), by paying money or delivering personal property to,

(a) the child, if the child has a legal obligation to support another person;

(b) a parent with whom the child resides; or

(c) a person who has lawful custody of the child.

Same

(1.1) The total of the amount of money paid and the value of personal property delivered under subsection (1) shall not exceed the prescribed amount or, if no amount is prescribed, $10,000.

Money payable under judgment

(2) Subsection (1) does not apply in respect of money payable under a judgment or order of a court.

Receipt for payment

(3) A receipt or discharge for money or personal property not in excess of the amount or value set out in subsection (1) received for a child by a parent with whom the child resides or a person who has lawful custody of the child has the same validity as if a court had appointed the parent or the person as a guardian of the property of the child.

Responsibility for money or property

(4) A parent with whom a child resides or a person who has lawful custody of a child who receives and holds money or personal property referred to in subsection (1) has the responsibility of a guardian for the care and management of the money or personal property.

Regulations

(5) The Lieutenant Governor in Council may, by regulation, prescribe an amount for the purpose of subsection (1.1).

Accounts

52. A guardian of the property of a child may be required to account or may voluntarily pass the accounts in respect of the care and management of the property of the child in the same manner as a trustee under a will may be required to account or may pass the accounts in respect of the trusteeship.

Transfer of property to child

53. A guardian of the property of a child shall transfer to the child all property of the child in the care of the guardian when the child attains the age of eighteen years.

Management fees and expenses

54. A guardian of the property of a child is entitled to payment of a reasonable amount for fees for and expenses of management of the property of the child.

Bond by guardian

55. (1) A court that appoints a guardian of the property of a child shall require the guardian to post a bond, with or without sureties, payable to the child in such amount as the court considers appropriate in respect of the care and management of the property of the child.

Where parent appointed guardian

(2) Subsection (1) does not apply where the court appoints a parent of a child as guardian of the property of the child and the court is of the opinion that it is appropriate not to require the parent to post a bond.

Where child has support obligation

56. Upon application by a child who has a legal obligation to support another person, the court that appointed a guardian of the property of the child or a co-ordinate court by order shall end the guardianship for the child.

Removal and resignation of guardian

Removal

57. (1) A guardian of the property of a child may be removed by a court for the same reasons for which a trustee may be removed.

Resignation

(2) A guardian of the property of a child, with the permission of a court, may resign as guardian upon such conditions as the court considers appropriate.

Notice to Estate Registrar for Ontario

58. A notice of every application to a court for appointment of a guardian of the property of a child shall be transmitted by the clerk of the court to the Estate Registrar for Ontario.

Disposition of Property

Court order re property of child

59. (1) Upon application by a child's parent or by any other person, on notice to the Children's Lawyer, the Superior Court of Justice by order may require or approve, or both,

(a) the disposition or encumbrance of all or part of the interest of the child in land;

(b) the sale of the interest of the child in personal property; or

(c) the payment of all or part of any money belonging to the child or of the income from any property belonging to the child, or both.

Criteria

(2) An order shall be made under subsection (1) only where the Court is of the opinion that the disposition, encumbrance, sale or payment is necessary or proper for the support or education of the child or will substantially benefit the child.

Conditions

(3) An order under subsection (1) may be made subject to such conditions as the Court considers appropriate.

Limitation

(4) The Court shall not require or approve a disposition or encumbrance of the interest of a child in land contrary to a term of the instrument by which the child acquired the interest.

Execution of documents

(5) The Court, where it makes an order under subsection (1), may order that the child or another person named in the order execute any documents necessary to carry out the disposition, encumbrance, sale or payment.

Directions

(6) The Court by order may give such directions as it considers necessary for the carrying out of an order made under subsection (1).

Validity of documents

(7) Every document executed in accordance with an order under this section is as effectual as if the child by whom it was executed was eighteen years of age or, if executed by another person in accordance with the order, as if the child had executed it and had been eighteen years of age at the time.

Liability

(8) No person incurs or shall be deemed to incur liability by making a payment in accordance with an order under clause (1)(c).

Order for maintenance where power of appointment in favour of children

60. (1) Upon application by or with the consent of a person who has an estate for life in property with power to devise or appoint the property to one or more of his or her children, the Superior Court of Justice may order that such part of the proceeds of the property as the Court considers proper be used for the support, education or benefit of one or more of the children.

Idem

(2) An order may be made under subsection (1) whether or not,

(a) there is a gift over in the event that there are no children to take under the power; or

(b) any person could dispose of the property in the event that there are no children to take under the power.

Testamentary Custody and Guardianship

Appointments by will

Custody

61. (1) A person entitled to custody of a child may appoint by will one or more persons to have custody of the child after the death of the appointor.

Guardianship

(2) A guardian of the property of a child may appoint by will one or more persons to be guardians of the property of the child after the death of the appointor.

Appointment by minor

(3) An unmarried parent who is a minor may make an appointment mentioned in subsection (1) or (2) by a written appointment signed by the parent.

Limitation

(4) An appointment under subsection (1), (2) or (3) is effective only,

(a) if the appointor is the only person entitled to custody of the child or who is the guardian of the property of the child, as the case requires, on the day immediately before the appointment is to take effect; or

(b) if the appointor and any other person entitled to custody of the child or who is the guardian of the property of the child, as the case requires, die at the same time or in circumstances that render it uncertain which survived the other.

Where more than one appointment

(5) Where two or more persons are appointed to have custody of or to be guardians of the property of a child by appointors who die as mentioned in clause (4)(b), only the appointments of the persons appointed by both or all of the appointors are effective.

Consent of appointee

(6) No appointment under subsection (1), (2) or (3) is effective without the consent of the person appointed.

Expiration of appointment

(7) An appointment under subsection (1), (2) or (3) for custody of a child or guardianship of the property of a child expires ninety days after the appointment becomes effective or, where the appointee applies under this Part for custody of the child or guardianship of the property of the child within the ninety-day period, when the application is disposed of.

Application or order under ss. 21, 47

(8) An appointment under this section does not apply to prevent an application for or the making of an order under section 21 or 47.

Application

(9) This section applies in respect of,

(a) any will made on or after the 1st day of October, 1982; and

(b) any will made before the 1st day of October, 1982, if the testator is living on that day.

Procedure

Procedure, general

Joinder of proceedings

62. (1) An application under this Part may be made in the same proceeding and in the same manner as an application under the Family Law Act, or in another proceeding.

Nature of order

(2) An application under this Part may be an original application or for the variance of an order previously given or to supersede an order of an extra-provincial tribunal.

Parties

(3) The parties to an application under this Part in respect of a child shall include,

(a) the mother and the father of the child;

(b) a person who has demonstrated a settled intention to treat the child as a child of his or her family;

(c) a person who had the actual care and upbringing of the child immediately before the application; and

(d) any other person whose presence as a party is necessary to determine the matters in issue.

Combining of applications

(4) Where, in an application under this Part, it appears to the court that it is necessary or desirable in the best interests of the child to have other matters first or simultaneously determined, the court may direct that the application stand over until such other proceedings are brought or determined as the court considers appropriate, subject to section 26.

Where identity of father not known

(5) Where there is no presumption of paternity and the identity of the father is not known or is not reasonably capable of being ascertained, the court may order substituted service or may dispense with service of documents upon the father in the proceeding.

Application or response by minor

63. (1) A minor who is a parent may make an application under this Part without a next friend and may respond without a litigation guardian.

Consent by minor

(2) A consent in respect of a matter provided for by this Part is not invalid by reason only that the person giving the consent is a minor.

Child entitled to be heard

64. (1) In considering an application under this Part, a court where possible shall take into consideration the views and preferences of the child to the extent that the child is able to express them.

Interview by court

(2) The court may interview the child to determine the views and preferences of the child.

Recording

(3) The interview shall be recorded.

Counsel

(4) The child is entitled to be advised by and to have his or her counsel, if any, present during the interview.

Where child is sixteen or more years old

65. Nothing in this Part abrogates the right of a child of sixteen or more years of age to withdraw from parental control.

All proceedings in one court

66. Except as otherwise provided, where an application is made to a court under this Part, no person who is a party to the proceeding shall make an application under this Part to any other court in respect of a matter in issue in the proceeding, but the court may order that the proceeding be transferred to a court having other jurisdiction where, in the opinion of the court, the court having other jurisdiction is more appropriate to determine the matters in issue that should be determined at the same time.

Consent and domestic contracts

Consent orders

67. (1) Upon the consent of the parties in an application under this Part, the court may make any order that the court is otherwise empowered to make by this Part, subject to the duty of the court to have regard to the best interests of the child.

Incorporation of contract in order

(2) Any matter provided for in this Part and in a domestic contract as defined in the *Family Law Act* may be incorporated in an order made under this Part.

Part subject to contracts

68. Where a domestic contract as defined in the *Family Law Act* makes provision in respect of a matter that is provided for in this Part, the contract prevails except as otherwise provided in Part IV of the *Family Law Act*.

Jurisdiction of Superior Court of Justice

69. This Part does not deprive the Superior Court of Justice of its parens patriae jurisdiction.

Confidentiality

70. (1) Where a proceeding includes an application under this Part, the court shall consider whether it is appropriate to order,

(a) that access to all or part of the court file be limited to,

(i) the court and authorized court employees,

(ii) the parties and their counsel,

(iii) counsel, if any, representing the child who is the subject of the application, and

(iv) any other person that the court may specify; or

(b) that no person shall publish or make public information that has the effect of identifying any person referred to in any document relating to the application that appears in the court file.

Considerations

(2) In determining whether to make an order under subsection (1), the court shall consider,

(a) the nature and sensitivity of the information contained in the documents relating to the application under this Part that appear in the court file; and

(b) whether not making the order could cause physical, mental or emotional harm to any person referred to in those documents.

Order on application

(3) Any interested person may make an application for an order under subsection (1).

Varying or discharging order

(4) The court may vary or discharge an order made under subsection (1).

Where to apply for interim orders and variations

Place of application for interim order

71. (1) An application for an interim order shall be made to the court in which the original proceeding was taken.

Place of application to vary order

(2) An application under this Part to vary an order may be made to the court in which the original proceeding was taken or to a co-ordinate court in another part of Ontario.

Interim order

72. In a proceeding under this Part, the court may make such interim order as the court considers appropriate.

Appeal from Ontario Court of Justice

73. An appeal from an order of the Ontario Court of Justice under this Part lies to the Superior Court of Justice.

Order effective pending appeal

74. An order under this Part is effective even if an appeal is taken from the order, unless the court that made the order or the court to which the appeal is taken orders otherwise.

Rule of construction, guardianship of person and property

75. (1) For the purposes of construing any instrument, Act or regulation, unless the contrary intention appears, a reference to a guardian with respect to the person of a child shall be construed to refer to custody of the child and a reference to a guardian with respect to property of a child shall be construed to refer to guardianship of the property of the child.

Application

(2) Subsection (1) applies to any instrument, any Act of the Legislature or any regulation, order or by-law made under an Act of the Legislature enacted or made before, on or after the 1st day of October, 1982.

76. Repealed.

77. Repealed.

78. Repealed.

79.–83. Repealed.

84. Omitted (provides for amendments to this Act).

85. Omitted (provides for coming into force of provisions of this Act).

Divorce Act

RSC 1985, c. 3 (2d Supp.)

SHORT TITLE

Short title

1. This Act may be cited as the *Divorce Act*.

INTERPRETATION

Definitions

2. (1) In this Act,

"age of majority," in respect of a child, means the age of majority as determined by the laws of the province where the child ordinarily resides, or, if the child ordinarily resides outside of Canada, eighteen years of age;

"appellate court," in respect of an appeal from a court, means the court exercising appellate jurisdiction with respect to that appeal;

"applicable guidelines" means

(a) where both spouses or former spouses are ordinarily resident in the same province at the time an application for a child support order or a variation order in respect of a child support order is made, or the amount of a child support order is to be recalculated pursuant to section 25.1, and that province has been designated by an order made under subsection (5), the laws of the province specified in the order, and

(b) in any other case, the Federal Child Support Guidelines;

"child of the marriage" means a child of two spouses or former spouses who, at the material time,

(a) is under the age of majority and who has not withdrawn from their charge, or

(b) is the age of majority or over and under their charge but unable, by reason of illness, disability or other cause, to withdraw from their charge or to obtain the necessaries of life;

"child support order" means an order made under subsection 15.1(1);

"corollary relief proceeding" means a proceeding in a court in which either or both former spouses seek a child support order, a spousal support order or a custody order;

"court," in respect of a province, means

(a) for the Province of Ontario, the Superior Court of Justice,

(a.1) for the Province of Prince Edward Island or Newfoundland, the trial division of the Supreme Court of the Province,

(b) for the Province of Quebec, the Superior Court,

(c) for the Provinces of Nova Scotia and British Columbia, the Supreme Court of the Province,

(d) for the Province of New Brunswick, Manitoba, Saskatchewan or Alberta, the Court of Queen's Bench for the Province, and

(e) for Yukon or the Northwest Territories, the Supreme Court, and in Nunavut, the Nunavut Court of Justice,

and includes such other court in the province the judges of which are appointed by the Governor General as is designated by the Lieutenant Governor in Council of the province as a court for the purposes of this Act;

"custody" includes care, upbringing and any other incident of custody;

"custody order" means an order made under subsection 16(1);

"divorce proceeding" means a proceeding in a court in which either or both spouses seek a divorce alone or together with a child support order, a spousal support order or a custody order;

"Federal Child Support Guidelines" means the guidelines made under section 26.1;

"provincial child support service" means any service, agency or body designated in an agreement with a province under subsection 25.1(1);

"spousal support order" means an order made under subsection 15.2(1);

"spouse" means either of a man or woman who are married to each other;

"support order" means a child support order or a spousal support order;

"variation order" means an order made under subsection 17(1);

"variation proceeding" means a proceeding in a court in which either or both former spouses seek a variation order.

Child of the marriage

(2) For the purposes of the definition "child of the marriage" in subsection (1), a child of two spouses or former spouses includes

(a) any child for whom they both stand in the place of parents; and

(b) any child of whom one is the parent and for whom the other stands in the place of a parent.

Term not restrictive

(3) The use of the term "application" to describe a proceeding under this Act in a court shall not be construed as limiting the name under which and the form and manner in which that proceeding may be taken in that court, and the name, manner and form of the proceeding in that court shall be such as is provided for by the rules regulating the practice and procedure in that court.

Idem

(4) The use in section 21.1 of the terms "affidavit" and "pleadings" to describe documents shall not be construed as limiting the name that may be used to refer to those documents in a court and the form of those documents, and the name and form of the documents shall be such as is provided for by the rules regulating the practice and procedure in that court.

Provincial child support guidelines

(5) The Governor in Council may, by order, designate a province for the purposes of the definition "applicable guidelines" in subsection (1) if the laws of the province establish comprehensive guidelines for the determination of child support that deal with the matters referred to in section 26.1. The order shall specify the laws of the province that constitute the guidelines of the province.

Amendments included

(6) The guidelines of a province referred to in subsection (5) include any amendments made to them from time to time.

JURISDICTION

Jurisdiction in divorce proceedings

3. (1) A court in a province has jurisdiction to hear and determine a divorce proceeding if either spouse has been ordinarily resident in the province for at least one year immediately preceding the commencement of the proceeding.

Jurisdiction where two proceedings commenced on different days

(2) Where divorce proceedings between the same spouses are pending in two courts that would otherwise have jurisdiction under subsection (1) and were commenced on different days and the proceeding that was commenced first is not discontinued within thirty days after it was commenced, the court in which a divorce proceeding was commenced first has exclusive jurisdiction to hear and determine any divorce proceeding then pending between the spouses and the second divorce proceeding shall be deemed to be discontinued.

Jurisdiction where two proceedings commenced on same day

(3) Where divorce proceedings between the same spouses are pending in two courts that would otherwise have jurisdiction under subsection (1) and were commenced on the same day and neither proceeding is discontinued within thirty days after it was commenced, the Federal Court has exclusive jurisdiction to hear and determine any divorce proceeding then pending between the spouses and the divorce proceedings in those courts shall be transferred to the Federal Court on the direction of that Court.

Jurisdiction in corollary relief proceedings

4. (1) A court in a province has jurisdiction to hear and determine a corollary relief proceeding if

(a) either former spouse is ordinarily resident in the province at the commencement of the proceeding; or

(b) both former spouses accept the jurisdiction of the court.

Jurisdiction where two proceedings commenced on different days

(2) Where corollary relief proceedings between the same former spouses and in respect of the same matter are pending in two courts that would otherwise have jurisdiction under subsection (1) and were commenced on different days and the proceeding that was commenced first is not discontinued within thirty days after it was commenced, the court in which a corollary relief proceeding was commenced first has exclusive jurisdiction to hear and determine any corollary relief proceeding then pending between the former spouses in respect of that matter and the second corollary relief proceeding shall be deemed to be discontinued.

Jurisdiction where two proceedings commenced on same day

(3) Where proceedings between the same former spouses and in respect of the same matter are pending in two courts that would otherwise have jurisdiction under subsection (1) and were commenced on the same day and neither proceeding is discontinued within thirty days after it was commenced,

the Federal Court has exclusive jurisdiction to hear and determine any corollary relief proceeding then pending between the former spouses in respect of that matter and the corollary relief proceedings in those courts shall be transferred to the Federal Court on the direction of that Court.

Jurisdiction in variation proceedings

5. (1) A court in a province has jurisdiction to hear and determine a variation proceeding if

(a) either former spouse is ordinarily resident in the province at the commencement of the proceeding; or

(b) both former spouses accept the jurisdiction of the court.

Jurisdiction where two proceedings commenced on different days

(2) Where variation proceedings between the same former spouses and in respect of the same matter are pending in two courts that would otherwise have jurisdiction under subsection (1) and were commenced on different days and the proceeding that was commenced first is not discontinued within thirty days after it was commenced, the court in which a variation proceeding was commenced first has exclusive jurisdiction to hear and determine any variation proceeding then pending between the former spouses in respect of that matter and the second variation proceeding shall be deemed to be discontinued.

Jurisdiction where two proceedings commenced on same day

(3) Where variation proceedings between the same former spouses and in respect of the same matter are pending in two courts that would otherwise have jurisdiction under subsection (1) and were commenced on the same day and neither proceeding is discontinued within thirty days after it was commenced, the Federal Court has exclusive jurisdiction to hear and determine any variation proceeding then pending between the former spouses in respect of that matter and the variation proceedings in those courts shall be transferred to the Federal Court on the direction of that Court.

Transfer of divorce proceeding where custody application

6. (1) Where an application for an order under section 16 is made in a divorce proceeding to a court in a province and is opposed and the child of the marriage in respect of whom the order is sought is most substantially connected with another province, the court may, on application by a spouse or on its own motion, transfer the divorce proceeding to a court in that other province.

Transfer of corollary relief proceeding where custody application

(2) Where an application for an order under section 16 is made in a corollary relief proceeding to a court in a province and is opposed and the child of the marriage in respect of whom the order is sought is most substantially connected with another province, the court may, on application by a former spouse or on its own motion, transfer the corollary relief proceeding to a court in that other province.

Transfer of variation proceeding where custody application

(3) Where an application for a variation order in respect of a custody order is made in a variation proceeding to a court in a province and is opposed and the child of the marriage in respect of whom the variation order is sought is most substantially connected with another province, the court may, on application by a former spouse or on its own motion, transfer the variation proceeding to a court in that other province.

Exclusive jurisdiction

(4) Notwithstanding sections 3 to 5, a court in a province to which a proceeding is transferred under this section has exclusive jurisdiction to hear and determine the proceeding.

Exercise of jurisdiction by judge

7. The jurisdiction conferred on a court by this Act to grant a divorce shall be exercised only by a judge of the court without a jury.

DIVORCE

Divorce

8. (1) A court of competent jurisdiction may, on application by either or both spouses, grant a divorce to the spouse or spouses on the ground that there has been a breakdown of their marriage.

Breakdown of marriage

(2) Breakdown of a marriage is established only if

(a) the spouses have lived separate and apart for at least one year immediately preceding the determination of the divorce proceeding and were living separate and apart at the commencement of the proceeding; or

(b) the spouse against whom the divorce proceeding is brought has, since celebration of the marriage,

(i) committed adultery, or

(ii) treated the other spouse with physical or mental cruelty of such a kind as to render intolerable the continued cohabitation of the spouses.

Calculation of period of separation

(3) For the purposes of paragraph (2)(a),

(a) spouses shall be deemed to have lived separate and apart for any period during which they lived apart and either of them had the intention to live separate and apart from the other; and

(b) a period during which spouses have lived separate and apart shall not be considered to have been interrupted or terminated

(i) by reason only that either spouse has become incapable of forming or having an intention to continue to live separate and apart or of continuing to live separate and apart of the spouse's own volition, if it appears to the court that the separation would probably have continued if the spouse had not become so incapable, or

(ii) by reason only that the spouses have resumed cohabitation during a period of, or periods totalling, not more than ninety days with reconciliation as its primary purpose.

Duty of legal adviser

9. (1) It is the duty of every barrister, solicitor, lawyer or advocate who undertakes to act on behalf of a spouse in a divorce proceeding

(a) to draw to the attention of the spouse the provisions of this Act that have as their object the reconciliation of spouses, and

(b) to discuss with the spouse the possibility of the reconciliation of the spouses and to inform the spouse of the marriage counselling or guidance facilities known to him or her that might be able to assist the spouses to achieve a reconciliation,

unless the circumstances of the case are of such a nature that it would clearly not be appropriate to do so.

Idem

(2) It is the duty of every barrister, solicitor, lawyer or advocate who undertakes to act on behalf of a spouse in a divorce proceeding to discuss with the spouse the advisability of negotiating the matters that may be the subject of a support order or a custody order and to inform the spouse of the mediation facilities known to him or her that might be able to assist the spouses in negotiating those matters.

Certification

(3) Every document presented to a court by a barrister, solicitor, lawyer or advocate that formally commences a divorce proceeding shall contain a statement by him or her certifying that he or she has complied with this section.

Duty of court—reconciliation

10. (1) In a divorce proceeding, it is the duty of the court, before considering the evidence, to satisfy itself that there is no possibility of the reconciliation of the spouses, unless the circumstances of the case are of such a nature that it would clearly not be appropriate to do so.

Adjournment

(2) Where at any stage in a divorce proceeding it appears to the court from the nature of the case, the evidence or the attitude of either or both spouses that there is a possibility of the reconciliation of the spouses, the court shall

(a) adjourn the proceeding to afford the spouses an opportunity to achieve a reconciliation; and

(b) with the consent of the spouses or in the discretion of the court, nominate

(i) a person with experience or training in marriage counselling or guidance, or

(ii) in special circumstances, some other suitable person,

to assist the spouses to achieve a reconciliation.

Resumption

(3) Where fourteen days have elapsed from the date of any adjournment under subsection (2), the court shall resume the proceeding on the application of either or both spouses.

Nominee not competent or compellable

(4) No person nominated by a court under this section to assist spouses to achieve a reconciliation is competent or compellable in any legal proceedings to disclose any admission or communication made to that person in his or her capacity as a nominee of the court for that purpose.

Evidence not admissible

(5) Evidence of anything said or of any admission or communication made in the course of assisting spouses to achieve a reconciliation is not admissible in any legal proceedings.

Duty of court—bars

11. (1) In a divorce proceeding, it is the duty of the court

(a) to satisfy itself that there has been no collusion in relation to the application for a divorce and to dismiss the application if it finds that there was collusion in presenting it;

(b) to satisfy itself that reasonable arrangements have been made for the support of any children of the marriage, having regard to the applicable guidelines, and, if such arrangements have not been made, to stay the granting of the divorce until such arrangements are made; and

(c) where a divorce is sought in circumstances described in paragraph 8(2)(b), to satisfy itself that there has been no condonation or connivance on the part of the spouse bringing the proceeding, and to dismiss the application for a divorce if that spouse has condoned or connived at the act or conduct complained of unless, in the opinion of the court, the public interest would be better served by granting the divorce.

Revival

(2) Any act or conduct that has been condoned is not capable of being revived so as to constitute a circumstance described in paragraph 8(2)(b).

Condonation

(3) For the purposes of this section, a continuation or resumption of cohabitation during a period of, or periods totalling, not more than ninety days with reconciliation as its primary purpose shall not be considered to constitute condonation.

Definition of "collusion"

(4) In this section, "collusion" means an agreement or conspiracy to which an applicant for a divorce is either directly or indirectly a party for the purpose of subverting the administration of justice, and includes any agreement, understanding or arrangement to fabricate or suppress evidence or to deceive the court, but does not include an agreement to the extent that it provides for separation between the parties, financial support, division of property or the custody of any child of the marriage.

Effective date generally

12. (1) Subject to this section, a divorce takes effect on the thirty-first day after the day on which the judgment granting the divorce is rendered.

Special circumstances

(2) Where, on or after rendering a judgment granting a divorce,

(a) the court is of the opinion that by reason of special circumstances the divorce should take effect earlier than the thirty-first day after the day on which the judgment is rendered, and

(b) the spouses agree and undertake that no appeal from the judgment will be taken, or any appeal from the judgment that was taken has been abandoned,

the court may order that the divorce takes effect at such earlier time as it considers appropriate.

Effective date where appeal

(3) A divorce in respect of which an appeal is pending at the end of the period referred to in subsection (1), unless voided on appeal, takes effect on the expiration of the time fixed by law for instituting an appeal from the decision on that appeal or any subsequent appeal, if no appeal has been instituted within that time.

Certain extensions to be counted

(4) For the purposes of subsection (3), the time fixed by law for instituting an appeal from a decision on an appeal includes any extension thereof fixed pursuant to law before the expiration of that time or fixed thereafter on an application instituted before the expiration of that time.

No late extensions of time for appeal

(5) Notwithstanding any other law, the time fixed by law for instituting an appeal from a decision referred to in subsection (3) may not be extended after the expiration of that time, except on an application instituted before the expiration of that time.

Effective date where decision of Supreme Court of Canada

(6) A divorce in respect of which an appeal has been taken to the Supreme Court of Canada, unless voided on the appeal, takes effect on the day on which the judgment on the appeal is rendered.

Certificate of divorce

(7) Where a divorce takes effect in accordance with this section, a judge or officer of the court that rendered the judgment granting the divorce or, where that judgment has been appealed, of the appellate court that rendered the judgment on the final appeal, shall, on request, issue to any person a certificate that a divorce granted under this Act dissolved the marriage of the specified persons effective as of a specified date.

Conclusive proof

(8) A certificate referred to in subsection (7), or a certified copy thereof, is conclusive proof of the facts so certified without proof of the signature or authority of the person appearing to have signed the certificate.

Legal effect throughout Canada

13. On taking effect, a divorce granted under this Act has legal effect throughout Canada.

Marriage dissolved

14. On taking effect, a divorce granted under this Act dissolves the marriage of the spouses.

COROLLARY RELIEF

Interpretation

Definition of "spouse"

15. In sections 15.1 to 16, "spouse" has the meaning assigned by subsection 2(1), and includes a former spouse.

Child Support Orders

Child support order

15.1 (1) A court of competent jurisdiction may, on application by either or both spouses, make an order requiring a spouse to pay for the support of any or all children of the marriage.

Interim order

(2) Where an application is made under subsection (1), the court may, on application by either or both spouses, make an interim order requiring a spouse to pay for the support of any or all children of the marriage, pending the determination of the application under subsection (1).

Guidelines apply

(3) A court making an order under subsection (1) or an interim order under subsection (2) shall do so in accordance with the applicable guidelines.

Terms and conditions

(4) The court may make an order under subsection (1) or an interim order under subsection (2) for a definite or indefinite period or until a specified event occurs, and may impose terms, conditions or restrictions in connection with the order or interim order as it thinks fit and just.

Court may take agreement, etc., into account

(5) Notwithstanding subsection (3), a court may award an amount that is different from the amount that would be determined in accordance with the applicable guidelines if the court is satisfied

(a) that special provisions in an order, a judgment or a written agreement respecting the financial obligations of the spouses, or the division or transfer of their property, directly or indirectly benefit a child, or that special provisions have otherwise been made for the benefit of a child; and

(b) that the application of the applicable guidelines would result in an amount of child support that is inequitable given those special provisions.

Reasons

(6) Where the court awards, pursuant to subsection (5), an amount that is different from the amount that would be determined in accordance with the applicable guidelines, the court shall record its reasons for having done so.

Consent orders

(7) Notwithstanding subsection (3), a court may award an amount that is different from the amount that would be determined in accordance with the applicable guidelines on the consent of both spouses if it is satisfied that reasonable arrangements have been made for the support of the child to whom the order relates.

Reasonable arrangements

(8) For the purposes of subsection (7), in determining whether reasonable arrangements have been made for the support of a child, the court shall have regard to the applicable guidelines. However, the court shall not consider the arrangements to be unreasonable solely because the amount of support agreed to is not the same as the amount that would otherwise have been determined in accordance with the applicable guidelines.

Spousal Support Orders

Spousal support order

15.2 (1) A court of competent jurisdiction may, on application by either or both spouses, make an order requiring a spouse to secure or pay, or to secure and pay, such lump sum or periodic sums, or such lump sum and periodic sums, as the court thinks reasonable for the support of the other spouse.

Interim order

(2) Where an application is made under subsection (1), the court may, on application by either or both spouses, make an interim order requiring a spouse to secure or pay, or to secure and pay, such lump sum or periodic sums, or such lump sum and periodic sums, as the court thinks reasonable for the support of the other spouse, pending the determination of the application under subsection (1).

Terms and conditions

(3) The court may make an order under subsection (1) or an interim order under subsection (2) for a definite or indefinite period or until a specified event occurs, and may impose terms, conditions or restrictions in connection with the order as it thinks fit and just.

Factors

(4) In making an order under subsection (1) or an interim order under subsection (2), the court shall take into consideration the condition, means, needs and other circumstances of each spouse, including

(a) the length of time the spouses cohabited;

(b) the functions performed by each spouse during cohabitation; and

(c) any order, agreement or arrangement relating to support of either spouse.

Spousal misconduct

(5) In making an order under subsection (1) or an interim order under subsection (2), the court shall not take into consideration any misconduct of a spouse in relation to the marriage.

Objectives of spousal support order

(6) An order made under subsection (1) or an interim order under subsection (2) that provides for the support of a spouse should

(a) recognize any economic advantages or disadvantages to the spouses arising from the marriage or its breakdown;

(b) apportion between the spouses any financial consequences arising from the care of any child of the marriage over and above any obligation for the support of any child of the marriage;

(c) relieve any economic hardship of the spouses arising from the breakdown of the marriage; and

(d) in so far as practicable, promote the economic self-sufficiency of each spouse within a reasonable period of time.

Priority

Priority to child support

15.3 (1) Where a court is considering an application for a child support order and an application for a spousal support order, the court shall give priority to child support in determining the applications.

Reasons

(2) Where, as a result of giving priority to child support, the court is unable to make a spousal support order or the court makes a spousal support order in an amount that is less than it otherwise would have been, the court shall record its reasons for having done so.

Consequences of reduction or termination of child support order

(3) Where, as a result of giving priority to child support, a spousal support order was not made, or the amount of a spousal support order is less than it otherwise would have been, any subsequent reduction or termination of that child support constitutes a change of circumstances for the purposes of applying for a spousal support order, or a variation order in respect of the spousal support order, as the case may be.

Custody Orders

Order for custody

16. (1) A court of competent jurisdiction may, on application by either or both spouses or by any other person, make an order respecting the custody of or the access to, or the custody of and access to, any or all children of the marriage.

Interim order for custody

(2) Where an application is made under subsection (1), the court may, on application by either or both spouses or by any other person, make an interim order respecting the custody of or the access to, or the custody of and access to, any or all children of the marriage pending determination of the application under subsection (1).

Application by other person

(3) A person, other than a spouse, may not make an application under subsection (1) or (2) without leave of the court.

Joint custody or access

(4) The court may make an order under this section granting custody of, or access to, any or all children of the marriage to any one or more persons.

Access

(5) Unless the court orders otherwise, a spouse who is granted access to a child of the marriage has the right to make inquiries, and to be given information, as to the health, education and welfare of the child.

Terms and conditions

(6) The court may make an order under this section for a definite or indefinite period or until the happening of a specified event and may impose such other terms, conditions or restrictions in connection therewith as it thinks fit and just.

Order respecting change of residence

(7) Without limiting the generality of subsection (6), the court may include in an order under this section a term requiring any person who has custody of a child of the marriage and who intends to change the place of residence of that child to notify, at least thirty days before the change or within such other period before the change as the court may specify, any person who is granted access to that child of the change, the time at which the change will be made and the new place of residence of the child.

Factors

(8) In making an order under this section, the court shall take into consideration only the best interests of the child of the marriage as determined by reference to the condition, means, needs and other circumstances of the child.

Past conduct

(9) In making an order under this section, the court shall not take into consideration the past conduct of any person unless the conduct is relevant to the ability of that person to act as a parent of a child.

Maximum contact

(10) In making an order under this section, the court shall give effect to the principle that a child of the marriage should have as much contact with each spouse as is consistent with the best interests of the child and, for that purpose, shall take into consideration the willingness of the person for whom custody is sought to facilitate such contact.

Variation, Rescission or Suspension of Orders

Order for variation, rescission or suspension

17. (1) A court of competent jurisdiction may make an order varying, rescinding or suspending, prospectively or retroactively,

(a) a support order or any provision thereof on application by either or both former spouses; or

(b) a custody order or any provision thereof on application by either or both former spouses or by any other person.

Application by other person

(2) A person, other than a former spouse, may not make an application under paragraph (1)(b) without leave of the court.

Terms and conditions

(3) The court may include in a variation order any provision that under this Act could have been included in the order in respect of which the variation order is sought.

Factors for child support order

(4) Before the court makes a variation order in respect of a child support order, the court shall satisfy itself that a change

of circumstances as provided for in the applicable guidelines has occurred since the making of the child support order or the last variation order made in respect of that order.

Factors for spousal support order

(4.1) Before the court makes a variation order in respect of a spousal support order, the court shall satisfy itself that a change in the condition, means, needs or other circumstances of either former spouse has occurred since the making of the spousal support order or the last variation order made in respect of that order, and, in making the variation order, the court shall take that change into consideration.

Factors for custody order

(5) Before the court makes a variation order in respect of a custody order, the court shall satisfy itself that there has been a change in the condition, means, needs or other circumstances of the child of the marriage occurring since the making of the custody order or the last variation order made in respect of that order, as the case may be, and, in making the variation order, the court shall take into consideration only the best interests of the child as determined by reference to that change.

Variation order

(5.1) For the purposes of subsection (5), a former spouse's terminal illness or critical condition shall be considered a change of circumstances of the child of the marriage, and the court shall make a variation order in respect of access that is in the best interests of the child.

Conduct

(6) In making a variation order, the court shall not take into consideration any conduct that under this Act could not have been considered in making the order in respect of which the variation order is sought.

Guidelines apply

(6.1) A court making a variation order in respect of a child support order shall do so in accordance with the applicable guidelines.

Court may take agreement, etc., into account

(6.2) Notwithstanding subsection (6.1), in making a variation order in respect of a child support order, a court may award an amount that is different from the amount that would be determined in accordance with the applicable guidelines if the court is satisfied

(a) that special provisions in an order, a judgment or a written agreement respecting the financial obligations of the spouses, or the division or transfer of their property, directly or indirectly benefit a child, or that special provisions have otherwise been made for the benefit of a child; and

(b) that the application of the applicable guidelines would result in an amount of child support that is inequitable given those special provisions.

Reasons

(6.3) Where the court awards, pursuant to subsection (6.2), an amount that is different from the amount that would be determined in accordance with the applicable guidelines, the court shall record its reasons for having done so.

Consent orders

(6.4) Notwithstanding subsection (6.1), a court may award an amount that is different from the amount that would be determined in accordance with the applicable guidelines on the consent of both spouses if it is satisfied that reasonable arrangements have been made for the support of the child to whom the order relates.

Reasonable arrangements

(6.5) For the purposes of subsection (6.4), in determining whether reasonable arrangements have been made for the support of a child, the court shall have regard to the applicable guidelines. However, the court shall not consider the arrangements to be unreasonable solely because the amount of support agreed to is not the same as the amount that would otherwise have been determined in accordance with the applicable guidelines.

Objectives of variation order varying spousal support order

(7) A variation order varying a spousal support order should

(a) recognize any economic advantages or disadvantages to the former spouses arising from the marriage or its breakdown;

(b) apportion between the former spouses any financial consequences arising from the care of any child of the marriage over and above any obligation for the support of any child of the marriage;

(c) relieve any economic hardship of the former spouses arising from the breakdown of the marriage; and

(d) in so far as practicable, promote the economic self-sufficiency of each former spouse within a reasonable period of time.

(8) Repealed.

Maximum contact

(9) In making a variation order varying a custody order, the court shall give effect to the principle that a child of the marriage should have as much contact with each former spouse as is consistent with the best interests of the child and, for that purpose, where the variation order would grant custody of the child to a person who does not currently have custody, the court shall take into consideration the willingness of that person to facilitate such contact.

Limitation

(10) Notwithstanding subsection (1), where a spousal support order provides for support for a definite period or until

a specified event occurs, a court may not, on an application instituted after the expiration of that period or the occurrence of the event, make a variation order for the purpose of resuming that support unless the court is satisfied that

(a) a variation order is necessary to relieve economic hardship arising from a change described in subsection (4.1) that is related to the marriage; and

(b) the changed circumstances, had they existed at the time of the making of the spousal support order or the last variation order made in respect of that order, as the case may be, would likely have resulted in a different order.

Copy of order

(11) Where a court makes a variation order in respect of a support order or a custody order made by another court, it shall send a copy of the variation order, certified by a judge or officer of the court, to that other court.

Variation order by affidavit, etc.

17.1 Where both former spouses are ordinarily resident in different provinces, a court of competent jurisdiction may, in accordance with any applicable rules of the court, make a variation order pursuant to subsection 17(1) on the basis of the submissions of the former spouses, whether presented orally before the court or by means of affidavits or any means of telecommunication, if both former spouses consent thereto.

Provisional Orders

Definitions

18. (1) In this section and section 19,

"Attorney General," in respect of a province, means

(a) for Yukon, the member of the Executive Council of Yukon designated by the Commissioner of Yukon,

(b) for the Northwest Territories, the member of the Executive Council of the Northwest Territories designated by the Commissioner of the Northwest Territories,

(b.1) for Nunavut, the member of the Executive Council of Nunavut designated by the Commissioner of Nunavut, and

(c) for the other provinces, the Attorney General of the province,

and includes any person authorized in writing by the member or Attorney General to act for the member or Attorney General in the performance of a function under this section or section 19;

"provisional order" means an order made pursuant to subsection (2).

Provisional order

(2) Notwithstanding paragraph 5(1)(a) and subsection 17(1), where an application is made to a court in a province for a variation order in respect of a support order and

(a) the respondent in the application is ordinarily resident in another province and has not accepted the jurisdiction of the court, or both former spouses have not consented to the application of section 17.1 in respect of the matter, and

(b) in the circumstances of the case, the court is satisfied that the issues can be adequately determined by proceeding under this section and section 19,

the court shall make a variation order with or without notice to and in the absence of the respondent, but such order is provisional only and has no legal effect until it is confirmed in a proceeding under section 19 and, where so confirmed, it has legal effect in accordance with the terms of the order confirming it.

Transmission

(3) Where a court in a province makes a provisional order, it shall send to the Attorney General for the province

(a) three copies of the provisional order certified by a judge or officer of the court;

(b) a certified or sworn document setting out or summarizing the evidence given to the court; and

(c) a statement giving any available information respecting the identification, location, income and assets of the respondent.

Idem

(4) On receipt of the documents referred to in subsection (3), the Attorney General shall send the documents to the Attorney General for the province in which the respondent is ordinarily resident.

Further evidence

(5) Where, during a proceeding under section 19, a court in a province remits the matter back for further evidence to the court that made the provisional order, the court that made the order shall, after giving notice to the applicant, receive further evidence.

Transmission

(6) Where evidence is received under subsection (5), the court that received the evidence shall forward to the court that remitted the matter back a certified or sworn document setting out or summarizing the evidence, together with such recommendations as the court that received the evidence considers appropriate.

Transmission

19. (1) On receipt of any documents sent pursuant to subsection 18(4), the Attorney General for the province in which the respondent is ordinarily resident shall send the documents to a court in the province.

Procedure

(2) Subject to subsection (3), where documents have been sent to a court pursuant to subsection (1), the court shall serve

on the respondent a copy of the documents and a notice of a hearing respecting confirmation of the provisional order and shall proceed with the hearing, in the absence of the applicant, taking into consideration the certified or sworn document setting out or summarizing the evidence given to the court that made the provisional order.

Return to Attorney General

(3) Where documents have been sent to a court pursuant to subsection (1) and the respondent apparently is outside the province and is not likely to return, the court shall send the documents to the Attorney General for that province, together with any available information respecting the location and circumstances of the respondent.

Idem

(4) On receipt of any documents and information sent pursuant to subsection (3), the Attorney General shall send the documents and information to the Attorney General for the province of the court that made the provisional order.

Right of respondent

(5) In a proceeding under this section, the respondent may raise any matter that might have been raised before the court that made the provisional order.

Further evidence

(6) Where, in a proceeding under this section, the respondent satisfies the court that for the purpose of taking further evidence or for any other purpose it is necessary to remit the matter back to the court that made the provisional order, the court may so remit the matter and adjourn the proceeding for that purpose.

Order of confirmation or refusal

(7) Subject to subsection (7.1), at the conclusion of a proceeding under this section, the court shall make an order

(a) confirming the provisional order without variation;
(b) confirming the provisional order with variation; or
(c) refusing confirmation of the provisional order.

Guidelines apply

(7.1) A court making an order under subsection (7) in respect of a child support order shall do so in accordance with the applicable guidelines.

Further evidence

(8) The court, before making an order confirming the provisional order with variation or an order refusing confirmation of the provisional order, shall decide whether to remit the matter back for further evidence to the court that made the provisional order.

Interim order for support of children

(9) Where a court remits a matter pursuant to this section in relation to a child support order, the court may, pending the making of an order under subsection (7), make an interim order in accordance with the applicable guidelines requiring a spouse to pay for the support of any or all children of the marriage.

Interim order for support of spouse

(9.1) Where a court remits a matter pursuant to this section in relation to a spousal support order, the court may make an interim order requiring a spouse to secure or pay, or to secure and pay, such lump sum or periodic sums, or such lump sum and periodic sums, as the court thinks reasonable for the support of the other spouse, pending the making of an order under subsection (7).

Terms and conditions

(10) The court may make an order under subsection (9) or (9.1) for a definite or indefinite period or until a specified event occurs, and may impose terms, conditions or restrictions in connection with the order as it thinks fit and just.

Provisions applicable

(11) Subsections 17(4), (4.1) and (6) to (7) apply, with such modifications as the circumstances require, in respect of an order made under subsection (9) or (9.1) as if it were a variation order referred to in those subsections.

Report and filing

(12) On making an order under subsection (7), the court in a province shall

(a) send a copy of the order, certified by a judge or officer of the court, to the Attorney General for that province, to the court that made the provisional order and, where that court is not the court that made the support order in respect of which the provisional order was made, to the court that made the support order;

(b) where an order is made confirming the provisional order with or without variation, file the order in the court; and

(c) where an order is made confirming the provisional order with variation or refusing confirmation of the provisional order, give written reasons to the Attorney General for that province and to the court that made the provisional order.

Definition of "court"

20. (1) In this section, "court," in respect of a province, has the meaning assigned by subsection 2(1) and includes such other court having jurisdiction in the province as is designated by the Lieutenant Governor in Council of the province as a court for the purposes of this section.

Legal effect throughout Canada

(2) Subject to subsection 18(2), an order made under any of sections 15.1 to 17 or subsection 19(7), (9) or (9.1) has legal effect throughout Canada.

Enforcement

(3) An order that has legal effect throughout Canada pursuant to subsection (2) may be

(a) registered in any court in a province and enforced in like manner as an order of that court; or

(b) enforced in a province in any other manner provided for by the laws of that province, including its laws respecting reciprocal enforcement between the province and a jurisdiction outside Canada.

Variation of orders

(4) Notwithstanding subsection (3), a court may only vary an order that has legal effect throughout Canada pursuant to subsection (2) in accordance with this Act.

Assignment of order

20.1 (1) A support order may be assigned to

(a) any minister of the Crown for Canada designated by the Governor in Council;

(b) any minister of the Crown for a province, or any agency in a province, designated by the Lieutenant Governor in Council of the province;

(c) any member of the Legislative Assembly of Yukon, or any agency in Yukon, designated by the Commissioner of Yukon;

(d) any member of the Legislative Assembly of the Northwest Territories, or any agency in the Northwest Territories, designated by the Commissioner of the Northwest Territories; or

(e) any member of the Legislative Assembly of Nunavut, or any agency in Nunavut, designated by the Commissioner of Nunavut.

Rights

(2) A minister, member or agency referred to in subsection (1) to whom an order is assigned is entitled to the payments due under the order, and has the same right to be notified of, and to participate in, proceedings under this Act to vary, rescind, suspend or enforce the order as the person who would otherwise be entitled to the payments.

APPEALS

Appeal to appellate court

21. (1) Subject to subsections (2) and (3), an appeal lies to the appellate court from any judgment or order, whether final or interim, rendered or made by a court under this Act.

Restriction on divorce appeals

(2) No appeal lies from a judgment granting a divorce on or after the day on which the divorce takes effect.

Restriction on order appeals

(3) No appeal lies from an order made under this Act more than thirty days after the day on which the order was made.

Extension

(4) An appellate court or a judge thereof may, on special grounds, either before or after the expiration of the time fixed by subsection (3) for instituting an appeal, by order extend that time.

Powers of appellate court

(5) The appellate court may

(a) dismiss the appeal; or

(b) allow the appeal and

(i) render the judgment or make the order that ought to have been rendered or made, including such order or such further or other order as it deems just, or

(ii) order a new hearing where it deems it necessary to do so to correct a substantial wrong or miscarriage of justice.

Procedure on appeals

(6) Except as otherwise provided by this Act or the rules or regulations, an appeal under this section shall be asserted, heard and decided according to the ordinary procedure governing appeals to the appellate court from the court rendering the judgment or making the order being appealed.

GENERAL

Definition of "spouse"

21.1 (1) In this section, "spouse" has the meaning assigned by subsection 2(1) and includes a former spouse.

Affidavit re removal of barriers to religious remarriage

(2) In any proceedings under this Act, a spouse (in this section referred to as the "deponent") may serve on the other spouse and file with the court an affidavit indicating

(a) that the other spouse is the spouse of the deponent;

(b) the date and place of the marriage, and the official character of the person who solemnized the marriage;

(c) the nature of any barriers to the remarriage of the deponent within the deponent's religion the removal of which is within the other spouse's control;

(d) where there are any barriers to the remarriage of the other spouse within the other spouse's religion the removal of which is within the deponent's control, that the deponent

(i) has removed those barriers, and the date and circumstances of that removal, or

(ii) has signified a willingness to remove those barriers, and the date and circumstances of that signification;

(e) that the deponent has, in writing, requested the other spouse to remove all of the barriers to the remarriage of the deponent within the deponent's religion the removal of which is within the other spouse's control;

(f) the date of the request described in paragraph (e); and

(g) that the other spouse, despite the request described in paragraph (e), has failed to remove all of the barriers referred to in that paragraph.

Powers of court where barriers not removed

(3) Where a spouse who has been served with an affidavit under subsection (2) does not

(a) within fifteen days after that affidavit is filed with the court or within such longer period as the court allows, serve on the deponent and file with the court an affidavit indicating that all of the barriers referred to in paragraph (2)(e) have been removed, and

(b) satisfy the court, in any additional manner that the court may require, that all of the barriers referred to in paragraph (2)(e) have been removed,

the court may, subject to any terms that the court considers appropriate,

(c) dismiss any application filed by that spouse under this Act, and

(d) strike out any other pleadings and affidavits filed by that spouse under this Act.

Special case

(4) Without limiting the generality of the court's discretion under subsection (3), the court may refuse to exercise its powers under paragraphs (3)(c) and (d) where a spouse who has been served with an affidavit under subsection (2)

(a) within fifteen days after that affidavit is filed with the court or within such longer period as the court allows, serves on the deponent and files with the court an affidavit indicating genuine grounds of a religious or conscientious nature for refusing to remove the barriers referred to in paragraph (2)(e); and

(b) satisfies the court, in any additional manner that the court may require, that the spouse has genuine grounds of a religious or conscientious nature for refusing to remove the barriers referred to in paragraph (2)(e).

Affidavits

(5) For the purposes of this section, an affidavit filed with the court by a spouse must, in order to be valid, indicate the date on which it was served on the other spouse.

Where section does not apply

(6) This section does not apply where the power to remove the barrier to religious remarriage lies with a religious body or official.

Recognition of foreign divorce

22. (1) A divorce granted, on or after the coming into force of this Act, pursuant to a law of a country or subdivision of a country other than Canada by a tribunal or other authority having jurisdiction to do so shall be recognized for all purposes of determining the marital status in Canada of any person, if either former spouse was ordinarily resident in that country or subdivision for at least one year immediately preceding the commencement of proceedings for the divorce.

Idem

(2) A divorce granted, after July 1, 1968, pursuant to a law of a country or subdivision of a country other than Canada by a tribunal or other authority having jurisdiction to do so, on the basis of the domicile of the wife in that country or subdivision determined as if she were unmarried and, if she was a minor, as if she had attained the age of majority, shall be recognized for all purposes of determining the marital status in Canada of any person.

Other recognition rules preserved

(3) Nothing in this section abrogates or derogates from any other rule of law respecting the recognition of divorces granted otherwise than under this Act.

Provincial laws of evidence

23. (1) Subject to this or any other Act of Parliament, the laws of evidence of the province in which any proceedings under this Act are taken, including the laws of proof of service of any document, apply to such proceedings.

Presumption

(2) For the purposes of this section, where any proceedings are transferred to the Federal Court under subsection 3(3) or 5(3), the proceedings shall be deemed to have been taken in the province specified in the direction of the Court to be the province with which both spouses or former spouses, as the case may be, are or have been most substantially connected.

Proof of signature or office

24. A document offered in a proceeding under this Act that purports to be certified or sworn by a judge or an officer of a court shall, unless the contrary is proved, be proof of the appointment, signature or authority of the judge or officer and, in the case of a document purporting to be sworn, of the appointment, signature or authority of the person before whom the document purports to be sworn.

Definition of "competent authority"

25. (1) In this section, "competent authority," in respect of a court, or appellate court, in a province means the body, person or group of persons ordinarily competent under the laws of that province to make rules regulating the practice and procedure in that court.

Rules

(2) Subject to subsection (3), the competent authority may make rules applicable to any proceedings under this Act in a court, or appellate court, in a province, including, without limiting the generality of the foregoing, rules

(a) regulating the practice and procedure in the court, including the addition of persons as parties to the proceedings;

(b) respecting the conduct and disposition of any proceedings under this Act without an oral hearing;

(b.1) respecting the application of section 17.1 in respect of proceedings for a variation order;

(c) regulating the sittings of the court;

(d) respecting the fixing and awarding of costs;

(e) prescribing and regulating the duties of officers of the court;

(f) respecting the transfer of proceedings under this Act to or from the court; and

(g) prescribing and regulating any other matter considered expedient to attain the ends of justice and carry into effect the purposes and provisions of this Act.

Exercise of power

(3) The power to make rules for a court or appellate court conferred by subsection (2) on a competent authority shall be exercised in the like manner and subject to the like terms and conditions, if any, as the power to make rules for that court conferred on that authority by the laws of the province.

Not statutory instruments

(4) Rules made pursuant to this section by a competent authority that is not a judicial or quasi-judicial body shall be deemed not to be statutory instruments within the meaning and for the purposes of the Statutory Instruments Act.

Agreements with provinces

25.1 (1) With the approval of the Governor in Council, the Minister of Justice may, on behalf of the Government of Canada, enter into an agreement with a province authorizing a provincial child support service designated in the agreement to

(a) assist courts in the province in the determination of the amount of child support; and

(b) recalculate, at regular intervals, in accordance with the applicable guidelines, the amount of child support orders on the basis of updated income information.

Effect of recalculation

(2) Subject to subsection (5), the amount of a child support order as recalculated pursuant to this section shall for all purposes be deemed to be the amount payable under the child support order.

Liability

(3) The former spouse against whom a child support order was made becomes liable to pay the amount as recalculated pursuant to this section thirty-one days after both former spouses to whom the order relates are notified of the recalculation in the manner provided for in the agreement authorizing the recalculation.

Right to vary

(4) Where either or both former spouses to whom a child support order relates do not agree with the amount of the order as recalculated pursuant to this section, either former spouse may, within thirty days after both former spouses are notified of the recalculation in the manner provided for in the agreement authorizing the recalculation, apply to a court of competent jurisdiction for an order under subsection 17(1).

Effect of application

(5) Where an application is made under subsection (4), the operation of subsection (3) is suspended pending the determination of the application, and the child support order continues in effect.

Withdrawal of application

(6) Where an application made under subsection (4) is withdrawn before the determination of the application, the former spouse against whom the order was made becomes liable to pay the amount as recalculated pursuant to this section on the day on which the former spouse would have become liable had the application not been made.

Regulations

26. (1) The Governor in Council may make regulations for carrying the purposes and provisions of this Act into effect and, without limiting the generality of the foregoing, may make regulations

(a) respecting the establishment and operation of a central registry of divorce proceedings in Canada; and

(b) providing for uniformity in the rules made pursuant to section 25.

Regulations prevail

(2) Any regulations made pursuant to subsection (1) to provide for uniformity in the rules prevail over those rules.

Guidelines

26.1 (1) The Governor in Council may establish guidelines respecting the making of orders for child support, including, but without limiting the generality of the foregoing, guidelines

(a) respecting the way in which the amount of an order for child support is to be determined;

(b) respecting the circumstances in which discretion may be exercised in the making of an order for child support;

(c) authorizing a court to require that the amount payable under an order for child support be paid in periodic payments, in a lump sum or in a lump sum and periodic payments;

(d) authorizing a court to require that the amount payable under an order for child support be paid or secured, or paid and secured, in the manner specified in the order;

(e) respecting the circumstances that give rise to the making of a variation order in respect of a child support order;

(f) respecting the determination of income for the purposes of the application of the guidelines;

(g) authorizing a court to impute income for the purposes of the application of the guidelines; and

(h) respecting the production of income information and providing for sanctions when that information is not provided.

Principle

(2) The guidelines shall be based on the principle that spouses have a joint financial obligation to maintain the children of the marriage in accordance with their relative abilities to contribute to the performance of that obligation.

Definition of "order for child support"

(3) In subsection (1), "order for child support" means

(a) an order or interim order made under section 15.1;

(b) a variation order in respect of a child support order; or

(c) an order or an interim order made under section 19.

Fees

27. (1) The Governor in Council may, by order, authorize the Minister of Justice to prescribe a fee to be paid by any person to whom a service is provided under this Act or the regulations.

Agreements

(2) The Minister of Justice may, with the approval of the Governor in Council, enter into an agreement with the government of any province respecting the collection and remittance of any fees prescribed pursuant to subsection (1).

Review and report

28. The Minister of Justice shall undertake a comprehensive review of the provisions and operation of the Federal Child Support Guidelines and the determination of child support under this Act and shall cause a report on the review to be laid before each House of Parliament within five years after the coming into force of this section. …

Family Law Act

RSO 1990, c. F.3
Current to January 1, 2012

Preamble

Whereas it is desirable to encourage and strengthen the role of the family; and whereas for that purpose it is necessary to recognize the equal position of spouses as individuals within marriage and to recognize marriage as a form of partnership; and whereas in support of such recognition it is necessary to provide in law for the orderly and equitable settlement of the affairs of the spouses upon the breakdown of the partnership, and to provide for other mutual obligations in family relationships, including the equitable sharing by parents of responsibility for their children;

Therefore, Her Majesty, by and with the advice and consent of the Legislative Assembly of the Province of Ontario, enacts as follows:

Definitions

1. (1) In this Act,

"child" includes a person whom a parent has demonstrated a settled intention to treat as a child of his or her family, except under an arrangement where the child is placed for valuable consideration in a foster home by a person having lawful custody;

"child support guidelines" means the guidelines established by the regulations made under subsections 69(2) and (3);

"cohabit" means to live together in a conjugal relationship, whether within or outside marriage;

"court" means the Ontario Court of Justice, the Family Court of the Superior Court of Justice or the Superior Court of Justice;

"domestic contract" means a domestic contract as defined in Part IV (Domestic Contracts);

"parent" includes a person who has demonstrated a settled intention to treat a child as a child of his or her family, except under an arrangement where the child is placed for valuable consideration in a foster home by a person having lawful custody;

"paternity agreement" means a paternity agreement as defined in Part IV (Domestic Contracts);

"spouse" means either of two persons who,

(a) are married to each other, or

(b) have together entered into a marriage that is voidable or void, in good faith on the part of a person relying on this clause to assert any right.

Polygamous marriages

(2) In the definition of "spouse," a reference to marriage includes a marriage that is actually or potentially polygamous, if it was celebrated in a jurisdiction whose system of law recognizes it as valid.

Procedural and other miscellaneous matters

Staying application

2. (1) If, in an application under this Act, it appears to the court that for the appropriate determination of the spouses' affairs it is necessary or desirable to have other matters determined first or simultaneously, the court may stay the application until another proceeding is brought or determined as the court considers appropriate.

All proceedings in one court

(2) Except as this Act provides otherwise, no person who is a party to an application under this Act shall make another application under this Act to another court, but the court may order that the proceeding be transferred to a court having other jurisdiction where, in the first court's opinion, the other court is more appropriate to determine the matters in issue that should be determined at the same time.

Applications in Superior Court of Justice

(3) In the Superior Court of Justice, an application under this Act may be made by action or application.

Statement re removal of barriers to remarriage

(4) A party to an application under section 7 (net family property), 10 (questions of title between spouses), 33 (support), 34 (powers of court) or 37 (variation) may serve on the other party and file with the court a statement, verified by oath or statutory declaration, indicating that,

(a) the author of the statement has removed all barriers that are within his or her control and that would prevent the other spouse's remarriage within that spouse's faith; and

(b) the other party has not done so, despite a request.

Idem

(5) Within ten days after service of the statement, or within such longer period as the court allows, the party served with a statement under subsection (4) shall serve on the other party and file with the court a statement, verified by oath or statutory declaration, indicating that the author of the statement has removed all barriers that are within his or her control and that would prevent the other spouse's remarriage within that spouse's faith.

Dismissal, etc.

(6) When a party fails to comply with subsection (5),

(a) if the party is an applicant, the proceeding may be dismissed;

(b) if the party is a respondent, the defence may be struck out.

Exception

(7) Subsections (5) and (6) do not apply to a party who does not claim costs or other relief in the proceeding.

Extension of times

(8) The court may, on motion, extend a time prescribed by this Act if it is satisfied that,

(a) there are apparent grounds for relief;

(b) relief is unavailable because of delay that has been incurred in good faith; and

(c) no person will suffer substantial prejudice by reason of the delay.

Incorporation of contract in order

(9) A provision of a domestic contract in respect of a matter that is dealt with in this Act may be incorporated in an order made under this Act.

Act subject to contracts

(10) A domestic contract dealing with a matter that is also dealt with in this Act prevails unless this Act provides otherwise.

Registration of orders

(11) An order made under this Act that affects real property does not affect the acquisition of an interest in the real property by a person acting in good faith without notice of the order, unless the order is registered in the proper land registry office.

Mediation

3. (1) In an application under this Act, the court may, on motion, appoint a person whom the parties have selected to mediate any matter that the court specifies.

Consent to act

(2) The court shall appoint only a person who,

(a) has consented to act as mediator; and

(b) has agreed to file a report with the court within the period of time specified by the court.

Duty of mediator

(3) The mediator shall confer with the parties, and with the children if the mediator considers it appropriate to do so, and shall endeavour to obtain an agreement between the parties.

Full or limited report

(4) Before entering into mediation, the parties shall decide whether,

(a) the mediator is to file a full report on the mediation, including anything that he or she considers relevant; or

(b) the mediator is to file a limited report that sets out only the agreement reached by the parties or states only that the parties did not reach agreement.

Filing and copies of report

(5) The mediator shall file with the clerk or registrar of the court a full or limited report, as the parties have decided, and shall give a copy to each of the parties.

Admissions, etc., in the course of mediation

(6) If the parties have decided that the mediator is to file a limited report, no evidence of anything said or of any admission or communication made in the course of the mediation is admissible in any proceeding, except with the consent of all parties to the proceeding in which the mediator was appointed.

Fees and expenses

(7) The court shall require the parties to pay the mediator's fees and expenses and shall specify in the order the proportions or amounts of the fees and expenses that each party is required to pay.

Idem, serious financial hardship

(8) The court may require one party to pay all the mediator's fees and expenses if the court is satisfied that payment would cause the other party or parties serious financial hardship.

PART I FAMILY PROPERTY

Definitions

4. (1) In this Part,

"court" means a court as defined in subsection 1(1), but does not include the Ontario Court of Justice;

"matrimonial home" means a matrimonial home under section 18 and includes property that is a matrimonial home under that section at the valuation date;

"net family property" means the value of all the property, except property described in subsection (2), that a spouse owns on the valuation date, after deducting,

(a) the spouse's debts and other liabilities, and

(b) the value of property, other than a matrimonial home, that the spouse owned on the date of the marriage, after deducting the spouse's debts and other liabilities, other than debts or liabilities related directly to the acquisition or significant improvement of a matrimonial home, calculated as of the date of the marriage;

"property" means any interest, present or future, vested or contingent, in real or personal property and includes,

(a) property over which a spouse has, alone or in conjunction with another person, a power of appointment exercisable in favour of himself or herself,

(b) property disposed of by a spouse but over which the spouse has, alone or in conjunction with another person, a power to revoke the disposition or a power to consume or dispose of the property, and

(c) in the case of a spouse's rights under a pension plan, the imputed value, for family law purposes, of the spouse's interest in the plan, as determined in accordance with section 10.1, for the period beginning with the date of the marriage and ending on the valuation date;

"valuation date" means the earliest of the following dates:

1. The date the spouses separate and there is no reasonable prospect that they will resume cohabitation.
2. The date a divorce is granted.
3. The date the marriage is declared a nullity.
4. The date one of the spouses commences an application based on subsection 5(3) (improvident depletion) that is subsequently granted.
5. The date before the date on which one of the spouses dies leaving the other spouse surviving.

Net family property, liabilities

(1.1) The liabilities referred to in clauses (a) and (b) of the definition of "net family property" in subsection (1) include any applicable contingent tax liabilities in respect of the property.

Excluded property

(2) The value of the following property that a spouse owns on the valuation date does not form part of the spouse's net family property:

1. Property, other than a matrimonial home, that was acquired by gift or inheritance from a third person after the date of the marriage.
2. Income from property referred to in paragraph 1, if the donor or testator has expressly stated that it is to be excluded from the spouse's net family property.
3. Damages or a right to damages for personal injuries, nervous shock, mental distress or loss of guidance, care and companionship, or the part of a settlement that represents those damages.
4. Proceeds or a right to proceeds of a policy of life insurance, as defined under the *Insurance Act*, that are payable on the death of the life insured.
5. Property, other than a matrimonial home, into which property referred to in paragraphs 1 to 4 can be traced.
6. Property that the spouses have agreed by a domestic contract is not to be included in the spouse's net family property.
7. Unadjusted pensionable earnings under the *Canada Pension Plan*.

Onus of proof re deductions and exclusions

(3) The onus of proving a deduction under the definition of "net family property" or an exclusion under subsection (2) is on the person claiming it.

Close of business

(4) When this section requires that a value be calculated as of a given date, it shall be calculated as of close of business on that date.

Net family property not to be less than zero

(5) If a spouse's net family property as calculated under subsections (1), (2) and (4) is less than zero, it shall be deemed to be equal to zero.

Equalization of net family properties

Divorce, etc.

5. (1) When a divorce is granted or a marriage is declared a nullity, or when the spouses are separated and there is no reasonable prospect that they will resume cohabitation, the spouse whose net family property is the lesser of the two net family properties is entitled to one-half the difference between them.

Death of spouse

(2) When a spouse dies, if the net family property of the deceased spouse exceeds the net family property of the surviving spouse, the surviving spouse is entitled to one-half the difference between them.

Improvident depletion of spouse's net family property

(3) When spouses are cohabiting, if there is a serious danger that one spouse may improvidently deplete his or her net family property, the other spouse may on an application under section 7 have the difference between the net family properties divided as if the spouses were separated and there were no reasonable prospect that they would resume cohabitation.

No further division

(4) After the court has made an order for division based on subsection (3), neither spouse may make a further application under section 7 in respect of their marriage.

Idem

(5) Subsection (4) applies even though the spouses continue to cohabit, unless a domestic contract between the spouses provides otherwise.

Variation of share

(6) The court may award a spouse an amount that is more or less than half the difference between the net family properties if the court is of the opinion that equalizing the net family properties would be unconscionable, having regard to,

(a) a spouse's failure to disclose to the other spouse debts or other liabilities existing at the date of the marriage;

(b) the fact that debts or other liabilities claimed in reduction of a spouse's net family property were incurred recklessly or in bad faith;

(c) the part of a spouse's net family property that consists of gifts made by the other spouse;

(d) a spouse's intentional or reckless depletion of his or her net family property;

(e) the fact that the amount a spouse would otherwise receive under subsection (1), (2) or (3) is disproportionately large in relation to a period of cohabitation that is less than five years;

(f) the fact that one spouse has incurred a disproportionately larger amount of debts or other liabilities than the other spouse for the support of the family;

(g) a written agreement between the spouses that is not a domestic contract; or

(h) any other circumstance relating to the acquisition, disposition, preservation, maintenance or improvement of property.

Purpose

(7) The purpose of this section is to recognize that child care, household management and financial provision are the joint responsibilities of the spouses and that inherent in the marital relationship there is equal contribution, whether financial or otherwise, by the spouses to the assumption of these responsibilities, entitling each spouse to the equalization of the net family properties, subject only to the equitable considerations set out in subsection (6).

Election

Spouse's will

6. (1) When a spouse dies leaving a will, the surviving spouse shall elect to take under the will or to receive the entitlement under section 5.

Spouse's intestacy

(2) When a spouse dies intestate, the surviving spouse shall elect to receive the entitlement under Part II of the *Succession Law Reform Act* or to receive the entitlement under section 5.

Spouse's partial intestacy

(3) When a spouse dies testate as to some property and intestate as to other property, the surviving spouse shall elect to take under the will and to receive the entitlement under Part II of the *Succession Law Reform Act*, or to receive the entitlement under section 5.

Property outside estate

(4) A surviving spouse who elects to take under the will or to receive the entitlement under Part II of the *Succession Law Reform Act*, or both in the case of a partial intestacy, shall also receive the other property to which he or she is entitled because of the first spouse's death.

Gifts by will

(5) The surviving spouse shall receive the gifts made to him or her in the deceased spouse's will in addition to the entitlement under section 5 if the will expressly provides for that result.

Amounts to be credited

(6) The rules in subsection (7) apply if a surviving spouse elects or has elected to receive an entitlement under section 5 and is,

(a) the beneficiary of a policy of life insurance, as defined in the *Insurance Act*, that was taken out on the life of the deceased spouse and owned by the deceased spouse or was taken out on the lives of a group of which he or she was a member;

(b) the beneficiary of a lump sum payment provided under a pension or similar plan on the death of the deceased spouse; or

(c) the recipient of property or a portion of property to which the surviving spouse becomes entitled by right of survivorship or otherwise on the death of the deceased spouse.

Same

(7) The following rules apply in the circumstances described in subsection (6):

1. The amount of every payment and the value of every property or portion of property described in that subsection, less any contingent tax liability in respect of the payment, property or portion of property, shall be credited against the surviving spouse's entitlement under section 5.
2. If the total amount of the credit under paragraph 1 exceeds the entitlement under section 5, the deceased spouse's personal representative may recover the excess amount from the surviving spouse.
3. Paragraphs 1 and 2 do not apply in respect of a payment, property or portion of property if,

i. the deceased spouse provided in a written designation, will or other written instrument, as the case may be, that the surviving spouse shall receive the payment, property or portion of property in addition to the entitlement under section 5, or

ii. in the case of property or a portion of property referred to in clause (6)(c), if the surviving spouse's entitlement to the property or portion of property was established by or on behalf of a third person, either the deceased spouse or the third person provided in a will or other written instrument that the surviving spouse shall receive the property or portion of property in addition to the entitlement under section 5.

Effect of election to receive entitlement under s. 5

(8) When a surviving spouse elects to receive the entitlement under section 5, the gifts made to him or her in the deceased spouse's will are revoked and the will shall be interpreted as if the surviving spouse had died before the other, unless the will expressly provides that the gifts are in addition to the entitlement under section 5.

Idem

(9) When a surviving spouse elects to receive the entitlement under section 5, the spouse shall be deemed to have disclaimed the entitlement under Part II of the *Succession Law Reform Act*.

Manner of making election

(10) The surviving spouse's election shall be in the form prescribed by the regulations made under this Act and shall be filed in the office of the Estate Registrar for Ontario within six months after the first spouse's death.

Deemed election

(11) If the surviving spouse does not file the election within that time, he or she shall be deemed to have elected to take under the will or to receive the entitlement under the *Succession Law Reform Act*, or both, as the case may be, unless the court, on application, orders otherwise.

Priority of spouse's entitlement

(12) The spouse's entitlement under section 5 has priority over,

(a) the gifts made in the deceased spouse's will, if any, subject to subsection (13);

(b) a person's right to a share of the estate under Part II (Intestate Succession) of the *Succession Law Reform Act*;

(c) an order made against the estate under Part V (Support of Dependants) of the *Succession Law Reform Act*, except an order in favour of a child of the deceased spouse.

Exception

(13) The spouse's entitlement under section 5 does not have priority over a gift by will made in accordance with a contract that the deceased spouse entered into in good faith and for valuable consideration, except to the extent that the value of the gift, in the court's opinion, exceeds the consideration.

Distribution within six months of death restricted

(14) No distribution shall be made in the administration of a deceased spouse's estate within six months of the spouse's death, unless,

(a) the surviving spouse gives written consent to the distribution; or

(b) the court authorizes the distribution.

Idem, notice of application

(15) No distribution shall be made in the administration of a deceased spouse's death after the personal representative has received notice of an application under this Part, unless,

(a) the applicant gives written consent to the distribution; or

(b) the court authorizes the distribution.

Extension of limitation period

(16) If the court extends the time for a spouse's application based on subsection 5(2), any property of the deceased spouse that is distributed before the date of the order and without notice of the application shall not be brought into the calculation of the deceased spouse's net family property.

Exception

(17) Subsections (14) and (15) do not prohibit reasonable advances to dependants of the deceased spouse for their support.

Definition

(18) In subsection (17),

"dependant" has the same meaning as in Part V of the *Succession Law Reform Act*.

Liability of personal representative

(19) If the personal representative makes a distribution that contravenes subsection (14) or (15), the court makes an order against the estate under this Part and the undistributed portion of the estate is not sufficient to satisfy the order, the personal representative is personally liable to the applicant for the amount that was distributed or the amount that is required to satisfy the order, whichever is less.

Order suspending administration

(20) On motion by the surviving spouse, the court may make an order suspending the administration of the deceased spouse's estate for the time and to the extent that the court decides.

Application to court

7. (1) The court may, on the application of a spouse, former spouse or deceased spouse's personal representative, determine any matter respecting the spouses' entitlement under section 5.

Personal action; estates

(2) Entitlement under subsections 5(1), (2) and (3) is personal as between the spouses but,

(a) an application based on subsection 5(1) or (3) and commenced before a spouse's death may be continued by or against the deceased spouse's estate; and

(b) an application based on subsection 5(2) may be made by or against a deceased spouse's estate.

Limitation

(3) An application based on subsection 5(1) or (2) shall not be brought after the earliest of,

(a) two years after the day the marriage is terminated by divorce or judgment of nullity;

(b) six years after the day the spouses separate and there is no reasonable prospect that they will resume cohabitation;

(c) six months after the first spouse's death.

Statement of property

8. In an application under section 7, each party shall serve on the other and file with the court, in the manner and form prescribed by the rules of the court, a statement verified by oath or statutory declaration disclosing particulars of,

(a) the party's property and debts and other liabilities,

(i) as of the date of the marriage,

(ii) as of the valuation date, and

(iii) as of the date of the statement;

(b) the deductions that the party claims under the definition of "net family property";

(c) the exclusions that the party claims under subsection 4(2); and

(d) all property that the party disposed of during the two years immediately preceding the making of the statement, or during the marriage, whichever period is shorter.

Powers of court

9. (1) In an application under section 7, the court may order,

(a) that one spouse pay to the other spouse the amount to which the court finds that spouse to be entitled under this Part;

(b) that security, including a charge on property, be given for the performance of an obligation imposed by the order;

(c) that, if necessary to avoid hardship, an amount referred to in clause (a) be paid in instalments during a period not exceeding ten years or that payment of all or part of the amount be delayed for a period not exceeding ten years; and

(d) that, if appropriate to satisfy an obligation imposed by the order,

(i) property be transferred to or in trust for or vested in a spouse, whether absolutely, for life or for a term of years, or

(ii) any property be partitioned or sold.

Financial information, inspections

(2) The court may, at the time of making an order for instalment or delayed payments or on motion at a later time, order that the spouse who has the obligation to make payments shall,

(a) furnish the other spouse with specified financial information, which may include periodic financial statements; and

(b) permit inspections of specified property of the spouse by or on behalf of the other spouse, as the court directs.

Variation

(3) If the court is satisfied that there has been a material change in the circumstances of the spouse who has the obligation to make instalment or delayed payments, the court may, on motion, vary the order, but shall not vary the amount to which the court found the spouse to be entitled under this Part.

Ten-year period

(4) Subsections (3) and 2(8) (extension of times) do not permit the postponement of payment beyond the ten-year period mentioned in clause (1)(c).

Determination of questions of title between spouses

10. (1) A person may apply to the court for the determination of a question between that person and his or her spouse or former spouse as to the ownership or right to possession of particular property, other than a question arising out of an equalization of net family properties under section 5, and the court may,

(a) declare the ownership or right to possession;

(b) if the property has been disposed of, order payment in compensation for the interest of either party;

(c) order that the property be partitioned or sold for the purpose of realizing the interests in it; and

(d) order that either or both spouses give security, including a charge on property, for the performance of an obligation imposed by the order,

and may make ancillary orders or give ancillary directions.

Estates

(2) An application based on subsection (1) may be made by or continued against the estate of a deceased spouse.

Interest in a pension plan

Imputed value for family law purposes

10.1 (1) The imputed value, for family law purposes, of a spouse's interest in a pension plan to which the *Pension Benefits Act* applies is determined in accordance with section 67.2 of that Act.

Same

(2) The imputed value, for family law purposes, of a spouse's interest in any other pension plan is determined, where reasonably possible, in accordance with section 67.2 of the *Pension Benefits Act* with necessary modifications.

Order for immediate transfer of a lump sum

(3) An order made under section 9 or 10 may provide for the immediate transfer of a lump sum out of a pension plan but, except as permitted under subsection (5), not for any other division of a spouse's interest in the plan.

Same

(4) In determining whether to order the immediate transfer of a lump sum out of a pension plan and in determining the amount to be transferred, the court may consider the following matters and such other matters as the court considers appropriate:

1. The nature of the assets available to each spouse at the time of the hearing.
2. The proportion of a spouse's net family property that consists of the imputed value, for family law purposes, of his or her interest in the pension plan.
3. The liquidity of the lump sum in the hands of the spouse to whom it would be transferred.
4. Any contingent tax liabilities in respect of the lump sum that would be transferred.
5. The resources available to each spouse to meet his or her needs in retirement and the desirability of maintaining those resources.

Order for division of pension payments

(5) If payment of the first instalment of a spouse's pension under a pension plan is due on or before the valuation date, an order made under section 9 or 10 may provide for the division of pension payments but not for any other division of the spouse's interest in the plan.

Same

(6) Subsections 9(2) and (4) do not apply with respect to an order made under section 9 or 10 that provides for the division of pension payments.

Restrictions re certain pension plans

(7) If the *Pension Benefits Act* applies to the pension plan, the restrictions under sections 67.3 and 67.4 of that Act apply with respect to the division of the spouse's interest in the plan by an order under section 9 or 10.

Transition, valuation date

(8) This section applies whether the valuation date is before, on or after the date on which this section comes into force.

Transition, previous orders

(9) This section does not apply to an order made before the date on which this section comes into force that requires one spouse to pay to the other spouse the amount to which that spouse is entitled under section 5.

Operating business or farm

11. (1) An order made under section 9 or 10 shall not be made so as to require or result in the sale of an operating business or farm or so as to seriously impair its operation, unless there is no reasonable alternative method of satisfying the award.

Idem

(2) To comply with subsection (1), the court may,

(a) order that one spouse pay to the other a share of the profits from the business or farm; and

(b) if the business or farm is incorporated, order that one spouse transfer or have the corporation issue to the other shares in the corporation.

Orders for preservation

12. In an application under section 7 or 10, if the court considers it necessary for the protection of the other spouse's interests under this Part, the court may make an interim or final order,

(a) restraining the depletion of a spouse's property; and

(b) for the possession, delivering up, safekeeping and preservation of the property.

Variation and realization of security

13. If the court has ordered security or charged a property with security for the performance of an obligation under this Part, the court may, on motion,

(a) vary or discharge the order; or

(b) on notice to all persons having an interest in the property, direct its sale for the purpose of realizing the security or charge.

Order regarding conduct

13.1 In making any order under this Part, the court may also make an interim order prohibiting, in whole or in part, a party from directly or indirectly contacting or communicating with another party, if the court determines that the order is necessary to ensure that an application under this Part is dealt with justly.

Presumptions

14. The rule of law applying a presumption of a resulting trust shall be applied in questions of the ownership of property between spouses, as if they were not married, except that,

(a) the fact that property is held in the name of spouses as joint tenants is proof, in the absence of evidence to the contrary, that the spouses are intended to own the property as joint tenants; and

(b) money on deposit in the name of both spouses shall be deemed to be in the name of the spouses as joint tenants for the purposes of clause (a).

Conflict of laws

15. The property rights of spouses arising out of the marital relationship are governed by the internal law of the place where both spouses had their last common habitual residence or, if there is no place where the spouses had a common habitual residence, by the law of Ontario.

Application of Part

16. (1) This Part applies to property owned by spouses,

(a) whether they were married before or after the 1st day of March, 1986; and

(b) whether the property was acquired before or after that day.

Application of s. 14

(2) Section 14 applies whether the event giving rise to the presumption occurred before or after the 1st day of March, 1986.

PART II MATRIMONIAL HOME

Definitions

17. In this Part,

"court" means a court as defined in subsection 1(1) but does not include the Ontario Court of Justice;

"property" means real or personal property.

Matrimonial home

18. (1) Every property in which a person has an interest and that is or, if the spouses have separated, was at the time of separation ordinarily occupied by the person and his or her spouse as their family residence is their matrimonial home.

Ownership of shares

(2) The ownership of a share or shares, or of an interest in a share or shares, of a corporation entitling the owner to occupy a housing unit owned by the corporation shall be deemed to be an interest in the unit for the purposes of subsection (1).

Residence on farmland, etc.

(3) If property that includes a matrimonial home is normally used for a purpose other than residential, the matrimonial home is only the part of the property that may reasonably be regarded as necessary to the use and enjoyment of the residence.

Possession of matrimonial home

19. (1) Both spouses have an equal right to possession of a matrimonial home.

Idem

(2) When only one of the spouses has an interest in a matrimonial home, the other spouse's right of possession,

(a) is personal as against the first spouse; and

(b) ends when they cease to be spouses, unless a separation agreement or court order provides otherwise.

Designation of matrimonial home

20. (1) One or both spouses may designate property owned by one or both of them as a matrimonial home, in the form prescribed by the regulations made under this Act.

Contiguous property

(2) The designation may include property that is described in the designation and is contiguous to the matrimonial home.

Registration

(3) The designation may be registered in the proper land registry office.

Effect of designation by both spouses

(4) On the registration of a designation made by both spouses, any other property that is a matrimonial home under section 18 but is not designated by both spouses ceases to be a matrimonial home.

Effect of designation by one spouse

(5) On the registration of a designation made by one spouse only, any other property that is a matrimonial home under section 18 remains a matrimonial home.

Cancellation of designation

(6) The designation of a matrimonial home is cancelled, and the property ceases to be a matrimonial home, on the registration or deposit of,

(a) a cancellation, executed by the person or persons who made the original designation, in the form prescribed by the regulations made under this Act;

(b) a decree absolute of divorce or judgment of nullity;

(c) an order under clause 23(e) cancelling the designation; or

(d) proof of death of one of the spouses.

Revival of other matrimonial homes

(7) When a designation of a matrimonial home made by both spouses is cancelled, section 18 applies again in respect of other property that is a matrimonial home.

Alienation of matrimonial home

21. (1) No spouse shall dispose of or encumber an interest in a matrimonial home unless,

(a) the other spouse joins in the instrument or consents to the transaction;

(b) the other spouse has released all rights under this Part by a separation agreement;

(c) a court order has authorized the transaction or has released the property from the application of this Part; or

(d) the property is not designated by both spouses as a matrimonial home and a designation of another property as a matrimonial home, made by both spouses, is registered and not cancelled.

Setting aside transaction

(2) If a spouse disposes of or encumbers an interest in a matrimonial home in contravention of subsection (1), the transaction may be set aside on an application under section 23, unless the person holding the interest or encumbrance at the time of the application acquired it for value, in good faith and without notice, at the time of acquiring it or making an agreement to acquire it, that the property was a matrimonial home.

Proof that property not a matrimonial home

(3) For the purpose of subsection (2), a statement by the person making the disposition or encumbrance,

(a) verifying that he or she is not, or was not, a spouse at the time of the disposition or encumbrance;

(b) verifying that the person is a spouse who is not separated from his or her spouse and that the property is not ordinarily occupied by the spouses as their family residence;

(c) verifying that the person is a spouse who is separated from his or her spouse and that the property was not ordinarily occupied by the spouses, at the time of their separation, as their family residence;

(d) where the property is not designated by both spouses as a matrimonial home, verifying that a designation of another property as a matrimonial home, made by both spouses, is registered and not cancelled; or

(e) verifying that the other spouse has released all rights under this Part by a separation agreement,

shall, unless the person to whom the disposition or encumbrance is made had notice to the contrary, be deemed to be sufficient proof that the property is not a matrimonial home.

Idem, attorney's personal knowledge

(4) The statement shall be deemed to be sufficient proof that the property is not a matrimonial home if it is made by the attorney of the person making the disposition or encumbrance, on the basis of the attorney's personal knowledge.

Liens arising by operation of law

(5) This section does not apply to the acquisition of an interest in property by operation of law or to the acquisition of a lien under section 48 of the *Legal Aid Services Act, 1998.*

Right of redemption and to notice

22. (1) When a person proceeds to realize upon a lien, encumbrance or execution or exercises a forfeiture against property that is a matrimonial home, the spouse who has a right of possession under section 19 has the same right of redemption or relief against forfeiture as the other spouse and is entitled to the same notice respecting the claim and its enforcement or realization.

Service of notice

(2) A notice to which a spouse is entitled under subsection (1) shall be deemed to be sufficiently given if served or given personally or by registered mail addressed to the spouse at his or her usual or last known address or, if none, the address of the matrimonial home, and, if notice is served or given by mail, the service shall be deemed to have been made on the fifth day after the day of mailing.

Idem: power of sale

(3) When a person exercises a power of sale against property that is a matrimonial home, sections 33 and 34 of the *Mortgages Act* apply and subsection (2) does not apply.

Payments by spouse

(4) If a spouse makes a payment in exercise of the right conferred by subsection (1), the payment shall be applied in satisfaction of the claim giving rise to the lien, encumbrance, execution or forfeiture.

Realization may continue in spouse's absence

(5) Despite any other Act, when a person who proceeds to realize upon a lien, encumbrance or execution or exercises a forfeiture does not have sufficient particulars of a spouse for the purpose and there is no response to a notice given under subsection (2) or under section 33 of the *Mortgages Act*, the realization or exercise of forfeiture may continue in the absence and without regard to the interest of the spouse and the spouse's rights under this section end on the completion of the realization or forfeiture.

Powers of court respecting alienation

23. The court may, on the application of a spouse or person having an interest in property, by order,

(a) determine whether or not the property is a matrimonial home and, if so, its extent;

(b) authorize the disposition or encumbrance of the matrimonial home if the court finds that the spouse whose consent is required,

(i) cannot be found or is not available,

(ii) is not capable of giving or withholding consent, or

(iii) is unreasonably withholding consent,

subject to any conditions, including provision of other comparable accommodation or payment in place of it, that the court considers appropriate;

(c) dispense with a notice required to be given under section 22;

(d) direct the setting aside of a transaction disposing of or encumbering an interest in the matrimonial home contrary to subsection 21(1) and the revesting of the interest or any part of it on the conditions that the court considers appropriate; and

(e) cancel a designation made under section 20 if the property is not a matrimonial home.

Order for possession of matrimonial home

24. (1) Regardless of the ownership of a matrimonial home and its contents, and despite section 19 (spouse's right of possession), the court may on application, by order,

(a) provide for the delivering up, safekeeping and preservation of the matrimonial home and its contents;

(b) direct that one spouse be given exclusive possession of the matrimonial home or part of it for the period that the court directs and release other property that is a matrimonial home from the application of this Part;

(c) direct a spouse to whom exclusive possession of the matrimonial home is given to make periodic payments to the other spouse;

(d) direct that the contents of the matrimonial home, or any part of them,

(i) remain in the home for the use of the spouse given possession, or

(ii) be removed from the home for the use of a spouse or child;

(e) order a spouse to pay for all or part of the repair and maintenance of the matrimonial home and of other liabilities arising in respect of it, or to make periodic payments to the other spouse for those purposes;

(f) authorize the disposition or encumbrance of a spouse's interest in the matrimonial home, subject to the other spouse's right of exclusive possession as ordered; and

(g) where a false statement is made under subsection 21(3), direct,

(i) the person who made the false statement, or

(ii) a person who knew at the time he or she acquired an interest in the property that the statement was false and afterwards conveyed the interest,

to substitute other real property for the matrimonial home, or direct the person to set aside money or security to stand in place of it, subject to any conditions that the court considers appropriate.

Temporary or interim order

(2) The court may, on motion, make a temporary or interim order under clause (1)(a), (b), (c), (d) or (e).

Order for exclusive possession: criteria

(3) In determining whether to make an order for exclusive possession, the court shall consider,

(a) the best interests of the children affected;

(b) any existing orders under Part I (Family Property) and any existing support orders;

(c) the financial position of both spouses;

(d) any written agreement between the parties;

(e) the availability of other suitable and affordable accommodation; and

(f) any violence committed by a spouse against the other spouse or the children.

Best interests of child

(4) In determining the best interests of a child, the court shall consider,

(a) the possible disruptive effects on the child of a move to other accommodation; and

(b) the child's views and preferences, if they can reasonably be ascertained.

Offence

(5) A person who contravenes an order for exclusive possession is guilty of an offence and upon conviction is liable,

(a) in the case of a first offence, to a fine of not more than $5,000 or to imprisonment for a term of not more than three months, or to both; and

(b) in the case of a second or subsequent offence, to a fine of not more than $10,000 or to imprisonment for a term of not more than two years, or to both.

Arrest without warrant

(6) A police officer may arrest without warrant a person the police officer believes on reasonable and probable grounds to have contravened an order for exclusive possession.

Existing orders

(7) Subsections (5) and (6) also apply in respect of contraventions, committed on or after the 1st day of March, 1986, of orders for exclusive possession made under Part III of the *Family Law Reform Act*, being chapter 152 of the Revised Statutes of Ontario, 1980.

Variation

Possessory order

25. (1) On the application of a person named in an order made under clause 24(1)(a), (b), (c), (d) or (e) or his or her personal representative, if the court is satisfied that there has been a material change in circumstances, the court may discharge, vary or suspend the order.

Conditions

(2) On the motion of a person who is subject to conditions imposed in an order made under clause 23(b) or (d) or 24(1)(g), or his or her personal representative, if the court is satisfied that the conditions are no longer appropriate, the court may discharge, vary or suspend them.

Existing orders

(3) Subsections (1) and (2) also apply to orders made under the corresponding provisions of Part III of the *Family Law Reform Act*, being chapter 152 of the Revised Statutes of Ontario, 1980.

Order regarding conduct

25.1 In making any order under this Part, the court may also make an interim order prohibiting, in whole or in part, a party from directly or indirectly contacting or communicating with another party, if the court determines that the order is necessary to ensure that an application under this Part is dealt with justly.

Spouse without interest in matrimonial home

Joint tenancy with third person

26. (1) If a spouse dies owning an interest in a matrimonial home as a joint tenant with a third person and not with the other spouse, the joint tenancy shall be deemed to have been severed immediately before the time of death.

Sixty-day period after spouse's death

(2) Despite clauses 19(2)(a) and (b) (termination of spouse's right of possession), a spouse who has no interest in a matrimonial home but is occupying it at the time of the other spouse's death, whether under an order for exclusive possession or otherwise, is entitled to retain possession against the spouse's estate, rent free, for sixty days after the spouse's death.

Registration of order

27. Orders made under this Part or under Part III of the *Family Law Reform Act*, being chapter 152 of the Revised Statutes of Ontario, 1980 are registrable against land under the *Registry Act* and the *Land Titles Act*.

Application of Part

28. (1) This Part applies to matrimonial homes that are situated in Ontario.

Idem

(2) This Part applies,

(a) whether the spouses were married before or after the 1st day of March, 1986; and

(b) whether the matrimonial home was acquired before or after that day.

PART III SUPPORT OBLIGATIONS

Definitions

29. In this Part,

"dependant" means a person to whom another has an obligation to provide support under this Part;

"spouse" means a spouse as defined in subsection 1(1), and in addition includes either of two persons who are not married to each other and have cohabited,

(a) continuously for a period of not less than three years, or

(b) in a relationship of some permanence, if they are the natural or adoptive parents of a child.

Obligation of spouses for support

30. Every spouse has an obligation to provide support for himself or herself and for the other spouse, in accordance with need, to the extent that he or she is capable of doing so.

Obligation of parent to support child

31. (1) Every parent has an obligation to provide support for his or her unmarried child who is a minor or is enrolled in a full time program of education, to the extent that the parent is capable of doing so.

Idem

(2) The obligation under subsection (1) does not extend to a child who is sixteen years of age or older and has withdrawn from parental control.

Obligation of child to support parent

32. Every child who is not a minor has an obligation to provide support, in accordance with need, for his or her parent who has cared for or provided support for the child, to the extent that the child is capable of doing so.

Order for support

33. (1) A court may, on application, order a person to provide support for his or her dependants and determine the amount of support.

Applicants

(2) An application for an order for the support of a dependant may be made by the dependant or the dependant's parent.

Same

(2.1) The *Limitations Act, 2002* applies to an application made by the dependant's parent or by an agency referred to in subsection (3) as if it were made by the dependant himself or herself.

Same

(3) An application for an order for the support of a dependant who is the respondent's spouse or child may also be made by one of the following agencies,

(a) the Ministry of Community and Social Services in the name of the Minister;

(b) a municipality, excluding a lower-tier municipality in a regional municipality;

(c) a district social services administration board under the *District Social Services Administration Boards Act*;

(d) Repealed.

(e) a delivery agent under the *Ontario Works Act, 1997*,

if the agency is providing or has provided a benefit under the *Family Benefits Act*, assistance under the *General Welfare Assistance Act* or the *Ontario Works Act, 1997* or income support under the *Ontario Disability Support Program Act, 1997* in respect of the dependant's support, or if an application for such a benefit or assistance has been made to the agency by or on behalf of the dependant.

Setting aside domestic contract

(4) The court may set aside a provision for support or a waiver of the right to support in a domestic contract and may determine and order support in an application under subsection (1) although the contract contains an express provision excluding the application of this section,

(a) if the provision for support or the waiver of the right to support results in unconscionable circumstances;

(b) if the provision for support is in favour of or the waiver is by or on behalf of a dependant who qualifies for an allowance for support out of public money; or

(c) if there is default in the payment of support under the contract at the time the application is made.

Adding party

(5) In an application the court may, on a respondent's motion, add as a party another person who may have an obligation to provide support to the same dependant.

Idem

(6) In an action in the Superior Court of Justice, the defendant may add as a third party another person who may have an obligation to provide support to the same dependant.

Purposes of order for support of child

(7) An order for the support of a child should,

(a) recognize that each parent has an obligation to provide support for the child;

(b) apportion the obligation according to the child support guidelines.

Purposes of order for support of spouse

(8) An order for the support of a spouse should,

(a) recognize the spouse's contribution to the relationship and the economic consequences of the relationship for the spouse;

(b) share the economic burden of child support equitably;

(c) make fair provision to assist the spouse to become able to contribute to his or her own support; and

(d) relieve financial hardship, if this has not been done by orders under Parts I (Family Property) and II (Matrimonial Home).

Determination of amount for support of spouses, parents

(9) In determining the amount and duration, if any, of support for a spouse or parent in relation to need, the court shall consider all the circumstances of the parties, including,

(a) the dependant's and respondent's current assets and means;

(b) the assets and means that the dependant and respondent are likely to have in the future;

(c) the dependant's capacity to contribute to his or her own support;

(d) the respondent's capacity to provide support;

(e) the dependant's and respondent's age and physical and mental health;

(f) the dependant's needs, in determining which the court shall have regard to the accustomed standard of living while the parties resided together;

(g) the measures available for the dependant to become able to provide for his or her own support and the length of time and cost involved to enable the dependant to take those measures;

(h) any legal obligation of the respondent or dependant to provide support for another person;

(i) the desirability of the dependant or respondent remaining at home to care for a child;

(j) a contribution by the dependant to the realization of the respondent's career potential;

(k) Repealed.

(l) if the dependant is a spouse,

(i) the length of time the dependant and respondent cohabited,

(ii) the effect on the spouse's earning capacity of the responsibilities assumed during cohabitation,

(iii) whether the spouse has undertaken the care of a child who is of the age of eighteen years or over and unable by reason of illness, disability or other cause to withdraw from the charge of his or her parents,

(iv) whether the spouse has undertaken to assist in the continuation of a program of education for a child eighteen years of age or over who is unable for that reason to withdraw from the charge of his or her parents,

(v) any housekeeping, child care or other domestic service performed by the spouse for the family, as if the spouse were devoting the time spent in performing that service in remunerative employment and were contributing the earnings to the family's support,

(v.1) Repealed.

(vi) the effect on the spouse's earnings and career development of the responsibility of caring for a child; and

(m) any other legal right of the dependant to support, other than out of public money.

Conduct

(10) The obligation to provide support for a spouse exists without regard to the conduct of either spouse, but the court may in determining the amount of support have regard to a course of conduct that is so unconscionable as to constitute an obvious and gross repudiation of the relationship.

Application of child support guidelines

(11) A court making an order for the support of a child shall do so in accordance with the child support guidelines.

Exception: special provisions

(12) Despite subsection (11), a court may award an amount that is different from the amount that would be determined in accordance with the child support guidelines if the court is satisfied,

(a) that special provisions in an order or a written agreement respecting the financial obligations of the parents, or the division or transfer of their property, directly or indirectly benefit a child, or that special provisions have otherwise been made for the benefit of a child; and

(b) that the application of the child support guidelines would result in an amount of child support that is inequitable given those special provisions.

Reasons

(13) Where the court awards, under subsection (12), an amount that is different from the amount that would be determined in accordance with the child support guidelines, the court shall record its reasons for doing so.

Exception: consent orders

(14) Despite subsection (11), a court may award an amount that is different from the amount that would be determined in accordance with the child support guidelines on the consent of both parents if the court is satisfied that,

(a) reasonable arrangements have been made for the support of the child to whom the order relates; and

(b) where support for the child is payable out of public money, the arrangements do not provide for an amount less than the amount that would be determined in accordance with the child support guidelines.

Reasonable arrangements

(15) For the purposes of clause (14)(a), in determining whether reasonable arrangements have been made for the support of a child,

(a) the court shall have regard to the child support guidelines; and

(b) the court shall not consider the arrangements to be unreasonable solely because the amount of support agreed to is not the same as the amount that would otherwise have been determined in accordance with the child support guidelines.

Powers of court

34. (1) In an application under section 33, the court may make an interim or final order,

(a) requiring that an amount be paid periodically, whether annually or otherwise and whether for an indefinite or limited period, or until the happening of a specified event;

(b) requiring that a lump sum be paid or held in trust;

(c) requiring that property be transferred to or in trust for or vested in the dependant, whether absolutely, for life or for a term of years;

(d) respecting any matter authorized to be ordered under clause 24(1)(a), (b), (c), (d) or (e) (matrimonial home);

(e) requiring that some or all of the money payable under the order be paid into court or to another appropriate person or agency for the dependant's benefit;

(f) requiring that support be paid in respect of any period before the date of the order;

(g) requiring payment to an agency referred to in subsection 33(3) of an amount in reimbursement for a benefit or assistance referred to in that subsection, including a benefit or assistance provided before the date of the order;

(h) requiring payment of expenses in respect of a child's prenatal care and birth;

(i) requiring that a spouse who has a policy of life insurance as defined under the *Insurance Act* designate the other spouse or a child as the beneficiary irrevocably;

(j) requiring that a spouse who has an interest in a pension plan or other benefit plan designate the other spouse or a child as beneficiary under the plan and not change that designation; and

(k) requiring the securing of payment under the order, by a charge on property or otherwise.

Limitation on jurisdiction of Ontario Court of Justice

(2) The Ontario Court of Justice shall not make an order under clause (1)(b), (c), (i), (j) or (k) except for the provision of necessities or to prevent the dependant from becoming or continuing to be a public charge, and shall not make an order under clause (d).

Assignment of support

(3) An order for support may be assigned to an agency referred to in subsection 33(3).

Same

(3.1) An agency referred to in subsection 33(3) to whom an order for support is assigned is entitled to the payments due under the order and has the same right to be notified of and to participate in proceedings under this Act to vary, rescind, suspend or enforce the order as the person who would otherwise be entitled to the payments.

Support order binds estate

(4) An order for support binds the estate of the person having the support obligation unless the order provides otherwise.

Indexing of support payments

(5) In an order made under clause (1)(a), other than an order for the support of a child, the court may provide that the amount payable shall be increased annually on the order's anniversary date by the indexing factor, as defined in subsection (6), for November of the previous year.

Definition

(6) The indexing factor for a given month is the percentage change in the Consumer Price Index for Canada for prices of all items since the same month of the previous year, as published by Statistics Canada.

Domestic contract, etc., may be filed with court

35. (1) A person who is a party to a domestic contract may file the contract with the clerk of the Ontario Court of Justice or of the Family Court of the Superior Court of Justice together with the person's affidavit stating that the contract is in effect and has not been set aside or varied by a court or agreement.

Interpretation

(1.1) For the purposes of subsection (1), a party to a domestic contract includes a party's guardian of property or attorney for property, if the guardian or attorney entered into the domestic contract on behalf of the party under the authority of subsection 55(3).

Effect of filing

(2) A provision for support or maintenance contained in a contract that is filed in this manner,

(a) may be enforced;

(b) may be varied under section 37; and

Note: On a day to be named by proclamation of the Lieutenant Governor, clause (b) is amended by striking out "and" at the end.

(c) except in the case of a provision for the support of a child, may be increased under section 38,

Note: On a day to be named by proclamation of the Lieutenant Governor, subsection (2) is amended by adding "and" at the end of clause (c), and by adding the following clause:

(d) in the case of a provision for the support of a child, may be recalculated under section 39.1,

See: 2009, c. 11, ss. 32(2), 53(2).

as if it were an order of the court where it is filed.

Setting aside available

(3) Subsection 33(4) (setting aside in unconscionable circumstances, etc.) applies to a contract that is filed in this manner.

Enforcement available despite waiver

(4) Subsection (1) and clause (2)(a) apply despite an agreement to the contrary.

Existing contracts, etc.

(5) Subsections (1) and (2) also apply to contracts made before the 1st day of March, 1986.

Existing arrears

(6) Clause (2)(a) also applies to arrears accrued before the 1st day of March, 1986.

Effect of divorce proceeding

36. (1) When a divorce proceeding is commenced under the *Divorce Act* (Canada), an application for support under this Part that has not been adjudicated is stayed, unless the court orders otherwise.

Arrears may be included in order

(2) The court that deals with a divorce proceeding under the *Divorce Act* (Canada) may determine the amount of arrears owing under an order for support made under this Part and make an order respecting that amount at the same time as it makes an order under the *Divorce Act* (Canada).

Idem

(3) If a marriage is terminated by divorce or judgment of nullity and the question of support is not adjudicated in the divorce or nullity proceedings, an order for support made under this Part continues in force according to its terms.

Application for variation

37. (1) An application to the court for variation of an order made or confirmed under this Part may be made by,

(a) a dependant or respondent named in the order;

(b) a parent of a dependant referred to in clause (a);

(c) the personal representative of a respondent referred to in clause (a); or

(d) an agency referred to in subsection 33(3).

Powers of court: spouse and parent support

(2) In the case of an order for support of a spouse or parent, if the court is satisfied that there has been a material change in the dependant's or respondent's circumstances or that evidence not available on the previous hearing has become available, the court may,

(a) discharge, vary or suspend a term of the order, prospectively or retroactively;

(b) relieve the respondent from the payment of part or all of the arrears or any interest due on them; and

(c) make any other order under section 34 that the court considers appropriate in the circumstances referred to in section 33.

Powers of court: child support

(2.1) In the case of an order for support of a child, if the court is satisfied that there has been a change in circumstances within the meaning of the child support guidelines or that evidence not available on the previous hearing has become available, the court may,

(a) discharge, vary or suspend a term of the order, prospectively or retroactively;

(b) relieve the respondent from the payment of part or all of the arrears or any interest due on them; and

(c) make any other order for the support of a child that the court could make on an application under section 33.

Application of child support guidelines

(2.2) A court making an order under subsection (2.1) shall do so in accordance with the child support guidelines.

Exception: special provisions

(2.3) Despite subsection (2.2), a court may award an amount that is different from the amount that would be determined in accordance with the child support guidelines if the court is satisfied,

(a) that special provisions in an order or a written agreement respecting the financial obligations of the parents, or the division or transfer of their property, directly or indirectly benefit a child, or that special provisions have otherwise been made for the benefit of a child; and

(b) that the application of the child support guidelines would result in an amount of child support that is inequitable given those special provisions.

Reasons

(2.4) Where the court awards, under subsection (2.3), an amount that is different from the amount that would be determined in accordance with the child support guidelines, the court shall record its reasons for doing so.

Exception: consent orders

(2.5) Despite subsection (2.2), a court may award an amount that is different from the amount that would be determined in accordance with the child support guidelines on the consent of both parents if the court is satisfied that,

(a) reasonable arrangements have been made for the support of the child to whom the order relates; and

(b) where support for the child is payable out of public money, the arrangements do not provide for an amount less than the amount that would be determined in accordance with the child support guidelines.

Reasonable arrangements

(2.6) For the purposes of clause (2.5)(a), in determining whether reasonable arrangements have been made for the support of a child,

(a) the court shall have regard to the child support guidelines; and

(b) the court shall not consider the arrangements to be unreasonable solely because the amount of support agreed to is not the same as the amount that would otherwise have been determined in accordance with the child support guidelines.

Limitation on applications for variation

(3) No application for variation shall be made within six months after the making of the order for support or the disposition of another application for variation in respect of the same order, except by leave of the court.

Indexing existing orders

Non-application to orders for child support

38. (1) This section does not apply to an order for the support of a child.

Application to have existing order indexed

(2) If an order made or confirmed under this Part is not indexed under subsection 34(5), the dependant, or an agency referred to in subsection 33(3), may apply to the court to have the order indexed in accordance with subsection 34(5).

Power of court

(3) The court shall, unless the respondent shows that his or her income, assets and means have not increased sufficiently to permit the increase, order that the amount payable be increased by the indexing factor, as defined in subsection 34(6), for November of the year before the year in which the application is made and be increased in the same way annually thereafter on the anniversary date of the order under this section.

Priority to child support

38.1 (1) Where a court is considering an application for the support of a child and an application for the support of a spouse, the court shall give priority to the support of the child in determining the applications.

Reasons

(2) Where as a result of giving priority to the support of a child, the court is unable to make an order for the support of a spouse or the court makes an order for the support of a spouse in an amount less than it otherwise would have, the court shall record its reasons for doing so.

Consequences of reduction or termination of child support

(3) Where as a result of giving priority to the support of a child, an order for the support of a spouse is not made or the amount of the order for the support of a spouse is less than it otherwise would have been, any material reduction or termination of the support for the child constitutes a material change of circumstances for the purposes of an application for the support of the spouse or for variation of an order for the support of the spouse.

(4) Repealed.

Existing orders

39. (1) Sections 36 to 38 also apply to orders for maintenance or alimony made before the 31st day of March, 1978 or in proceedings commenced before the 31st day of March, 1978 and to orders for support made under Part II of the *Family Law Reform Act*, being chapter 152 of the Revised Statutes of Ontario, 1980.

Combined support orders

(2) Where an application is made under section 37 to vary an order that provides a single amount of money for the combined support of one or more children and a spouse, the court shall rescind the order and treat the application as an application for an order for the support of a child and an application for an order for the support of a spouse.

Existing proceedings

(3) Where an application for the support of a child, including an application under section 37 to vary an order for the support of a child, is made before the day the *Uniform Federal and Provincial Child Support Guidelines Act, 1997* comes into force and the court has not considered any evidence in the application, other than in respect of an interim order, before that day, the proceeding shall be deemed to be an application under the *Family Law Act* as amended by the *Uniform Federal and Provincial Child Support Guidelines Act, 1997*, subject to such directions as the court considers appropriate.

Note: On a day to be named by proclamation of the Lieutenant Governor, the Act is amended by adding the following section:

Recalculation of child support

39.1 (1) The amount payable for the support of a child under an order may be recalculated in accordance with this Act and the regulations made under this Act, by the child support service established by the regulations, in order to reflect updated income information.

Effect of recalculation

(2) Subject to any review or appeal process established by the regulations made under this Act, if the child support service recalculates an amount payable for the support of a child under an order, the recalculated amount is, 31 days after the date on which the parties to the order are notified of the recalculation in accordance with the regulations, deemed to be the amount payable under the order.

See: 2009, c. 11, ss. 33, 53(2).

Restraining orders

40. The court may, on application, make an interim or final order restraining the depletion of a spouse's property that would impair or defeat a claim under this Part.

Financial statement

41. In an application under section 33 or 37, each party shall serve on the other and file with the court a financial statement verified by oath or statutory declaration in the manner and form prescribed by the rules of the court.

Obtaining information

Order for return by employer

42. (1) In an application under section 33 or 37, the court may order the employer of a party to the application to make a written return to the court showing the party's wages or other remuneration during the preceding twelve months.

Return as evidence

(2) A return purporting to be signed by the employer may be received in evidence as proof, in the absence of evidence to the contrary, of its contents.

Order for access to information

(3) The court may, on motion, make an order under subsection (4) if it appears to the court that, in order to make an application under section 33 or 37, the moving party needs to learn or confirm the proposed respondent's whereabouts.

Idem

(4) The order shall require the person or public body to whom it is directed to provide the court or the moving party with any information that is shown on a record in the person's or public body's possession or control and that indicates the proposed respondent's place of employment, address or location.

Crown bound

(5) This section binds the Crown in right of Ontario.

Arrest of absconding debtor

43. (1) If an application is made under section 33 or 37 and the court is satisfied that the respondent is about to leave Ontario and that there are reasonable grounds for believing that the respondent intends to evade his or her responsibilities under this Act, the court may issue a warrant for the respondent's arrest for the purpose of bringing him or her before the court.

Bail

(2) Section 150 (interim release by justice of the peace) of the *Provincial Offences Act* applies with necessary modifications to an arrest under the warrant.

Provisional orders

44. (1) In an application under section 33 or 37 in the Ontario Court (Provincial Division) or the Unified Family Court, the court shall proceed under this section, whether or not the respondent in the application files a financial statement, if,

(a) the respondent fails to appear;

(b) it appears to the court that the respondent resides in a locality in Ontario that is more than 150 kilometres away from the place where the court sits; and

(c) the court is of the opinion, in the circumstances of the case, that the issues can be adequately determined by proceeding under this section.

Idem

(2) If the court determines that it would be proper to make a final order, were it not for the respondent's failure to appear, the court shall make an order for support that is provisional only and has no effect until it is confirmed by the Ontario Court (Provincial Division) or the Unified Family Court sitting nearest the place where the respondent resides.

Transmission for hearing

(3) The court that makes a provisional order shall send to the court in the locality in which the respondent resides copies of such documents and records, certified in such manner, as are prescribed by the rules of the court.

Show cause

(4) The court to which the documents and records are sent shall cause them to be served upon the respondent, together with a notice to file with the court the financial statement required by section 41, and to appear and show cause why the provisional order should not be confirmed.

Confirmation of order

(5) At the hearing, the respondent may raise any defence that might have been raised in the original proceeding, but if the respondent fails to satisfy the court that the order ought not to be confirmed, the court may confirm the order without variation or with the variation that the court considers proper having regard to all the evidence.

Adjournment for further evidence

(6) If the respondent appears before the court and satisfies the court that for the purpose of a defence or for the taking of further evidence or otherwise it is necessary to remit the case to the court where the applicant resides, the court may remit the case and adjourn the proceeding for that purpose.

Where order not confirmed

(7) If the respondent appears before the court and the court, having regard to all the evidence, is of the opinion that the order ought not to be confirmed, the court shall remit the case to the court sitting where the order was made with a statement of the reasons for doing so, and the court sitting where the order was made shall dispose of the application in accordance with the statement.

Certificates as evidence

(8) A certificate certifying copies of documents or records for the purpose of this section and purporting to be signed by the clerk of the court is, without proof of the clerk's office or signature, admissible in evidence in a court to which it is transmitted under this section as proof, in the absence of evidence to the contrary, of the copy's authenticity.

Right of appeal

(9) No appeal lies from a provisional order made under this section, but a person bound by an order confirmed under this section has the same right of appeal as he or she would have had if the order had been made under section 34.

Necessities of life

Pledging credit of spouse

45. (1) During cohabitation, a spouse has authority to render himself or herself and his or her spouse jointly and severally liable to a third party for necessities of life, unless the spouse has notified the third party that he or she has withdrawn the authority.

Liability for necessities of minor

(2) If a person is entitled to recover against a minor in respect of the provision of necessities for the minor, every parent who has an obligation to support the minor is liable for them jointly and severally with the minor.

Recovery between persons jointly liable

(3) If persons are jointly and severally liable under this section, their liability to each other shall be determined in accordance with their obligation to provide support.

Common law supplanted

(4) This section applies in place of the rules of common law by which a wife may pledge her husband's credit.

Restraining order

46. (1) On application, the court may make an interim or final restraining order against a person described in subsection (2) if the applicant has reasonable grounds to fear for his or her own safety or for the safety of any child in his or her lawful custody.

Same

(2) A restraining order under subsection (1) may be made against,

(a) a spouse or former spouse of the applicant; or

(b) a person other than a spouse or former spouse of the applicant, if the person is cohabiting with the applicant or has cohabited with the applicant for any period of time.

Provisions of order

(3) A restraining order made under subsection (1) shall be in the form prescribed by the rules of court and may contain one or more of the following provisions, as the court considers appropriate:

1. Restraining the respondent, in whole or in part, from directly or indirectly contacting or communicating with the applicant or any child in the applicant's lawful custody.
2. Restraining the respondent from coming within a specified distance of one or more locations.
3. Specifying one or more exceptions to the provisions described in paragraphs 1 and 2.
4. Any other provision that the court considers appropriate.

Transition

(4) This section, as it read immediately before the day section 35 of the *Family Statute Law Amendment Act, 2009* came into force, continues to apply to,

(a) any prosecution or other proceeding begun under this section before that day; and

(b) any order made under this section that was in force immediately before that day.

Application for custody

47. The court may direct that an application for support stand over until an application for custody under the *Children's Law Reform Act* has been determined.

Order regarding conduct

47.1 In making any order under this Part, other than an order under section 46, the court may also make an interim order prohibiting, in whole or in part, a party from directly or indirectly contacting or communicating with another party, if the court determines that the order is necessary to ensure that an application under this Part is dealt with justly.

Appeal from Ontario Court of Justice

48. An appeal lies from an order of the Ontario Court of Justice under this Part to the Superior Court of Justice.

Contempt of orders of Ontario Court of Justice

49. (1) In addition to its powers in respect of contempt, the Ontario Court of Justice may punish by fine or imprisonment, or by both, any wilful contempt of or resistance to its process, rules or orders under this Act, but the fine shall not exceed $5,000 nor shall the imprisonment exceed ninety days.

Conditions of imprisonment

(2) An order for imprisonment under subsection (1) may be conditional upon default in the performance of a condition set out in the order and may provide for the imprisonment to be served intermittently.

50. Repealed.

PART IV DOMESTIC CONTRACTS

Definitions

51. In this Part,

"cohabitation agreement" means an agreement entered into under section 53;

"domestic contract" means a marriage contract, separation agreement, cohabitation agreement, paternity agreement or family arbitration agreement;

"family arbitration" means an arbitration that,

(a) deals with matters that could be dealt with in a marriage contract, separation agreement, cohabitation agreement or paternity agreement under this Part, and

(b) is conducted exclusively in accordance with the law of Ontario or of another Canadian jurisdiction;

"family arbitration agreement" and "family arbitration award" have meanings that correspond to the meaning of "family arbitration";

"marriage contract" means an agreement entered into under section 52;

"paternity agreement" means an agreement entered into under section 59;

"separation agreement" means an agreement entered into under section 54.

Marriage contracts

52. (1) Two persons who are married to each other or intend to marry may enter into an agreement in which they agree on their respective rights and obligations under the marriage or on separation, on the annulment or dissolution of the marriage or on death, including,

(a) ownership in or division of property;

(b) support obligations;

(c) the right to direct the education and moral training of their children, but not the right to custody of or access to their children; and

(d) any other matter in the settlement of their affairs.

Rights re matrimonial home excepted

(2) A provision in a marriage contract purporting to limit a spouse's rights under Part II (Matrimonial Home) is unenforceable.

Cohabitation agreements

53. (1) Two persons who are cohabiting or intend to cohabit and who are not married to each other may enter into an agreement in which they agree on their respective rights and obligations during cohabitation, or on ceasing to cohabit or on death, including,

(a) ownership in or division of property;

(b) support obligations;

(c) the right to direct the education and moral training of their children, but not the right to custody of or access to their children; and

(d) any other matter in the settlement of their affairs.

Effect of marriage on agreement

(2) If the parties to a cohabitation agreement marry each other, the agreement shall be deemed to be a marriage contract.

Separation agreements

54. Two persons who cohabited and are living separate and apart may enter into an agreement in which they agree on their respective rights and obligations, including,

(a) ownership in or division of property;

(b) support obligations;

(c) the right to direct the education and moral training of their children;

(d) the right to custody of and access to their children; and

(e) any other matter in the settlement of their affairs.

Form and capacity

Form of contract

55. (1) A domestic contract and an agreement to amend or rescind a domestic contract are unenforceable unless made in writing, signed by the parties and witnessed.

Capacity of minor

(2) A minor has capacity to enter into a domestic contract, subject to the approval of the court, which may be given before or after the minor enters into the contract.

Guardian, attorney

(3) If a mentally incapable person has a guardian of property or an attorney under a continuing power of attorney for property, and the guardian or attorney is not his or her spouse, the guardian or attorney may enter into a domestic contract or give any waiver or consent under this Act on the person's behalf, subject to the court's prior approval.

P.G.T.

(4) In all other cases of mental incapacity, the Public Guardian and Trustee has power to act on the person's behalf in accordance with subsection (3).

Provisions that may be set aside or disregarded

Contracts subject to best interests of child

56. (1) In the determination of a matter respecting the education, moral training or custody of or access to a child, the court may disregard any provision of a domestic contract pertaining to the matter where, in the opinion of the court, to do so is in the best interests of the child.

Contracts subject to child support guidelines

(1.1) In the determination of a matter respecting the support of a child, the court may disregard any provision of a domestic contract pertaining to the matter where the provision is unreasonable having regard to the child support guidelines, as well as to any other provision relating to support of the child in the contract.

Clauses requiring chastity

(2) A provision in a domestic contract to take effect on separation whereby any right of a party is dependent upon remaining chaste is unenforceable, but this subsection shall not be construed to affect a contingency upon marriage or cohabitation with another.

Idem

(3) A provision in a domestic contract made before the 1st day of March, 1986 whereby any right of a party is dependent upon remaining chaste shall be given effect as a contingency upon marriage or cohabitation with another.

Setting aside domestic contract

(4) A court may, on application, set aside a domestic contract or a provision in it,

(a) if a party failed to disclose to the other significant assets, or significant debts or other liabilities, existing when the domestic contract was made;

(b) if a party did not understand the nature or consequences of the domestic contract; or

(c) otherwise in accordance with the law of contract.

Barriers to remarriage

(5) The court may, on application, set aside all or part of a separation agreement or settlement, if the court is satisfied that the removal by one spouse of barriers that would prevent the other spouse's remarriage within that spouse's faith was a consideration in the making of the agreement or settlement.

Idem

(6) Subsection (5) also applies to consent orders, releases, notices of discontinuance and abandonment and other written or oral arrangements.

Application of subss. (4, 5, 6)

(7) Subsections (4), (5) and (6) apply despite any agreement to the contrary.

Provisions re pension plan

Family law valuation date

56.1 (1) In this section,

"family law valuation date" means, with respect to the parties to a domestic contract,

(a) the valuation date under Part I (Family Property) that applies in respect of the parties, or

(b) for parties to whom Part I does not apply, the date on which they separate and there is no reasonable prospect that they will resume cohabitation.

Immediate transfer of lump sum

(2) A domestic contract may provide for the immediate transfer of a lump sum out of a pension plan, but, except as permitted under subsection (3), not for any other division of a party's interest in the plan.

Division of pension payments

(3) If payment of the first instalment of a party's pension under a pension plan is due on or before the family law valuation date, the domestic contract may provide for the division of pension payments, but not for any other division of the party's interest in the plan.

Restrictions re certain pension plans

(4) If the *Pension Benefits Act* applies to the pension plan, the restrictions under sections 67.3 and 67.4 of that Act apply with respect to the division of the party's interest in the plan under a domestic contract.

Valuation

(5) Subsections 10.1(1) and (2) apply, with necessary modifications, with respect to the valuation of a party's interest in a pension plan.

Transition, family law valuation date

(6) This section applies whether the family law valuation date is before, on or after the date on which this section comes into force.

Transition, previous domestic contracts

(7) This section does not apply to a domestic contract that provided, before the date on which this section comes into force, for the division of a party's interest in a pension plan.

Rights of donors of gifts

57. If a domestic contract provides that specific gifts made to one or both parties may not be disposed of or encumbered without the consent of the donor, the donor shall be deemed to be a party to the contract for the purpose of enforcement or amendment of the provision.

Contracts made outside Ontario

58. The manner and formalities of making a domestic contract and its essential validity and effect are governed by the proper law of the contract, except that,

(a) a contract of which the proper law is that of a jurisdiction other than Ontario is also valid and enforceable in Ontario if entered into in accordance with Ontario's internal law;

(b) subsection 33(4) (setting aside provision for support or waiver) and section 56 apply in Ontario to contracts for which the proper law is that of a jurisdiction other than Ontario; and

(c) a provision in a marriage contract or cohabitation agreement respecting the right to custody of or access to children is not enforceable in Ontario.

Paternity agreements

59. (1) If a man and a woman who are not spouses enter into an agreement for,

(a) the payment of the expenses of a child's prenatal care and birth;

(b) support of a child; or

(c) funeral expenses of the child or mother,

on the application of a party, or a children's aid society, to the Ontario Court of Justice or the Family Court of the Superior Court of Justice, the court may incorporate the agreement in an order, and Part III (Support Obligations) applies to the order in the same manner as if it were an order made under that Part.

Child support guidelines

(1.1) A court shall not incorporate an agreement for the support of a child in an order under subsection (1) unless the court is satisfied that the agreement is reasonable having regard to the child support guidelines, as well as to any other provision relating to support of the child in the agreement.

Absconding respondent

(2) If an application is made under subsection (1) and a judge of the court is satisfied that the respondent is about to leave Ontario and that there are reasonable grounds to believe that the respondent intends to evade his or her responsibilities under the agreement, the judge may issue a warrant in the form prescribed by the rules of the court for the respondent's arrest.

Bail

(3) Section 150 (interim release by justice of the peace) of the *Provincial Offences Act* applies with necessary modifications to an arrest under the warrant.

Capacity of minor

(4) A minor has capacity to enter into an agreement under subsection (1) that is approved by the court, whether the approval is given before or after the minor enters into the agreement.

Application to existing agreements

(5) This section applies to paternity agreements that were made before the 1st day of March, 1986.

Transitional provision

(6) A paternity agreement that is made before the day section 4 of the *Family Statute Law Amendment Act, 2006* comes into force is not invalid for the reason only that it does not comply with subsection 55(1).

Family arbitrations, agreements and awards

59.1 (1) Family arbitrations, family arbitration agreements and family arbitration awards are governed by this Act and by the *Arbitration Act, 1991*.

Conflict

(2) In the event of conflict between this Act and the *Arbitration Act, 1991*, this Act prevails.

Other third-party decision-making processes in family matters

59.2 (1) When a decision about a matter described in clause (a) of the definition of "family arbitration" in section 51 is made by a third person in a process that is not conducted exclusively in accordance with the law of Ontario or of another Canadian jurisdiction,

(a) the process is not a family arbitration; and

(b) the decision is not a family arbitration award and has no legal effect.

Advice

(2) Nothing in this section restricts a person's right to obtain advice from another person.

Contracting out

59.3 Any express or implied agreement by the parties to a family arbitration agreement to vary or exclude any of sections 59.1 to 59.7 is without effect.

No agreement in advance of dispute

59.4 A family arbitration agreement and an award made under it are unenforceable unless the family arbitration agreement is entered into after the dispute to be arbitrated has arisen.

Award re pension plan

Family law valuation date

59.4.1 (1) In this section,

"family law valuation date" means, with respect to the parties to an arbitration,

(a) the valuation date under Part I (Family Property) that applies in respect of the parties, or

(b) for parties to whom Part I does not apply, the date on which they separate and there is no reasonable prospect that they will resume cohabitation.

Immediate transfer of lump sum

(2) A family arbitration award may provide for the immediate transfer of a lump sum out of a pension plan, but, except as permitted under subsection (3), not for any other division of a party's interest in the plan.

Division of pension payments

(3) If payment of the first instalment of a party's pension under a pension plan is due on or before the family law valuation date, the family arbitration award may provide for the division of pension payments, but not for any other division of the party's interest in the plan.

Restrictions re certain pension plans

(4) If the *Pension Benefits Act* applies to the pension plan, the restrictions under sections 67.3 and 67.4 of that Act apply with respect to the division of the party's interest in the plan under a family arbitration award.

Valuation

(5) Subsections 10.1(1) and (2) apply, with necessary modifications, with respect to the valuation of a party's interest in a pension plan.

Transition, family law valuation date

(6) This section applies whether the family law valuation date is before, on or after the date on which this section comes into force.

Transition, previous family arbitration awards

(7) This section does not apply to a family arbitration award made before the date on which this section comes into force that requires one party to pay to the other party the amount to which that party is entitled under section 5 (equalization of net family properties).

59.5 Repealed.

Conditions for enforceability

59.6 (1) A family arbitration award is enforceable only if,

(a) the family arbitration agreement under which the award is made is made in writing and complies with any regulations made under the *Arbitration Act, 1991*;

(b) each of the parties to the agreement receives independent legal advice before making the agreement;

(c) the requirements of section 38 of the *Arbitration Act, 1991* are met (formal requirements, writing, reasons, delivery to parties); and

(d) the arbitrator complies with any regulations made under the *Arbitration Act, 1991*.

Certificate of independent legal advice

(2) When a person receives independent legal advice as described in clause (1)(b), the lawyer who provides the advice shall complete a certificate of independent legal advice, which may be in a form approved by the Attorney General.

Secondary arbitration

59.7 (1) The following special rules apply to a secondary arbitration and to an award made as the result of a secondary arbitration:

1. Despite section 59.4, the award is not unenforceable for the sole reason that the separation agreement was entered into or the court order or earlier award was made before the dispute to be arbitrated in the secondary arbitration had arisen.

2. Despite clause 59.6(1)(b), it is not necessary for the parties to receive independent legal advice before participating in the secondary arbitration.
3. Despite clause 59.6(1)(c), the requirements of section 38 of the *Arbitration Act, 1991* need not be met.

Definition

(2) In this section,

"secondary arbitration" means a family arbitration that is conducted in accordance with a separation agreement, a court order or a family arbitration award that provides for the arbitration of possible future disputes relating to the ongoing management or implementation of the agreement, order or award.

Enforcement

59.8 (1) A party who is entitled to the enforcement of a family arbitration award may make an application to the Superior Court of Justice or the Family Court to that effect.

Application or motion

(2) If there is already a proceeding between the parties to the family arbitration agreement, the party entitled to enforcement shall make a motion in that proceeding rather than an application.

Notice, supporting documents

(3) The application or motion shall be made on notice to the person against whom enforcement is sought and shall be supported by,

(a) the original award or a certified copy;
(b) a copy of the family arbitration agreement; and
(c) copies of the certificates of independent legal advice.

Order

(4) If the family arbitration award satisfies the conditions set out in subsection 59.6(1), the court shall make an order in the same terms as the award, unless,

(a) the period for commencing an appeal or an application to set the award aside has not yet elapsed;

(b) there is a pending appeal, application to set the award aside or application for a declaration of invalidity; or

(c) the award has been set aside or the arbitration is the subject of a declaration of invalidity.

Pending proceeding

(5) If clause (4)(a) or (b) applies, the court may,

(a) make an order in the same terms as the award; or

(b) order, on such conditions as are just, that enforcement of the award is stayed until the period has elapsed without an appeal or application being commenced or until the pending proceeding is finally disposed of.

Unusual remedies

(6) If the family arbitration award gives a remedy that the court does not have jurisdiction to grant or would not grant in a proceeding based on similar circumstances, the court may,

(a) make an order granting a different remedy, if the applicant requests it; or

(b) remit the award to the arbitrator with the court's opinion, in which case the arbitrator may award a different remedy.

Application of Act to existing contracts

60. (1) A domestic contract validly made before the 1st day of March, 1986 shall be deemed to be a domestic contract for the purposes of this Act.

Contracts entered into before the 1st day of March, 1986

(2) If a domestic contract was entered into before the 1st day of March, 1986 and the contract or any part would have been valid if entered into on or after that day, the contract or part is not invalid for the reason only that it was entered into before that day.

Idem

(3) If property is transferred, under an agreement or understanding reached before the 31st day of March, 1978, between spouses who are living separate and apart, the transfer is effective as if made under a domestic contract.

PART V DEPENDANTS' CLAIM FOR DAMAGES

Right of dependants to sue in tort

61. (1) If a person is injured or killed by the fault or neglect of another under circumstances where the person is entitled to recover damages, or would have been entitled if not killed, the spouse, as defined in Part III (Support Obligations), children, grandchildren, parents, grandparents, brothers and sisters of the person are entitled to recover their pecuniary loss resulting from the injury or death from the person from whom the person injured or killed is entitled to recover or would have been entitled if not killed, and to maintain an action for the purpose in a court of competent jurisdiction.

Damages in case of injury

(2) The damages recoverable in a claim under subsection (1) may include,

(a) actual expenses reasonably incurred for the benefit of the person injured or killed;

(b) actual funeral expenses reasonably incurred;

(c) a reasonable allowance for travel expenses actually incurred in visiting the person during his or her treatment or recovery;

(d) where, as a result of the injury, the claimant provides nursing, housekeeping or other services for the person, a reasonable allowance for loss of income or the value of the services; and

(e) an amount to compensate for the loss of guidance, care and companionship that the claimant might reasonably have expected to receive from the person if the injury or death had not occurred.

Contributory negligence

(3) In an action under subsection (1), the right to damages is subject to any apportionment of damages due to contributory fault or neglect of the person who was injured or killed.

(4) Repealed.

Offer to settle for global sum

62. (1) The defendant may make an offer to settle for one sum of money as compensation for his or her fault or neglect to all plaintiffs, without specifying the shares into which it is to be divided.

Apportionment

(2) If the offer is accepted and the compensation has not been otherwise apportioned, the court may, on motion, apportion it among the plaintiffs.

Payment before apportionment

(3) The court may direct payment from the fund before apportionment.

Payment may be postponed

(4) The court may postpone the distribution of money to which minors are entitled.

Assessment of damages, insurance

63. In assessing damages in an action brought under this Part, the court shall not take into account any sum paid or payable as a result of the death or injury under a contract of insurance.

PART VI AMENDMENTS TO THE COMMON LAW

Unity of legal personality abolished

64. (1) For all purposes of the law of Ontario, a married person has a legal personality that is independent, separate and distinct from that of his or her spouse.

Capacity of married person

(2) A married person has and shall be accorded legal capacity for all purposes and in all respects as if he or she were an unmarried person and, in particular, has the same right of action in tort against his or her spouse as if they were not married.

Purpose of subss. (1, 2)

(3) The purpose of subsections (1) and (2) is to make the same law apply, and apply equally, to married men and married women and to remove any difference in it resulting from any common law rule or doctrine.

Actions between parent and child

65. No person is disentitled from bringing an action or other proceeding against another for the reason only that they are parent and child.

Recovery for prenatal injuries

66. No person is disentitled from recovering damages in respect of injuries for the reason only that the injuries were incurred before his or her birth.

Domicile of minor

67. The domicile of a person who is a minor is,

(a) if the minor habitually resides with both parents and the parents have a common domicile, that domicile;

(b) if the minor habitually resides with one parent only, that parent's domicile;

(c) if the minor resides with another person who has lawful custody of him or her, that person's domicile; or

(d) if the minor's domicile cannot be determined under clause (a), (b) or (c), the jurisdiction with which the minor has the closest connection.

68. Repealed.

General

Regulations

69. (1) The Lieutenant Governor in Council may make regulations respecting any matter referred to as prescribed by the regulations.

Same

(2) The Lieutenant Governor in Council may make regulations establishing,

(a) guidelines respecting the making of orders for child support under this Act; and

(b) guidelines that may be designated under subsection 2(5) of the *Divorce Act* (Canada).

Same

(3) Without limiting the generality of subsection (2), guidelines may be established under subsection (2),

(a) respecting the way in which the amount of an order for child support is to be determined;

(b) respecting the circumstances in which discretion may be exercised in the making of an order for child support;

(c) respecting the circumstances that give rise to the making of a variation order in respect of an order for the support of a child;

(d) respecting the determination of income for the purposes of the application of the guidelines;

(e) authorizing a court to impute income for the purposes of the application of the guidelines;

(f) respecting the production of income information and providing for sanctions when that information is not provided.

Same

(4) The Lieutenant Governor in Council may make regulations respecting the production of information, including income information, relating to child support obligations created by domestic contracts or by written agreements that are not domestic contracts, and providing for enforcement procedures when that information is not provided.

Note: On a day to be named by proclamation of the Lieutenant Governor, section 69 is amended by adding the following subsection:

Same

(5) The Lieutenant Governor in Council may make regulations governing the recalculation of the amount payable for the support of a child for the purposes of section 39.1, including regulations,

(a) establishing a child support service, governing its structure and prescribing its powers, duties and functions;

(b) governing procedures respecting the recalculation of child support amounts;

(c) governing the recalculation of child support amounts by the child support service;

(d) providing for review or appeal processes respecting recalculated child support amounts;

(e) excluding specified classes of provisions for child support from recalculation.

See: 2009, c. 11, ss. 40(2), 53(2).

Transition

Application of ss. 5-8

70. (1) Sections 5 to 8 apply unless,

(a) an application under section 4 of the *Family Law Reform Act*, being chapter 152 of the Revised Statutes of Ontario, 1980 was adjudicated or settled before the 4th day of June, 1985; or

(b) the first spouse's death occurred before the 1st day of March, 1986.

Application of Part II

(2) Part II (Matrimonial Home) applies unless a proceeding under Part III of the *Family Law Reform Act*, being chapter 152 of the Revised Statutes of Ontario, 1980 to determine the rights between spouses in respect of the property concerned was adjudicated or settled before the 4th day of June, 1985.

Interpretation of existing contracts

(3) A separation agreement or marriage contract that was validly made before the 1st day of March, 1986 and that excludes a spouse's property from the application of sections 4 and 8 of the *Family Law Reform Act*, being chapter 152 of the Revised Statutes of Ontario, 1980,

(a) shall be deemed to exclude that property from the application of section 5 of this Act; and

(b) shall be read with necessary modifications.

Family Law Rules

Ontario Regulation 114/99
Current to January 1, 2014

RULE 1: GENERAL

Citation

1. (1) These rules may be cited as the *Family Law Rules*.

Cases and courts to which rules apply

(2) These rules apply to all family law cases in the Family Court of the Superior Court of Justice, in the Superior Court of Justice and in the Ontario Court of Justice,

(a) under,

(i) the *Change of Name Act*,

(ii) Parts III, VI and VII of the *Child and Family Services Act*,

(iii) the *Children's Law Reform Act*, except sections 59 and 60,

(iv) the *Divorce Act* (Canada),

(v) the *Family Law Act*, except Part V,

(vi) the *Family Responsibility and Support Arrears Enforcement Act, 1996*,

(vii) sections 6 and 9 of the *Marriage Act*, and

(viii) the *Interjurisdictional Support Orders Act, 2002*;

(b) for the interpretation, enforcement or variation of a marriage contract, cohabitation agreement, separation agreement, paternity agreement, family arbitration agreement or family arbitration award;

(c) for a constructive or resulting trust or a monetary award as compensation for unjust enrichment between persons who have cohabited; and

(d) for annulment of a marriage or a declaration of validity or invalidity of a marriage; and

(e) for appeals of family arbitration awards under the *Arbitration Act, 1991*.

(2.1) Revoked.

Case management in Family Court of Superior Court of Justice

(3) Despite subrule (2), rule 39 (case management in the Family Court of the Superior Court of Justice) applies only to cases in the Family Court of the Superior Court of Justice, which has jurisdiction in the following municipalities:

Regional Municipality of Durham
County of Frontenac
County of Haliburton
City of Hamilton
County of Lanark
United Counties of Leeds and Grenville
County of Lennox and Addington
County of Middlesex
Territorial District of Muskoka
The part of The Regional Municipality of Niagara that was the County of Lincoln as it existed on December 31, 1969
County of Northumberland
City of Ottawa
County of Peterborough
United Counties of Prescott and Russell
County of Simcoe
United Counties of Stormont, Dundas and Glengarry
City of Kawartha Lakes
Regional Municipality of York.

Case management in Ontario Court of Justice

(4) Despite subrule (2), rule 40 (case management in the Ontario Court of Justice) applies only to cases in the Ontario Court of Justice.

Case management in the Superior Court of Justice

(4.1) Despite subrule (2), rule 41 (case management in the Superior Court of Justice, other than the Family Court of the Superior Court of Justice) applies only to cases in the Superior Court of Justice that are not in the Family Court of the Superior Court of Justice.

Family law case combined with other matter

(5) If a case in the court combines a family law case to which these rules apply with another matter to which these rules would not otherwise apply, the parties may agree or the court on motion may order that these rules apply to the combined case or part of it.

Conditions and directions

(6) When making an order, the court may impose conditions and give directions as appropriate.

Matters not covered in rules

(7) If these rules do not cover a matter adequately, the court may give directions, and the practice shall be decided by analogy to these rules, by reference to the *Courts of Justice Act* and the Act governing the case and, if the court considers it appropriate, by reference to the Rules of Civil Procedure.

Failure to obey order

(8) If a person fails to obey an order in a case or a related case, the court may deal with the failure by making any order that it considers necessary for a just determination of the matter, including,

(a) an order for costs;
(b) an order dismissing a claim;
(c) an order striking out any application, answer, notice of motion, motion to change, response to motion to change, financial statement, affidavit, or any other document filed by a party;
(d) an order that all or part of a document that was required to be provided but was not, may not be used in the case;
(e) if the failure to obey was by a party, an order that the party is not entitled to any further order from the court unless the court orders otherwise;
(f) an order postponing the trial or any other step in the case; and
(g) on motion, a contempt order.

Failure to follow rules

(8.1) If a person fails to follow these rules, the court may deal with the failure by making any order described in subrule (8), other than a contempt order under clause (8)(g).

Document that may delay or is inflammatory, etc.

(8.2) The court may strike out all or part of any document that may delay or make it difficult to have a fair trial or that is inflammatory, a waste of time, a nuisance or an abuse of the court process.

Power to make order under subrule (8), (8.1) or (8.2)

(8.3) For greater certainty, a court may make an order under subrule (8), (8.1) or (8.2) at any time during a case, and the power to make such an order exists unless these rules expressly provide otherwise.

Consequences of striking out certain documents

(8.4) If an order is made striking out a party's application, answer, motion to change or response to motion to change in a case, the following consequences apply unless a court orders otherwise:

1. The party is not entitled to any further notice of steps in the case, except as provided by subrule 25(13) (service of order).
2. The party is not entitled to participate in the case in any way.
3. The court may deal with the case in the party's absence.
4. A date may be set for an uncontested trial of the case.

Reference to forms

(9) In these rules, when a form is referred to by number, the reference is to the form with that number that is described in the Table of Forms at the end of these rules and is available on the Internet through www.ontariocourtforms.on.ca.

Use of forms

(9.1) The forms authorized by these rules and set out in the Table of Forms shall be used where applicable and may be adjusted as needed to fit the situation.

Format of written documents

(10) Every written document in a case,

(a) shall be legibly typed or printed;
(b) shall be on white paper, or on white or nearly white paper with recycled paper content; and
(c) may appear on one or both sides of the page.

Practice directions

(11) In subrules (12), (12.1) and (12.2),

"practice direction" means a direction, notice, memorandum or guide for the purpose of governing, subject to these rules, the conduct of cases in any area.

Requirements for practice direction

(12) A practice direction shall be approved in advance by the Chief Justice or Chief Judge of the court, filed with the secretary of the Family Rules Committee and posted on the Ontario Courts website, and notice of the practice direction shall be published in the *Ontario Reports*.

Effective date of practice direction

(12.1) A practice direction does not come into effect before it is filed and posted and notice of it is published as described in subrule (12).

Old practice directions

(12.2) Practice directions that were issued before these rules take effect no longer apply.

Transitional provision

(13) If a case was started in the Superior Court of Justice, other than in the Family Court of the Superior Court of Justice, before July 1, 2004, the following applies:

1. The case or a step in the case shall be carried on under these rules on or after July 1, 2004.
2. If the case was not governed by the Family Case Management Rules for the Superior Court of Justice in Toronto or by the Essex Family Case Management Rules before July 1, 2004 and a step in the case is taken on or after that date, the timetable set out in subrule 41(5) and subrules 41(6), (7) and (8) apply as if the case started on the date on which the step was taken.
3. If the case was governed by the Family Case Management Rules for the Superior Court of Justice in Toron-

to before July 1, 2004, the timetable established for the case when it was started applies to the case on or after July 1, 2004.

4. If the case was governed by the Essex Family Case Management Rules before July 1, 2004 and a family consent timetable was made by the court before that date, the family consent timetable continues to apply to the case on or after July 1, 2004.
5. If the case was governed by the Essex Family Case Management Rules before July 1, 2004 but no family consent timetable was made by the court before that date,
   i. the case management order expires on July 1, 2004, and
   ii. if a step in the case is taken on or after July 1, 2004, the timetable set out in subrule 41(5) and subrules 41(6), (7) and (8) apply to the case as if the case started on the date on which the step was taken.

(14) Revoked.

RULE 2: INTERPRETATION

Definitions

2. (1) In these rules,

"address" means a person's street or municipal address, mailing address, telephone number, fax number and electronic mail address;

"appellant" means a person who starts an appeal;

"applicant" means a person who starts an application;

"application" means, as the context requires, the document that starts a case or the procedure by which new cases are brought to the court for a final order or provisional order;

"arbitration agreement" means an agreement by which two or more persons agree to submit to arbitration a dispute that has arisen or may arise between them;

"bond" includes a recognizance, and expressions that refer to the posting of a bond include the act of entering into a recognizance;

"case" means an application or any other method allowed in law for bringing a matter to the court for a final order or provisional order, and includes all motions, enforcements and appeals;

"change," when used to refer to an order or agreement, means to vary, suspend or discharge, or a variation, suspension or discharge (depending on whether the word is used as a verb or as a noun);

"child" means a child as defined in the Act governing the case or, if not defined in that Act, a person under the age of 18 years, and in a case under the *Divorce Act* (Canada) includes a "child of the marriage" within the meaning of that Act;

"child protection case" means a case under Part III of the *Child and Family Services Act*;

"clerk" means a person who has the authority of a clerk or a registrar of the court;

"contempt motion" means a motion for a contempt order;

"contempt order" means an order finding a person in contempt of court;

"continuing record" means the record made under Rule 9 containing, in accordance with these rules, written documents in a case that are filed with the court;

"corporation" *French version only.*

"court" means the court in which a case is being heard;

"default hearing" means a hearing under section 41 of the *Family Responsibility and Support Arrears Enforcement Act, 1996* in which a payor is required to come to court to explain why payment has not been made as required by a support order;

"Director of the Family Responsibility Office" means the Director of the Family Responsibility Office under the *Family Responsibility and Support Arrears Enforcement Act, 1996*, and "Director" has the same meaning, unless the context requires otherwise;

"document" means information, sound or images recorded by any method;

"enforcement" means the use of one or more remedies mentioned in rule 26 (enforcement of orders) to enforce an order;

"family arbitration" means an arbitration that,

(a) deals with matters that could be dealt with in a marriage contract, separation agreement, cohabitation agreement or paternity agreement under Part IV of the *Family Law Act*, and

(b) is conducted exclusively in accordance with the law of Ontario or of another Canadian jurisdiction;

"family arbitration agreement" and "family arbitration award" have meanings that correspond to the meaning of "family arbitration";

"file" means to file with proof of service in the court office in the municipality,

(a) where the case or enforcement is started, or

(b) to which the case or enforcement is transferred;

"final order" means an order, other than a temporary order, that decides a claim in an application, including,

(a) an order made on motion that changes a final order,

(b) a judgment, and

(c) an order that decides a party's rights, in an issue between the parties or between a party and a non-party;

"government agency" means the Crown, a Crown agency, a municipal government or agency, a children's aid society or any other public body;

"income source" has the same meaning as in the *Family Responsibility and Support Arrears Enforcement Act, 1996*;

"lawyer" means a person authorized under the *Law Society Act* to practise law in Ontario;

"legal aid rate" means the rate payable by the Ontario Legal Aid Plan on an account submitted by a lawyer for copying in the lawyer's office;

"mail," when used as a noun, means ordinary or regular mail, and when used as a verb means to send by ordinary or regular mail;

"municipality" means a county, district, district municipality, regional municipality, the City of Toronto or a municipal corporation formed from the amalgamation of all the municipalities of a county, district, district municipality or regional municipality, and includes,

(a) an Indian reserve within the territorial area of a municipality, and

(b) the part of The Regional Municipality of Niagara that was the County of Lincoln as it existed on December 31, 1969;

"on motion" means on motion of a party or a person having an interest in the case;

"payment order" means a temporary or final order, but not a provisional order, requiring a person to pay money to another person, including,

(a) an order to pay an amount under Part I or II of the *Family Law Act* or the corresponding provisions of a predecessor Act,

(b) a support order,

(c) a support deduction order,

(d) an order under section 60 or subsection 154(2) of the *Child and Family Services Act*, or under the corresponding provision of a predecessor Act,

(e) a payment order made under rules 26 to 32 (enforcement measures) or under section 41 of the *Family Responsibility and Support Arrears Enforcement Act, 1996*,

(f) a fine for contempt of court,

(g) an order of forfeiture of a bond or recognizance,

(h) an order requiring a party to pay the fees and expenses of,

(i) an assessor, mediator or other expert named by the court, or

(ii) a person conducting a blood test to help determine a child's parentage, and

(i) the costs and disbursements in a case;

"payor" means a person required to pay money under an order or agreement, and includes the estate trustee of a payor who died;

"periodic payment" means an amount payable at regular intervals and includes an amount payable in instalments;

"property claim" means a claim,

(a) under Part I of the *Family Law Act*,

(b) for a constructive or resulting trust, or

(c) for a monetary award as compensation for unjust enrichment;

"provisional order" means an order that is not effective until confirmed by a court;

"recipient" means a person entitled to receive money or costs under a payment order or agreement, including,

(a) a guardian or person with custody of a child who is entitled to money for the child's benefit under an order,

(b) in the case of a support order made under the *Family Law Act*, an agency referred to in subsection 33(3) of that Act,

(c) in the case of a support order made under the *Divorce Act* (Canada), an agency referred to in subsection 20.1(1) of that Act,

(d) a children's aid society entitled to money under an order made under section 60 or subsection 154(2) of the *Child and Family Services Act*, or the corresponding provision in a predecessor Act,

(e) an assessor, mediator or other expert entitled to fees and expenses from the party named in the order, and

(f) the estate trustee of a person who was entitled to money under an order at the time of his or her death;

"Registrar General" means the Registrar General under the *Vital Statistics Act*;

"respondent" means a person against whom a claim is made in an application, answer or appeal;

"special party" means a party who is a child or who is or appears to be mentally incapable for the purposes of the *Substitute Decisions Act, 1992* in respect of an issue in the case and who, as a result, requires legal representation, but does not include a child in a custody, access, child protection, adoption or child support case;

"support deduction order" means a support deduction order as defined in section 1 of the *Family Responsibility and Support Arrears Enforcement Act, 1996*;

"support order" means an order described in subsection 34(1) of the *Family Law Act* or a support order as defined in subsection 2(1) of the *Divorce Act* (Canada) or in section 1 of the *Family Responsibility and Support Arrears Enforcement Act, 1996*;

"temporary order" means an order that says it is effective only for a limited time, and includes an interim order;

"transcript" includes an electronic recording;

"trial" includes a hearing;

"uncontested trial" means a trial at which only the party making the claim provides evidence and submissions.

Primary objective

(2) The primary objective of these rules is to enable the court to deal with cases justly.

Dealing with cases justly

(3) Dealing with a case justly includes,

(a) ensuring that the procedure is fair to all parties;
(b) saving expense and time;
(c) dealing with the case in ways that are appropriate to its importance and complexity; and
(d) giving appropriate court resources to the case while taking account of the need to give resources to other cases.

Duty to promote primary objective

(4) The court is required to apply these rules to promote the primary objective, and parties and their lawyers are required to help the court to promote the primary objective.

Duty to manage cases

(5) The court shall promote the primary objective by active management of cases, which includes,

(a) at an early stage, identifying the issues, and separating and disposing of those that do not need full investigation and trial;
(b) encouraging and facilitating use of alternatives to the court process;
(c) helping the parties to settle all or part of the case;
(d) setting timetables or otherwise controlling the progress of the case;
(e) considering whether the likely benefits of taking a step justify the cost;
(f) dealing with as many aspects of the case as possible on the same occasion; and
(g) if appropriate, dealing with the case without parties and their lawyers needing to come to court, on the basis of written documents or by holding a telephone or video conference.

RULE 3: TIME

Counting days

3. (1) In these rules or an order, the number of days between two events is counted as follows:

1. The first day is the day after the first event.
2. The last day is the day of the second event.

Counting days—Short periods

(2) If a rule or order provides a period of less than seven days for something to be done, Saturdays, Sundays and other days when all court offices are closed do not count as part of the period.

Day when court offices closed

(3) If the last day of a period of time under these rules or an order falls on a day when court offices are closed, the period ends on the next day they are open.

Counting days—Examples

(4) The following are examples of how time is counted under these rules:

1. Notice of a motion must be served not later than four days before the motion date (see subrule 14(11)). Saturday and Sunday are not counted, because the notice period is less than seven days (see subrule (2)). Service on the day set out in the left column below is in time for the motion to be heard on the day set out in the right column below.

Service on	Motion may be heard on the following
Monday	Friday
Tuesday	Monday
Wednesday	Tuesday
Thursday	Wednesday
Friday	Thursday
Saturday	Friday
Sunday	Friday

2. A respondent who is served with an application in Canada has 30 days to serve an answer (see subrule 10(1)). A respondent who is served with an application on October 1 is in time if the answer is served on or before October 31. A respondent served on November 1 is in time if the answer is served on or before December 1.
3. If the last day for doing something under these rules or an order is New Year's Day, January 1, which is a day when court offices are closed, the time expires on January 2. If January 2 is a Saturday, Sunday or other day when court offices are closed, the time expires on January 3. If January 3 is a day when court offices are closed, the time expires on January 4.

Order to lengthen or shorten time

(5) The court may make an order to lengthen or shorten any time set out in these rules or an order, except that it may lengthen a time set out in subrule 33(1) (timetable for child protection cases) only if the best interests of the child require it.

Written consent to change time

(6) The parties may, by consent in writing, change any time set out in these rules, except that they may not change a time set out in,

(a) clause 14(11)(c) (confirmation of motion);
(b) subrules 17(14) and (14.1) (confirmation of conference, late briefs);
(c) subrule 33(1) (timetable for child protection cases);
(d) rule 39 (case management in Family Court of Superior Court of Justice);

(e) rule 40 (case management in Ontario Court of Justice); or

(f) rule 41 (case management in the Superior Court of Justice (other than the Family Court of the Superior Court of Justice)).

Late documents refused by court office

(7) The staff at a court office shall refuse to accept a document that a person asks to file after,

(a) the time specified in these rules; or

(b) the later time specified in a consent under subrule (6), a statute that applies to the case, or a court order.

RULE 4: REPRESENTATION

Definition

4. (0.1) In this rule,

"limited scope retainer" means the provision of legal services by a lawyer for part, but not all, of a party's case by agreement between the lawyer and the party.

Representation for a party

(1) A party may,

(a) act in person;

(b) be represented by a lawyer; or

(c) be represented by a person who is not a lawyer, but only if the court gives permission in advance.

Interpretation, acting in person

(1.1) Where a party acts in person, anything these rules require or permit a lawyer or other representative to do shall be done by the party.

Limited scope retainer

(1.2) Clause (1)(b) permits a party to be represented by a lawyer acting under a limited scope retainer.

Interpretation, limited scope retainer

(1.3) A party who is represented by a lawyer acting under a limited scope retainer is considered for the purposes of these rules to be acting in person, unless the lawyer is acting as the party's lawyer of record.

Private representation of special party

(2) The court may authorize a person to represent a special party if the person is,

(a) appropriate for the task; and

(b) willing to act as representative.

Public law officer to represent special party

(3) If there is no appropriate person willing to act as a special party's representative, the court may authorize the Children's Lawyer or the Public Guardian and Trustee to act as representative, but only with that official's consent.

Service of authorization to represent

(4) An order under subrule (2) or (3) shall be served immediately, by the person who asked for the order or by any other person named by the court,

(a) on the representative; and

(b) on every party in the case.

Representation of party who dies

(5) If a party dies after the start of a case, the court may make the estate trustee a party instead, on motion without notice.

Authorizing representative for party who dies

(6) If the party has no estate trustee, the court may authorize an appropriate person to act as representative, with that person's consent, given in advance.

Lawyer for child

(7) In a case that involves a child who is not a party, the court may authorize a lawyer to represent the child, and then the child has the rights of a party, unless the court orders otherwise.

Child's rights subject to statute

(8) Subrule (7) is subject to section 38 (legal representation of child, protection hearing) and subsection 114(6) (legal representation of child, secure treatment hearing) of the *Child and Family Services Act*.

Choice of lawyer

(9) A party who is acting in person may choose a lawyer by serving on every other party and filing a notice of change in representation (Form 4) containing the lawyer's consent to act.

Non-application

(9.1) Subrule (9) does not apply if the party chooses a lawyer acting under a limited scope retainer and that lawyer is not the lawyer of record for the party.

Change in representation

(10) Except as subrule (10.1) provides, a party represented by a lawyer may, by serving on every other party and filing a notice of change in representation (Form 4),

(a) change lawyers; or

(b) act in person.

Exception, child protection case scheduled for trial

(10.1) In a child protection case that has been scheduled for trial or placed on a trial list, a party may act under clause (10)(b) only with the court's permission, obtained in advance by motion made with notice.

Notice of change in representation

(11) A notice of change in representation shall,

(a) contain the party's address for service, if the party wants to appear without a lawyer; or

(b) show the name and address of the new lawyer, if the party wants to change lawyers.

Lawyer's removal from the case

(12) A lawyer may make a motion for an order to be removed from the case, with notice to the client and to,

(a) the Children's Lawyer, if the client is a child;

(b) the Public Guardian and Trustee, if the client is or appears to be mentally incapable in respect of an issue in the case.

Notice of motion to remove lawyer

(13) Notice of a motion to remove a lawyer shall also be served on the other parties to the case, but the evidence in support of the motion shall not be served on them, shall not be put into the continuing record and shall not be kept in the court file after the motion is heard.

Affidavit in support of motion to remove lawyer

(14) The affidavit in support of the motion shall indicate what stage the case is at, the next event in the case and any scheduled dates.

Contents and service of order removing lawyer

(15) The order removing the lawyer from the case shall,

(a) set out the client's last known address for service; and

(b) be served on all other parties, served on the client by mail, fax or electronic mail at the client's last known address and filed immediately.

RULE 5: WHERE A CASE STARTS AND IS TO BE HEARD

Where case starts

5. (1) Subject to sections 21.8 and 21.11 of the *Courts of Justice Act* (territorial jurisdiction—Family Court), a case shall be started,

(a) in the municipality where a party resides;

(b) if the case deals with custody of or access to a child, in the municipality where the child ordinarily resides, except for cases described in,

(i) section 22 (jurisdiction of an Ontario court) of the *Children's Law Reform Act*, and

(ii) subsection 48(2) (place for child protection hearing) and subsection 150(1) (place for adoption proceeding) of the *Child and Family Services Act*; or

(c) in a municipality chosen by all parties, but only with the court's permission given in advance in that municipality.

Starting case—Danger to child or party

(2) Subject to sections 21.8 and 21.11 of the *Courts of Justice Act*, if there is immediate danger that a child may be removed from Ontario or immediate danger to a child's or party's health or safety, a party may start a case in any municipality and a motion may be heard in that municipality, but the case shall be transferred to a municipality referred to in subrule (1) immediately after the motion is heard, unless the court orders otherwise.

Clerk to refuse documents if case in wrong place

(3) The clerk shall refuse to accept an application for filing unless,

(a) the case is started in the municipality where a party resides;

(b) the case deals with custody of or access to a child and is started in the municipality where the child ordinarily resides;

(c) the case is started in a municipality chosen by all parties and the order permitting the case to be started there is filed with the application; or

(d) the lawyer or party asking to file the application says in writing that the case is one that is permitted by clause (1)(b) or subrule (2) to be started in that municipality.

Place for steps other than enforcement

(4) All steps in the case, other than enforcement, shall take place in the municipality where the case is started or transferred.

Place for enforcement—Payment orders

(5) All steps in enforcement of a payment order, including a motion to suspend a support deduction order, shall take place,

(a) in the municipality where the recipient resides;

(b) if the recipient does not reside in Ontario, in the municipality where the order is filed with the court for enforcement;

(c) if the person enforcing the order so chooses, in the municipality where the payor resides; or

(d) in a motion under section 26 (income source dispute) of the *Family Responsibility and Support Arrears Enforcement Act, 1996*, in the municipality where the income source resides.

Place for enforcement—Other orders

(6) All steps in the enforcement of an order other than a payment order shall take place,

(a) if the order involves custody of or access to a child,

(i) in the municipality where the child ordinarily resides, or

(ii) if the child does not ordinarily reside in Ontario, in the municipality to which the child has the closest connection;

(b) if the order involves property, in the municipality where the person enforcing the order resides or the municipality where the property is located; or

(c) in a municipality chosen by all parties, but only with the court's permission given in advance in that municipality.

Alternative place for enforcement—Order enforced by contempt motion

(7) An order, other than a payment order, that is being enforced by a contempt motion may also be enforced in the municipality in which the order was made.

Transfer to another municipality

(8) If it is substantially more convenient to deal with a case or any step in the case in another municipality, the court may, on motion, order that the case or step be transferred there.

Change of place for child protection case

(9) Notice of a motion under subsection 48(3) of the *Child and Family Services Act* to transfer a case to a place within the jurisdiction of another children's aid society shall be served on the parties and the other children's aid society, with the evidence in support of the motion.

RULE 6: SERVICE OF DOCUMENTS

Methods of service

6. (1) Service of a document under these rules may be carried out by regular service or by special service in accordance with this rule, unless an Act, rule or order provides otherwise.

Age restriction

(1.1) No person shall serve a document under these rules unless he or she is at least 18 years of age.

Regular service

(2) Regular service of a document on a person is carried out by,

(a) mailing a copy to the person's lawyer or, if none, to the person;

(b) sending a copy by courier to the person's lawyer or, if none, to the person;

(c) depositing a copy at a document exchange to which the person's lawyer belongs;

(d) faxing a copy to the person's lawyer or, if none, to the person; or

(e) carrying out special service.

Special service

(3) Special service of a document on a person is carried out by,

(a) leaving a copy,

(i) with the person to be served,

(ii) if the person is or appears to be mentally incapable in respect of an issue in the case, with the person and with the guardian of the person's property or, if none, with the Public Guardian and Trustee,

(iii) if the person is a child, with the child and with the child's lawyer, if any,

(iv) if the person is a corporation, with an officer, director or agent of the corporation, or with a person at any place of business of the corporation who appears to be managing the place, or

(v) if the person is a children's aid society, with an officer, director or employee of the society;

(b) leaving a copy with the person's lawyer of record in the case, or with a lawyer who accepts service in writing on a copy of the document;

(c) mailing a copy to the person, together with an acknowledgment of service in the form of a prepaid return postcard (Form 6), all in an envelope that is addressed to the person and has the sender's return address (but service under this clause is not valid unless the return postcard, signed by the person, is filed in the continuing record); or

(d) leaving a copy at the person's place of residence, in an envelope addressed to the person, with anyone who appears to be an adult person resident at the same address and, on the same day or on the next, mailing another copy to the person at that address.

Special service—Documents that could lead to imprisonment

(4) Special service of the following documents shall be carried out only by a method set out in clause (3)(a), unless the court orders otherwise:

1. A notice of contempt motion.
2. A summons to witness.
3. A notice of motion or notice of default hearing in which the person to be served faces a possibility of imprisonment.

Special service—Restriction on who may serve

(4.1) Subject to subrule (4.2), special service of the following documents shall be carried out by a person other than the party required to serve the document:

1. An application (Form 8, 8A, 8B, 8B.1, 8B.2, 8C, 8D, 8D.1, 34L or 34N).
2. A motion to change (Form 15) and change information form (Form 15A) or affidavit permitted under subrule 15(22), with required attachments.
3. A document listed in subrule (4).

Exceptions

(4.2) Subrule (4.1) does not apply if,

(a) the party required to serve the document or the person being served is a person referred to in clause 8(6)(c) (officials, agencies, etc.); or

(b) the court orders otherwise.

Regular service at address on latest document

(5) Regular service may be carried out at the address for service shown on the latest document filed by the person to be served.

Notice of address change

(6) A party whose address for service changes shall immediately serve notice of the change on the other parties and file it.

Service outside business hours

(7) If a document is served by any method after 4 p.m. on a day when court offices are open or at any time on a day when they are not open, service is effective on the next day when they are open.

Hours of fax service

(8) Service of a document by fax may be carried out only before 4 p.m. on a day when court offices are open, unless the parties consent or the court orders otherwise.

Effective date, service by mail

(9) Service of a document by mail is effective on the fifth day after it was mailed.

Effective date, service by courier

(10) Service of a document by courier is effective on the day after the courier picks it up.

Effective date, service by document exchange

(11) Service by deposit at a document exchange is effective only if the copy deposited and an additional copy of the document are date-stamped by the document exchange in the presence of the person depositing the copy, and then service is effective on the day after the date on the stamp.

Information to be included with document served by fax

(12) A document that is served by fax shall show, on its first page,

(a) the sender's name, address, telephone number and fax number;
(b) the name of the person or lawyer to be served;
(c) the date and time of the fax;
(d) the total number of pages faxed; and
(e) the name and telephone number of a person to contact in case of transmission difficulties.

Maximum length of document that may be faxed

(13) Service of a document or documents relating to a single step in a case may be carried out by fax only if the total number of pages (including any cover page or back sheet) is not more than 16, unless the parties consent in advance or the court orders otherwise.

Documents that may not be faxed

(14) A trial record, appeal record, factum or book of authorities may not be served by fax at any time unless the person to be served consents in advance.

Substituted service

(15) The court may order that a document be served by substituted service, using a method chosen by the court, if the party making the motion,

(a) provides detailed evidence showing,

(i) what steps have been taken to locate the person to be served, and

(ii) if the person has been located, what steps have been taken to serve the document on that person; and

(b) shows that the method of service could reasonably be expected to bring the document to the person's attention.

Same, notice

(15.1) An order under subrule (15) may be obtained on motion without notice, except where the person to be served is a government agency.

Service not required

(16) The court may, on motion without notice, order that service is not required if,

(a) reasonable efforts to locate the person to be served have not been or would not be successful; and
(b) there is no method of substituted service that could reasonably be expected to bring the document to the person's attention.

Service by advertisement

(17) If the court orders service by advertisement, Form 6A shall be used.

Approving irregular service

(18) When a document has been served by a method not allowed by these rules or by an order, the court may make an order approving the service if the document,

(a) came to the attention of the person to be served; or
(b) would have come to the person's attention if the person had not been evading service.

Proof of service

(19) Service of a document may be proved by,

(a) an acceptance or admission of service, written by the person to be served or the person's lawyer;
(b) an affidavit of service (Form 6B);
(c) the return postcard mentioned in clause (3)(c); or
(d) the date stamp on a copy of the document served by deposit at a document exchange.

RULE 7: PARTIES

Who are parties—Case

7. (1) A person who makes a claim in a case or against whom a claim is made in a case is a party to the case.

Who are parties—Motion

(2) For purposes of a motion only, a person who is affected by a motion is also a party, but this does not apply to a child affected by a motion relating to custody, access, child protection, adoption or child support.

Persons who must be named as parties

(3) A person starting a case shall name,

(a) as an applicant, every person who makes a claim;
(b) as a respondent,

(i) every person against whom a claim is made, and
(ii) every other person who should be a party to enable the court to decide all the issues in the case.

Parties in cases involving children

(4) In any of the following cases, every parent or other person who has care and control of the child involved, except a foster parent under the *Child and Family Services Act*, shall be named as a party, unless the court orders otherwise:

1. A case about custody of or access to a child.
2. A child protection case.
3. A secure treatment case (Part VI of the *Child and Family Services Act*).

Motion to change order under s. 57.1 of the *Child and Family Services Act*

(4.1) In a motion to change an order made under section 57.1 of the *Child and Family Services Act*, the children's aid society that was a party to the case in which the order was made is not a party to the motion to change the order, unless the court orders otherwise.

Party added by court order

(5) The court may order that any person who should be a party shall be added as a party, and may give directions for service on that person.

Permanent case name and court file number

(6) The court file number given to a case and the description of the parties as applicants and respondents in the case shall remain the same on a motion to change an order, a status review application, an application (general) for *Child and Family Services Act* cases other than child protection and status review, an application for an openness order, an enforcement or an appeal, no matter who starts it, with the following exceptions:

1. In an enforcement of a payment order, the parties may be described instead as payors, recipients and garnishees.
2. In an appeal, the parties shall also be described as appellants and respondents.
3. When a case is transferred to another municipality, it may be given a new court file number.
4. An application under section 153.1 of the *Child and Family Services Act* to change or terminate an openness order shall be given a new court file number.
5. In a motion to change an order made under section 57.1 of the *Child and Family Services Act*,
   i. the person making the motion shall be named as the applicant and every other party to the motion shall be named as the respondents, and
   ii. the motion shall be given a new court file number.
6. In an application brought under section 145.1.2 of the Child and Family Services Act, the person bringing the application shall be named as the applicant and the children's aid society and any other party entitled to notice shall be named as the respondents.

RULE 8: STARTING A CASE

Filing an application

8. (1) To start a case, a person shall file an application (Form 8, 8A, 8B, 8B.1, 8B.2, 8C, 8D, 8D.1, 34L or 34N).

Enforcement of family arbitration award

(1.1) Despite subrule (1), a person who is entitled to the enforcement of a family arbitration award and who wants to ask the court to enforce the award under section 59.8 of the *Family Law Act* may do so by filing a request to enforce a family arbitration award (Form 32.1) under rule 32.1.

When required to proceed by motion

(1.2) Despite subrules (1) and (1.1), if there is already a family law case to which these rules apply between the parties to the family arbitration agreement in the Superior Court of Justice or the Family Court of the Superior Court of Justice, the party entitled to enforcement shall make a motion in that case rather than an application under this rule or a request under rule 32.1, and subrule 14(24) applies in respect of the motion.

Change to final order or agreement

(2) Subject to subrule 25(19) (changing order—fraud, mistake, lack of notice), a party who wants to ask the court to change a final order or an agreement for support filed under section 35 of the *Family Law Act* may do so only by a motion under rule 15 (if permitted to do so by that rule).

Exception

(2.1) Despite subrule (2), if a party who wants to ask the court to change a final order or agreement to which rule 15 applies also wants to make one or more related claims to which rule 15 does not apply, the party may file an application under subrule (1) to deal with the request for a change together with the related claim or claims and, in that case, subrules 15(11) to (13) apply with necessary modifications to the request.

Claims in application

(3) An application may contain,

(a) a claim against more than one person; and
(b) more than one claim against the same person.

Claim for custody or access

(3.1) An application containing a claim for custody of or access to a child shall be accompanied by the applicable documents referred to in rule 35.1.

Claim relating to family arbitration

(3.2) An application containing a claim under the *Arbitration Act, 1991* or the *Family Law Act* relating to a family arbitration, family arbitration agreement or family arbitration award shall be accompanied by,

(a) copies of the certificates of independent legal advice required by the *Family Law Act* for the parties;

(b) a copy of the family arbitration agreement; and

(c) if an award has been made, the original award or a certified copy.

Court date set when application filed

(4) When an application is filed, the clerk shall,

(a) set a court date, except as provided by subrule 39(7) (case management, standard track) and subrule 41(4) (case management, clerk's role); and

(b) seal the application with the court seal.

Service of application

(5) The application shall be served immediately on every other party, and special service shall be used unless the party is listed in subrule (6).

Service on officials, agencies, etc.

(6) The application may be served by regular service,

(a) on a foster parent, at the foster parent's residence;

(b) on a representative of a band or native community, by serving the chief or other person who appears to be in charge of its management;

(c) on any of the following persons, at their place of business:

1. A Director appointed under section 5 of the *Child and Family Services Act.*
2. A local director appointed under section 16 of the *Child and Family Services Act.*
3. An administrator in charge of a secure treatment program under Part VI of the *Child and Family Services Act.*
4. A children's aid society.
5. The Minister of Community and Social Services.
6. An agency referred to in subsection 33(3) of the *Family Law Act* or subsection 20.1(1) of the *Divorce Act* (Canada).
7. The Director of the Family Responsibility Office.
8. The Children's Lawyer.
9. The Public Guardian and Trustee.
10. The Registrar General.

Serving protection application on child

(7) In a child protection case in which the child is entitled to notice, the application shall be served on the child by special service.

Serving secure treatment application on child

(8) An application for secure treatment (Part VI of the *Child and Family Services Act*) shall be served on the child by special service.

Serving application on child's lawyer

(9) If an order has been made for legal representation of a child under section 38 or subsection 114(6) of the *Child and Family Services Act* or under subrule 4(7), the applicant, or another party directed by the court, shall serve all documents in the continuing record and any status review application on the child's lawyer by regular service.

Serving protection application before start of case

(10) If a child is brought to a place of safety (section 40, 42 or 43 of the *Child and Family Services Act*) or a homemaker remains or is placed on premises (subsection 78(2) of that Act), an application may be served without being sealed by the clerk, if it is filed on or before the court date.

Application not served on or before court date

(11) If an application is not served on a respondent on or before the court date, at the applicant's request the clerk shall set a new court date for that respondent and the applicant shall make the necessary change to the application and serve it immediately on that respondent.

RULE 8.1: MANDATORY INFORMATION PROGRAM

Application of rule

8.1 (1) This rule applies to cases started after August 31, 2011 that deal with any of the following:

1. A claim for custody of or access to a child under the *Divorce Act* (Canada) or Part III of the *Children's Law Reform Act.*
2. A claim respecting net family property under Part I of the *Family Law Act.*
3. A claim respecting a matrimonial home under Part II of the *Family Law Act.*
4. A claim for support under the *Divorce Act* (Canada) or Part III of the *Family Law Act.*
5. A restraining order under the *Family Law Act* or the *Children's Law Reform Act.*
6. A motion to change a final order or agreement under rule 15, except motions that deal only with changing child or spousal support.

Exception

(2) Subrules (4) to (7) do not apply to,

(a) a person or agency referred to in subsection 33(3) of the *Family Law Act*;

(b) the Director of the Family Responsibility Office;

(c) parties in cases that are proceeding on consent;

(d) parties in cases in which the only claims made are for a divorce, costs or the incorporation of the terms of an agreement or prior court order;

(d.1) parties to an application in which the only claims made in the application and any answer relate to a family arbitration, family arbitration agreement or family arbitration award, unless the court orders otherwise; or

(e) parties who have already attended a mandatory information program.

Content of program

(3) The program referred to in this rule shall provide parties to cases referred to in subrule (1) with information about

separation and the legal process, and may include information on topics such as,

(a) the options available for resolving differences, including alternatives to going to court;

(b) the impact the separation of parents has on children; and

(c) resources available to deal with problems arising from separation.

Attendance compulsory

(4) Each party to a case shall attend the program no later than 45 days after the case is started.

Appointments to attend

(5) The applicant shall arrange his or her own appointment to attend the program, obtain an appointment for the respondent from the person who conducts the program, and serve notice of the respondent's appointment with the application.

Certificate

(6) The person who conducts the program shall provide for each party who attends a certificate of attendance, which shall be filed as soon as possible, and in any event not later than 2 p.m. on the second day before the day of the case conference, if one is scheduled.

No other steps

(7) A party shall not take any step in the case before his or her certificate of attendance is filed, except that a respondent may serve and file an answer and a party may make an appointment for a case conference.

Exception

(8) The court may, on motion, order that any or all of subrules (4) to (7) do not apply to the party because of urgency or hardship or for some other reason in the interest of justice.

(9) Revoked.

RULE 9: CONTINUING RECORD

Continuing record created

9. (1) A person starting a case shall,

(a) prepare a single continuing record of the case, to be the court's permanent record of the case; and

(b) serve it on all other parties and file it, along with the affidavits of service or other documents proving that the continuing record was served.

(2) Revoked.

Support enforcement continuing record

(3) If a support order is filed with the Director of the Family Responsibility Office, the person bringing the case before the court shall prepare the continuing record, and the continuing record shall be called the support enforcement continuing record.

Child protection continuing record

(4) In an application for a child protection order or an application for a status review of a child protection order, the continuing record shall be called the child protection continuing record.

(5) Revoked.

Formal requirements of continuing record

(6) In preparing and maintaining a continuing record and support enforcement continuing record under this rule, the parties shall meet the requirements set out in the document entitled "Formal Requirements of the Continuing Record under the *Family Law Rules*," dated October 21, 2013, published by the Family Rules Committee and available on the Internet through www.ontariocourtforms.on.ca.

Formal requirements of child protection continuing record

(6.1) In preparing and maintaining a child protection continuing record under this rule, the parties shall meet the requirements set out in the document entitled "Formal Requirements of the Child Protection Continuing Record under the *Family Law Rules*," dated November 1, 2005, published by the Family Rules Committee and available on the Internet through www.ontariocourtforms.on.ca.

Separation of single record

(7) Instead of the single continuing record mentioned in subrule (1), the continuing record may be separated into separate records for the applicant and the respondent, in accordance with the following:

1. In a case other than a child protection case, the court may order separate records on its own initiative or at the request of either party on motion or at a case conference, settlement conference or trial management conference.
2. Revoked.
3. If the court orders separate records and there is more than one applicant and respondent, the court may order separate records for each applicant and respondent.
4. If the record consists of separate records, the separate records are called the applicant's record and the respondent's record.

Combining separated records

(8) If the continuing record has been separated, the court may order the records to be combined into a single record on its own initiative or at the request of either party at a case conference, settlement conference or trial management conference.

Combining separated records on consent

(9) If the continuing record has been separated, the parties may, if they agree, combine the separate records into a single continuing record, in which case the parties shall arrange together for the combining of the records.

By whom record is separated or combined

(10) If the court orders that the continuing record,

(a) be separated or combined on its own initiative, the court shall give directions as to which party shall separate or combine the record, as the case requires;

(b) be separated or combined at the request of a party at a case conference, settlement conference or trial management conference, the party that makes the request shall separate or combine the record, as the case requires, unless the court orders otherwise.

Maintaining continuing record

(11) The parties are responsible, under the clerk's supervision, for adding to a continuing record that has not been separated all documents filed in the case and, in the case of separated records, each party is responsible, under the clerk's supervision, for adding the documents the party files to the party's own record.

Duties of party serving documents

(12) A party serving documents shall,

(a) if the continuing record has not been separated,

(i) serve and file any documents that are not already in the continuing record, and

(ii) serve with the documents an updated cumulative table of contents listing the documents being filed; and

(b) if the continuing record has been separated,

(i) serve and file any documents that are not already in the party's separate record, and

(ii) serve with the documents an updated cumulative table of contents listing the documents being filed in the party's separate record.

No service or filing of documents already in record

(13) A party shall not serve or file any document that is already in the record, despite any requirement in these rules that the document be served and filed.

(14) Revoked.

Documents referred to by tab in record

(15) A party who is relying on a document in the record shall refer to it by its tab in the record, except in a support enforcement continuing record.

Documents not to be removed from record

(16) No document shall be removed from the continuing record except by order.

Written reasons for order

(17) If the court gives written reasons for making an order,

(a) they may be endorsed by hand on an endorsement sheet, or the endorsement may be a short note on the endorsement sheet saying that written reasons are being given separately;

(b) the clerk shall add a copy of the reasons to the endorsements section of the record; and

(c) the clerk shall send a copy to the parties by mail, fax or electronic mail.

(18) Revoked.

Appeal

(19) If a final order is appealed, only the notice of appeal and any order of the appeal court (and no other appeal document) shall be added to the record.

Transfer of record if case transferred

(20) If the court transfers a case to another municipality the clerk shall, on request, transfer the record to the clerk at the court office in the other municipality, and the record shall be used there as if the case had started in the other municipality.

Confirmation of support order

(21) When a provisional support order or a provisional change to a support order is sent to a court in Ontario for confirmation,

(a) if the provisional order or change was made in Ontario, the clerk shall send the continuing record to the court office where the confirmation is to take place and the respondent shall update it as this rule requires; and

(b) if the provisional order or change was not made in Ontario, the clerk shall prepare the continuing record and the respondent shall update it as this rule requires.

Cases started before January 1, 2007

(22) Despite this rule, if a case was started before January 1, 2007, the version of this rule that applied to the case on December 31, 2006 as its application may have been modified by the court continues, subject to subrule (23), to apply to the case unless the court orders otherwise.

Exception, cases started before January 1, 2007

(23) If a motion to change a final order is made on or after January 1, 2007 in respect of a case started before that date, this rule shall apply to the motion and to all documents filed afterwards.

(24) Revoked.

RULE 10: ANSWERING A CASE

Serving and filing answer

10. (1) A person against whom an application is made shall serve an answer (Form 10, 33B, 33B.1 or 33B.2) on every other party and file it within 30 days after being served with the application.

Time for answer—Application served outside Canada or U.S.A.

(2) If an application is served outside Canada or the United States of America, the time for serving and filing an answer is 60 days.

Exception—Placement for adoption

(2.1) In an application to dispense with a parent's consent before adoption placement, (Form 8D.1), the time for serving the answer is,

(a) 20 days, if the application is served in Canada or the United States of America;

(b) 40 days, if the application is served outside Canada or the United States of America.

Answer may include claim

(3) A respondent may include in the answer,

(a) a claim against the applicant;

(b) a claim against any other person, who then also becomes a respondent in the case.

Answer by added respondent

(4) Subrules (1) to (3) apply to a respondent added under subrule (3), except that the time for serving and filing an answer is 14 days after service on the added respondent, or 30 days if the added respondent is served outside Canada or the United States of America.

Claim for custody or access

(4.1) An answer that includes a claim for custody of or access to a child shall be accompanied by the applicable documents referred to in rule 35.1.

No answer

(5) The consequences set out in paragraphs 1 to 4 of subrule 1(8.4) apply, with necessary modifications, if a respondent does not serve and file an answer.

Reply

(6) A party may, within 10 days after being served with an answer, serve and file a reply (Form 10A) in response to a claim made in the answer.

RULE 11: AMENDING AN APPLICATION, ANSWER OR REPLY

Amending application without court's permission

11. (1) An applicant may amend the application without the court's permission as follows:

1. If no answer has been filed, by serving and filing an amended application in the manner set out in rule 8 (starting a case).
2. If an answer has been filed, by serving and filing an amended application in the manner set out in rule 8 and also filing the consent of all parties to the amendment.

Amending answer without court's permission

(2) A respondent may amend the answer without the court's permission as follows:

1. If the application has been amended, by serving and filing an amended answer within 14 days after being served with the amended application.
2. If the application has not been amended, by serving and filing an amended answer and also filing the consent of all parties to the amendment.

Child protection, amendments without court's permission

(2.1) In a child protection case, if a significant change relating to the child happens after the original document is filed,

(a) the applicant may serve and file an amended application, an amended plan of care or both; and

(b) the respondent may serve and file an amended answer and plan of care.

Amending application or answer with court's permission

(3) On motion, the court shall give permission to a party to amend an application, answer or reply, unless the amendment would disadvantage another party in a way for which costs or an adjournment could not compensate.

Claim for custody or access

(3.1) If an application or answer is amended to include a claim for custody of or access to a child that was not in the original application or answer, the amended application or amended answer shall be accompanied by the applicable documents referred to in rule 35.1.

How amendment is shown

(4) An amendment shall be clearly shown by underlining all changes, and the rule or order permitting the amendment and the date of the amendment shall be noted in the margin of each amended page.

RULE 12: WITHDRAWING, COMBINING OR SPLITTING CASES

Withdrawing application, answer or reply

12. (1) A party who does not want to continue with all or part of a case may withdraw all or part of the application, answer or reply by serving a notice of withdrawal (Form 12) on every other party and filing it.

Withdrawal—Special party's application, answer or reply

(2) A special party's application, answer or reply may be withdrawn (whether in whole or in part) only with the court's permission, and the notice of motion for permission shall be served on every other party and on,

(a) the Children's Lawyer, if the special party is a child;

(b) the Public Guardian and Trustee, if the special party is not a child.

Costs payable on withdrawal

(3) A party who withdraws all or part of an application, answer or reply shall pay the costs of every other party in relation to the withdrawn application, answer, reply or part, up to the date of the withdrawal, unless the court orders or the parties agree otherwise.

Costs on withdrawal by government agency

(4) Despite subrule (3), if the party is a government agency, costs are in the court's discretion.

Combining and splitting cases

(5) If it would be more convenient to hear two or more cases, claims or issues together or to split a case into two or more separate cases, claims or issues, the court may, on motion, order accordingly.

Splitting divorce from other issues

(6) The court may, on motion, make an order splitting a divorce from the other issues in a case if,

(a) neither spouse will be disadvantaged by the order; and

(b) reasonable arrangements have been made for the support of any children of the marriage.

RULE 13: FINANCIAL STATEMENTS

Financial statement with application, answer or motion

13. (1) If an application, answer or motion contains a claim for support, a property claim, or a claim for exclusive possession of the matrimonial home and its contents,

(a) the party making the claim shall serve and file a financial statement (Form 13 or 13.1) with the document that contains the claim; and

(b) the party against whom the claim is made shall serve and file a financial statement within the time for serving and filing an answer, reply or affidavit or other document responding to the motion, whether the party is serving an answer, reply or affidavit or other document responding to the motion or not.

Form 13 for support claim without property claim

(1.1) If the application, answer or motion contains a claim for support but does not contain a property claim or a claim for exclusive possession of the matrimonial home and its contents, the financial statement used by the parties under these rules shall be in Form 13.

Form 13.1 for property claim with or without support claim

(1.2) If the application, answer or motion contains a property claim or a claim for exclusive possession of the matrimonial home and its contents, the financial statement used by the parties under these rules shall be in Form 13.1, whether a claim for support is also included or not.

Exception, certain support claims

(1.3) If the only claim for support contained in the application, answer or motion is a claim for child support in the amount specified in the table of the applicable child support guidelines, the party making the claim is not required to file a financial statement, unless the application, answer or motion also contains a property claim or a claim for exclusive possession of the matrimonial home and its contents.

Exception, family arbitration claim

(1.4) If the only claim contained in the application, answer or motion is a claim under the *Arbitration Act, 1991* or the *Family Law Act* relating to a family arbitration, family arbitration agreement or family arbitration award, the party making the claim is not required to file a financial statement, unless the court orders otherwise.

Claim for payment order under CFSA

(2) If an application, answer or notice of motion contains a claim for a payment order under section 60 of the *Child and Family Services Act*, clause (1)(a) does not apply to the children's aid society but clause (1)(b) applies to the party against whom the claim is made.

Financial statements in custody and access cases

(3) If an application, answer or motion contains a claim for custody of or access to a child and this rule does not otherwise require the parties to serve and file financial statements, the court may order each party to serve and file a financial statement in Form 13 within the time decided by the court.

Financial statement with motion to change temporary support order

(4) Subject to subrule (1.3), the following requirements apply if a motion contains a request for a change in a temporary support order:

1. The party making the motion shall serve and file a financial statement (Form 13 or 13.1) with the notice of motion.
2. The party responding to the motion shall serve and file a financial statement as soon as possible after being served with the notice of motion, but in any event no later than two days before the motion date. Any affidavit in response to the motion shall be served and filed at the same time as the financial statement.

Exception—by consent

(4.1) Parties to a consent motion to change a temporary support order do not need to serve and file financial statements if they file a consent agreeing not to serve and file them.

Financial statement with motion to change final support order or support agreement

(4.2) Subject to subrule (1.3), the following rules apply if a motion is made under rule 15 requesting a change to a final support order or a support agreement:

1. The party making the motion shall serve and file a financial statement (Form 13 or 13.1) with the motion to change (Form 15).
2. The party responding to the motion shall serve and file a financial statement within the time for serving and filing the response to motion to change (Form 15B) or

returning the consent motion to change (Form 15C) to the party making the motion, as set out in subrule 15(10). Any response to motion to change (Form 15B) shall be served and filed at the same time as the financial statement.

3. Parties who bring the motion by filing a consent motion to change (Form 15C) shall each file a financial statement with the form, unless they indicate in the form that they agree not to do so.
4. Parties who bring the motion by filing a consent motion to change child support (Form 15D) do not need to serve or file financial statements.

Financial statement required by response

(4.3) Subrule (4) or (4.2), as the case may be, applies with necessary modifications if a party makes a motion to change an order or agreement for which the party is not required by this rule to file a financial statement, and the party responding to the motion requests a change to a support order or support agreement.

No financial statement from assignee

(5) The assignee of a support order is not required to serve and file a financial statement under subrule (4) or (4.2).

Financial statement with motion to refrain

(5.1) A payor who makes a motion to require the Director of the Family Responsibility Office to refrain from suspending the payor's driver's licence shall, in accordance with subsection 35(7) of the *Family Responsibility and Support Arrears Enforcement Act, 1996*, serve and file with the notice of motion,

(a) a financial statement (Form 13 or 13.1) or a financial statement incorporated as Form 4 in Ontario Regulation 167/97 (General) made under that Act; and

(b) the proof of income specified in section 15 of the regulation referred to in clause (a).

Full disclosure in financial statement

(6) A party who serves and files a financial statement shall,

(a) make full and frank disclosure of the party's financial situation;

(b) attach any documents to prove the party's income that the financial statement requires;

(c) follow the instructions set out in the form; and

(d) fully complete all portions of the statement.

Requirements for filing

(7) The clerk shall not accept a party's financial statement for filing unless the following are attached to the form:

1. Proof of the party's current income.
2. One of the following, as proof of the party's income for the three previous years:
   i. For each of the three previous taxation years,
      A. the party's notice of assessment and, if any, notice of reassessment, or
      B. if a notice of assessment and a notice of reassessment are unavailable for a taxation year, a copy of the Income and Deductions printout provided by the Canada Revenue Agency for the party for the taxation year.
   ii. If the party swears or affirms a statement in the form that he or she is not required to and has chosen not to file an income tax return because of the *Indian Act* (Canada), some other proof of income for the three previous years.

Exception

(7.0.1) Subrule (7) does not apply to a financial statement filed under subrule (5.1).

Income tax returns

(7.1) Except in the case of a filing under subrule (5.1), income tax returns submitted in accordance with these rules are not required to be filed in the continuing record unless the court orders otherwise.

No financial statement by consent—Spousal support in divorce

(8) Parties to a claim for spousal support under the *Divorce Act* (Canada) do not need to serve and file financial statements if they file a consent,

(a) agreeing not to serve and file financial statements; or

(b) agreeing to a specified amount of support, or to no support.

(9) Revoked.

Documents not to be filed without financial statement

(10) The clerk shall not accept a document for filing without a financial statement if these rules require the document to be filed with a financial statement.

Additional financial information

(11) If a party believes that another party's financial statement does not contain enough information for a full understanding of the other party's financial circumstances,

(a) the party shall ask the other party to give the necessary additional information; and

(b) if the other party does not give it within seven days, the court may, on motion, order the other party to give the information or to serve and file a new financial statement.

Updating financial statement

(12) Before any case conference, motion, settlement conference or trial, each party shall update the information in any financial statement that is more than 30 days old by serving and filing,

(a) a new financial statement; or

(b) an affidavit saying that the information in the last statement has not changed and is still true.

Minor changes

(12.1) If there have been minor changes but no major changes to the information in a party's past statement, the party may serve and file, instead of a new financial statement, an affidavit with details of the changes.

Time for updating

(12.2) The material described in subrules (12) and (12.1) shall be served and filed as follows:

1. For a case conference or settlement conference requested by a party, the requesting party shall serve and file at least seven days before the conference date and the other party shall serve and file at least four days before that date.
2. For a case conference or settlement conference that is not requested by a party, the applicant shall serve and file at least seven days before the conference date and the respondent shall serve and file at least four days before that date.
3. For a motion, the party making the motion shall serve and file at least seven days before the motion date and the other party shall serve and file at least four days before that date.
4. For a trial, the applicant shall serve and file at least seven days before the trial date and the respondent shall serve and file at least four days before that date.

Questioning on financial statement

(13) A party may be questioned under rule 20 on a financial statement provided under this rule, but only after a request for information has been made under clause (11)(a).

Net family property statement

(14) Each party to a property claim under Part I of the *Family Law Act* shall serve and file a net family property statement (Form 13B) or, if the party has already served a net family property statement, an affidavit saying that the information in that statement has not changed and is still true,

(a) not less than seven days before a settlement conference; and

(b) not more than 30 days and not less than seven days before a trial.

Exception, family arbitration claim

(14.1) Subrule (14) does not apply if the property claim arises within a claim under the *Arbitration Act, 1991* or the *Family Law Act* relating to a family arbitration, family arbitration agreement or family arbitration award.

Correcting and updating statement or answer

(15) As soon as a party discovers that information in the party's financial statement or net family property statement or in a response the party gave under this rule is incorrect or incomplete, or that there has been a material change in the information provided, the party shall immediately serve on every other party to the claim and file the correct information or a new statement containing the correct information, together with any documents substantiating it.

Order to file statement

(16) If a party has not served and filed a financial statement or net family property statement or information as required by this rule or an Act, the court may, on motion without notice, order the party to serve and file the document or information and, if it makes that order, shall also order the party to pay costs.

(17) Revoked.

RULE 14: MOTIONS FOR TEMPORARY ORDERS

When to make motion

14. (1) A person who wants any of the following may make a motion:

1. A temporary order for a claim made in an application.
2. Directions on how to carry on the case.
3. A change in a temporary order.

Who may make motion

(2) A motion may be made by a party to the case or by a person with an interest in the case.

Parties to motion

(3) A person who is affected by a motion is also a party, for purposes of the motion only, but this does not apply to a child affected by a motion relating to custody, access, child protection, adoption or child support.

No motion before case conference on substantive issues completed

(4) No notice of motion or supporting evidence may be served and no motion may be heard before a conference dealing with the substantive issues in the case has been completed.

(4.1) Revoked.

Urgency, hardship etc.

(4.2) Subrule (4) does not apply if the court is of the opinion that there is a situation of urgency or hardship or that a case conference is not required for some other reason in the interest of justice.

(5) Revoked.

Other motions

(6) Subrule (4) does not apply to a motion,

(a) to change a temporary order under subrule 25(19) (fraud, mistake, lack of notice);

(b) for a contempt order under rule 31 or an order striking out a document under subrule (22);

(c) for summary judgment under rule 16;

(d) to require the Director of the Family Responsibility Office to refrain from suspending a licence;

(e) to limit or stay a support order, the enforcement of arrears under a support order, or an alternative payment order under the *Family Responsibility and Support Arrears Enforcement Act, 1996*;

(e.1) in a child protection case;

(e.2) made without notice, made on consent, that is unopposed or that is limited to procedural, uncomplicated or unopposed matters (Form 14B);

(e.3) made in an appeal;

(f) for an oral hearing under subrule 32.1(10), 37(8) or 37.1(8); or

(g) to set aside the registration of an interjurisdictional support order made outside Canada.

Motion involving complicated matters

(7) The judge who hears a motion involving complicated matters may,

(a) order that the motion or any part of it be heard as a trial; and

(b) give any directions that are necessary.

Motion by telephone or video conference

(8) A party who wants a motion to be heard by telephone or video conference shall,

(a) obtain an appointment from the clerk for the hearing of the motion;

(b) make the necessary arrangements;

(c) serve a notice of the appointment and arrangements on all other parties, and file it; and

(d) participate in the motion as the notice specifies.

Documents for a motion

(9) A motion, whether made with or without notice,

(a) requires a notice of motion (Form 14) and an affidavit (Form 14A); and

(b) may be supported by additional evidence.

Procedural, uncomplicated or unopposed matters—Motion form

(10) If a motion is limited to procedural, uncomplicated or unopposed matters, the party making the motion may use a motion form (Form 14B) instead of a notice of motion and affidavit.

Response to motion form

(10.1) If a party uses a motion form (Form 14B) and no person served with the motion form serves and files a response within four days after being served, the motion shall be dealt with by the court as an unopposed motion.

Where no reply permitted

(10.2) A party who uses a motion form (Form 14B) and who is served with a response to it may not serve or file a reply.

Motion with notice

(11) A party making a motion with notice shall,

(a) serve the documents mentioned in subrule (9) or (10) on all other parties, not later than four days before the motion date;

(b) file the documents as soon as possible after service, but not later than two days before the motion date; and

(c) file a confirmation (Form 14C) not later than 2 p.m. two days before the motion date.

No late documents

(11.1) No documents for use on the motion may be served or filed after 2 p.m. two days before the motion date.

Motion without notice

(12) A motion may be made without notice if,

(a) the nature or circumstances of the motion make notice unnecessary or not reasonably possible;

(b) there is an immediate danger of a child's removal from Ontario, and the delay involved in serving a notice of motion would probably have serious consequences;

(c) there is an immediate danger to the health or safety of a child or of the party making the motion, and the delay involved in serving a notice of motion would probably have serious consequences; or

(d) service of a notice of motion would probably have serious consequences.

Filing for motion without notice

(13) The documents for use on a motion without notice shall be filed on or before the motion date, unless the court orders otherwise.

Order made on motion without notice

(14) An order made on motion without notice (Form 14D) shall require the matter to come back to the court and, if possible, to the same judge, within 14 days or on a date chosen by the court.

Service of order made without notice

(15) An order made on motion without notice shall be served immediately on all parties affected, together with all documents used on the motion, unless the court orders otherwise.

Withdrawing a motion

(16) A party making a motion may withdraw it in the same way as an application or answer is withdrawn under rule 12.

Evidence on a motion

(17) Evidence on a motion may be given by any one or more of the following methods:

1. An affidavit or other admissible evidence in writing.
2. A transcript of the questions and answers on a questioning under rule 20.
3. With the court's permission, oral evidence.

Affidavit based on personal knowledge

(18) An affidavit for use on a motion shall, as much as possible, contain only information within the personal knowledge of the person signing the affidavit.

Affidavit based on other information

(19) The affidavit may also contain information that the person learned from someone else, but only if,

(a) the source of the information is identified by name and the affidavit states that the person signing it believes the information is true; and

(b) in addition, if the motion is a contempt motion under rule 31, the information is not likely to be disputed.

Restrictions on evidence

(20) The following restrictions apply to evidence for use on a motion, unless the court orders otherwise:

1. The party making the motion shall serve all the evidence in support of the motion with the notice of motion.
2. The party responding to the motion shall then serve all the evidence in response.
3. The party making the motion may then serve evidence replying to any new matters raised by the evidence served by the party responding to the motion.
4. No other evidence may be used.

No motions without court's permission

(21) If a party tries to delay the case or add to its costs or in any other way to abuse the court's process by making numerous motions without merit, the court may order the party not to make any other motions in the case without the court's permission.

(22), (23) Revoked.

Motion relating to family arbitration

(24) A party who wishes to make a claim under the *Arbitration Act, 1991* or the *Family Law Act* relating to a family arbitration, family arbitration agreement or family arbitration award that must or may be commenced by way of a motion may do so under this rule, even if the order being sought is a final order and, for the purpose, this rule applies with the following and any other necessary modifications:

1. In addition to the documents referred to in subrule (9) or (10), the motion also requires,
   i. copies of the certificates of independent legal advice required by the *Family Law Act* for the parties,
   ii. a copy of the family arbitration agreement, and
   iii. if an award has been made, the original award or a certified copy.
2. The documents referred to in subparagraphs 1 i, ii and iii shall be served and filed in accordance with subrule (11).
3. In the case of a motion to enforce a family arbitration award under section 59.8 of the *Family Law Act*, subrules (12) to (15) do not apply.

RULE 15: MOTIONS TO CHANGE A FINAL ORDER OR AGREEMENT

Definition

15. (1) In this rule,

"assignee" means an agency or person to whom a support order or agreement that is the subject of a motion under this rule is assigned under the *Family Law Act* or the *Divorce Act* (Canada).

Application

(2) Subject to subrule (3), this rule only applies to a motion to change,

(a) a final order; or

(b) an agreement for support filed under section 35 of the *Family Law Act*.

Exception

(3) This rule does not apply to a motion or application to change an order made under the *Child and Family Services Act*, other than a final order made under section 57.1 of that Act.

Place of motion

(4) Rule 5 (where a case starts) applies to a motion to change a final order or agreement as if the motion were a new case.

Motion to change

(5) Subject to subrules (17) and (18), a party who wants to ask the court to change a final order or agreement shall serve and file,

(a) a motion to change (Form 15); and

(b) a change information form (Form 15A), with all required attachments.

Claim for custody or access

(5.1) If the motion includes a claim for custody of or access to a child, the documents referred to in subrule (5) shall be accompanied by the applicable documents referred to in rule 35.1.

Service to include blank forms

(6) The party making the motion shall serve on the other party a blank response to motion to change (Form 15B) and a blank consent motion to change (Form 15C) together with the documents referred to in subrule (5).

Special service

(7) The documents referred to in subrules (5), (5.1) and (6) shall be served by special service (subrule 6(3)), and not by regular service.

Exception

(8) Despite subrule (7), service on the persons mentioned in subrule 8(6) (officials, agencies, etc.) may be made by regular service.

Response or consent to motion

(9) The following rules apply to a party who is served with a motion to change a final order or agreement:

1. If the party does not agree to the change or if the party wants to ask the court to make an additional or a different change to the final order or agreement, the party shall serve and file a response to motion to change (Form 15B), with all required attachments, within the time set out in clause (10)(a) or (b), as the case may be.
2. If the party agrees to the change or if the parties agree to a different change, the party shall complete the applicable portions of the consent motion to change (Form 15C) and shall, within the time set out in clause (10)(a) or (b), as the case may be,
    i. return a signed copy of the consent motion to change to the party making the motion, and
    ii. provide a copy of the signed consent motion to change to the assignee, if any.

Same

(10) The documents referred to in paragraphs 1 and 2 of subrule (9) shall be served and filed or returned and provided,

(a) no later than 30 days after the party responding to the motion receives the motion to change and the supporting documents, if that party resides in Canada or the United States of America; or

(b) no later than 60 days after the party responding to the motion receives the motion to change and the supporting documents, in any other case.

Service on assignee required

(11) In a motion to change a final order or agreement that has been assigned to an assignee, a party shall, in serving documents under subrule (5) or paragraph 1 of subrule (9), serve the documents on the assignee as if the assignee were also a party.

Assignee may become party

(12) On serving and filing a notice claiming a financial interest in the motion, an assignee becomes a respondent to the extent of the financial interest.

Sanctions if assignee not served

(13) If an assignee is not served as required by subrule (11), the following rules apply:

1. The court may at any time, on motion by the assignee with notice to the other parties, set aside the changed order to the extent that it affects the assignee's financial interest.
2. The party who asked for the change has the burden of proving that the changed order should not be set aside.
3. If the changed order is set aside, the assignee is entitled to full recovery of its costs of the motion to set aside, unless the court orders otherwise.

No response or consent

(14) The consequences set out in paragraphs 1 to 4 of subrule 1(8.4) apply, with necessary modifications, if a party does not serve and file a response to motion to change (Form 15B) or return a consent motion to change (Form 15C) to the party making the motion as required under subrule (9).

Request for order

(15) If a party does not serve and file a response to motion to change (Form 15B) or return a consent motion to change (Form 15C) to the party making the motion as required under subrule (9), or if the party's response is struck out by an order, the party making the motion to change may file a motion form (Form 14B) asking that the court make the order requested in the materials filed by the party, unless an assignee has filed a notice of financial interest in the motion and opposes the change.

Consent to motion

(16) If a party returns to the party making the motion a consent motion to change (Form 15C) in accordance with subparagraph 2 i of subrule (9), the party making the motion shall complete and file the consent motion to change and, unless any assignee refuses to consent to the change being requested, the party making the motion shall file with the consent motion to change,

(a) a motion form (Form 14B) asking that the court make the order described in the consent motion to change;

(b) five copies of a draft order;

(c) a stamped envelope addressed to each party and to the assignee, if any; and

(d) if the order that is agreed on relates in whole or in part to a support obligation,

(i) a support deduction order information form prescribed under the *Family Responsibility and Support Arrears Enforcement Act, 1996*, and

(ii) a draft support deduction order.

Motion to change on consent

(17) Subject to subrule (18), if the parties to a final order or agreement want to ask the court to change the final order or agreement and the parties and any assignee agree to the change, the parties shall file,

(a) a change information form (Form 15A), with all required attachments;

(b) a consent motion to change (Form 15C);

(c) a motion form (Form 14B) asking that the court make the order described in the consent motion to change;

(d) five copies of a draft order;

(e) a stamped envelope addressed to each party and to the assignee, if any; and

(f) if the order that is agreed on relates in whole or in part to a support obligation,

(i) a support deduction order information form prescribed under the *Family Responsibility and Support Arrears Enforcement Act, 1996*, and

(ii) a draft support deduction order.

Motion to change on consent—Child support only

(18) If the parties to a final order or agreement want to ask the court to change the final order or agreement in relation only to a child support obligation, and the parties and any assignee agree to the change, the parties shall file,

(a) a consent motion to change child support (Form 15D), with all required attachments;

(b) five copies of a draft order;

(c) a stamped envelope addressed to each party and to the assignee, if any;

(d) a support deduction order information form prescribed under the *Family Responsibility and Support Arrears Enforcement Act, 1996*; and

(e) a draft support deduction order.

Consent after response filed

(19) If, at any time after a party has served and filed a response under paragraph 1 of subrule (9) and before the motion to change is heard, the parties and any assignee agree to an order that changes the final order or agreement that is the subject of the motion, the parties may proceed on consent by filing,

(a) a consent motion to change (Form 15C);

(b) a motion form (Form 14B) asking that the court make the order described in the consent motion to change;

(c) five copies of a draft order;

(d) a stamped envelope addressed to each party and to the assignee, if any; and

(e) if the order that is agreed on relates in whole or in part to a support obligation,

(i) a support deduction order information form prescribed under the *Family Responsibility and Support Arrears Enforcement Act, 1996*, and

(ii) a draft support deduction order.

Order, agreement to be attached

(20) A copy of any existing order or agreement that deals with custody, access or support shall be attached to every change information form (Form 15A) or consent motion to change child support (Form 15D).

Change not in accordance with child support guidelines

(21) Unless a motion to change a child support order or agreement is proceeding on the consent of the parties and any assignee, if a party asks that an order be made under this rule that is not in accordance with the tables in the applicable child support guidelines, the support recipient and the support payor shall each serve and file the evidence required by the following sections of the applicable child support guidelines, or the evidence that is otherwise necessary to satisfy the court that it should make the order asked for:

1. Section 4 (income over $150,000).
2. Section 5 (step-parent).
3. Section 7 (special expenses).
4. Section 8 (split custody).
5. Section 9 (shared custody).
6. Section 10 (undue hardship).
7. Section 21 (income and financial information).

Affidavit may be filed

(22) A party or parties who want to ask the court to change a final order or agreement may, instead of using a change information form (Form 15A), use an affidavit containing evidence necessary to satisfy the court that it should make the order asked for and, in that case, these rules apply to the affidavit as if it were a change information form.

Same

(23) A party who responds to a motion to change a final order or agreement by serving and filing a response to motion to change (Form 15B) may use an affidavit to provide evidence supporting his or her position instead of relying on the relevant portions of the form to provide the evidence or in addition to those portions of the form and, in that case, the affidavit is deemed to be part of the form.

Requirements for affidavit

(24) Subrules 14(18) and (19) apply with necessary modifications to an affidavit provided in accordance with subrule (22) or (23).

Powers of court—Motion on consent or unopposed

(25) If a motion to change a final order or agreement proceeds on the consent of the parties and any assignee or is unopposed, the clerk shall present the filed materials to a judge and the judge may,

(a) make the order asked for;

(b) require one or both parties to file further material;

or

(c) require one or both parties to come to court.

Powers of court—Directions

(26) If the court is of the opinion that a motion, whether proceeding on consent or not, cannot be properly dealt with because of the material filed, because of the matters in dispute or for any other reason, the court may give directions, including directions for a trial.

Application of subrule 14(21)

(27) Subrule 14(21) applies with necessary modifications to a motion to change a final order or agreement.

Motion under rule 14

(28) A motion under rule 14 may be made on a motion to change a final order or agreement.

Access to listed documents

(29) Subrule 19(2) (access to listed documents) applies with necessary modifications to a document mentioned in a form or affidavit used under this rule.

RULE 16: SUMMARY JUDGMENT

When available

16. (1) After the respondent has served an answer or after the time for serving an answer has expired, a party may make a motion for summary judgment for a final order without a trial on all or part of any claim made or any defence presented in the case.

Available in any case except divorce

(2) A motion for summary judgment under subrule (1) may be made in any case (including a child protection case) that does not include a divorce claim.

Divorce claim

(3) In a case that includes a divorce claim, the procedure provided in rule 36 (divorce) for an uncontested divorce may be used, or the divorce claim may be split from the rest of the case under subrule 12(6).

Evidence required

(4) The party making the motion shall serve an affidavit or other evidence that sets out specific facts showing that there is no genuine issue requiring a trial.

Evidence of responding party

(4.1) In response to the affidavit or other evidence served by the party making the motion, the party responding to the motion may not rest on mere allegations or denials but shall set out, in an affidavit or other evidence, specific facts showing that there is a genuine issue for trial.

Evidence not from personal knowledge

(5) If a party's evidence is not from a person who has personal knowledge of the facts in dispute, the court may draw conclusions unfavourable to the party.

No issue for trial

(6) If there is no genuine issue requiring a trial of a claim or defence, the court shall make a final order accordingly.

Only issue amount of entitlement

(7) If the only genuine issue is the amount to which a party is entitled, the court shall order a trial to decide the amount.

Only issue question of law

(8) If the only genuine issue is a question of law, the court shall decide the issue and make a final order accordingly.

Order giving directions

(9) If the court does not make a final order, or makes an order for a trial of an issue, the court may also,

(a) specify what facts are not in dispute, state the issues and give directions about how and when the case will go to trial (in which case the order governs how the trial proceeds, unless the trial judge orders otherwise to prevent injustice);

(b) give directions; and

(c) impose conditions (for example, require a party to pay money into court as security, or limit a party's pretrial disclosure).

Costs of unsuccessful motion

(10) If the party who made the motion has no success on the motion, the court shall decide the amount of the other party's costs of the motion on a full recovery basis and order the party who made the motion to pay them immediately, unless the motion was justified, although unsuccessful.

Costs—Bad faith

(11) If a party has acted in bad faith, the court shall decide the costs of the motion on a full recovery basis and shall order the party to pay them immediately.

Motion for summary decision on legal issue

(12) The court may, on motion,

(a) decide a question of law before trial, if the decision may dispose of all or part of the case, substantially shorten the trial or save substantial costs;

(b) strike out an application, answer or reply because it sets out no reasonable claim or defence in law; or

(c) dismiss or suspend a case because,

(i) the court has no jurisdiction over it,

(ii) a party has no legal capacity to carry on the case,

(iii) there is another case going on between the same parties about the same matter, or

(iv) the case is a waste of time, a nuisance or an abuse of the court process.

Evidence on motion for summary decision of legal issue

(13) On a motion under subrule (12), evidence is admissible only if the parties consent or the court gives permission.

RULE 17: CONFERENCES

Conferences in defended cases

17. (1) Subject to subrule (1.1), in each case in which an answer is filed, a judge shall conduct at least one conference.

Exception, case conference optional in child protection case

(1.1) In a child protection case, a case conference may be conducted if,

(a) a party requests it; or

(b) the court considers it appropriate.

Undefended cases

(2) If no answer is filed,

(a) the clerk shall, on request, schedule a case conference or set a date for an uncontested trial or, in an uncontested divorce case, prepare the documents for a judge; and

(b) a settlement conference or trial management conference shall be conducted only if the court orders it.

Motions to change final order or agreement

(3) Subrule (1) applies, with necessary changes, to a motion to change a final order or agreement under rule 15, unless the motion is proceeding on the consent of the parties and any assignee or is unopposed.

Purposes of case conference

(4) The purposes of a case conference include,

(a) exploring the chances of settling the case;

(b) identifying the issues that are in dispute and those that are not in dispute;

(c) exploring ways to resolve the issues that are in dispute;

(d) ensuring disclosure of the relevant evidence;

(d.1) identifying any issues relating to any expert evidence or reports on which the parties intend to rely at trial;

(e) noting admissions that may simplify the case;

(f) setting the date for the next step in the case;

(g) setting a specific timetable for the steps to be taken in the case before it comes to trial;

(h) organizing a settlement conference, or holding one if appropriate; and

(i) giving directions with respect to any intended motion, including the preparation of a specific timetable for the exchange of material for the motion and ordering the filing of summaries of argument, if appropriate.

Case conference notice

(4.1) A party who asks for a case conference shall serve and file a case conference notice (Form 17).

Purposes of settlement conference

(5) The purposes of a settlement conference include,

(a) exploring the chances of settling the case;

(b) settling or narrowing the issues in dispute;

(c) ensuring disclosure of the relevant evidence;

(c.1) settling or narrowing any issues relating to any expert evidence or reports on which the parties intend to rely at trial;

(d) noting admissions that may simplify the case;

(e) if possible, obtaining a view of how the court might decide the case;

(f) considering any other matter that may help in a quick and just conclusion of the case;

(g) if the case is not settled, identifying the witnesses and other evidence to be presented at trial, estimating the time needed for trial and scheduling the case for trial; and

(h) organizing a trial management conference, or holding one if appropriate.

Purposes of trial management conference

(6) The purposes of a trial management conference include,

(a) exploring the chances of settling the case;

(b) arranging to receive evidence by a written report, an agreed statement of facts, an affidavit or another method, if appropriate;

(c) deciding how the trial will proceed;

(c.1) exploring the use of expert evidence or reports at trial, including the timing requirements for service and filing of experts' reports;

(d) ensuring that the parties know what witnesses will testify and what other evidence will be presented at trial;

(e) estimating the time needed for trial; and

(f) setting the trial date, if this has not already been done.

Combined conference

(7) At any time on the direction of a judge, part or all of a case conference, settlement conference and trial management conference may be combined.

Orders at conference

(8) At a case conference, settlement conference or trial management conference the judge may, if it is appropriate to do so,

(a) make an order for document disclosure (rule 19), questioning (rule 20) or filing of summaries of argument on a motion, set the times for events in the case or give directions for the next step or steps in the case;

(a.0.1) make an order respecting the use of expert witness evidence at trial or the service and filing of experts' reports;

(a.1) order that the evidence of a witness at trial be given by affidavit;

(b) make an order requiring one or more parties to attend,

(i) a mandatory information program,

(ii) a case conference or settlement conference conducted by a person named under subrule (9),

(iii) an intake meeting with a court-affiliated mediation service, or

(iv) a program offered through any other available community service or resource;

(b.1) if notice has been served, make a final order or any temporary order, including any of the following temporary orders to facilitate the preservation of the rights of the parties until a further agreement or order is made:

(i) an order relating to the designation of beneficiaries under a policy of life insurance, registered retirement savings plan, trust, pension, annuity or a similar financial instrument,

(ii) an order preserving assets generally or particularly,

(iii) an order prohibiting the concealment or destruction of documents or property,

(iv) an order requiring an accounting of funds under the control of one of the parties,

(v) an order preserving the health and medical insurance coverage for one of the parties and the children of the relationship, and

(vi) an order continuing the payment of periodic amounts required to preserve an asset or a benefit to one of the parties and the children;

(c) make an unopposed order or an order on consent; and

(d) on consent, refer any issue for alternative dispute resolution.

Conferences with a non-judge

(9) A case conference or settlement conference may be conducted by a person who has been named by the appropriate senior judge, unless a party requests a conference with a judge.

Settlement conference with judge before case set for trial

(10) A case shall not be scheduled for trial unless,

(a) a judge has conducted a settlement conference; or

(b) a judge has ordered that the case be scheduled for trial.

(11) Revoked.

When conferences optional

(12) A case conference, settlement conference or trial management conference is not required, but may be held at a party's request or on a judge's direction in the following circumstances:

1. In an enforcement.
2. In a request to enforce a family arbitration award under rule 32.1.

Parties to serve briefs

(13) For each conference, each party shall serve and file a case conference brief (Form 17A or Form 17B), settlement conference brief (Form 17C or Form 17D) or trial management conference brief (Form 17E), as appropriate.

Case conference brief in child protection case

(13.0.1) In a child protection case, a case conference brief shall be served and filed only if a case conference is being held under subrule (1.1).

Time for service of briefs

(13.1) The party requesting the conference (or, if the conference is not requested by a party, the applicant) shall serve and file a brief not later than seven days before the date scheduled for the conference and the other party shall do so not later than four days before that date.

Parties to confirm attendance

(14) Not later than 2 p.m. two days before the date scheduled for the conference, each party shall file a confirmation (Form 14C).

No late briefs

(14.1) No brief or other document for use at the conference may be served or filed after 2 p.m. two days before the date scheduled for the conference.

Parties and lawyers to come to conference

(15) The following shall come to each conference:

1. The parties, unless the court orders otherwise.
2. For each represented party, the lawyer with full knowledge of and authority in the case.

Participation by telephone or video conference

(16) With permission obtained in advance from the judge who is to conduct a conference, a party or lawyer may participate in the conference by telephone or video conference.

Setting up telephone or video conference

(17) A party or lawyer who has permission to participate by telephone or video conference shall,

(a) make the necessary arrangements;

(b) serve a notice of the arrangements on all other parties and file it; and

(c) participate in the conference as the notice specifies.

Costs of adjourned conference

(18) If a conference is adjourned because a party is not prepared, has not served the required brief, has not made the required disclosure or has otherwise not followed these rules, the judge shall,

(a) order the party to pay the costs of the conference immediately;

(b) decide the amount of the costs; and

(c) give any directions that are needed.

Conference agreement

(19) No agreement reached at a conference is effective until it is signed by the parties, witnessed and, in a case involving a special party, approved by the court.

Agreement filed in continuing record

(20) The agreement shall be filed as part of the continuing record, unless the court orders otherwise.

Continuing record, trial management conference briefs

(21) Trial management conference briefs form part of the continuing record.

Continuing record, case conference briefs

(22) Case conference briefs do not form part of the continuing record unless the court orders otherwise and shall be returned at the end of the conference to the parties who filed them or be destroyed by court staff immediately after the conference.

Deletions from case conference brief included in record

(22.1) If the court orders that a case conference brief form part of the continuing record, that portion of the brief that deals with settlement of the case shall be deleted.

Continuing record, settlement conference briefs

(22.2) Settlement conference briefs do not form part of the continuing record and shall be returned at the end of the conference to the parties who filed them or be destroyed by the court staff immediately after the conference.

Confidentiality of settlement conference

(23) No brief or evidence prepared for a settlement conference and no statement made at a settlement conference shall be disclosed to any other judge, except in,

(a) an agreement reached at a settlement conference; or

(b) an order.

Settlement conference judge cannot hear issue

(24) A judge who conducts a settlement conference about an issue shall not hear the issue, except as subrule (25) provides.

Exception, child protection case

(25) In a child protection case, if a finding that the child is in need of protection is made without a trial and a trial is needed to determine which order should be made under section 57 of the *Child and Family Services Act*, any judge who has not conducted a settlement conference on that issue may conduct the trial.

RULE 18: OFFERS TO SETTLE

Definition

18. (1) In this rule,

"offer" means an offer to settle one or more claims in a case, motion, appeal or enforcement, and includes a counter-offer.

Application

(2) This rule applies to an offer made at any time, even before the case is started.

Making an offer

(3) A party may serve an offer on any other party.

Offer to be signed by party and lawyer

(4) An offer shall be signed personally by the party making it and also by the party's lawyer, if any.

Withdrawing an offer

(5) A party who made an offer may withdraw it by serving a notice of withdrawal, at any time before the offer is accepted.

Time-limited offer

(6) An offer that is not accepted within the time set out in the offer is considered to have been withdrawn.

Offer expires when court begins to give decision

(7) An offer may not be accepted after the court begins to give a decision that disposes of a claim dealt with in the offer.

Confidentiality of offer

(8) The terms of an offer,

(a) shall not be mentioned in any document filed in the continuing record; and

(b) shall not be mentioned to the judge hearing the claim dealt with in the offer, until the judge has dealt with all the issues in dispute except costs.

Accepting an offer

(9) The only valid way of accepting an offer is by serving an acceptance on the party who made the offer, at any time before,

(a) the offer is withdrawn; or

(b) the court begins to give a decision that disposes of a claim dealt with in the offer.

Offer remains open despite rejection or counter-offer

(10) A party may accept an offer in accordance with subrule (9) even if the party has previously rejected the offer or made a counter-offer.

Costs not dealt with in offer

(11) If an accepted offer does not deal with costs, either party is entitled to ask the court for costs.

Court approval, offer involving special party

(12) A special party may make, withdraw and accept an offer, but another party's acceptance of a special party's offer and a special party's acceptance of another party's offer are not binding on the special party until the court approves.

Failure to carry out terms of accepted offer

(13) If a party to an accepted offer does not carry out the terms of the offer, the other party may,

(a) make a motion to turn the parts of the offer within the court's jurisdiction into an order; or

(b) continue the case as if the offer had never been accepted.

Costs consequences of failure to accept offer

(14) A party who makes an offer is, unless the court orders otherwise, entitled to costs to the date the offer was served and full recovery of costs from that date, if the following conditions are met:

1. If the offer relates to a motion, it is made at least one day before the motion date.
2. If the offer relates to a trial or the hearing of a step other than a motion, it is made at least seven days before the trial or hearing date.

3. The offer does not expire and is not withdrawn before the hearing starts.
4. The offer is not accepted.
5. The party who made the offer obtains an order that is as favourable as or more favourable than the offer.

Costs consequences—Burden of proof

(15) The burden of proving that the order is as favourable as or more favourable than the offer to settle is on the party who claims the benefit of subrule (14).

Costs—Discretion of court

(16) When the court exercises its discretion over costs, it may take into account any written offer to settle, the date it was made and its terms, even if subrule (14) does not apply.

RULE 19: DOCUMENT DISCLOSURE

Affidavit listing documents

19. (1) Subject to subrule (1.1), every party shall, within 10 days after another party's request, give the other party an affidavit listing every document that is,

(a) relevant to any issue in the case; and

(b) in the party's control, or available to the party on request.

Exceptions

(1.1) Subrule (1) does not apply to the Office of the Children's Lawyer or to children's aid societies.

Access to listed documents

(2) The other party is entitled, on request,

(a) to examine any document listed in the affidavit, unless it is protected by a legal privilege; and

(b) to receive, at the party's own expense at the legal aid rate, a copy of any document that the party is entitled to examine under clause (a).

Access to documents mentioned in court papers

(3) Subrule (2) also applies, with necessary changes, to a document mentioned in a party's application, answer, reply, notice of motion, affidavit, financial statement or net family property statement.

Documents protected by legal privilege

(4) If a party claims that a document is protected by a legal privilege, the court may, on motion, examine it and decide the issue.

Use of privileged documents

(5) A party who claims that a document is protected by a legal privilege may use it at trial only,

(a) if the other party has been allowed to examine the document and been supplied with a copy, free of charge, at least 30 days before the settlement conference; or

(b) on the conditions the trial judge considers appropriate, including an adjournment if necessary.

Documents of subsidiary or affiliated corporation

(6) The court may, on motion, order a party to give another party an affidavit listing the documents that are,

(a) relevant to any issue in the case; and

(b) in the control of, or available on request to a corporation that is controlled, directly or indirectly, by the party or by another corporation that the party controls directly or indirectly.

Documents of Office of the Children's Lawyer or children's aid society

(6.1) The court may, on motion, order the Office of the Children's Lawyer or a children's aid society to give another party an affidavit listing the documents that are,

(a) relevant to any issue in the case; and

(b) in the control of, or available on request to, the Office of the Children's Lawyer or the children's aid society.

Access to listed documents

(7) Subrule (2) also applies, with necessary changes, to any document listed in an affidavit ordered under subrule (6) or (6.1).

Documents omitted from affidavit or found later

(8) A party who, after serving an affidavit required under subrule (1), (6) or (6.1), finds a document that should have been listed in it, or finds that the list is not correct or not complete, shall immediately serve on the other party a new affidavit listing the correct information.

Access to additional documents

(9) The other party is entitled, on request,

(a) to examine any document listed in an affidavit served under subrule (8), unless it is protected by a legal privilege; and

(b) to receive, free of charge, a copy of any document that the party is entitled to examine under clause (a).

Failure to follow rule 19 or obey order

(10) If a party does not follow this rule or obey an order made under this rule, the court may, in addition to any power to make an order under subrule 1(8) or (8.1),

(a) order the party to give another party an affidavit, let the other party examine a document or supply the other party with a copy free of charge;

(b) order that a document favourable to the party's case may not be used except with the court's permission; or

(c) order that the party is not entitled to obtain disclosure under these rules until the party follows the rule or obeys the order.

Document in non-party's control

(11) If a document is in a non-party's control, or is available only to the non-party, and is not protected by a legal privilege, and it would be unfair to a party to go on with the case

without the document, the court may, on motion with notice served on every party and served on the non-party by special service,

(a) order the non-party to let the party examine the document and to supply the party with a copy at the legal aid rate; and

(b) order that a copy be prepared and used for all purposes of the case instead of the original.

RULE 20: QUESTIONING A WITNESS AND DISCLOSURE

Questioning—Procedure

20. (1) Questioning under this rule shall take place orally under oath or affirmation.

Cross-examination

(2) The right to question a person includes the right to cross-examine.

Child protection case—Available as of right

(3) In a child protection case, a party is entitled to obtain information from another party about any issue in the case,

(a) by questioning the other party, in which case the party shall serve the other party with a summons to witness (Form 23) by special service in accordance with subrule 6(4); or

(b) by affidavit or by another method, in which case the party shall serve the other party with a request for information (Form 20).

Other cases—Consent or order

(4) In a case other than a child protection case, a party is entitled to obtain information from another party about any issue in the case,

(a) with the other party's consent; or

(b) by an order under subrule (5).

Order for questioning or disclosure

(5) The court may, on motion, order that a person (whether a party or not) be questioned by a party or disclose information by affidavit or by another method about any issue in the case, if the following conditions are met:

1. It would be unfair to the party who wants the questioning or disclosure to carry on with the case without it.
2. The information is not easily available by any other method.
3. The questioning or disclosure will not cause unacceptable delay or undue expense.

Questioning special party

(6) If a person to be questioned is a special party, the court may, on motion, order that someone else be questioned in addition to or in place of the person.

Questioning about affidavit or net family property statement

(7) The court may make an order under subrule (5) that a person be questioned or disclose details about information in an affidavit or net family property statement.

Questioning or disclosure—Preconditions

(8) A party who wants to question a person or obtain information by affidavit or by another method may do so only if the party,

(a) has served and filed any answer, financial statement or net family property statement that these rules require; and

(b) promises in writing not to serve or file any further material for the next step in the case, except in reply to the answers or information obtained.

Notice and summons to non-party

(9) The court may make an order under this rule affecting a non-party only if the non-party has been served with the notice of motion, a summons to witness (Form 23) and the witness fee required by subrule 23(4), all by special service (subrules 6(3) and (4)).

Penalty for failure to obey summons

(10) Subrule 23(7) (failure to obey summons to witness) applies, with necessary changes, if a person summoned under subrule (9) fails to obey the summons.

Place of questioning

(11) The questioning shall take place in the municipality in which the person to be questioned lives, unless that person and the party who wants to do the questioning agree to hold it in another municipality.

Other arrangements for questioning

(12) If the person to be questioned and the party who wants to do the questioning do not agree on one or more of the following matters, the court shall, on motion, make an order to decide the matter:

1. The date and time for the questioning.
2. The person responsible for recording the questioning.
3. The method for recording the questioning.
4. Payment of the expenses of the person to be questioned, if a non-party.

Notice to parties

(13) The parties shall, not later than three days before the questioning, be served with notice of the name of the person to be questioned and the address, date and time of the questioning.

Questioning person outside Ontario

(14) If a person to be questioned lives outside Ontario and will not come to Ontario for questioning, the court may decide,

(a) the date, time and place for the questioning;

(b) how much notice the person should be given;

(c) the person before whom the questioning will be held;

(d) the amount of the witness fee to be paid to the person to be questioned;

(e) the method for recording the questioning;

(f) where necessary, that the clerk shall issue,

(i) an authorization to a commissioner (Form 20A) who is to supervise the questioning outside Ontario, and

(ii) a letter of request (Form 20B) to the appropriate court or authorities outside Ontario, asking for their assistance in getting the person to be questioned to come before the commissioner; and

(g) any other related matter.

Commissioner's duties

(15) A commissioner authorized under subrule (14) shall,

(a) supervise the questioning according to the terms of the court's authorization, these rules and Ontario's law of evidence, unless the law of the place where the questioning is to be held requires some other manner of questioning;

(b) make and keep a copy of the record of the questioning and, if possible, of the exhibits, if any;

(c) deliver the original record, any exhibits and the authorization to the clerk who issued it; and

(d) notify the party who asked for the questioning that the record has been delivered to the clerk.

Order to bring documents or things

(16) An order for questioning and a summons to witness may also require the person to bring any document or thing that is,

(a) relevant to any issue in the case; and

(b) in the person's control or available to the person on request.

Other rules apply

(17) Subrules 19(2), (4) and (5) (right to examine document and obtain copy, documents protected by legal privilege, use of privileged documents) apply, with necessary changes, to the documents mentioned in the order.

Scope of questions

(18) A person to be questioned may be asked about,

(a) the names of persons who might reasonably be expected to know about the claims in the case and, with the court's permission, their addresses;

(b) the names of the witnesses whom a party intends to call at trial and, with the court's permission, their addresses;

(c) the names, addresses, findings, conclusions and opinions of expert witnesses whom a party intends to call or on whose reports the party intends to rely at trial;

(d) if it is relevant to the case, the existence and details of any insurance policy under which the insurance company may be required to pay all or part of an order for the payment of money in the case or to pay back to a party money that the party has paid under an order; and

(e) any other matter in dispute in the case.

Refusal to answer question

(19) If a person being questioned refuses to answer a question,

(a) the court may, on motion,

(i) decide whether the question is proper,

(ii) give directions for the person's return to the questioning, and

(iii) make a contempt order against the person; and

(b) if the person is a party or is questioned on behalf or in place of a party, the party shall not use the information that was refused as evidence in the case, unless the court gives permission under subrule (20).

Court's permission

(20) The court shall give permission unless the use of the information would cause harm to another party or an unacceptable delay in the trial, and may impose any appropriate conditions on the permission, including an adjournment if necessary.

Duty to correct or update answers

(21) A person who has been questioned or who has provided information in writing by affidavit or by another method and who finds that an answer or information given was incorrect or incomplete, or is no longer correct or complete, shall immediately provide the correct and complete information in writing to all parties.

Lawyer answering

(22) If there is no objection, questions may be answered by the lawyer for a person being questioned, and the answer shall be taken as the person's own answer unless the person corrects or changes it before the questioning ends.

Method for recording questioning

(23) All the questions and answers at a questioning shall be recorded electronically or manually.

Obligation to keep information confidential

(24) When a party obtains evidence under this rule, rule 13 (financial statements) or rule 19 (document disclosure), the party and the party's lawyer may use the evidence and any information obtained from it only for the purposes of the case in which the evidence was obtained, subject to the exceptions in subrule (25).

Use of information permitted

(25) Evidence and any information obtained from it may be used for other purposes,

(a) if the person who gave the evidence consents;
(b) if the evidence is filed with the court, given at a hearing or referred to at a hearing;
(c) to impeach the testimony of a witness in another case; or
(d) in a later case between the same parties or their successors, if the case in which the evidence was obtained was withdrawn or dismissed.

Court may lift obligation of confidentiality

(26) The court may, on motion, give a party permission to disclose evidence or information obtained from it if the interests of justice outweigh any harm that would result to the party who provided the evidence.

RULE 20.1: EXPERTS

Duty of expert

20.1 (1) It is the duty of every expert who provides evidence in relation to a case under these rules,

(a) to provide opinion evidence that is fair, objective and non-partisan;
(b) to provide opinion evidence that is related only to matters that are within the expert's area of expertise; and
(c) to provide such additional assistance as the court may reasonably require to determine a matter in issue.

Duty prevails

(2) In the case of an expert engaged by or on behalf of a party, the duty in subrule (1) prevails over any obligation owed by the expert to that party.

Court appointed experts

(3) The court may, on motion or on its own initiative, appoint one or more independent experts to inquire into and report on any question of fact or opinion relevant to an issue in a case.

Expert to be named

(4) An order under subrule (3) appointing an expert shall name the expert and, where possible, the expert shall be a person agreed on by the parties.

Instructions

(5) An order under subrule (3) appointing an expert shall contain the instructions to be given to the expert, and the court may make any further orders that it considers necessary to enable the expert to carry out the instructions.

Fees and expenses

(6) The court shall require the parties to pay the fees and expenses of an expert appointed under subrule (3), and shall specify the proportions or amounts of the fees and expenses that each party is required to pay.

Security

(7) If a motion by a party for the appointment of an expert under subrule (3) is opposed, the court may, as a condition of making the appointment, require the party seeking the appointment to give such security for the expert's fees and expenses as is just.

Serious financial hardship

(8) The court may relieve a party from responsibility for payment of any of the expert's fees and expenses, if the court is satisfied that payment would cause serious financial hardship to the party.

Report

(9) The expert shall prepare a report of the results of his or her inquiry, and shall,

(a) file the report with the clerk of the court; and
(b) provide a copy of the report to each of the parties.

Content of report

(10) A report provided by an expert shall contain the following information:

1. The expert's name, address and area of expertise.
2. The expert's qualifications, including his or her employment and educational experiences in his or her area of expertise.
3. The instructions provided to the expert in relation to the proceeding.
4. The nature of the opinion being sought and each issue in the proceeding to which the opinion relates.
5. The expert's opinion respecting each issue and, where there is a range of opinions given, a summary of the range and the reasons for the expert's own opinion within that range.
6. The expert's reasons for his or her opinion, including,
   i. a description of the factual assumptions on which the opinion is based,
   ii. a description of any research conducted by the expert that led him or her to form the opinion, and
   iii. a list of every document relied on by the expert in forming the opinion.
7. An acknowledgement of expert's duty (Form 20.1) signed by the expert.

Admissibility

(11) The expert's report is admissible in evidence in the case.

Cross-examination

(12) Any party may cross-examine the expert at the trial.

Non-application

(13) For greater certainty, subrules (3) to (12) do not apply in respect of,

(a) appointments of persons by the court under subsection 54(1.2) of the *Child and Family Services Act* or subsection 30(1) of the *Children's Law Reform Act*; or

(b) requests by the court that the Children's Lawyer act under subsection 112(1) of the *Courts of Justice Act*.

RULE 21: REPORT OF CHILDREN'S LAWYER

Report of Children's Lawyer

21. When the Children's Lawyer investigates and reports on custody of or access to a child under section 112 of the *Courts of Justice Act*,

(a) the Children's Lawyer shall first serve notice on the parties and file it;

(b) the parties shall, from the time they are served with the notice, serve the Children's Lawyer with every document in the case that involves the child's custody, access, support, health or education, as if the Children's Lawyer were a party in the case;

(c) the Children's Lawyer has the same rights as a party to document disclosure (rule 19) and questioning witnesses (rule 20) about any matter involving the child's custody, access, support, health or education;

(d) within 90 days after serving the notice under clause (a), the Children's Lawyer shall serve a report on the parties and file it;

(e) within 30 days after being served with the report, a party may serve and file a statement disputing anything in it; and

(f) the trial shall not be held and the court shall not make a final order in the case until the 30 days referred to in clause (e) expire or the parties file a statement giving up their right to that time.

RULE 22: ADMISSION OF FACTS

Meaning of admission that document genuine

22. (1) An admission that a document is genuine is an admission,

(a) if the document is said to be an original, that it was written, signed or sealed as it appears to have been;

(b) if it is said to be a copy, that it is a complete and accurate copy; and

(c) if it is said to be a copy of a document that is ordinarily sent from one person to another (for example, a letter, fax or electronic message), that it was sent as it appears to have been sent and was received by the person to whom it is addressed.

Request to admit

(2) At any time, by serving a request to admit (Form 22) on another party, a party may ask the other party to admit, for purposes of the case only, that a fact is true or that a document is genuine.

Copy of document to be attached

(3) A copy of any document mentioned in the request to admit shall be attached to it, unless the other party already has a copy or it is impractical to attach a copy.

Response required within 20 days

(4) The party on whom the request to admit is served is considered to have admitted, for purposes of the case only, that the fact is true or that the document is genuine, unless the party serves a response (Form 22A) within 20 days,

(a) denying that a particular fact mentioned in the request is true or that a particular document mentioned in the request is genuine; or

(b) refusing to admit that a particular fact mentioned in the request is true or that a particular document mentioned in the request is genuine, and giving the reasons for each refusal.

Withdrawing admission

(5) An admission that a fact is true or that a document is genuine (whether contained in a document served in the case or resulting from subrule (4)), may be withdrawn only with the other party's consent or with the court's permission.

RULE 23: EVIDENCE AND TRIAL

Trial record

23. (1) At least 30 days before the start of the trial, the applicant shall serve and file a trial record containing a table of contents and the following documents:

1. The application, answer and reply, if any.
2. Any agreed statement of facts.
3. If relevant to an issue at trial, financial statements and net family property statements by all parties, completed not more than 30 days before the record is served.

3.1 If the trial involves a claim for custody of or access to a child, the applicable documents referred to in rule 35.1.

4. Any assessment report ordered by the court or obtained by consent of the parties.
5. Any temporary order relating to a matter still in dispute.
6. Any order relating to the trial.
7. The relevant parts of any transcript on which the party intends to rely at trial.
8. Revoked.

Respondent may add to trial record

(2) Not later than seven days before the start of the trial, a respondent may serve, file and add to the trial record any document referred to in subrule (1) that is not already in the trial record.

Summons to witness

(3) A party who wants a witness to give evidence in court or to be questioned and to bring documents or other things shall serve on the witness a summons to witness (Form 23)

by special service in accordance with subrule 6(4), together with the witness fee set out in subrule (4).

Witness fee

(4) A person summoned as a witness shall be paid, for each day that the person is needed in court or to be questioned,

(a) $50 for coming to court or to be questioned;
(b) travel money in the amount of,

(i) $5, if the person lives in the city or town where the person gives evidence,
(ii) 30 cents per kilometre each way, if the person lives elsewhere but within 300 kilometres of the court or place of questioning,
(iii) the cheapest available air fare plus $10 a day for airport parking and 30 cents per kilometre each way from the person's home to the airport and from the airport to the court or place of questioning, if the person lives 300 or more kilometres from the court or place of questioning; and

(c) $100 per night for meals and overnight stay, if the person does not live in the city or town where the trial is held and needs to stay overnight.

Meaning of "city or town"

(4.1) For the purposes of subrule (4), a municipality shall be considered a city or town if it was a city or town on December 31, 2002.

Continuing effect of summons

(5) A summons to witness remains in effect until it is no longer necessary to have the witness present.

Summons for original document

(6) If a document can be proved by a certified copy, a party who wants a witness to bring the original shall not serve a summons on the witness for that purpose without the court's permission.

Failure to obey summons

(7) The court may issue a warrant for arrest (Form 32B) to bring a witness before the court if,

(a) the witness has been served as subrule (3) requires, but has not obeyed the summons; and
(b) it is necessary to have the witness present in court or at a questioning.

Interprovincial summons to witness

(8) A summons to a witness outside Ontario under the *Interprovincial Summonses Act* shall be in Form 23A.

Setting aside summons to witness

(9) The court may, on motion, order that a summons to witness be set aside.

Attendance of a prisoner

(10) If it is necessary to have a prisoner come to court or to be questioned, the court may order (Form 23B) the prisoner's custodian to deliver the prisoner on payment of the fee set out in the regulations under the *Administration of Justice Act*.

Calling opposing party as witness

(11) A party may call the opposing party as a witness and may cross-examine the opposing party.

Attendance of opposing party

(11.1) A party who wishes to call an opposing party as a witness may have the opposing party attend,

(a) by serving a summons under subrule (3) on the opposing party; or
(b) by serving on the opposing party's lawyer, at least 10 days before the start of the trial, a notice of intention to call the opposing party as a witness.

Opposing party disobeying summons

(12) When an opposing party has been served with a summons under subrule (3), the court may make a final order in favour of the party calling the witness, adjourn the case or make any other appropriate order, including a contempt order, if the opposing party,

(a) does not come to or remain in court as required by the summons; or
(b) refuses to be sworn or to affirm, to answer any proper question or to bring any document or thing named in the summons.

Reading opposing party's answers into evidence

(13) An answer or information given under rule 20 (questioning) by an opposing party may be read into evidence at trial if it is otherwise proper evidence, even if the opposing party has already testified at trial.

Reading other person's answers into evidence

(14) Subrule (13) also applies, with necessary changes, to an answer or information given by a person questioned on behalf of or in place of an opposing party, unless the trial judge orders otherwise.

Using answers—Special circumstances

(15) Subrule (13) is subject to the following:

1. If the answer or information is being read into evidence to show that a witness's testimony at trial is not to be believed, answers or information given by the witness earlier must be put to the witness as sections 20 and 21 of the *Evidence Act* require.
2. At the request of an opposing party, the trial judge may direct the party reading the answer or information into evidence to read in, as well, any other answer or information that qualifies or explains what the party has read into evidence.
3. A special party's answer or information may be read into evidence only with the trial judge's permission.

Rebutting answers

(16) A party who has read answers or information into evidence at trial may introduce other evidence to rebut the answers or information.

Using answers of witness not available for trial

(17) The trial judge may give a party permission to read into evidence all or part of the answers or information given under rule 20 (questioning) by a person who is unable or unwilling to testify at the trial, but before doing so the judge shall consider,

(a) the importance of the evidence;

(b) the general principle that trial evidence should be given orally in court;

(c) the extent to which the person was cross-examined; and

(d) any other relevant factor.

Taking evidence before trial

(18) The court may order that a witness whose evidence is necessary at trial may give evidence before trial at a place and before a person named in the order, and then may accept the transcript as evidence.

Taking evidence before trial outside Ontario

(19) If a witness whose evidence is necessary at trial lives outside Ontario, subrules 20(14) and (15) (questioning person outside Ontario, commissioner's duties) apply, with necessary changes.

Evidence by affidavit or electronic recording

(20) The court may allow a witness to give evidence at trial by affidavit or electronic recording if,

(a) the parties consent;

(b) the witness is ill or unavailable to come to court for some other good reason;

(c) the evidence concerns minor or uncontroversial issues; or

(d) it is in the interests of justice to do so.

Direction, evidence by affidavit

(20.1) A direction made at a conference that the evidence of a witness be given by affidavit shall be followed at trial unless the trial judge orders otherwise.

Conditions for use of affidavit or electronic recording

(21) Evidence at trial by affidavit or electronic recording may be used only if,

(a) the use is in accordance with an order under subrule (20);

(b) the evidence is served at least 30 days before the start of the trial; and

(c) the evidence would have been admissible if given by the witness in court.

Affidavit evidence at uncontested trial

(22) At an uncontested trial, evidence by affidavit in Form 14A or Form 23C and, if applicable, Form 35.1 may be used without an order under subrule (20), unless the court directs that oral evidence must be given.

Expert witness reports

(23) A party who wants to call an expert witness at trial shall serve on all other parties a report signed by the expert and containing the information listed in subrule (25),

(a) at least 90 days before the start of the trial; or

(b) in the case of a child protection case, at least 30 days before the start of the trial.

Same, response

(24) A party who wants to call an expert witness at trial to respond to the expert witness of another party shall serve on all other parties a report signed by the expert and containing the information listed in subrule (25),

(a) at least 60 days before the start of the trial; or

(b) in the case of a child protection case, at least 14 days before the start of the trial.

Same, contents

(25) A report provided for the purposes of subrule (1) or (2) shall contain the following information:

1. The expert's name, address and area of expertise.
2. The expert's qualifications and employment and educational experiences in his or her area of expertise.
3. The substance of the expert's proposed evidence.

Supplementary report

(26) Any supplementary expert witness report shall be signed by the expert and served on all other parties,

(a) at least 30 days before the start of the trial; or

(b) in the case of a child protection case, at least 14 days before the start of the trial.

Failure to serve expert witness report

(27) A party who has not followed a requirement under subrule (23), (24), or (26) to serve and file an expert witness report, may not call the expert witness unless the trial judge allows otherwise.

RULE 24: COSTS

Successful party presumed entitled to costs

24. (1) There is a presumption that a successful party is entitled to the costs of a motion, enforcement, case or appeal.

No presumption in child protection case or if party is government agency

(2) The presumption does not apply in a child protection case or to a party that is a government agency.

Court's discretion—Costs for or against government agency

(3) The court has discretion to award costs to or against a party that is a government agency, whether it is successful or unsuccessful.

Successful party who has behaved unreasonably

(4) Despite subrule (1), a successful party who has behaved unreasonably during a case may be deprived of all or part of the party's own costs or ordered to pay all or part of the unsuccessful party's costs.

Decision on reasonableness

(5) In deciding whether a party has behaved reasonably or unreasonably, the court shall examine,

(a) the party's behaviour in relation to the issues from the time they arose, including whether the party made an offer to settle;

(b) the reasonableness of any offer the party made; and

(c) any offer the party withdrew or failed to accept.

Divided success

(6) If success in a step in a case is divided, the court may apportion costs as appropriate.

Absent or unprepared party

(7) If a party does not appear at a step in the case, or appears but is not properly prepared to deal with the issues at that step, the court shall award costs against the party unless the court orders otherwise in the interests of justice.

Bad faith

(8) If a party has acted in bad faith, the court shall decide costs on a full recovery basis and shall order the party to pay them immediately.

Costs caused by fault of lawyer or agent

(9) If a party's lawyer or agent has run up costs without reasonable cause or has wasted costs, the court may, on motion or on its own initiative, after giving the lawyer or agent an opportunity to be heard,

(a) order that the lawyer or agent shall not charge the client fees or disbursements for work specified in the order, and order the lawyer or agent to repay money that the client has already paid toward costs;

(b) order the lawyer or agent to repay the client any costs that the client has been ordered to pay another party;

(c) order the lawyer or agent personally to pay the costs of any party; and

(d) order that a copy of an order under this subrule be given to the client.

Costs to be decided at each step

(10) Promptly after each step in the case, the judge or other person who dealt with that step shall decide in a summary manner who, if anyone, is entitled to costs, and set the amount of costs.

Factors in costs

(11) A person setting the amount of costs shall consider,

(a) the importance, complexity or difficulty of the issues;

(b) the reasonableness or unreasonableness of each party's behaviour in the case;

(c) the lawyer's rates;

(d) the time properly spent on the case, including conversations between the lawyer and the party or witnesses, drafting documents and correspondence, attempts to settle, preparation, hearing, argument, and preparation and signature of the order;

(e) expenses properly paid or payable; and

(f) any other relevant matter.

Payment of expenses

(12) The court may make an order that a party pay an amount of money to another party to cover part or all of the expenses of carrying on the case, including a lawyer's fees.

Order for security for costs

(13) A judge may, on motion, make an order for security for costs that is just, based on one or more of the following factors:

1. A party ordinarily resides outside Ontario.
2. A party has an order against the other party for costs that remains unpaid, in the same case or another case.
3. A party is a corporation and there is good reason to believe it does not have enough assets in Ontario to pay costs.
4. There is good reason to believe that the case is a waste of time or a nuisance and that the party does not have enough assets in Ontario to pay costs.
5. A statute entitles the party to security for costs.

Amount and form of security

(14) The judge shall determine the amount of the security, its form and the method of giving it.

Effect of order for security

(15) Until the security has been given, a party against whom there is an order for security for costs may not take any step in the case, except to appeal from the order, unless a judge orders otherwise.

Failure to give security

(16) If the party does not give the security as ordered and, as a result, a judge makes an order dismissing the party's case or striking out the party's answer or any other document filed by the party, then subrule (15) no longer applies.

Security may be changed

(17) The amount of the security, its form and the method of giving it may be changed by order at any time.

RULE 25: ORDERS

Consent order

25. (1) If the parties agree, the court may make an order under these rules or an Act without having the parties or their lawyers come to court.

Successful party prepares draft order

(2) The party in whose favour an order is made shall prepare a draft of the order (Form 25, 25A, 25B, 25C or 25D), unless the court orders otherwise.

Other party may prepare draft order

(3) If the party in whose favour an order is made does not have a lawyer or does not prepare a draft order within 10 days after the order is made, any other party may prepare the draft order, unless the court orders otherwise.

Approval of draft order

(4) A party who prepares an order shall serve a draft, for approval of its form and content, on every other party who was in court or was represented when the order was made (including a child who has a lawyer).

Settling contents of disputed order

(5) Unless the court orders otherwise, a party who disagrees with the form or content of a draft order shall serve, on every party who was served under subrule (4) and on the party who served the draft order,

(a) a notice disputing approval (Form 25E);

(b) a copy of the order, redrafted as proposed; and

(c) notice of a time and date at which the clerk will settle the order by telephone conference.

Time and date

(6) The time and date shall be set by the clerk and shall be within five days after service of the notice disputing approval.

Disputed order—Settlement by judge

(7) If unable to settle the order at the telephone conference, the clerk shall, as soon as possible, refer the order to the judge who made it, to be settled at a further telephone conference, unless the judge orders the parties to come to court for settlement of the order.

No approval required if no response from other party

(8) If no approval or notice disputing approval (Form 25E) is served within 10 days after the draft order is served for approval, it may be signed without approval.

No approval required for certain orders

(9) If an order dismisses a motion, case or appeal, without costs, or is prepared by the clerk under subrule (11), it may be signed without approval.

No approval required in emergencies

(10) If the delay involved in getting an order approved would have serious consequences, the judge who made it may sign it without approval.

When clerk prepares order

(11) The clerk shall prepare the order for signature,

(a) within 10 days after it is made, if no party has a lawyer;

(b) as soon as it is made,

(i) if it is a support deduction order or alternative payment order under the *Family Responsibility and Support Arrears Enforcement Act, 1996* or an order under the *Interjurisdictional Support Orders Act, 2002*,

(i.1) if it is a restraining order under section 35 of the *Children's Law Reform Act* or section 46 of the *Family Law Act*,

(i.2) if it is an order terminating a restraining order referred to in subclause (i.1), or

(ii) if the judge directs the clerk to do so.

Restraining orders

(11.1) A restraining order referred to in subclause 11(b)(i.1) shall be in Form 25F or 25G.

(11.2) An order terminating a restraining order referred to in subclause 11(b)(i.1) shall be in Form 25H.

Who signs order

(12) An order may be signed by the judge who made it or by the clerk.

Service of order

(13) Unless the court orders otherwise, the person who prepared an order shall serve it, by regular service (subrule 6(2)) or by mail, fax or electronic mail to the person's last known address,

(a) on every other party, including a party to whom paragraph 1 of subrule 1(8.4) (no notice to party) applies;

(b) if a child involved in the case has a lawyer, on the lawyer; and

(c) on any other person named by the court.

Support deduction order not served

(14) A support deduction order under the *Family Responsibility and Support Arrears Enforcement Act, 1996* does not have to be served.

Service of Crown wardship order

(15) An order for Crown wardship under Part III of the *Child and Family Services Act* shall be served on the following persons, in addition to the ones mentioned in subrule (13):

1. The child, if that Act requires notice to the child.
2. Any foster parent or other person who is entitled to notice under subsection 39(3) of that Act.
3. A Director appointed under that Act.

Service of secure treatment order

(16) An order for secure treatment under Part VI of the *Child and Family Services Act* shall be served on the administrator of the secure treatment program, in addition to the persons mentioned in subrule (13).

Service of adoption order

(17) An adoption order shall be served on the following persons, in addition to the ones mentioned in subrule (13):

1. The adopted child, if the child gave consent under subsection 137(6) of the *Child and Family Services Act*.
2. The persons mentioned in subsection 162(3) of that Act.

Effective date

(18) An order is effective from the date on which it is made, unless it states otherwise.

Changing order—Fraud, mistake, lack of notice

(19) The court may, on motion, change an order that,

(a) was obtained by fraud;

(b) contains a mistake;

(c) needs to be changed to deal with a matter that was before the court but that it did not decide;

(d) was made without notice; or

(e) was made with notice, if an affected party was not present when the order was made because the notice was inadequate or the party was unable, for a reason satisfactory to the court, to be present.

Same

(20) Rule 14 applies with necessary modifications to a motion to change a final order under subrule (19) and, for the purpose, clause 14(6)(a) shall be read as if the reference to a temporary order were a reference to a final order.

RULE 25.1: PAYMENT INTO AND OUT OF COURT

Definition

25.1 (1) In this rule,

"Accountant" means the Accountant of the Superior Court of Justice.

Non-application of rule

(2) This rule does not apply to,

(a) money paid or to be paid into court for the enforcement of an order for the payment or recovery of money, including enforcement by garnishment; or

(b) money for the support of a child or spouse that is paid or to be paid into court by the payor on behalf of a recipient.

Payment into court, filing in person with clerk or accountant

(3) Subject to subrule (9), a party who is required to pay money into court shall do so in accordance with subrules (4) to (8).

Documents to be filed

(4) The party shall file with the clerk or Accountant a written request for payment into court and a copy of the order under which the money is payable.

Direction

(5) On receiving the documents filed under subrule (4), the clerk or Accountant shall give the party a direction to receive the money, addressed to a bank listed in Schedule I or II to the *Bank Act* (Canada) and specifying the account in the Accountant's name into which the money is to be paid.

Clerk to forward documents

(6) If the documents are filed with the clerk, the clerk shall forward the documents to the Accountant.

Payment

(7) On receiving from the clerk or Accountant the direction referred to in subrule (5), the party shall pay the money into the specified bank account in accordance with the direction.

Bank's duties

(8) On receiving the money, the bank shall give a receipt to the party paying the money and immediately send a copy of the receipt to the Accountant.

Payment into court, payment by mail to accountant

(9) A party may pay money into court by mailing to the Accountant the documents referred to in subrule (4), together with the money that is payable.

Accountant to provide receipt

(10) On receiving money under subrule (9), the Accountant shall give a receipt to the party paying the money.

Payment out of court, authority

(11) Money may only be paid out of court under an order or on consent of all parties.

Payment out under an order

(12) A person who seeks payment of money out of court under an order shall file with the Accountant,

(a) a written request for payment out naming the person to whom the money is to be paid under the order;

(b) the original order for payment out or a copy certified by an official of the court, unless one or the other has already been filed with the Accountant; and

(c) an affidavit stating that the order for payment out is not under appeal and that the time for appealing the order has expired, or that any appeal of the order has been disposed of.

Children's Lawyer, Public Guardian and Trustee

(13) If the person seeking payment out under an order is the Children's Lawyer or the Public Guardian and Trustee, the documents referred to in clauses (12)(a) and (c) are not required to be filed.

Payment out on consent

(14) A person who seeks payment of money out of court on consent shall file with the Accountant,

(a) a written request for payment out naming the person to whom the money is to be paid, and an affidavit stating that neither the person making the request nor the person to whom the money is to be paid is a special party or a child under the age of 18 years who is not a party, with copies of the following attached as exhibits:

(i) photo identification of the requesting person,
(ii) proof of that person's date of birth,
(iii) proof of that person's current address; and

(b) the affidavit of each party or each of the other parties, as the case may be, stating that the party consents to the payment out as set out in the request and that neither the party nor the person to whom the money is to be paid is a special party or a child under the age of 18 years who is not a party, with copies of the documents referred to in subclauses (a) (i), (ii) and (iii), as they relate to the party providing the affidavit, attached as exhibits.

Accountant's duties

(15) If the requirements of subrule (12) or (14), as the case may be, are met, the Accountant shall pay the money to the person named in the order or request for payment out, and the payment shall include any accrued interest, unless a court orders otherwise.

Order for payment out, special party or non-party child

(16) The court may, on motion, order payment out of court of money for or on behalf of a special party or a child who is not a party.

Where notice is not required

(17) A motion under subrule (16) by the Children's Lawyer or the Public Guardian and Trustee may be made without notice, unless the court orders otherwise.

Costs

(18) In making an order under subrule (16), the court may order that costs payable to the person who made the motion be paid directly to that person's representative out of the money in court.

Application

(19) This rule applies to the payment into and out of court of money paid into court on and after the day on which Ontario Regulation 389/12 comes into force.

RULE 26: ENFORCEMENT OF ORDERS

Where to enforce an order

26. (1) The place for enforcement of an order is governed by subrules 5(5) and (6) (place for starting enforcement).

How to enforce an order

(2) An order that has not been obeyed may, in addition to any other method of enforcement provided by law, be enforced as provided by subrules (3) and (4).

Payment orders

(3) A payment order may be enforced by,

(a) a request for a financial statement (subrule 27(1));
(b) a request for disclosure from an income source (subrule 27(7));
(c) a financial examination (subrule 27(11));
(d) seizure and sale (rule 28);
(e) garnishment (rule 29);
(f) a default hearing (rule 30), if the order is a support order;
(g) the appointment of a receiver under section 101 of the *Courts of Justice Act*; and
(h) registration under section 42 of the *Family Responsibility and Support Arrears Enforcement Act, 1996*.

Other orders

(4) An order other than a payment order may be enforced by,

(a) a writ of temporary seizure of property (subrule 28(10));
(b) a contempt order (rule 31); and
(c) the appointment of a receiver under section 101 of the *Courts of Justice Act*.

Statement of money owed

(5) A statement of money owed shall be in Form 26, with a copy of the order that is in default attached.

Special forms for statement of money owed

(6) Despite subrule (5),

(a) if the *Family Responsibility and Support Arrears Enforcement Act, 1996* applies, a statement of arrears in the form used by the Director may be used instead of Form 26;
(b) if the *Interjurisdictional Support Orders Act, 2002* applies, a document receivable under section 49 of that Act may be used instead of Form 26.

Recipient's or Director's entitlement to costs

(7) Unless the court orders otherwise, the recipient or the Director is entitled to the costs,

(a) of carrying out a financial examination; and
(b) of issuing, serving, filing and enforcing a writ of seizure and sale, a writ of temporary seizure and a notice of garnishment and of changing them by statutory declaration.

Enforcement of administrative costs

(8) For the purpose of subrule (7), the recipient or the Director may collect under a writ of seizure and sale, a notice of garnishment or a statutory declaration changing either of them,

(a) the amounts set out in the regulations under the *Administration of Justice Act* and awarded under rule 24 (costs) for filing and renewing with the sheriff a writ of seizure and sale or a writ of temporary seizure;

(b) payments made to a sheriff, clerk, official examiner, court reporter or other public officer in accordance with the regulations under the *Administration of Justice Act* and awarded under rule 24 (costs), on filing with the sheriff or clerk a copy of a receipt for each payment or an affidavit setting out the payments made; and

(c) the actual expense for carrying out a financial examination, or any other costs to which the recipient or the Director is entitled under subrule (7), on filing with the sheriff or clerk an affidavit (Form 26A) setting out the items of expense in detail.

Affidavit for filing domestic contract or paternity agreement

(9) An affidavit for filing a domestic contract or paternity agreement under subsection 35(1) of the *Family Law Act* shall be in Form 26B.

Director's status

(10) If the Director enforces an order under the *Family Responsibility and Support Arrears Enforcement Act, 1996*, anything in these rules relating to enforcement by the person in whose favour the order was made applies to the Director.

Filing and refiling with the Director

(11) A person who files or refiles a support order in the Director's office shall immediately send notice of the filing, by mail, fax or electronic mail, to the clerk at any court office where the recipient is enforcing the order.

Transferring enforcement from recipient to Director

(12) A recipient who files a support order in the Director's office shall, on the Director's request, assign to the Director any enforcement that the recipient has started, and then the Director may continue with the enforcement as if the Director had started it.

Transferring enforcement from Director to recipient

(13) If the parties withdraw a support order from the Director's office, the Director shall, on the recipient's request, given to the Director at the same time as the notice of withdrawal, assign to the recipient any enforcement that the Director has started, and then the recipient may continue with the enforcement as if the recipient had started it.

Notice of transfer of enforcement

(14) A person who continues an enforcement under subrule (12) or (13) shall immediately send a notice of transfer of enforcement (Form 26C), by mail, fax or electronic mail to,

(a) all parties to the enforcement;

(b) the clerk at every court office where the enforcement is being carried on; and

(c) every sheriff who is involved with the enforcement at the time of transfer.

Place of registration of support order under the Divorce Act (Canada)

(15) If a person wants to enforce an order for support made outside Ontario under the *Divorce Act* (Canada), the order shall be registered in a court, as defined in subsection 20(1) of that Act, as follows:

1. If the recipient resides in Ontario, in the municipality where the recipient resides.
2. If the recipient does not reside in Ontario, in the municipality where the payor resides.
3. If neither the recipient nor the payor resides in Ontario, in the municipality where any property owned by the payor is located or, if the payor doesn't have any property, in any municipality.

Place of registration of custody or access order under the Divorce Act (Canada)

(16) If a person wants to enforce an order involving custody of or access to a child that is made outside Ontario under the *Divorce Act* (Canada), the order shall be registered in a court, as defined in subsection 20(1) of that Act, in accordance with clause 5(6)(a) of these rules.

Registration requirements

(17) The person requesting the registration shall send to the court a certified copy of the order and a written request that the order be registered under paragraph 20(3)(a) of the *Divorce Act* (Canada).

RULE 27: REQUIRING FINANCIAL INFORMATION

Request for financial statement

27. (1) If a payment order is in default, a recipient may serve a request for a financial statement (Form 27) on the payor.

Effect of request for financial statement

(2) Within 15 days after being served with the request, the payor shall send a completed financial statement (Form 13) to the recipient by mail, fax or electronic mail.

Frequency of requests for financial statements

(3) A recipient may request a financial statement only once in a six-month period, unless the court gives the recipient permission to do so more often.

Application of rule 13

(4) If a party is required under this rule to give a financial statement, the following subrules apply with necessary changes:

13(6) (full disclosure)
13(7) or (7.1) (income tax documents)
13(11) (additional information)
13(12) (updating financial statement)
13(15) (correcting and updating)
13(16) (order to file statement).

Order for financial statement

(5) The court may, on motion, order a payor to serve and file a financial statement.

Failure to obey order

(6) If the payor does not serve and file a financial statement within 10 days after being served with the order, the court may, on motion with special service (subrule 6(3)), order that the payor be imprisoned continuously or intermittently for not more than 40 days.

Request for statement of income from income source

(7) If a payment order is in default, the recipient may serve a request for a statement of income (Form 27A) on an income source of the payor, requiring the income source to prepare and send to the recipient, by mail, fax or electronic mail, a statement of income (Form 27B).

Frequency of requests for statement of income

(8) A recipient may request a statement of income from an income source only once in a six-month period, unless the court gives the recipient permission to do so more often.

Order for statement of income

(9) The court may, on the recipient's motion, order an income source to serve and file a statement of income.

Income source's failure to obey order

(10) If the income source does not serve and file a statement of income within 10 days after being served with the order, the court may, on the recipient's motion, order the income source to post a bond (Form 32).

Appointment for financial examination

(11) If a payment order is in default, the recipient may serve on the payor, by special service (subrule 6(3)), an appointment for a financial examination (Form 27C), requiring the payor to,

(a) come to a financial examination;

(b) bring to the examination any document or thing named in the appointment that is in the payor's control or available to the payor on request, relevant to the enforcement of the order, and not protected by a legal privilege; and

(c) serve a financial statement (Form 13) on the recipient, not later than seven days before the date of the examination.

Financial examination of person other than payor

(12) If a payment order is in default and a person other than the payor may know about the matters listed in subrule (17), the recipient may require that person to come to a financial examination by serving a summons to witness (Form 23) and the witness fee (subrule 23(4)) on the person by special service (subrules 6(3) and (4)).

Place where financial examination held

(13) A financial examination shall be held,

(a) in a place where the parties and the person to be examined agree;

(b) where the person to be examined lives in Ontario, in the municipality where the person lives; or

(c) in a place chosen by the court.

Other rules apply

(14) Subrules 19(4), (5) and (8) (documents protected by legal privilege, use of privileged documents, documents omitted from affidavit) and 23(7) (failure to obey summons) apply to a financial examination, with necessary changes.

Notice of time and place of examination

(15) A payor who is served with an appointment or a person who is served with a summons for a financial examination shall have at least 10 days' notice of the time and place of the examination.

Before whom examination is held, method of recording

(16) A financial examination shall be held under oath or affirmation, before a person chosen by agreement of the payor and recipient or in accordance with subrule 20(12) (other arrangements for questioning), and shall be recorded by a method chosen in the same way.

Scope of examination

(17) On a financial examination, the payor or other person may be questioned about,

(a) the reason for the payor's default;

(b) the payor's income and property;

(c) the debts owed to and by the payor;

(d) the disposal of any property by the payor either before or after the making of the order that is in default;

(e) the payor's past, present and future ability to pay under the order;

(f) whether the payor intends to obey the order, and any reason for not doing so; and

(g) any other matter relevant to the enforcement of the order.

Resistance to examination

(18) Subrule (19) applies if a payor who is served with an appointment or a person who is served with a summons for a financial examination,

(a) does not come to the examination as required by the appointment or summons;

(b) does not serve on the recipient a financial statement as required by the appointment;

(c) comes to the examination, but does not bring a document or thing named in the appointment or summons; or

(d) comes to the examination, but refuses to take an oath or affirm or to answer a question.

Order for another examination

(19) The court may, on motion, make an order and give directions for another financial examination of the payor or other person and may in addition require the payor or person to post a bond (Form 32).

Imprisonment

(20) If a payor or other person, without sufficient excuse, fails to obey an order or direction made under subrule (19), the court may, on motion with special service (subrule 6(3)), order that the payor or person be imprisoned continuously or intermittently for not more than 40 days.

Imprisonment power is additional

(21) The court may exercise its power under subrule (20) in addition to or instead of its power of forfeiture under rule 32 (bonds, recognizances and warrants).

Frequency of examinations

(22) A recipient may conduct only one financial examination of a payor and one financial examination of any other person in a six-month period, or more often with the court's permission.

RULE 28: SEIZURE AND SALE

Issue of writ of seizure and sale

28. (1) The clerk shall issue a writ of seizure and sale (Form 28) if a recipient files,

(a) a request for a writ of seizure and sale (Form 28A); and

(b) a statement of money owed (subrules 26(5) and (6)).

Statutory declaration to change amount owed

(2) The statutory declaration to sheriff mentioned in section 44 of the *Family Responsibility and Support Arrears Enforcement Act, 1996* shall be in Form 28B.

Statutory declaration if order changed

(3) If a court changes a payment order that is being enforced by a writ of seizure and sale, a statutory declaration to sheriff (Form 28B) may be filed with the sheriff and once filed, it has the same effect as a declaration mentioned in subrule (2).

Duration of writ

(4) A writ of seizure and sale continues in effect until,

(a) the recipient withdraws it under subrule (7); or

(b) the court orders otherwise under subrule (8).

Writ issued under former rules

(5) A writ directing the sheriff to seize and sell a payor's property that was issued by the court under the rules that applied before these rules take effect has the same legal effect as a writ of seizure and sale issued under these rules, and does not expire except as subrule (4) provides.

Notifying sheriff of payment received

(6) If a writ of seizure and sale has been filed with a sheriff,

(a) the recipient shall, on the sheriff's request, provide a statutory declaration setting out details of all payments received by or on behalf of the recipient; and

(b) the sheriff shall update the writ accordingly.

Withdrawing writ

(7) The person who obtained a writ to enforce an order shall immediately withdraw it from every sheriff's office where it has been filed if,

(a) the person no longer wants to enforce the order by a writ;

(b) in the case of a payment order, the payor's obligation to make periodic payments under the order has ended and all other amounts owing under it have been paid; or

(c) in the case of any other order, the person against whom the writ was issued has obeyed the order.

Order changing, withdrawing or suspending writ

(8) The court may, on motion, make an order changing the terms of a writ, withdrawing it or temporarily suspending it, even if the writ was issued by another court in Ontario.

Service of order

(9) The person making the motion, or another person named by the court, shall serve a copy of the order on,

(a) every sheriff in whose office the writ has been filed; and

(b) if the writ was issued by the court in another place, or by another court, on the clerk of the court in the other place or the clerk of the other court.

Writ of temporary seizure of property

(10) The court may, on motion with special service (subrule 6(3)), give permission to issue a writ of temporary seizure (Form 28C) directing the sheriff to take possession of and hold all or part of the land and other property of a person against whom an order has been made and to hold any income from the property until the writ is withdrawn or the court orders otherwise.

Electronic writs

(11) If a recipient is entitled to the issue of a writ of seizure and sale by the Superior Court of Justice, the recipient is entitled to the electronic issue and filing of the writ in accordance with the Rules of Civil Procedure.

RULE 29: GARNISHMENT

Issue of notice or notices of garnishment

29. (1) The clerk shall issue as many notices of garnishment (Form 29A or 29B) as a recipient requests if the recipient files,

(a) a request for garnishment (Form 29) or an extra-provincial garnishment process referred to in section 50 of the *Family Responsibility and Support Arrears Enforcement Act, 1996*; and

(b) a statement of money owed (subrules 26(5) and (6)).

One recipient and one garnishee per notice

(2) Each notice of garnishment shall name only one recipient and one garnishee.

Service on payor and garnishee

(3) The notice of garnishment shall be served on the payor and on the garnishee but the payor shall, in addition, be served with the documents filed under subrule (1).

Effect of notice of garnishment

(4) A notice of garnishment attaches,

(a) every debt that is payable by the garnishee to the payor at the time the notice is served; and

(b) every debt that is payable by the garnishee to the payor,

(i) after the notice is served, or

(ii) on the fulfilment of a condition after the notice is served.

Duration

(5) The notice of garnishment continues in effect from the time of service on the garnishee until it is withdrawn or stopped under this rule or until the court orders otherwise under this rule.

Financial institution

(6) If the garnishee is a financial institution, the notice of garnishment and all further notices required to be served under this rule shall be served at the branch of the institution where the debt to the payor is payable, unless subrule (6.1) applies.

Federally regulated financial institution—Garnishment re support

(6.1) If the garnishee is a financial institution to which the *Bank Act* (Canada), the *Cooperative Credit Associations Act* (Canada) or the *Trust and Loan Companies Act* (Canada) applies and the garnishment enforces a support order, the notice of garnishment and all further notices required to be served under this rule,

(a) shall be served at the designated office of the institution established for this purpose; and

(b) shall be accompanied by a statement to garnishee financial institution re support (Form 29J).

New accounts

(6.2) Subrules (4) and (5) do not apply to money in an account opened after a notice of garnishment is served as described in subrule (6) or (6.1).

Joint debts garnishable

(7) Subrules (4) and (5) also apply to debts owed to the payor and another person jointly.

Procedure when joint debt garnished

(8) If a garnishee has been served with a notice of garnishment and the garnishee owes a debt to which subrules (4) and (5) apply to the payor and another person jointly,

(a) the garnishee shall pay, in accordance with subrule (11), half of the debt, or the larger or smaller amount that the court orders;

(b) the garnishee shall immediately send the other person a notice to co-owner of debt (Form 29C) by mail, fax or electronic mail, to the person's address in the garnishee's records; and

(c) the garnishee shall immediately serve the notice to co-owner of debt on the recipient or the Director, depending on who is enforcing the order, and on the sheriff or clerk if the sheriff or clerk is to receive the money under subrule (11) or (12).

Joint debt—Money to be held

(9) Despite subrule (12), if served with notice under clause (8)(c), the sheriff, clerk or Director shall hold the money received for 30 days, and may pay it out when the 30 days expire, unless the other person serves and files a dispute within the 30 days.

Payment of arrears does not end garnishment

(10) A notice of garnishment continues to attach future periodic payments even though the total amount owed when it was served is fully paid up.

Persons to whom garnishee makes payments

(11) A garnishee who has been served with a notice of garnishment shall make the required payments to,

(a) the Director, if the notice of garnishment relates to an order being enforced by the Director;

(b) the clerk, if the notice of garnishment does not relate to an order being enforced by the Director.

Clerk or Director to pay out money

(12) On receiving money under a notice of garnishment, the Director or clerk shall, even if a dispute has been filed, but subject to subrules (9) and (13), immediately pay,

(a) to the recipient, any part of the money that comes within the priority created by subsection 2(3) of the *Creditors' Relief Act, 2010*; and

(b) to the sheriff, any part of the money that exceeds that priority.

Order that subrule (12) does not apply

(13) The court may, at a garnishment hearing or on a motion to change the garnishment under this rule, order that subrule (12) does not apply.

Change in garnishment, indexed support

(14) If a notice of garnishment enforces a support order that indexes periodic payments for inflation, the recipient may serve on the garnishee and on the payor a statutory declaration of indexed support (Form 29D) setting out the new amount to be paid under the order, and file the declaration with the court.

Effect of statutory declaration of indexed support

(15) A statutory declaration of indexed support requires the garnishee to pay the new amount set out in the declaration from the time it is served on the garnishee.

Garnishment dispute

(16) Within 10 days after being served with a notice of garnishment or a statutory declaration of indexed support, a payor, garnishee or co-owner of a debt may serve on the other parties and file a dispute (Form 29E, 29F or 29G).

Notice of garnishment hearing

(17) The clerk shall, on request, issue a notice of garnishment hearing (Form 29H),

(a) within 10 days after a dispute is served and filed; or

(b) if the recipient says that the garnishee has not paid any money or has not paid enough money.

Service of notice

(18) The clerk shall serve and file the notice not later than 10 days before the hearing.

Garnishment hearing

(19) At a garnishment hearing, the court may make one or more of the following temporary or final orders:

1. An order dismissing the dispute.
2. An order that changes how much is being garnished on account of a periodic payment order. The court may make an order under this paragraph even if it does not have the authority to change the payment order itself.

2.1 An order that changes how much is being garnished on account of a periodic payment order and that, at the same time, changes the payment order itself. The court may make an order under this paragraph only if,

   i. the payment order is one that the court has the authority to change, and

   ii. the parties to the payment order agree to the change, or one of those parties has served and filed notice of a motion to have the change made.

3. An order changing how much is being garnished on account of a non-periodic payment order.
4. An order suspending the garnishment or any term of it, while the hearing is adjourned or until the court orders otherwise.
5. An order setting aside the notice of garnishment or any statutory declaration of indexed support.
6. An order that garnished money held or received by the clerk, Director or sheriff be held in court.
7. An order that garnished money that has been paid out in error to the recipient be paid into and held in court, returned to the garnishee or sent to the payor or to the co-owner of the debt.
8. An order that garnished money held in court be returned to the garnishee or be sent to the payor, the co-owner of the debt, the sheriff, the clerk or the Director.
9. An order deciding how much remains owing under a payment order that is being enforced by garnishment against the payor or garnishee.
10. If the garnishee has not paid what was required by the notice of garnishment or statutory declaration of indexed support, an order that the garnishee pay all or part of what was required.
11. An order deciding who is entitled to the costs of the garnishment hearing and setting the amount of the costs.

Changing garnishment at other times

(20) The court may also use the powers listed in subrule (19), on motion or on its own initiative, even if the notice of garnishment was issued by another court,

(a) on a motion under section 7 of the *Wages Act;*

(b) if the court replaces a temporary payment order with a final payment order;

(c) if the court indexes or changes a payment order; or

(d) if the court allows an appeal.

Changing garnishment when ability to pay changes

(21) If there has been a material change in the payor's circumstances affecting the payor's ability to pay, the court may, on motion, use the powers listed in subrule (19).

Garnishee's payment pays debt

(22) Payment of a debt by a garnishee under a notice of garnishment or statutory declaration of indexed support pays off the debt between the garnishee and the payor to the extent of the payment.

Notice by garnishee—Payor not working or receiving money

(23) Within 10 days after a payor stops working for or is no longer receiving any money from a garnishee, the garnishee shall send a notice as subrule (27) requires,

(a) saying that the payor is no longer working for or is no longer receiving any money from the garnishee;

(b) giving the date on which the payor stopped working for or receiving money from the garnishee and the date of the last payment to the payor from the garnishee; and

(c) giving the name and address of any other income source of the payor, if known.

Notice by garnishee—Payor working or receiving money again

(24) Within 10 days after the payor returns to work for or starts to receive money again from the garnishee, the garnishee shall send another notice as subrule (27) requires, saying that the payor has returned to work for or started to receive money again from the garnishee.

Notice by payor—Working or receiving money again

(25) Within 10 days after returning to work for or starting to receive money again from the garnishee, the payor shall send a notice as subrule (27) requires, saying that the payor has returned to work for or started to receive money again from the garnishee.

Notice by payor—New income source

(26) Within 10 days after starting to work for or receive money from a new income source, the payor shall send a notice as subrule (27) requires, saying that the payor has started to work for or to receive money from the new income source.

Notice sent to clerk and recipient or Director

(27) A notice referred to in subrule (23), (24), (25) or (26) shall be sent to the clerk, and to the recipient or the Director (depending on who is enforcing the order), by mail, fax or electronic mail.

Notice by clerk

(28) When the clerk receives a notice under subrule (26), the clerk shall immediately notify the recipient or the Director (depending on who is enforcing the order) by mail, fax or electronic mail.

New notice of garnishment

(29) If no written objection is received within 10 days of the clerk notifying the recipient or the Director that a notice under subrule (26) was received, the clerk shall,

(a) issue a new notice of garnishment directed to the new garnishee, requiring the same deductions as were required to be made, under the previous notice of garnishment or statutory declaration of indexed support, on the day that the notice under subrule (26) was received; and

(b) send a copy of the new notice of garnishment to the payor and the new garnishee, by mail, fax or electronic mail.

Effect of new notice of garnishment

(30) Issuing a new notice of garnishment under clause (29)(a) does not cancel any previous notice of garnishment or statutory declaration of indexed support.

Notice to stop garnishment

(31) The recipient shall immediately send a notice to stop garnishment (Form 29I), by mail, fax or electronic mail, to the garnishee and payor and file it with the clerk if,

(a) the recipient no longer wants to enforce the order by garnishment; or

(b) the requirement to make periodic payments under the order has ended and all other amounts owing under the order have been paid.

Old orders

(32) This rule applies, with necessary changes, to,

(a) an attachment order made under section 30 of the *Family Law Reform Act* (chapter 152 of the Revised Statutes of Ontario, 1980); and

(b) a garnishment order issued by the court under the rules that were in effect before January 1, 1985.

RULE 30: DEFAULT HEARING

Issuing notice of default hearing

30. (1) The clerk shall issue a notice of default hearing (Form 30),

(a) if the support order is being enforced by the recipient, when the recipient files a request for a default hearing (Form 30A) and a statement of money owed (subrule 26(5));

(b) if it is being enforced by the Director, when the Director files a statement of money owed.

Serving notice of default hearing

(2) The notice of default hearing shall be served on the payor by special service in accordance with subrule 6(4) and filed.

Payor's dispute

(3) Within 10 days after being served with the notice, the payor shall serve on the recipient and file,

(a) a financial statement (Form 13); and

(b) a default dispute (Form 30B).

Updating statement of money owed

(4) The recipient shall serve and file a new statement of money owed (subrule 26(5)) not more than seven days before the default hearing.

When Director to update statement

(5) Despite subrule 26(10), subrule (4) applies to the Director only if,

(a) the amount the Director is asking the court to enforce is greater than the amount shown in the notice of default hearing; or

(b) the court directs it.

Statement of money owed presumed correct

(6) The payor is presumed to admit that the recipient's statement of money owed is correct, unless the payor has filed a default dispute stating that the statement of money owed is not correct and giving detailed reasons.

Arrears enforceable to date of hearing

(7) At the default hearing, the court may decide and enforce the amount owing as of the date of the hearing.

Conditional imprisonment

(8) The court may make an order under clause 41(10)(h) or (i) of the *Family Responsibility and Support Arrears Enforcement Act, 1996*, suspending the payor's imprisonment on appropriate conditions.

Issuing warrant of committal

(9) If the recipient, on a motion with special service in accordance with subrule 6(4) on the payor, states by affidavit (or by oral evidence, with the court's permission) that the payor has not obeyed a condition that was imposed under subrule (8), the court may issue a warrant of committal against the payor, subject to subsection 41(15) (power to change order) of the *Family Responsibility and Support Arrears Enforcement Act, 1996*.

RULE 31: CONTEMPT OF COURT

When contempt motion available

31. (1) An order, other than a payment order, may be enforced by a contempt motion made in the case in which the order was made, even if another penalty is available.

Notice of contempt motion

(2) The notice of contempt motion (Form 31) shall be served together with a supporting affidavit, by special service in accordance with subrule 6(4), unless the court orders otherwise.

Affidavit for contempt motion

(3) The supporting affidavit may contain statements of information that the person signing the affidavit learned from someone else, but only if the requirements of subrule 14(19) are satisfied.

Warrant to bring to court

(4) To bring before the court a person against whom a contempt motion is made, the court may issue a warrant for the person's arrest if,

(a) the person's attendance is necessary in the interest of justice; and

(b) the person is not likely to attend voluntarily.

Contempt orders

(5) If the court finds a person in contempt of the court, it may order that the person,

(a) be imprisoned for any period and on any conditions that are just;

(b) pay a fine in any amount that is appropriate;

(c) pay an amount to a party as a penalty;

(d) do anything else that the court decides is appropriate;

(e) not do what the court forbids;

(f) pay costs in an amount decided by the court; and

(g) obey any other order.

Writ of temporary seizure

(6) The court may also give permission to issue a writ of temporary seizure (Form 28C) against the person's property.

Limited imprisonment or fine

(7) In a contempt order under one of the following provisions, the period of imprisonment and the amount of a fine may not be greater than the relevant Act allows:

1. Section 38 of the *Children's Law Reform Act.*
2. Section 49 of the *Family Law Act.*
3. Section 53 of the *Family Responsibility and Support Arrears Enforcement Act, 1996.*

Conditional imprisonment or fine

(8) A contempt order for imprisonment or for the payment of a fine may be suspended on appropriate conditions.

Issuing warrant of committal

(9) If a party, on a motion with special service (subrule 6(3)) on the person in contempt, states by an affidavit in Form 32C (or by oral evidence, with the court's permission) that the person has not obeyed a condition imposed under subrule (8), the court may issue a warrant of committal against the person.

Payment of fine

(10) A contempt order for the payment of a fine shall require the person in contempt to pay the fine,

(a) in a single payment, immediately or before a date that the court chooses; or

(b) in instalments, over a period of time that the court considers appropriate.

Corporation in contempt

(11) If a corporation is found in contempt, the court may also make an order under subrule (5), (6) or (7) against any officer or director of the corporation.

Change in contempt order

(12) The court may, on motion, change an order under this rule, give directions and make any other order that is just.

RULE 32: BONDS, RECOGNIZANCES AND WARRANTS

Warrant to bring a person to court

32. (1) If a person does not come to court after being served with notice of a case, enforcement or motion that may result in an order requiring the person to post a bond,

(a) the court may issue a warrant for the person's arrest, to bring the person before the court, and adjourn the case to await the person's arrival; or

(b) the court may,

(i) hear and decide the case in the person's absence and, if appropriate, make an order requiring the person to post a bond, and

(ii) if the person has been served with the order and does not post the bond by the date set out in the order, issue a warrant for the person's arrest, on motion without notice, to bring the person before the court.

Form of bond and other requirements

(2) A bond shall be in Form 32, does not need a seal, and shall,

(a) have at least one surety, unless the court orders otherwise;

(b) list the conditions that the court considers appropriate;

(c) set out an amount of money to be forfeited if the conditions are not obeyed;

(d) shall require the person posting the bond to deposit the money with the clerk immediately, unless the court orders otherwise; and

(e) name the person to whom any forfeited money is to be paid out.

Person before whom recognizance to be entered into

(3) A recognizance shall be entered into before a judge, a justice of the peace or the clerk.

Change of conditions in a bond

(4) The court may, on motion, change any condition in a bond if there has been a material change in a party's circumstances since the date of the order for posting the bond or the date of an order under this subrule, whichever is more recent.

Change in bond under Children's Law Reform Act

(5) In the case of a bond under the *Children's Law Reform Act*, subrule (4) also applies to a material change in circumstances that affects or is likely to affect the best interests of the child.

Removal or replacement of surety

(6) The court may, on motion, order that a surety be removed or be replaced by another person as surety, in which case as soon as the order is made, the surety who is removed or replaced is free from any obligation under the bond.

Motion to enforce bond

(7) A person requesting the court's permission to enforce a bond under subsection 143(1) (enforcement of recognizance or bond) of the *Courts of Justice Act* shall serve a notice of forfeiture motion (Form 32A), with a copy of the bond attached, on the person said to have broken the bond and on each surety.

Forfeiture if no deposit made

(8) If an order of forfeiture of a bond is made and no deposit was required, or a deposit was required but was not made, the order shall require the payor or surety to pay the required amount to the person to whom the bond is payable,

(a) in a single payment, immediately or before a date that the court chooses; or

(b) in instalments, over a period of time that the court considers appropriate.

Change in payment schedule

(9) If time is allowed for payment under subrule (8), the court may, on a later motion by the payor or a surety, allow further time for payment.

Order for forfeiture of deposit

(10) If an order of forfeiture of a bond is made and a deposit was required and was made, the order shall direct the clerk to pay the required amount immediately to the person to whom the bond is made payable.

Cancelling bond

(11) The court may, on motion, make an order under subrule (4), or an order cancelling the bond and directing a refund of all or part of the deposit, if,

(a) a payor or surety made a deposit under the bond;

(b) the conditions of the bond have not been broken; and

(c) the conditions have expired or, although they have not expired or do not have an expiry date, the payor or surety has good reasons for getting the conditions of the bond changed.

Form of warrant for arrest

(12) A warrant for arrest issued against any of the following shall be in Form 32B:

1. A payor who does not file a financial statement ordered under subsection 40(4) of the *Family Responsibility and Support Arrears Enforcement Act, 1996* or under these rules.
2. A payor who does not come to a default hearing under section 41 of the *Family Responsibility and Support Arrears Enforcement Act, 1996.*
3. An absconding respondent under subsection 43(1) or 59(2) of the *Family Law Act.*
4. An absconding payor under subsection 49(1) of the *Family Responsibility and Support Arrears Enforcement Act, 1996.*
5. A witness who does not come to court or remain in attendance as required by a summons to witness.
6. A person who does not come to court in a case that may result in an order requiring the person to post a bond under these rules.
7. A person who does not obey an order requiring the person to post a bond under these rules.
8. A person against whom a contempt motion is made.
9. Any other person liable to arrest under an order.
10. Any other person liable to arrest for committing an offence.

Bail on arrest

(13) Section 150 (interim release by justice of the peace) of the *Provincial Offences Act* applies, with necessary chang-

es, to an arrest made under a warrant mentioned in paragraph 1, 2, 3 or 4 of subrule (12).

Affidavit for warrant of committal

(14) An affidavit in support of a motion for a warrant of committal shall be in Form 32C.

Form of warrant of committal

(15) A warrant of committal issued to enforce an order of imprisonment shall be in Form 32D.

RULE 32.1: ENFORCEMENT OF FAMILY ARBITRATION AWARDS

Requesting enforcement

32.1 (1) A party who is entitled to the enforcement of a family arbitration award and who wants to ask the court to enforce the award under section 59.8 of the *Family Law Act* may file a request to enforce a family arbitration award (Form 32.1), together with,

(a) copies of the certificates of independent legal advice required by the *Family Law Act* for the parties to the family arbitration agreement;
(b) a copy of the family arbitration agreement; and
(c) the original award or a certified copy.

When required to proceed by motion

(2) Despite subrule (1), if there is already a family law case to which these rules apply between the parties to the family arbitration agreement in the Superior Court of Justice or the Family Court of the Superior Court of Justice, the party entitled to enforcement shall make a motion in that case rather than a request under this rule, and subrule 14(24) applies in respect of the motion.

Application of other rules

(3) The rules that apply to an application apply to a request to enforce a family arbitration award that is proceeding under this rule, unless these rules provide otherwise.

Hearing date

(4) When a request to enforce a family arbitration award is filed, the clerk shall set a hearing date.

Service

(5) The request shall be served immediately on every other party.

Request not served on or before hearing date

(6) If a request to enforce a family arbitration award is not served on a respondent on or before the hearing date, the clerk shall, at the applicant's request, set a new hearing date for that respondent, and the applicant shall make the necessary change to the request and serve it immediately on that respondent.

Opposing a request

(7) Despite subrule 10(1) (serving and filing answer), a respondent who wants to oppose a request to enforce a family arbitration award shall serve a dispute of request for enforcement (Form 32.1A) on every other party and file it,

(a) no later than 30 days after being served with the request; or
(b) if the request is served outside Canada or the United States of America, no later than 60 days after being served with the request.

Written hearing

(8) Unless the court orders otherwise under subrule (10), the request shall be dealt with on the basis of written documents without the parties or their lawyers needing to come to court.

Request for oral hearing

(9) A respondent may request an oral hearing by filing a motion (Form 14B) within seven days after being served with the request to enforce a family arbitration award.

Order for oral hearing

(10) The court may order an oral hearing, on motion or on its own initiative, if it is satisfied that an oral hearing is necessary to deal with the case justly.

RULE 33: CHILD PROTECTION

Timetable

33. (1) Every child protection case, including a status review application, is governed by the following timetable:

Step in the case	Maximum time for completion, from start of case
First hearing, if child has been apprehended	5 days
Service and filing of answers and plans of care	30 days
Temporary care and custody hearing	35 days
Settlement conference	80 days
Hearing	120 days

Case management judge

(2) Wherever possible, at the start of the case a judge shall be assigned to manage it and monitor its progress.

Court may lengthen times only in best interests of child

(3) The court may lengthen a time shown in the timetable only if the best interests of the child require it.

Parties may not lengthen times

(4) The parties may not lengthen a time shown in the timetable by consent under subrule 3(6).

Plan of care or supervision to be served

(5) A party who wants the court to consider a plan of care or supervision shall serve it on the other parties and file it not later than seven days before a conference, even if that is sooner than the timetable would require.

Temporary care and custody hearing—Affidavit evidence

(6) The evidence at a temporary care and custody hearing shall be given by affidavit, unless the court orders otherwise.

Status review

(6.1) A status review application under clause 64(2)(a) or (b) of the *Child and Family Services Act* shall be served at least 30 days before the date the order for society supervision or society wardship expires.

Forms for child protection cases

(7) In a child protection case,

(a) an information for a warrant to apprehend a child shall be in Form 33;

(b) a warrant to apprehend a child shall be in Form 33A;

(c) an applicant's plan of care for a child shall be,

(i) if the applicant is a children's aid society, in Form 33B, and

(ii) if the applicant is not a children's aid society, in Form 33B.1;

(c.1) a respondent's answer and plan of care for a child shall be,

(i) if the respondent is not a children's aid society, in Form 33B.1,

(ii) if the respondent is a children's aid society, in Form 10 and Form 33B;

(d) an agreed statement of facts in a child protection case shall be in Form 33C; and

(e) an agreed statement of facts in a status review application shall be in Form 33D.

Forms for secure treatment cases

(8) In an application under Part VI (secure treatment) of the *Child and Family Services Act*, a consent signed by the child shall be in Form 33E and a consent signed by any other person shall be in Form 33F.

RULE 34: ADOPTION

CFSA definitions apply

34. (1) The definitions in the *Child and Family Services Act* apply to this rule and, in particular,

"Director" means a Director within the meaning of the Act.

Meaning of "act"

(2) In this rule,

"Act" means the *Child and Family Services Act*.

Use of initials in documents

(2.1) An applicant or respondent may be referred to by only the first letter of his or her surname in any document in the case, except that,

(a) the applicant's full names shall appear in the adoption order; and

(b) the child's full names shall appear in the adoption order, unless the court orders that the child's first name and the first letter of his or her surname be used.

Certified copy of order from outside Ontario

(3) When this rule requires a copy of an order to be filed and the order in question was made outside Ontario, it shall be a copy that is certified by an official of the court or other authority that made it.

Material to be filed with adoption applications

(4) The following shall be filed with every application for an adoption:

1. A certified copy of the statement of live birth of the child, or an equivalent that satisfies the court.
2. If required, the child's consent to adoption (Form 34) or a notice of motion and supporting affidavit for an order under subsection 137(9) of the Act dispensing with the child's consent.
3. If the child is not a Crown ward, an affidavit of parentage (Form 34A) or any other evidence about parentage that the court requires from the child's parent or a person named by the court.
4. If the applicant has a spouse who has not joined in the application, a consent to the child's adoption by the spouse (Form 34B).
5. If required by the Act or by an order, a Director's or local director's statement on adoption (Form 34C) under subsection 149(1) or (6) of the Act.
6. An affidavit signed by the applicant (Form 34D) that includes details about the applicant's education, employment, health, background and ability to support and care for the child, a history of the relationship between the parent and the child and any other evidence relating to the best interests of the child, and states whether the child is an Indian or a native person.

Report of child's adjustment

(5) A report under subsection 149(5) or (6) of the Act of the child's adjustment in the applicant's home shall also be filed with the application if the child is under 16 years of age, or is 16 years of age or older but has not withdrawn from parental control and has not married.

Additional material—Crown ward

(6) If the child is a Crown ward, the following shall also be filed with the application:

1. A Director's consent to adoption (Form 34E).

1.1 If an access order was made under subsection 58(1) of the Act,

   i. copies of each notice of intention to place a child for adoption (Form 8D.2) or of the notice to child of intention to place for adoption (Form 8D.3) that was sent to a person who was granted an access order,

   ii. copies of each notice of termination of access (Form 8D.4) that was sent to a person who was the subject of an access order but was not entitled to bring an application for an openness order,

   iii. for each notice,

      A. proof of service of the notice in accordance with subsection 145.1.1(4) of the Act,

      B. a copy of an order permitting another method of service under subsection 145.1.1(5) of the Act and proof of such service, or

      C. a copy of an order under subsection 145.1.1(6) of the Act that notice is not required, and

   iv. an affidavit (Form 34G.1) signed by an employee of a children's aid society stating that,

      A. no application for an openness order has been filed, or

      B. if any applications for openness orders have been filed, the status of those applications, including details of any openness orders that have been made.

2. A copy of any order under subsection 58(1) of the Act ending access to the child.
3. A copy of the order of Crown wardship.
4. Proof of service of the orders referred to in paragraphs 2 and 3, or a copy of any order dispensing with service.
5. An affidavit (Form 34G.1), signed by a person delegated by the local director of the children's aid society that has placed the child for adoption, stating that there is no appeal in progress from an order referred to in paragraph 2 or 3, or that the appeal period has expired without an appeal being filed, or that an appeal was filed but has been withdrawn or finally dismissed.
6. If the child is an Indian or native person, proof of 30 days written notice to the child's band or native community of the intention to place the child for adoption.

Additional material—Child not Crown ward

(7) If the child is not a Crown ward and is placed for adoption by a licensee or children's aid society, the following shall also be filed with the application:

1. A copy of any custody or access order that is in force and is known to the person placing the child, or to an applicant.
2. Revoked.
3. A consent to adoption (Form 34F) under section 137 of the Act from every parent, other than the applicant, of whom the person placing the child or an applicant is aware. An order under section 138 of the Act dispensing with a parent's consent may be filed instead of the consent.
4. An affidavit (Form 34G) signed by the licensee or by an authorized employee of the children's aid society (depending on who is placing the child).
5. If the child is placed by a licensee, a copy of the licensee's licence to make the placement at the time of placing the child for adoption.
6. If the child is an Indian or native person, proof of 30 days written notice to the child's band or native community of the intention to place the child for adoption.

Additional material—Relative or step-parent

(8) If the applicant is the child's relative or the spouse of the child's parent, an affidavit from each applicant (Form 34H) shall also be filed with the application.

Application by step-parent or relative

(9) An application by a relative of the child or the spouse of the child's parent,

(a) shall not be commenced until the 21-day period referred to in subsection 137(8) of the Act has expired; and

(b) shall be accompanied by the applicant's affidavit confirming that he or she did not receive a withdrawal of consent during the 21-day period.

Step-parent adoption, parent's consent

(10) An application by the spouse of the child's parent shall be accompanied by the parent's consent (Form 34I).

Independent legal advice, child's consent

(11) The consent of a child to be adopted (Form 34) shall be witnessed by a representative of the Children's Lawyer, who shall complete the affidavit of execution and independent legal advice contained in the form.

Independent legal advice, consent of parent under 18

(11.1) The consent of a person under the age of 18 years who is a parent of the child to be adopted (Form 34F) shall be witnessed by a representative of the Children's Lawyer, who shall complete an affidavit of execution and independent legal advice (Form 34J).

Independent legal advice, adult parent's consent

(12) The consent of an adult parent of the child to be adopted shall be witnessed by an independent lawyer, who shall complete the affidavit of execution and independent legal advice.

Copy of consent for person signing

(13) A person who signs a consent to an adoption shall be given a copy of the consent and of the affidavit of execution and independent legal advice.

Withdrawal of consent by parent

(13.1) A parent who has given consent to an adoption under subsection 137(2) of the Act may withdraw the consent under subsection 137(8) of the Act in accordance with the following:

1. If the child is placed for adoption by a children's aid society, the parent who wishes to withdraw the consent shall ensure that the children's aid society receives the written withdrawal within 21 days after the consent was given.
2. If the child is placed for adoption by a licensee, the parent who wishes to withdraw the consent shall ensure that the licensee receives the written withdrawal within 21 days after the consent was given.
3. If a relative of the child or a spouse of a parent proposes to apply to adopt the child, the parent who wishes to withdraw the consent shall ensure that the relative or spouse receives the written withdrawal within 21 days after the consent was given.

Withdrawal of consent by child aged seven or older

(13.2) A child who has given consent to an adoption under subsection 137(6) of the Act may withdraw the consent under subsection 137(8) of the Act in accordance with the following:

1. The withdrawal shall be signed within 21 days after the consent was given, and witnessed by the person who witnessed the consent under subrule (11) or by another representative of the Children's Lawyer.
2. The person who witnesses the withdrawal shall give the original withdrawal document to the child and promptly serve a copy on the children's aid society, licensee, relative or spouse, as the case may be, by regular service.

Motion to withdraw consent

(14) Despite subrule 5(4) (place for steps other than enforcement), a motion to withdraw a consent to an adoption under subsection 139(1) of the Act shall be made in,

(a) the municipality where the person who gave the consent lives; or

(b) in any other place that the court decides.

Clerk to check adoption application

(15) Before the application is presented to a judge, the clerk shall,

(a) review the application and other documents filed to see whether they are in order; and

(b) prepare a certificate (Form 34K).

Dispensing with consent before placement

(16) In an application to dispense with a parent's consent before placement for adoption,

(a) the applicant may be the licensee, a parent, the children's aid society or the person who wants to adopt;

(b) the respondent is the person who has not given consent;

(c) if an order that service is not required is sought, the request shall be made in the application and not by motion;

(d) if the application is being served, the applicant shall serve and file with it an affidavit (Form 14A) setting out the facts of the case;

(e) if the application is not being served, the applicant shall file with it an affidavit (Form 14A) setting out the facts of the case, and the clerk shall send the case to a judge for a decision on the basis of affidavit evidence.

Forms for openness applications

(17) In a case about an openness order under Part VII of the Act,

(a) an application for an openness order shall be in Form 34L;

(b) a consent to an openness order under section 145.1 of the Act shall be in Form 34M;

(b.1) a consent to an openness order under section 145.1.2 of the Act shall be in Form 34M.1;

(c) an application to change or terminate an openness order shall be in Form 34N; and

(d) an answer to an application for an openness order or an answer to an application to change or terminate an openness order shall be in Form 33B.2.

(e) the notice of intention to place a child for adoption to be served on persons entitled to access, other than the child, shall be in Form 8D.2;

(f) the notice to a child who is entitled to access that he or she will be placed for adoption shall be in Form 8D.3; and

(g) the notice of termination of access to be served on a person who is the subject of an access order and not entitled to bring an application for an openness order shall be in Form 8D.4.

Service of notice of intention to place a child for adoption

(18) In an application for an order under subsection 145.1.1(5) of the Act to allow another method of service of the notice of intention to place a child for adoption or of the notice of termination of access (Form 8D.4), or for an order under subsection 145.1.1 (6) of the Act that notice is not required,

(a) the applicant is the children's aid society;

(b) the respondent is the person who is entitled to have access to, or contact with, the child;

(c) the application shall be made using Form 8B.2—Application (general) (*Child and Family Services Act* cases other than child protection and status review);

(d) the application shall be filed in the same court file as the child protection case in which the child was made a Crown ward;

(e) the applicant shall file an affidavit (Form 14A) setting out the facts in support of the order being requested and the clerk shall send the case to a judge for a decision on the basis of the affidavit evidence.

Timelines for openness applications

(19) Every application for an openness order is governed by the following timetable:

Step in the case	Maximum time for completion, from the date the application is filed
Service and filing of answers	30 days
First hearing or settlement conference	50 days
Hearing	90 days

RULE 35: CHANGE OF NAME

Time for application

35. (1) An application under subsection 7(3) (application to court for change of name) of the *Change of Name Act* shall be made within 30 days after the applicant is notified that the Registrar General has refused to make the requested change of name.

Service on the registrar general

(2) The applicant shall serve the application and any supporting material on the Registrar General by delivering or mailing a copy of the documents to the Deputy Registrar General.

Registrar general's reasons for refusal

(3) Within 15 days after being served under subrule (2), the Registrar General may file reasons for refusing to make the requested change of name.

RULE 35.1: CUSTODY AND ACCESS

Definition

35.1 (1) In this rule,

"parent" means,

(a) a biological parent of a child,

(b) an adoptive parent of a child,

(c) an individual declared under Part II of the *Children's Law Reform Act* to be a parent of a child, and

(d) an individual presumed under section 8 of the *Children's Law Reform Act* to be the father of a child.

Affidavit in support of custody or access claim

(2) If an application, answer or motion to change a final order contains a claim for custody of or access to a child, the party making the claim shall serve and file an affidavit in support of claim for custody or access (Form 35.1), together with any other documents required by this rule, with the document that contains the claim.

Police records check

(3) Every person who makes a claim for custody of a child and who is not a parent of the child shall attach to the affidavit in support of claim for custody or access,

(a) a police records check obtained not more than 60 days before the person starts the claim; or

(b) if the person requested the police records check for the purposes of the claim but has not received it by the time he or she starts the claim, proof of the request.

Same

(4) If clause (3)(b) applies, the person shall serve and file the police records check no later than 10 days after receiving it.

Request for report from children's aid society

(5) Every person required to submit a request under subsection 21.2(2) of the *Children's Law Reform Act* for a report from a children's aid society shall provide to the court a copy of the request together with the affidavit in support of claim for custody or access.

Documents shall be refused

(6) If these rules require a document to be accompanied by the applicable documents referred to in this rule, the clerk shall not accept the document for filing without,

(a) an affidavit in support of claim for custody or access; and

(b) the documents referred to in subrules (3) and (5), if applicable.

Corrections and updates

(7) As soon as a person discovers that information in his or her affidavit in support of claim for custody or access is incorrect or incomplete, or that there has been a change in the information provided in the affidavit, he or she shall immediately serve and file,

(a) a new affidavit in support of claim for custody or access (Form 35.1) containing the correct or updated information; or

(b) if the correction or change is minor, an affidavit in Form 14A describing the correction or change and indicating any effect it has on the person's plan for the care and upbringing of the child.

Associated cases

(8) If the clerk provides to a person making a claim for custody of a child information in writing under subsection 21.3(1) of the *Children's Law Reform Act* respecting any current or previous family proceedings involving the child or any person who is a party to the claim and who is not a parent of the child, the person shall serve a copy of the written information on every other party.

Same

(9) If the written information provided by the clerk contains information indicating that the person making the claim was or is involved in family proceedings in which he or she was or is not involved, the person making the claim may serve with the copy of the written information an affidavit identifying those proceedings.

RULE 36: DIVORCE

Application for divorce

36. (1) Either spouse may start a divorce case by,

(a) filing an application naming the other spouse as a respondent; or

(b) filing a joint application with no respondent.

Joint application

(2) In a joint application, the divorce and any other order sought shall be made only with the consent of both spouses.

Allegation of adultery

(3) In an application for divorce claiming that the other spouse committed adultery with another person, that person does not need to be named, but if named, shall be served with the application and has all the rights of a respondent in the case.

Marriage certificate and central divorce registry certificate

(4) The court shall not grant a divorce until the following have been filed:

1. A marriage certificate or marriage registration certificate, unless the application states that it is impractical to obtain a certificate and explains why.
2. A report on earlier divorce cases started by either spouse, issued under the *Central Registry of Divorce Proceedings Regulations* (Canada).

Divorce based on affidavit evidence

(5) If the respondent files no answer, or files one and later withdraws it, the applicant shall file an affidavit (Form 36) that,

(a) confirms that all the information in the application is correct, except as stated in the affidavit;

(b) if no marriage certificate or marriage registration certificate has been filed, provides sufficient information to prove the marriage;

(c) contains proof of any previous divorce or the death of a party's previous spouse, unless the marriage took place in Canada;

(d) contains the information about arrangements for support of any children of the marriage required by paragraph 11(1)(b) of the *Divorce Act* (Canada), and attaches as exhibits the income and financial information required by section 21 of the child support guidelines; and

(e) contains any other information necessary for the court to grant the divorce.

Draft divorce order

(6) The applicant shall file with the affidavit,

(a) three copies of a draft divorce order (Form 25A);

(b) a stamped envelope addressed to each party; and

(c) if the divorce order is to contain a support order,

(i) an extra copy of the draft divorce order for the clerk to file with the Director of the Family Responsibility Office, and

(ii) two copies of a draft support deduction order.

Clerk to present papers to judge

(7) When the documents mentioned in subrules (4) to (6) have been filed, the clerk shall prepare a certificate (Form 36A) and present the documents to a judge, who may,

(a) grant the divorce as set out in the draft order;

(b) have the clerk return the documents to the applicant to make any needed corrections; or

(c) grant the divorce but make changes to the draft order, or refuse to grant the divorce, after giving the applicant a chance to file an additional affidavit or come to court to explain why the order should be made without change.

Divorce certificate

(8) When a divorce takes effect, the clerk shall, on either party's request,

(a) check the continuing record to verify that,

(i) no appeal has been taken from the divorce order, or any appeal from it has been disposed of, and

(ii) no order has been made extending the time for an appeal, or any extended time has expired without an appeal; and

(b) if satisfied of those matters, issue a divorce certificate (Form 36B) and mail it to the parties, unless the court orders otherwise.

(9) Revoked.

RULE 37: INTERJURISDICTIONAL SUPPORT ORDERS ACT, 2002

Application

37. (1) This rule applies to cases under the Act.

Definitions

(2) In this rule,

"Act" means the *Interjurisdictional Support Orders Act, 2002*;

"appropriate authority" has the same meaning as in the Act;

"designated authority" has the same meaning as in the Act;

"general regulation" means Ontario Regulation 55/03;

"send," when used in reference to a person, means to,

(a) mail to the person's lawyer or, if none, to the person,

(b) send by courier to the person's lawyer or, if none, to the person,

(c) deposit at a document exchange to which the person's lawyer belongs, or

(d) fax to the person's lawyer or, if none, to the person.

Notice of hearing

(3) When the court receives a support application or a support variation application the clerk shall, under section 10 or 33 of the Act,

(a) serve on the respondent, by special service,

(i) the notice of hearing mentioned in clause 10(b) or 33(b) of the Act (Form 37),

(ii) a copy of the documents sent by the designated authority, and

(iii) blank response forms; and

(b) send to the designated authority a copy of the notice of hearing and an information sheet (Form 37A).

Information and documents to be provided by respondent

(4) The respondent shall file, within 30 days after service of the notice of hearing,

(a) an answer in Form N under the general regulation,

(i) identifying any issues the respondent intends to raise with respect to the support application, and

(ii) containing the financial information referred to in subsection 21(1) of Ontario Regulation 391/97 (Child Support Guidelines), if the support application includes a claim for child support;

(b) an affidavit (Form 14A) setting out the evidence on which the respondent relies; and

(c) a financial statement in Form K under the general regulation.

Respondent's financial statement

(5) The respondent is required to file a financial statement whether he or she intends to dispute the claim or not.

Applicant's financial statement

(6) The fact that the applicant has provided financial information in a form different than that required by these rules does not affect the case.

Written hearing

(7) Unless the court orders otherwise under subrule (9), the application shall be dealt with on the basis of written documents without the parties or their lawyers needing to come to court.

Request for oral hearing

(8) The respondent may request an oral hearing by filing a motion (Form 14B) within 30 days after being served with the notice of hearing.

Order for oral hearing

(9) The court may order an oral hearing, on the respondent's motion or on its own initiative, if it is satisfied that an oral hearing is necessary to deal with the case justly.

Direction to request further information or documents

(10) A direction to request further information or documents under clause 11(2)(a) or 34(2)(a) of the Act shall be in Form 37B, and a statement of the court's reasons for requesting further evidence shall be attached to the direction.

Direction to be sent to respondent

(11) When a direction is sent to the designated authority under clause 11(2)(a) of the Act, the clerk shall also send a copy to the respondent.

Adjournment

(12) When the court adjourns the hearing under clause 11(2)(b) or 34(2)(b) of the Act, it shall specify the date on which the hearing is to continue.

Copies of further information or documents

(13) When the court receives the further information or documents, the clerk shall promptly prepare a notice of continuation of hearing (Form 37C) and send it, with copies of the information or documents, to the respondent and to the designated authority.

Respondent's affidavit

(14) If the respondent wishes to respond to the further information or documents, he or she shall file an affidavit (Form 14A) containing the response with the court, within 30 days after receiving the notice of continuation of hearing.

Preparation of order

(15) The clerk shall prepare the order for signature as soon as it is made, in accordance with subrule 25(11).

Sending copies of order to respondent and designated authority

(16) The court shall send,

(a) a copy of the order to the respondent, addressed to the respondent's last known address if sent by mail; and

(b) a certified copy of the order to the designated authority.

Sending copy of order to appropriate authority

(17) The designated authority shall send the certified copy of the order to the appropriate authority.

Notice of registration, order made outside Canada

(18) For the purpose of subsection 20(1) of the Act, the clerk of the Ontario court shall give notice of the registration of an order made outside Canada by providing a notice in

Form 37D, as described in subrule (19), to any party to the order who is believed to ordinarily reside in Ontario.

Sending or special service

(19) If the party to whom notice is to be provided applied for the order in Ontario, the clerk shall send the notice to the party, but in any other case, the clerk shall serve the notice on the party by special service.

Motion to set aside registration

(20) For the purpose of subsection 20(3) of the Act, a party shall give notice of a motion to set aside the registration of an order made outside Canada by,

(a) filing in the Ontario court a notice of motion (Form 14) setting out the grounds for the motion;

(b) sending the notice of motion and supporting documents to the claimant at the address shown in the order; and

(c) serving the notice of motion and supporting documents on the designated authority by regular service at least 10 days before the motion hearing date.

Designated authority need not appear on motion

(21) The designated authority is not required to appear on the motion to set aside registration.

Notice of decision or order

(22) When the court makes a decision or order under section 20 of the Act, the clerk shall send copies of the order, with the court's reasons, if any,

(a) to each party, addressed to the party's last known address if sent by mail; and

(b) to the designated authority.

Party in reciprocating jurisdiction

(23) If a party ordinarily resides in a reciprocating jurisdiction and the order was originally sent to Ontario for registration by the appropriate authority there, the clerk may send it to that appropriate authority rather than sending it to the party as set out in clause (22)(a).

Provisional orders

(24) When the court makes a provisional order under section 7 or 30 of the Act, the clerk shall send the following to the designated authority, to be sent to the reciprocating jurisdiction:

1. One copy of,
   i. the application (Form A under the general regulation),
   ii. the applicant's financial statement (Form K under the general regulation), and
   iii. a statement giving any information about the respondent's identification, whereabouts, income, assets and liabilities.
2. Three certified copies of,
   i. the applicant's evidence and, if reasonably possible, the exhibits, and
   ii. the provisional order.

Further evidence

(25) When the court that made a provisional order receives a request for further evidence from the confirming court under subsection 7(4) or 30(4) of the Act, the clerk shall send to the applicant a notice for taking further evidence (Form 37E) and a copy of the documents sent by the confirming court.

RULE 37.1: PROVISIONAL ORDERS AND CONFIRMATION OF PROVISIONAL ORDERS—DIVORCE ACT, FAMILY LAW ACT

Application

37.1 (1) This rule applies to orders made under sections 18 and 19 of the *Divorce Act* (Canada) and under section 44 of the *Family Law Act.*

Definitions

(2) In this rule,

"confirming court" means,

(a) in the case of an order under section 19 of the *Divorce Act* (Canada), the court in Ontario or another province or territory of Canada that has jurisdiction to confirm a provisional variation of the order, or

(b) for the purpose of section 44 of the *Family Law Act,*

(i) the Ontario Court of Justice sitting in the municipality where the respondent resides, or

(ii) the Family Court of the Superior Court of Justice, if the respondent resides in an area where that court has jurisdiction;

"originating court" means,

(a) in the case of an order under section 18 of the *Divorce Act* (Canada), the court in Ontario or another province or territory of Canada that has jurisdiction under section 5 of that Act to deal with an application for a provisional variation of the order, or

(b) for the purpose of section 44 of the *Family Law Act,*

(i) the Ontario Court of Justice sitting in the municipality where the provisional order is made, or

(ii) the Family Court of the Superior Court of Justice when it makes the provisional order;

"send," when used in reference to a person, means to,

(a) mail to the person's lawyer or, if none, to the person,

(b) send by courier to the person's lawyer or, if none, to the person,

(c) deposit at a document exchange to which the person's lawyer belongs, or

(d) fax to the person's lawyer or, if none, to the person.

Documents to be sent to confirming court

(3) When the court makes a provisional order under section 18 of the *Divorce Act* (Canada) or section 44 of the *Family Law Act,* the clerk shall send the following to the confirming court (if it is in Ontario) or to the Attorney General to be sent to the confirming court (if it is outside Ontario):

1. One copy of,
   i. the application (Form 8),
   ii. the applicant's financial statement (Form 13),
   iii. a statement giving any information about the respondent's identification, whereabouts, income, assets and liabilities, and
   iv. if the confirming court is in another municipality in Ontario, proof that the application was served on the respondent.
2. Three certified copies of,
   i. the applicant's evidence and, if reasonably possible, the exhibits, and
   ii. the provisional order.

No financial statement from foreign applicant

(4) When a confirming court in Ontario receives a provisional order made outside Ontario, the applicant does not have to file a financial statement.

Notice of confirmation hearing

(5) A clerk of a confirming court in Ontario who receives a provisional order shall,

(a) serve on the respondent, by special service (subrule 6(3)),

(i) a notice of hearing (Form 37),

(ii) a copy of the documents sent by the originating court, and

(iii) blank response forms; and

(b) send a notice of hearing and an information sheet (Form 37A) to,

(i) the applicant,

(ii) the clerk of the originating court, and

(iii) the Attorney General, if the provisional order was made outside Ontario.

Respondent's financial statement

(6) A respondent at a confirmation hearing under section 19 of the *Divorce Act* (Canada) shall serve and file a financial statement (Form 13) within 30 days after service of the notice of confirmation hearing.

Written hearing

(7) Unless the court orders otherwise under subrule (9), the application shall be dealt with on the basis of written documents without the parties or their lawyers needing to come to court.

Request for oral hearing

(8) The respondent may request an oral hearing by filing a motion (Form 14B) within 30 days after being served with the notice of hearing.

Order for oral hearing

(9) The court may order an oral hearing, on the applicant's motion or on its own initiative, if it is satisfied that an oral hearing is necessary to deal with the case justly.

Court receives request for further evidence

(10) When an originating court in Ontario receives a request for further evidence from the confirming court, the clerk shall send to the applicant a notice for taking further evidence (Form 37E) and a copy of the documents sent by the confirming court.

Court sends request for further evidence

(11) When a confirming court in Ontario requests further evidence from the originating court,

(a) the confirming court shall adjourn the confirmation hearing to a new date; and

(b) the clerk shall send to the originating court two certified copies of the evidence taken in the confirming court.

Continuing the Confirmation Hearing

(12) When a confirming court in Ontario receives further evidence from the originating court, the clerk shall promptly prepare a notice of continuation of hearing (Form 37C) and send it, with copies of the evidence, to the respondent and, if the provisional order was made outside Ontario, to the Attorney General.

Respondent's affidavit

(13) If the respondent wishes to respond to the further evidence, he or she shall file an affidavit containing the response with the court, within 30 days after receiving the notice of continuation of hearing.

RULE 38: APPEALS

Rules that apply in appeals to Divisional Court and Court of Appeal

38. (1) Rules 61, 62 and 63 of the Rules of Civil Procedure apply with necessary modifications, including those modifications set out in subrules (2) and (3),

(a) if an appeal lies to the Divisional Court or the Court of Appeal;

(b) if leave to appeal to the Divisional Court or the Court of Appeal is required,

in a family law case as described in subrule 1(2).

Modifications in child protection appeals

(2) If the appeal is brought in a case under the *Child and Family Services Act*, the following time periods apply instead of the time periods mentioned in the referenced provisions of the Rules of Civil Procedure:

1. The time period referred to in clause 61.09(1)(a) shall be 14 days after filing the notice of appeal if there is no transcript.
2. The time period referred to in clause 61.09(1)(b) shall be 30 days after receiving notice that the evidence has been transcribed.
3. The time period referred to in clause 61.12(2) shall be 30 days after service of the appeal book and compendium, exhibit book, transcript of evidence, if any, and appellant's factum.
4. The time period referred to in clause 61.13(2)(a) shall be 30 days after the registrar receives notice that the evidence has been transcribed.
5. The time period referred to in clause 61.13(2)(b) shall be six months after filing the notice of appeal.
6. The time period referred to in subrule 62.02(2) for serving the notice of motion for leave to appeal shall be 30 days.

Appeal of temporary order in *Child and Family Services Act* case

(3) In an appeal of a temporary order made in a case under the *Child and Family Services Act* and brought to the Divisional Court under clause 19(1)(b) of the *Courts of Justice Act*, the motion for leave to appeal shall be combined with the notice of appeal and heard together with the appeal.

Appeals to the superior court of justice

(4) Subrules (5) to (45) apply to an appeal from an order of the Ontario Court of Justice to the Superior Court of Justice under,

(a) section 48 of the *Family Law Act*;

(b) section 73 of the *Children's Law Reform Act*;

(c) sections 69 and 156 of the *Child and Family Services Act*;

(d) section 40 of the *Interjurisdictional Support Orders Act, 2002*;

(e) section 40 of the *Courts of Justice Act*; and

(f) any other statute to which these rules apply, unless the statute provides for another procedure.

How to start appeal

(5) To start an appeal from a final order of the Ontario Court of Justice to the Superior Court of Justice under any of the provisions listed in subrule (4), a party shall,

(a) within 30 days after the date of the order or decision being appealed from, serve a notice of appeal (Form 38) by regular service on,

(i) every other party affected by the appeal or entitled to appeal,

(ii) the clerk of the court in the place where the order was made, and

(iii) if the appeal is under section 69 of the *Child and Family Services Act*, every other person entitled to notice under subsection 39(3) of that Act who appeared at the hearing; and

(b) within 10 days after serving the notice of appeal, file it.

Starting appeal of temporary order

(6) Subrule (5) applies to the starting of an appeal from a temporary order of the Ontario Court of Justice to the Superior Court of Justice except that the notice of appeal shall be served within seven days after the date of the temporary order.

Same, *Child and Family Services Act* case

(7) To start an appeal from a temporary order of the Ontario Court of Justice to the Superior Court of Justice in a case under the *Child and Family Services Act*, subrule (5) applies and the notice of appeal shall be served within 30 days after the date of the temporary order.

Name of case unchanged

(8) The name of a case in an appeal shall be the same as the name of the case in the order appealed from and shall identify the parties as appellant and respondent.

Appeal by respondent

(9) If the respondent in an appeal also wants to appeal the same order, this rule applies, with necessary modifications, to the respondent's appeal, and the two appeals shall be heard together.

Grounds stated in notice of appeal

(10) The notice of appeal shall state the order that the appellant wants the appeal court to make and the legal grounds for the appeal.

Other grounds

(11) At the hearing of the appeal, no grounds other than the ones stated in the notice of appeal may be argued unless the court gives permission.

Transcript of evidence

(12) If the appeal requires a transcript of evidence, the appellant shall, within 30 days after filing the notice of appeal, file proof that the transcript has been ordered.

Consultation with respondent

(13) The appellant shall determine if the appeal requires a transcript of evidence in consultation with the respondent.

Agreement on evidence to be transcribed

(14) If the appellant and respondent agree about what evidence needs to be transcribed, the appellant shall order the agreed evidence transcribed.

No agreement

(15) If the appellant and respondent cannot agree, the appellant shall order a transcript of all of the oral evidence from the hearing of the decision under appeal unless the court orders otherwise.

Court reporter's duty

(16) When the court reporter has completed the transcript, he or she shall promptly notify the appellant, the respondent and the court office in the court where the appeal will be heard.

Contents of appellant's appeal record

(17) The appellant's appeal record shall contain a copy of the following documents, in the following order:

1. A table of contents describing each document, including each exhibit, by its nature and date and, for an exhibit, by exhibit number or letter.
2. The notice of appeal.
3. The order being appealed, as signed, and any reasons given by the court appealed from, as well as a further printed copy of the reasons if they are handwritten.
4. A transcript of the oral evidence.
5. Any other material that was before the court appealed from and that is necessary for the appeal.

Contents of appellant's factum

(18) The appellant's factum shall be not more than 30 pages long, shall be signed by the appellant's lawyer or, if none, by the appellant and shall consist of the following parts, containing paragraphs numbered consecutively from the beginning to the end of the factum:

1. Part 1: Identification. A statement identifying the appellant and respondent and the court appealed from, and stating the result in that court.
2. Part 2: Overview. A brief overview of the case and the issues on the appeal.
3. Part 3: Facts. A brief summary of the facts relevant to the appeal, with reference to the evidence by page and line as necessary.
4. Part 4: Issues. A brief statement of each issue, followed by a brief argument referring to the law relating to that issue.
5. Part 5: Order. A precise statement of the order the appeal court is asked to make, including any order for costs.
6. Part 6: Time estimate. An estimate of how much time will be needed for the appellant's oral argument, not including reply to the respondent's argument.
7. Part 7: List of authorities. A list of all statutes, regulations, rules, cases and other authorities referred to in the factum.
8. Part 8: Legislation. A copy of all relevant provisions of statutes, regulations and rules.

Respondent's factum and appeal record

(19) The respondent shall, within the timeline set out in subrule (21) or (22), serve on every other party to the appeal and file,

(a) a respondent's factum (subrule (20)); and

(b) if applicable, a respondent's appeal record containing a copy of any material that was before the court appealed from which are necessary for the appeal but are not included in the appellant's appeal record.

Contents of respondent's factum

(20) The respondent's factum shall be not more than 30 pages long, shall be signed by the respondent's lawyer or, if none, by the respondent and shall consist of the following parts, containing paragraphs numbered consecutively from the beginning to the end of the factum:

1. Part 1: Overview. A brief overview of the case and the issues on the appeal.
2. Part 2: Facts. A brief statement of the facts in the appellant's factum that the respondent accepts as correct and the facts that the respondent says are incorrect, and a brief summary of any additional facts relied on by the respondent, with reference to the evidence by page and line as necessary.
3. Part 3: Issues. A statement of the respondent's position on each issue raised by the appellant, followed by a brief argument referring to the law relating to that issue.
4. Part 4: Additional issues. A brief statement of each additional issue raised by the respondent, followed by a brief argument referring to the law relating to that issue.
5. Part 5: Order. A precise statement of the order the appeal court is asked to make, including any order for costs.
6. Part 6: Time estimate. An estimate of how much time will be needed for the respondent's oral argument.
7. Part 7: List of authorities. A list of all statutes, regulations, rules, cases and other authorities referred to in the factum.
8. Part 8: Legislation. A copy of all relevant provisions of statutes, regulations and rules not included in the appellant's factum.

Timelines for serving and filing of records and factums other than in *Child and Family Services Act* cases

(21) Except for appeals in cases under the *Child and Family Services Act*, the following timelines for serving appeal records and factums apply:

1. If a transcript is required, the appellant's appeal record and factum shall be served on the respondent and any other person entitled to be heard in the appeal and

filed within 60 days from the date of receiving notice that evidence has been transcribed.

2. If no transcript is required, the appellant's appeal record and factum shall be served on the respondent and any other person entitled to be heard in the appeal and filed within 30 days of filing of the notice of appeal.
3. The respondent's appeal record and factum shall be served on the appellant and any other person entitled to be heard on the appeal and filed within 60 days from the serving of the appellant's appeal record and factum.

Timelines for serving and filing of records and factums in *Child and Family Services Act* cases

(22) For appeals of cases under the *Child and Family Services Act*, the following timelines for serving appeal records and factums apply:

1. If a transcript is required, the appellant's appeal record and factum shall be served on the respondent and any other person entitled to be heard in the appeal and filed within 30 days from the date of receiving notice that evidence has been transcribed.
2. If no transcript is required, the appellant's appeal record and factum shall be served on the respondent and any other person entitled to be heard in the appeal and filed within 14 days of filing of the notice of appeal.
3. The respondent's appeal record and factum shall be served on the appellant and any other person entitled to be heard on the appeal and filed within 30 days from the serving of the appellant's appeal record and factum.

Scheduling of hearing

(23) When the appellant's appeal record and factum have been filed and the respondent's factum and appeal record, if any, have been filed, or the time for their filing has expired, the clerk shall schedule the appeal for hearing.

Prompt hearing of CFSA appeals

(24) An appeal under the *Child and Family Services Act* shall be heard within 60 days after the appellant's factum and appeal record are filed.

Motions in appeals

(25) If a person needs to bring a motion in an appeal, rule 14 applies with necessary modifications to the motion.

Security for costs of appeal

(26) On a motion by the respondent for security for costs, the court may make an order for security for costs that is just, if it is satisfied that,

(a) there is good reason to believe that the appeal is a waste of time, a nuisance, or an abuse of the court process and that the appellant has insufficient assets in Ontario to pay the costs of the appeal;

(b) an order for security for costs could be made against the appellant under subrule 24(13); or

(c) for other good reason, security for costs should be ordered.

Dismissal for failure to obey order

(27) If an appellant does not obey an order under subrule (26), the court may on motion dismiss the appeal.

Motion for summary judgment in appeal

(28) After the notice of appeal is filed, the respondent or any other person who is entitled to be heard on the appeal may make a motion for summary judgment or for summary decision on a legal issue without a hearing of the appeal, and rule 16 applies to the motion with necessary modifications.

Motion to receive further evidence

(29) Any person entitled to be heard in the appeal may bring a motion to admit further evidence under clause 134(4)(b) of the *Courts of Justice Act*.

Motion for dismissal for delay

(30) If the appellant has not,

(a) filed proof that a transcript of evidence was ordered under subrule (12);

(b) served and filed the appeal record and factum within the timelines set out in subrule (21) or (22) or such longer time as may have been ordered by the court,

the respondent may file a procedural motion (Form 14B) to have the appeal dismissed for delay.

Withdrawal of appeal

(31) The appellant may withdraw an appeal by serving a notice of withdrawal (Form 12) on every other party and filing it.

Deemed withdrawal

(32) If a person serves a notice of appeal and does not file it within 10 days as required by clause (5)(b), the appeal shall be deemed to be withdrawn unless the court orders otherwise.

Automatic stays pending appeal, support orders

(33) The service of a notice of appeal from a temporary or final order does not stay a support order or an order that enforces a support order.

Other payment orders

(34) The service of a notice of appeal from a temporary or final order stays, until the disposition of the appeal, any other payment order made under the temporary or final order.

Stay by order of court

(35) A temporary or final order may be stayed on any conditions that the court considers appropriate,

(a) by an order of the court that made the order;

(b) by an order of the Superior Court of Justice.

Expiry of stay granted by court that made order

(36) A stay granted under clause (35)(a) expires if no notice of appeal is served and the time for service has expired.

Powers of superior court of justice

(37) A stay granted under subrule (35) may be set aside or changed by the Superior Court of Justice.

Effect of stay generally

(38) If an order is stayed, no steps may be taken under the order or for its enforcement, except,

(a) by order of the Superior Court of Justice; or
(b) as provided in subrules (39) and (40).

Settling of order

(39) A stay does not prevent the settling or signing of the order.

Writ of execution

(40) A stay does not prevent the issue of a writ of seizure and sale or the filing of the writ in a sheriff's office or land registry office, but no instruction or direction to enforce the writ shall be given to a sheriff while the stay remains in effect.

Certificate of stay

(41) If an order is stayed, the clerk of the court that granted the stay shall, if requested by a party to the appeal, issue a certificate of stay in Form 63A under the Rules of Civil Procedure with necessary modifications.

Stay of support order

(42) A party who obtains a stay of a support order shall obtain a certificate of stay under subrule (41) and file it immediately in the office of the Director of the Family Responsibility Office if the stay relates to a support order being enforced by the Director.

Certificate filed with sheriff's office

(43) If a certificate of stay is filed with the sheriff's office, the sheriff shall not begin or continue enforcement of the order until satisfied that the stay is no longer in effect.

Request for certificate

(44) A request for a certificate of stay under subrule (41) shall state whether the stay is under subrule (34) or by order under subrule (35) and, if under subrule (35), shall set out the particulars of the order.

Setting aside writ of execution

(45) The court may set aside the issue or filing of a writ of seizure and sale if the party making the motion or the appellant gives security satisfactory to the court.

Appeals, family arbitration awards

(46) Subrules (5), (8) to (21), (23) and (25) to (32) apply, with necessary modifications, including the modifications set out in subrules (47) to (55), to the appeal of a family arbitration award under section 45 of the *Arbitration Act, 1991* and, for the purpose,

(a) a reference to the Ontario Court of Justice or to the court being appealed from shall be read as a reference to the arbitrator who made the family arbitration award; and

(b) a reference to the order or decision being appealed from shall be read as a reference to the family arbitration award.

Same, service

(47) In addition to the persons listed under clause (5)(a), the appellant shall serve the notice of appeal on the arbitrator.

Same, contents of appellant's appeal record

(48) The material referred to in paragraph 5 of subrule (17) shall include,

(a) copies of the certificates of independent legal advice required by the *Family Law Act* for the parties;
(b) a copy of the family arbitration agreement; and
(c) the original family arbitration award or a certified copy.

Same, if leave required

(49) If the appeal of a family arbitration award requires the leave of the court, rule 14 applies, with necessary modifications, including the modifications set out in subrules (50) to (55), to the motion for leave to appeal, other than subrules 14(4), (4.2), (6), (7), (10) to (15) and (17).

Same

(50) The notice of motion (Form 14) shall,

(a) be served on every other party affected by the appeal or entitled to appeal and on the arbitrator no later than 15 days after the making of the family arbitration award; and
(b) be filed no later than five days after service.

Same

(51) The affidavit (Form 14A) and any additional evidence mentioned in clause 14(9)(b) shall be served and filed no later than 30 days after the filing of the notice of motion for leave to appeal, together with,

(a) a copy of the notice of motion;
(b) the documents listed in subrule (48); and
(c) a factum consisting of a concise argument stating the facts and law relied on by the party making the motion.

Same

(52) The notice of motion and factum shall set out the specific questions that it is proposed the court should answer on appeal if leave to appeal is granted.

Same

(53) Any response to the motion for leave to appeal by a party shall be served and filed no later than 15 days after the materials referred to in subrule (51) were served on the party.

Same

(54) The clerk shall fix a date for the hearing of the motion, which shall not, except with the consent of the party responding to the motion, be earlier than 15 days after the filing of the materials referred to in subrule (51).

Same

(55) If leave to appeal is granted,

(a) the notice of appeal shall be served no later than seven days after the granting of leave; and

(b) the 30-day deadline set out in clause (5)(a) does not apply, but the filing deadline set out in clause (5)(b) continues to apply.

RULE 39: CASE MANAGEMENT IN FAMILY COURT OF SUPERIOR COURT OF JUSTICE

Case management in certain areas only

39. (1) This rule applies only to cases in the Family Court of the Superior Court of Justice, which has jurisdiction in the municipalities listed in subrule 1(3).

Excluded cases

(2) This rule does not apply to,

(a) enforcements;
(b) cases under rule 32.1, 37 or 37.1; or
(c) cases under the *Child and Family Services Act*.

Parties may not lengthen times

(3) A time set out in this rule may be lengthened only by order of the case management judge and not by the parties' consent under subrule 3(6).

Fast track

(4) Applications to which this rule applies, except the ones mentioned in subrule (7), and motions to change a final order or agreement are fast track cases (subrules (5) and (6)).

Fast track—First court date

(5) In a fast track case the clerk shall, on or before the first court date,

(a) confirm that all necessary documents have been served and filed;

(b) refer the parties to sources of information about the court process, alternatives to court (including mediation), the effects of separation and divorce on children and community resources that may help the parties and their children;

(c) if an answer has been filed in response to an application, or if a response to motion to change (Form 15B) or a notice of financial interest has been filed in a motion to change a final order or agreement under rule 15, confirm that the case is ready for a hearing, case conference or settlement conference and schedule it accordingly;

(d) if no answer has been filed in response to an application, send the case to a judge for a decision on the basis of affidavit evidence or, on request of the applicant, schedule a case conference; and

(e) if no response to motion to change (Form 15B), consent motion to change (Form 15C) or notice of financial interest is filed in response to a motion to change a final order or agreement under rule 15, send the case to a judge for a decision on the basis of the evidence filed in the motion.

Fast track—Case management judge assigned at start

(6) In a fast track case, a case management judge shall be assigned by the first time the case comes before a judge.

Standard track

(7) Applications in which the applicant makes any of the following claims are standard track cases (subrule (8)).

1. A claim for divorce.
2. A property claim.
3. A claim under the *Arbitration Act, 1991* or the *Family Law Act* relating to a family arbitration, family arbitration agreement or family arbitration award.

Features of standard track

(8) In a standard track case,

(a) the clerk shall not set a court date when the application is filed;

(b) a case management judge shall be assigned when a case conference or a motion is scheduled, whichever comes first; and

(c) the clerk shall schedule a case conference on any party's request.

Functions of case management judge

(9) The case management judge assigned to a case,

(a) shall generally supervise its progress;

(b) shall conduct the case conference and the settlement conference;

(c) may schedule a case conference or settlement conference at any time, on the judge's own initiative; and

(d) shall hear motions in the case, when available to hear motions.

(e) Revoked.

Substitute case management judge

(10) If the case management judge is, for any reason, unavailable to continue as the case management judge, another case management judge may be assigned for part or all of the case.

Notice of approaching dismissal after 365 days

(11) The clerk shall serve a notice of approaching dismissal (Form 39) for a case on the parties by mail, fax or electronic mail if the case has not been settled, withdrawn or scheduled or adjourned for trial before the 365th day after the date the case was started, and that time has not been lengthened by an order under subrule (3).

Exception

(11.1) Despite subrule (11), if a case conference or settlement conference is arranged before the 365th day after the date the case was started for a date on or later than the 365th day, the clerk shall not serve a notice of approaching dismissal except as set out in subrule (11.2).

Notice sent if conference does not take place

(11.2) If a case conference or settlement conference is arranged for a date on or later than the 365th day after the date the case was started, but the hearing does not take place on that date and is not adjourned by a judge, the clerk shall serve the notice of approaching dismissal on the parties by mail, fax or electronic mail.

Dismissal of case

(12) A case for which a notice of approaching dismissal has been served shall be dismissed without further notice, unless one of the parties, within 60 days after the notice is served,

(a) obtains an order under subrule (3) to lengthen that time;

(b) files an agreement signed by all parties and their lawyers, if any, for a final order disposing of all issues in the case, and a notice of motion for an order carrying out the agreement;

(c) serves on all parties and files a notice of withdrawal (Form 12) that discontinues all outstanding claims in the case;

(d) schedules or adjourns the case for trial; or

(e) arranges a case conference or settlement conference for the first available date.

Same

(12.1) If a case conference or settlement conference is arranged for a date as described in clause (12)(e), but the hearing does not take place on that date and is not adjourned by a judge, the case shall be dismissed without further notice.

Dismissal after notice

(12.2) The clerk shall dismiss a case under subrule (12) or (12.1) by preparing and signing an order dismissing the case, with no costs payable by any party.

Service of dismissal order by clerk

(13) The clerk shall serve the order on each party by mail, fax or electronic mail.

Service of dismissal order by lawyer on client

(14) A lawyer who is served with a dismissal order on behalf of a client shall serve it on the client by mail, fax or electronic mail and file proof of service of the order.

Judge may set clerk's order aside

(14.1) The case management judge or another judge may, on motion, set aside an order of the clerk under subrule (12).

(15) Revoked.

RULE 40: CASE MANAGEMENT IN ONTARIO COURT OF JUSTICE

Case management in certain areas only

40. (1) This rule applies only to cases in the Ontario Court of Justice.

Excluded cases

(2) This rule does not apply to,

(a) enforcements;

(b) cases under rule 37 or 37.1; or

(c) cases under the *Child and Family Services Act*.

Parties may not lengthen times

(3) A time set out in this rule may be lengthened only by order and not by the parties' consent under subrule 3(6).

First court date

(4) The clerk shall, on or before the first court date,

(a) confirm that all necessary documents have been served and filed;

(b) refer the parties to sources of information about the court process, alternatives to court (including mediation), the effects of separation and divorce on children and community resources that may help the parties and their children;

(c) if an answer has been filed in response to an application, or if a response to motion to change (Form 15B) or a notice of financial interest has been filed in a motion to change a final order or agreement under rule 15, confirm that the case is ready for a hearing, case conference or settlement conference and schedule it accordingly;

(d) if no answer has been filed in response to an application, send the case to a judge for a decision on the basis of affidavit evidence or, on request of the applicant, schedule a case conference; and

(e) if no response to motion to change (Form 15B), consent motion to change (Form 15C) or notice of financial interest is filed in response to a motion to change a final order or agreement under rule 15, send the case to a judge for a decision on the basis of the evidence filed in the motion.

Notice of approaching dismissal after 365 days

(5) The clerk shall serve a notice of approaching dismissal (Form 39) for a case on the parties by mail, fax or electronic mail if the case has not been settled, withdrawn or scheduled or adjourned for trial before the 365th day after the date the case was started, and that time has not been lengthened by an order under subrule (3).

Exception

(5.1) Despite subrule (5), if a case conference or settlement conference is arranged before the 365th day after the date the case was started for a date on or later than the 365th day, the clerk shall not serve a notice of approaching dismissal except as set out in subrule (5.2).

Notice sent if conference does not take place

(5.2) If a case conference or settlement conference is arranged for a date on or later than the 365th day after the date the case was started, but the hearing does not take place on that date and is not adjourned by a judge, the clerk shall serve the notice of approaching dismissal on the parties by mail, fax or electronic mail.

Dismissal of case

(6) A case for which a notice of approaching dismissal has been served shall be dismissed without further notice, unless one of the parties, within 60 days after the notice is served,

(a) obtains an order under subrule (3) to lengthen that time;

(b) files an agreement signed by all parties and their lawyers, if any, for a final order disposing of all issues in the case, and a notice of motion for an order carrying out the agreement;

(c) serves on all parties and files a notice of withdrawal (Form 12) that discontinues all outstanding claims in the case;

(d) schedules or adjourns the case for trial; or

(e) arranges a case conference or settlement conference for the first available date.

Same

(6.1) If a case conference or settlement conference is arranged for a date as described in clause (6)(e), but the hearing does not take place on that date and is not adjourned by a judge, the case shall be dismissed without further notice.

Dismissal after notice

(6.2) The clerk shall dismiss a case under subrule (6) or (6.1) by preparing and signing an order dismissing the case, with no costs payable by any party.

Service of dismissal order by clerk

(7) The clerk shall serve the order on each party by mail, fax or electronic mail.

Service of dismissal order by lawyer on client

(8) A lawyer who is served with a dismissal order on behalf of a client shall serve it on the client by mail, fax or electronic mail and file proof of service of the order.

Judge may set clerk's order aside

(9) A judge may, on motion, set aside an order of the clerk under subrule (6).

(10) Revoked.

RULE 41: CASE MANAGEMENT IN THE SUPERIOR COURT OF JUSTICE (OTHER THAN THE FAMILY COURT OF THE SUPERIOR COURT OF JUSTICE)

Case management

41. (1) This rule applies only to cases in the Superior Court of Justice, other than cases in the Family Court of the Superior Court of Justice, started on or after July 1, 2004.

Excluded cases

(2) This rule does not apply to,

(a) enforcements; or

(b) cases under rule 32.1, 37 or 37.1.

Parties may not lengthen times

(3) A time set out in this rule may be lengthened only by order of the court and not by the parties' consent under subrule 3(6).

Clerk's role

(4) The clerk shall not set a court date when the application is filed, and the case shall come before the court when a case conference or a motion is scheduled, whichever comes first, and the clerk shall schedule a case conference on any party's request.

Notice of approaching dismissal after 365 days

(5) The clerk shall serve a notice of approaching dismissal (Form 39) for a case on the parties by mail, fax or electronic mail if the case has not been settled, withdrawn or scheduled or adjourned for trial before the 365th day after the date the case was started, and that time has not been lengthened by an order under subrule (3).

Exception

(5.1) Despite subrule (5), if a case conference or settlement conference is arranged before the 365th day after the date the case was started for a date on or later than the 365th day, the clerk shall not serve a notice of approaching dismissal except as set out in subrule (5.2).

Notice sent if conference does not take place

(5.2) If a case conference or settlement conference is arranged for a date on or later than the 365th day after the date the case was started, but the hearing does not take place on that date and is not adjourned by a judge, the clerk shall serve the notice of approaching dismissal on the parties by mail, fax or electronic mail.

Dismissal of case

(6) A case for which a notice of approaching dismissal has been served shall be dismissed without further notice, unless one of the parties, within 60 days after the notice is served,

(a) obtains an order under subrule (3) to lengthen that time;

(b) files an agreement signed by all parties and their lawyers, if any, for a final order disposing of all issues in the case, and a notice of motion for an order carrying out the agreement;

(c) serves on all parties and files a notice of withdrawal (Form 12) that discontinues all outstanding claims in the case;

(d) schedules or adjourns the case for trial; or

(e) arranges a case conference or settlement conference for the first available date.

Same

(6.1) If a case conference or settlement conference is arranged for a date as described in clause (6)(e), but the hearing does not take place on that date and is not adjourned by a judge, the case shall be dismissed without further notice.

Dismissal after notice

(6.2) The clerk shall dismiss a case under subrule (6) or (6.1) by preparing and signing an order dismissing the case, with no costs payable by any party.

Service of dismissal order

(7) The clerk shall serve the order on each party by mail, fax or electronic mail.

Service of dismissal order by lawyer on client

(8) A lawyer who is served with a dismissal order on behalf of a client shall serve it on the client by mail, fax or electronic mail and file proof of service of the order.

Judge may set clerk's order aside

(9) A judge may, on motion, set aside an order of the clerk under subrule (6).

(10) Revoked.

RULE 42: APPOINTMENT OF FAMILY CASE MANAGER IN THE FAMILY COURT OF THE SUPERIOR COURT OF JUSTICE IN OTTAWA

Scope

42. (1) This rule applies to cases in the Family Court of the Superior Court of Justice in the City of Ottawa if the cases relate to matters under the following Acts:

1. The *Child and Family Services Act*, subject to subrule (6).
2. The *Children's Law Reform Act*.
3. The *Divorce Act* (Canada).
4. The *Family Law Act*.
5. The *Family Responsibility and Support Arrears Enforcement Act, 1996*.

Purpose

(2) The purpose of this rule is to promote the active management, in accordance with subrule 2(5), of cases to which this rule applies by conferring specified family law jurisdiction on a Family Case Manager.

Definition

(3) In this rule,

"Family Case Manager" means a person appointed under section 86.1 of the *Courts of Justice Act* by the Lieutenant Governor in Council as a case management master who is assigned to manage cases for the purposes of this rule.

Family case manager, powers and duties

(4) In a case to which this rule applies,

(a) the Family Case Manager may only exercise the powers and carry out the duties and functions that are specified in this rule; and

(b) the exercise of those powers and the performance of those duties and functions are subject to the restrictions specified in subrules (5) and (6).

No jurisdiction

(5) The Family Case Manager has no jurisdiction in respect of,

(a) a power, duty or function that is conferred exclusively on a judge of a superior court by law or expressly on a judge by an Act;

(b) a case involving a special party;

(c) the determination of a right or interest of a party in real property; or

(d) the making of an order or hearing of a motion for an order,

(i) to change, set aside, stay or confirm an order of a judge,

(ii) to find a person in contempt of court,

(iii) to restrain the liberty of a person, including an order for imprisonment, a warrant for arrest or a warrant of committal,

(iv) to dismiss all or part of a party's case for a failure by the party to follow these rules or obey an order in the case or a related case, if the *Family Responsibility and Support Arrears Enforcement Act, 1996* applies to the party's case,

(v) to split a divorce from other issues in a case under subrule 12(6),

(vi) to request the Children's Lawyer to act in accordance with subsection 89(3.1) or 112(2) of the *Courts of Justice Act*, or

(vii) to grant summary judgment.

Limited jurisdiction, *Child and Family Services Act*

(6) With respect to cases under the *Child and Family Services Act*,

(a) the Family Case Manager has jurisdiction only with respect to Part III of that Act (child protection case); and

(b) the jurisdiction of the Family Case Manager with respect to cases under Part III of that Act is not as broad as it is with respect to cases under the other Acts to which this rule applies but is subject to such further limitations as are specified in this rule.

Motions under rule 14

(7) The Family Case Manager may hear motions under rule 14 relating to matters over which he or she has jurisdiction and, for the purpose, may exercise any power under that rule, other than a power under subrule 14(21).

Orders on motion under rule 14

(8) If a motion under rule 14 is made in a case under an Act to which this rule applies other than the *Child and Fam-*

ily Services Act, the Family Case Manager may make only the following orders:

0.1 Subject to subclause (5)(d)(iv), an order under subrule 1(8), other than a contempt order under clause 1(8)(g), and an order under subrule 1(8.1).
0.2 An order under subrule 1(8.2).
0.3 An order under subrule 1(8.4), if the Family Case Manager made the order striking out the document.
1. An order under rules 3, 4, 5, 6, 7, 9, 10, 11, 12, 13, 18, 19 and 20.
2. An order for costs under rule 24 relating to a step in the case that the Family Case Manager dealt with.
3. An order under rule 25 relating to an order made by the Family Case Manager.
4. An order to change a temporary order made by the Family Case Manager.
5. An order under section 10 (Leave for blood tests and DNA tests) of the *Children's Law Reform Act.*
6. A temporary order for or relating to custody of or access to a child under section 21, 23, 25, 28, 29, 30, 32, 34, 39 or 40 of the *Children's Law Reform Act.*
7. A temporary order for custody of or access to a child under section 16 of the *Divorce Act* (Canada).
8. An order appointing a mediator under section 31 of the *Children's Law Reform Act* or section 3 (Mediation) of the *Family Law Act.*
9. A temporary order for or relating to support under section 33, clause 34(1)(a), (e), (f), (g) or (h), subsection 34(5) or section 37, 42 or 47 of the *Family Law Act.*
10. A temporary order for support under section 15.1 (Child support order) or 15.2 (Spousal support order) of the *Divorce Act* (Canada).
11. A temporary order under section 40 of the *Family Law Act.*
12. A temporary order dealing with property other than real property.
13. A support deduction order under section 10 (Support deduction orders to be made) of the *Family Responsibility and Support Arrears Enforcement Act, 1996.*
14. An order limiting or suspending a support deduction order.
15. An order under section 8 (Director to cease enforcement, termination of support obligation) of the *Family Responsibility and Support Arrears Enforcement Act, 1996* that terminates a support obligation or orders repayment from a person who received support.
16. An order that is necessary and incidental to the power to make a temporary order that is within the jurisdiction of the Family Case Manager.

Same, *Child and Family Services Act*

(9) If a motion under rule 14 is made in a case under the *Child and Family Services Act*, the Family Case Manager may make only the following orders:

1. An order under subrule 3(5) (order to lengthen or shorten time), if the motion is made on consent.
2. An order under rule 5 (where a case starts and is to be heard), if the motion is unopposed or made on consent.
3. An order under rule 6 (service of documents).
4. An order under subrule 7(5) (adding a party), if the motion is unopposed or made on consent.
5. An order under section 39 (parties and notice) or under subsection 48(3) (transfer of a proceeding) of the *Child and Family Services Act*, if the motion is unopposed or made on consent.
6. A finding that there is no person who should be presumed to be, or recognized in law as, the father of a child under section 8 of the *Children's Law Reform Act.*
7. An order granting an adjournment, if the motion is made on consent.

Temporary order to be continued

(10) An order for adjournment made under paragraph 7 of subrule (9) in a child protection case shall provide for the continuation of any temporary order made under subsection 51(2) (custody during adjournment) of the *Child and Family Services Act* that applies in respect of the case being adjourned.

(11) Revoked.

Conferences

(12) Subject to subrule (13), the Family Case Manager may conduct a case conference, settlement conference or trial management conference instead of a judge under rule 17.

Same, *Child and Family Services Act*

(13) In a case under Part III of the *Child and Family Services Act*, the Family Case Manager shall not conduct a settlement conference without the consent of the parties and of the child's representative.

Application of Rule 17

(14) At a case conference, settlement conference or trial management conference conducted by the Family Case Manager, rule 17 applies subject to the following changes:

1. In a case to which this rule applies other than the *Child and Family Services Act*, the Family Case Manager may make any order described in rule 17 and, with respect to the temporary and final orders referred to in clause 17(8)(b),
   i. the only temporary or final orders that the Family Case Manager may make are those described in subrule (8) of this rule, and
   ii. the Family Case Manager shall not make a final order unless the parties consent to the order.

2. In a case under Part III of the *Child and Family Services Act*, the Family Case Manager,
   i. may make any order described in rule 17 other than an order under subrule 17(18), and
   ii. the only temporary or final orders that the Family Case Manager may make under clause 17(8)(b) are those described in subrule (9) of this rule.
3. A party to the conference may not request that the conference be conducted by a judge under subrule 17(9).
4. Despite clause 17(10)(a), a case may be scheduled for trial if the Family Case Manager conducted a settlement conference.

Enforcement powers

(15) The Family Case Manager may exercise,

(a) any power that a court may exercise under rule 27 (requiring financial information) other than a power to order a person imprisoned under subrule 27(6), (20) or (21); and

(b) the powers relating to garnishment orders set out in subrules 29(5) and (19).

Sending case to judge

(16) Despite anything to the contrary in this rule, the Family Case Manager may at any time order that a matter assigned to him or her be adjourned and sent to a judge.

Appeal from temporary order

(17) Subrules 38(5) to (45) apply with necessary modifications to an appeal from a temporary order of the Family Case Manager.

Appeal from final order

(18) Subrules 38(1), (2) and (3) apply with necessary modifications to an appeal from a final order of the Family Case Manager.

Revocation

(19) This rule is revoked on July 1, 2016.

43. Omitted (provides for coming into force of provisions of this Regulation).

TABLE OF FORMS

Form Number	Form Title	Date of Form
4	Notice of change in representation	October 21, 2013
6	Acknowledgment of service	September 1, 2005
6A	Advertisement	September 1, 2005
6B	Affidavit of service	November 15, 2009
8	Application (general)	October 1, 2012
8A	Application (divorce)	June 15, 2007
8B	Application (child protection and status review)	October 1, 2006
8B.1	Application (status review for Crown ward and former Crown ward)	October 1, 2006
8B.2	Application (general) (*Child and Family Services Act* cases other than child protection and status review)	October 1, 2006
8C	Application (secure treatment)	November 15, 2009
8D	Application (adoption)	April 23, 2012
8D.1	Application (dispense with parent's consent to adoption before placement)	September 1, 2005
8D.2	Notice of intention to place a child for adoption	August 2, 2011
8D.3	Notice to child of intention to place for adoption	August 2, 2011
8D.4	Notice of termination of access	August 2, 2011
8E	Revoked.	
10	Answer	October 1, 2012
10A	Reply	September 1, 2005
12	Notice of withdrawal	September 1, 2005
13	Financial statement (support claims)	February 1, 2010

Form Number	Form Title	Date of Form
13.1	Financial statement (property and support claims)	February 1, 2010
13A	Revoked.	September 1, 2005
13B	Net family property statement	May 15, 2009
14	Notice of motion	June 15, 2007
14A	Affidavit (general)	September 1, 2005
14B	Motion form	September 1, 2005
14C	Confirmation	September 1, 2005
14D	Order on motion without notice	September 1, 2005
15	Motion to change	April 1, 2008
15A	Change information form	April 1, 2008
15B	Response to motion to change	April 1, 2008
15C	Consent motion to change	April 1, 2008
15D	Consent motion to change child support	April 1, 2008
17	Conference notice	September 1, 2005
17A	Case conference brief—General	November 15, 2009
17B	Case conference brief for protection application or status review	November 15, 2009
17C	Settlement conference brief—General	November 15, 2009
17D	Settlement conference brief for protection application or status review	November 15, 2009
17E	Trial management conference brief	November 15, 2009
20	Request for information	September 1, 2005
20.1	Acknowledgement of expert's duty	August 2, 2011
20A	Authorization to commissioner	September 1, 2005
20B	Letter of request	September 1, 2005
22	Request to admit	September 1, 2005
22A	Response to request to admit	September 1, 2005
23	Summons to witness	September 1, 2005
23A	Summons to witness outside Ontario	September 1, 2005
23B	Order for prisoner's attendance	September 1, 2005
23C	Affidavit for uncontested trial	September 1, 2009
25	Order (general)	September 1, 2005
25A	Divorce order	September 1, 2005
25B	Secure treatment order	September 1, 2005
25C	Adoption order	April 23, 2012
25D	Order (uncontested trial)	September 1, 2005
25E	Notice disputing approval of order	September 1, 2005
25F	Restraining order	September 1, 2009
25G	Restraining order on motion without notice	September 1, 2009

Form Number	Form Title	Date of Form
25H	Order terminating restraining order	September 1, 2009
26	Statement of money owed	September 1, 2005
26A	Affidavit of enforcement expenses	September 1, 2005
26B	Affidavit for filing domestic contract or paternity agreement with court	September 1, 2005
26C	Notice of transfer of enforcement	September 1, 2005
27	Request for financial statement	September 1, 2005
27A	Request for statement of income	September 1, 2005
27B	Statement of income from income source	September 1, 2005
27C	Appointment for financial examination	September 1, 2005
28	Writ of seizure and sale	September 1, 2005
28A	Request for writ of seizure and sale	September 1, 2005
28B	Statutory declaration to sheriff	June 15, 2007
28C	Writ of temporary seizure	September 1, 2005
29	Request for garnishment	September 1, 2005
29A	Notice of garnishment (lump-sum debt)	September 1, 2005
29B	Notice of garnishment (periodic debt)	September 1, 2005
29C	Notice to co-owner of debt	September 1, 2005
29D	Statutory declaration of indexed support	September 1, 2005
29E	Dispute (payor)	September 1, 2005
29F	Dispute (garnishee)	September 1, 2005
29G	Dispute (co-owner of debt)	September 1, 2005
29H	Notice of garnishment hearing	September 1, 2005
29I	Notice to stop garnishment	September 1, 2005
29J	Statement to garnishee financial institution re support	September 1, 2005
30	Notice of default hearing	September 1, 2005
30A	Request for default hearing	September 1, 2005
30B	Default dispute	September 1, 2005
31	Notice of contempt motion	September 1, 2005
32	Bond (recognizance)	September 1, 2005
32A	Notice of forfeiture motion	September 1, 2005
32B	Warrant for arrest	September 1, 2005
32C	Affidavit for warrant of committal	September 1, 2005
32D	Warrant of committal	September 1, 2005
32.1	Request to enforce a family arbitration award	October 1, 2012
32.1A	Dispute of request for enforcement	October 1, 2012
33	Information for warrant to apprehend child	September 1, 2005
33A	Warrant to apprehend child	September 1, 2005

Form Number	Form Title	Date of Form
33B	Plan of care for child(ren) (Children's Aid Society)	October 1, 2006
33B.1	Answer and plan of care (parties other than Children's Aid Society)	October 1, 2006
33B.2	Answer (*Child and Family Services Act* cases other than child protection and status review)	August 2, 2011
33C	Statement of agreed facts (child protection)	September 1, 2005
33D	Statement of agreed facts (status review)	September 1, 2005
33E	Child's consent to secure treatment	September 1, 2005
33F	Consent to secure treatment (person other than child)	September 1, 2005
34	Child's consent to adoption	April 1, 2009
34A	Affidavit of parentage	September 1, 2005
34B	Non-parent's consent to adoption by spouse	June 15, 2007
34C	Director's or local director's statement on adoption	September 1, 2005
34D	Affidavit of adoption applicant(s), sworn/affirmed	April 1, 2009
34E	Director's consent to adoption	August 2, 2011
34F	Parent's or custodian's consent to adoption	April 1, 2009
34G	Affidavit of adoption licensee or society employee	September 1, 2005
34G.1	Affidavit of society employee for adoption of a Crown ward	August 2, 2011
34H	Affidavit of adopting relative or stepparent	April 1, 2009
34I	Parent's consent to adoption by spouse	April 1, 2009
34J	Affidavit of execution and independent legal advice (Children's Lawyer)	April 1, 2009
34K	Certificate of clerk (adoption)	August 2, 2011
34L	Application for openness order	August 2, 2011
34M	Consent to openness order under s. 145.1 of the *Child and Family Services Act*	August 2, 2011
34M.1	Consent to openness order under s. 145.1.2 of the *Child and Family Services Act*	August 2, 2011
34N	Application to change or terminate openness order	October 1, 2006
35.1	Affidavit in support of claim for custody or access	November 15, 2009
36	Affidavit for divorce	September 1, 2005
36A	Certificate of clerk (divorce)	September 1, 2005
36B	Certificate of divorce	September 1, 2005
37	Notice of hearing	September 1, 2005
37A	Information sheet	September 1, 2005
37B	Direction to request further information	September 1, 2005
37C	Notice of continuation of hearing	September 1, 2005
37D	Notice of registration of order	September 1, 2005
37E	Notice for taking further evidence	September 1, 2005
38	Notice of appeal	September 1, 2005
39	Notice of approaching dismissal	June 15, 2007

FORMS 4-39 Revoked.

Family Responsibility and Support Arrears Enforcement Act, 1996

SO 1996, c. 31
Current to December 12, 2013

PART I INTERPRETATION

Definitions

1. (1) In this Act,

"Director" means the Director of the Family Responsibility Office;

"income source" means an individual, corporation or other entity that owes or makes any payment, whether periodically or in a lump sum, to or on behalf of a payor of,

(a) wages, wage supplements or salary, or draws or advances on them,

(b) a commission, bonus, piece-work allowance or similar payment,

(c) a payment made under a contract for service,

(d) a benefit under an accident, disability or sickness plan,

(e) a disability, retirement or other pension,

(f) an annuity,

(g) vacation pay, termination pay and severance pay,

(h) an employee loan,

(i) a shareholder loan or dividends on shares, if the corporation that issued the shares is effectively controlled by the payor or the payor and the payor's parent, spouse, child or other relative or a body corporate which the payor and his or her parent, spouse, child or other relative effectively control, directly or indirectly,

(j) refunds under the *Income Tax Act* (Canada),

(k) lump sum payments under the *Family Orders and Agreements Enforcement Assistance Act* (Canada),

(l) income of a type described in the regulations;

"payor" means a person who is required to pay support under a support order;

"provisional order" means an order that has no effect until it is confirmed by another court and includes orders made under subsection 18(2) of the *Divorce Act* (Canada), sections 7 and 30 of the *Interjurisdictional Support Orders Act, 2002* and section 44 of the *Family Law Act*;

"recipient" means a person entitled to support under a support order or the parent, other than the payor, of a child entitled to support under a support order;

"reciprocating jurisdiction" has the same meaning as in the *Interjurisdictional Support Orders Act, 2002*;

"regulations" means the regulations made under this Act;

"spouse" means,

(a) a spouse as defined in section 1 of the *Family Law Act*, or

(b) either of two persons who live together in a conjugal relationship outside marriage;

"support deduction order" means a support deduction order made or deemed to have been made under this Act or its predecessor;

"support order" means a provision in an order made in or outside Ontario and enforceable in Ontario for the payment of money as support or maintenance, and includes a provision for,

(a) the payment of an amount periodically, whether annually or otherwise and whether for an indefinite or limited period, or until the happening of a specified event,

(b) a lump sum to be paid or held in trust,

(c) payment of support or maintenance in respect of a period before the date of the order,

(d) payment to an agency of an amount in reimbursement for a benefit or assistance provided to a party under a statute, including a benefit or assistance provided before the date of the order,

(e) payment of expenses in respect of a child's prenatal care and birth,

(e.1) payment of expenses in respect of DNA testing to establish parentage,

(f) the irrevocable designation, by a spouse who has a policy of life insurance or an interest in a benefit plan, of the other spouse or a child as the beneficiary, or

(g) interest or the payment of legal fees or other expenses arising in relation to support or maintenance,

and includes such a provision in a domestic contract or paternity agreement that is enforceable under section 35 of the *Family Law Act*.

Interpretation—income source

(2) An individual, corporation or other entity continues to be an income source despite temporary interruptions in the payments owed to a payor.

Same—related orders

(3) A support deduction order is related to the support order on which it is based and a support order is related to the support deduction order that is based on it.

PART II DIRECTOR OF THE FAMILY RESPONSIBILITY OFFICE

Director of Family Responsibility Office

2. There shall be a Director of the Family Responsibility Office who shall be appointed by the Lieutenant Governor in Council.

Delegation

3. (1) The Director may, in writing, authorize a person or class of persons employed in the Director's office to exercise any of the powers or perform any of the duties of the Director.

Decisions

(2) A decision made by a person exercising the Director's powers or performing the Director's duties under subsection (1) shall be deemed to be a decision of the Director.

Assignment of Director's powers, etc.

4. (1) The Attorney General may, subject to the approval of the Lieutenant Governor in Council, assign to any person, agency or body, or class thereof, any of the powers, duties or functions of the Director under this Act, subject to the limitations, conditions and requirements set out in the assignment.

Same

(2) An assignment may include powers, duties or functions that are not purely administrative in nature, including statutory powers of decision and discretionary powers given to the Director under this Act, and may provide that an assignee may be a party in any action or proceeding instead of the Director.

Fees, etc.

(3) An assignment may, subject to any regulation made under clause 63(1), set out the fees, costs, disbursements, surcharges and other charges that the assignee may charge to the payor, or a method for determining them, how and when they may be collected, and may exempt the assignee from clause 22(a) of the *Collection Agencies Act*.

Note: On a day to be named by proclamation of the Lieutenant Governor, subsection (3) is amended by striking out "*Collection Agencies Act*" at the end and substituting "*Collection and Debt Settlement Services Act*." (See: 2013, c. 13, Sched. 1, ss. 13, 19)

Same

(4) An assignee may charge fees, costs, disbursements, surcharges and other charges as set out in the assignment and such fees, costs, disbursements, surcharges and other charges may,

(a) be in respect of services for which the Director may not charge anything;

(b) be higher than a fee, cost, disbursement, surcharge or other charge that the Director is permitted to charge for the same service; and

(c) be applied in a manner other than that provided in section 57.

Same

(5) Any fees, costs, disbursements, surcharges or other charges charged by an assignee must be charged to the payor and may be added to the amount of arrears owing by the payor and may be collected in like manner as arrears.

Interest

(6) For the purposes of subsections (3), (4) and (5),

"other charges" includes interest at a rate prescribed by regulation.

Use of information restricted

(7) An assignee shall not use or disclose the information it has collected in carrying out any power, duty or function assigned to the assignee under subsection (1) except for the purposes of this Act.

Duty of Director

5. (1) It is the duty of the Director to enforce support orders where the support order and the related support deduction order, if any, are filed in the Director's office and to pay the amounts collected to the person to whom they are owed.

Transition

(2) Subject to subsection (4), a support order or support deduction order that is filed in the office of the Director of the

Family Support Plan immediately before the day this section comes into force shall be deemed to be filed in the Director's office on the day this section comes into force.

Same

(3) If a support deduction order is filed in the office of the Director of the Family Support Plan immediately before the day this section comes into force and the related support order was never filed in his or her office before that day, it is the duty of the Director to enforce the support deduction order so long as it is filed in the Director's office.

Same

(4) If a support deduction order is filed in the office of the Director of the Family Support Plan immediately before the day this section comes into force and the related support order was withdrawn from his or her office before that day, either when the support order was made or later, the support deduction order shall be deemed to be withdrawn from the Director's office on the day this section comes into force.

Powers

6. (1) The Director shall carry out his or her duties in the manner, if any, that appears practical to the Director and, for the purpose, may commence and conduct a proceeding and take any steps in the Director's name for the benefit of recipients, including,

(a) enforcing support deduction orders that are filed in the Director's office, as provided by this Act;

(b) employing any other enforcement mechanisms expressly provided for in this Act;

(c) employing any other enforcement mechanisms not expressly provided for in this Act.

Policies and procedures

(1.1) The Director may establish policies and procedures respecting subsection (1) and the policies and procedures shall be considered in the exercise of the Director's powers and the performance of the Director's duties under that subsection.

Transition

(2) The Director may enforce the payment of arrears of support under a support order although they were incurred before the order was filed in the Director's office or before July 2, 1987.

Same

(3) The Director may enforce the payment of the arrears of support owed on the day this section comes into force under an order that,

(a) is not a support order as defined in subsection 1(1) but was a support order within the meaning of the *Family Support Plan Act*, as it read immediately before its repeal by this Act; and

(b) is filed in the office of the Director of the Family Support Plan immediately before such repeal.

Same

(4) For the purpose of subsection (3), an order described in that subsection shall be deemed to be a support order as defined in subsection 1(1).

(5) Repealed. See: Table of Public Statute Provisions Repealed Under Section 10.1 of the *Legislation Act, 2006*—December 31, 2011.

Enforcement alternatives

(6) Enforcement of a support order or support deduction order by one means does not prevent enforcement by other means at the same time or different times.

Enforcement by Director exclusive

(7) Subject to section 4, no person other than the Director shall enforce a support order that is filed in the Director's office.

Same

(8) Subject to section 4, no person other than the Director shall enforce a support deduction order, whether the order is filed in the Director's office or not.

Director may refuse to enforce

7. (1) Despite section 5, the Director may at any time refuse to enforce a support order or support deduction order that is filed in the Director's office if, in his or her opinion,

(a) the amount of the support is nominal;

(b) the amount of the support cannot be determined from the face of the order because it is expressed as a percentage of the payor's income or it is dependent on another variable that does not appear on the order;

(c) the meaning of the order is unclear or ambiguous;

(d) the recipient has not complied with reasonable requests to provide the Director with accurate or sufficient information as may be needed in order to enforce the order or respecting the amount of arrears owed under the order;

(e) the whereabouts of the recipient cannot be determined after reasonable efforts have been made;

(f) the payor is in prison serving a sentence of five years or longer and has no assets or income available to satisfy the support order and any arrears under the order;

(g) the payor is receiving benefits under the *Family Benefits Act*, assistance under the *General Welfare Assistance Act* or the *Ontario Works Act, 1997* or income support under the *Ontario Disability Support Program Act, 1997* and has no assets or income available to satisfy the support order and any arrears under the order;

(h) the recipient repeatedly accepts payment of support directly from the payor;

(i) the recipient consents to a limitation of enforcement of the support order by the Director;

(j) enforcement of the support order has been stayed by a court; or

(k) enforcement of the order is otherwise unreasonable or impractical.

Policies and procedures

(2) The Director may establish policies and procedures respecting subsection (1) and the policies and procedures shall be considered in the exercise of the Director's discretion under that subsection.

Order deemed withdrawn

(3) If the Director refuses to enforce an order under subsection (1), the Director shall notify the payor and the recipient and the support order and the related support deduction order, if any, shall be deemed to be withdrawn from the Director's office on the date set out in the notice.

Cost of living clauses

(4) The Director shall not enforce a cost of living clause in a support order or support deduction order made in Ontario unless it is calculated in accordance with subsection 34(5) of the *Family Law Act* or in a manner prescribed by regulation.

Same

(5) The Director shall not enforce a cost of living clause in a support order or a support deduction order if the support order was made outside Ontario unless it is calculated in a manner that the Director considers similar to that provided in subsection 34(5) of the *Family Law Act* or in a manner prescribed by regulation.

Same

(6) Where the cost of living clause in an order is not calculated in accordance with subsection 34(5) of the *Family Law Act* or in a manner prescribed by regulation or, if the order was made outside Ontario, in a manner that the Director considers similar, the Director shall, subject to subsection (1), enforce the order as if it contained no cost of living clause.

Transition

(7) Despite subsections (5) and (6), if an order contains a cost of living clause that is not calculated in accordance with subsection 34(5) of the *Family Law Act* or in a manner prescribed by regulation or, if the order was made outside Ontario, in a manner that the Director considers similar, which became effective before this section came into force,

(a) the Director shall continue to enforce the order and the cost of living clause at the same amount at which the Director of the Family Support Plan was enforcing them immediately before this section came into force; and

(b) the Director shall not make any further adjustments under the cost of living clause after this section comes into force.

Same

(8) This section applies even if the order was filed in the Director's office before this section comes into force.

Note: On a day to be named by proclamation of the Lieutenant Governor, the Act is amended by the Statutes of Ontario, 2005, chapter 16, section 2 by adding the following section:

Interest

7.1 (1) If the recipient under a support order is entitled to interest on arrears, the Director may add interest to the arrears and collect the interest in the same manner as the arrears.

Rate of interest and manner of calculation

(2) Interest added and collected under subsection (1) shall be calculated,

(a) by the Director, at the rate and in the manner prescribed by the regulations; or

(b) by the recipient, at the rate and in the manner required by the support order.

When interest begins to accrue

(3) Interest added and collected under subsection (1) begins to accrue on the latest of the following:

1. The date the support becomes payable.
2. The date the arrears become payable.
3. The date the support order or support deduction order is filed with the Director.
4. The day section 2 of the *Family Responsibility and Support Arrears Enforcement Amendment Act, 2005* comes into force.

Exception

(4) No interest is payable on support that is paid within 30 days after the day on which it becomes payable.

Non-application of *Courts of Justice Act*, s. 129

(5) Section 129 of the *Courts of Justice Act* does not apply to interest calculated by the Director under clause (2)(a).

See: 2005, c. 16, ss. 2, 42(2).

Director to cease enforcement

Termination of support obligation

8. (1) Subject to section 8.3, the Director shall cease enforcement of a support obligation provided for in a support order or support deduction order filed in the Director's office if the support obligation has terminated.

How termination is determined

(2) For the purpose of subsection (1), a support obligation is terminated if,

(a) the parties to the support order or support deduction order agree, in the manner prescribed by the regulations, that the support obligation has terminated;

(b) the support order or support deduction order states that the support obligation terminates on a set calendar date, and that date arrives; or

(c) a court orders that the obligation has terminated; or

(d) in the case of an obligation for the support of a child, the Director receives notice, in accordance with the regulations, of the child's death.

Payor's death

(3) The Director shall not enforce a support order or support deduction order against the estate of a payor after he or she is notified, in accordance with the regulations, of the payor's death.

Notice to Director

(4) For the purposes of clause (2)(a), if a support order or related support deduction order is filed in the Director's office, each party to the support order shall give the Director notice of a termination of a support obligation under the order, in the manner and at the time prescribed by the regulations.

Director's discretion

8.1 (1) Despite section 5 and subject to section 8.3, the Director has discretion to discontinue enforcement of a support order or support deduction order that is filed in the Director's office if,

(a) the payor notifies the Director in accordance with subsection 8(4) that the support obligation has terminated;

(b) the Director serves on the recipient a request to confirm or deny that the support obligation has terminated; and

(c) the recipient does not respond within 20 days after being served.

Written response

(1.1) For the purposes of clause (1)(c), the response must be in writing.

Reinstatement

(2) If, after enforcement has been discontinued in accordance with subsection (1), the Director receives a written notice from the recipient denying that the support obligation has terminated, the Director may resume enforcement.

Discretion to enforce for lesser amount if child's entitlement ceases

8.2 (1) Subject to section 8.3, if the conditions set out in subsection (2) are satisfied with respect to a support order or support deduction order, the Director may exercise discretion to enforce a lesser amount of support in accordance with the table set out in the applicable child support guidelines.

Conditions

(2) The conditions referred to in subsection (1) are:

1. The order was made in accordance with the table set out in the applicable child support guidelines.
2. One of the following applies:
   i. It has been agreed under clause 8(2)(a) that the support obligation under the order has terminated with respect to a child.
   ii. The payor notifies the Director in accordance with subsection 8(4) that the support obligation has terminated, the Director serves on the recipient a request to confirm or deny that the support obligation has terminated, and the recipient does not respond within 20 days after being served.
3. The support obligation under the order still continues with respect to another child.
4. The order states,
   i. the number of children, and
   ii. the total amount of support determined in accordance with the table.

Written response

(3) For the purposes of subparagraph 2 ii of subsection (2), the response must be in writing.

Reinstatement

(4) If, after the Director exercises the discretion to enforce a lesser amount in reliance on subparagraph 2 ii of subsection (2), the Director receives a written notice from the recipient denying that the support obligation has terminated, the Director may reinstate the amount enforced before the reduction.

Agency's consent required

8.3 If a support order has been assigned to an agency described in subsection 33(3) of the *Family Law Act*, the Director shall not cease, discontinue or reduce enforcement of the support order without the agency's consent.

Disputes

8.4 (1) If the parties to a support order do not agree that a support obligation has terminated or if the agency referred to in section 8.3 does not provide its consent under that section, the court that made the support order shall, on the motion of a party to the support order or of the agency,

(a) decide whether the support obligation has terminated; and

(b) make an order to that effect.

Same

(2) If the support order was not made by a court, the order described in subsection (1) shall be made by the Ontario Court of Justice or the Family Court.

Same

(3) If an issue as to whether the support obligation has terminated arises within an application between the parties, it is not necessary to make a separate motion under subsection (1).

Order to repay

(4) A court that finds that a support obligation has terminated may order repayment in whole or in part from a person who received support after the obligation was terminated if the court is of the opinion that the person ought to have notified the Director that the support obligation had terminated.

Same

(5) In determining whether to make an order under subsection (4), the court shall consider the circumstances of each of the parties to the support order.

Role of Director

(6) An order under subsection (4) is not a support order and shall not be enforced by the Director.

Continued enforcement

(7) The Director shall continue to enforce the support obligation until he or she receives a copy of the court's order terminating the support obligation.

Same

(8) Despite the termination of a support obligation, the Director shall continue to enforce the support obligation in respect of any arrears that have accrued.

Director not a party

(9) The Director is not a party to,

(a) a proceeding to determine a person's entitlement to support under a support order; or

(b) a motion to decide whether a support obligation has terminated.

PART III SUPPORT ORDERS AND SUPPORT DEDUCTION ORDERS—MAKING AND FILING

Contents of support order

9. (1) Every support order made by an Ontario court, other than a provisional order, shall state in its operative part that unless the order is withdrawn from the Director's office, it shall be enforced by the Director and that amounts owing under the order shall be paid to the Director, who shall pay them to the person to whom they are owed.

Court may require that order may not be withdrawn

(2) If the court considers it appropriate to do so, it may state in the operative part of the order, instead of the wording prescribed by subsection (1), that the order and the related support deduction order shall be enforced by the Director and that they cannot be withdrawn from the Director's office.

Director retains discretion to not enforce orders

(3) Section 7 applies to every support order worded as provided in subsection (1) or (2), whether the order was made before or after this section comes into force and despite the wording of an order made under subsection (2).

Support deduction orders to be made

10. (1) An Ontario court that makes a support order, as defined in subsection 1(1), shall also make a support deduction order.

New orders to be made

(2) When a support order is changed and the changed order is a support order as defined in subsection 1(1), the court shall also make a support deduction order to reflect the change.

Transition

(3) When a support order, within the meaning of the *Family Support Plan Act* as it read immediately before its repeal by this Act, is changed and the changed order is a support order as defined in subsection 1(1), the court shall also make a support deduction order to reflect the change.

Order mandatory

(4) A support deduction order shall be made even though the court cannot identify an income source in respect of the payor at the time the support order is made.

Exception

(5) A support deduction order shall not be made in respect of a provisional order.

Form of support deduction order

11. (1) A support deduction order shall be in the form prescribed by the regulations.

Information re payor, income source

(2) Before making a support deduction order, the court shall make such inquiries of the parties as it considers necessary to determine the names and addresses of each income source of the payor and the amounts paid to the payor by each income source and shall make such other inquiries to obtain information as may be prescribed by the regulations.

Same

(3) If the support order is sought on consent or by way of motion for judgment or if the making of the support order is uncontested, the parties shall give the court the particulars described in subsection (2) and such other information as may be prescribed by the regulations.

Completion of form, etc.

(4) The support deduction order shall be completed and signed by the court, or by the clerk or registrar of the court, at the time the support order is made and shall be entered in the court records promptly after it is signed, even if the support order may not have been settled or signed at that time.

Precedence of orders

11.1 In the event of a conflict between a support order and the support deduction order made in relation to the support order, the support order prevails.

Court to file orders

Support orders

12. (1) The clerk or registrar of the court that makes a support order shall file it with the Director's office promptly after it is signed.

Support deduction orders

(2) The clerk or registrar of the court that makes a support deduction order shall file it with the Director's office promptly after it is signed, even if the related support order may not have been settled or signed at the time.

Orders of other jurisdictions

13. (1) When a support order made by a court outside Ontario is registered under subsection 19(1) of the *Interjurisdictional Support Orders Act, 2002*, the clerk who registers the order shall promptly file it with the Director's office, unless the order is accompanied by a notice signed by the person seeking enforcement stating that he or she does not want the order enforced by the Director.

Same — *Divorce Act* (Canada) orders

(2) A support order made by a court outside Ontario under the *Divorce Act* (Canada) may be filed in the Director's office by the recipient under the order and, for the purpose of subsection 20(3) of the *Divorce Act* (Canada), the order becomes enforceable by the Director upon its filing in the Director's office without it having been registered in a court in Ontario.

Orders filed by Minister, etc.

14. (1) If a recipient has applied and is eligible for, or has received, a benefit under the *Family Benefits Act* or assistance under the *General Welfare Assistance Act* or the *Ontario Works Act, 1997* or income support under the *Ontario Disability Support Program Act, 1997*, a support order may be filed in the Director's office, whether or not the payor and recipient have given a notice to withdraw under subsection 16(1.1), by the following:

1. The Ministry of Community and Social Services in the name of the Minister.
2. A municipality, excluding a lower-tier municipality in a regional municipality.
3. A district social services administration board under the *District Social Services Administration Boards Act*.
4. A band approved under section 15 of the *General Welfare Assistance Act*.
5. A delivery agent under the *Ontario Works Act, 1997*.

Same, reciprocating jurisdiction

(1.1) If a recipient has applied and is eligible for, or has received, social assistance benefits in a reciprocating jurisdiction, or if a support order has been assigned to a social assistance provider in a reciprocating jurisdiction, the support order may be filed in the Director's office by the social assistance provider in the reciprocating jurisdiction, whether or not the payor and recipient have given a notice to withdraw under subsection 16(1.1).

Same

(2) If a support order is filed under subsection (1) or (1.1), the related support deduction order, if any, shall be deemed to be filed in the Director's office at the same time.

Payors, recipients may file support orders

15. Subject to sections 12, 13 and 14, a support order may be filed in the Director's office only by the payor or recipient under the order.

Withdrawal of orders

16. (1) A support order or support deduction order filed in the office of the Director may be withdrawn at any time, as described in subsection (1.1), unless the support order states that it and the related support deduction order cannot be withdrawn from the Director's office.

Method

(1.1) Withdrawal is effected by a written notice signed by,

(a) the recipient and the payor, if the payor is in compliance as defined in the regulations; or

(b) the recipient, if the payor is not in compliance as defined in the regulations.

Consent of agency filing order

(2) A support order and related support deduction order, if any, that have been assigned to an agency referred to in subsection 14(1) may not be withdrawn under subsection (1) except by the agency or with the consent of the agency so long as the orders are under assignment.

Effect of withdrawal

(3) The Director shall cease enforcement of an order upon its withdrawal from the Director's office.

Same

(4) If there are arrears owing to an agency referred to in subsection 14(1) from a past assignment, the Director may continue to enforce the support order and related support deduction order, if any, to collect the arrears owed to the agency, even if the payor and recipient have withdrawn the orders under this section.

Support and support deduction order must be withdrawn together

(5) A support order cannot be withdrawn under subsection (1) unless the related support deduction order, if any, is also withdrawn and a support deduction order cannot be withdrawn under subsection (1) unless the related support order, if any, is also withdrawn.

Filing after withdrawal

(6) A support order or support deduction order that has been withdrawn under subsection (1) or that has been deemed to have been withdrawn under subsection 7(3) may be filed in the office of the Director at any time by a written notice signed by either the payor or the recipient.

Effect

(7) Filing under subsection (6) has the same effect for all purposes, including the purposes of subsection 6(2), as filing under sections 12 to 15.

Application

(7.1) Subsection (7) applies whether the order was filed under subsection (6) before or after the day the *Government Efficiency Act, 2001* receives Royal Assent.

Support and support deduction orders, filing together after withdrawal

(7.2) A support order cannot be filed under subsection (6) unless the related support deduction order, if any, is also filed and a support deduction order cannot be filed under subsection (6) unless the related support order is also filed.

Transition

(8) Despite subsection 6(4), subsection (7) does not apply to an order that is not a support order as defined in subsection 1(1), but was a support order within the meaning of the *Family Support Plan Act*, as it read immediately before its repeal by this Act, and was filed in the office of the Director of the Family Support Plan immediately before this section came into force.

Notice of filings and withdrawals

17. The Director shall give notice of the filing or withdrawal of a support order or support deduction order to all the parties to the order, and at the request of any agency referred to in subsection 14(1), to the agency.

Duty to advise re unfiled support orders

18. Where a support deduction order that was made before this section came into force is filed in the Director's office but the related support order was never filed in the Director's office, the recipient shall inform the Director in writing of,

(a) the amount of money received on account of the support order other than by means of the support deduction order; and

(b) any changes in the amount to be paid under the support order.

Updating contact information

19. A payor or recipient under a support order or support deduction order that is filed in the Director's office shall advise the Director of any changes to the following, within 10 days after the change:

1. Any name or alias used by the payor or recipient, including any spelling variation of any name or alias.
2. The payor's or recipient's home address, and the mailing address if different from the home address.
3. Any telephone number of the payor or recipient.
4. Other contact information, such as the payor's or recipient's work address, fax number or e-mail address, if the payor or recipient has previously provided that contact information to the Director.

PART IV SUPPORT DEDUCTION ORDERS—ENFORCEMENT

Director to enforce support deduction orders

20. (1) The Director shall enforce a support deduction order that is filed in the Director's office, subject to section 7, to any change made to the support deduction order and to any alternative payment order made under section 28, until the related support order is terminated and there are no arrears owing or until the support order and support deduction order are withdrawn.

Notice of support deduction order to income sources

(2) The Director may serve a notice of a support deduction order to each income source from whom the Director is seeking payment, and may serve new notices when the amount to be paid under a support order changes or arrears are owing.

Contents of notice

(3) The notice shall set out the amount of support owed by the payor under the support order and may also set out any amount in arrears under the support order and the amount required to be paid by the income source to the Director.

Notice to payor

(4) The Director shall send to the payor a copy of every notice sent under subsection (2).

Notice deemed garnishment for *Family Orders and Agreements Enforcement Assistance Act* (Canada)

(5) A notice of a support deduction order shall be deemed to be a notice of garnishment made under provincial garnishment law for the purposes of the *Family Orders and Agreements Enforcement Assistance Act* (Canada).

Support deduction order not affected by stay of enforcement of support order

(6) The operation or enforcement of a support deduction order is not affected by an order staying the enforcement of the related support order unless the support order is also stayed.

Support deduction order deemed to be made

21. (1) A support deduction order shall be deemed to have been made in respect of a support order described in subsection (8) if,

(a) the recipient requests that the Director enforce the support order under this Part and the Director considers it practical to do so; or

(b) the Director considers it advisable to enforce the support order under this Part.

Notice to payor

(2) The Director shall give notice to the payor of the Director's intention to enforce the support order under this Part.

When and by what court deemed order is made

(3) The support deduction order shall, 30 days after the notice is served on the payor, be deemed to have been made by the court that made the support order or,

(a) if the support order was made under the *Divorce Act* (Canada) by a court outside Ontario, by the Superior Court of Justice or, where applicable, the Family Court;

(b) if the support order (other than an order under the *Divorce Act* (Canada)) was made by a court outside Ontario, by a court in Ontario that is the same level as the court that has the jurisdiction to make the order enforceable in Ontario;

(c) if the support order is a domestic contract or paternity agreement, by the Ontario Court of Justice or the Family Court.

Alternative payment order

(4) The payor may, within 30 days after being served with the notice under subsection (2), make a motion for an alternative payment order under section 28, in the court that is deemed to have made the support deduction order.

Delay of effective date

(5) If a motion is made under subsection (4), a deemed support deduction order does not come into force until the motion is determined.

Withdrawal of support deduction order

(6) Section 16 applies to a deemed support deduction order.

No form required

(7) Subsection 11(1) does not apply to a deemed support deduction order.

Application of this section

(8) This section applies only to support orders filed in the Director's office that are,

(a) support orders made by an Ontario court before March 1, 1992;

(b) domestic contracts or paternity agreements that are enforceable under section 35 of the *Family Law Act*;

(c) support orders made by a court outside Ontario that are enforceable in Ontario.

Duty of income source

22. (1) An income source that receives notice of a support deduction order, whether or not the income source is named in the order, shall, subject to section 23, deduct from the money the income source owes to the payor the amount of the support owed by the payor, or such other amount that is set out in the notice, and shall pay that amount to the Director.

First payment

(2) The income source shall begin making payments to the Director not later than the day the first payment is to be paid to the payor that falls at least 14 days after the day on which the income source is served with the notice.

Electronic payment

(2.1) The income source may make the payments by a prescribed method of electronic transmission.

Payor's duty to pay

(3) Until an income source begins deducting support payments in respect of a support deduction order or if payments by an income source are interrupted or terminated, the payor shall pay the amounts owing under the support order to the Director, if the support order is filed in the Director's office, or to the recipient, if the support order is not filed in the Director's office.

Maximum deduction by income source

23. (1) The total amount deducted by an income source and paid to the Director under a support deduction order shall not exceed 50 per cent of the net amount owed by the income source to the payor.

(2) Repealed. See: Table of Public Statute Provisions Repealed Under Section 10.1 of the *Legislation Act, 2006*—December 31, 2011.

Exception for certain federal payments

(3) Despite subsection (1), up to 100 per cent of a payor's income tax refund or other lump sum payment that is attachable under the *Family Orders and Agreements Enforcement Assistance Act* (Canada) may be deducted and paid to the Director under a support deduction order.

(4) Repealed. See: Table of Public Statute Provisions Repealed Under Section 10.1 of the *Legislation Act, 2006*—December 31, 2011.

Interpretation—net amount

(5) For the purposes of this section,

"net amount" means the total amount owed by the income source to the payor at the time payment is to be made to the Director, less the total of the following deductions:

1. Income Tax.
2. Canada Pension Plan.
3. Employment Insurance.
4. Union dues.
5. Such other deductions as may be prescribed by the regulations.

Same

(6) Despite any other provision of this Act, no deduction shall be made under a support deduction order in respect of amounts owing to a payor as reimbursement for expenses covered by a medical, health, dental or hospital insurance contract or plan.

Crown bound by support deduction order

24. (1) A support deduction order is effective against the Crown only in respect of amounts payable on behalf of the administrative unit served with notice of the support deduction order to the payor named in the notice.

Social assistance benefits

(2) Despite subsection (1), no amounts shall be deducted from any amount payable to a payor as a benefit under the *Family Benefits Act* or as assistance under the *General Welfare Assistance Act* or the *Ontario Works Act, 1997* or as income support under the *Ontario Disability Support Program Act, 1997*, in order to comply with a support deduction order unless authorized under the *Ontario Works Act, 1997* or the *Ontario Disability Support Program Act, 1997*.

Definition

(3) In subsection (1),

"administrative unit" means a ministry of the Government of Ontario, a Crown agency within the meaning of the *Crown Agency Act* or the Office of the Assembly.

Duty to inform re payment interruption

25. (1) Within 10 days after the termination or beginning of an interruption of payments by an income source to a payor, both the income source and the payor shall give written notice of the termination or interruption to the Director, together with such other information as may be required by the regulations.

Same

(2) If notice has been or should have been given under subsection (1),

(a) the payor and the income source, within 10 days after the resumption of payments that have been interrupted, shall give written notice to the Director of the resumption;

(b) the payor, within 10 days of beginning employment with another income source or of becoming entitled to payments from another income source, shall give written notice to the Director of the new employment or entitlement and of the name and address of the income source.

Disputes re income source

26. (1) If an individual, corporation or other entity served with notice of a support deduction order is not an income source of the payor named in the notice, the individual, corporation or other entity shall give written notice in the prescribed form of that fact to the Director within 10 days after the service of the notice.

Same

(2) The Director or an individual, corporation or other entity who has notified the Director under subsection (1) may, on notice to each other, make a motion to the court that made or is deemed to have made the support deduction order to determine whether the individual, corporation or other entity is an income source.

Same

(3) The Director or an income source may, on notice to each other, make a motion to the court that made or is deemed to have made the support deduction order to determine,

(a) whether the income source has failed to comply with the order; or

(b) whether the amount the income source is deducting and paying to the Director under the order is correct.

Determination by court

(4) In a motion under subsection (2) or (3), the court shall determine the issue in a summary manner and make such order as it considers appropriate in the circumstances.

Limitation

(5) A motion shall not be made under subsection (2) by an individual (other than the Director), corporation or other entity until at least 14 days after the individual, corporation or other entity gave written notice to the Director as required by subsection (1).

Same

(6) A motion shall not be made by an income source under subsection (3) unless the income source has given written particulars of the proposed motion to the Director at least 14 days before serving the Director with notice of the motion.

Liability

(7) An income source is liable to pay to the Director any amount that it failed without proper reason to deduct and pay to the Director after receiving notice of a support deduction order and, in a motion under subsection (3), the court may order the income source to pay the amount that it ought to have deducted and paid to the Director.

Other enforcement

(8) In addition to any other method available to enforce an order in a civil proceeding, any order made under subsection (4) or (7) may be enforced under this Act in the same manner and with the same remedies as a support order.

Disputes, etc., by payor

27. (1) A payor, on motion in the court that made or is deemed to have made the support deduction order,

(a) may dispute the amount being deducted by an income source under a support deduction order if he or she is of the opinion that because of a mistake of fact more is being deducted than is required under this Act;

(b) may dispute whether he or she has defaulted in paying support after an alternative payment order has been made under section 28;

(c) may seek relief regarding the amount that is being deducted by an income source under a support deduction order for arrears under a support order.

Motion to increase deductions for arrears

(2) If an order has been made on a motion under clause (1)(c), the Director may, on motion in the court that made the order, request that the amount to be deducted by an income source be increased if there has been an improvement in the payor's financial circumstances.

Dispute over entitlement

(3) On a motion under subsection (1) or (2), the payor shall not dispute the entitlement of a person to support under a support order.

Necessary party

(4) The Director is a necessary party to a motion under subsection (1) and the payor is a necessary party to a motion under subsection (2).

Determination by court

(5) The court shall determine the issue in a motion under subsection (1) or (2) in a summary manner and make such order as it considers appropriate in the circumstances.

Same

(6) On a motion under clause (1)(c), the payor shall be presumed to have the ability to pay the amount being deducted for arrears and the court may change the amount being deducted only if it is satisfied that the payor is unable for valid reasons to pay that amount, but this does not affect the accruing of arrears.

Variation of support deduction order

(7) A court shall not change the amount to be paid under a support deduction order except under subsection (5) or 23(4) or if the related support order is changed.

Alternative payment order

28. (1) A court that makes a support deduction order may make an order requiring the payor to make payments directly to the Director, at the same time as it makes the support deduction order, or subsequently on motion.

Same

(2) A court that is deemed to have made a support deduction order may, on a motion made under subsection 21(4), make an order requiring the payor to make payments directly to the Director.

Effect on support order and support deduction order

(3) An alternative payment order made under subsection (1) or (2) suspends the support deduction order, but it does not affect the payor's obligations under the support order nor does it affect any other means of enforcing the support order.

Criteria

(4) The court may make an alternative payment order under subsection (1) or (2) only if,

(a) it finds that it would be unconscionable, having regard to all of the circumstances, to require the payor to make support payments by means of a support deduction order; or

(b) the parties to the support order agree that they do not want support payments collected by means of a support deduction order and the court requires the payor to post such security as it considers adequate and in accordance with the regulations.

Agency's consent required

(5) If the support order has been assigned to an agency described in subsection 33(3) of the *Family Law Act* or if there are arrears owing to the agency from a past assignment, the court shall not make an alternative payment order in the circumstances described in clause (4)(b) without the agency's consent.

Unconscionable, determination

(6) The following shall not be considered by a court in determining whether it would be unconscionable to require a payor to make support payments by means of a support deduction order:

1. The fact that the payor has demonstrated a good payment history in respect of his or her debts, including support obligations.
2. The fact that the payor has had no opportunity to demonstrate voluntary compliance in respect of support obligations.
3. The fact that the parties have agreed to the making of an alternative payment order.
4. The fact that there are grounds upon which a court might find that the amount payable under the support order should be changed.

Security

(7) For the purposes of clause (4)(b), security shall be in a minimum amount equal to the support payable for four months and the security shall be in money or in such other form as may be prescribed in the regulations.

When Director is a party

(8) The Director is not a party to a motion made to obtain an alternative payment order, but if the motion relates to a support deduction order deemed to have been made under section 21, the Director,

(a) shall also be served with notice of the motion; and

(b) may be added as a party.

When agency is a party

(9) If the support order was filed in the Director's office by an agency under subsection 14(1), or has been assigned to an agency referred to in that subsection, the agency,

(a) shall also be served with notice of the motion; and
(b) may be added as a party.

Completion of form, etc.

(10) An alternative payment order shall be completed and signed by the court or by the clerk or registrar of the court at the time it is made and shall be entered in the court records promptly after it is signed.

Prompt filing

(11) The clerk or registrar of the court that makes an alternative payment order shall file it in the Director's office promptly after it is made.

Form and effective date

(12) An alternative payment order shall be in the form prescribed by the regulations and takes effect only when it is filed in the Director's office and every income source affected by the alternative payment order has received notice of it and of its effect on the support deduction order.

Termination of alternative payment order

(13) An alternative payment order is automatically terminated if the payor fails to post security of the type or within the time period set out in the alternative payment order or if the payor fails to comply with the support order.

Effect of termination

(14) When an alternative payment order is terminated under subsection (13), the support deduction order is reinstated and the Director may immediately realize on any security that was posted.

Effect of withdrawing support order and support deduction order

(15) If the support order and the related support deduction order are withdrawn from the Director's office while an alternative payment order is in effect, the alternative payment order is terminated and the Director shall repay to the payor any security that was posted.

Effect of changing support order or support deduction order

(16) If the support order or the related support deduction order is changed while an alternative payment order is in effect, the alternative payment order is terminated and the Director shall repay to the payor any security that was posted.

Transition

(17) A suspension order made under this section as it read on the day before section 15 of the *Family Responsibility and Support Arrears Enforcement Amendment Act, 2005* came into force has the same effect as an alternative payment order, and this Act applies to the suspension order as if it were an alternative payment order.

Income source to keep information confidential

29. Information about a payor obtained as a result of the application of this Part by an income source or an individual, corporation or other entity believed to be an income source shall not be disclosed by the income source or the individual, corporation or other entity, as the case may be, or any director, officer, employee or agent thereof, except for the purposes of complying with a support deduction order or this Act.

Priority of support deduction orders

30. (1) Despite any other Act, a support deduction order has the same priority over other judgment debts as a support order has under the *Creditors' Relief Act, 2010* and all support orders and support deduction orders rank equally with each other.

Same

(2) If an income source is required to make payments to the Director under a support deduction order and the income source receives a garnishment notice related to the same support obligation, the income source shall make full payment under the support deduction order and the garnishment shall be of no effect until the income source has received notice from the Director that an alternative payment order has been made or that the support deduction order is terminated or withdrawn from the Director's office.

Anti-avoidance

31. An agreement by the parties to a support order to change enforcement of a support deduction order that is filed in the Director's office and any agreement or arrangement to avoid or prevent enforcement of a support deduction order that is filed in the Director's office are of no effect.

Conflict with other Acts

32. A support deduction order may be enforced despite any provision in any other Act protecting any payment owed by an income source to a payor from attachment or other process for the enforcement of a judgment debt.

PART V SUSPENSION OF DRIVERS' LICENCES

Definition, Part V

33. In this Part,

"driver's licence" has the same meaning as in subsection 1(1) of the *Highway Traffic Act*.

First notice

34. When a support order that is filed in the Director's office is in default, the Director may serve a first notice on the payor, informing the payor that his or her driver's licence may be suspended unless, within 30 days after the day the first notice is served,

(a) the payor makes an arrangement satisfactory to the Director for complying with the support order and for paying the arrears owing under the support order;

(b) the payor obtains an order to refrain under subsection 35(1) and files the order in the Director's office; or

(c) the payor pays all arrears owing under the support order.

Order to refrain

35. (1) If a payor is served with a first notice under section 34 and makes a motion to change the support order, the payor may also, on notice to the Director, make a motion for an order that the Director refrain from directing the suspension of the payor's driver's licence under subsection 37(1), on the terms that the court considers just, which may include payment terms.

Interjurisdictional Support Orders Act, 2002

(2) For the purposes of this section, submitting a support variation application to the designated authority in Ontario under the *Interjurisdictional Support Orders Act, 2002* has the same effect as making a motion to change a support order.

Effect on arrears

(3) Payment terms that are included in an order to refrain do not affect the accruing of arrears, nor do they affect any other means of enforcing the support order.

Exceptions

(4) Despite subsection (1), a motion for an order to refrain may be made,

(a) before making a motion to change the support order, on the undertaking of the payor or the payor's lawyer to obtain, within 20 days after the date of the order to refrain, a court date for the motion to change the support order; or

(b) without making a motion to change the support order, if the payor has started an appeal of the support order and the appeal has not been determined.

Court with jurisdiction to change support order

(5) A motion for an order to refrain shall be made in the court that has jurisdiction to change the support order.

Same

(6) The court that has jurisdiction to change a support order is,

(a) in the case of a support order that was made in Ontario,

(i) the court that made the support order, unless subclause (ii) applies,

(ii) if the support order is a provision in a domestic contract or paternity agreement, the Ontario Court of Justice or the Family Court; and

(b) in the case of a support order that was made outside Ontario,

(i) if the support order was made under the *Divorce Act* (Canada), the Superior Court of Justice or the Family Court,

(ii) if the support order is registered under the *Interjurisdictional Support Orders Act, 2002*, the court in Ontario that has jurisdiction under that Act to vary the support order.

Financial statement and proof of income

(7) A payor who makes a motion for an order to refrain shall serve and file,

(a) a financial statement, in the form prescribed by the regulations or in the form prescribed by the rules of court; and

(b) such proof of income as may be prescribed by the regulations.

Exception, undertaking

(8) Despite clause (7)(b), if the payor is unable to serve and file the proof of income before the motion is heard, the court may make the order to refrain subject to the undertaking of the payor or the payor's lawyer to serve and file the proof of income within 20 days.

Court may change or terminate order to refrain

(9) When an undertaking is made under subsection (8), the court may change or terminate the order to refrain, without proof of a material change in circumstances, on motion by the Director, if,

(a) the 20-day period has expired and the proof of income has not been served and filed; or

(b) the proof of income has been served and filed and the court is satisfied that a different order would have been made if the proof of income had been available when the motion for the order to refrain was heard.

Time limits and changing order to refrain

(10) A court shall not make an order to refrain after the 30-day period referred to in the first notice, but an order to refrain may be changed, on motion by the payor or the Director, at any time before the motion to change support is determined if there is a material change in the payor's circumstances.

Same

(11) A court may make an order to refrain only within the 30-day period referred to in the first notice and may make only one order to refrain in respect of any first notice.

Same

(12) For greater certainty, the 30-day period referred to in the first notice can not be extended for the purposes of subsections (10) and (11).

Same

(13) For greater certainty, if the 30-day period referred to in the first notice expires on a day when court offices are

closed, the last day for making an order to refrain is the last day on which court offices are open before the 30-day period expires.

Order re arrears

(14) When a court that has determined a motion for an order to refrain also determines the related motion to change support, the court,

(a) shall state the amount of the arrears owing, after any change to the support order; and

(b) may make an order respecting payment of the arrears.

Same

(15) For the purpose of clause (14)(b), the court may make any order that may be made under clause 41(10)(a), (b), (c), (e), (h) or (i) or subsection 41(19) and, in the case of an order provided by clause 41(10)(h) or (i), imprisonment does not discharge arrears under the support order.

When Director is a party

(16) The Director is not a party to a motion to change a support order referred to in subsection (1), but the Director and the payor are the only parties to a motion under subsection (1) for an order to refrain.

Filing with Director's office

(17) The court shall file a copy of the order in the Director's office promptly after the order is signed.

Form and effective date

(18) An order to refrain shall be in the form prescribed by the regulations and takes effect only when it is filed in the Director's office.

Duration of order

(19) An order to refrain terminates on the earliest of,

(a) the day the order to refrain is terminated under subsection (9);

(b) the day the motion to change or the appeal is determined;

(c) the day the support order is withdrawn from the Director's office; and

(d) the day that is six months after the order to refrain is made.

Exception

(20) Despite subsection (19), an order to refrain made before the making of a motion to change the support order is automatically terminated if the payor does not, within 20 days after the date of the order to refrain, obtain a court date for the motion to change the support order.

Extension of order

(21) The court that made an order to refrain may, on a motion made by the payor with notice to the Director, extend the order for one further period of,

(a) three months, unless clause (b) applies; or

(b) six months, if the motion to change is being dealt with under section 44 of the *Family Law Act*, sections 18 and 19 of the *Divorce Act* (Canada) or the *Interjurisdictional Support Orders Act, 2002*.

Time for extending order

(22) An extending order under subsection (21) shall not be made after the order to refrain has terminated.

Same

(23) For greater certainty, if the order to refrain terminates on a day when court offices are closed, the last day for making an extending order is the last day on which court offices are open before the order terminates.

Application of order

(24) An order to refrain is applicable only to the notice in respect of which the motion for an order to refrain was made under subsection (1).

Final notice

36. (1) The Director may serve a final notice on the payor if, at any time in the 24 months after the payor made an arrangement under clause 34(a) or obtained an order under subsection 35(1) or clause 35(14)(b), the payor fails to comply with,

(a) the terms of the arrangement made with the Director in response to the first notice;

(b) the terms of an order to refrain under subsection 35(1); or

(c) the terms of the changed support order and an order respecting payment of arrears under clause 35(14)(b).

Contents

(2) The final notice shall inform the payor that his or her driver's licence may be suspended,

(a) unless, within 15 days after the day the final notice is served,

(i) the payor complies with clause (1)(a), (b) or (c), or

(ii) the payor pays all arrears owing under the support order; or

(b) if, within 24 months after the payor makes an arrangement under clause (1)(a) or obtains an order under subsection 35(1) or clause 35(14)(b), the payor fails to comply with the arrangement or order.

Interpretation: arrangement in response to notice

(3) For the purposes of this section, an arrangement is made in response to a first notice if it is made within the time referred to in the first notice.

Same

(4) An arrangement that is made in response to a first notice and is then amended by agreement in writing remains an arrangement made in response to the first notice.

Direction to suspend

After first notice

37. (1) The Director may direct the Registrar of Motor Vehicles to suspend a payor's driver's licence if, within the 30-day period referred to in the first notice, the payor does not,

(a) make an arrangement satisfactory to the Director for complying with the support order;

(b) obtain an order to refrain under subsection 35(1) and file the order in the Director's office; or

(c) pay all arrears owing under the support order.

After final notice

(2) The Director may direct the Registrar of Motor Vehicles to suspend a payor's driver's licence if, within the 15-day period referred to in the final notice or at any time in the 24-month period referred to in the final notice, the payor does not,

(a) comply with clause 36(1)(a), (b) or (c); or

(b) pay all arrears owing under the support order.

Form of direction

(3) A direction under this section shall be in a form approved by the Director and the Registrar of Motor Vehicles.

Direction to reinstate

38. (1) The Director shall direct the Registrar of Motor Vehicles to reinstate a driver's licence suspended as a result of a direction under section 37 if,

(a) the payor pays all the arrears owing under the support order;

(b) the payor is complying with the terms of the arrangement made with the Director in response to the first notice;

(c) the payor is complying with the terms of an order to refrain that has not expired;

(d) the support order has been changed and the payor is complying with the terms of the changed support order, including the terms of any order under clause 35(14)(b) that relates to the support order;

(d.1) the payor makes an arrangement satisfactory to the Director for complying with the support order and for paying the arrears owing under the support order; or

(e) the support order is withdrawn under section 16.

Notice revived if payor breaches arrangement or order

(2) If the Director directs the Registrar of Motor Vehicles to reinstate a driver's licence under clause (1)(b), (c) or (d) and the payor subsequently defaults within 24 months from the date of reinstatement or if the payor subsequently defaults within 24 months after the payor entered into an arrangement under clause 34(a) or obtained an order under clause 35(14)(b), the Director may proceed to act in accordance with the most recent notice that was served on the payor under this Part.

More than one order in default

(3) If the payor is in default on one or more other support orders, the Director shall not direct the Registrar of Motor Vehicles to reinstate the driver's licence unless,

(a) all arrears under all the support orders are paid;

(b) an arrangement or arrangements have been made, on terms satisfactory to the Director, to pay all arrears under all the support orders, and the payor is in compliance with the arrangement or arrangements; or

(c) all arrears under all the support orders are the subject of a court order or orders for payment and the payor is in compliance with the court order or orders.

Discretion to reinstate

(4) The Director may direct the Registrar of Motor Vehicles to reinstate a driver's licence suspended as a result of a direction under section 37 if, in the opinion of the Director, it would be unconscionable not to do so.

Form of direction

(5) A direction under this section shall be in a form approved by the Director and the Registrar of Motor Vehicles.

Anti-avoidance

39. An agreement by the parties to a support order to avoid or prevent its enforcement under this Part is of no effect.

Note: On a day to be named by proclamation of the Lieutenant Governor, the Act is amended by the Statutes of Ontario, 2005, chapter 16, section 22 by adding the following Part:

PART V.1 SUSPENSION OF LICENCES UNDER FISH AND WILDLIFE CONSERVATION ACT, 1997

Definition, Part V.1

39.1 In this Part,

"licences," when used with respect to a payor, means any hunting and sport fishing licences that,

(a) have been issued to the payor under the *Fish and Wildlife Conservation Act, 1997*, and

(b) belong to a class that is prescribed by the regulations.

Suspension

Notice

39.2 (1) When a support order that is filed in the Director's office is in default, the Director may serve a notice on the payor, informing the payor that his or her licences may be suspended unless, within 30 days after the day the notice is served,

(a) the payor makes an arrangement satisfactory to the Director for complying with the support order and for paying the arrears owing under the support order; or

(b) the payor pays all arrears owing under the support order.

Request

(2) The Director may request that the Minister of Natural Resources suspend a payor's licences if, within the 30-day period referred to in the notice, the payor does not,

(a) make an arrangement satisfactory to the Director for complying with the support order; or

(b) pay all arrears owing under the support order.

Form

(3) A request under this section shall be in a form approved by the Director and the Minister of Natural Resources.

Reinstatement

Request

39.3 (1) The Director shall request that the Minister of Natural Resources reinstate a payor's licences that were suspended as a result of a request under section 39.2 if,

(a) the payor pays all the arrears owing under the support order;

(b) the payor is complying with the terms of the arrangement made with the Director in response to the notice;

(c) the support order has been changed and the payor is complying with the terms of the changed support order;

(d) the payor makes an arrangement satisfactory to the Director for complying with the support order and for paying the arrears owing under the support order; or

(e) the support order is withdrawn under section 16.

Notice revived if payor breaches arrangement or order

(2) If the Director requests that the Minister of Natural Resources reinstate a payor's licences under clause (1)(b), (c) or (d) and the payor subsequently defaults within 24 months from the date of reinstatement or if the payor subsequently defaults within 24 months after the payor entered into an arrangement under clause 39.2(1)(a), the Director may again request that the Minister of Natural Resources suspend the payor's licences in accordance with the notice served under section 39.2.

More than one order in default

(3) If the payor is in default on one or more other support orders, the Director shall not request that the Minister of Natural Resources reinstate the payor's licences unless,

(a) all arrears under all the support orders are paid;

(b) an arrangement or arrangements have been made, on terms satisfactory to the Director, to pay all arrears under all the support orders, and the payor is in compliance with the arrangement or arrangements; or

(c) all arrears under all the support orders are the subject of a court order or orders for payment and the payor is in compliance with the court order or orders.

Discretion to request reinstatement

(4) The Director may request that the Minister of Natural Resources reinstate a payor's licences that were suspended as a result of a request under section 39.2 if, in the opinion of the Director, it would be unconscionable not to do so.

Form

(5) A request under this section shall be in a form approved by the Director and the Minister of Natural Resources.

Anti-avoidance

39.4 An agreement by the parties to a support order to avoid or prevent its enforcement under this Part is of no effect.

See: 2005, c. 16, ss. 22, 42(2).

PART VI OTHER ENFORCEMENT MECHANISMS

Financial statements

40. (1) The Director may request that a payor who is in default under a support order, where the support order or related support deduction order is filed in the Director's office, complete and deliver to the Director a financial statement in the form prescribed by the regulations together with such proof of income as may be required by the regulations.

Same

(2) The payor shall deliver the completed financial statement to the Director within 15 days after he or she was served with the request to complete the form.

Changes in information

(3) If a payor discovers that any information was incomplete or wrong at the time he or she completed the financial statement, he or she shall, within 10 days of the discovery, deliver the corrected information to the Director.

Failure to comply

(4) The Ontario Court of Justice or the Family Court, on the motion of the Director, may order a payor to comply with a request under subsection (1) and subsections 41(6) and (7) apply with necessary modifications.

Limitation

(5) The Director may request a financial statement under this section once in any six-month period but this does not

restrict the Director's right to obtain a financial statement under section 41.

Default hearing

41. (1) When a support order that is filed in the Director's office is in default, the Director may prepare a statement of the arrears and, by notice served on the payor together with the statement of arrears, may require the payor to deliver to the Director a financial statement and such proof of income as may be required by the regulations and to appear before the court to explain the default.

Same

(2) When a support order that is not filed in the Director's office is in default, the recipient may file a request with the court, together with a statement of arrears, and, on such filing, the clerk of the court shall, by notice served on the payor together with the statement of arrears, require the payor to file a financial statement and appear before the court to explain the default.

Persons financially connected to payor

(3) The Director or the recipient may, at any time during a default hearing under subsection (1) or (2), request that the court make an order under subsection (4) or (5) or both.

Financial statement

(4) The court may, by order, require a person to file a financial statement and any other relevant documents with the court if the court is satisfied that the person is financially connected to the payor.

Adding party

(5) The court may, by order, add a person as a party to the hearing if the court,

(a) has made or could make an order under subsection (4); and

(b) is satisfied on considering all the circumstances, including the purpose and effect of the dealings between the person and the payor and their benefit or expected benefit to the payor, that there is some evidence that the person has sheltered assets or income of the payor such that enforcement of the support order against the payor may be frustrated.

Form of statements

(6) A financial statement and statement of arrears required by subsection (2) shall be in the form prescribed by the rules of the court and a financial statement required by subsection (1) or (4) shall be in the form prescribed by the regulations.

Arrest of payor

(7) If the payor fails to file the financial statement or to appear as the notice under subsection (1) or (2) requires, the court may issue a warrant for the payor's arrest for the purpose of bringing him or her before the court.

Bail

(8) Section 150 (interim release by justice of the peace) of the *Provincial Offences Act* applies with necessary modifications to an arrest under the warrant.

Presumptions at hearing

(9) At the default hearing, unless the contrary is shown, the payor shall be presumed to have the ability to pay the arrears and to make subsequent payments under the order, and the statement of arrears prepared and served by the Director shall be presumed to be correct as to arrears accruing while the order is filed in the Director's office.

Powers of court

(10) The court may, unless it is satisfied that the payor is unable for valid reasons to pay the arrears or to make subsequent payments under the order, order that the payor,

(a) pay all or part of the arrears by such periodic payments as the court considers just, but an order for partial payment does not rescind any unpaid arrears;

(b) discharge the arrears in full by a specified date;

(c) comply with the order to the extent of the payor's ability to pay;

(d) make a motion to change the support order;

(e) provide security in such form as the court directs for the arrears and subsequent payment;

(f) report periodically to the court, the Director or a person specified in the order;

(g) provide to the court, the Director or a person specified in the order particulars of any future change of address or employment as soon as they occur;

(h) be imprisoned continuously or intermittently until the period specified in the order, which shall not be more than 180 days, has expired, or until the arrears are paid, whichever is sooner; and

(i) on default in any payment ordered under this subsection, be imprisoned continuously or intermittently until the period specified in the order, which shall not be more than 180 days, has expired, or until the payment is made, whichever is sooner.

No effect on accruing of arrears or other means of enforcement

(11) An order under subsection (10) does not affect the accruing of arrears, nor does it affect any other means of enforcing the support order.

Order against person financially connected to payor

(12) If the court is satisfied that a person who was made a party to the hearing under subsection (5) sheltered assets or income of the payor such that enforcement of the support order against the payor has been frustrated, the court may, having regard to all the circumstances, including the purpose and effect of the dealings and the benefit or expected benefit therefrom to the payor, make any order against the person that it

may make against the payor under clauses (10)(a), (b), (c), (e), (f) and (g) and subsection (19), to the extent of the value of the sheltered assets or income and, for the purpose, in clause (10)(c), "payor's" shall be read as "person's."

Same

(13) Subsections (7) and (8) apply with necessary modifications to a person with respect to whom an order is made under subsection (4) or (5).

Temporary orders

(14) The court may make a temporary order against the payor, or a person who was made a party to the hearing under subsection (5), that includes any order that may be made under subsection (10) or (12), as the case may be.

Power to change order

(15) The court that made an order under subsection (10) or (12) may change the order on motion if there is a material change in the payor's or other person's circumstances, as the case may be.

Enforcement of order

(16) The Director may enforce an order against a person made under subsection (12), (14) or (15) in the same manner as he or she may enforce an order against the payor.

Imprisonment does not discharge arrears

(17) Imprisonment of a payor under clause (10)(h) or (i) does not discharge arrears under an order.

No early release

(18) Section 28 of the *Ministry of Correctional Services Act* does not apply to the imprisonment of a payor under clause (10)(h) or (i).

Realizing on security

(19) An order for security under clause (10)(e) or a subsequent order of the court may provide for the realization of the security by seizure, sale or other means, as the court directs.

Proof of service not necessary

(20) Proof of service of a support order or a changed support order is not necessary for the purpose of a default hearing.

Joinder of default and change hearings

(21) A default hearing under this section and a hearing on a motion to change the support order may be held together or separately.

Effect of change on default hearing

(22) If an order changing a support order is made while a default hearing under this section in relation to the support order is under way,

(a) the default hearing continues;

(b) it is not necessary to serve fresh documents under subsection (1) or (2); and

(c) the payment terms of the changed support order shall be incorporated into any subsequent order made under subsection (10).

Spouses compellable witnesses

(23) Spouses are competent and compellable witnesses against each other on a default hearing.

Records sealed

(24) A financial statement or other document filed under subsection (4) shall be sealed in the court file and shall not be disclosed except as permitted by the order or a subsequent order or as necessary to enforce an order made under subsection (12) or (14) against a person other than the payor.

Definition

(25) In this section,

"court" means the Ontario Court of Justice or the Family Court.

Registration against land

42. (1) A support order may be registered in the proper land registry office against the payor's land and on registration the obligation under the order becomes a charge on the property.

Sale of property

(2) A charge created by subsection (1) may be enforced by sale of the property against which it is registered in the same manner as a sale to realize on a mortgage.

Discharge or postponement of charge

(3) A court may order the discharge, in whole or in part, or the postponement, of a charge created by subsection (1), on such terms as to security or other matters as the court considers just.

Notice

(4) An order under subsection (3) may be made only after notice to the Director, if the support order or a related support deduction order is filed with the Director's office for enforcement.

Registration under the *Personal Property Security Act*

43. (1) Arrears owing from time to time under a support order are, upon registration by the Director or the recipient with the registrar under the *Personal Property Security Act* of a notice claiming a lien and charge under this section, a lien and charge on any interest in all the personal property in Ontario owned or held at the time of registration or acquired afterwards by the payor.

Amounts included and priority

(2) The lien and charge is in respect of the arrears owed by the payor under a support order at the time of registration of the notice and the arrears owed by the payor under the support order which accrue afterwards while the notice remains

registered and, upon registration of a notice of lien and charge, the lien and charge has priority over,

(a) any perfected security interest registered after the notice is registered;

(b) any security interest perfected by possession after the notice is registered; and

(c) any encumbrance or other claim that is registered against or that otherwise arises and affects the payor's property after the notice is registered.

Exception

(3) For the purpose of subsection (2), the notice of lien and charge does not have priority over a perfected purchase money security interest in collateral or its proceeds and shall be deemed to be a security interest perfected by registration for the purpose of the priority rules under section 28 of the *Personal Property Security Act*.

Effective period

(4) The notice of lien and charge is effective from the time assigned to its registration by the registrar or branch registrar until its discharge or expiry.

Secured party

(5) In addition to any other rights and remedies, if any arrears under a support order remain unpaid, the Director or recipient, as the case may be, has, in respect of the lien and charge,

(a) all the rights, remedies and duties of a secured party under sections 17, 59, 61, 62, 63 and 64, subsections 65(4), (5), (6) and (7) and section 66 of the *Personal Property Security Act*;

(b) a security interest in the collateral for the purpose of clause 63(4)(c) of that Act; and

(c) a security interest in the personal property for the purposes of sections 15 and 16 of the *Repair and Storage Liens Act*, if it is an article as defined in that Act.

Registration of documents

(6) The notice of lien and charge shall be in the form of a financing statement as prescribed by regulation under the *Personal Property Security Act* and may be tendered for registration at a branch office as provided in Part IV of that Act.

Errors in documents

(7) The notice of lien and charge is not invalidated nor its effect impaired by reason only of an error or omission in the notice or in its execution or registration, unless a reasonable person is likely to be materially misled by the error or omission.

Bankruptcy and Insolvency Act (Canada) unaffected

(8) Subject to Crown rights provided under section 87 of the *Bankruptcy and Insolvency Act* (Canada), nothing in this section affects or purports to affect the rights and obligations of any person under that Act.

Writs of seizure and sale

44. (1) If a writ of seizure and sale is filed with a sheriff in respect of a support order, the person who filed the writ may at any time file with the sheriff a statutory declaration specifying,

(a) the amount currently owing under the order; or

(b) any name, alias or spelling variation of any name or alias used by the payor.

Same

(2) When a statutory declaration is filed under clause (1)(a), the writ of seizure and sale shall be deemed to be amended to specify the amount owing in accordance with the statutory declaration.

Same

(2.1) When a statutory declaration is filed under clause (1)(b), the writ of seizure and sale shall be deemed to be amended to include the names specified on the statutory declaration.

Notice from sheriff of opportunity to amend writ

(3) A sheriff who comes into possession of money to be paid out under a writ of seizure and sale in respect of a support order shall, not later than seven days after making the entry required by subsection 4(1) of the *Creditors' Relief Act, 2010*, give notice to the person who filed the writ of the opportunity to file a statutory declaration under clause (1)(a).

Same

(4) A sheriff who receives a request for information about the amount owing under a writ of seizure and sale in respect of a support order from a person seeking to have the writ removed from the sheriff's file shall promptly give notice to the person who filed the writ of the opportunity to file a statutory declaration under clause (1)(a).

Removal of writ from sheriff's file

(5) A sheriff shall not remove a writ of seizure and sale in respect of a support order from his or her file unless,

(a) the writ has expired and has not been renewed;

(b) the sheriff receives written notice from the person who filed the writ to the effect that the writ should be withdrawn;

(c) notice is given under subsection (3) or (4), a statutory declaration is subsequently filed under clause (1)(a) and the writ, as deemed to be amended under subsection (2), has been fully satisfied; or

(d) notice is given under subsection (3) or (4), 10 days have elapsed since the notice was given, no statutory declaration has been filed under clause (1)(a) since the giving of the notice and the writ has been fully satisfied.

Delivery of statutory declaration to land registrar

(6) If a copy of a writ of seizure and sale has been delivered by the sheriff to a land registrar under section 136 of the *Land Titles Act* and a statutory declaration is filed under subsection (1) in respect of the writ, the sheriff shall promptly deliver a copy of the statutory declaration to the land registrar and the amendment deemed to be made to the writ under subsection (2) or (2.1) does not bind land registered under the *Land Titles Act* until a copy of the statutory declaration has been received and recorded by the land registrar.

Garnishment of joint accounts

45. (1) Upon being served on a financial institution, a notice of garnishment issued by the Director to enforce a support order against a payor attaches 50 per cent of the money credited to a deposit account held in the financial institution in the name of the payor together with one or more other persons as joint or joint and several deposit account holders, and the financial institution shall pay up to 50 per cent of the money credited to the deposit account to the Director in accordance with the notice of garnishment.

Duties of financial institution

(2) The financial institution shall, within 10 days of being served with the notice of garnishment,

(a) pay the money to the Director and, at the same time, notify the Director if the account is held jointly or jointly and severally in the name of two or more persons; and

(b) notify the co-holders of the account who are not named in the notice of garnishment of the garnishment.

Dispute by co-holder

(3) Within 30 days after the financial institution notified the Director under clause (2)(a), a co-holder of the deposit account may file a dispute to the garnishment in the Ontario Court of Justice or the Family Court claiming ownership of all or part of the money that the financial institution paid to the Director.

Director to hold money for 30 days

(4) If the financial institution notifies the Director under clause (2)(a), the Director shall not release the money received under subsection (1) until 30 days after the financial institution so notified the Director, and the Director may release the money after the 30 days unless a co-holder of the deposit account first serves on the Director a copy of the dispute to the garnishment that the co-holder filed under subsection (3).

Determination by court

(5) In a hearing to determine the dispute to the garnishment, the money paid to the Director shall be presumed to be owned by the payor and the court shall order,

(a) that the garnishment be limited to the payor's interest in the money that was paid to the Director; and

(b) that all or part of the money that was paid to the Director be returned to the co-holder only if it is satisfied that the co-holder owns that money.

Payment by Director

(6) Upon receipt of a copy of the court's order, the Director shall return to the co-holder any money determined by the court to belong to the co-holder and may release any remaining money, if any, to the recipient.

Action by joint account co-holder against payor

(7) A co-holder may bring an action against the payor in a court of competent jurisdiction,

(a) to recover any money owned by the co-holder that was paid to the Director under subsection (1);

(b) to recover any interest that the co-holder would have earned on the money owned by the co-holder that was paid to the Director under subsection (1).

Director and recipient are not parties

(8) The Director and the recipient are not parties to an action under subsection (7).

Definition

(9) In this section,

"deposit account" includes a deposit as defined in the *Deposits Regulation Act* and a demand account, time account, savings account, passbook account, checking account, current account and other similar accounts in,

(a) a bank listed in Schedule I or II to the *Bank Act* (Canada),

(b) a loan corporation or trust corporation as defined in the *Loan and Trust Corporations Act*,

(c) a credit union as defined in the *Credit Unions and Caisses Populaires Act, 1994*, or

(d) a similar institution.

(e) Repealed.

Garnishment of lottery prizes

46. (1) In this section,

"Corporation" means the Ontario Lottery Corporation;

"lottery" means a lottery scheme, as defined in section 1 of the *Ontario Lottery Corporation Act*, that is conducted by the Corporation in Ontario and involves the issuance and sale of tickets;

"prize" means a prize in a lottery.

Deduction of arrears from prize

(2) If a payor who owes arrears under a support order that is filed in the Director's office is entitled to a single monetary prize of $1,000 or more from the Corporation, the Corporation shall,

(a) deduct from the prize the amount of the arrears or the amount of the prize, whichever is less;

(b) pay the amount deducted to the Director; and

(c) pay any balance to the payor.

Non-monetary prize

(3) If a payor who owes arrears under a support order that is filed in the Director's office is entitled to a non-monetary prize from the Corporation that the Corporation values at $1,000 or more, the Corporation shall promptly disclose to the Director,

(a) any identifying information about the payor from the Corporation's records, including his or her name and address; and

(b) a complete description of the prize.

Exchange of information

(4) For the purposes of subsections (2) and (3),

(a) the Director shall disclose to the Corporation any identifying information about payors from the Director's records, including their names and addresses and the status and particulars of their support obligations; and

(b) the Corporation shall disclose to the Director any identifying information about prize winners from its records, including their names and addresses.

Reporting default to consumer reporting agency

47. The Director may disclose the information set out in section 47.2 to a consumer reporting agency registered under the *Consumer Reporting Act*.

Reporting default to prescribed entity

47.1 (1) The Director may disclose the information set out in section 47.2 to a prescribed entity that is,

(a) a professional or occupational organization;

(b) the governing body of a self-governing or regulated profession; or

(c) an entity that is responsible for licensing or registering individuals for occupational purposes.

Presumption

(2) In the absence of evidence to the contrary, it shall be presumed that the amount disclosed with respect to arrears as described in clause 47.2(d) is correct.

Information that may be disclosed

47.2 The information that may be disclosed under section 47 or 47.1 is,

(a) the name of a payor who is in default on a support order filed in the Director's office;

(b) the date of the support order;

(c) the amount and frequency of the payor's support obligation under the support order;

(d) the amount of the arrears owing under the support order at the time of the disclosure; and

(e) such other information as may be prescribed.

Restraining order

48. A court, including the Ontario Court of Justice, may make an order restraining the disposition or wasting of assets that may hinder or defeat the enforcement of a support order or support deduction order.

Arrest of absconding payor

49. (1) The Ontario Court of Justice or the Family Court may issue a warrant for a payor's arrest for the purpose of bringing him or her before the court if the court is satisfied that the payor is about to leave Ontario and that there are reasonable grounds for believing that the payor intends to evade his or her obligations under the support order.

Bail

(2) Section 150 (interim release by justice of the peace) of the *Provincial Offences Act* applies with necessary modifications to an arrest under the warrant.

Powers of court

(3) When the payor is brought before the court, it may make any order provided for in subsection 41(10).

Recognition of extra-provincial garnishments

50. (1) On the filing of a garnishment process that,

(a) is issued outside Ontario and is directed to a garnishee in Ontario;

(b) states that it is issued in respect of support or maintenance; and

(c) is written in or accompanied by a sworn or certified translation into English or French,

the clerk of the Ontario Court of Justice or Family Court shall issue a notice of garnishment to enforce the support or maintenance obligation.

Foreign currencies

(2) If the garnishment process refers to an obligation in a foreign currency, section 44 of the *Interjurisdictional Support Orders Act, 2002* applies with necessary modifications.

PART VII OFFENCES AND PENALTIES

Offences — payors, income sources, etc.

Payors

51. (1) A payor who knowingly contravenes or knowingly fails to comply with section 19 or subsection 25(1) or (2) or 40(2) or (3) is guilty of an offence and on conviction is liable to a fine of not more than $10,000.

Income sources

(2) An income source who knowingly contravenes or knowingly fails to comply with subsection 22(2) or 25(1) or (2) or section 29 is guilty of an offence and on conviction is liable to a fine of not more than $10,000.

Individuals, etc., believed to be an income source

(3) An individual, corporation or other entity that knowingly contravenes or knowingly fails to comply with subsection 26(1) or section 29 is guilty of an offence and on conviction is liable to a fine of not more than $10,000.

Offences—assignees

52. (1) An assignee under section 4 who knowingly contravenes or knowingly fails to comply with this Act or its regulations or the limitations, conditions or requirements set out in the assignment is guilty of an offence and on conviction is liable to a fine of not more than $10,000.

Same—directors, officers, employees, agents

(2) A director, officer, employee or agent of an assignee who commits an offence described in subsection (1) on conviction is liable to a fine of not more than $10,000.

Same—directors, officers

(3) A director or officer of an assignee is guilty of an offence if he or she,

(a) knowingly causes, authorizes, permits or participates in the commission of an offence described in subsection (1); or

(b) fails to take reasonable care to prevent the commission of an offence described in subsection (1).

Penalty

(4) A person who is convicted of an offence under subsection (3) is liable to a fine of not more than $10,000.

Contempt

53. (1) In addition to its powers in respect of contempt, a court, including the Ontario Court of Justice, may punish by fine or imprisonment, or by both, any wilful contempt of, or resistance to, its process, rules or orders under this Act, but the fine shall not exceed $10,000 nor shall the imprisonment exceed 90 days.

Conditions of imprisonment

(2) An order for imprisonment under subsection (1) may be conditional upon default in the performance of a condition set out in the order and may provide for the imprisonment to be served intermittently.

PART VIII MISCELLANEOUS

Director's access to information

Definitions

54. (1) In this section,

"enforcement-related information" means information that indicates any of the following about a payor:

0.1 name, alias or spelling variation of any name or alias,
1. employer or place of employment,
2. wages, salary or other income,
2.1 indexing factors applied to the payor's wages, salary, pension or other income,
3. assets or liabilities,
4. home, work or mailing address, or location,
5. telephone number, fax number or e-mail address;

"recipient information" means information that indicates any of the following about a recipient:

0.1 name, alias or spelling variation of any name or alias,
1. home, work or mailing address, or location,
2. telephone number, fax number or e-mail address.

Power of Director

(2) The Director may, for the purpose of enforcing a support order or support deduction order filed in the Director's office or for the purpose of assisting an office or person in another jurisdiction performing similar functions to those performed by the Director,

(a) demand enforcement-related information or recipient information from any person, public body or other entity from a record in the possession or control of the person, public body or other entity;

(b) subject to subsections (4) and (5), have access to all records that may contain enforcement-related information or recipient information and that are in the possession or control of any ministry, agency, board or commission of the Government of Ontario in order to search for and obtain the information from the records;

(c) subject to subsections (4) and (5), enter into an agreement with any person, public body or other entity, including the Government of Canada, a Crown corporation, the government of another province or territory or any agency, board or commission of such government, to permit the Director to have access to records in the possession or control of the person, public body or other entity that may contain enforcement-related information or recipient information, in order to search for and obtain the information from the records; and

(d) disclose information obtained under clause (a), (b) or (c) to a person performing similar functions to those of the Director in another jurisdiction.

10-day period for response

(3) When the Director demands information under clause (2)(a), the person, public body or other entity shall provide the information within 10 days after being served with the demand.

Access to part of record

(4) Where the record referred to in clause (2)(b) or (c) is part of a larger record, the Director,

(a) may have access to the part of the record that may contain enforcement-related information or recipient information; and

(b) may have incidental access to any other information contained in that part of the record, but may not use or disclose that other information.

Restriction on access to health information

(5) Despite subsection (4), if a record described in clause (2)(b) or (c) contains health information, as defined in the regulations, the Director shall not have access to the health information but shall have access only to the part of the rec-

ord that may contain enforcement-related information or recipient information.

Information confidential

(6) Information obtained under subsection (2) shall not be disclosed except,

(a) to the extent necessary for the enforcement of the support order or support deduction order;

(b) as provided in clause (2)(d); or

(c) to a police officer who needs the information for a criminal investigation that is likely to assist the enforcement of the support order or support deduction order.

Court order for access to information

(7) A court may, on motion, make an order requiring any person, public body or other entity to provide the court or the person whom the court names with any enforcement-related information or recipient information that is shown on a record in the possession or control of the person, public body or other entity if it appears that,

(a) the Director has been refused information after making a demand under clause (2)(a);

(b) the Director has been refused access to a record under clause (2)(b); or

(c) a person needs an order under this subsection for the enforcement of a support order that is not filed in the Director's office.

Court order re agreement

(8) A court may, on motion, make an order requiring any person, public body or other entity to enter into an agreement described in clause (2)(c) with the Director if it appears that the person, public body or other entity has unreasonably refused to enter into such an agreement.

Costs

(9) If the Director obtains an order under clause (7)(a) or (b) or under subsection (8), the court shall award the costs of the motion to the Director.

Information confidential

(10) Information obtained under an order under clause (7)(c) shall be sealed in the court file and shall not be disclosed except,

(a) as permitted by the order or a subsequent order;

(b) to the extent necessary for the enforcement of the support order or support deduction order;

(c) as provided in clause (2)(d); or

(d) to a police officer who needs the information for a criminal investigation that is likely to assist the enforcement of the support order or support deduction order.

Section governs

(11) This section applies despite any other Act or regulation and despite any common law rule of confidentiality.

Federal-provincial agreement

55. (1) The Attorney General may, on behalf of the Government of Ontario, enter into an agreement with the Government of Canada concerning the searching for and the release of information under Part I of the *Family Orders and Agreements Enforcement Assistance Act* (Canada).

Information obtained from federal government

(2) The Director shall not disclose information obtained under the *Family Orders and Agreements Enforcement Assistance Act* (Canada) for the enforcement of a support order, except,

(a) to the extent necessary for the enforcement of the order; or

(b) as permitted by the *Freedom of Information and Protection of Privacy Act.*

Payments pending court decisions

56. (1) The Director shall pay any money he or she receives in respect of a support order or a support deduction order to the recipient despite the commencement of any court proceeding in respect of the support obligation or its enforcement, in the absence of a court order to the contrary.

Exception

(2) If a court orders the Director to hold any of the money received in respect of a support order or a support deduction order pending the disposition of the proceeding, the Director shall, upon receipt of a copy of the order, hold any money he or she receives to the extent required by the court.

Application of payments

57. (1) Money paid to the Director on account of a support order or support deduction order shall be credited as prescribed by the regulations.

Same

(2) Despite anything in this Act, the payor shall not be credited with making a payment until the money for that payment is received by the Director and if a payment is made but not honoured, the amount of the payment shall be added to the support arrears owed by the payor.

Fees

58. (1) The Director shall not charge any fee to any person for his or her services except as provided by regulation.

Enforcement of orders to collect fees, etc.

(2) The Director may continue to enforce a support order or support deduction order to collect an amount described in subsection (3), even if,

(a) the support order or support deduction order to which the amount relates has been withdrawn from the Director's office;

(b) there is no current support obligation, and there are no arrears, or any arrears are rescinded by a changed support order; or

(c) the support obligation has terminated and there are no arrears, or any arrears are rescinded by a changed support order.

Same

(3) Subsection (2) applies with respect to,

(a) fees;

(b) costs awarded to the Director by a court;

(c) any amount owed to the Director as reimbursement for money paid to a recipient; and

(d) any amount similar to the ones described in clauses (a), (b) and (c) that is owed to a support enforcement program in a reciprocating jurisdiction, if the support order to which the amount relates is registered in Ontario under the *Interjurisdictional Support Orders Act, 2002.*

Protection from personal liability

59. (1) No action or other proceeding for damages shall be instituted against the Director or any employee of the Director's office for any act done in good faith in the execution or intended execution of any duty or authority under this Act or for any alleged neglect or default in the execution in good faith of any duty or authority under this Act.

Crown not relieved of liability

(2) Despite subsections 5(2) and (4) of the *Proceedings Against the Crown Act*, subsection (1) does not relieve the Crown of liability in respect of a tort committed by a person mentioned in subsection (1) to which it would otherwise be subject.

Acting by lawyer

60. Anything that this Act requires to be signed or done by a person, or that is referred to in this Act as signed or done by a person, may be signed or done by a lawyer acting on the person's behalf.

Disclosure of personal information

61. (1) The Director shall collect, disclose and use personal information about an identifiable individual for the purpose of enforcing a support order or a support deduction order under this Act.

Same

(2) Any person, public body or other entity that is referred to in clause 54(2)(a) shall disclose personal information about an identifiable individual to the Director for the purpose of section 54, within 10 days after being served with the Director's demand.

Notice to individual not required

(3) Subsection 39(2) of the *Freedom of Information and Protection of Privacy Act* does not apply to the collection of personal information about an identifiable individual under this Act.

Act prevails over confidentiality provisions

(4) This Act prevails over a confidentiality provision in another Act that would, if not for this Act, prohibit the disclosure of information to the Director.

Law enforcement

(5) The Director shall be deemed to be engaged in law enforcement for the purposes of section 14 of the *Freedom of Information and Protection of Privacy Act* when collecting information, under section 54 or otherwise, for the purpose of enforcing a support order or support deduction order under this Act.

Obtaining information about payor by means of Internet posting

Director's discretion

61.1 (1) The Director may post a payor's name and other prescribed information relating to the payor on a website on the Internet if,

(a) the payor is in default under a support order;

(b) the support order or a related support deduction order is filed in the Director's office;

(c) the Director has been unsuccessful in locating the payor; and

(d) the prescribed conditions are satisfied.

Purpose of posting

(2) The sole purpose of posting information under subsection (1) is to assist the Director in locating the payor.

Confidentiality of information obtained as a result of posting

(3) Subsection 54(6) applies, with necessary modifications, to any information obtained by the Director as a result of the posting.

Act binds Crown

62. This Act binds the Crown.

Regulations

63. (1) The Lieutenant Governor in Council may make regulations,

(a) prescribing forms and providing for their use;

(b) prescribing types of income for the purposes of clause (l) of the definition of "income source" in subsection 1(1);

(c) prescribing the manner of calculating a cost of living clause for the purposes of subsections 7(4), (5), (6) and (7);

(d) prescribing classes of persons and information to be supplied to the court and the manner in which information is to be supplied for the purposes of subsections 11(2) and (3);

(e) prescribing practices and procedures related to the filing and withdrawal of support orders and support deduction orders and to the enforcement, suspension and termination of such orders filed in the Director's office;

(e.1) defining "in compliance" for the purposes of subsection 16(1.1);

(e.2) prescribing methods of electronic transmission for the purpose of subsection 22(2.1);

(f) prescribing deductions for the purposes of subsection 23(5);

(g) prescribing information that shall be supplied under subsection 25(1);

(g.1) prescribing practices and procedures relating to the filing and withdrawal of alternative payment orders under section 28;

(h) governing the form and posting of security by a payor under section 28 and the realization thereon;

Note: On a day to be named by proclamation of the Lieutenant Governor, section 63 is amended by the Statutes of Ontario, 2005, chapter 16, subsection 36(3) by adding the following clause:

(h.1) prescribing classes of licences for the purposes of Part V.1;

See: 2005, c. 16, ss. 36(3), 42(2).

(i) respecting proof of income for the purposes of sections 35, 40 and 41;

(j) prescribing, for the purposes of clause 47.2(e), other information that may be disclosed under section 47 or 47.1;

(k) prescribing,

(i) fees to be charged by the Director for administrative services, including preparing and photocopying documents on request, and

(ii) fees for any steps taken by the Director to enforce a support order in response to the persistent or wilful default by a payor;

(k.1) prescribing fees for the repeated filing of a support order or support deduction order, and specifying what constitutes repeated filing;

(l) prescribing the maximum fees, costs, disbursements, surcharges and other charges, or a method for determining the maximum fees, costs, disbursements, surcharges and other charges, that an assignee under section 4 may charge a payor, including fees, costs, disbursements, surcharges and other charges for services for which the Director is not permitted to charge and including fees, costs, disbursements, surcharges or other charges that are higher than the fees, costs, disbursements, surcharges and other charges that the Director may charge for the same service, prescribing how and when such fees, costs, disbursements, surcharges and other charges may be collected, prescribing the manner in which they may be applied and prescribing the rate of interest to be charged on any of them;

(m) prescribing methods of and rules respecting service, filing and notice for the purposes of this Act, including different methods and rules for different provisions and different methods and rules for service on or notice to the Crown;

(n) providing that a support deduction order is not effective against the Crown unless a statement of particulars in the prescribed form is served with the notice of the order;

(o) defining "health information" for the purposes of subsection 54(5);

(p) prescribing the manner in which payments received by the Director are to be credited;

(p.1) governing the delivery of payments to recipients, including requiring recipients to provide the Director with the information and authorization required to enable the Director to make direct deposits into the recipients' accounts with financial institutions;

(p.2) setting out recommended standard terms for support orders;

(q) prescribing anything that is required or authorized by this Act to be prescribed.

Repeated filing

(2) A fee prescribed under clause (1)(k.1) may be charged against both the payor and the recipient, regardless of which one of them files the order.

64. Repealed. See: Table of Public Statute Provisions Repealed Under Section 10.1 of the *Legislation Act, 2006*—December 31, 2011.

65.-70. Omitted (amends or repeals other Acts).

71. Repealed. See: Table of Public Statute Provisions Repealed Under Section 10.1 of the *Legislation Act, 2006*—December 31, 2011.

72., 73. Omitted (amends or repeals other Acts).

74. Omitted (provides for coming into force of provisions of this Act).

75. Omitted (enacts short title of this Act).

Child Support Guidelines

O. Reg. 391/97
Current to December 31, 2011

OBJECTIVES

Objectives

1. The objectives of this Regulation are,

(a) to establish a fair standard of support for children that ensures that they benefit from the financial means of their parents and, in the case of divorce, from the financial means of both spouses after separation;

(b) to reduce conflict and tension between parents or spouses by making the calculation of child support more objective;

(c) to improve the efficiency of the legal process by giving courts, and parents and spouses, guidance in setting the levels of child support and encouraging settlement; and

(d) to ensure consistent treatment of parents or spouses and their children who are in similar circumstances.

INTERPRETATION

Definitions

2. (1) In this Regulation,

"child" means, other than in Schedule II to this Regulation,

(a) a child who is a dependant under the Act, or

(b) in cases where the *Divorce Act* (Canada) applies, a child of the marriage under that Act;

"income" means the annual income determined under sections 15 to 20;

"order assignee" means,

(a) an agency to whom an order is assigned under subsection 34(3) of the Act, or

(b) a minister, member or agency referred to in subsection 20.1(1) of the *Divorce Act* (Canada) to whom an order for the support of a child is assigned in accordance with that subsection;

"parent," in a case to which the Act applies, means a parent to whom section 31 of the Act applies;

"spouse," in a case to which the *Divorce Act* (Canada) applies, has the meaning assigned by subsection 2(1) of that Act, and includes a former spouse;

"table" means,

(a) if the parent or spouse against whom an order is sought ordinarily resides in Ontario at the time of the application, the Child Support Table for Ontario set out in Schedule I to this Regulation,

(b) if the parent or spouse against whom an order is sought ordinarily resides elsewhere in Canada, the table set out in the Federal Child Support Guidelines for the province or territory in which the parent or spouse ordinarily resides at the time of the application,

(c) if the court is satisfied that the province or territory in which the parent or spouse against whom an order is sought ordinarily resides has changed since the time of the application, the table set out in the Federal Child Support Guidelines for the province or territory in which the parent or spouse ordinarily resides at the time the amount of support is determined,

(d) if the court is satisfied that the parent or spouse against whom an order is sought will, in the near future after the amount of support is determined, ordinarily reside in another province or territory than the one in which he or she ordinarily resides at the time the amount of support is determined, the table set out in the Federal Child Support Guidelines for that other province or territory,

(e) if the parent or spouse against whom an order is sought ordinarily resides outside of Canada or if the ordinary residence of the parent or spouse is unknown,

(i) the Child Support Table for Ontario set out in Schedule I to this Regulation if the other parent or spouse applying for the order resides in Ontario, or

(ii) the table set out in the Federal Child Support Guidelines for the province or territory in which the parent or spouse applying for the order ordinarily resides.

"universal child care benefit" means a benefit provided under section 4 of the *Universal Child Care Benefit Act* (Canada).

Income Tax Act (Canada)

(2) Words and expressions that are used in sections 15 to 21 and that are not defined in this section have the meanings assigned to them under the *Income Tax Act* (Canada).

Most current information

(3) Where, for the purposes of the child support guidelines, any amount is determined on the basis of specified information, the most current information must be used.

Application of guidelines

(4) In addition to their application to orders for support of a child, the child support guidelines apply, with such modifications as the circumstances require, to,

(a) interim orders under subsection 34(1) of the Act or subsections 15.1(2) and 19(9) of the *Divorce Act* (Canada);

(b) orders varying a child support order; and

(c) orders referred to in subsection 19(7) of the *Divorce Act* (Canada).

AMOUNT OF CHILD SUPPORT

Presumptive rule

3. (1) Unless otherwise provided under these guidelines, the amount of an order for the support of a child for children under the age of majority is,

(a) the amount set out in the applicable table, according to the number of children under the age of majority to whom the order relates and the income of the parent or spouse against whom the order is sought; and

(b) the amount, if any, determined under section 7.

Child the age of majority or over

(2) Unless otherwise provided under these guidelines, where a child to whom an order for the support of a child relates is the age of majority or over, the amount of an order for the support of a child is,

(a) the amount determined by applying these guidelines as if the child were under the age of majority; or

(b) if the court considers that approach to be inappropriate, the amount that it considers appropriate, having regard to the condition, means, needs and other circumstances of the child and the financial ability of each parent or spouse to contribute to the support of the child.

Incomes over $150,000

4. Where the income of the parent or spouse against whom an order for the support of a child is sought is over $150,000, the amount of an order for the support of a child is,

(a) the amount determined under section 3; or

(b) if the court considers that amount to be inappropriate,

(i) in respect of the first $150,000 of the parent's or spouse's income, the amount set out in the table for the number of children under the age of majority to whom the order relates,

(ii) in respect of the balance of the parent's or spouse's income, the amount that the court considers appropriate, having regard to the condition, means, needs and other circumstances of the children who are entitled to support and the financial ability of each parent or spouse to contribute to the support of the children, and

(iii) the amount, if any, determined under section 7.

Spouse in place of a parent

5. Where the spouse against whom an order for the support of a child is sought stands in the place of a parent for a child or the parent is not a natural or adoptive parent of the child, the amount of the order is, in respect of that parent or spouse, such amount as the court considers appropriate, having regard to these guidelines and any other parent's legal duty to support the child.

Medical and dental insurance

6. In making an order for the support of a child, where medical or dental insurance coverage for the child is available to either parent or spouse through his or her employer or otherwise at a reasonable rate, the court may order that coverage be acquired or continued.

Special or extraordinary expenses

7. (1) In an order for the support of a child, the court may, on the request of either parent or spouse or of an applicant under section 33 of the Act, provide for an amount to cover all or any portion of the following expenses, which expenses may be estimated, taking into account the necessity of the expense in relation to the child's best interests and the reasonableness of the expense in relation to the means of the parents or spouses and those of the child and to the spending pattern of the parents or spouses in respect of the child during cohabitation:

(a) child care expenses incurred as a result of the custodial parent's employment, illness, disability or education or training for employment;

(b) that portion of the medical and dental insurance premiums attributable to the child;

(c) health-related expenses that exceed insurance reimbursement by at least $100 annually, including orthodontic treatment, professional counselling provided by a psychologist, social worker, psychiatrist or any other person, physiotherapy, occupational therapy, speech therapy, prescription drugs, hearing aids, glasses and contact lenses;

(d) extraordinary expenses for primary or secondary school education or for any other educational programs that meet the child's particular needs;

(e) expenses for post-secondary education; and

(f) extraordinary expenses for extracurricular activities.

Definition, "extraordinary expenses"

(1.1) For the purposes of clauses (1)(d) and (f), "extraordinary expenses" means

(a) expenses that exceed those that the parent or spouse requesting an amount for the extraordinary expenses can reasonably cover, taking into account that parent's or spouse's income and the amount that the parent or spouse would receive under the applicable table or, where the court has determined that the table amount is inappropriate, the amount that the court has otherwise determined is appropriate, or

(b) where clause (a) is not applicable, expenses that the court considers are extraordinary taking into account,

(i) the amount of the expense in relation to the income of the parent or spouse requesting the amount, including the amount that the parent or spouse would receive under the applicable table or, where the court has determined that the table amount is inappropriate, the amount that the court has otherwise determined is appropriate,

(ii) the nature and number of the educational programs and extracurricular activities,

(iii) any special needs and talents of the child,

(iv) the overall cost of the programs and activities, and

(v) any other similar factors that the court considers relevant.

Sharing of expense

(2) The guiding principle in determining the amount of an expense referred to in subsection (1) is that the expense is shared by the parents or spouses in proportion to their respective incomes after deducting from the expense, the contribution, if any, from the child.

Subsidies, tax deductions, etc.

(3) Subject to subsection (4), in determining the amount of an expense referred to in subsection (1), the court must take into account any subsidies, benefits or income tax deductions or credits relating to the expense, and any eligibility to claim a subsidy, benefit or income tax deduction or credit relating to the expense.

Universal child care benefit

(4) In determining the amount of an expense referred to in subsection (1), the court shall not take into account any universal child care benefit or any eligibility to claim that benefit.

Split custody

8. Where each parent or spouse has custody of one or more children, the amount of an order for the support of a child is the difference between the amount that each parent or spouse would otherwise pay if such an order were sought against each of the parents or spouses.

Shared custody

9. Where a parent or spouse exercises a right of access to, or has physical custody of, a child for not less than 40 per cent of the time over the course of a year, the amount of the order for the support of a child must be determined by taking into account,

(a) the amounts set out in the applicable tables for each of the parents or spouses;

(b) the increased costs of shared custody arrangements; and

(c) the condition, means, needs and other circumstances of each parent or spouse and of any child for whom support is sought.

Undue hardship

10. (1) On the application of either spouse or an applicant under section 33 of the Act, a court may award an amount of child support that is different from the amount determined under any of sections 3 to 5, 8 or 9 if the court finds that the parent or spouse making the request, or a child in respect of whom the request is made, would otherwise suffer undue hardship.

Circumstances that may cause undue hardship

(2) Circumstances that may cause a parent, spouse or child to suffer undue hardship include,

(a) the parent or spouse has responsibility for an unusually high level of debts reasonably incurred to support the parents or spouses and their children during cohabitation or to earn a living;

(b) the parent or spouse has unusually high expenses in relation to exercising access to a child;

(c) the parent or spouse has a legal duty under a judgment, order or written separation agreement to support any person;

(d) the spouse has a legal duty to support a child, other than a child of the marriage, who is,

(i) under the age of majority, or

(ii) the age of majority or over but is unable, by reason of illness, disability or other cause, to obtain the necessaries of life;

(e) the parent has a legal duty to support a child, other than the child who is the subject of this application, who is under the age of majority or who is enrolled in a full time course of education;

(f) the parent or spouse has a legal duty to support any person who is unable to obtain the necessaries of life due to an illness or disability.

Standards of living must be considered

(3) Despite a determination of undue hardship under subsection (1), an application under that subsection must be denied by the court if it is of the opinion that the household of the parent or spouse who claims undue hardship would, after determining the amount of child support under any of sections 3 to 5, 8 or 9, have a higher standard of living than the household of the other parent or spouse.

Standards of living test

(4) In comparing standards of living for the purpose of subsection (3), the court may use the comparison of household standards of living test set out in Schedule II.

Reasonable time

(5) Where the court awards a different amount of child support under subsection (1), it may specify, in the order for child support, a reasonable time for the satisfaction of any obligation arising from circumstances that cause undue hardship and the amount payable at the end of that time.

Reasons

(6) Where the court makes an order for the support of a child in a different amount under this section, it must record its reasons for doing so.

ELEMENTS OF AN ORDER FOR THE SUPPORT OF A CHILD

Form of payments

11. Where the child support guidelines apply to orders made under the *Divorce Act* (Canada), section 34 of the Act applies.

Security

12. The court may require in the order for the support of a child that the amount payable under the order be paid or secured, or paid and secured, in the manner specified in the order.

Information to be specified in order

13. An order for the support of a child must include,

(a) the name and birth date of each child to whom the order relates;

(b) the income of any parent or spouse whose income is used to determine the amount of the order;

(c) the amount determined under clause 3(1)(a) for the number of children to whom the order relates;

(d) the amount determined under clause 3(2)(b) for a child the age of majority or over;

(e) the particulars of any expense described in subsection 7(1), the child to whom the expense relates and the amount of the expense or, where that amount cannot be determined, the proportion to be paid in relation to the expense;

(f) the date on which the lump sum or first payment is payable and the day of the month or other time period on which all subsequent payments are to be made; and

(g) reference to the obligation under subsection 24.1(1) to provide updated income information no later than 30 days after the anniversary of the date on which the order is made in every year in which the child is a child within the meaning of this Regulation, unless the parties agree that the obligation shall not apply, as provided for in that subsection.

VARIATION OF ORDERS FOR THE SUPPORT OF A CHILD

Circumstances for variation

14. For the purposes of subsection 37(2.2) of the Act and subsection 17(4) of the *Divorce Act* (Canada), any one of the following constitutes a change of circumstances that gives rise to the making of a variation order:

1. In the case where the amount of child support includes a determination made in accordance with the table, any change in circumstances that would result in a different order for the support of a child or any provision thereof.
2. In the case where the amount of child support does not include a determination made in accordance with a table, any change in the condition, means, needs or other circumstances of either parent or spouse or of any child who is entitled to support.
3. In the case of an order made under the *Divorce Act* (Canada) before May 1, 1997, the coming into force of section 15.1 of that Act, enacted by section 2 of chapter 1 of the Statutes of Canada, (1997).
4. In the case of an order made under the Act, the coming into force of subsection 33(11) of the Act.

INCOME

Determination of annual income

15. (1) Subject to subsection (2), a parent's or spouse's annual income is determined by the court in accordance with sections 16 to 20.

Agreement

(2) Where both parents or spouses agree in writing on the annual income of a parent or spouse, the court may consider that amount to be the parent's or spouse's income for the purposes of these guidelines if the court thinks that the amount is reasonable having regard to the income information provided under section 21.

Calculation of annual income

16. Subject to sections 17 to 20, a parent's or spouse's annual income is determined using the sources of income set out under the heading "Total income" in the T1 General form issued by the Canada Revenue Agency and is adjusted in accordance with Schedule III.

Pattern of income

17. (1) If the court is of the opinion that the determination of a parent's or spouse's annual income under section 16 would not be the fairest determination of that income, the court may have regard to the parent's or spouse's income over the last three years and determine an amount that is fair and reasonable in light of any pattern of income, fluctuation in income or receipt of a non-recurring amount during those years.

Non-recurring losses

(2) Where a parent or spouse has incurred a non-recurring capital or business investment loss, the court may, if it is of the opinion that the determination of the parent's or spouse's annual income under section 16 would not provide the fairest determination of the annual income, choose not to apply sections 6 and 7 of Schedule III, and adjust the amount of the loss, including related expenses and carrying charges and interest expenses, to arrive at such amount as the court considers appropriate.

Shareholder, director or officer

18. (1) Where a parent or spouse is a shareholder, director or officer of a corporation and the court is of the opinion that the amount of the parent's or spouse's annual income as determined under section 16 does not fairly reflect all the money available to the parent or spouse for the payment of child support, the court may consider the situations described in section 17 and determine the parent's or spouse's annual income to include,

(a) all or part of the pre-tax income of the corporation, and of any corporation that is related to that corporation, for the most recent taxation year; or

(b) an amount commensurate with the services that the parent or spouse provides to the corporation, provided that the amount does not exceed the corporation's pre-tax income.

Adjustment to corporation's pre-tax income

(2) In determining the pre-tax income of a corporation for the purposes of subsection (1), all amounts paid by the corporation as salaries, wages or management fees, or other payments or benefits, to or on behalf of persons with whom the corporation does not deal at arm's length must be added to the pre-tax income, unless the parent or spouse establishes that the payments were reasonable in the circumstances.

Imputing income

19. (1) The court may impute such amount of income to a parent or spouse as it considers appropriate in the circumstances, which circumstances include,

(a) the parent or spouse is intentionally under-employed or unemployed, other than where the under-employment or unemployment is required by the needs of any child or by the reasonable educational or health needs of the parent or spouse;

(b) the parent or spouse is exempt from paying federal or provincial income tax;

(c) the parent or spouse lives in a country that has effective rates of income tax that are significantly lower than those in Canada;

(d) it appears that income has been diverted which would affect the level of child support to be determined under these guidelines;

(e) the parent's or spouse's property is not reasonably utilized to generate income;

(f) the parent or spouse has failed to provide income information when under a legal obligation to do so;

(g) the parent or spouse unreasonably deducts expenses from income;

(h) the parent or spouse derives a significant portion of income from dividends, capital gains or other sources that are taxed at a lower rate than employment or business income or that are exempt from tax; and

(i) the parent or spouse is a beneficiary under a trust and is or will be in receipt of income or other benefits from the trust.

Reasonableness of expenses

(2) For the purpose of clause (1)(g), the reasonableness of an expense deduction is not solely governed by whether the deduction is permitted under the *Income Tax Act* (Canada).

Non-resident

20. (1) Subject to subsection (2), where a parent or spouse is a non-resident of Canada, the parent's or spouse's annual income is determined as though the parent or spouse were a resident of Canada.

Non-resident taxed at higher rates

(2) Where a parent or spouse is a non-resident of Canada and resides in a country that has effective rates of income tax that are significantly higher than those applicable in the province or territory in which the other parent or spouse ordinarily resides, the non-resident parent's or spouse's annual income is the amount which the court determines to be appropriate taking the higher rates into consideration.

INCOME INFORMATION

Obligation of applicant

21. (1) A parent or spouse who is applying for an order for the support of a child and whose income information is necessary to determine the amount of the order must include with the application,

(a) a copy of every personal income tax return filed by the parent or spouse including any materials that were filed with the return for each of the three most recent taxation years;

(b) a copy of every notice of assessment and reassessment issued to the parent or spouse for each of the three most recent taxation years;

(c) where the parent or spouse is an employee, the most recent statement of earnings indicating the total earnings paid in the year to date, including overtime, or, where such a statement is not provided by the employer, a letter from the parent's or spouse's employer setting out that information including the parent's or spouse's rate of annual salary or remuneration;

(d) where the parent or spouse is self-employed, for the three most recent taxation years,

(i) the financial statements of the parent's or spouse's business or professional practice, other than a partnership, and

(ii) a statement showing a breakdown of all salaries, wages, management fees or other payments or benefits paid to, or on behalf of, persons or corporations with whom the parent or spouse does not deal at arm's length;

(e) where the parent or spouse is a partner in a partnership, confirmation of the parent's or spouse's income and draw from, and capital in, the partnership for its three most recent taxation years;

(f) where the parent or spouse controls a corporation, for its three most recent taxation years,

(i) the financial statements of the corporation and its subsidiaries, and

(ii) a statement showing a breakdown of all salaries, wages, management fees or other payments or benefits paid to, or on behalf of, persons or corporations with whom the corporation, and every related corporation, does not deal at arm's length;

(g) where the parent or spouse is a beneficiary under a trust, a copy of the trust settlement agreement and copies of the trust's three most recent financial statements; and

(h) in addition to any information that must be included under clauses (c) to (g), where the parent or spouse receives income from employment insurance, social assistance, a pension, workers compensation, disability payments or any other source, the most recent statement of income indicating the total amount of income from the applicable source during the current year or, if such a statement is not provided, a letter from the appropriate authority stating the required information.

Obligation of respondent

(2) A parent or spouse who is served with an application for an order for the support of a child and whose income information is necessary to determine the amount of the order, must, within 30 days after the application is served if the parent or spouse resides in Canada or the United States or within 60 days if the parent or spouse resides elsewhere, or such other time limit as the court specifies, provide the court, as well as the other spouse, an applicant under section 33 of the Act or the order assignee with the documents referred to in subsection (1).

Special expenses or undue hardship

(3) Where, in the course of proceedings in respect of an application for an order for the support of a child, a parent or spouse requests an amount to cover expenses referred to in subsection 7(1) or pleads undue hardship, the parent or spouse who would be receiving the amount of child support must, within 30 days after the amount is sought or undue hardship is pleaded if the parent or spouse resides in Canada or the United States or within 60 days if the parent or spouse resides elsewhere, or such other time limit as the court specifies, provide the court and the other parent or spouse with the documents referred to in subsection (1).

Income over $150,000

(4) Where, in the course of proceedings in respect of an application for an order for the support of a child, it is established that the income of the parent or spouse who would be paying the amount of child support is greater than $150,000, the other parent or spouse must, within 30 days after the income is established to be greater than $150,000 if the other parent or spouse resides in Canada or the United States or within 60 days if the other parent or spouse resides elsewhere, or such other time limit as the court specifies, provide the court and the other parent or spouse with the documents referred to in subsection (1).

Failure to comply

22. (1) Where a parent or spouse fails to comply with section 21, the other spouse, an applicant under section 33 of the Act or an order assignee may apply,

(a) to have the application for an order for the support of a child set down for a hearing, or move for judgment; or

(b) for an order requiring the parent or spouse who failed to comply to provide the court, as well as the other parent or spouse or order assignee, as the case may be, with the required documents.

Costs of the proceedings

(2) Where a court makes an order under clause (1)(a) or (b), the court may award costs in favour of the other spouse, the applicant under section 33 of the Act or an order assignee up to an amount that fully compensates the other spouse, the applicant or order assignee for all costs incurred in the proceedings.

Adverse inference

23. Where the court proceeds to a hearing on the basis of an application under clause 22(1)(a), the court may draw an adverse inference against the parent or spouse who failed to comply and impute income to that parent or spouse in such amount as it considers appropriate.

Failure to comply with court order

24. Where a parent or spouse fails to comply with an order issued on the basis of an application under clause 22(1)(b), the court may,

(a) strike out any of the parent's or spouse's pleadings;

(b) make a contempt order against the parent or spouse;

(c) proceed to a hearing, in the course of which it may draw an adverse inference against the parent or spouse and impute income to that parent or spouse in such amount as it considers appropriate; and

(d) award costs in favour of the other spouse, an applicant under section 33 of the Act or an order assignee up to an amount that fully compensates the other spouse, the applicant or assignee for all costs incurred in the proceedings.

Annual obligation to provide income information

24.1 (1) Every person whose income or other financial information is used to determine the amount of an order for the support of a child shall, no later than 30 days after the anniversary of the date on which the order was made in every year in which the child is a child within the meaning of this Regulation, provide every party to the order with the following, unless the parties have agreed otherwise:

1. For the most recent taxation year, a copy of the person's,
   - i. personal income tax return, including any materials that were filed with the return, and
   - ii. notice of assessment and, if any, notice of reassessment.
2. As applicable, any current information in writing about,
   - i. the status and amount of any expenses included in the order pursuant to subsection 7(1), and
   - ii. any loan, scholarship or bursaries the child has received or will receive in the coming year that affect or will affect the expenses referred to in subparagraph i.

Notices of assessment

(2) If the person has not received his or her notice of assessment or notice of reassessment for the most recent taxation year by the date referred to in subsection (1), the person shall provide every party to the order with a copy of the notice as soon as possible after the person receives the notice.

Change in address

(3) If the address at which a party receives documents changes, the party shall, at least 30 days before the next anniversary of the date on which the order was made, give written notice of his or her updated address information to every person required to provide documents and information under subsection (1).

Failure to comply

(4) If a person required to provide a document or information under this section fails to do so, a court may, on application by the party who did not receive the document or information, make one or more of the following orders:

1. An order finding the person to be in contempt of court.
2. An order awarding costs in favour of the applicant up to an amount that fully compensates the applicant for all costs incurred in the proceedings.
3. An order requiring the person to provide the document or information to,
   - i. the court,
   - ii. the applicant, and
   - iii. any other party to whom the person did not provide the document or information when required to do so.

Exception

(5) Subsection (4) does not apply if the person who fails to provide the document or information is a child who is not a party to the order for support.

Transition

(6) In the case of an order to which subsection (1) applies that is in existence on the day section 5 of Ontario Regulation 25/10 comes into force, if the first date by which a person must provide documents and information under that subsection occurs less than six months after the day on which the person provided documents and information under section 25, the person is not required to provide documents and information under subsection (1) in the first year in which he or she would otherwise have been required to provide them.

Continuing obligation to provide income information

25. (1) Every parent or spouse against whom an order for the support of a child has been made must, on the written request of the other spouse or the person or agency entitled to payment under the order not more than once a year after the making of the order and as long as the child is a child within the meaning of this Regulation, provide that other spouse, or the person or agency entitled to payment under the order, with,

(a) the documents referred to in subsection 21(1) for any of the three most recent taxation years for which the parent or spouse has not previously provided the documents;

(b) as applicable, any current information in writing about,

(i) the status and amount of any expenses included in the order pursuant to subsection 7(1), and

(ii) any loan, scholarship or bursaries the child has received that affect the expenses referred to in subclause (i); and

(c) as applicable, any current information, in writing, about the circumstances relied on by the court in a determination of undue hardship.

Below minimum income

(2) Where a court has determined that the parent or spouse against whom an order for the support of a child is sought does not have to pay child support because his or her income level is below the minimum amount required for application of the tables, that parent or spouse must, on the written request of the other spouse or the applicant under section 33 of the Act, not more than once a year after the determination and as long as the child is a child within the meaning of this Regulation, provide the other spouse or the applicant with the documents referred to in subsection 21(1) for any of the three most recent taxation years for which the parent or spouse has not previously provided the documents.

Obligation of receiving parent or spouse

(3) Where the income information of the parent or spouse in favour of whom an order for the support of a child is made is used to determine the amount of the order, the parent or spouse must, not more than once a year after the making of the order and as long as the child is a child within the meaning of this Regulation, on the written request of the other parent or spouse, provide the other parent or spouse with the documents and information referred to in subsection (1).

Information requests

(4) Where a parent or spouse requests information from the other parent or spouse under any of subsections (1) to (3) and the income information of the requesting parent or spouse is used to determine the amount of the order for the support of a child, the requesting parent or spouse must include the documents and information referred to in subsection (1) with the request.

Time limit

(5) A parent or spouse who receives a request made under any of subsections (1) to (3) must provide the required documents within 30 days after the request's receipt if the parent or spouse resides in Canada or the United States and within 60 days after the request's receipt if the parent or spouse resides elsewhere.

Deemed receipt

(6) A request made under any of subsections (1) to (3) is deemed to have been received 10 days after it is sent.

Failure to comply

(7) A court may, on application by either spouse, an applicant under section 33 of the Act or an order assignee, where the parent or spouse has failed to comply with any of subsections (1) to (3),

(a) consider the parent or spouse to be in contempt of court and award costs in favour of the applicant up to an amount that fully compensates the applicant for all costs incurred in the proceedings; or

(b) make an order requiring the parent or spouse to provide the required documents to the court, as well as to the spouse, order assignee or applicant under section 33 of the Act, as the case may be.

Unenforceable provision

(8) A provision in a judgment, order or agreement purporting to limit a parent's or spouse's obligation to provide documents under this section is unenforceable.

PROVIDING INCOME INFORMATION FOR DOMESTIC CONTRACTS AND OTHER AGREEMENTS

Annual obligation to provide income information

25.1 (1) Every person whose income or other financial information is used to determine the amount of a child support obligation under a domestic contract or other written agreement shall, no later than 30 days after the anniversary of the date on which the contract or agreement was entered into in every year in which the child is a child within the meaning of this Regulation, provide every party to the contract or agreement with the following, unless the parties have agreed otherwise in a domestic contract or other agreement:

1. For the most recent taxation year, a copy of the person's,
   i. personal income tax return, including any materials that were filed with the return, and
   ii. notice of assessment and, if any, notice of reassessment.
2. If the contract or agreement provides for the payment of any of the expenses referred to in clauses 7(1)(a) to (f), any current information in writing about,
   i. the status and amount of the expenses, and
   ii. any loan, scholarship or bursaries the child has received or will receive in the coming year that affect or will affect the expenses referred to in subparagraph i.

Notices of assessment

(2) If the person has not received his or her notice of assessment or notice of reassessment for the most recent taxation year by the date referred to in subsection (1), the person shall provide every party to the contract or agreement with a copy of the notice as soon as possible after the person receives the notice.

Change in address

(3) If the address at which a party to the domestic contract or agreement receives documents changes, the party shall, at least 30 days before the next anniversary of the date on which the contract or agreement was entered into, give written notice of his or her updated address information to every person required to provide documents and information under subsection (1).

Failure to comply

(4) If a person required to provide a document or information under this section fails to do so, a court may, on application by the person who did not receive the document or information, make one or more of the following orders:

1. An order awarding costs in favour of the applicant up to an amount that fully compensates the applicant for all costs incurred in the proceedings.
2. An order requiring the person to provide the document or information to,
   i. the court,
   ii. the applicant, and
   iii. any other party to the domestic contract or other written agreement to whom the person did not provide the document or information when required to do so.

Exception

(5) Subsection (4) does not apply if the person who fails to provide the document or information is a child who is not a party to the domestic contract or other written agreement.

Transition

(6) This section applies in respect of a domestic contract or other written agreement only if the contract or agreement was entered into on or after the day section 7 of Ontario Regulation 25/10 comes into force.

26. Omitted (provides for coming into force of provisions of this Regulation).

Note: The child support guidelines come into force with respect to cases to which the *Family Law Act* applies on the day the *Uniform Federal and Provincial Child Support Guidelines Act, 1997* is proclaimed in force. Proclamation date is December 1, 1997. See: O. Reg. 391/97, s. 26(1).

Note: The child support guidelines come into force with respect to cases to which the *Divorce Act* (Canada) applies on the day the guidelines are specified by order of the Governor in Council as "applicable guidelines" within the meaning of that Act under subsection 2(5) of that Act. See: O. Reg. 391/97, s. 26(2).

SCHEDULE I

Child Support Table For Ontario (Subsection 2(1))

Notes:

1. The child support table for Ontario sets out the amount of monthly child support payments for Ontario on the basis of the annual income of the parent or spouse ordered to pay child support (the "support payor") and the number of children for whom a table amount is payable. Refer to these guidelines to determine whether special measures apply.
2. There is a threshold level of income below which no amount of child support is payable. Child support amounts are specified for incomes up to $150,000 per year. Refer to section 4 of this Regulation to determine the amount of child support payments for support payors with annual incomes over $150,000.
3. Income is set out in the tables in intervals of $1,000. Monthly amounts are determined by adding the basic amount and the amount calculated by multiplying the applicable percentage by the portion of the income that exceeds the lower amount within that interval of income.
4. The amounts in the tables are based on economic studies of average spending on children in families at different income levels in Canada. They are calculated on the basis that child support payments are no longer taxable in the hands of the receiving parent and no longer deductible by the paying parent. They are calculated using a mathematical formula and generated by a computer program.
5. The formula referred to in note 4 sets support amounts to reflect average expenditures on children by a parent or spouse with a particular number of children and level of income. The calculation is based on the support payor's income. The formula uses the basic personal amount for non-refundable tax credits to recognize personal expenses, and takes other federal and provincial income taxes and credits into account. Federal Child Tax benefits and Goods and Services Tax credits for children are excluded from the calculation. At lower income levels, the formula sets the amounts to take into account the combined impact of taxes and child support payments on the support payor's limited disposable income.

Child Support Table for Ontario: One Child

Income ($)		Monthly Award ($)			Income ($)		Monthly Award ($)			Income ($)		Monthly Award ($)		
From	**To**	Basic Amount	Plus (%)	of Income over	**From**	**To**	Basic Amount	Plus (%)	of Income over	**From**	**To**	Basic Amount	Plus (%)	of Income over
0	**10819**	0			**58000**	**58999**	527	0.94	58000	**107000**	**107999**	935	0.74	107000
10820	**10999**	0	1.90	10820	**59000**	**59999**	536	0.98	59000	**108000**	**108999**	942	0.76	108000
11000	**11999**	21	1.90	11000	**60000**	**60999**	546	0.92	60000	**109000**	**109999**	950	0.76	109000
12000	**12999**	40	1.90	12000	**61000**	**61999**	555	0.96	61000	**110000**	**110999**	958	0.78	110000
13000	**13999**	59	1.90	13000	**62000**	**62999**	565	0.90	62000	**111000**	**111999**	966	0.80	111000
14000	**14999**	78	1.88	14000	**63000**	**63999**	574	0.96	63000	**112000**	**112999**	974	0.80	112000
15000	**15999**	97	1.88	15000	**64000**	**64999**	584	1.00	64000	**113000**	**113999**	982	0.82	113000
16000	**16999**	116	1.88	16000	**65000**	**65999**	594	0.94	65000	**114000**	**114999**	990	0.84	114000
17000	**17999**	135	0.66	17000	**66000**	**66999**	603	0.98	66000	**115000**	**115999**	998	0.74	115000
18000	**18999**	142	0.88	18000	**67000**	**67999**	613	0.82	67000	**116000**	**116999**	1005	0.76	116000
19000	**19999**	151	0.92	19000	**68000**	**68999**	621	0.86	68000	**117000**	**117999**	1013	0.78	117000
20000	**20999**	160	0.80	20000	**69000**	**69999**	630	0.90	69000	**118000**	**118999**	1021	0.80	118000
21000	**21999**	168	0.80	21000	**70000**	**70999**	639	0.82	70000	**119000**	**119999**	1029	0.80	119000
22000	**22999**	176	0.82	22000	**71000**	**71999**	647	0.96	71000	**120000**	**120999**	1037	0.82	120000
23000	**23999**	184	0.82	23000	**72000**	**72999**	657	0.74	72000	**121000**	**121999**	1045	0.84	121000
24000	**24999**	192	0.82	24000	**73000**	**73999**	664	0.92	73000	**122000**	**122999**	1053	0.74	122000
25000	**25999**	200	1.02	25000	**74000**	**74999**	673	0.88	74000	**123000**	**123999**	1060	0.76	123000
26000	**26999**	210	0.86	26000	**75000**	**75999**	682	0.88	75000	**124000**	**124999**	1068	0.78	124000
27000	**27999**	219	0.90	27000	**76000**	**76999**	691	0.88	76000	**125000**	**125999**	1076	0.78	125000
28000	**28999**	228	0.92	28000	**77000**	**77999**	700	0.88	77000	**126000**	**126999**	1084	0.80	126000
29000	**29999**	237	0.84	29000	**78000**	**78999**	709	0.78	78000	**127000**	**127999**	1092	0.72	127000
30000	**30999**	245	1.18	30000	**79000**	**79999**	717	0.72	79000	**128000**	**128999**	1099	0.78	128000
31000	**31999**	257	1.18	31000	**80000**	**80999**	724	0.72	80000	**129000**	**129999**	1107	0.72	129000
32000	**32999**	269	1.18	32000	**81000**	**81999**	731	0.72	81000	**130000**	**130999**	1114	0.78	130000
33000	**33999**	281	1.12	33000	**82000**	**82999**	738	0.78	82000	**131000**	**131999**	1122	0.74	131000
34000	**34999**	292	1.08	34000	**83000**	**83999**	746	0.80	83000	**132000**	**132999**	1129	0.70	132000
35000	**35999**	303	1.16	35000	**84000**	**84999**	754	0.82	84000	**133000**	**133999**	1136	0.76	133000

Child Support Table for Ontario: One Child Concluded

Income ($)		Monthly Award ($)			Income ($)		Monthly Award ($)			Income ($)		Monthly Award ($)		
From	**To**	Basic Amount	Plus (%)	of Income over	**From**	**To**	Basic Amount	Plus (%)	of Income over	**From**	**To**	Basic Amount	Plus (%)	of Income over
36000	**36999**	315	1.02	36000	**85000**	**85999**	762	0.82	85000	**134000**	**134999**	1144	0.70	134000
37000	**37999**	325	1.08	37000	**86000**	**86999**	770	0.74	86000	**135000**	**135999**	1151	0.76	135000
38000	**38999**	336	1.16	38000	**87000**	**87999**	777	0.76	87000	**136000**	**136999**	1159	0.72	136000
39000	**39999**	348	1.18	39000	**88000**	**88999**	785	0.78	88000	**137000**	**137999**	1166	0.78	137000
40000	**40999**	360	0.96	40000	**89000**	**89999**	793	0.78	89000	**138000**	**138999**	1174	0.72	138000
41000	**41999**	370	0.90	41000	**90000**	**90999**	801	0.80	90000	**139000**	**139999**	1181	0.78	139000
42000	**42999**	379	0.92	42000	**91000**	**91999**	809	0.82	91000	**140000**	**140999**	1189	0.74	140000
43000	**43999**	388	0.94	43000	**92000**	**92999**	817	0.82	92000	**141000**	**141999**	1196	0.70	141000
44000	**44999**	397	0.94	44000	**93000**	**93999**	825	0.74	93000	**142000**	**142999**	1203	0.76	142000
45000	**45999**	406	0.94	45000	**94000**	**94999**	832	0.76	94000	**143000**	**143999**	1211	0.70	143000
46000	**46999**	415	0.94	46000	**95000**	**95999**	840	0.76	95000	**144000**	**144999**	1218	0.76	144000
47000	**47999**	424	0.94	47000	**96000**	**96999**	848	0.78	96000	**145000**	**145999**	1226	0.72	145000
48000	**48999**	433	0.78	48000	**97000**	**97999**	856	0.80	97000	**146000**	**146999**	1233	0.78	146000
49000	**49999**	441	0.94	49000	**98000**	**98999**	864	0.82	98000	**147000**	**147999**	1241	0.74	147000
50000	**50999**	450	0.98	50000	**99000**	**99999**	872	0.82	99000	**148000**	**148999**	1248	0.78	148000
51000	**51999**	460	0.92	51000	**100000**	**100999**	880	0.74	100000	**149000**	**149999**	1256	0.74	149000
52000	**52999**	469	0.96	52000	**101000**	**101999**	887	0.76	101000	**150000**	**or greater**	1263	0.74	150000
53000	**53999**	479	0.92	53000	**102000**	**102999**	895	0.76	102000					
54000	**54999**	488	0.96	54000	**103000**	**103999**	903	0.78	103000					
55000	**55999**	498	1.00	55000	**104000**	**104999**	911	0.80	104000					
56000	**56999**	508	0.94	56000	**105000**	**105999**	919	0.80	105000					
57000	**57999**	517	0.98	57000	**106000**	**106999**	927	0.82	106000					

Child Support Table for Ontario: Two Children

Income ($)		Monthly Award ($)			Income ($)		Monthly Award ($)			Income ($)		Monthly Award ($)		
From	**To**	Basic Amount	Plus (%)	of Income over	**From**	**To**	Basic Amount	Plus (%)	of Income over	**From**	**To**	Basic Amount	Plus (%)	of Income over
0	**10819**	0			**58000**	**58999**	862	1.52	58000	**107000**	**107999**	1501	1.26	107000
10820	**10999**	0	4.80	10820	**59000**	**59999**	877	1.54	59000	**108000**	**108999**	1514	1.24	108000
11000	**11999**	50	4.40	11000	**60000**	**60999**	892	1.44	60000	**109000**	**109999**	1526	1.22	109000
12000	**12999**	94	3.64	12000	**61000**	**61999**	906	1.46	61000	**110000**	**110999**	1538	1.20	110000
13000	**13999**	130	3.50	13000	**62000**	**62999**	921	1.48	62000	**111000**	**111999**	1550	1.18	111000
14000	**14999**	165	3.04	14000	**63000**	**63999**	936	1.48	63000	**112000**	**112999**	1562	1.26	112000
15000	**15999**	195	3.00	15000	**64000**	**64999**	951	1.50	64000	**113000**	**113999**	1575	1.24	113000
16000	**16999**	225	3.12	16000	**65000**	**65999**	966	1.50	65000	**114000**	**114999**	1587	1.20	114000
17000	**17999**	256	2.06	17000	**66000**	**66999**	981	1.52	66000	**115000**	**115999**	1599	1.18	115000
18000	**18999**	277	1.42	18000	**67000**	**67999**	996	1.44	67000	**116000**	**116999**	1611	1.26	116000
19000	**19999**	291	1.46	19000	**68000**	**68999**	1010	1.34	68000	**117000**	**117999**	1624	1.24	117000
20000	**20999**	306	1.36	20000	**69000**	**69999**	1023	1.36	69000	**118000**	**118999**	1636	1.22	118000
21000	**21999**	320	1.34	21000	**70000**	**70999**	1037	1.36	70000	**119000**	**119999**	1648	1.20	119000
22000	**22999**	333	1.32	22000	**71000**	**71999**	1051	1.48	71000	**120000**	**120999**	1660	1.18	120000
23000	**23999**	346	1.28	23000	**72000**	**72999**	1066	1.14	72000	**121000**	**121999**	1672	1.26	121000
24000	**24999**	359	1.36	24000	**73000**	**73999**	1077	1.40	73000	**122000**	**122999**	1685	1.22	122000
25000	**25999**	373	1.34	25000	**74000**	**74999**	1091	1.36	74000	**123000**	**123999**	1697	1.20	123000
26000	**26999**	386	1.06	26000	**75000**	**75999**	1105	1.36	75000	**124000**	**124999**	1709	1.18	124000
27000	**27999**	397	1.14	27000	**76000**	**76999**	1119	1.36	76000	**125000**	**125999**	1721	1.26	125000
28000	**28999**	408	1.48	28000	**77000**	**77999**	1133	1.36	77000	**126000**	**126999**	1734	1.24	126000
29000	**29999**	423	1.50	29000	**78000**	**78999**	1147	1.26	78000	**127000**	**127999**	1746	1.12	127000
30000	**30999**	438	1.44	30000	**79000**	**79999**	1160	1.22	79000	**128000**	**128999**	1757	1.16	128000
31000	**31999**	452	1.48	31000	**80000**	**80999**	1172	1.24	80000	**129000**	**129999**	1769	1.20	129000
32000	**32999**	467	1.40	32000	**81000**	**81999**	1184	1.24	81000	**130000**	**130999**	1781	1.14	130000
33000	**33999**	481	1.40	33000	**82000**	**82999**	1196	1.24	82000	**131000**	**131999**	1792	1.18	131000
34000	**34999**	495	1.34	34000	**83000**	**83999**	1208	1.22	83000	**132000**	**132999**	1804	1.12	132000
35000	**35999**	508	1.38	35000	**84000**	**84999**	1220	1.18	84000	**133000**	**133999**	1815	1.16	133000

Child Support Table for Ontario: Two Children Concluded

Income ($)		Monthly Award ($)			Income ($)		Monthly Award ($)			Income ($)		Monthly Award ($)		
From	**To**	Basic Amount	Plus (%)	of Income over	**From**	**To**	Basic Amount	Plus (%)	of Income over	**From**	**To**	Basic Amount	Plus (%)	of Income over
36000	**36999**	522	1.22	36000	**85000**	**85999**	1232	1.26	85000	**134000**	**134999**	1827	1.10	134000
37000	**37999**	534	1.20	37000	**86000**	**86999**	1245	1.24	86000	**135000**	**135999**	1838	1.16	135000
38000	**38999**	546	1.68	38000	**87000**	**87999**	1257	1.22	87000	**136000**	**136999**	1850	1.20	136000
39000	**39999**	563	1.64	39000	**88000**	**88999**	1269	1.20	88000	**137000**	**137999**	1862	1.14	137000
40000	**40999**	579	1.76	40000	**89000**	**89999**	1281	1.18	89000	**138000**	**138999**	1873	1.18	138000
41000	**41999**	597	1.68	41000	**90000**	**90999**	1293	1.26	90000	**139000**	**139999**	1885	1.12	139000
42000	**42999**	614	1.62	42000	**91000**	**91999**	1306	1.22	91000	**140000**	**140999**	1896	1.16	140000
43000	**43999**	630	1.68	43000	**92000**	**92999**	1318	1.20	92000	**141000**	**141999**	1908	1.20	141000
44000	**44999**	647	1.72	44000	**93000**	**93999**	1330	1.18	93000	**142000**	**142999**	1920	1.14	142000
45000	**45999**	664	1.64	45000	**94000**	**94999**	1342	1.26	94000	**143000**	**143999**	1931	1.18	143000
46000	**46999**	680	1.66	46000	**95000**	**95999**	1355	1.24	95000	**144000**	**144999**	1943	1.14	144000
47000	**47999**	697	1.78	47000	**96000**	**96999**	1367	1.22	96000	**145000**	**145999**	1954	1.18	145000
48000	**48999**	715	1.34	48000	**97000**	**97999**	1379	1.20	97000	**146000**	**146999**	1966	1.12	146000
49000	**49999**	728	1.50	49000	**98000**	**98999**	1391	1.28	98000	**147000**	**147999**	1977	1.16	147000
50000	**50999**	743	1.52	50000	**99000**	**99999**	1404	1.24	99000	**148000**	**148999**	1989	1.20	148000
51000	**51999**	758	1.54	51000	**100000**	**100999**	1416	1.22	100000	**149000**	**149999**	2001	1.14	149000
52000	**52999**	773	1.44	52000	**101000**	**101999**	1428	1.20	101000	**150000**	**or greater**	2012	1.14	150000
53000	**53999**	787	1.46	53000	**102000**	**102999**	1440	1.18	102000					
54000	**54999**	802	1.48	54000	**103000**	**103999**	1452	1.26	103000					
55000	**55999**	817	1.48	55000	**104000**	**104999**	1465	1.24	104000					
56000	**56999**	832	1.50	56000	**105000**	**105999**	1477	1.22	105000					
57000	**57999**	847	1.50	57000	**106000**	**106999**	1489	1.18	106000					

Child Support Table for Ontario: Three Children

Income ($)		Monthly Award ($)			Income ($)		Monthly Award ($)			Income ($)		Monthly Award ($)		
From	**To**	Basic Amount	Plus (%)	of Income over	**From**	**To**	Basic Amount	Plus (%)	of Income over	**From**	**To**	Basic Amount	Plus (%)	of Income over
0	**10819**	0			**58000**	**58999**	1130	1.92	58000	**107000**	**107999**	1955	1.54	107000
10820	**10999**	0	5.20	10820	**59000**	**59999**	1149	1.90	59000	**108000**	**108999**	1970	1.56	108000
11000	**11999**	54	4.72	11000	**60000**	**60999**	1168	1.88	60000	**109000**	**109999**	1986	1.58	109000
12000	**12999**	101	3.92	12000	**61000**	**61999**	1187	1.88	61000	**110000**	**110999**	2002	1.62	110000
13000	**13999**	140	3.70	13000	**62000**	**62999**	1206	1.86	62000	**111000**	**111999**	2018	1.54	111000
14000	**14999**	177	3.26	14000	**63000**	**63999**	1225	1.96	63000	**112000**	**112999**	2033	1.58	112000
15000	**15999**	210	3.20	15000	**64000**	**64999**	1245	1.94	64000	**113000**	**113999**	2049	1.60	113000
16000	**16999**	242	3.38	16000	**65000**	**65999**	1264	1.92	65000	**114000**	**114999**	2065	1.52	114000
17000	**17999**	276	4.08	17000	**66000**	**66999**	1283	1.92	66000	**115000**	**115999**	2080	1.56	115000
18000	**18999**	317	4.30	18000	**67000**	**67999**	1302	1.80	67000	**116000**	**116999**	2096	1.58	116000
19000	**19999**	360	4.40	19000	**68000**	**68999**	1320	1.80	68000	**117000**	**117999**	2112	1.62	117000
20000	**20999**	404	3.74	20000	**69000**	**69999**	1338	1.78	69000	**118000**	**118999**	2128	1.54	118000
21000	**21999**	441	1.80	21000	**70000**	**70999**	1356	1.78	70000	**119000**	**119999**	2143	1.56	119000
22000	**22999**	459	1.74	22000	**71000**	**71999**	1374	1.86	71000	**120000**	**120999**	2159	1.60	120000
23000	**23999**	476	1.70	23000	**72000**	**72999**	1393	1.40	72000	**121000**	**121999**	2175	1.52	121000
24000	**24999**	493	1.76	24000	**73000**	**73999**	1407	1.86	73000	**122000**	**122999**	2190	1.56	122000
25000	**25999**	511	1.80	25000	**74000**	**74999**	1426	1.80	74000	**123000**	**123999**	2206	1.58	123000
26000	**26999**	529	1.56	26000	**75000**	**75999**	1444	1.80	75000	**124000**	**124999**	2222	1.60	124000
27000	**27999**	545	1.54	27000	**76000**	**76999**	1462	1.80	76000	**125000**	**125999**	2238	1.54	125000
28000	**28999**	560	1.58	28000	**77000**	**77999**	1480	1.80	77000	**126000**	**126999**	2253	1.56	126000
29000	**29999**	576	1.52	29000	**78000**	**78999**	1498	1.60	78000	**127000**	**127999**	2269	1.50	127000
30000	**30999**	591	1.96	30000	**79000**	**79999**	1514	1.56	79000	**128000**	**128999**	2284	1.50	128000
31000	**31999**	611	1.90	31000	**80000**	**80999**	1530	1.60	80000	**129000**	**129999**	2299	1.52	129000
32000	**32999**	630	1.86	32000	**81000**	**81999**	1546	1.62	81000	**130000**	**130999**	2314	1.52	130000
33000	**33999**	649	1.80	33000	**82000**	**82999**	1562	1.52	82000	**131000**	**131999**	2329	1.54	131000
34000	**34999**	667	1.80	34000	**83000**	**83999**	1577	1.56	83000	**132000**	**132999**	2344	1.44	132000
35000	**35999**	685	1.80	35000	**84000**	**84999**	1593	1.58	84000	**133000**	**133999**	2358	1.46	133000

Child Support Table for Ontario: Three Children Concluded

Income ($)		Monthly Award ($)			Income ($)		Monthly Award ($)			Income ($)		Monthly Award ($)		
From	**To**	Basic Amount	Plus (%)	of Income over	**From**	**To**	Basic Amount	Plus (%)	of Income over	**From**	**To**	Basic Amount	Plus (%)	of Income over
36000	**36999**	703	1.60	36000	**85000**	**85999**	1609	1.62	85000	**134000**	**134999**	2373	1.48	134000
37000	**37999**	719	1.46	37000	**86000**	**86999**	1625	1.54	86000	**135000**	**135999**	2388	1.48	135000
38000	**38999**	734	1.54	38000	**87000**	**87999**	1640	1.58	87000	**136000**	**136999**	2403	1.50	136000
39000	**39999**	749	1.54	39000	**88000**	**88999**	1656	1.60	88000	**137000**	**137999**	2418	1.50	137000
40000	**40999**	764	1.66	40000	**89000**	**89999**	1672	1.52	89000	**138000**	**138999**	2433	1.52	138000
41000	**41999**	781	1.56	41000	**90000**	**90999**	1687	1.56	90000	**139000**	**139999**	2448	1.52	139000
42000	**42999**	797	2.04	42000	**91000**	**91999**	1703	1.58	91000	**140000**	**140999**	2463	1.54	140000
43000	**43999**	817	2.02	43000	**92000**	**92999**	1719	1.62	92000	**141000**	**141999**	2478	1.44	141000
44000	**44999**	837	2.08	44000	**93000**	**93999**	1735	1.54	93000	**142000**	**142999**	2492	1.46	142000
45000	**45999**	858	2.02	45000	**94000**	**94999**	1750	1.56	94000	**143000**	**143999**	2507	1.48	143000
46000	**46999**	878	2.08	46000	**95000**	**95999**	1766	1.60	95000	**144000**	**144999**	2522	1.48	144000
47000	**47999**	899	2.14	47000	**96000**	**96999**	1782	1.52	96000	**145000**	**145999**	2537	1.50	145000
48000	**48999**	920	1.78	48000	**97000**	**97999**	1797	1.56	97000	**146000**	**146999**	2552	1.50	146000
49000	**49999**	938	2.14	49000	**98000**	**98999**	1813	1.58	98000	**147000**	**147999**	2567	1.52	147000
50000	**50999**	959	2.18	50000	**99000**	**99999**	1829	1.60	99000	**148000**	**148999**	2582	1.52	148000
51000	**51999**	981	2.20	51000	**100000**	**100999**	1845	1.54	100000	**149000**	**149999**	2597	1.44	149000
52000	**52999**	1003	2.14	52000	**101000**	**101999**	1860	1.56	101000	**150000**	**or greater**	2611	1.44	150000
53000	**53999**	1024	2.18	53000	**102000**	**102999**	1876	1.60	102000					
54000	**54999**	1046	2.20	54000	**103000**	**103999**	1892	1.62	103000					
55000	**55999**	1068	2.14	55000	**104000**	**104999**	1908	1.54	104000					
56000	**56999**	1089	2.18	56000	**105000**	**105999**	1923	1.58	105000					
57000	**57999**	1111	1.92	57000	**106000**	**106999**	1939	1.60	106000					

Child Support Table for Ontario: Four Children

Income ($)		Monthly Award ($)			Income ($)		Monthly Award ($)			Income ($)		Monthly Award ($)		
From	**To**	Basic Amount	Plus (%)	of Income over	**From**	**To**	Basic Amount	Plus (%)	of Income over	**From**	**To**	Basic Amount	Plus (%)	of Income over
0	**10819**	0			**58000**	**58999**	1332	2.46	58000	**107000**	**107999**	2326	1.84	107000
10820	**10999**	0	5.58	10820	**59000**	**59999**	1357	2.46	59000	**108000**	**108999**	2344	1.88	108000
11000	**11999**	58	5.02	11000	**60000**	**60999**	1382	2.48	60000	**109000**	**109999**	2363	1.82	109000
12000	**12999**	108	4.20	12000	**61000**	**61999**	1407	2.48	61000	**110000**	**110999**	2381	1.86	110000
13000	**13999**	150	4.00	13000	**62000**	**62999**	1432	2.50	62000	**111000**	**111999**	2400	1.90	111000
14000	**14999**	190	3.50	14000	**63000**	**63999**	1457	2.50	63000	**112000**	**112999**	2419	1.84	112000
15000	**15999**	225	3.40	15000	**64000**	**64999**	1482	2.52	64000	**113000**	**113999**	2437	1.90	113000
16000	**16999**	259	3.66	16000	**65000**	**65999**	1507	2.32	65000	**114000**	**114999**	2456	1.84	114000
17000	**17999**	296	4.42	17000	**66000**	**66999**	1530	2.30	66000	**115000**	**115999**	2474	1.88	115000
18000	**18999**	340	4.64	18000	**67000**	**67999**	1553	2.14	67000	**116000**	**116999**	2493	1.82	116000
19000	**19999**	386	4.62	19000	**68000**	**68999**	1574	2.18	68000	**117000**	**117999**	2511	1.86	117000
20000	**20999**	432	4.16	20000	**69000**	**69999**	1596	2.14	69000	**118000**	**118999**	2530	1.90	118000
21000	**21999**	474	4.20	21000	**70000**	**70999**	1617	2.18	70000	**119000**	**119999**	2549	1.84	119000
22000	**22999**	516	4.14	22000	**71000**	**71999**	1639	2.22	71000	**120000**	**120999**	2567	1.88	120000
23000	**23999**	557	4.16	23000	**72000**	**72999**	1661	1.74	72000	**121000**	**121999**	2586	1.82	121000
24000	**24999**	599	2.50	24000	**73000**	**73999**	1678	2.22	73000	**122000**	**122999**	2604	1.88	122000
25000	**25999**	624	2.20	25000	**74000**	**74999**	1700	2.12	74000	**123000**	**123999**	2623	1.82	123000
26000	**26999**	646	1.96	26000	**75000**	**75999**	1721	2.08	75000	**124000**	**124999**	2641	1.86	124000
27000	**27999**	666	2.02	27000	**76000**	**76999**	1742	2.16	76000	**125000**	**125999**	2660	1.90	125000
28000	**28999**	686	1.94	28000	**77000**	**77999**	1764	2.14	77000	**126000**	**126999**	2679	1.84	126000
29000	**29999**	705	1.96	29000	**78000**	**78999**	1785	1.92	78000	**127000**	**127999**	2697	1.78	127000
30000	**30999**	725	1.98	30000	**79000**	**79999**	1804	1.86	79000	**128000**	**128999**	2715	1.72	128000
31000	**31999**	745	2.00	31000	**80000**	**80999**	1823	1.88	80000	**129000**	**129999**	2732	1.76	129000
32000	**32999**	765	2.14	32000	**81000**	**81999**	1842	1.88	81000	**130000**	**130999**	2750	1.80	130000
33000	**33999**	786	2.16	33000	**82000**	**82999**	1861	1.88	82000	**131000**	**131999**	2768	1.74	131000
34000	**34999**	808	2.20	34000	**83000**	**83999**	1880	1.82	83000	**132000**	**132999**	2785	1.78	132000
35000	**35999**	830	2.14	35000	**84000**	**84999**	1898	1.86	84000	**133000**	**133999**	2803	1.72	133000

Child Support Table for Ontario: Four Children Concluded

Income ($)		Monthly Award ($)			Income ($)		Monthly Award ($)			Income ($)		Monthly Award ($)		
From	**To**	Basic Amount	Plus (%)	of Income over	**From**	**To**	Basic Amount	Plus (%)	of Income over	**From**	**To**	Basic Amount	Plus (%)	of Income over
36000	**36999**	851	1.96	36000	**85000**	**85999**	1917	1.80	85000	**134000**	**134999**	2820	1.76	134000
37000	**37999**	871	1.80	37000	**86000**	**86999**	1935	1.86	86000	**135000**	**135999**	2838	1.80	135000
38000	**38999**	889	1.84	38000	**87000**	**87999**	1954	1.90	87000	**136000**	**136999**	2856	1.74	136000
39000	**39999**	907	1.92	39000	**88000**	**88999**	1973	1.84	88000	**137000**	**137999**	2873	1.78	137000
40000	**40999**	926	2.08	40000	**89000**	**89999**	1991	1.88	89000	**138000**	**138999**	2891	1.72	138000
41000	**41999**	947	1.90	41000	**90000**	**90999**	2010	1.82	90000	**139000**	**139999**	2908	1.76	139000
42000	**42999**	966	1.84	42000	**91000**	**91999**	2028	1.86	91000	**140000**	**140999**	2926	1.72	140000
43000	**43999**	984	1.88	43000	**92000**	**92999**	2047	1.90	92000	**141000**	**141999**	2943	1.76	141000
44000	**44999**	1003	1.88	44000	**93000**	**93999**	2066	1.84	93000	**142000**	**142999**	2961	1.80	142000
45000	**45999**	1022	1.88	45000	**94000**	**94999**	2084	1.88	94000	**143000**	**143999**	2979	1.74	143000
46000	**46999**	1041	2.26	46000	**95000**	**95999**	2103	1.84	95000	**144000**	**144999**	2996	1.78	144000
47000	**47999**	1064	2.44	47000	**96000**	**96999**	2121	1.88	96000	**145000**	**145999**	3014	1.72	145000
48000	**48999**	1088	1.98	48000	**97000**	**97999**	2140	1.82	97000	**146000**	**146999**	3031	1.76	146000
49000	**49999**	1108	2.48	49000	**98000**	**98999**	2158	1.86	98000	**147000**	**147999**	3049	1.80	147000
50000	**50999**	1133	2.48	50000	**99000**	**99999**	2177	1.90	99000	**148000**	**148999**	3067	1.74	148000
51000	**51999**	1158	2.50	51000	**100000**	**100999**	2196	1.84	100000	**149000**	**149999**	3084	1.78	149000
52000	**52999**	1183	2.50	52000	**101000**	**101999**	2214	1.88	101000	**150000**	**or greater**	3102	1.78	150000
53000	**53999**	1208	2.52	53000	**102000**	**102999**	2233	1.82	102000					
54000	**54999**	1233	2.52	54000	**103000**	**103999**	2251	1.86	103000					
55000	**55999**	1258	2.54	55000	**104000**	**104999**	2270	1.82	104000					
56000	**56999**	1283	2.54	56000	**105000**	**105999**	2288	1.86	105000					
57000	**57999**	1308	2.44	57000	**106000**	**106999**	2307	1.90	106000					

Child Support Table for Ontario: Five Children

Income ($)		Monthly Award ($)			Income ($)		Monthly Award ($)			Income ($)		Monthly Award ($)		
From	**To**	Basic Amount	Plus (%)	of Income over	**From**	**To**	Basic Amount	Plus (%)	of Income over	**From**	**To**	Basic Amount	Plus (%)	of Income over
0	**10819**	0			**58000**	**58999**	1499	2.80	58000	**107000**	**107999**	2635	2.12	107000
10820	**10999**	0	5.58	10820	**59000**	**59999**	1527	2.74	59000	**108000**	**108999**	2656	2.14	108000
11000	**11999**	58	5.02	11000	**60000**	**60999**	1554	2.78	60000	**109000**	**109999**	2677	2.14	109000
12000	**12999**	108	4.20	12000	**61000**	**61999**	1582	2.72	61000	**110000**	**110999**	2698	2.14	110000
13000	**13999**	150	4.00	13000	**62000**	**62999**	1609	2.76	62000	**111000**	**111999**	2719	2.14	111000
14000	**14999**	190	3.50	14000	**63000**	**63999**	1637	2.80	63000	**112000**	**112999**	2740	2.04	112000
15000	**15999**	225	3.40	15000	**64000**	**64999**	1665	2.74	64000	**113000**	**113999**	2760	2.06	113000
16000	**16999**	259	3.66	16000	**65000**	**65999**	1692	2.78	65000	**114000**	**114999**	2781	2.06	114000
17000	**17999**	296	4.42	17000	**66000**	**66999**	1720	2.72	66000	**115000**	**115999**	2802	2.06	115000
18000	**18999**	340	4.64	18000	**67000**	**67999**	1747	2.66	67000	**116000**	**116999**	2823	2.06	116000
19000	**19999**	386	4.62	19000	**68000**	**68999**	1774	2.60	68000	**117000**	**117999**	2844	2.06	117000
20000	**20999**	432	4.16	20000	**69000**	**69999**	1800	2.66	69000	**118000**	**118999**	2865	2.08	118000
21000	**21999**	474	4.20	21000	**70000**	**70999**	1827	2.60	70000	**119000**	**119999**	2886	2.08	119000
22000	**22999**	516	4.14	22000	**71000**	**71999**	1853	2.76	71000	**120000**	**120999**	2907	2.08	120000
23000	**23999**	557	4.16	23000	**72000**	**72999**	1881	2.22	72000	**121000**	**121999**	2928	2.08	121000
24000	**24999**	599	4.20	24000	**73000**	**73999**	1903	2.54	73000	**122000**	**122999**	2949	2.08	122000
25000	**25999**	641	4.54	25000	**74000**	**74999**	1928	2.42	74000	**123000**	**123999**	2970	2.10	123000
26000	**26999**	686	4.60	26000	**75000**	**75999**	1952	2.40	75000	**124000**	**124999**	2991	2.10	124000
27000	**27999**	732	4.70	27000	**76000**	**76999**	1976	2.40	76000	**125000**	**125999**	3012	2.10	125000
28000	**28999**	779	3.44	28000	**77000**	**77999**	2000	2.42	77000	**126000**	**126999**	3033	2.10	126000
29000	**29999**	813	2.36	29000	**78000**	**78999**	2024	2.22	78000	**127000**	**127999**	3054	2.00	127000
30000	**30999**	837	2.32	30000	**79000**	**79999**	2046	2.20	79000	**128000**	**128999**	3074	2.02	128000
31000	**31999**	860	2.30	31000	**80000**	**80999**	2068	2.14	80000	**129000**	**129999**	3094	1.94	129000
32000	**32999**	883	2.26	32000	**81000**	**81999**	2089	2.20	81000	**130000**	**130999**	3113	1.96	130000
33000	**33999**	906	2.14	33000	**82000**	**82999**	2111	2.12	82000	**131000**	**131999**	3133	1.96	131000
34000	**34999**	927	2.30	34000	**83000**	**83999**	2132	2.12	83000	**132000**	**132999**	3153	1.98	132000
35000	**35999**	950	2.48	35000	**84000**	**84999**	2153	2.14	84000	**133000**	**133999**	3173	2.00	133000
36000	**36999**	975	2.20	36000	**85000**	**85999**	2174	2.14	85000	**134000**	**134999**	3193	2.02	134000

Child Support Table for Ontario: Five Children Concluded

Income ($)		Monthly Award ($)			Income ($)		Monthly Award ($)			Income ($)		Monthly Award ($)		
From	**To**	Basic Amount	Plus (%)	of Income over	**From**	**To**	Basic Amount	Plus (%)	of Income over	**From**	**To**	Basic Amount	Plus (%)	of Income over
37000	**37999**	997	2.06	37000	**86000**	**86999**	2195	2.14	86000	**135000**	**135999**	3213	2.02	135000
38000	**38999**	1018	2.14	38000	**87000**	**87999**	2216	2.14	87000	**136000**	**136999**	3233	1.94	136000
39000	**39999**	1039	2.22	39000	**88000**	**88999**	2237	2.04	88000	**137000**	**137999**	3252	1.96	137000
40000	**40999**	1061	2.40	40000	**89000**	**89999**	2257	2.06	89000	**138000**	**138999**	3272	1.98	138000
41000	**41999**	1085	2.10	41000	**90000**	**90999**	2278	2.06	90000	**139000**	**139999**	3292	1.98	139000
42000	**42999**	1106	2.16	42000	**91000**	**91999**	2299	2.06	91000	**140000**	**140999**	3312	2.00	140000
43000	**43999**	1128	2.20	43000	**92000**	**92999**	2320	2.06	92000	**141000**	**141999**	3332	2.02	141000
44000	**44999**	1150	2.22	44000	**93000**	**93999**	2341	2.06	93000	**142000**	**142999**	3352	2.04	142000
45000	**45999**	1172	2.22	45000	**94000**	**94999**	2362	2.08	94000	**143000**	**143999**	3372	1.94	143000
46000	**46999**	1194	2.22	46000	**95000**	**95999**	2383	2.08	95000	**144000**	**144999**	3391	1.96	144000
47000	**47999**	1216	2.32	47000	**96000**	**96999**	2404	2.08	96000	**145000**	**145999**	3411	1.98	145000
48000	**48999**	1239	1.82	48000	**97000**	**97999**	2425	2.08	97000	**146000**	**146999**	3431	2.00	146000
49000	**49999**	1257	2.34	49000	**98000**	**98999**	2446	2.10	98000	**147000**	**147999**	3451	2.00	147000
50000	**50999**	1280	2.60	50000	**99000**	**99999**	2467	2.10	99000	**148000**	**148999**	3471	2.02	148000
51000	**51999**	1306	2.74	51000	**100000**	**100999**	2488	2.10	100000	**149000**	**149999**	3491	1.94	149000
52000	**52999**	1333	2.78	52000	**101000**	**101999**	2509	2.10	101000	**150000**	**or greater**	3510	1.94	150000
53000	**53999**	1361	2.72	53000	**102000**	**102999**	2530	2.10	102000					
54000	**54999**	1388	2.76	54000	**103000**	**103999**	2551	2.12	103000					
55000	**55999**	1416	2.80	55000	**104000**	**104999**	2572	2.12	104000					
56000	**56999**	1444	2.74	56000	**105000**	**105999**	2593	2.12	105000					
57000	**57999**	1471	2.78	57000	**106000**	**106999**	2614	2.12	106000					

Child Support Table for Ontario: Six or More Children

Income ($)		Monthly Award ($)			Income ($)		Monthly Award ($)			Income ($)		Monthly Award ($)		
From	**To**	Basic Amount	Plus (%)	of Income over	**From**	**To**	Basic Amount	Plus (%)	of Income over	**From**	**To**	Basic Amount	Plus (%)	of Income over
0	**10819**	0			**58000**	**58999**	1640	3.02	58000	**107000**	**107999**	2896	2.28	107000
10820	**10999**	0	5.58	10820	**59000**	**59999**	1670	3.02	59000	**108000**	**108999**	2919	2.28	108000
11000	**11999**	58	5.02	11000	**60000**	**60999**	1700	3.04	60000	**109000**	**109999**	2942	2.28	109000
12000	**12999**	108	4.20	12000	**61000**	**61999**	1730	2.94	61000	**110000**	**110999**	2965	2.28	110000
13000	**13999**	150	4.00	13000	**62000**	**62999**	1759	2.96	62000	**111000**	**111999**	2988	2.28	111000
14000	**14999**	190	3.50	14000	**63000**	**63999**	1789	2.96	63000	**112000**	**112999**	3011	2.28	112000
15000	**15999**	225	3.40	15000	**64000**	**64999**	1819	2.98	64000	**113000**	**113999**	3034	2.28	113000
16000	**16999**	259	3.66	16000	**65000**	**65999**	1849	2.98	65000	**114000**	**114999**	3057	2.28	114000
17000	**17999**	296	4.42	17000	**66000**	**66999**	1879	3.00	66000	**115000**	**115999**	3080	2.30	115000
18000	**18999**	340	4.64	18000	**67000**	**67999**	1909	2.92	67000	**116000**	**116999**	3103	2.30	116000
19000	**19999**	386	4.62	19000	**68000**	**68999**	1938	2.84	68000	**117000**	**117999**	3126	2.30	117000
20000	**20999**	432	4.16	20000	**69000**	**69999**	1966	2.86	69000	**118000**	**118999**	3149	2.30	118000
21000	**21999**	474	4.20	21000	**70000**	**70999**	1995	2.88	70000	**119000**	**119999**	3172	2.30	119000
22000	**22999**	516	4.14	22000	**71000**	**71999**	2024	2.90	71000	**120000**	**120999**	3195	2.30	120000
23000	**23999**	557	4.16	23000	**72000**	**72999**	2053	2.36	72000	**121000**	**121999**	3218	2.30	121000
24000	**24999**	599	4.20	24000	**73000**	**73999**	2077	2.90	73000	**122000**	**122999**	3241	2.30	122000
25000	**25999**	641	4.54	25000	**74000**	**74999**	2106	2.96	74000	**123000**	**123999**	3264	2.32	123000
26000	**26999**	686	4.60	26000	**75000**	**75999**	2136	2.94	75000	**124000**	**124999**	3287	2.32	124000
27000	**27999**	732	4.70	27000	**76000**	**76999**	2165	2.92	76000	**125000**	**125999**	3310	2.32	125000
28000	**28999**	779	4.64	28000	**77000**	**77999**	2194	2.92	77000	**126000**	**126999**	3333	2.32	126000
29000	**29999**	825	4.68	29000	**78000**	**78999**	2223	2.70	78000	**127000**	**127999**	3356	2.22	127000
30000	**30999**	872	4.62	30000	**79000**	**79999**	2250	2.38	79000	**128000**	**128999**	3378	2.14	128000
31000	**31999**	918	4.66	31000	**80000**	**80999**	2274	2.38	80000	**129000**	**129999**	3399	2.16	129000
32000	**32999**	965	4.38	32000	**81000**	**81999**	2298	2.40	81000	**130000**	**130999**	3421	2.20	130000
33000	**33999**	1009	2.42	33000	**82000**	**82999**	2322	2.30	82000	**131000**	**131999**	3443	2.22	131000
34000	**34999**	1033	2.40	34000	**83000**	**83999**	2345	2.32	83000	**132000**	**132999**	3465	2.14	132000
35000	**35999**	1057	2.46	35000	**84000**	**84999**	2368	2.32	84000	**133000**	**133999**	3486	2.16	133000

Child Support Table for Ontario: Six or More Children Concluded

Income ($)		Monthly Award ($)			Income ($)		Monthly Award ($)			Income ($)		Monthly Award ($)		
From	**To**	Basic Amount	Plus (%)	of Income over	**From**	**To**	Basic Amount	Plus (%)	of Income over	**From**	**To**	Basic Amount	Plus (%)	of Income over
36000	**36999**	1082	2.24	36000	**85000**	**85999**	2391	2.32	85000	**134000**	**134999**	3508	2.20	134000
37000	**37999**	1104	2.26	37000	**86000**	**86999**	2414	2.32	86000	**135000**	**135999**	3530	2.22	135000
38000	**38999**	1127	2.32	38000	**87000**	**87999**	2437	2.32	87000	**136000**	**136999**	3552	2.14	136000
39000	**39999**	1150	2.46	39000	**88000**	**88999**	2460	2.32	88000	**137000**	**137999**	3573	2.16	137000
40000	**40999**	1175	2.68	40000	**89000**	**89999**	2483	2.32	89000	**138000**	**138999**	3595	2.18	138000
41000	**41999**	1202	2.44	41000	**90000**	**90999**	2506	2.32	90000	**139000**	**139999**	3617	2.22	139000
42000	**42999**	1226	2.34	42000	**91000**	**91999**	2529	2.34	91000	**140000**	**140999**	3639	2.14	140000
43000	**43999**	1249	2.46	43000	**92000**	**92999**	2552	2.34	92000	**141000**	**141999**	3660	2.16	141000
44000	**44999**	1274	2.42	44000	**93000**	**93999**	2575	2.34	93000	**142000**	**142999**	3682	2.18	142000
45000	**45999**	1298	2.48	45000	**94000**	**94999**	2598	2.34	94000	**143000**	**143999**	3704	2.20	143000
46000	**46999**	1323	2.42	46000	**95000**	**95999**	2621	2.34	95000	**144000**	**144999**	3726	2.14	144000
47000	**47999**	1347	2.58	47000	**96000**	**96999**	2644	2.34	96000	**145000**	**145999**	3747	2.16	145000
48000	**48999**	1373	2.02	48000	**97000**	**97999**	2667	2.34	97000	**146000**	**146999**	3769	2.18	146000
49000	**49999**	1393	2.62	49000	**98000**	**98999**	2690	2.24	98000	**147000**	**147999**	3791	2.20	147000
50000	**50999**	1419	2.62	50000	**99000**	**99999**	2712	2.26	99000	**148000**	**148999**	3813	2.14	148000
51000	**51999**	1445	2.62	51000	**100000**	**100999**	2735	2.26	100000	**149000**	**149999**	3834	2.16	149000
52000	**52999**	1471	2.62	52000	**101000**	**101999**	2758	2.26	101000	**150000**	**or greater**	3856	2.16	150000
53000	**53999**	1497	2.62	53000	**102000**	**102999**	2781	2.26	102000					
54000	**54999**	1523	2.72	54000	**103000**	**103999**	2804	2.26	103000					
55000	**55999**	1550	3.00	55000	**104000**	**104999**	2827	2.26	104000					
56000	**56999**	1580	3.00	56000	**105000**	**105999**	2850	2.26	105000					
57000	**57999**	1610	3.02	57000	**106000**	**106999**	2873	2.26	106000					

SCHEDULE II
Comparison of Household Standards of Living Test (Subsection 10(4))

Definitions

1. The definitions in this section apply in this Schedule.

"child" means,

(a) in cases where the *Divorce Act* (Canada) applies, a child of the marriage or a child who,

(i) is under the age of majority, or

(ii) is the age of majority or over but is unable, by reason of illness, disability or other cause to obtain the necessaries of life, or

(b) in cases where the Act applies, a child who is a dependant under the Act;

"household" means a parent or spouse and any of the following persons residing with him or her,

(a) any person who has a legal duty to support the parent or spouse or whom the parent or spouse has a legal duty to support,

(b) any person who shares living expenses with the parent or spouse or from whom the parent or spouse otherwise receives an economic benefit as a result of living with that person, if the court considers it reasonable for that person to be considered part of the household, and

(c) any child whom the parent or spouse or the person described in clause (a) or (b) has a legal duty to support;

"taxable income" means the annual taxable income determined using the calculations required to determine "Taxable Income" in the T1 General form issued by the Canada Revenue Agency.

Test

2. The comparison of household standards of living test is as follows:

STEP 1

Establish the annual income of each person in each household by applying the formula

A – B – C

where

A is the person's income determined under sections 15 to 20 of this Regulation,

B is the federal and provincial taxes payable on the person's taxable income, and

C is the person's source deductions for premiums paid under the *Employment Insurance Act* and contributions made to the *Canada Pension Plan* and the *Quebec Pension Plan.*

Where the information on which to base the income determination is not provided, the court may impute income in the amount it considers appropriate.

STEP 2

Adjust the annual income of each person in each household by

(a) deducting the following amounts, calculated on an annual basis:

(i) any amount relied on by the court as a factor that resulted in a determination of undue hardship, except any amount attributable to the support of a member of the household that is not incurred due to a disability or serious illness of that member,

(ii) the amount that would otherwise be payable by the person in respect of a child to whom the order relates, if the pleading of undue hardship was not made,

(A) under the applicable table, or

(B) as considered by the court to be appropriate, where the court considers the table amount to be inappropriate,

(iii) any amount of support that is paid by the person under a judgment, order or written separation agreement, except,

(A) an amount already deducted under subclause (i), and

(B) an amount paid by the person in respect of a child to whom the order referred to in subclause (ii) relates; and

(b) adding the following amounts, calculated on an annual basis:

(i) any amount that would otherwise be receivable by the person in respect of a child to whom the order relates, if the pleading of undue hardship was not made,

(A) under the applicable table, or

(B) as considered by the court to be appropriate, where the court considers the table amount to be inappropriate, and

(ii) any amount of child support that the person has received for any child under a judgment, order or written separation agreement.

STEP 3

Add the amounts of adjusted annual income for all the persons in each household to determine the total household income for each household.

STEP 4

Determine the applicable low-income measures amount for each household based on the following:

Low-income Measures

Household Size	Low-income Measures Amount
One person	
1 adult	$10,382
Two persons	
2 adults	$14,535
1 adult and 1 child	14,535
Three persons	
3 adults	$18,688
2 adults and 1 child	17,649
1 adult and 2 children	17,649
Four persons	
4 adults	$22,840
3 adults and 1 child	21,802
2 adults and 2 children	20,764
1 adult and 3 children	20,764
Five persons	
5 adults	$26,993
4 adults and 1 child	25,955
3 adults and 2 children	24,917
2 adults and 3 children	23,879
1 adult and 4 children	23,879
Six persons	
6 adults	$31,145
5 adults and 1 child	30,108
4 adults and 2 children	29,070
3 adults and 3 children	28,031
2 adults and 4 children	26,993
1 adult and 5 children	26,993
Seven persons	
7 adults	$34,261
6 adults and 1 child	33,222
5 adults and 2 children	32,184
4 adults and 3 children	31,146
3 adults and 4 children	30,108
2 adults and 5 children	29,070
1 adult and 6 children	29,070
Eight persons	
8 adults	$38,413
7 adults and 1 child	37,375
6 adults and 2 children	36,337
5 adults and 3 children	35,299
4 adults and 4 children	34,261
3 adults and 5 children	33,222
2 adults and 6 children	32,184
1 adult and 7 children	32,184

STEP 5
Divide the household income amount (Step 3) by the low-income measures amount (Step 4) to get a household income ratio for each household.

STEP 6
Compare the household income ratios. The household that has the higher ratio has the higher standard of living.

SCHEDULE III

Adjustments to Income (Section 16)

Employment expenses

1. Where the parent or spouse is an employee, the parent's or spouse's applicable employment expenses described in the following provisions of the *Income Tax Act* (Canada) are deducted:

(a) Revoked.

(b) paragraph 8(1)(d) concerning expenses of teacher's exchange fund contribution;

(c) paragraph 8(1)(e) concerning expenses of railway employees;

(d) paragraph 8(1)(f) concerning sales expenses;

(e) paragraph 8(1)(g) concerning transport employee's expenses;

(f) paragraph 8(1)(h) concerning travel expenses;

(f.1) paragraph 8(1)(h.1) concerning motor vehicle travel expenses;

(g) paragraph 8(1)(i) concerning dues and other expenses of performing duties;

(h) paragraph 8(l)(j) concerning motor vehicle and aircraft costs;

(i) paragraph 8(1)(l.1) concerning *Canada Pension Plan* contributions and *Employment Insurance Act* (Canada) premiums paid in respect of another employee who acts as an assistant or substitute for the parent or spouse;

(j) paragraph 8(1)(n) concerning salary reimbursement;

(k) paragraph 8(1)(o) concerning forfeited amounts;

(l) paragraph 8(1)(p) concerning musical instrument costs; and

(m) paragraph 8(1)(q) concerning artists' employment expenses.

Child support

2. Deduct any child support received that is included to determine total income in the T1 General form issued by the Canada Revenue Agency.

Support other than child support and universal child care benefit

3. To calculate income for the purpose of determining an amount under an applicable table, deduct,

(a) the support, not including child support, received from the other parent or spouse; and

(b) any universal child care benefit that is included to determine the parent or spouse's total income in the T1 General form issued by the Canada Revenue Agency.

Special or extraordinary expenses

3.1 To calculate income for the purpose of determining an amount under section 7 of this Regulation, deduct the support, not including child support, paid to the other parent or spouse and, as applicable, make the following adjustment in respect of universal child care benefits:

(a) deduct benefits that are included to determine the parent or spouse's total income in the T1 General form issued by the Canada Revenue Agency and that are for a child for whom special or extraordinary expenses are not being requested; or

(b) include benefits that are not included to determine the parent or spouse's total income in the T1 General form issued by the Canada Revenue Agency and that are received by the parent or spouse for a child for whom special or extraordinary expenses are being requested.

Social assistance

4. Deduct any amount of social assistance income that is not attributable to the parent or spouse.

Dividends from taxable Canadian corporations

5. Replace the taxable amount of dividends from taxable Canadian corporations received by the parent or spouse by the actual amount of those dividends received by the parent or spouse.

Capital gains and capital losses

6. Replace the taxable capital gains realized in a year by the parent or spouse by the actual amount of capital gains realized by the parent or spouse in excess of the parent's or spouse's actual capital losses in that year.

Business investment losses

7. Deduct the actual amount of business investment losses suffered by the parent or spouse during the year.

Carrying charges

8. Deduct the parent's or spouse's carrying charges and interest expenses that are paid by the parent or spouse and that would be deductible under the *Income Tax Act* (Canada).

Net self-employment income

9. Where the parent's or spouse's net self-employment income is determined by deducting an amount for salaries, benefits, wages or management fees, or other payments, paid to or on behalf of persons with whom the parent or spouse does not deal at arm's length, include that amount, unless the parent or spouse establishes that the payments were necessary to earn the self-employment income and were reasonable in the circumstances.

Additional amount

10. Where the parent or spouse reports income from self-employment that, in accordance with sections 34.1 and 34.2 of the *Income Tax Act* (Canada), includes an additional amount earned in a prior period, deduct the amount earned in the prior period, net of reserves.

Capital cost allowance for property

11. Include the parent's or spouse's deduction for an allowable capital cost allowance with respect to real property.

Partnership or sole proprietorship income

12. Where the parent or spouse earns income through a partnership or sole proprietorship, deduct any amount included in income that is properly required by the partnership or sole proprietorship for purposes of capitalization.

Employee stock options with a Canadian-controlled private corporation

13. (1) Where the parent or spouse has received, as an employee benefit, options to purchase shares of a Canadian-controlled private corporation or a publicly traded corporation that is subject to the same tax treatment with reference to stock options as a Canadian-controlled private corporation, and has exercised those options during the year, add the difference between the value of the shares at the time the options are exercised and the amount paid by the parent or spouse for the shares and any amount paid by the parent or spouse to acquire the options to purchase the shares, to the income for the year in which the options are exercised.

Disposal of shares

(2) If the parent or spouse has disposed of the shares during a year, deduct from the income for that year the difference determined under subsection (1).

Formal Requirements of the Continuing Record Under the Family Law Rules

Published by: The Family Rules Committee
Version Date: October 21, 2013
Effective Date: January 1, 2014
Available at: http://www.ontariocourtforms.on.ca

I. Introduction

The "Formal Requirements of the Continuing Record under the *Family Law Rules*" is published by the Family Rules Committee and available at the following website: http://www.ontariocourtforms.on.ca. These requirements must be followed in all cases, governed by the *Family Law Rules*, except child protection cases The Family Rules Committee has the authority to make court rules for the practice and procedure in family cases, subject to the approval of the Attorney General.

The formal requirements of the continuing record for child protection cases are set out in the "Formal Requirements of the Child Protection Continuing Record under the *Family Law Rules*," published by the Family Rules Committee and available at http://www.ontariocourtforms.on.ca.

The substantive requirements of the continuing record are set out in Rule 9. There are provisions in Rules 13 and 17 that set out the types of documents that may be excluded from the record. The formal requirements for the preparation and maintenance of the continuing record are set out in this document, and in the following appendices:

Appendix A – Summary of Contents
Appendix B – Sample Cover
Appendix C – Sample Table of Contents

II. Formal Requirements

1. Contents of the record

Unless otherwise indicated, a continuing record includes: an endorsements volume and documents volume.

The endorsements volume will contain a cumulative table of contents, an endorsements section, which would also contain reasons for judgment and minutes of settlement, and an orders section.

The documents volume will contain documents filed in the case, including applications, answers, replies, affidavits of service, financial statements, motions, affidavits and trial management conference briefs.

The applicant will file the endorsement volume at the same time as filing volume 1 of the documents volume of the continuing record. However, it is not necessary to start a separate endorsements volume in the following types of cases:

- Joint applications for divorce;
- Uncontested divorces in which the only claim is for divorce, when the respondent does not file an answer;
- When the applicant files a change information form (Form 15) and the respondent does not file an affidavit;
- Support enforcement proceedings;
- A consent motion for a final order.

The continuing records for these cases must include a separate section for endorsements and a minimum of three blank sheet on which the judge dealing with the case will note the disposition and the date.

The same endorsements volume must be used for all applications and motions to change that are filed in the same court file. Where a motion to change a final order is made a separate endorsements volume should not be created, unless there is no endorsements volume already in the court file.

A support enforcement continuing record consists of one volume, split into two sections, one called "Documents" which contains the table of contents and documents filed in the case. The second called "Endorsements" and contains endorsements, orders, reasons for judgment and minutes of settlement made in the enforcement proceeding, in the order in which they were made.

A summary of the contents of the continuing record is set out in a chart at Appendix A.

2. Preparation of the Record

(a) Volumes

Each new application or motion to change a final order starts a new volume to the continuing record.

Where a new volume is started when a motion to change a final order is made, the new volume shall be numbered sequentially after the last volume filed. Only documents related to the motion to change shall be filed in the motion to change volume.

If the clerk determines that a volume is full, the party filing the next document must create a new volume, which will be numbered sequentially.

(b) Record Cover

The endorsements volume will have a yellow cover, which will include the court file number and names of the parties to the case.

The documents volume will have a red cover. A sample record cover is attached at Appendix B. All elements of the sample cover must appear on a party's record cover. The title of the record (e.g. "Continuing Record") must appear in bold, font size 20, or an equivalent size, below the names of the parties to the case. The cover must identify the volume number of the record.

The support enforcement continuing record will have a green cover.

If separate continuing records are ordered, the respondent's document record will have a blue cover.

For the volume(s) of the record containing documents relating to a motion to change a final order, the cover must identify the order that is the subject of the motion. Below the title of the record state: "Motion to Change Final Order of Mr./Madam Justice………………., dated ……………, with respect to ……………".

(c) Filing Documents

Documents must be filed in chronological order, with the most recently filed document at the back. All documents filed in the record must be punched in standard three-hole format.

Other than in a support enforcement continuing record, a numbered tab must identify each document filed. Tabs must be in sequential order. A new volume must start with a new tab sequence starting with tab 1.

Pages between numbered tabs must be numbered consecutively. Page numbers are not required to appear in the table of contents, unless there are no tabs as in the support enforcement continuing record.

(d) Contents of Continuing Record

(i) Table of Contents

A sample table of contents is attached at Appendix C. There will be one cumulative table of contents located in the endorsements volume or in the support enforcement continuing record. It will be used to list all documents filed, including documents filed in the motion to change a final order volume. The table of contents must list documents in the order in which they are filed, indicate the volume in which the document is located, the tab number or page number that locates the document, the kind of document, which party filed it, and the date it was filed. For an affidavit or transcript of evidence, the name of the person who gave the affidavit or the evidence must also be shown.

Affidavits of service must be listed in the table of contents including a notation as to the document(s) served and the party who was served.

For documents filed in the volume containing a motion to change a final order, the table of contents must clearly identify that the documents relate to the motion to change.

The table of contents must be updated every time a document is filed.

(ii) Endorsements

The endorsements section of the endorsements volume, or of the support enforcement continuing record, must be identified by a tab or divider. The endorsements section must contain a minimum of three (3) blank sheets, on which the judge dealing with any step in the case will note the disposition of that step and the date. Any written reasons for judgment and minutes of settlement that form the basis of an order must be put in the endorsements section.

(iii) Orders

The orders section of the endorsements volume must be identified by a tab or divider, except for the support enforcement continuing record. The court's file copy of each order made in the case must be put into the orders section.

(iv) Documents

Documents filed in the case, including applications, answers, replies, financial statements, motions, affidavits and trial management conference briefs must be filed in the documents volume.

If the court has ordered separate records for the applicant and respondent, a report ordered by the court must be filed in the applicant's record. A report requested by a party must be filed in the record of the party who requested it.

A financial statement must be filed under its own numbered tab or page number in the support enforcement continuing record. Copies of income tax returns are not required to be attached to the financial statement in the continuing record, unless the court orders otherwise.

A motion for an order to refrain under s. 35(1) of the *Family Responsibility and Support Arrears Enforcement Act, 1996* must be filed in the volume containing the motion to change a final order.

(v) Affidavits of Service

Affidavits of service must be filed within the tab of the document to which the affidavit of service relates, behind the document. If the affidavit of service relates to more than one document, it must be filed within the tab of the first document to which it relates (usually the main document in the package of documents, or the document claiming the relief).

(e) Separate or combined records

Where the court orders that the continuing record be separated, or that separate court records be combined,

- court staff must supervise the separation or the combination of separate records;
- if the record is separated, the party requesting the separate records shall prepare an updated cumulative table of contents reflecting the contents of both records unless otherwise ordered by the court; and
- if separated records are combined, the party directed to combine the record, or the party that requested the combination, shall prepare an updated cumulative table of contents that reflects the contents of the combined record.

3. Additional requirements for support enforcement continuing record

The support enforcement continuing record will have its own cumulative table of contents, listing each document filed in the case. The support enforcement continuing record will be split into two sections: a documents section and an endorsements section.

The documents section must contain each document filed in the case, numbered consecutively and arranged in order, with the most recently filed document at the back. All affidavits of service must be filed in this section.

Endorsements, orders, reasons for judgment and minutes of settlement made in the enforcement proceeding are all filed in the support enforcement record, in numerical order under the second section.

APPENDIX A – SUMMARY OF CONTENTS

CONTINUING RECORD		
SINGLE RECORD	**SEPARATE RECORDS IF ORDERED**	
	Applicant's Record	**Respondent's Record**
Endorsements Volume	**Endorsements Volume**	**Endorsements Volume**
Yellow cover	Yellow cover	N/A
- Table of Contents - Endorsements, incl. Reasons for Judgment and Minutes of Settlement - Orders	- Table of Contents - Endorsements, incl. Reasons for Judgment and Minutes of Settlement - Orders	
Documents	**Documents**	**Documents**
Red cover	Red cover	Blue cover
- All documents, including affidavits of service, in chronological order	- All applicant documents, including affidavits of service, in chronological order	- All respondent documents, including affidavits of service, in chronological order

SUPPORT ENFORCEMENT CONTINUING RECORD		
SINGLE RECORD	**SEPARATE RECORDS IF ORDERED**	
	Director's Enforcement Record	**Payor's Enforcement Record**
Documents and Endorsements	**Documents and Endorsements**	**Documents and Endorsements**
Green cover	Green cover	Green cover
- Documents (including affidavits of service) - Endorsements, incl. Reasons for Judgment and Minutes of Settlement - Orders	- Documents (including affidavits of service) - Endorsements, incl. Reasons for Judgment and Minutes of Settlement - Orders	- Documents (including affidavits of service) - Endorsements, incl. Reasons for Judgment and Minutes of Settlement - Orders

APPENDIX B – SAMPLE COVER

ONTARIO

Court File Number / *Numéro de dossier du greffe*

(Name of court / *Nom du tribunal*)

at / *situé(e) au* ______________________
Court office address / *Adresse du greffe*

Volume / *Volume* : ____________

Applicant(s) / *Requérant(e)(s)*

Full legal name & address for service — street & number, municipality, postal code, telephone & fax numbers and e-mail address (if any). *Nom et prénom officiels et adresse aux fins de signification — numéro et rue, municipalité, code postal, numéros de téléphone et de télécopieur et adresse électronique (le cas échéant).*	Lawyer's name & address — street & number, municipality, postal code, telephone & fax numbers and e-mail address (if any). *Nom et adresse de l'avocat(e) — numéro et rue, municipalité, code postal, numéros de téléphone et de télécopieur et adresse électronique (le cas échéant).*

Respondent(s) / *Intimé(e)(s)*

Full legal name & address for service — street & number, municipality, postal code, telephone & fax numbers and e-mail address (if any). *Nom et prénom officiels et adresse aux fins de signification — numéro et rue, municipalité, code postal, numéros de téléphone et de télécopieur et adresse électronique (le cas échéant).*	Lawyer's name & address — street & number, municipality, postal code, telephone & fax numbers and e-mail address (if any). *Nom et adresse de l'avocat(e) — numéro et rue, municipalité, code postal, numéros de téléphone et de télécopieur et adresse électronique (le cas échéant).*

Children's Lawyer / *Avocat des enfants*

Name & address of Children's Lawyer's agent for service (street & number, municipality, postal code, telephone & fax numbers and e-mail address (if any) and name of person represented. *Nom et adresse de la personne qui représente l'avocat(e) des enfants aux fins de signification (numéro et rue, municipalité, code postal, numéros de téléphone et de télécopieur et adresse électronique (le cas échéant) et nom de la personne représentée.*

Continuing Record

(Title of record in bold, font size 20 or equivalent / *Intitulé du dossier en caractères gras; police de taille 20 ou l'équivalent*)

APPENDIX C – SAMPLE TABLE OF CONTENTS

ONTARIO

Court File Number

____
(Name of court)

at ____
Court office address

Cumulative Table of Contents
Continuing Record

Applicant(s)

Full legal name & address for service — street & number, municipality, postal code, telephone & fax numbers and e-mail address (if any).	*Lawyer's name & address — street & number, municipality, postal code, telephone & fax numbers and e-mail address (if any).*

Respondent(s)

Full legal name & address for service — street & number, municipality, postal code, telephone & fax numbers and e-mail address (if any).	*Lawyer's name & address — street & number, municipality, postal code, telephone & fax numbers and e-mail address (if any).*

Document *(For an affidavit or transcript of evidence, include the name of the person who gave the affidavit or the evidence.)*	**Filed by** *(A = applicant or R = respondent)*	**Date of Document** *(d, m, y)*	**Date of Filing** *(d, m, y)*	**Volume/Tab**
Application	A	11/10/06	20/10/06	Volume 1, Tab 1 (page # in support enforcement continuing record)
Affidavit of Service of Application on Respondent	A	18/10/06	20/10/06	Volume 1, Tab 1
Financial Statement	A	11/10/06	20/10/06	Volume 1, Tab 2
Answer	R	6/12/06	6/12/06	Volume 1, Tab 3
Affidavit of Service of Answer on Applicant	R	6/12/06	6/12/06	Volume 1, Tab 3
Financial Statement	R	6/12/06	6/12/06	Volume 1, Tab 4
Notice of Motion	R	5/6/07	5/6/07	Volume 1, Tab 5
Affidavit of Service of Notice of Motion on Applicant	R	5/7/07	5/6/07	Volume 1, Tab 5
Affidavit (name of person)	R	5/6/07	5/6/07	Volume 1, Tab 6
Affidavit in Response (name of person)	A	4/7/07	4/7/07	Volume 2, Tab 1
Affidavit of Service of Affidavit in response on Respondent	A	4/7/07	4/7/07	Volume 2, Tab 1
Notice of Motion to change final order dated 1/08/07	R	1/02/09	10/02/09	Volume 3, Tab 1
Affidavit of Service of Notice of Motion on Applicant	R	5/02/09	10/02/09	Volume 3, Tab 1
Financial Statement	R	1/02/09	10/02/09	Volume 3, Tab 2

☐ *Continued on next sheet*

(Français au verso)

Marriage Act

RSO 1990, c. M.3, as amended
Current to June 20, 2012

Definitions

1. (1) In this Act,

"band" means a band as defined in the *Indian Act* (Canada);

"church" includes chapel, meeting-house or place set aside for religious worship;

"Indian" means a person who is registered as an Indian or entitled to be registered as an Indian under the *Indian Act* (Canada);

"issuer" means a person authorized under this Act to issue marriage licences;

"judge" means a provincial judge or a judge of the Superior Court of Justice;

"licence" means a marriage licence issued under this Act;

"Minister" means the Minister of Consumer and Business Services;

> **Note: On a day to be named by proclamation of the Lieutenant Governor, the definition of "Minister" is repealed and the following substituted:**
>
> "Minister" means the minister responsible for the administration of this Act;
>
> **See: 2012, c. 8, Sched. 32, ss. 1, 9.**

"prescribed" means prescribed by the regulations;

"regulations" means the regulations made under this Act;

"reserve" means a reserve as defined in the *Indian Act* (Canada).

Application of Act to subsequent ceremonies

(2) This Act does not apply in respect of any ceremony or form of marriage gone through by two persons who are married to each other by a marriage previously solemnized in accordance with this Act or recognized as valid in Ontario.

Administration

2. The administration of this Act is under the direction of the Minister.

Delegation of powers and duties

3. (1) The Minister may delegate any of his or her powers or duties under this Act to the Deputy Minister of Consumer and Business Services or to any persons employed in the Ministry of Consumer and Business Services.

Same

(2) The delegation shall be in writing and may be made subject to such conditions as are set out in it.

> **Note: On a day to be named by proclamation of the Lieutenant Governor, section 3 is repealed and the following substituted:**
>
> **Delegation of powers and duties**
>
> **3.** The Minister may delegate in writing any or all of his or her powers and duties under this Act to any person, subject to any restrictions set out in the delegation.
>
> **See: 2012, c. 8, Sched. 32, ss. 2, 9.**

Authority to marry

4. No marriage may be solemnized except under the authority of a licence issued in accordance with this Act or the publication of banns.

Who may marry

5. (1) Any person who is of the age of majority may obtain a licence or be married under the authority of the publication of banns, provided no lawful cause exists to hinder the solemnization.

Idem

(2) No person shall issue a licence to a minor, or solemnize the marriage of a minor under the authority of the publication of banns, except where the minor is of the age of sixteen years or more and has the consent in writing of both parents in the form prescribed by the regulations.

Giving of consent

(3) The consent referred to in subsection (2) is not required in respect of a minor who was previously married and whose marriage was terminated by death or divorce.

Idem

(4) Where one of the parents of a minor is dead or both parents are living apart, the consent required by subsection (2) may be given by the parent having actual or legal custody of the minor.

Idem

(5) Where both parents of a minor are dead or are voluntary or involuntary patients in a psychiatric facility, the consent required by subsection (2) may be given by a lawfully appointed guardian or an acknowledged guardian who has brought up or who for the three years immediately preceding the intended marriage has supported the minor.

Idem

(6) Where a minor is made a ward of someone other than a parent by order of a court or under any Act, the consent required by subsection (2) may be given by the lawful guardian of the minor or person responsible for exercising the rights and duties of a guardian of the minor.

Application to dispense with consent

6. (1) Where a person whose consent is required by section 5 is not available or unreasonably or arbitrarily withholds consent, the person in respect of whose marriage the consent is required may apply to a judge without the intervention of a litigation guardian for an order dispensing with the consent.

Powers of judge

(2) The judge shall hear the application in a summary manner and may, in his or her discretion, make an order dispensing with the consent required by section 5.

Persons lacking mental capacity

7. No person shall issue a licence to or solemnize the marriage of any person who, based on what he or she knows or has reasonable grounds to believe, lacks mental capacity to marry by reason of being under the influence of intoxicating liquor or drugs or for any other reason.

Where dissolution of former marriage recognized in Ontario

8. (1) An applicant for a licence who has been previously married is entitled to be issued a licence if such marriage has been dissolved or annulled and such dissolution or annulment is recognized under the law of Ontario and the applicant otherwise complies with the requirements of this Act.

Proof of divorce, etc.

(2) Subject to subsection (6), an issuer shall not issue a licence to a person whose previous marriage has been dissolved or annulled in Canada unless the person produces for inspection by the issuer,

(a) the final decree or judgment dissolving or annulling the previous marriage;

(b) a copy of the final decree, judgment or Act dissolving or annulling the previous marriage certified by the proper officer; or

(c) a certificate of divorce issued by the registrar under the Rules of Civil Procedure.

Same

(2.1) Before issuing a licence, an issuer may require a person to whom subsection (2) applies to deposit with the issuer such material as the issuer considers relevant to the proof of the divorce or annulment.

Where dissolution, etc., outside Canada

(3) Subject to subsection (6), no issuer shall issue a licence to a person whose previous marriage has been dissolved or annulled elsewhere than in Canada, unless the authorization in writing of the Minister is obtained upon the deposit of such material as the Minister may require.

Review of refusal to issue licence

(4) Where an issuer refuses to issue a licence, or the Minister refuses to issue an authorization under subsection (3), the applicant may apply to the Divisional Court for judicial review under the *Judicial Review Procedure Act* and for an order directing that a licence be issued to the applicant and if the court finds that the applicant is so entitled it may make such an order.

Parties

(5) The applicant, the Minister and such other persons as the court may order are parties to an application under subsection (4).

Issue of licence under court order

(6) Where an applicant for a licence files with an issuer, together with his or her application, an order of the Divisional Court made on an application under subsection (4) directing that a licence be issued to the applicant, the issuer shall issue the licence.

Order under *Declarations of Death Act, 2002*

9. (1) If an order has been made under the *Declarations of Death Act, 2002* declaring that a married person has died, the person to whom the deceased was married may, subject to the provisions of this Act, obtain a licence or be married under the authority of the publication of banns upon depositing a certified copy of the order with the person issuing the licence or solemnizing the marriage together with an affidavit in the required form.

Exception

(2) Subsection (1) does not apply if the order is limited, under subsection 2(6) of the *Declarations of Death Act, 2002*, to specified purposes other than remarriage.

Discretionary power of Minister

10. Despite anything in this Act, if the Minister considers that circumstances justify the issue of a licence in any particular case, the Minister may, in his or her absolute discretion, authorize the issue of the licence.

Issuers

11. (1) Marriage licences may be issued by the clerk of every local municipality except a township.

Interpretation

(1.1) In subsection (1) and clause (2)(a), "township" means a local municipality that had the status of a township on December 31, 2002 and, but for the enactment of the *Municipal Act, 2001*, would have had the status of a township on January, 1, 2003.

Same

(2) If the Minister considers it expedient for the public convenience, the Minister may in writing appoint as an issuer,

(a) the clerk of a township, or a resident of a county or township adjacent thereto;

(b) a resident of a territorial district; or

Note: On a day to be named by proclamation of the Lieutenant Governor, subsection (2) is amended by striking out "or" at the end of clause (b). See: 2012, c. 8, Sched. 32, ss. 3, 9.

(c) a member of a band, on the band council's recommendation.

Note: On a day to be named by proclamation of the Lieutenant Governor, subsection (2) is amended by adding "or" at the end of clause (c). See: 2012, c. 8, Sched. 32, ss. 3, 9.

Note: On a day to be named by proclamation of the Lieutenant Governor, subsection (2) is amended by adding the following clause:

(d) any other person.

See: 2012. c. 8, Sched. 32, ss. 3, 9.

Deputy issuers

(3) An issuer may, with the approval in writing of the Minister or of the head of the council of the local municipality of which he or she is clerk, appoint in writing one or more deputies to act for him or her, and any such deputy while so acting has the power of the issuer appointing him or her.

Notice of appointment of deputy

(4) The issuer shall, upon appointing a deputy, forthwith transmit to the Minister a notice of the appointment, and of the name and official position of the person by whom the appointment has been approved, and the Minister may at any time cancel the appointment.

(5) Repealed.

Evidence on applications

12. (1) An issuer or the Minister may require evidence to identify any applicant or to establish his or her status and may examine, under oath if required, any applicant or other person as to any matter pertaining to the issue of a licence.

Untrue information

(2) Where an issuer has reason to believe that any information set out in an application for a licence is untrue, he or she shall not issue the licence unless, on the production of such further evidence as the issuer may require, he or she is satisfied as to the truth of the information.

Record of licences

13. (1) Every issuer shall keep in his or her office a record of the serial number and the date of issue of every licence issued by him or her, and the names and addresses of the parties to the intended marriage.

Note: On a day to be named by proclamation of the Lieutenant Governor, subsection (1) is repealed and the following substituted:

Record of licences

(1) Every issuer shall keep in his or her office a record of every licence he or she issues and the record shall contain any particulars required by the regulations.

See: 2012, c. 8, Sched. 32, ss. 4, 9.

Searches

(2) Any person is entitled, upon application, to have a search made respecting any licence issued within three months immediately preceding the date of application.

Information disclosed

(3) The search shall not disclose any information other than whether or not a licence has been issued and, if so, the date of issue of the licence.

Material to be forwarded to Registrar General

14. Every issuer immediately upon issuing a licence and every person registered as authorized to solemnize marriage upon publishing banns shall forward to the Registrar General,

(a) any consent under section 5;

(b) any judge's order under section 6;

(c) any affidavit or judge's order under section 9;

(d) any documentary or other material filed on the application for a licence under section 8;

(e) any affidavit as to age;

(f) any documentary material obtained under section 12.

Note: On a day to be named by proclamation of the Lieutenant Governor, section 14 is repealed and the following substituted:

Documents to be forwarded to Registrar General

14. (1) Every issuer shall immediately upon issuing a licence and every person registered as authorized to solemnize marriage shall upon publishing banns forward to the Registrar General any documents required by the regulations.

Interpretation

(2) In this section,

"Registrar General" means the Registrar General under the *Vital Statistics Act*.

See: 2012, c. 8, Sched. 32, ss. 5, 9.

Oaths

15. Issuers may administer oaths for the purposes of this Act.

Note: On a day to be named by proclamation of the Lieutenant Governor, section 15 is repealed and the following substituted:

Oaths and affirmations

15. Issuers may administer oaths and affirmations for the purposes of this Act.

See: 2012, c. 8, Sched. 32, ss. 6, 9.

Indians

16. Where both parties to an intended marriage are Indians ordinarily resident on a reserve in Ontario or on Crown lands in Ontario, no fee shall be charged for the licence.

Publication of banns

17. (1) Where a marriage is to be solemnized under the authority of the publication of banns, the intention to marry shall be proclaimed openly in an audible voice during divine service,

(a) where the parties are in the habit of attending worship at the same church, being within Canada, at that church; or

(b) where the parties are in the habit of attending worship in different churches, being within Canada, in each such church.

Method and time of publication

(2) The banns shall be published according to the usage of the denomination, faith or creed of the church in which they are published and during divine Sunday service.

Exception

(3) Where the usage of any denomination, faith or creed substitutes any other day as the usual and principal day of the week for the celebration of divine service, the banns shall be published on such other day.

Proof

(4) The person or persons who publish banns shall certify proof thereof in the prescribed form.

Where banns not to be published

18. Banns shall not be published where either of the parties to the intended marriage has been married and the marriage has been dissolved or annulled.

Prohibited degrees

19. If the regulations prescribe a form setting out the relationships by consanguinity or adoption that, under the *Marriage (Prohibited Degrees) Act* (Canada), bar the lawful solemnization of marriage, the form shall be endorsed on the licence and on the proof of publication of banns.

Who may solemnize marriage

20. (1) No person shall solemnize a marriage unless he or she is authorized by or under section 24 or is registered under this section as a person authorized to solemnize marriage.

Application for registration

(2) Upon application the Minister may, subject to subsection (3), register any person as a person authorized to solemnize marriage.

Who may be registered

(3) No person shall be registered unless it appears to the Minister,

(a) that the person has been ordained or appointed according to the rites and usages of the religious body to which he or she belongs, or is, by the rules of that religious body, deemed ordained or appointed;

(b) that the person is duly recognized by the religious body to which he or she belongs as entitled to solemnize marriage according to its rites and usages;

(c) that the religious body to which the person belongs is permanently established both as to the continuity of its existence and as to its rites and ceremonies; and

(d) that the person is resident in Ontario or has his or her parish or pastoral charge in whole or in part in Ontario; provided that in the case of a person who is in Ontario temporarily and who, if resident in Ontario, might be registered under this section, the Minister may register him or her as authorized to solemnize marriage during a period to be fixed by the Minister.

Where no person authorized to solemnize marriage

(4) Despite subsection (1), where it appears to the Minister that the doctrines of a religious body described in clause (3)(c) do not recognize any person as authorized to solemnize marriage, the Minister may register a person duly designated by the governing authority of the religious body who shall, in respect of marriages performed according to the rites, usages and customs of the religious body, perform all the duties imposed by this Act upon a person solemnizing a marriage, other than solemnizing the marriage.

Idem

(5) Where a person registered under subsection (4) performs the duties imposed by subsection (4), every marriage solemnized according to the rites, usages and customs of the religious body is valid.

Rights of person registered

(6) A person registered under this section is not required to solemnize a marriage, to allow a sacred place to be used for solemnizing a marriage or for an event related to the solemnization of a marriage, or to otherwise assist in the solemnization of a marriage, if to do so would be contrary to,

(a) the person's religious beliefs; or

(b) the doctrines, rites, usages or customs of the religious body to which the person belongs.

Definition

(7) In subsection (6),

"sacred place" includes a place of worship and any ancillary or accessory facilities.

Register

21. (1) The Minister shall keep a register of the name of every person registered as a person authorized to solemnize marriage, the date of such registration, and such other particulars as the Minister considers advisable.

Certificate of registration

(2) The Minister may issue a certificate of registration under this section in the prescribed form.

Cancellation of registration

22. (1) Where it appears to the Minister that any person registered as authorized to solemnize marriage has ceased to possess the qualifications entitling him or her to be so registered, or for any other cause, the Minister may cancel the registration.

Notice of change

(2) Every religious body, members of which are registered under this Act, shall notify the Minister of the name of every such member so registered who has died or has ceased to reside in Ontario or has ceased to be associated with such religious body.

Publication of registration and cancellation

23. When a person is registered under this Act as authorized to solemnize marriage, and when any such registration is cancelled, the Minister shall publish notice thereof in *The Ontario Gazette*.

Civil marriage

24. (1) A judge, a justice of the peace or any other person of a class designated by the regulations may solemnize marriages under the authority of a licence.

(2) Repealed.

Form of ceremony

(3) No particular form of ceremony is required except that in some part of the ceremony, in the presence of the person solemnizing the marriage and witnesses, each of the parties shall declare:

> I do solemnly declare that I do not know of any lawful impediment why I, AB, may not be joined in matrimony to CD,
>
> Je déclare solennellement que moi, AB, je ne connais aucun empêchement légal à mon mariage avec CD,

and each of the parties shall say to the other:

> I call upon these persons here present to witness that I, AB, do take you, CD, to be my lawful wedded wife (*or* to be my lawful wedded husband *or* to be my lawful wedded partner *or* to be my lawful wedded spouse),
>
> Je demande aux personnes qui sont ici présentes d'être témoins que moi, AB, je prends CD comme légitime épouse (*ou* comme légitime époux *ou* comme partenaire conjugal légitime *ou* comme légitime conjoint(e)),

after which the person solemnizing the marriage shall say:

> I, EF, by virtue of the powers vested in me by the *Marriage Act*, do hereby pronounce you AB and CD to be married,
>
> En vertu des pouvoirs qui me sont conférés par la *Loi sur le mariage*, moi, EF, je vous déclare mariés(ées), AB et CD.

Language

(4) For the purposes of subsection (3), it is sufficient to use only the English or only the French language.

Attendance of parties and witnesses

25. Every marriage shall be solemnized in the presence of the parties and at least two witnesses who shall affix their names as witnesses to the entry in the register made under section 28.

Proof of publication

26. No marriage shall be solemnized under the authority of the publication of banns unless proof of publication by the person or persons publishing the banns has been deposited with the person solemnizing the marriage.

Time for solemnization

27. (1) Repealed.

Idem: under banns

(2) A marriage shall not be solemnized under the authority of the publication of banns, earlier than the fifth day after the date of the publication of banns.

Time within which marriage to be solemnized

(3) A marriage shall be solemnized only within the three months immediately following the issue of the licence or the publication of banns, as the case may be.

Entry in marriage register

28. (1) Every person shall immediately after he or she has solemnized a marriage,

(a) where the marriage was solemnized in a church, enter in the church register kept for the purpose; or

(b) where the marriage was solemnized elsewhere than in the church, enter in a register kept by him or her for the purpose,

the particulars prescribed by the regulations, and the entry shall be authenticated by his or her signature and those of the parties and witnesses.

Record of marriage

(2) Every person who solemnizes a marriage shall, at the time of the marriage, if required by either of the parties, give a record of solemnization of the marriage specifying the names of the parties, the date of the marriage, the names of the witnesses, and whether the marriage was solemnized under the authority of a licence or publication of banns.

Supply of marriage registers

29. (1) Every person or religious body authorized to solemnize marriages may apply to the Minister for a marriage register, and the Minister shall thereupon supply the register.

Property of Crown

(2) Every register supplied by the Minister is the property of the Crown.

Protection of persons solemnizing marriage in good faith

30. No person who solemnizes or purports to solemnize a marriage is subject to any action or liability by reason of there having been any legal impediment to the marriage unless, at the time the person performed the ceremony, he or she was aware of the impediment.

Marriages solemnized in good faith

31. If the parties to a marriage solemnized in good faith and intended to be in compliance with this Act are not under a legal disqualification to contract such marriage and after such solemnization have lived together and cohabited as a married couple, such marriage shall be deemed a valid marriage, although the person who solemnized the marriage was not authorized to solemnize marriage, and despite the absence of or any irregularity or insufficiency in the publication of banns or the issue of the licence.

Breach of promise of marriage abolished

32. (1) No action shall be brought for a breach of a promise to marry or for any damages resulting therefrom.

Application of subs. (1)

(2) Subsection (1) does not apply in respect of actions for breach of promise to marry or damages resulting therefrom commenced before the 1st day of August, 1978.

Recovery of gifts made in contemplation of marriage

33. Where one person makes a gift to another in contemplation of or conditional upon their marriage to each other and the marriage fails to take place or is abandoned, the question of whether or not the failure or abandonment was caused by or was the fault of the donor shall not be considered in determining the right of the donor to recover the gift.

Note: On a day to be named by proclamation of the Lieutenant Governor, the Act is amended by adding the following section:

Powers of Minister

33.1 (1) The Minister may by order,

(a) set and collect fees for services that the Minister provides under this Act; and

(b) provide for the waiver of payment of those fees in favour of any person or class of persons.

Orders are not regulations

(2) An order made under this section is not a regulation for the purposes of Part III (Regulations) of the *Legislation Act, 2006*.

See: 2012, c. 8, Sched. 32, ss. 7, 9.

Regulations

34. The Lieutenant Governor in Council may make regulations,

(a) Repealed.

Note: On a day to be named by proclamation of the Lieutenant Governor, section 34 is amended by adding the following clause:

(a) prescribing any matter required or permitted by this Act to be prescribed by the regulations;

See: 2012, c. 8, Sched. 32, ss. 8 (1), 9.

(b) prescribing any matter required by this Act to be prescribed by the regulations;

Note: On a day to be named by proclamation of the Lieutenant Governor, clause (b) is repealed and the following substituted:

(b) requiring the payment of fees in respect of any matter required or authorized to be done under this Act, other than for services provided by the Minister;

See: 2012, c. 8, Sched. 32, ss. 8 (2), 9.

(c) requiring the payment of fees in respect of any matter required or authorized to be done under this Act, and providing for the retention of fees or any portion thereof by issuers and persons solemnizing marriages or any class of them and for the commutation of such fees;

Note: On a day to be named by proclamation of the Lieutenant Governor, clause (c) is repealed and the following substituted:

(c) providing for the retention of fees or a portion of the fees by issuers and persons solemnizing marriages or any class of either of them and for the commutation of such fees;

See: 2012, c. 8, Sched. 32, ss. 8 (2), 9.

(d) prescribing the duties of issuers;

Note: On a day to be named by proclamation of the Lieutenant Governor, section 34 is amended by adding the following clauses:

(d.1) respecting the particulars that shall be contained in a record under subsection 13(1);

(d.2) respecting the documents that shall be forwarded to the Registrar General under subsection 14(1);

See: 2012, c. 8, Sched. 32, ss. 8 (3), 9.

(e) requiring persons authorized to solemnize marriages to furnish such information and returns as are prescribed;

(f) Repealed.

(g) designating classes of persons authorized to solemnize marriages under section 24.

Penalty: false statements

35. (1) Every person who knowingly makes any false statement in any document required under this Act, in addition to any other penalty or punishment to which the person may be liable, is guilty of an offence and on conviction is liable to a fine of not more than $1,000 or to imprisonment for a term of not more than one year, or to both.

Idem: general

(2) Every person who contravenes any provision of this Act for which no other penalty is provided is guilty of an offence and on conviction is liable to a fine of not more than $500.

Form Repealed.

Civil Marriage Act

SC 2005, c. 33
Current to June 26, 2013
An Act respecting certain aspects of legal capacity for marriage for civil purposes

Preamble

WHEREAS the Parliament of Canada is committed to upholding the Constitution of Canada, and section 15 of the *Canadian Charter of Rights and Freedoms* guarantees that every individual is equal before and under the law and has the right to equal protection and equal benefit of the law without discrimination;

WHEREAS the courts in a majority of the provinces and in one territory have recognized that the right to equality without discrimination requires that couples of the same sex and couples of the opposite sex have equal access to marriage for civil purposes;

WHEREAS the Supreme Court of Canada has recognized that many Canadian couples of the same sex have married in reliance on those court decisions;

WHEREAS only equal access to marriage for civil purposes would respect the right of couples of the same sex to equality without discrimination, and civil union, as an institution other than marriage, would not offer them that equal access and would violate their human dignity, in breach of the *Canadian Charter of Rights and Freedoms*;

WHEREAS the Supreme Court of Canada has determined that the Parliament of Canada has legislative jurisdiction over marriage but does not have the jurisdiction to establish an institution other than marriage for couples of the same sex;

WHEREAS everyone has the freedom of conscience and religion under section 2 of the *Canadian Charter of Rights and Freedoms*;

WHEREAS nothing in this Act affects the guarantee of freedom of conscience and religion and, in particular, the freedom of members of religious groups to hold and declare their religious beliefs and the freedom of officials of religious groups to refuse to perform marriages that are not in accordance with their religious beliefs;

WHEREAS it is not against the public interest to hold and publicly express diverse views on marriage;

WHEREAS, in light of those considerations, the Parliament of Canada's commitment to uphold the right to equality without discrimination precludes the use of section 33 of the *Canadian Charter of Rights and Freedoms* to deny the right of couples of the same sex to equal access to marriage for civil purposes;

WHEREAS marriage is a fundamental institution in Canadian society and the Parliament of Canada has a responsibility to support that institution because it strengthens commitment in relationships and represents the foundation of family life for many Canadians;

AND WHEREAS, in order to reflect values of tolerance, respect and equality consistent with the *Canadian Charter of Rights and Freedoms*, access to marriage for civil purposes should be extended by legislation to couples of the same sex;

NOW, THEREFORE, Her Majesty, by and with the advice and consent of the Senate and House of Commons of Canada, enacts as follows:

Short title

1. This Act may be cited as the *Civil Marriage Act*.

PART 1 MARRIAGE

Marriage — certain aspects of capacity

2. Marriage, for civil purposes, is the lawful union of two persons to the exclusion of all others.

Religious officials

3. It is recognized that officials of religious groups are free to refuse to perform marriages that are not in accordance with their religious beliefs.

Freedom of conscience and religion and expression of beliefs

3.1 For greater certainty, no person or organization shall be deprived of any benefit, or be subject to any obligation or sanction, under any law of the Parliament of Canada solely by reason of their exercise, in respect of marriage between persons of the same sex, of the freedom of conscience and religion guaranteed under the *Canadian Charter of Rights and Freedoms* or the expression of their beliefs in respect of marriage as the union of a man and woman to the exclusion of all others based on that guaranteed freedom.

Marriage not void or voidable

4. For greater certainty, a marriage is not void or voidable by reason only that the spouses are of the same sex.

Marriage of non-resident persons

5. (1) A marriage that is performed in Canada and that would be valid in Canada if the spouses were domiciled in Canada is valid for the purposes of Canadian law even though either or both of the spouses do not, at the time of the marriage, have the capacity to enter into it under the law of their respective state of domicile.

Retroactivity

(2) Subsection (1) applies retroactively to a marriage that would have been valid under the law that was applicable in the province where the marriage was performed but for the lack of capacity of either or both of the spouses to enter into it under the law of their respective state of domicile.

Order dissolving marriage

(3) Any court order, made in Canada or elsewhere before the coming into force of this subsection, that declares the marriage to be null and void or that grants a divorce to the spouses dissolves the marriage, for the purposes of Canadian law, as of the day on which the order takes effect.

PART 2 DISSOLUTION OF MARRIAGE FOR NON-RESIDENT SPOUSES

Definition of "court"

6. In this Part, "court," in respect of a province, means

(a) for Ontario, the Superior Court of Justice;
(b) for Quebec, the Superior Court;
(c) for Nova Scotia and British Columbia, the Supreme Court of the province;
(d) for New Brunswick, Manitoba, Saskatchewan and Alberta, the Court of Queen's Bench for the province;
(e) for Prince Edward Island and Newfoundland and Labrador, the trial division of the Supreme Court of the province; and
(f) for Yukon and the Northwest Territories, the Supreme Court, and in Nunavut, the Nunavut Court of Justice.

It also means any other court in the province whose judges are appointed by the Governor General and that is designated by the Lieutenant Governor in Council of the province as a court for the purposes of this Part.

Divorce—non-resident spouses

7. (1) The court of the province where the marriage was performed may, on application, grant the spouses a divorce if

(a) there has been a breakdown of the marriage as established by the spouses having lived separate and apart for at least one year before the making of the application;
(b) neither spouse resides in Canada at the time the application is made; and
(c) each of the spouses is residing—and for at least one year immediately before the application is made, has resided—in a state where a divorce cannot be granted because that state does not recognize the validity of the marriage.

Application

(2) The application may be made by both spouses jointly or by one of the spouses with the other spouse's consent or, in the absence of that consent, on presentation of an order from the court or a court located in the state where one of the spouses resides that declares that the other spouse

(a) is incapable of making decisions about his or her civil status because of a mental disability;
(b) is unreasonably withholding consent; or
(c) cannot be found.

Exception if spouse is found

(3) Despite paragraph (2)(c), the other spouse's consent is required if that spouse is found in connection with the service of the application.

No corollary relief

8. For greater certainty, the *Divorce Act* does not apply to a divorce granted under this Act.

Effective date generally

9. (1) A divorce takes effect on the day on which the judgment granting the divorce is rendered.

Certificate of divorce

(2) After a divorce takes effect, the court must, on request, issue to any person a certificate that a divorce granted under this Act dissolved the marriage of the specified persons effective as of a specified date.

Conclusive proof

(3) The certificate, or a certified copy of it, is conclusive proof of the facts so certified without proof of the signature or authority of the person appearing to have signed the certificate.

Legal effect throughout Canada

10. On taking effect, a divorce granted under this Act has legal effect throughout Canada.

Marriage dissolved

11. On taking effect, a divorce granted under this Act dissolves the marriage of the spouses.

11.1 Repealed.

Definition of "competent authority"

12. (1) In this section, "competent authority", in respect of a court in a province, means the body, person or group of persons ordinarily competent under the laws of that province to make rules regulating the practice and procedure in that court.

Rules

(2) Subject to subsection (3), the competent authority may make rules applicable to any applications made under this Part in a court in a province, including rules

(a) regulating the practice and procedure in the court;

(b) respecting the conduct and disposition of any applications that are made under this Part without an oral hearing;

(c) prescribing and regulating the duties of the officers of the court; and

(d) prescribing and regulating any other matter considered expedient to attain the ends of justice and carry into effect the purposes and provisions of this Part.

Exercise of power

(3) The power of a competent authority to make rules for a court must be exercised in the like manner and subject to the like terms and conditions, if any, as the power to make rules for that court that are conferred on that authority by the laws of the province.

Not statutory instruments

(4) Rules that are made under this section by a competent authority that is not a judicial or quasi-judicial body are deemed not to be statutory instruments within the meaning and for the purposes of the *Statutory Instruments Act*.

Regulations

13. (1) The Governor in Council may make regulations for carrying out the purposes and provisions of this Part, including regulations providing for uniformity in the rules made under section 12.

Regulations prevail

(2) Any regulations that are made to provide for uniformity in the rules prevail over those rules.

14. Repealed.

15. Repealed.

Spousal Support Advisory Guidelines

July 2008

EXECUTIVE SUMMARY

The **Spousal Support Advisory Guidelines** were developed to bring more certainty and predictability to the determination of spousal support under the federal *Divorce Act*. The Advisory Guidelines project has been supported by the federal Department of Justice. The Advisory Guidelines were released three years ago, in January 2005, in the form of a Draft Proposal and have been used across Canada since then. Comments and feedback were provided and some revisions made. This document is the final version.

The *Spousal Support Advisory Guidelines* are very different from the *Federal Child Support Guidelines*. They **have not been legislated** by the federal government. They are informal guidelines that will operate on **an advisory basis only**. The Advisory Guidelines will be used to determine the amount and duration of spousal support within the existing legal framework of the *Divorce Act* and the judicial decisions interpreting its provisions. The Guidelines are not legally binding and their adoption and use will be voluntary. They are intended as a practical tool to assist spouses, lawyers, mediators and judges in determining the amount and duration of spousal support in typical cases. The various components of the Guidelines—the basic formulas, restructuring, and exceptions—are intended to build upon current practice, reflecting best practices and emerging trends across the country. The process of developing the Advisory Guidelines is described in Chapter 2.

An overview of the structure of the Guidelines is found in Chapter 3.

The Advisory Guidelines do **not** deal with **entitlement**, just amount and duration once entitlement has been found. A mere disparity of income that would generate an amount under the Guidelines does not automatically lead to entitlement. As is set out in Chapter 4, there must be a finding (or an agreement) on entitlement, on a compensatory or non-compensatory or contractual basis, *before* the formulas and the rest of the Guidelines are applied. The basis of entitlement is important, not only as a threshold issue, but also to determine location within the formula ranges or to justify departure from the ranges as an exception. Entitlement issues also arise frequently on review and variation, especially applications to terminate support.

Some limitations on the application of the Guidelines are dealt with in Chapter 5. The Advisory Guidelines have been developed specifically for use under the federal *Divorce Act*. **Provincial/territorial laws** differ in some respects and any use of these Guidelines in the provincial/territorial context must take account of these distinctive statutes, especially on matters of entitlement for unmarried couples and agreements. A **prior agreement** may limit the application of the Guidelines, as the Advisory Guidelines cannot be used to override existing agreements, especially agreements that time limit or waive spousal support.

There are two basic formulas in the proposal: the ***without child support*** **formula** and the ***with child support*** **formula**. The dividing line between the two is the absence or presence of a dependent child or children of the marriage, and a concurrent child support obligation, at the time spousal support is determined. Both formulas use **income sharing** as the method for determining the amount of spousal support, not budgets. The formulas produce **ranges** for the amount and duration of support, not just a single number. The precise number chosen within that range is a matter for negotiation or adjudication, depending upon the facts of a particular case.

The starting point under both formulas is the definition of **income** used in the *Federal Child Support Guidelines*, subject to some minor adjustments for spousal support purposes, explained in Chapter 6.

The ***without child support*** **formula**, set out below, is built around two crucial factors: the **gross income difference** between the spouses and the **length of the marriage**. Both the amount and the duration of support increase incrementally with the length of the marriage, as can be seen in the summary box below. The idea that explains this formula is **merger over time**: as a marriage lengthens, spouses more deeply merge their economic and non-economic lives, with each spouse making countless decisions to mould his or her skills, behaviours and finances around those of the other spouse.

The gross income difference measures their differential loss of the marital standard of living at the end of the marriage. The formulas for both amount and duration reflect the idea that the longer the marriage, the more the lower income spouse should be protected against such a differential loss. Merger over time captures both the compensatory and non-compensatory spousal support objectives that have been recognized by our law since *Moge* and *Bracklow*.

> **The *Without Child Support* Formula**
>
> **Amount** ranges from 1.5 to 2 percent of the difference between the spouses' gross incomes (the **gross income difference**) for each year of marriage (or, more precisely, years of cohabitation), up to a maximum of 50 percent. The maximum range remains fixed for marriages 25 years or longer at 37.5 to 50 percent of income difference. (The upper end of this maximum range is capped at the amount that would result in equalization of the spouses' net incomes—the **net income cap**.)
>
> **Duration** ranges from .5 to 1 year for each year of marriage. However, support will be **indefinite (duration not specified)** if the marriage is **20 years or longer** in duration *or*, if the marriage has lasted 5 years or longer, when the years of marriage and age of the support recipient (at separation) added together total 65 or more (the **rule of 65**).

Chapter 7 contains examples of the application of the *without child support* formula and the ranges it produces for marriages of different lengths and incomes.

Cases with dependent children and concurrent child support obligations require a different formula, the ***with child support* formula**, set out in Chapter 8. These cases raise different considerations: priority must be given to child support; there is usually reduced ability to pay; and particular tax and benefit issues arise. The rationale for spousal support is also different. Where there are dependent children, the primary rationale is compensatory, as both *Moge* and *Bracklow* made clear. What drives support is not the length of the marriage, or marital interdependency, or merger over time, but the presence of dependent children and the need to provide care and support for those children. This **parental partnership** rationale looks at not just past loss, but also at the continuing economic disadvantage that flows from present and future child care responsibilities, anchored in s. 15.2(6)(b) of the *Divorce Act*.

There are three important differences between the *without child support* formula and the *with child support* formula. First, the *with child support* formula uses the **net incomes** of the spouses, not their gross incomes. Second, this formula divides the **pool** of combined net incomes between the two spouses, not the gross income difference. Third, the upper and lower percentage limits of net income division in the *with child support* formula **do not change with the length of the marriage**.

Set out below is a summary version of the **basic *with child support* formula**, used to determine the amount of spousal support to be paid where the payor spouse pays both child and spousal support to the lower income recipient spouse who is also the parent with custody or primary care of the children.

> **The Basic *With Child Support* Formula for Amount**
>
> (1) Determine the individual net disposable income (INDI) of each spouse:
> - Guidelines Income *minus* Child Support *minus* Taxes and Deductions = Payor's INDI
> - Guidelines Income *minus* Notional Child Support *minus* Taxes and Deductions *Plus* Government Benefits and Credits = Recipient's INDI
>
> (2) Add together the individual net disposable incomes. By iteration, determine the range of spousal support amounts that would be required to leave the lower income recipient spouse with between 40 and 46 percent of the combined INDI.

Net income computations like these require computer software. Basic to this formula is the concept of **individual net disposable income**, an attempt to isolate a **pool** of net disposable income available after adjustment for each spouse's child support obligations. This is done by deducting or backing out their respective **contributions to child support**. The details of these calculations are set out in Chapter 8, along with several examples.

Duration under this basic *with child support* formula also reflects the underlying parental partnership rationale. Initial orders are **indefinite (duration not specified)**, subject to the usual process of review or variation. The formula does, however, provide a **durational range** which is intended to structure the process of review and variation and to limit the cumulative duration of spousal support. The durational limits under this formula can be thought of as "soft" time limits. There are two tests for duration and whichever produces the longer duration at each end of the range is to be employed:

- First is the **length-of-marriage** test, which is modelled on the duration under the *without child support* formula, i.e. one-half to one year of support for every year of marriage, and which will likely govern for most marriages of ten years or more.

- Second is the **age-of-children** test. The lower end of the durational range is until the youngest child starts full-time school. The upper end of the durational range is until the last or youngest child finishes high school. This test will typically apply to marriages of less than ten years.

Shared and split custody situations require slight variations in the computation of individual net disposable income, as the backing out of child support obligations is a bit more complicated. There is also a different, hybrid formula for cases where **spousal support is paid by the custodial parent**. Under this formula, the spouses' Guidelines incomes are reduced by the grossed-up amount of child support (actual or notional) and then the *without child support* formula is applied to determine amount and duration. Finally, there is one more hybrid formula for those spousal support cases where the child support for **adult children** is determined under section 3(2)(b) of the *Child Support Guidelines*.

The formulas provide ranges for the amount and duration of spousal support. The location of a precise amount or duration within those ranges—what we refer to as **using the ranges**—will be driven by the **factors** detailed in Chapter 9: the strength of any compensatory claim; the recipient's needs; the age, number, need and standard of living of any children; the needs and ability to pay or the payor; work incentives for the payor; property division and debts; and self-sufficiency incentives.

Restructuring allows the amount and duration under the formulas to be traded off against each other, so long as the overall value of the restructured award remains within the total or global amounts generated by the formula when amount and duration are combined. Chapter 10 shows how restructuring can be used in three different ways:

- to **front-end load** awards by increasing the amount beyond the formula's range and shortening duration;
- to **extend duration** beyond the formula's range by lowering the monthly amount; or
- to formulate a **lump sum** by combining amount and duration.

"Ceilings" and "floors" in Chapter 11 define the boundaries of the typical incomes to which the formulas can be applied. The **ceiling** is the income level for the payor spouse above which any formula gives way to discretion, set here at **a gross annual income for the payor of $350,000**. The **floor** is the income level for the payor below which no support is usually paid, here set at **$20,000**. To avoid a cliff effect, there is an **exception** for cases where the payor spouse's gross income is **more than $20,000 but less than $30,000**, where spousal support may not be awarded or may be reduced below the low end of the range. An additional **exception** is also necessary, to allow an award of spousal support **below the income floor** in particular cases.

Any formula, even with restructuring, will have its limits and there will always be exceptional cases. Because the Guidelines are only advisory, departures are always possible on a case-by-case basis where the formula outcomes are inappropriate. The Guidelines do contain a short list of **exceptions** in Chapter 12, intended to identify common categories of departures:

- compelling financial circumstances in the interim period;
- debt payment;
- prior support obligations;
- illness and disability;
- the compensatory exception in short marriages without children;
- reapportionment of property (British Columbia);
- basic needs/hardship under the *without child support* and *custodial payor* formulas;
- non-taxable payor income;
- non-primary parent to fulfil parenting role under the *custodial payor* formula;
- special needs of a child; and
- section 15.3 for small amounts and inadequate compensation under the *with child support* formula.

Self-sufficiency is a central concept in the law of spousal support and Chapter 13 draws together in one place all the aspects of the Advisory Guidelines that promote self-sufficiency, one of the objectives of the *Divorce Act*.

The formulas are intended to apply to initial orders and to the negotiation of initial agreements, including interim arrangements. Given the uncertain state of the current law, it is not possible to make the Advisory Guidelines apply to the full range of issues that can arise on **variation and review**, issues that are considered in Chapter 14. The Advisory Guidelines can be applied on applications to reduce spousal support because of changes in income, for example, when the payor spouse's income goes down or the recipient spouse's income goes up (or ought to have gone up). In some cases, one spouse may wish to apply to vary to **cross over** between the two formulas, mostly in longer marriages once the children are no longer dependent, where the *without child support* formula produces higher ranges.

More difficult issues arise where the payor's income increases or the recipient's income is reduced after separation. The most the formula can do is to establish an upper limit upon any increase in spousal support in such cases. At the present time, no formula can be constructed to resolve issues around the recipient spouse's remarriage or re-partnering, or subsequent children.

Quebec has different guidelines for determining child support, which have an impact on spousal support determinations. The application of the Advisory Guidelines to *Divorce Act* cases in Quebec raises special issues that are dealt with in Chapter 15.

3 AN OVERVIEW OF THE ADVISORY GUIDELINES

Spousal support guidelines can be structured in many different ways. For those who are interested, the Background Paper reviews in detail other models of spousal support guidelines. This chapter presents a structural overview of this scheme of Advisory Guidelines. Some of what you will find here has already been touched on, in a less systematic way, in Chapter 2. As well, many of the individual components of the Advisory Guidelines will be discussed more extensively in subsequent chapters. However, we thought it would be helpful for readers to have a sense of the big picture at the beginning.

We begin with a discussion of the basic concept of income sharing on which the Advisory Guidelines are constructed and then move into an organized, step-by-step review of the specific components of the Advisory Guidelines. We have divided this review into three main sections. First, we deal with the preliminary issues that arise *before* any consideration of the formulas—what might be called issues of application. Then we deal with the basic structure of the income-sharing formulas for determination of amount and duration of support that are at the heart of the proposed approach. The outcomes generated by the formulas are not necessarily determinative, however. The final section deals with the steps that can be taken *after* the formula calculations: locating a specific amount or duration within the ranges, restructuring the formula outcomes (by trading off amount against duration), and departing from the amounts and durations generated by the formulas, through exceptions.

3.1 Income Sharing

The core concept on which the Spousal Support Advisory Guidelines are built is **income sharing**. Under the Advisory Guidelines, budgets play a diminished role in determining spousal support outcomes. Instead the Advisory Guidelines look primarily to the incomes of the parties and rely on a mathematical formula to determine the portion of spousal incomes to be shared. Contrary to common perception, **income sharing does not mean equal sharing**. There are many ways of sharing income; it all depends on the formula that is adopted.

You will see below that other factors are also relevant in determining support outcomes under the Advisory Guidelines, such as the presence of dependent children or the length of the marriage. But the income levels of the parties and, and more specifically the income disparity between them, become the primary determinants of support outcomes. Under the Spousal Support Advisory Guidelines, as under the *Child Support Guidelines*, the precise determination of income, including the imputing of income, becomes a much more significant issue than it has been in the past.

Income sharing here is a method, and not a new theory of spousal support. As we have noted earlier, the Advisory Guidelines project has not been driven by a desire to theoretically reorder the law of spousal support. Rather it has been driven by the practical needs of family law practitioners and judges who deal with the daily dilemmas of advising, negotiating, litigating and deciding spousal support.

It is therefore important to emphasize that **the use of income sharing as a method** for determining the amount of spousal support does not necessarily imply adoption of the income-sharing theories of spousal support identified in the Background Paper. Some of these theories, which are admittedly contentious, rest upon a view of marriage as a relationship of trust and community, which justifies treating marital incomes as joint incomes.

The method of income sharing can be used, however, as a practical and efficient way of implementing many support objectives such as compensation for the economic advantages and disadvantages of the marriage or the recognition of need and economic dependency. Such use of proxy measures already exists in spousal support law—think of the prevalent use of standard of living and a "needs and means" analysis to quantify compensatory support.

The Guidelines do not commit to any particular theory of spousal support. As will become clear in the discussion of the different formulas under these Advisory Guidelines, they aim to accommodate the multiple theories that now inform our law and, to generate results that are in broad conformity with existing patterns in the law.

We now move on to an overview of the basic framework of the specific scheme of income sharing found in the Advisory Guidelines.

3.2 Preliminary Issues—The Applicability of the Advisory Guidelines

3.2.1 Form and force

Unlike the *Federal Child Support Guidelines*, the Spousal Support Advisory Guidelines **have not been legislated**. Following the practice in some American jurisdictions, these are **informal guidelines. They are not legally binding. Their use is completely voluntary.** They have been and will be adopted by lawyers and judges to the extent they find them useful, and will operate as a practical tool within **the existing legal framework**. As non-legislated, informal guidelines, these Guidelines are **advisory only**. They are intended as a **starting point** for negotiation and adjudication.

3.2.2 Entitlement

The Advisory Guidelines do **not** deal with entitlement. The informal status of the Guidelines means that they must remain subject to the entitlement provisions of the *Divorce Act*, notably ss. 15.2(4) and (6) as interpreted by the courts. Entitlement therefore remains a threshold issue to be determined before the guidelines will be applicable.

On its own, a mere disparity of income that would generate an amount under the Advisory Guidelines formulas, does not automatically lead to entitlement. There must be a finding (or an agreement) on entitlement, on a compensatory or non-compensatory or contractual basis, *before* the formulas and the rest of the Guidelines are applied.

The Advisory Guidelines were drafted on the assumption that the current law of spousal support, post-*Bracklow*, continues to offer a very expansive basis for entitlement to spousal support. Effectively any significant income disparity generates an entitlement to some support, leaving amount and duration as the main issues to be determined in spousal support cases. However, the Guidelines leave the issue of when an income disparity is significant, in the sense of signalling entitlement, to the courts. It is open to a court to find no entitlement on a particular set of facts, despite income disparity, and the Advisory Guidelines do not speak to that issue.

The basis of entitlement is important, not only as a threshold issue, but also to determine location within the formula ranges or to justify departure from the ranges as an exception. Entitlement issues also arise frequently on review and variation, especially applications to terminate support.

Entitlement is dealt with in Chapter 4.

3.2.3 Application to provincial/territorial law

The Advisory Guidelines have specifically been developed under the federal *Divorce Act* and are intended for use under that legislation. Provincial/territorial support law is governed by distinct statutory regimes. However, in practice there is much overlap between federal and provincial/territorial support laws.

The broad conceptual framework for spousal support articulated by the Supreme Court of Canada in *Moge* and *Bracklow* has been relied upon under both provincial and federal legislation. Indeed *Bracklow*, which combined claims under the *Divorce Act* and provincial legislation, made no real distinction between the two. Given this overlap, the Advisory Guidelines have been used under provincial/territorial support legislation.

There are some distinctive features of provincial/territorial spousal support laws that need to be taken into account when using the Advisory Guidelines. Many provincial/territorial laws have specific provisions governing entitlement, for example provisions determining which non-marital relationships give rise to a spousal support obligation. Like other issues of entitlement discussed above, this must be a threshold determination before the Advisory Guidelines are applied to determine amount and duration of support. We also note that the list of specific factors to be considered in determining spousal support does vary from statute to statute, with some provincial/territorial legislation making explicit reference, for example, to factors such as property and conduct, although the impact of these differences in wording on spousal support outcomes is unclear.

Provincial laws differ from the *Divorce Act* in their application to unmarried couples but this should not cause any difficulties with respect to the operation of the Advisory Guidelines. Although we conveniently refer to "length of marriage" as a relevant factor in the operation of the formulas, the formulas actually rely upon the period of spousal cohabitation (including any periods of pre-marital cohabitation), thus easily meshing with provincial/territorial legislation.

The application of the Advisory Guidelines under provincial/territorial legislation is dealt with in Chapter 5.

3.2.4 Application to agreements

The Advisory Guidelines **do not confer any power to re-open or override final agreements on spousal support**. This issue, like entitlement, is outside the scope of the Advisory Guidelines and will continue to be dealt with under the common law doctrine of unconscionability, provincial/territorial statutes and the evolving interpretation of the Supreme Court of Canada's recent decision in *Miglin*.[33] Agreements limiting or waiving spousal support may therefore preclude the application of the Guidelines.

If a final agreement is set aside or overridden under existing law, the Advisory Guidelines *may* be of assistance in determining the amount and duration of support, although the intentions of the parties as reflected in the agreement may also continue to influence the outcome.

As well, the Advisory Guidelines *may* be applicable if a spousal support agreement provides for review or variation.

Further discussion of the application of the Advisory Guidelines in the cases where there are spousal support agreements can be found in Chapters 5 and 14.

3.2.5 Interim orders

The Advisory Guidelines are intended to apply to interim orders as well as final orders. We anticipate, in fact, that they will be particularly valuable at the interim stage, which is now dominated by a needs-and-means analysis—budgets, expenses and deficits that require individualized decision making.

Any periods of interim support clearly have to be included within the durational limits set by the Advisory Guidelines. Otherwise, if duration were only to be fixed in final orders, there would be incentives in both directions—for some to drag out proceedings and for others to speed them up—and general inequity. Interim support is discussed in Chapter 5.

The Advisory Guidelines do recognize that the amount may need to be set differently during the interim period while parties are sorting out their financial situation immediately after

33 *Miglin v. Miglin*, [2003] 1 S.C.R. 303.

separation. To accommodate these short-term concerns, the Guidelines recognize an exception for compelling financial circumstances in the interim period, considered in Chapter 12.

3.2.6 Review and variation

The primary application of the Advisory Guidelines is to **initial determinations** of spousal support at the point of separation or divorce, whether through negotiated agreements or court orders. Ideally a truly comprehensive set of guidelines would apply not only to the initial determination of support but also to subsequent reviews and variations over time. However, these issues have proven the most difficult to reduce to a formula given the uncertainty in the current law concerning the effect of post-separation income changes, remarriage and repartnering, and subsequent children.

In the end, we chose a more modest course, identifying certain situations where the Advisory Guidelines can apply on reviews and variations, including increases in the recipient's income and decreases in the payor's income. We have left others, such as post-separation increases in the payor's income, re-partnering, remarriage and second families, to more discretionary determinations under the evolving framework of current law.

The application of the Advisory Guidelines in the context of review and variation is dealt with more extensively in Chapter 14.

3.3 The Formulas

3.3.1 Two basic formulas

The Advisory Guidelines are constructed around **two basic formulas**, rather than just one formula: the ***without child support* formula** and the ***with child support* formula**. The dividing line between the two is the absence or presence of a dependent child or children of the marriage, and a concurrent child support obligation, at the time spousal support is determined.

3.3.2 Determining income

Both formulas use **income sharing** as the method for determining the amount of spousal support, not budgets. Income-sharing formulas work directly from income, as income levels essentially determine the amount of support to be paid. Under the Advisory Guidelines, the accurate determination of income becomes a much more significant issue in spousal support cases than it has in the past, and there may be more incentives to dispute income. However, because the Advisory Guidelines generate ranges and not specific amounts, absolute precision in the determination of income may not be as crucial as under the *Federal Child Support Guidelines*. Many cases will involve combined claims for child and spousal support, where a precise determination of income is already required for child support purposes.

The starting point for the determination of income under both formulas is the definition of income under the *Federal Child Support Guidelines*, including the Schedule III adjustments. More details on the determination of income are found in Chapter 6.

The Advisory Guidelines do not solve the complex issues of income determination that arise in cases involving self-employment income and other forms of non-employment income. In determining income it may be necessary, as under the *Federal Child Support Guidelines*, to **impute income** in situations where a spouse's actual income does not appropriately reflect his or her earning capacity. In some cases the issue will be imputing income to the payor spouse. On variation and review the issue may be imputing income to the recipient spouse if it is established that the he or she has failed to make appropriate efforts towards self-sufficiency.

3.3.3 The *without child support* formula

In cases where there are no dependent children, the ***without child support* formula** applies. This formula relies heavily upon length of marriage—or more precisely, the length of relationship, including periods of pre-marital cohabitation—to determine both the amount and duration of support. Both amount and duration increase with the length of the relationship. This formula is constructed around the concept of **merger over time** which offers a useful tool for implementing both compensatory and non-compensatory support objectives in cases where there are no dependent children in a way that reflects general patterns in the current law.

Under the basic *without child support* formula:

- The *amount* of spousal support is 1.5 to 2 percent of the difference between the spouses' gross incomes for each year of marriage, to a maximum range of 37.5 to 50 per cent of the gross income difference for marriages of 25 years or more (The upper end of this maximum range is capped at the amount that would result in equalization of the spouses' net incomes—the net income cap.)
- *Duration* is .5 to 1 year of support for each year of marriage, with duration becoming indefinite (duration not specified) after 20 years *or*, if the marriage has lasted 5 years or longer, when the years of marriage and age of the support recipient (at separation) added together total 65 or more (the "rule of 65").

The *without child support* formula is discussed in detail in Chapter 7.

3.3.4 The *with child support* formula

In cases where there are dependent children, the ***with child support* formula** applies. The distinctive treatment of marriages with dependent children and concurrent child support obligations is justified by both theoretical and practical considerations and is reflected in current case law.

On the theoretical front, marriages with dependent children raise strong compensatory claims based on the economic disadvantages flowing from assumption of primary responsibility for child care, not only during the marriage, *but also after separation*. We have identified this aspect of the compensatory principle as it operates in cases involving dependent children as the **parental partnership principle**, and have drawn on this concept in structuring the *with child support* formula. For marriages with dependent children, length of marriage is not the most important determinant of support outcomes as compared to post-separation child-care responsibilities.

On the practical front, child support must be calculated first and given priority over spousal support. As well, the differential tax treatment of child and spousal support must be taken into account, complicating the calculations. The *with child support* formula thus works with computer software calculations of net disposable incomes

Under the basic *with child support* formula:

- Spousal support is an *amount* that will leave the recipient spouse with between 40 and 46 percent of the spouses' net incomes *after child support has been taken out*. (We refer to the spouses' net income after child support has been taken out as Individual Net Disposable Income or INDI).
- The approach to *duration* under this formula is more complex and flexible than under the *without child support* formula; orders are initially indefinite in form (duration not specified) but the formula also establishes durational ranges which are intended to structure the process of review and variation and which limit the cumulative duration of awards under this formula. These durational limits rely upon both length of marriage and the ages of the children.

The *with child support* formula is really a cluster of formulas dealing with different custodial arrangements. **Shared and split custody** situations require slight variations in the computation of individual net disposable income, as the backing out of child support obligations is a bit more complicated. There is also a different, hybrid formula for cases where **spousal support is paid by the custodial parent**. Under this formula, the spouses' Guidelines incomes are reduced by the grossed-up amount of child support (actual or notional) and then the *without child support* formula is applied to determine amount and duration. Finally, there is one more hybrid formula for those spousal support cases where the child support for **adult children** is determined under section 3(2)(b) of the *Child Support Guidelines.*

The *with child support* formula is discussed in detail in Chapter 8.

3.3.5 Length of marriage

Under the Advisory Guidelines length of marriage is a primary determinant of support outcomes in cases *without* dependent children. Under the *without child support* formula the percentage of income sharing increases with length of the marriage; the same is true for duration of support.

Length of marriage is much less relevant under the *with child support* formula, although it still plays a significant role in determining duration under that formula.

Given the relevance of length of marriage under the Advisory Guidelines, it is important to clarify its meaning. **While we use the convenient term length of marriage, the more accurate description is the length of the cohabitation, which includes periods of pre-marital cohabitation, and ends with separation.**

3.3.6 Ranges

The Advisory Guidelines do not generate a fixed figure for either amount or duration, but instead produce **a range of outcomes** that provide a starting point for negotiation or adjudication.

Ranges create scope for more individualized decision-making, allowing for argument about where a particular case should fall within the range in light of the *Divorce Act*'s multiple support objectives and factors. Ranges can also accommodate some of the variations in current practice, including local variations in spousal support cultures.

3.3.7 Ceilings and floors

As with the *Federal Child Support Guidelines*, the Spousal Support Advisory Guidelines establish ceilings and floors in terms of the income levels to which they are applicable. Both the ceiling and the floor have been set by reference to the annual gross income of the payor. The ceiling has been set at a gross annual income for the payor of $350,000 and the floor at a gross annual income of $20,000. Ceiling and floors are dealt with more extensively in Chapter 11.

3.4 After the Formulas Have Been Applied

Under the Advisory Guidelines there is still much room for flexibility to respond to the facts of particular cases. First, there is considerable room for discretion in the fixing of precise amounts and durations within the ranges generated by the formulas. Second, there is the ability to restructure the formula outcomes by trading off amount against duration. Third the other is the possibility of departing from the formula outcomes by relying upon exceptions.

3.4.1 Using the ranges

The location of a precise amount or duration within those ranges will be driven by the factors detailed in Chapter 9: the strength of any compensatory claim, the recipient's needs, the age, number, needs and standard of living of any children, the needs and ability to pay of the payor, work incentives for the payor, property division and debts, and self-sufficiency incentives.

3.4.2 Restructuring

Although the formulas generate separate figures for amount and duration, the Advisory Guidelines explicitly recognize that these awards can be restructured by trading off amount against duration.

In *Bracklow* the Supreme Court of Canada explicitly recognized that the amount and duration of awards can be configured in different ways to yield awards of similar value (what the Court called quantum). Thus the Court noted that an order for a smaller amount paid out over a long period of time can be equivalent to an order for a higher amount paid out over a shorter period of time.

Restructuring can be used in three ways:

- to **front-end load** awards by increasing the amount beyond the formulas' ranges and shortening duration;
- to **extend duration** beyond the formulas' ranges by lowering the monthly amount; and
- to formulate a **lump sum** payment by combining amount and duration.

When restructuring is relied upon to resolve issues of inappropriate formula outcomes, awards remain consistent with the overall or global amounts generated by the Advisory Guidelines. **Restructuring thus does not involve an exception or departure from the formulas.**

Restructuring works best when duration is clearly defined, and will thus have its primary application under the *without child support* formula.

Restructuring is dealt with in more detail in Chapter 10.

3.4.3 Exceptions

The formulas are intended to generate appropriate outcomes in the majority of cases. We recognize, however, that there will be cases where the formula outcomes, even after consideration of restructuring, will not generate results consistent with the support objectives and factors under the *Divorce Act*. The informal, advisory nature of the Guidelines means that the formula outcomes are never binding and departures are always possible on a case-by-case basis where the formula outcomes are found to be inappropriate. The Advisory Guidelines do, however, itemize a series of exceptions which, although clearly not exhaustive, are intended to assist lawyers and judges in framing and assessing departures from the formulas. The exceptions create room both for the operation of competing theories of spousal support and for consideration of the particular factual circumstances in individual cases where these may not be sufficiently accommodated by restructuring.

The exceptions are listed and explained in Chapter 12:

- compelling financial circumstances in the interim period;
- debt payments;
- prior support obligations;
- illness or disability of a recipient spouse;
- a compensatory exception for shorter marriages under the *with child support* formula;
- reapportionment of property (British Columbia);
- basic needs/hardship under the *without child support* and *custodial payor* formulas;
- non-taxable payor income;
- non-primary parent to fulfil a parenting role under the *custodial payor* formula;
- special needs of a child; and
- section 15.3 for small amounts and inadequate compensation under the *with child support* formula.

7 THE WITHOUT CHILD SUPPORT FORMULA

Here we examine the first of the two basic formulas that lie at the core of the Advisory Guidelines—the ***without child support* formula**. This formula applies in cases where there are no dependent children and hence no concurrent child support obligations. Assuming entitlement, the formula generates ranges for amount and duration of spousal support.

The *without child support* formula covers a diverse range of fact situations, the only unifying factor being the absence of a concurrent child support obligation for a child or children of the marriage.[61] It covers marriages of all lengths where the spouses never had children. It also applies to long marriages where there were children, but they are no longer dependent.[62] The support claims in these cases involve a mix of compensatory and non-compensatory rationales.

It might seem impossible to develop one formula that could yield appropriate support outcomes over such a wide array of marital situations. In developing the formula we turned to the concept of **merger over time**, which incorporates both compensatory and non-compensatory rationales for spousal support. Put simply, the idea is that as a marriage lengthens, spouses more deeply merge their economic and non-economic lives, resulting in greater claims to the marital standard of living.[63] Using that concept, which relates support outcomes

61 Support obligations to children or spouses from prior relationships are dealt with as exceptions under both formulas; see Chapter 11.

62 Some medium length marriages with dependent children in which support is initially determined under the *with child support* formula may cross-over to the *without child support* formula for a re-determination of amount after child support ceases. Crossover is discussed in Chapter 14, Variation and Review, below.

63 In developing this formula we drew in part on the American Law Institute (ALI) proposals referred to in Chapter 1, including the concept of merger over time. As we discuss further below, this concept—although not the terminology—is strongly anchored in our current law of spousal support.

to the length of the marriage, we developed a formula that surprisingly generates results consistent with much of current practice, while bringing some much-needed structure.

In what follows we first introduce the basic structure of the *without child support* formula and provide an example of its operation. We then discuss the concept of merger over time that underlies the formula and its relation to existing rationales for spousal support. This is followed by a more detailed examination of the different parts of the formula and a series of further examples illustrating the formula's application in a variety of factual contexts.

The *Without Child Support* Formula

Amount ranges from 1.5 to 2 percent of the difference between the spouses' gross incomes (the **gross income difference**) for each year of marriage (or more precisely, year of cohabitation), up to a maximum of 50 percent. The range remains fixed for marriages 25 years or longer, at 37.5 to 50 percent of income difference. (The upper end of this maximum range is capped at the amount that would result in equalization of the spouses' net incomes—the **net income cap**).

Duration ranges from .5 to 1 year for each year of marriage. However support will be **indefinite (duration not specified)** if the marriage is **20 years or longer** in duration *or*, if the marriage has lasted five years or longer, when years of marriage and age of the support recipient (at separation) added together total 65 or more (the **rule of 65**).

7.1 The Basic Structure of the *Without Child Support* Formula

The *without child support* formula is set out in the box below in its most basic form. The formula is in fact two formulas—one for amount and one for duration. The formula generates **ranges** for amount and duration, rather than fixed numbers.

There are two crucial factors under the formula:

- the **gross income difference** between the spouses, and
- the **length of the marriage**, or more precisely, as will be explained below, the length of the period of cohabitation.

Both amount and duration increase incrementally with the length of marriage.

A simple example illustrating the basic operation of the *without child support* formula will be helpful at this point before we venture further into its more complex details. The primary purpose of this example is to show the basic calculations required under the formula and to give a sense of the outcomes the formula generates.

Example 7.1

Arthur and Ellen have separated after a 20-year marriage and one child. During the marriage Arthur, who had just finished his commerce degree when the two met, worked for a bank, rising through the ranks and eventually becoming a branch manager. He was transferred several times during the course of the marriage. His gross annual income is now $90,000. Ellen worked for a few years early in the marriage as a bank teller, then stayed home until their son was in school full time. She worked part time as a store clerk until he finished high school. Their son is now independent. Ellen now works full time as a receptionist earning $30,000 gross per year. Both Arthur and Ellen are in their mid forties.

Assuming entitlement has been established in this case, here is how support would be determined under the *without child support* formula.

To determine the **amount** of support:

- Determine the **gross income difference** between the parties:

  $90,000 – $30,000 = $60,000
- Determine the **applicable percentage** by multiplying the length of the marriage by 1.5–2 percent per year:

  1.5 × 20 years = **30 percent**

  to

  2 × 20 years = **40 percent**
- Apply the applicable percentage to the income difference:

  30 percent × $60,000 = $18,000/year (**$1,500/month**)

  to

  40 percent × $60,000 = $24,000/year (**$2,000/month**)

Duration would be indefinite (duration not specified) in this case because the length of the marriage was 20 years.

Thus, assuming entitlement, spousal support under the formula would be in the range of $1,500 to $2,000 per month for an indefinite (not specified) duration. This formula amount assumes the usual tax consequences, i.e. deductible to the payor and taxable to the recipient. It would also be open to the normal process of variation and review.

An award of $1,500 per month, at the low end of the range, would leave Ellen with a gross annual income of $48,000 and Arthur with one of $72,000. An award of $2,000 per month, at the high end of the range, would leave Ellen with a gross annual income of $54,000 and Arthur with one of $66,000. In

Chapter 9 we deal with the factors that determine the setting of a precise amount within that range.

On first glance, this formula no doubt looks like an entirely new approach to spousal support, far removed both from the *Divorce Act* and its spousal support objectives and factors and from the principles of compensatory and non-compensatory support that the Supreme Court of Canada articulated in *Moge* and *Bracklow*. Before we examine the operation and application of this formula in more detail, we explain the concept of "merger over time" that underlies this formula and how it relates to existing theories of spousal support and the current law. We will show that the formula is a "proxy measure" for factors such as economic disadvantage, need, and standard of living that are currently used to determine spousal support outcomes.

7.2 Merger over Time and Existing Theories of Spousal Support

The idea that underlies the *without child support* formula and explains sharing income in proportion to the length of the marriage is **merger over time**. We use this term[64] to capture the idea that as a marriage lengthens, spouses merge their economic and non-economic lives more deeply, with each spouse making countless decisions to mould his or her skills, behaviour and finances around those of the other spouse. Under the *without child support* formula, the income difference between the spouses represents their differential loss of the marital standard of living. The formulas for both amount and duration reflect the idea that the longer the marriage, the more the lower-income spouse should be protected against such a differential loss.

Under this formula, short marriages without children will generate very modest awards, both in terms of amount and duration. In cases where there are adequate resources, the support could be paid out in a single lump sum. Medium length marriages will generate transitional awards of varying lengths and in varying amounts, increasing with the length of the relationship. Long marriages will generate generous spousal support awards on an indefinite basis that will provide the spouses with something approaching equivalent standards of living after marriage breakdown. The formula generates the same ranges for long marriages in which the couple have never had children as for long marriages in which there have been children who are now grown.

While the label may be unfamiliar, the concept of merger over time, which relates the extent of the spousal support claim to the length of the marriage, underlies much of our current law. Its clearest endorsement can be found in Justice L'Heureux-Dubé's much-quoted passage from *Moge*:

> Although the doctrine of spousal support which focuses on equitable sharing does not guarantee to either party the marital standard of living enjoyed during the marriage, this standard is far from irrelevant to support entitlement … . As marriage should be regarded as a joint endeavour, the longer the relationship endures, the closer the economic union, the greater will be the presumptive claim to equal standards of living upon its dissolution.[65]

Merger over time offers an effective way of capturing both the compensatory and non-compensatory spousal support objectives that have been recognized by our law since *Moge* and *Bracklow*. Under our current law, both kinds of support claims have come to be analyzed in terms of loss of the marital standard of living. Budgets, and more specifically budgetary deficits, now play a central role in quantifying this drop in standard of living. Under the *without child support* formula, the spousal income difference serves as a convenient and efficient **proxy measure** for loss of the marital standard of living, replacing the uncertainty and imprecision of budgets. The length of marriage then determines the extent of the claim to be protected against this loss of the marital standard of living.

Merger over time can have a significant compensatory component. One of the common ways in which spouses merge their economic lives is by dividing marital roles to accommodate the responsibilities of child-rearing. Compensatory claims will loom large in one significant segment of marriages covered by the *without child support* formula—long marriages in which there were children of the marriage who are now independent

Compensatory claims, in theory, focus on the lower income spouse's loss of earning capacity, career development, pension benefits etc. as a result of having assumed primary responsibility for child care. However in practice, after *Moge*, courts began to respond to the difficulties of quantifying such losses with any accuracy, particularly in longer marriages, by developing proxy measures of economic loss that focussed on the marital standard of living. When awarding spousal support in cases involving long traditional marriages, courts began to articulate their goal as providing the lower income spouse with a reasonable standard of living as assessed against the marital standard of living. And increasingly the standard for determining spousal support in long marriages has become a rough equivalency of standards of living.

Merger over time also has a significant non-compensatory component. In cases of long traditional marriages where the children are grown, it is now common to see spousal support justified on a dual basis. Non-compensatory support claims based on dependency over a long period of time are commonly relied upon to supplement compensatory claims

64 We have taken this term from the American Law Institute (ALI) proposals which are referred to in Chapter 1 above and discussed in more detail in the Background Paper.

65 *Moge v. Moge*, [1992] 3 S.C.R. 813 at 870.

based on earning-capacity loss. In marriages where the spouses have never had children—the other segment of marriages covered by the *without child support* formula—spousal support claims are usually non-compensatory in nature, based on need, dependency, and loss of the marital standard of living. Merger over time addresses these non-compensatory claims.

Giving precise content to the concept of non-compensatory or needs-based support has been one of the main challenges in spousal support law since *Bracklow*. One reading of *Bracklow* suggests that non-compensatory support is grounded in the economic dependency or, in Justice McLachlin's words, the "interdependency" of the spouses. It recognizes the difficulties of disentangling lives that have been intertwined in complex ways over lengthy periods of time. On this broad reading of *Bracklow*, which many courts have accepted, need is not confined to situations of absolute economic necessity, but is a relative concept related to the previous marital standard of living.[66] On this view entitlement to non-compensatory support arises whenever a lower income spouse experiences a significant drop in standard of living after marriage breakdown as a result of loss of access to the other spouse's income, with amount and duration resolved by an individual judge's sense of fairness.

Merger over time incorporates this broad view of non-compensatory support and provides some structure for quantifying awards made on this basis.[67] It takes account not just of obvious economic losses occasioned by the marriage, but also of the elements of reliance and expectation that develop in spousal relationships and increase with the length of the relationship.

The *without child support* formula generates the same ranges for long marriages in which the couple have never had children as for long marriages in which there have been children who are now grown. This result, which flows from the merger over time principle, mirrors what we find in the current law—lengthy marriages involving economic dependency give rise to significant spousal support obligations without regard to the source of the dependency.

We recognize that in some specific situations the *without child support* formula, based as it is on the concept of merger over time which gives significant weight to the length of the marriage, may not adequately satisfy either compensatory or non-compensatory (needs-based) support objectives. Rather than modifying the formula, which in general works well across a wide-range of fact situations and incomes, we have dealt with these problems through exceptions—the exception for disproportionate compensatory claims in shorter marriages; the illness and disability exception, and the basic needs/undue hardship exception in short marriages. These exceptions are discussed in Chapter 12, below.

We now turn to a more detailed examination of the operation and application of the formula.

7.3 Determining the Length of the Relationship

The *without child support* formula relies upon length of marriage for determining both amount and duration of support. While we use the convenient term "length of marriage," the actual measure under the Advisory Guidelines is the **period of cohabitation**. This includes pre-marital cohabitation and ends with separation. Inclusion of pre-marital cohabitation in determining length of marriage is consistent with what most judges do now in determining spousal support. This way of defining length of marriage also makes the Advisory Guidelines more easily used under provincial spousal support laws, which apply to non-marital relationships.

We have not set precise rules for determining the length of marriage. The simplest approach would be to round up or down to the nearest full year, and this is what we have done in our examples. Another, slightly more complicated, approach would be to allow for half years and round up or down to that. Because the formula generates ranges and not a fixed number, absolute precision in the calculation of the length of the marriage is not required. Addition or subtraction of half a year will likely make little or no difference to the outcome.

7.4 The Formula for Amount

Several aspects of the formula for amount should be noted. First, this formula uses **gross income** (i.e. before tax) figures rather than net (i.e. after tax). (The determination of income is dealt with more fully in Chapter 6.) While net income figures may be marginally more accurate, familiarity and ease of calculation tipped the scales in favour of using gross income figures.[68] As you will see in Chapter 8, net income figures are

66 Some read *Bracklow* as grounding non-compensatory support in a "basic social obligation" theory of spousal support. This somewhat questionable theory, which is discussed in more detail in the Background Paper, understands need in the absolute sense of an inability to meet basic needs and grounds the obligation to meet that need in the status of marriage itself.

67 Building as it does on the concept of merger over time, the *without child support* formula does not directly incorporate the "basic social obligation" theory of non-compensatory support that some read *Bracklow* as supporting, see footnote immediately above. The *without child support* formula produces awards that will go some way toward meeting basic needs where they exist, but limits the extent of any basic social obligation by the length of the marriage. However, some of the exceptions identified in Chapter 12, such as the illness/disability exception and the basic needs/hardship exception in short marriages do provide some accommodation for elements of basic social obligation.

68 In the revision process we introduced one small element of a net income calculation—an "equalization of net income" cap on the formula, which is discussed below.

used under the *with child support* formula because of the need to deal with the differential tax treatment of spousal and child support.

Second, this formula applies a specified percentage to the **income difference** between the spouses rather than allocating specified percentages of the pool of combined spousal incomes. In applying income sharing to the spousal income difference this formula once again differs from the *with child support* formula where the use of net income figures requires a model of income sharing that applies to a combined pool of spousal incomes.

Third, the formula for amount does not use a fixed or flat percentage for sharing the income differential. Instead, drawing on the underlying concept of merger of time, the formula incorporates a **durational factor** to increase the percentage of income shared as the marriage increases in length.[69] The durational factor is 1.5 to 2 percent of the gross income difference for each year of marriage.

The **ranges for amount** were developed by first determining the point when maximum sharing would be reached, which we set at 25 years. We also started with the assumption that maximum sharing would involve something close to equalization of incomes, or sharing 50 percent of the gross income difference. We then essentially worked backwards to determine what level of income sharing per year would be required to reach maximum sharing at year 25. The answer was 2 percent per year. In the course of developing the formula, we experimented with different percentage ranges, but the range of 1.5 to 2 percent provided the best fit with outcomes under current practice.

We chose income equalization (50 per cent of the gross income difference) as the **maximum level of income sharing**, potentially reached after 25 years of marriage and representing the full merger of the spouses' lives. Much time was spent considering the arguments for a somewhat lower maximum to take into account incentive effects and the costs of going out to work in situations where only the payor is employed. However, we also recognized that there would be cases where equalization of income would be appropriate. For example where only pension income is being shared after a very long marriage, where both spouses are low income, or perhaps where both spouses are employed after a long marriage, but with a significant income disparity. We drafted the formula to allow for that possibility.

After the release of the Draft Proposal we sought feedback on the issue of whether the maximum level of sharing should be set lower than 50 percent of the gross income difference.

69 The concept of the durational factor is drawn from the ALI and Maricopa County guidelines; see Chapter 1.

We concluded that income equalization should be retained as the maximum level of sharing, but that it should be expressed as equalization of *net* incomes rather than of gross incomes. The formula has therefore been adjusted by capping the upper end of the maximum range at equalization of the spouses' net incomes—the **net income cap**.

7.4.1 The equalization of net income cap

In long marriages where the formula generates the maximum range of 37.5 to 50 percent of the gross income difference the recipient can end up with more than 50 per cent of the spouses' *net* income, notably where the payor spouse is still employed and subject to tax and employment deductions, and the recipient has little or no income. This result should never occur.

To avoid this result, shortly after the release of the Draft Proposal we began advising lawyers and judges to look closely at the net incomes of the spouses in these longer marriages when determining an appropriate amount within the range. We have now decided to modify the *without child support* formula itself by introducing a **net income cap. The recipient of spousal support should never receive an amount of spousal support that will leave him or her with more than 50 percent of the couple's net disposable income or monthly cash flow.**

Effectively, the introduction of the net income cap retains income equalization as the maximum level of sharing under the *without child support* formula. It simply provides for a more accurate calculation of income equalization. As for lowering the high end of the maximum range below equalization of net income, we concluded that the arguments that supported the initial choice of income equalization as the maximum level of sharing continued to be persuasive. As well, there was no obvious consensus around a lower percentage cap.

The software programs can calculate the "50 percent of net income" limit with precision and the formula range presented on the screen will reflect this limit at the upper end of the range. In computing "net income" for purposes of this cap, the permitted deductions would be federal and provincial income taxes, employment insurance premiums, Canada Pension Plan contributions, and any deductions that benefit the recipient spouse (e.g. medical or dental insurance, group life insurance and other benefit plans). Mandatory pension deductions are not permitted, for the same reasons as under the basic *with child support* formula, explained below in Chapter 8. Union dues and professional fees are already deducted from the spouses' gross incomes, consistent with the *Federal Child Support Guidelines* (see Chapter 6).

One of the advantages of the *without child support* formula is that the calculations can be done without a computer. For those without software, or more precise net income calculations, this net income cap can be calculated crudely by hand, at 48 percent of the gross income difference. This "48 percent" method is a second-best, but adequate, alternative.[70]

In thinking about the maximum level of sharing under this formula it is important to keep in mind that the formula does not **require** an award that would equalize spousal incomes after 25 years, but rather **permits** awards in the range of between 37.5 to 50 percent of the gross income difference (capped at net income equalization). Consistent with current law, the formula does not generate a general rule of income equalization; it simply provides for the possibility of equalization.

7.4.2 The problem of amount in short marriages

The feedback we received after the release of the Draft Proposal, combined with our continued reading of Guidelines cases, has confirmed that the ranges for amount generated by the *without child support* formula are "about right" and require no major adjustment beyond the net income cap.

We have generally found that the *without child support* formula works well, generating a reasonable range of outcomes across a wide range of cases from short to long marriages with varying incomes. The formula works extremely well for long marriages, which constitute the majority of the cases in which this formula is applied.[71] For medium length marriages, in some cases the monthly amounts need to be adjusted (i.e. increased) through restructuring (see Chapter 10), but we were well aware of this when we developed the formula. We placed heavy emphasis on restructuring to render the results of the formula consistent with current practice. These are also the cases—medium-length marriages without children—that frequently give rise to exceptions.

During the feedback process we did hear criticisms in some parts of the country that the amounts produced by the formula in shorter marriage cases were "too low."

In some of these cases, there was a failure to consider the **compensatory exception**—the exception for disproportionate compensatory claims in shorter marriages. In these cases, one spouse may have experienced a significant economic loss as a result of the marriage, by moving or by giving up employment, for example. Or, one spouse may have conferred an economic benefit on the other spouse by funding his or her pursuit of a professional degree or other education and training. This exception is considered in more detail in Chapter 12.

In other, non-compensatory cases, the formula was criticized as not providing enough support for the transition from the marital standard of living back to a lower standard of living based upon the recipient's earning ability. In these cases, involving marriages of less than 6 or 7 years, there is also little scope for much restructuring. This raised the issue of whether the structure of the formula needed to be fundamentally changed by increasing the percentage level of income-sharing in shorter marriages.

In the end, we concluded against any change to the basic structure of the formula. In the majority of cases across the country the formula works well for short marriages without children, which under current law typically give rise to very limited support obligations, if entitlement is found at all. The modest amounts generated by the formula are typically restructured into a lump sum or into a very short transitional award. In most of these cases, the recipient has a base income, which is supplemented by spousal support. In some parts of the country one does find more generous transitional awards providing the marital standard of living even after short marriages. This is a limited, regional pattern that is difficult to justify under the current principles that govern spousal support.

We do recognize, however, that there is a specific problem for shorter marriages where the recipient has little or no income. In these shorter marriage cases, the formula may generate too little support for the low income recipient even to meet her or his basic needs for a transitional period. The amount required to meet those basic needs will vary from big city to small city to town to rural area. Whether restructuring provides a satisfactory outcome, i.e. more support for a shorter time, will depend upon where the recipient lives. Thus the problem for these short-to-medium-marriage-low-income cases is most acute in big cities.

We did not wish to change the structure of the formula itself for this one sub-set of cases. The best approach to these cases was to create a carefully-tailored exception—the **basic needs/undue hardship exception for short marriages**—discussed further in Chapter 12 on Exceptions below.

7.5 The Formula for Duration

As with amount, duration under the *without child support* formula increases with the length of marriage. Subject to the provisions for indefinite support (duration not specified), the formula generates ranges for duration with the ends of the ranges determined as follows:

- **a minimum duration of half the length of the marriage and**
- **a maximum duration of the length of the marriage**.

70 The "48 percent" cap will work well in cases where the payor is working and the recipient is not. It will not necessarily be a good proxy for the equalization of net income cap where both parties are working; that will depend upon the spouses' respective tax rates and deductions.

71 This is true not only for long marriages/relationships in which there were children who are now adults, but also long marriages/relationships in which the parties had no children. See *Foley v. Girard*, [2006] O.J. No. 2496 (S.C.J.) which involved a 20 year same-sex relationship and *Long-Beck v. Beck*, [2006] N.B.J. No. 398, 2006 NBQB 317 which involved a 22 year marriage without children in which the wife quit work with the husband's consent.

It is important to remember, as discussed in Chapter 5 on application, that any periods of interim support are to be included in the durational ranges.

The ranges for duration under the *without child support* formula are admittedly very broad, allowing for an award at the top end of the range that is effectively double in value that at the bottom end. This will be particularly significant in medium-length marriages. Given the uncertainties in the current law on duration, it was not possible to come up with tighter ranges.

The formula also provides for indefinite support (duration not specified) in two circumstances:

- when the marriage has been 20 years or longer in length; or
- when the marriage has lasted five years or longer, **if the years of marriage plus the *age* of the support recipient *at the time of separation* equals or exceeds 65 and (the rule of 65)**.

The "rule of 65" recognizes that length of marriage cannot be the only factor in determining the duration of spousal support in marriages without dependent children. Age is also a significant factor as it affects the ability to become self-supporting.

7.5.1 The tendency to ignore duration

Our monitoring of the use of the Advisory Guidelines since the release of the Draft Proposal has shown that **in practice the durational aspect of the *without child support* formula is often ignored**. The formula is used to determine the amount of spousal support, but not duration. In some cases awards are for shorter periods of time than the formula suggests. In other cases the durational limits are ignored in favour of indefinite orders.

To ignore duration is to misapply the *without child support* formula. Amount and duration are interrelated parts of the formula—they are a package deal. Using one part of the formula without the other undermines its integrity and coherence. If the durational limits were to be systematically increased, for example, by lowering the threshold for indefinite support, the formula would have to be redesigned and the amounts decreased. Within the scheme of the Advisory Guidelines itself, adjustment of duration beyond the formula requires restructuring and will involve a corresponding adjustment of amount.

In what follows we discuss in more detail four aspects of the formula for duration under the *without child support* formula: indefinite support, the "rule of 65," time limits in short marriages, and time limits in medium-length marriages. The real problem of duration under this formula has proven to be this last aspect, the use of time limits in marriages that are neither long nor short.

7.5.2 The meaning of "indefinite" support

In using the term "indefinite" we simply adopted a word that had been used for years in spousal support law to mean "an order for support without a time limit at the time it is made." Under the Advisory Guidelines **an order for indefinite support does not necessarily mean permanent support, and it certainly does not mean that support will continue indefinitely at the level set by the formula**.

Under the current law, orders for indefinite support are open to variation as the parties' circumstances change over time and may also have review conditions attached to them. The Advisory Guidelines do nothing to change this: **"indefinite" support means support that is subject to the normal process of variation and review**.

Through the process of review and variation the amount of spousal support may be reduced, for example if the recipient's income increases or if the recipient fails to make reasonable efforts to earn income and income is imputed. Support may even be terminated if the basis for entitlement disappears. It is true that current law supports the idea that after long marriages spousal support will often be permanent, even if the amount is subject to reduction to reflect the recipient's obligation to pursue self-sufficiency.

In practice, however, most orders for indefinite support after long marriages will be significantly modified, if not eliminated, after the retirement of the payor and the receipt of pension income by the payor and the recipient. "Indefinite" often means "until the payor reaches 65." Variation and review in the context of the Advisory Guidelines are discussed in more detail in Chapter 14.

After the release of the Draft Proposal we were very surprised to learn from our feedback sessions that the term "indefinite" in the Advisory Guidelines was being misinterpreted by many as meaning "infinite" or "permanent."

We realized that we would have to develop a new term to express the concept that indefinite orders are not necessarily permanent, that they are subject to review and variation and, through that process, even to time limits and termination. Our solution has been to add "duration not specified" as a parenthetical explanation whenever the term "indefinite" is used in the formulas, i.e. **indefinite (duration not specified)**.

7.5.3 The "rule of 65": the age factor and indefinite support

The *without child support* formula provides that indefinite (duration not specified) support will be available even in cases where the marriage is shorter than 20 years **if the years of marriage plus the *age* of the support recipient *at the time of separation* equals or exceeds 65**. In a shorthand expression, we described this as the **"rule of 65."**

Thus, if a 10-year marriage ends when the recipient is 55, indefinite (duration not specified) support will be available because years of marriage (10) plus age (55) equals 65. Note that this is only a "rule" about duration, as the amount of support would be limited by the length of the marriage, i.e. 1.5 to 2 percent per year or 15 to 20 percent of the gross income difference in a 10-year marriage.

In reality, given the ages of the parties in the cases covered by the rule of 65, there will likely be significant changes in the amount of support ordered upon the retirement of one or both of the spouses. This refinement to the formula for duration is intended to respond to the situation of older spouses who were economically dependent during a medium length marriage and who may have difficulty becoming self-sufficient given their age.

The "rule of 65" for indefinite (duration not specified) support is not available in short marriages (under 5 years in length). The assumption in the current law is that short marriages generate only limited support obligations.

In the Draft Proposal, we struggled with the issue of whether an age component should always be required for indefinite (duration not specified) support—i.e. whether the "rule of 65" should apply even in long marriages. Under a 20-year rule with no age requirement, for example, a 38-year-old spouse leaving a 20-year marriage would be entitled to indefinite (duration not specified) support. Some would argue that indefinite (duration not specified) support is not appropriate for a spouse who is still relatively young and capable of becoming self-sufficient. If the "rule of 65" were generally applicable, support would not become indefinite (duration not specified) even after a 20-year marriage unless the recipient were 45 years of age or older.

Several considerations led us to the conclusion that a 20-year rule without any age requirement was the more appropriate choice. First, a spouse who married young and spent the next 20 years caring for children could be more disadvantaged than someone who married when they were older and had been able to acquire some job skills before withdrawing from the labour force. As well, under the current law it would be very difficult to impose a time-limit on support after a 20-year marriage, even if self-sufficiency and an eventual termination of support were contemplated at some point in the future. The typical order would be an indefinite order subject to review and/or variation. An order for indefinite support (duration not specified) under the Advisory Guidelines is no different.

Despite the frequent misinterpretation of the meaning of "indefinite," there was no pressure to change either of the conditions for indefinite support. Most of the feedback about the "rule of 65" focussed on technical issues of its application, as there was general agreement on the "rule."

7.5.4 Time limits in short marriages

The current law of spousal support has no difficulty with time limits in short marriages without children. Time limits, or lump sum orders, are common in these cases. Even in those jurisdictions where appeal courts have discouraged the use of time-limited support, discussed below, short marriages without children are identified as permissible exceptions. In practice, we were told in the feedback phase, these cases are not a problem.

7.5.5 Lowering the threshold for indefinite support?

In some parts of the country, it is very difficult to time limit spousal support, by reason of appellate decisions or local practices. For marriages of less than 20 years, the Draft Proposal incorporated time limits, although these were generous time limits. During the feedback phase, we did canvass the possibility of lowering the threshold for indefinite support, below 20 years.

We found little support for such a change. Even those who wanted to lower the threshold could not agree on what that new threshold should be. Many lawyers, mediators and judges expressed their frustration with the current law on duration, especially their perceived inability to use time limits in a sensible way. The durational limits in the Advisory Guidelines were seen as providing some structure for negotiations, initial decisions and variation or review. Lowering the threshold for indefinite support would not solve the problem and would in practice undermine the usefulness of the Guidelines.

7.5.6 The problem of time limits in medium length marriages

The real "problems" for time limits under the *without child support* formula are concentrated in marriages that are neither "long" (20 years or more) or "short" (under 5 years). For marriages that last 6 to 19 years, in every jurisdiction we were told, it becomes increasingly difficult to impose time limits on initial support orders as the marriage lengthens. At some point, in each jurisdiction, the time limits were seen as inconsistent with the current law on duration. At the same time, as we explained above, many lawyers, mediators and judges wanted to see more use of time limits.

It is certainly true that after *Moge* time limits fell into disfavour because of the associated problems of "crystal ball gazing" and arbitrary terminations of spousal support where self-sufficiency was "deemed" rather than actually achieved. Time-limited orders became less common. However, since *Bracklow*, some judges have brought back time limits, at least for non-compensatory support orders. While time limits are frequently negotiated by parties in agreements and consent orders, the law on time limits remains uncertain. In some parts of the country trial courts feel bound by appellate court rulings confining time-limited orders to a narrow range of exceptional cases, primarily short marriages without children.

It is in marriages of medium length that duration remains uncertain. Here practice varies and depends upon many factors—regional support cultures and the governing provincial appellate court jurisprudence; whether the context is negotiation or court-ordered support; and whether the support claim is compensatory or non-compensatory in nature. The most that can be said is that current law is inconsistent on the issue of time limits in medium-length marriages.

In practice the issue of duration in medium-length marriages is often put off to the future, to be dealt with through ongoing reviews and variations. In some cases this process of review and variation may eventually generate a time-limited order leading to termination. Under current practice uncertainty about duration can generate low monthly awards, as judges or lawyers fear that any monthly amount of support could continue for a long time, even permanently.

In developing the Draft Proposal, it was our view that reasonable time limits for medium length marriages would be an essential element of the scheme, under both the *without child support* and *with child support* formulas, especially if the Guidelines were to generate reasonable monthly amounts. *Bracklow* emphasized this interrelationship between amount and duration, recognizing that a low award paid out over a lengthy period of time is equivalent to an award for a higher amount paid out over a shorter period of time. As well, we were aware of the importance of providing structure in this area to facilitate negotiation and settlement. Recognizing that this was an area of law in flux, we saw a role for the Advisory Guidelines in helping to shape the developing law.

In assessing the compatibility of the time limits generated by the *without child support* formula with current law it is important to keep in mind that they are potentially very generous; in medium length marriages they can extend for up to 19 years. These time limits are thus very different from the short and arbitrary time limits, typically of between three to five years, that became standard under the clean-break model of spousal support for medium-to-long marriages and which *Moge* rejected. The time limits generated by the formula should be assessed in context—they are potentially for lengthy periods of time and, once marriages are of any significant length, operate in conjunction with generous monthly amounts.

As well, it is important to keep in mind that in the context of the *without child support* formula, support claims in medium-length marriages will typically be non-compensatory. In non-compensatory support cases, one strand of the post-*Bracklow* case law recognizes the appropriateness of time limited orders when the purpose of the support order is to provide a period of transition to a lower standard of living rather than compensation for lost career opportunities. Such use of time limits does not involve "crystal-ball gazing" and the making of arbitrary assumptions about future developments, but rather reflects the basis of entitlement.

In Chapter 8 you will see that we dealt with the issue of time limits in short and medium-length marriages with children somewhat differently, because of the strong compensatory claims in such cases and the need for individualized assessment of recipients' challenges in over-coming disadvantage resulting from the assumption of the child-rearing role.

We recognize that some provincial appellate court jurisprudence may at this point create barriers to the use of the formula's time-limits by trial judges. We also recognize that the lengthy time limits potentially generated under the *without child support* formula—up to 19 years in duration—are very different from the typical kinds of time limits with which our law of spousal support is familiar and raise some distinct problems of foreseeability. In our view, the law around time limits will continue to develop and to respond to the durational ranges under the formula. We already see signs of this in the Guidelines case law since the release of the Draft Proposal which offers several examples of judges making somewhat novel time-limited orders for the lengthy durations generated by the *without child support* formula.[72] In assessing the feasibility of these orders, it is important to remember that time-limited orders are subject to variation. It is thus possible to avoid some of the problems of arbitrary "crystal ball gazing" while reinforcing expectations with respect to the eventual termination of the support order.[73]

As well, in cases where it is not feasible for courts to impose the time limits generated by the formula in initial orders, the time limits can still be used in a "softer," more indirect way to structure the on-going process of review and variation and to reinforce expectations of the eventual termination of the order. This is not dissimilar to the use of the time limits under the *with child support* formula where they establish the outside limit for indefinite (duration not specified) orders. The fact that courts are reluctant to make time limited orders on initial applications does not preclude the eventual use of time limits on subsequent reviews or variations. The Guidelines case law already offers several examples of this "softer" use of

72 See for example, *Hance v. Carbone*, 2006 CarswellOnt 7063 (Ont.S.C.J.) (17½ yr. marriage; spousal support ordered for 15 years in addition to 6 years time-limited provided under separation agreement) and *Bishop v. Bishop*, [2005] N.S.J. No. 324, 2005 NSSC 220 (N.S.S.C.) (13 year marriage; final order spousal support for 10 years in addition to 1 year interim). For an example under the *with child support* formula, discussed in Chapter 8, see *Fewer v. Fewer*, [2005] N.J. No. 303, 2005 NLTD 163 (N.L.S.C.) (16½ yr. marriage; 1 child 15 with wife; spousal support ordered for 16½ yrs from separation, subject to variation).

73 The variation of time-limited orders is explicitly discussed in *Fewer, ibid.*

time limits in subsequent variations or reviews to bring an eventual termination to what was initially an indefinite order.[74]

Finally, if the durational limits under this formula, even in their "softer" form, are found to be inappropriate in cases close to the 20 year threshold for indefinite support, restructuring can be used to extend duration. As is explained in Chapter 10, duration can be extended by restructuring so long as an appropriate downward adjustment is made to amount so as to keep the total value of the award within the global ranges generated by the formula.

7.6 Making the Formula Concrete—Some Examples

7.6.1 A short-marriage example

In cases of short marriages, marriages of less than 5 years, the *without child support* formula generates very small amounts for a very short duration. The formula will always generate time-limits in these cases.[75]

Example 7.2

Karl and Beth were married for only four years. They had no children. Beth was 25 when they met and Karl was 30. When they married, Beth was a struggling artist. Karl is a music teacher with a gross annual income of $60,000. Beth now earns $20,000 per year, selling her work and giving art lessons to children. Entitlement is a threshold issue before the Advisory Guidelines apply. On these facts, given the disparity in income and Beth's limited income at the point of marriage breakdown, entitlement is likely to be found.

The conditions for indefinite (duration not specified) support do not apply and duration would be calculated on the basis of .5 to 1 year of support for each year of marriage.

To determine the **amount** of support under the formula:

- Determine the **gross income difference** between the parties:

  $60,000 – $20,000 = $40,000
- Determine the **applicable percentage** by multiplying the length of the marriage by 1.5–2 percent per year:

  1.5 × 4 years = **6 percent**

  to

  2 × 4 years = **8 percent**
- Apply the applicable percentage to the income difference:

  6 percent × $40,000 = $2,400/year (**$200/month**)

  to

  8 percent × $40,000 = $3,200/year (**$267/month**)

Duration of spousal support = (.5–1) × 4 years of marriage = 2 to 4 years

The result under the formula is support in the range of $200 to $267 per month for a duration of 2 to 4 years.

In practice, this modest award would likely be converted into a lump sum using **restructuring**, discussed in Chapter 10.

7.6.2 Some medium-length marriage examples

In medium-length marriages (5 to 19 years), the formula generates increasing amounts of support as the marriage increases in length, moving from relatively small percentages at the shorter end of the spectrum to relatively generous amounts after 15 years, when awards of 30 percent of the gross income difference become possible. Except where the rule of 65 is applicable, the formula generates time limits of varying lengths depending on the length of the marriage. The ranges for duration are, however, very wide, leaving much opportunity to respond to the facts of particular cases.

This category covers a diverse array of cases raising a variety of support objectives. Current law is at its most inconsistent in its handling of these cases. This area posed the greatest challenges to developing a single formula that would yield appropriate results. We concluded that our formula based on merger over time provided the best starting point. But not surprisingly, it is in these cases that there will be the most frequent need to rely upon restructuring to massage the formula outcomes and where there will likely be the greatest resort to exceptions.

74 One of the best examples is *Kelly v. Kelly*, [2007] B.C.J. No. 324, 2007 BCSC 227 (17 year relationship, no children, support paid for 9 years; wife remarried; on variation application support recognized as non-compensatory; time-limited to further 19 months, 10 years total.) Another good example under the *custodial payor* formula is *Puddifant v. Puddifant*, [2005] N.S.J. No. 558, 2005 NSSC 340 (S.C.F.D.) (12 year marriage, 1 child with husband, wife mental illness, support paid for 9 years; on husband's application to terminate support ordered for further 3 years, total 12 years.)

75 The "rule of 65," which allows for indefinite support to older spouses in marriages of less than 20 years in length, does not apply to short marriages (under 5 years).

Example 7.3

Bob and Susan have been married 10 years. They married in their late twenties and Sue is now 38. Bob is employed as a computer salesman and Sue is a hairdresser. Both worked throughout the marriage. There were no children. Bob's gross annual income is $65,000; Sue's is $25,000.

Entitlement is a threshold issue before the Advisory Guidelines are applicable. An argument might be made that there is no entitlement to support: Sue is employed full time and could support herself, and there is no compensatory basis for support. However, Sue will suffer a significant drop in standard of living as result of the marriage breakdown and, at an income of $25,000, will likely experience some economic hardship. Current law would suggest an entitlement to at least transitional support on a non-compensatory basis to allow Sue to adjust to a lower standard of living.

The case does not satisfy the conditions for indefinite (duration not specified) support. The marriage is under 20 years and the case does not fall within the "rule of 65" for indefinite support because Sue's age at separation plus years of marriage is below 65 (38 + 10 = 48).

To determine the amount of support under the formula:

- Determine the **gross income difference** between the parties:

  $65,000 – $25,000 = $40,000

- Determine the **applicable percentage** by multiplying the length of the marriage by 1.5–2 percent per year:

  1.5 × 10 years = **15 percent**

  to

  2 × 10 years = **20 percent**

- Apply the **applicable percentage** to the income difference:

  15 percent × $40,000 = $6,000/year (**$500/month**)

  to

  20 percent × $40,000 = $8,000/year (**$667/month**)

Duration of spousal support = (.5–1) × 10 years of marriage = 5 to 10 years

The result under the formula is support in the range of $500 to $667 per month for a duration of 5 to 10 years.

Consistent with current law, the formula essentially generates modest top-up support for a transitional period to assist Sue in adjusting from the marital standard of living.

An award of $500 per month, at the low end of the range, would leave Sue with a gross annual income of $31,000 and Bob with one of $59,000. An award of $667 per month, at the high end of the range, would leave Sue with a gross annual income of $33,000 and Bob with one of $57,000. In a marriage of this length the formula does not equalize incomes.

Some might find the amounts generated by the formula too low, even at the high end of the range. An argument could be made that, consistent with current law, any transitional order should put Sue somewhat closer to the marital standard of living for the period of gearing down. As will be discussed in Chapter 10, a **restructuring** of the formula outcome is possible to produce larger amounts for a shorter duration.

Example 7.4

David and Jennifer were married for 12 years. It was a second marriage for both. David was 50 when they met. He is a businessman whose gross annual income is now $100,000 per year. Now 62, he is in good health, loves his work, and has no immediate plans to retire. Jennifer was 45 when they met, while Jennifer was working in his office. She had been a homemaker for 20 years during her first marriage and had received time-limited support. When they met she was working in a low-level clerical position earning $20,000 gross per year. Jennifer, now 57, did not work outside the home during the marriage.

Entitlement is a threshold issue before the Advisory Guidelines are applicable. Given the length of the marriage and Jennifer's lack of income, entitlement to support on non-compensatory grounds would be relatively uncontentious.

The **amount** of support on an income difference of $100,000 and a 12 year marriage would be calculated as follows:

18 percent × $100,000 = $18,000/year (**$1,500/month**)

to

24 percent × $100,000 = $24,000/year (**$2,000/month**)

This is a case where the "rule of 65" would govern duration. Because Jennifer's age at separation plus years of marriage is 65 or over (57 + 12 = 69), the formula provides for indefinite (duration not specified) support, rather than the durational range of 6 to 12 years based on length of marriage alone. A variation in amount would, however, be likely when David retires.

The result under the formula is support in the range of $1,500 to $2,000 a month on an indefinite (duration not specified) basis, subject to variation and possibly review.

Support at the low end of the range would leave Jennifer with a gross annual income of $18,000 and David with one of $72,000. Support at the high end of the range would leave Jennifer with a gross annual income of $24,000 and David with one of $66,000. Again, because of the length of the marriage (12 years), the formula does not generate results that approach income equalization.

7.6.3 Some long-marriage examples

In cases of long marriages (20 years or longer) the formula generates generous levels of spousal support for indefinite periods, reflecting the fairly full merger of the spouses' lives. The long marriages covered by the *without child support* formula fall into two categories: those where there have been children who are no longer dependent and those where the couple did not have children.

Example 7.1 provides an example of the formula's application to a long marriage with children where the wife was a secondary earner. *Example 7.5*, presented below, involves the familiar scenario of a very long traditional marriage.

Example 7.5

John and Mary were married for 28 years. Theirs was a traditional marriage in which John worked his way up the career ladder and now earns $100,000 gross per year, while Mary stayed home and raised their two children, both of whom are now grown up and on their own. Mary is 50 years of age and has no income. John is 55.

Entitlement to spousal support is clear on these facts and thus the Advisory Guidelines are applicable. Because the length of the marriage is over 25 years, the maximum range for amount applies—37.5 to 50 percent of the gross income difference (capped at equalization of net incomes).

The range for amount on an income difference of $100,000 after a 28 year marriage would be:

37.5 percent × $100,000 = $37,500/year (**$3,125/month**)

to

50 percent × $100,000 = $50,000/year (**$4,167/month, capped at $4048**[76])

Duration is indefinite (duration not specified) because the marriage is 20 years or over in length.

The formula results in a range for support of $3,125 to $4,048 per month for an indefinite (unspecified) duration, subject to variation and possibly review.

An award of $3,125 per month, at the low end of the range, would leave Mary with a gross income of $37,500 per year and John with one of $62,500. An award of $4,048 per month, at the high end of the range, would equalize the net incomes of the parties.

As will be discussed further in Chapter 14, the order is open to variation over time in response to changes in the parties' circumstances, including increases in Mary's income or the imputation of income to her if she fails to make reasonable efforts to contribute to her own support. John's retirement would also likely be grounds for variation.

Example 7.6 involves a long marriage without children.

Example 7.6

Richard is a teacher with a gross annual income of $75,000. He is in his late forties. His wife, Judy, is the same age. She trained as a music teacher but has worked as a freelance violinist for most of the marriage, with a present gross income of $15,000 a year. Judy has also been responsible for organizing their active social life and extensive vacations. They were married 20 years. They had no children.

Entitlement will easily be established in this case given the significant income disparity, Judy's limited employment income, and the length of the marriage.

The range for amount under the formula, based on income difference of $60,000 and a 20 year marriage is:

30 percent × $60,000 = $18,000/year (**$1,500/month**)

to

40 percent × $60,000 = $24,000/year (**$2,000/month**)

Duration would be indefinite (duration not specified) because the marriage was 20 years in length.

The result under the formula is support in the range from of $1,500 to $2,000 per month for an indefinite (unspecified) duration, subject to variation and possibly review.

An award at the lower end of the range would leave Judy with a gross annual income of $33,000 and Richard with one of $57,000. An award at the high end of the range would leave

76 This is based on an assumption of Ontario residence and the applicable tax rates and mandatory deductions in November 2007.

Judy with a gross annual income of $39,000 and Richard with one of $51,000.

Judy will certainly be expected to increase her income and contribute to her own support. The issue in applying the formula will be whether a gross income of $30,000 a year, for example, should be attributed to Judy for the purposes of an initial determination of support. If so, support under the formula would be lowered to a range of $1,125 to $1,500 per month (or $13,500 to $18,000 per year).

More likely, Judy would be given some period of time (for example one or two years) before she would be expected to earn at that level, with support to be adjusted at that point, after a review.

7.7 After the Formula

As the examples in this chapter indicate, many issues remain after the application of the *without child support* formula—issues of choosing an amount and duration within the ranges, restructuring, and exceptions, all addressed in separate chapters below. It is important to keep these other parts of the Advisory Guidelines in mind, particularly in cases involving the *without child support* formula where restructuring and exceptions will frequently need to be used.

8 THE WITH CHILD SUPPORT FORMULA

The dividing line between the two proposed formulas under the Advisory Guidelines is the presence of a child support obligation.[77] Where the spouses have not had children or the children have grown up and are on their own, the *without child support* formula will apply. Where a spouse is paying child support, the *with child support* formula will apply.

From a technical perspective, there must be a different formula for spousal support in these cases, a formula that takes into account the payment of child support and its priority over spousal support as set out in s. 15.3 of the *Divorce Act*. Further, because of tax and benefit issues, we have to use net rather than gross incomes. Practically, the payment of child support usually means reduced ability to pay spousal support. And, theoretically, there are different rationales for the amount and duration of spousal support where there are still dependent children to be cared for and supported.

This category of cases dominates in practice, in support statistics and in jurisprudence. Any guidelines must generate a workable formula for amount and duration for this category, a formula that can adjust across a wide range of incomes and family circumstances. For the most part, marriages with dependent children will involve spousal support paid by a parent who is also paying child support to the recipient spouse. The basic formula in this chapter is constructed around this typical situation. Variations on the basic formula are required to accommodate cases of shared and split custody. There are also a sizeable number of cases where the spouse paying spousal support has primary parental responsibility for the children. In these custodial payor situations, an alternative formula must be constructed. Finally, we have added one more hybrid formula, applicable in cases where the only remaining children are away at university or otherwise have their child support determined under section 3(2)(b) of the *Child Support Guidelines*.

The *with child support* formula is thus really a family of formulas, adjusted for different parenting arrangements.

8.1 The Compensatory Rationale for Spousal Support

Where there are dependent children, the primary rationale for spousal support is compensatory. After *Moge*, spouses must, as Chief Justice McLachlin put it in *Bracklow*, "compensate each other for foregone careers and missed opportunities during the marriage upon the breakdown of their union."[78] The main reason for those foregone careers and missed opportunities is the assumption of primary responsibility by one spouse for the care of children during the marriage. Where one spouse, in a marriage with children, has become a full-time homemaker or has worked outside the home part time or has worked as a secondary earner, there will be disadvantage and loss at the end of the marriage, usually warranting compensatory support. This compensatory rationale is encompassed by the first of the four objectives of spousal support, in s. 15.2(6)(a) of the *Divorce Act*.

Under compensatory theory, it is usually necessary to estimate the spouse's disadvantage or loss by determining what the recipient's career or employment path might have been, had the recipient not adopted his or her role during the marriage—not an easy task. The ideal evidence would be individualized economic evidence of earning capacity loss, but few litigants can afford such evidence and often it would be highly speculative. Some spouses never establish a career or employment history. For others, their pre-marital and marital choices were shaped by their future expected role during marriage. And there are short marriages, where past losses are relatively small and most of the spouse's child-rearing and any associated losses are still to come in the future.

As was explained in Chapter 1, after *Moge*, courts had to develop proxies to measure that loss where there was no clear and specific career or employment path. Need became the most common proxy, calculated through the conventional budget analysis. Sometimes standard of living was used, with

77 The child support obligation must be for a child of the marriage. A child support obligation to a child from a prior marriage or relationship is dealt with as an exception under both formulas, explained in more detail in Chapter 12 on Exceptions below.

78 *Bracklow v. Bracklow*, [1999] 1 S.C.R. 420 at para. 1.

the post-separation position of the recipient spouse measured against the marital standard or some reasonable standard of living. In practice, crude compromises were made in applying the compensatory approach.

More recently, what we have called the **parental partnership** rationale has emerged in the literature and in the case law. On this approach, the obligation for spousal support flows from parenthood rather than the marital relationship itself. It is not the length of the marriage, or marital interdependency, or merger over time, that drives this theory of spousal support, but the presence of dependent children and the need to provide care and support for those children. Unlike the conventional compensatory approach, parental partnership looks at not just past loss, but also the continuing economic disadvantage that flows from present and future child-care responsibilities. For shorter marriages with younger children, these present and future responsibilities are more telling. Further, the parental partnership rationale better reflects the reality that many women never acquire a career before marriage, or mould their pre-marital employment in expectation of their primary parental role after marriage.

The parental partnership rationale is firmly anchored in one of the four statutory objectives in s. 15.2(6) of the *Divorce Act*, where clause (b) states a spousal support order should:

> apportion between the spouses any financial consequences arising from the care of any child of the marriage over and above any obligation for the support of any child of the marriage.

The 1997 implementation of the *Federal Child Support Guidelines* has reinforced this rationale. Under the Guidelines, only the direct costs of child-rearing—and not even all of them—are included in child support. The indirect costs of child-rearing were left to be compensated through spousal support, as was recognized by the 1995 Family Law Committee's *Report and Recommendations on Child Support*. Principal amongst these indirect costs is the custodial parent's reduced ability to maximize his or her income because of child-care responsibilities. Now that child support is fixed under the *Child Support Guidelines* and determined by a different method than before 1997, spousal support has to be adjusted to reflect the concerns identified by the parental partnership model.

With the implementation of the *Federal Child Support Guidelines* came the increased use of computer software. The software regularly and graphically displays information like net disposable income, monthly cash flow and household standards of living. This information has made spouses, lawyers, mediators and courts more conscious of the financial implications of child and spousal support, in turn reflected in the use of these concepts in determining the amount of spousal support. Before the *Federal Child Support Guidelines*, and even afterwards for a while, most courts were not prepared to award more than 50 percent of the family's net disposable income to the recipient spouse and children, leaving the single payor spouse with the other 50 percent. With the new software, many courts began consciously to allocate more than 50 percent of a family's net disposable income to the recipient spouse and children, and even as much as 60 percent, as in the Ontario Court of Appeal decision in *Andrews v. Andrews*[79] and in numerous trial decisions across the country.[80]

These cases also reveal a non-compensatory element found in some decisions where both child and spousal support are paid to the same parent. There is a household standard of living element within the parental partnership rationale that should be openly acknowledged. Both child and spousal support go into the same household, to support the standard of living of both parent and child. In some cases, spousal support is used as a residual financial remedy to shore up the standard of living that the children experience in the recipient's household.

8.2 Background to the Basic Formula

There is no simple way to construct a formula for spousal support where the support payor is also paying child support. First, child support must be determined, as it takes priority over spousal support in assessing the payor's ability to pay. Second, child support is not taxable or deductible, but spousal support is taxable to the recipient and deductible for the payor. Third, child and spousal support must be determined separately, but it is very difficult in any formula to isolate spousal finances cleanly from support of children.

This formula for cases with child support—the *with child support* formula—differs from the *without child support* formula set out in Chapter 7. First, the *with child support* formula uses the **net incomes** of the spouses, not their gross incomes. Second, the *with child support* formula divides the **pool** of combined net incomes between the two spouses, not just the difference between the spouses' gross incomes. Third, in the *with child support* formula, the upper and lower percentage limits for net income division **do not change with the length of the marriage**.

Unlike the *without child support* formula, this formula must use **net income**. While gross income would be simpler to understand, calculate and implement, nothing remains simple once child support has to be considered. Different tax treatment demands more detailed after-tax calculations, and

79 *Andrews v. Andrews* (1999), 50 R.F.L. (4th) 1 (Ont. C.A.).

80 See for example *Gale v. Gale* (2000), 6 R.F.L. (5th) 157 (Man. Q.B.), *Bastedo v. Bastedo*, [2000] P.E.I.J. No. 49 (S.C.T.D.), *Lyttle v. Bourget*, [1999] N.S.J. No. 298 (S.C.), *Tedham v. Tedham*, [2002] B.C.J. No. 1635 (S.C.), *Clark v. Cooper-Clark*, [2002] N.B.J. No. 41 (Q.B.).

ability to pay must be more accurately assessed. Net income computations will usually require computer software, another unavoidable complication.

Thanks to that same computer software, many lawyers had become familiar with net disposable income or monthly cash flow calculations before the release of the Draft Proposal. Judges were using such calculations to underpin their spousal support decisions. In the software programs, these numbers included child and spousal support to produce what can be called **family net disposable income** or monthly cash flow. This larger pool of net income is then divided between the spouses. Often, more than 50 percent of this family net disposable income is allocated to the recipient spouse and children by way of combined child and spousal support, or sometimes as much as 60 percent and occasionally even more. Under the formula proposed here for spousal support, we divide a different and smaller pool of net income, after removing the spouses' respective child support obligations—what we call **individual net disposable income** or **INDI**.

We considered using the more familiar family net disposable income as the basis for the *with child support* formula, rather than this newer variation of individual net disposable income. In the end we opted for individual net disposable income. First, the family net disposable income of the recipient spouse includes both child and spousal support, bulking up the recipient's income in a somewhat misleading fashion and masking the impact of spousal support upon the recipient parent's individual income. Second, allocating family NDI between spouses blurs the distinction between child and spousal support, between child and adult claims upon income. Individual NDI attempts to back out the child support contributions of each spouse, to obtain a better estimate of the income pool that remains to be divided between the adults. Third, after separation, the spouses see themselves, not as one family, but more as individuals with distinct relationships with their children and their former spouses. Fourth, separating out each spouse's individual net disposable income, after removal of child support obligations, produced a more robust and sophisticated formula, one that adjusted better across income levels and numbers of children.

8.3 The Basic Formula

Set out in the box below is a summary of how this basic *with child support* formula works. Remember that this formula applies where the higher income spouse is paying both child and spousal support to the lower income spouse who is also the primary parent. By primary parent, we mean the spouse with sole custody or the spouse with primary care of the children in a joint custody arrangement.

The Basic *With Child Support* Formula for Amount

(1) Determine the **individual net disposable income (INDI)** of each spouse:

- Guidelines Income *minus* Child Support *minus* Taxes and Deductions = Payor's INDI
- Guidelines Income *minus* Notional Child Support *minus* Taxes and Deductions *plus* Government Benefits and Credits = Recipient's INDI

(2) Add together the individual net disposable incomes. By iteration, determine the range of spousal support amounts that would be required to leave the lower income recipient spouse with between 40 and 46 per cent of the combined INDI.

8.3.1 Calculating individual net disposable income

Basic to this formula is the concept of **individual net disposable income**, an attempt to isolate a **pool** of net disposable income available after adjustment for child support obligations.

The starting point is the Guidelines income of each spouse as is explained in Chapter 6 above. In the interests of uniformity and efficiency, we basically use the same definition of income as that found in the *Federal Child Support Guidelines*. Next, we deduct or back out from each spouse's income their respective **contributions to child support**.

For the child support **payor**, that is usually the table amount, plus any contributions to special or extraordinary expenses, or any other amount fixed under any other provisions of the *Federal Child Support Guidelines*. For the child support **recipient**, a **notional table amount** is deducted, plus any contributions by the recipient spouse to s. 7 expenses. In reality, the recipient will likely spend more than these amounts through direct spending for the children in her or his care. But by this means we make an adjustment, however imperfect, for the recipient's child support obligation. A formula could be constructed without this notional child support number, but such a formula would have adjusted to the number of children and income levels with less precision and with less transparency about the role of the recipient parent.

Second, **income taxes and other deductions** must be subtracted from the incomes of both the payor and the recipient to obtain net incomes. As spousal support is transferred from one spouse to another, because of tax effects, the size of the total pool of individual net disposable income actually changes slightly, which complicates these calculations. The current software does these calculations automatically, as differing hypothetical amounts of spousal support are transferred, a process called "iteration."

Clearly permissible **deductions** are federal and provincial income taxes, as well as employment insurance premiums and Canada Pension Plan contributions. Union dues and professional fees are already deducted from Guidelines income under the adjustments of Schedule III to the *Federal Child Support Guidelines*. Deductions should be recognized for certain benefits, e.g. medical or dental insurance, group life insurance, and other benefit plans, especially those that provide immediate or contingent benefits to the former spouse or the children of the marriage.

More contentious are **deductions for mandatory pension contributions**. We concluded that there should **not** be an automatic deduction for such pension contributions, but the size of these mandatory deductions may sometimes be used as a factor to justify fixing an amount towards the lower end of the spousal support range.

We reached this conclusion after considerable discussion. Like EI, CPP and other deductions, pension contributions are mandatory deductions, in that the employee has no control over, and no access to, that money. But, unlike other deductions, pension contributions are a form of forced saving that permit the pension member to accumulate an asset. Further, after separation, the spouse receiving support does not usually share in the further pension value being accumulated by post-separation contributions. Finally, there are serious problems of horizontal equity in allowing a deduction for mandatory pension contributions by employees. What about payors with non-contributory pension plans or RRSPs or those without any pension scheme at all? And what about the recipient spouse—would we have to allow a notional or actual deduction for the recipient too, to reflect her or his saving for retirement? In the end, we decided it was fairer and simpler **not** to allow an automatic deduction for pension contributions.

Third, we **do include** in each spouse's income the amounts identified for **government benefits and refundable credits**. Included are the Child Tax Benefit, the National Child Benefit Supplement, the GST credit, the refundable medical credit, the Child Disability Benefit, the various provincial benefit and credit schemes, and the new Universal Child Care Benefit. Under the *Federal Child Support Guidelines* these benefits and credits are generally **not** treated as income. For the reasons set out in Chapter 6 on Income above, a different approach is warranted for spousal support purposes.

8.3.2 The Basic Formula: Dividing Individual Net Disposable Income

Once the individual net disposable income (INDI) of each spouse has been determined, the next step is to add together these individual net disposable incomes. Then we have to iterate, i.e. to estimate hypothetical spousal support repeatedly, in order to determine the amount of spousal support that will leave the lower income recipient spouse with between 40 and 46 percent of the combined pool of individual net disposable income.

How did we arrive at the percentages for the range, from 40 to 46 percent of the individual net disposable income? This was a critical issue in the construction of this formula. In our earlier Sneak Preview in the summer of 2004, we had suggested a higher range, from 44 to 50 percent of INDI. We ultimately opted for a lower range, after much discussion with the Advisory Working Group, some limited feedback from the Sneak Preview, further reviews of the case law in various provinces, and some more hard thought about the upper and lower bounds for these ranges. Since the release of the Draft Proposal and after our meetings across Canada, we can confirm that this percentage range is appropriate.

We found that a range of 40 to 46 percent of individual net disposable income typically covered spousal support outcomes in the **middle** of the very wide range of outcomes now observed in most Canadian provinces. To capture the middle of the range on a national basis means that some areas will find the upper bound (46 percent) a bit low and other areas will consider even the lower bound (40 percent) at the higher end of their local range.

Prior to the Sneak Preview, we had experimented with a range of 40 to 50 percent of INDI. But that produced far too broad a range in absolute dollar terms. One of the objectives of the Advisory Guidelines is to develop more predictability and consistency in spousal support outcomes and a ten-percentage point range simply failed to do that. A narrower five or six percentage point range is about right.

The lower boundary of this range—40 percent of INDI—does ensure that the recipient spouse will receive not less than 50 percent of the family net disposable income in all cases involving two or more children, and slightly below that in one-child cases.

The upper end of this range—46 percent of INDI—falls short of an equal split, which would leave both spouses in the same individual position. Despite the intellectual attraction of a 50/50 split, there are a number of practical problems that convinced us that it was not appropriate to set the upper limit of the range there. First, very few courts are currently prepared to push spousal support amounts that high. Second, there is a live concern for the access-related expenses of the payor spouse, expenses that are not otherwise reflected in the formula. Most payors are exercising access and most are spending directly upon their children during the time they spend with their children. Third, there are concerns for the payor in the situation where the payor has employment-related expenses and the recipient spouse is at home full time and receiving large spousal support.

We should repeat here a central difference between this formula and the *without child support* formula: **the length of the marriage does not affect the upper and lower percentages in this *with child support* formula**.

We also wish to stress the inter-relationship between the percentage limits and the precise elements of our version of individual net disposable income. If a notional table amount were not removed from the recipient spouse's income, or if government benefits and refundable credits were excluded, then the formula percentages would have to change. Our objective throughout has been to develop formulas that can capture the bulk of current outcomes, while at the same time demonstrating robustness in adjusting across incomes and child support amounts and custodial situations.

As a result of computer software, lawyers and courts became accustomed to calculating net disposable income or monthly cash flow on a *family* basis: the payor's net disposable income after deduction of child and spousal support and taxes, and the recipient's after addition of child and spousal support (and deduction of taxes). How do these more familiar family net disposable income percentages compare to our range of individual net disposable income divisions? Typically, the 46 percent of INDI at the upper end of our proposed formula generates a family net disposable income for the primary parent spouse of 56 to 58 percent where there are two children. At the lower end of the range, a spousal support amount that leaves the recipient spouse with 40 percent of INDI will typically leave that spouse and the two children with 52 or 53 percent of the family net disposable income. For comparison purposes, we have provided family net disposable income proportions in the examples below.

We recognize that Quebec has a different scheme of determining child support, which in turn has implications for fixing spousal support. The application of the Advisory Guidelines in divorce cases in Quebec is dealt with in more detail in Chapter 15.

8.4 Amounts of Spousal Support: Examples of the Basic Formula

At this point it helps to give a few examples of the ranges of monthly spousal support generated by this basic formula. Then we will move to the issue of duration. For illustration purposes, we assume that these parents and children all live in Ontario, as the use of one jurisdiction simplifies the exposition of the formula's operation.

In the earlier Draft Proposal, the formula calculations were done partially with software and partially by hand. With the release of the Draft Proposal, Canada's three major family law software suppliers incorporated the Spousal Support Advisory Guidelines into their programs, so that the calculations can be done easily and with greater precision. In addition, the ranges for amount have changed since the January 2005 release of the Draft Proposal, due to changes in child support table amounts in May 2006, various changes to federal and provincial taxes and changes in child benefits. The result is that the numbers in these examples are different from those set out in the Draft Proposal.

Example 8.1

Ted and Alice have separated after 11 years together. Ted works at a local manufacturing plant, earning $80,000 gross per year. Alice has been home with the two children, now aged 8 and 10, who continue to reside with her after separation. After the separation, Alice found work, less than full time, earning $20,000 gross per year. Alice's mother provides lunch and after-school care for the children, for nothing, when Alice has to work. Ted will pay the table amount for child support, $1,159 per month. Alice's notional table amount would be $308. There are no s. 7 expenses (if there were, the spousal amounts would be lower).

Under the formula, Ted would pay spousal support in the range of $474 to $1,025 per month.

Using the family net disposable income figures (or the similar monthly cash flow figures) more familiar to current software users, spousal support of $1,025 monthly along with the child support would leave Alice and the children with $4,003 per month and Ted with $2,976 per month, or 57.4 per cent of the family's net disposable income in favour of Alice and the children. At the lower end of the range, with spousal support of $474 per month, the net disposable income of the family would be split 52.6/47.4 in favour of Alice and the children, leaving Ted with $3,326 monthly and Alice and the children with $3,684. The amount of spousal support is obviously affected by the **number of children**. If Ted and Alice had only one child, the spousal support range would be higher, from $888 to $1,463 per month. If the couple had three children, Ted's ability to pay would be reduced, bringing the range down to $79 to $626 monthly. Four children would lower that range even further, down to a range from zero to $222 per month.

The spousal support range will also be lowered by any payment of section 7 expenses. In our *Example 8.1*, if Alice were paying child care expenses of $8,000 per year for the two children and Ted paid his proportionate share of the net cost, the formula range would reduce to $319 to $925 per month for spousal support.

Example 8.2

Bob and Carol have separated after eight years of marriage and two children, now aged 4 and 6, who are both living with Carol. Bob earns $40,000 gross annually at a local building supply company, while Carol has found part-time work, earning $10,000 per year. Carol's mother lives with Carol and provides care for the children when needed. Bob pays the table amount of $601 per month for the children. Carol's notional table amount of child support would be $61 per month. There are no s. 7 expenses.

Under the formula, Bob would pay spousal support in the range of zero to $34 per month.

Again, by way of comparison to the more familiar numbers, if Bob were to pay child support of $601 and spousal support of $34 monthly, at the upper end of the range, he would be left with $1,951 per month, while Carol and the two children would have *family* net disposable income of $2,325 monthly, or 54.4 percent of the family's net disposable income.

Example 8.3

Drew and Kate have been married for four years. Drew earns $70,000 gross per year working for a department store. Kate used to work as a clerk in the same store, but she has been home since their first child was born. The children are now 1 and 3, living with Kate. Kate has no Guidelines income (and hence there is no notional table amount for her). Drew will pay the table amount of $1,043 per month for the two children.

Under the formula, Drew would pay spousal support to Kate in the range of $908 to $1,213 per month.

If Drew were to pay spousal support of $1,213 monthly, he would have $2,394 per month, while Kate and the children would have *family* net disposable income of $3,084 monthly, or 56.3 percent of the total family NDI. At the lower end of the range, spousal support of $908 per month would leave Drew with $2,604 in family NDI, while Kate and the children would have $2,780 monthly, or 51.6 percent of the family's NDI.

The formula generates ranges for the amount of spousal support. Chapter 9 below discusses the factors to be considered in fixing a particular amount within the ranges.

8.5 Duration under the Basic Formula

In most cases where there are dependent children, the courts order "indefinite" spousal support, usually subject to review or sometimes just left to variation. Even when the recipient spouse is expected to become self-sufficient in the foreseeable future, courts typically have not often imposed time limits in initial support orders. Where the recipient spouse is not employed outside the home, or is employed part-time, the timing of any review is tied to the age of the children, or to some period of adjustment after separation, or to the completion of a program of education or training. As the recipient spouse becomes employed or more fully employed, spousal support will eventually be reduced, to top up the recipient's employment earnings, or support may even be terminated. In other cases, support is reduced or terminated if the recipient spouse remarries or re-partners.

In practice, where there are dependent children, few "indefinite" orders are permanent. Many intervening events will lead to changes or even termination. Some of these issues are canvassed in Chapter 14, which deals with variation, review, remarriage, second families, etc. By making initial orders indefinite, the current law simply postpones many of the difficult issues relating to duration and recognizes the fact-specific nature of these determinations.

Under the *without child support* formula, discussed in Chapter 7, there are time limits keyed to the length of the marriage, i.e. .5 to 1 year of spousal support for each year the spouses have cohabited, subject to the exceptions for indefinite (duration not specified) support.

Under the *with child support* formula, one option was simply to leave duration indefinite in all cases, with no durational limits of any kind, thereby avoiding all of the difficult issues of duration where there are dependent children. Such an approach would, however, be inconsistent with our durational approach under the *without child support* formula. It would also be inconsistent with the underlying parental partnership rationale for spousal support. This rationale emphasizes the ongoing responsibilities for child-care after separation and the resulting limitations on the custodial or residential parent's earning abilities. When those responsibilities cease, there must be some other reason for support to continue, such as the length of the marriage.

Our approach to duration for marriages with dependent children maintains current practices, while introducing the general idea of a range for duration. **Initial orders continue to be indefinite (duration not specified) in form**, subject to the usual processes of review or variation. That does not change. What our approach adds is the acceptance of generally understood **outside limits** on the cumulative duration of spousal support that will inform the process of review and variation.[81]

The durational limits under this formula combine the factors of length of marriage and length of the remaining child-rearing period, under two different tests for duration. For longer marriages, it makes sense that a recipient spouse should get the benefit of the time limits based upon length of marriage that might be obtained under the *without child support* formula, as these will typically run well beyond the end

81 The approach to duration under this formula involves fairly extensive reliance upon review orders. We discuss review orders and the leading Supreme Court of Canada decision, *Leskun v. Leskun*, [2006] 1 S.C.R. 920 in more detail in Chapters 13 and 14. In our view, the role contemplated for review orders under this formula is not inconsistent with *Leskun*.

of any child-rearing period. More difficult are shorter marriages where the recipient parent has the care of young children. To deal with these cases we have, under this formula, developed additional durational limits based on the responsibilities of child-rearing and the age of the children.

In what follows we explain in more detail the different elements of the admittedly complex approach to duration under this formula, and then draw these elements together in a concise summation in s. 8.5.4.

8.5.1 The creation of a range for duration in the basic formula

In this final version we have made some changes to the language used to describe and present the two tests for duration under this formula. More importantly, we have also added a lower end for the range under the basic *with child support* formula.

In the Draft Proposal, we did not propose any minimum duration or lower end of the range for duration under the *with child support* formula, only a maximum outside duration. Through the feedback process, we became convinced that some range for duration was required, for three reasons. First, absent a lower end of the range, the maximum duration was not treated as an outside time limit, but instead as a default time limit, i.e. a recipient was seen as possessing an entitlement to receive spousal support for the length of the marriage or until the youngest child finished high school, no matter what. That was never our intention. Second, absent a lower end and following upon the default approach just described, there was no room created for negotiation around duration between the spouses, unlike under the *without child support* formula. Third, after further feedback across Canada and further research, we did get a strong sense of what the lower end of the range could be under the current law.

The real crux of any range is for shorter marriages with pre-school children, where we feared that these recipients might be seriously disadvantaged by creating a lower end of the range. This remains a concern, especially since it appears that the duration of support in these cases is lengthening, as the courts continue to develop an appreciation of the serious continuing disadvantage flowing from a spouse's on-going child care obligations.

We emphasise that the durational limits under this formula must be seen as "softer," more flexible than under the *without child support* formula given the prominence of the compensatory rationale under this formula. First, the durational limits are not intended to be implemented as time limits on initial orders, but rather to give structure to an on-going process of review and variation. Second, determinations of duration in cases with dependent children are very fact-specific and vary enormously based upon the education, skills and work-experience of the dependent spouse, the ages of the children and the available arrangements for child-care. Our suggested durational range is at best a typical range that will not be appropriate in all cases. And third, this is an area of law in flux. We see the law over time giving increased emphasis to what we have termed the "parental partnership" concept, which recognizes the ongoing responsibilities for child-care after separation and the resulting limitations on the custodial or residential parent's earning abilities.

As we explain in more detail below, there are two tests that establish the range for duration under the basic *with child support* formula. We have renamed these test to clarify their rational and operation: the *length-of-marriage* test and the *age-of-children* test. Under these two tests the upper and lower end of the range in each case will be the **longer duration** produced by either test.

Before we explain the two tests for duration, it is import to remember that **the durational limits under the *with child support* formula include any period of spousal support paid at the interim stage**, the same treatment as under the *without child support* formula.

8.5.2 The *length-of-marriage* test for duration

The first test for duration is the same as the test for duration under the *without child support* formula. It will typically be the applicable test for longer marriages, marriage of ten years or more. The **upper end** is one year of support for each year of marriage, subject to the provisions under the *without child support* formula for indefinite (duration not specified) support after 20 years of marriage. The **lower end** is one-half year of support for each year of marriage. If the children are already in school at the time of separation, then the lower end of the range will always be determined by this *length-of-marriage* test.

Once again, we emphasize that these "softer" time limits are intended to structure the process of review and variation of initial orders that are indefinite in form; they are not intended to give rise to time-limited orders, at least not initially.

We can use *Example 8.1* above to explain this test. Ted and Alice cohabited for 11 years during their marriage and are now in their late thirties or early forties, with two children, aged 8 and 10 at separation. The initial support order would be indefinite (duration not specified), but it would be expected that the ultimate, cumulative duration of the award would fall somewhere within the range of 5.5 years (lower end) to 11 years (upper end). The maximum outside time limit would be 11 years. Reviews and variations in the meantime may bring support to an end before 11 years, and certainly the amount may have been reduced significantly during this period. But if support is still in pay after 11 years, there would be an expectation, barring exceptional circumstances, that support would be terminated at that point on an application for review or variation.

In the longer marriage cases under the *with child support* formula, where the *length-of-marriage* test defines the durational range, most cases will tend towards the longer end of the durational range and few cases should see support terminate at the lower end, given the strong compensatory claims that are typically present in these cases. The age of the children will be a critical factor in location with the range. Consider *Example 8.1* again: if support terminated for Alice at lower end of 5.5 years, the children would be only 13 and 15, an age at which the demands of child care can still have considerable impact upon Alice's income-earning abilities. By contrast, if Ted and Alice had been married for 14 years, and the children were 10 and 12 at separation, the lower end of the durational range would see support last until the children were 17 and 19. The choice of a particular duration within this range would be affected by these and other factors set out in Chapter 9.

8.5.3 The *age-of-children* test for duration

The second test for duration under the basic *with child support* formula is driven by the age of the children of the marriage. It usually operates where the period of time until the last or youngest child finishes high school is greater than the length of the marriage. These are mostly short or short-to-medium marriages, typically (but not always) under 10 years in length. The current case law is inconsistent and erratic on duration for these marriages, ranging from indefinite orders without conditions, to indefinite orders with short review periods and sometimes stringent review conditions, and even occasionally to time limits. Despite the language of indefinite support, the reality in most cases is that support does not continue for long, as re-employment, retraining, remarriage and other changes often intervene to bring spousal support to an end.

We too have struggled with duration for this category of cases. On the one hand, many of these custodial parents face some of the most serious disadvantages of all spouses, especially mothers with little employment history who have very young children in their care, all of which militates in favour of no time limits or very long time limits. On the other hand, many recipient spouses do have good education and employment backgrounds, are younger, and are emerging from shorter marriages and briefer periods out of the paid labour market, all indicators of quicker recovery of earning capacity. Inevitably, as under the current law, this means that reviews are a critical means of sorting out the individual circumstances of the recipient spouses.

The **upper end of the range** for spousal support under this test is **the date when the last or youngest child finishes high school**. Relatively few cases will reach this outside time limit and those that do will likely involve reduced amounts of top-up support by that date. Hence, extensions beyond that date would involve cases that fall within any of the exceptions described in Chapter 12, like the exception for the special needs of a child or the exception under s. 15.3 of the *Divorce Act*.

The **lower end of the range** under this test is also tied to the age of the youngest child and schooling, once again reflecting the parental partnership model. In shorter marriages, spousal support should continue at least until **the date the youngest child starts attending school full-time**. The school date will vary from province to province and from school district to school district, based upon the availability of junior kindergarten, the age rules governing school registration and the program the child takes.

Keep in mind that these tests for duration say nothing about the proper *amount* of spousal support during this period. That will be a function of the recipient's income-earning ability, her or his ability to undertake part-time or full-time employment. The amount of support may be significantly reduced over the course of any order, or even reduced to zero.

As with longer marriages with dependent children, **the initial support order in these shorter marriage cases will still be indefinite (duration not specified)**, as the determination of self-sufficiency remains an individualized decision. Any time limit will typically only appear after a review or variation hearing, especially in these cases involving young children. This appears to be the pattern in the current Canadian practice, as best as we can discern from the few reported decisions, the feedback we received since the Draft Proposal and the Advisory Working Group.

Take our *Example 8.3* where Drew and Kate have only been married four years, with two pre-school children aged 1 and 3 and Kate at home with them. The upper end of the range for duration would be 17 years, while the lower end would be 5 years, the latter assuming that children in their area start full-time school at age 6. In this typical case, any initial order would likely include a review provision, the review to occur at some point before the youngest child starts school.

8.5.4 The use of the two tests for duration: whichever is longer

In most cases, only one of the two tests, either the *length-of-marriage* test or the *age-of-children* test, will apply to determine both the upper and lower ends of the range. In general, the *length-of-marriage* test applies for longer marriages, marriages of ten years or more, while the *age-of-children* test applies for shorter marriages, those under ten years. But the two tests must be used together, **as it is the longer of the two tests that applies for each end of the range**. Remember that this is a **range** for duration, and that the actual outcome in any particular case will be worked out within that range over a series of orders or agreements, by way or review or variation of an initial order or agreement.

The Basic *With Child Support* Formula for Duration

Initial orders indefinite (duration not specified)
Subject to cumulative durational limits implemented by review or variation:

Upper End of the Range: the longer of

- the length of marriage, or
- the date the last or youngest child finishes high school

Lower End of the Range: the longer of

- one-half the length of marriage, or
- the date the youngest child starts full-time school

Take our *Example 8.2* where Bob and Carol have been married for 8 years, with two children aged 4 and 6. The *length-of-marriage* test suggests a durational range of 4 to 8 years, while the *age-of-children* test would suggest a range of 2 to 14 years. The result for Bob and Carol would be a durational range where the lower end of the range is 4 years (from the *length-of-marriage* test) and of the upper end of the range is 14 years (from the *age-of-children* test). As can be seen, much turns upon the interaction of the length of the marriage and the age of the children.

8.5.5 The problem of short marriages with young children

Applying the two tests for duration under the *with child support* formula, the range for duration will be determined by whichever test produces the longer duration at both the lower and upper ends of the range. Where those bounds are determined by the *length-of-marriage* test, there seems to be little difficulty. The range is the same as that under the *without child support* formula. A durational range of half the length of the marriage to the length of the marriage is intuitively understandable.

The *age-of-children* test is not as simple. It is tied to the presence of children in the marriage, and the economic disadvantages that come with the obligation to care for children. Length of marriage alone no longer provides a measure of the duration of the spousal support obligation, as the case law increasingly demonstrates, even if some spouses think it should. The *age-of-children* test will usually apply in shorter marriages. For shorter marriages with young children, this test will generate a long potential duration at the upper end of the range, one that *can* run as long as the date that the last or youngest child finishes high school, an outcome that raised some concerns during the feedback process. For very short marriages with very young children, the lower end of the range under the *age-of-children* test, added in the revision process, has also raised some concerns.

Critical to understanding these durational issues is the compensatory rationale for spousal support in these shorter marriage cases. Most of the economic disadvantage in these cases is not in the past, but in the future; it is the continuing disadvantage that flows from the obligations of child care and their impact upon the ability of the recipient parent to obtain and maintain employment. Hence the importance of the age of the children in fashioning durational limits. Our understanding of the current law, based both upon reported cases and discussions with lawyers and judges in our cross-country consultations, is that the law applicable to these cases is in flux, showing increasing recognition over time of the on-going economic disadvantage flowing from post-separation child-care responsibilities.

The upper end of the range for duration under the *age-of-children* test—up until the last or youngest child finishes high school—may appear long in a shorter marriage case. Consider Bob and Carol again in *Example 8.2*, where spousal support could potentially last as long as 14 years after an 8-year marriage, if the children are 4 and 6 in Carol's primary care at the date of separation. If duration were tied to the length of the marriage alone, spousal support would otherwise terminate when the children were 12 and 14 years old. But at this point, Carol's employment position may still reflect continuing economic disadvantage and limitations placed on her ability to achieve full-self-sufficiency by her post-separation custodial responsibilities. It may only be as the children reach their teenage years that she can focus more on improving her employment position. Termination at this point might also fail, depending on the facts, to recognize Carol's continuing child care obligations. A good way to test this outside durational limit is to think about the labour market position of the primary parent if one of those children had special needs or developed problems in their teenage years.

Slightly different problems are raised by the lower end of the durational range under the *age-of-children* test—until the youngest child starts attending school full-time. In the majority of cases, as our consultations revealed, this lower end of the durational range will not be contentious. In marriages of even four or five years, the *age-of-children* test will begin to yield results similar to the lower end of the durational range under the *length-of-marriage* test. Indeed, the major concern raised by the introduction of the lower end of the durational range in cases of shorter marriages with children, whether defined by length of marriage or age of youngest child starting full-time school, has been that it will create a "ceiling" and stunt the progressive development of the law in this area.

However, in some cases, of very short marriages, the *age-of-children* test has raised concerns that it sets the lower end of the durational range too high—i.e., that it establishes a "minimum duration" that is too long because it exceeds the length of the marriage. The kind of case that raises this concern is a fairly extreme set of facts: a marriage as brief as one or two years, with an infant less than a year old. In this hypothetical case, assuming the child would start full-time school at age 6, the lower end of the range for duration under the *age-of-children* test would be five years, which some would suggest is too long for such a short marriage.

In responding to this concern, we note that there are a number of other important dimensions to spousal support in these cases, in addition to duration, that soften the impact of this lower end of the range for duration. First, the lower end of the range for duration does not guarantee any particular *amount* of support. The formula range is driven by the number and age of the children, the spousal incomes, the child custody arrangements, child support amounts, section 7 contributions and tax positions. Much will turn upon the employment status of the recipient, and the recipient's ability to return to the paid labour market. A recipient is always under an obligation to make reasonable efforts towards self-sufficiency, and, on particular facts, those efforts may be subject to scrutiny in a review scheduled well before the youngest child starts full-time school. Second, in some situations, income will have to be imputed to the recipient, either part-time or full-time, on an individualized basis, often through the process of review. Third, entitlement is always an issue, before reaching the questions of amount and duration under the Advisory Guidelines. In some cases of strong facts—i.e. a recipient with a strong connection to the work-force—there may even be a finding of no entitlement so that the lower end of the range for duration is not engaged. The lower end of the durational range does not create a "minimum entitlement." Finally, we have said all along that the durational limits under the *with child support* formula are "softer," less formulaic, than those under the *without child support* formula. In *Moge*, the Supreme Court of Canada emphasized the need for individualized decision-making on self-sufficiency in compensatory support cases and duration under the *with child support* formula must therefore not be too rigidly applied.

8.6 Shared Custody

The basic formula is constructed around the typical fact situation, where the higher income spouse pays child and spousal support to the lower income spouse who has the primary care of the children. Here we address custodial variations, the first being shared custody.

Where the spouses have **shared custody**, the starting point for the calculation of child support under s. 9(a) of the *Federal Child Support Guidelines* is the straight set-off of table amounts for the number of children subject to shared custody, as set out in the Supreme Court decision in *Contino v. Leonelli-Contino*.[82] That amount is then adjusted, usually upwards, but occasionally downwards, based upon s. 9(b) (increased costs of shared custody and actual spending on children by the spouses) and s. 9(c) (other circumstances, including relative incomes, income levels, assets and debts, household standards of living, any reliance upon previous levels of child support paid). The *Contino* decision was handed down after the release of the Draft Proposal, but the shared custody formula anticipated that outcome. The majority in *Contino* emphasised that there is no presumption in favour of the full table amount for the payor, nor is there any presumption in favour of the straight set-off, under section 9.

Under the basic *with child support* formula, child support is deducted from the payor's income and then that child support amount plus a notional amount for child support is deducted from the recipient's income, to obtain individual net disposable income. Shared custody requires some changes to this basic formula.

Assume for the moment that the payor is paying only the straight set-off amount of child support in a shared custody case. If we were only to deduct the smaller set-off amount of child support for the payor spouse in a shared custody situation, that would misrepresent and understate the payor parent's contribution to child support. Shared custody assumes that both parents spend directly upon the child in their shared care. The full table amount (plus any s. 7 contributions) is thus deducted from the payor spouse's net disposable income. For the recipient, the notional table amount (plus any contribution to s. 7 expenses) is deducted from his or her income. This would be done in the calculation of INDI, even though the child support paid by the payor and received by the recipient would be the straight set-off amount.

If the straight set-off of child support is calculated as above, it turns out that the spousal support ranges are basically the same in these shared custody situations as in sole custody situations. Shared custody arrangements do not result in any automatic lowering of spousal support. It was important that the shared custody formula not provide any false financial incentives to encourage shared custody litigation, while at the same time providing ample room within the range to adjust for the realities of shared parenting.

Example 8.4

Peter and Cynthia have separated after nine years together. Peter works as a reporter at the local television station, earning $65,000 gross per year, while his wife Cynthia works for a local arts organization, earning $39,000 gross per year.

Peter and Cynthia share custody of their two children, aged 8 and 7 on a week about, 50/50 basis. In these circumstances, there could be entitlement issues, but we will assume entitlement here for exposition purposes.

82 [2005] 3 S.C.R. 217, 19 R.F.L. (6th) 272.

First, assume Peter only pays the straight set-off amount of child support, i.e. $972 – $584 = $388. We would deduct from Peter's income the full table amount of $972, of which $584 is spent by him directly for the children in his care and $388 is paid as child support to Cynthia. Cynthia's income would still be reduced by her notional table amount of $584. If Cynthia receives the full amount of the child benefits, and assuming entitlement, then the range for spousal support would be **zero to $142 per month**.

8.6.1 Adjusting for rotating child benefits

Since the release of the Draft Proposal, there has been a change in policy governing the receipt of the Child Tax Benefit and the child portion of the GST/HST Credit. The Canada Revenue Agency (CRA) decided that parents in shared custody cases "will have their benefits rotated between them *only* on a six-month on, six-month off basis." According to the CRA policy, it is possible for only one shared custody parent to receive the full child benefits provided that the parents do not self-identify or otherwise come to CRA's attention. The same approach has now been extended to the Universal Child Care Benefit (UCCB) in shared custody situations. As with all tax matters, the CRA policy cannot be altered by the parents' agreement or by a court order.

Under the *with child support* formula, these child benefits are treated as income and thus the allocation of the Child Tax Benefit, GST Credit and UCCB can affect the spousal support range for amount. It is therefore critical to be clear on this income issue.

In our *Example 8.4*, if the child benefits are rotated, thereby reducing Cynthia's income, the formula range would be higher, **from zero to $289 per month**.

8.6.2 Adjusting the ranges for child support that departs from the set-off

To make matters more difficult, in some shared custody cases, the amount of support is increased beyond the straight set-off amount, for various reasons: to reflect the increased costs of shared custody (or the respective abilities of the parents to incur those increased costs); to adjust for the recipient parent's larger share of actual child care costs; to reflect a parent's reliance upon a previous higher amount of child support, as in *Contino*; or to reduce disparities in the standards of living between the parental households. A central concern expressed in *Contino* was that the children not experience any dramatic change in standards of living as they move between the two parental households.

To return to *Example 8.4*, what if Peter pays more than the straight set-off amount of $388 per month? Much depends upon why Peter pays more. If Peter pays a higher amount of child support because Cynthia spends more on the children or because of the increased costs of shared custody, no adjustment should be made.

On the other hand, if Peter pays more child support simply to reduce the disparity in household standards of living, an adjustment should probably be made to the ranges for spousal support, as there is less need for the same function to be performed by spousal support. For example, if Peter were to pay child support of $569 per month on this standard-of-living rationale, rather than $388, then the range for spousal support would be **zero to zero** after adjustment (assuming the full child benefits are paid to Cynthia). At child support of $569 per month, Cynthia would have noticeably more of the family's net disposable income than Peter, leaving no room for spousal support under the *with child support* formula.

Contino emphasized the discretionary nature of child support in shared custody cases. Departures from the set-off can even sometimes go below the set-off amount. There can be a number of reasons for departing from the set-off amount, either above or below. A careful analysis of those reasons is thus necessary, to determine whether any adjustment should be made in calculating the formula ranges and, eventually, in choosing the appropriate amount within the ranges.

8.6.3 Adjusting the limits of the range

We received much feedback from mediators and lawyers working with shared custody parents, stating that these parents often opt for a 50/50 split of the couple's family net disposable income or monthly cash flow after the payment of child and spousal support (remember that this is a broader and different measure from INDI or individual net disposable income). This option leaves the children with roughly the same resources and standard of living in each household. We agree that this equal split of net income should be available as one of the normal range of outcomes—not mandated, just available—in every shared custody case.

The shared custody formula for spousal support usually includes this 50/50 split within the range, but in some cases this 50/50 split falls just outside the upper or lower end of the range. In these cases, the shared custody range has been broadened to include this 50/50 split. Take *Example 8.4* which shows a range of zero to $142 per month where Peter pays the set-off amount of $388 as child support (and assuming that Cynthia receives the full child benefits). At the upper end of the range, Cynthia would be left with 49.7 per cent of the family net disposable income. To increase her share to 50 per cent, the upper end of the spousal support range would have to be $179. Under our revised shared custody formula, the range here would become zero to $179 per month, to ensure that the 50/50 split falls within the range.

In what cases has the formula range been adjusted? In cases where parental incomes are lower or not that far apart (like Peter and Cynthia), the upper end of the range has been adjusted upwards a bit. In cases where the recipient parent has little or no income and there are two or more children subject to shared custody, then the lower end of the range has been adjusted downwards, to ensure that the 50/50 split falls within the range. These adjustments are made automatically by the software programs.

In these latter cases, where there are two or more children subject to shared custody and the recipient has little or no income, the formula will produce a range with a lower end that leaves the lower-income recipient with 50 per cent of the family's net disposable income and the rest of the range will obviously go higher. During the feedback process, some criticized this range of outcomes, suggesting that a shared custody recipient should never receive spousal support that would give her or him more than 50 per cent of the family's net disposable income. After all, they suggested, under this arrangement, both parents face the same ongoing obligations of child care going into the future, with neither parent experiencing more disadvantage.

The answer to these criticisms is that the past *is* relevant in these cases, as there is a reason the recipient has little or no income, usually explained by that parent's past shouldering of the bulk of child care responsibilities. In most shared custody cases, both parents have shared parenting during the relationship, so that there is less disadvantage and less disparity in their incomes at the end of the marriage. Where the recipient has little or no income, she or he will have a greater need for increased support in the short run. But the shared custody arrangement will reduce the impact of ongoing child care upon the recipient's employment prospects, such that progress towards self-sufficiency should occur more quickly. In these cases, spousal support will likely be reduced in the near future on review or variation, and the duration of support may be shorter.

8.7 Split custody

In a **split custody** situation, more significant changes to the basic formula are required. If each parent has one or more children in their primary care or custody, then s. 8 of the *Federal Child Support Guidelines* requires a set-off of table amounts, with each spouse paying the table amount for the number of children in the other spouse's custody. But this means that each parent will also be considered to support the child or children in their care directly, out of their remaining income. Thus, in the split custody situation, a notional table amount must be deducted from *each* parent, not just the recipient but the payor as well.

Since there is one child in each household, there are no economies of scale and accordingly larger proportions of their incomes are devoted to child support, leaving a smaller pool of INDI to be divided by way of spousal support. Again, as with shared custody, this would be done in the calculation of INDI, even though the child support paid by the payor and received by the recipient would be the set-off amount directed by the s. 8 formula.

Example 8.5

Take the case of Peter and Cynthia again, and assume that each parent has custody of one child, same incomes, same facts. Peter's one child table amount would be $601 per month, Cynthia's $358 per month. Under s. 8 of the *Federal Child Support Guidelines*, these table amounts would be offset, with Peter paying Cynthia $243 per month. In calculating Peter's individual net disposable income, for spousal support purposes, the full one child amount is deducted, twice, once for the table amount effectively paid to Cynthia and once for the notional amount spent directly on the child in his care. Similarly, in calculating Cynthia's INDI, a double deduction of her one-child table amount is made, once for the amount effectively paid to Peter for the child in his care, plus a notional table amount for the child in Cynthia's own care.

The actual child support paid by Peter to Cynthia would be $243, the one-child set-off amount under s. 8. Using the split custody formula for spousal support, Peter would pay spousal support to Cynthia in the range of **zero to $445 per month**.

8.8 Step-Children

Under the *Divorce Act* and provincial family law statutes, a spouse can be found to stand in the place of a parent towards a child who is not his or her biological or adoptive child.[83] With that finding, a step-parent becomes liable to pay child support, in an amount that is "appropriate" under section 5 of the *Child Support Guidelines*, "having regard to these Guidelines and any other parent's legal duty to support the child." For the most part, the threshold for finding step-parent status is fairly high, not easily satisfied in short marriages except for very young children.[84] After the Supreme Court decision in *Chartier*,[85] some courts have lowered that threshold, making it more likely that a spouse will be found to stand in the place of a parent after a shorter marriage. In British Columbia, the *Family Relations Act* imposes a step-parent child

83 *Divorce Act*, s. 2(2).

84 Carol Rogerson, "The Child Support Obligations of Step-Parents" (2001), 18 Can.J.Fam.L. 9; Nick Bala, "Who is a 'Parent'? 'Standing in the Place of a Parent' and Section 5 of the Child Support Guidelines" in Law Society of Upper Canada, *Special Lectures 2006: Family Law* (Toronto: Irwin Law, 2007) at 71.

85 *Chartier v. Chartier*, [1999] 1 S.C.R. 242.

support obligation if "the step-parent contributed to the support and maintenance of the child for at least one year."[86]

During the feedback phase, especially in British Columbia, there were questions about which formula is appropriate to apply in short-marriage step-parent situations or whether there should be an exception under the *with child support* formula for step-parent cases. There were concerns that this formula generated spousal support obligations that were too substantial in such cases.

In the vast majority of step-parent cases, the *with child support* formula will apply with no difficulty. In many cases, the step-parent will treat the children as his or her own after the breakdown of the marriage. In some of these cases, there will be both step-children and biological children, with all of them treated alike. In other cases, the threshold for the finding of step-parent status will be high enough that the marriage will be a medium-to-long one, with substantial spousal support obligations.

In our view, the short marriage concerns are now resolved by the creation of a range for duration under this formula. Upon closer analysis, the difficulty in these step-parent cases was not the range for amount, but the potentially long duration under the *age-of-children* test for the upper end of the range and its use as a "default rule." An example can demonstrate how the addition of a lower end for the durational range allows for a reasonable range of outcomes in step-parent cases.

Example 8.6

Art and Kathie have been married for 5 years. Art earns $80,000 per year and Kathie earns $20,000. Kathie had two children from a previous relationship at the time she and Art got married, two girls who are now 10 and 12. Assume that Kathie does not receive any child support from the girls' father and that she has sole custody of the girls.

Under the *Federal Child Support Guidelines*, Art could be required to pay as much as the table amount of child support, $1,159 per month. If Art pays the full table amount, **the basic *with child support* formula would produce an amount for spousal support in the range of $474 to $1,025 per month**.

As for the duration of spousal support, the order would be **indefinite (duration not specified), with a cumulative durational range of 2.5 years at the lower end to 8 years at the upper end**. The upper end of the durational range here is determined by the *age-of-children* test, i.e. when the youngest daughter (now 10) finishes high school at age 18, or 8 years. The lower end, however, is fixed by the *length-of-marriage* test, as both children are older and in full-time school, i.e. one-half the length of the marriage, or 2½ years. Upon a future review or a variation application, a court could put a relatively short time limit on spousal support, depending upon the facts.

The facts of this simple example can be modified to strengthen or weaken the spousal support claim. If the girls are younger during their relationship with Art, so that they are only 6 and 8 at separation, then the durational range would be 2½ to 12 years and there would be strong factors pushing towards the upper end of the range. Contrast the effect of the low British Columbia threshold under the *Family Relations Act*. The girls are 6 and 8 at separation, but assume that Art was only married to Kathie for two years. The upper end of the durational range would still be 12 years, but the lower end would be reduced to one year, i.e. one-half year for each year of marriage.

Under section 8 of the *Child Support Guidelines*, it is possible for a step-parent to pay less than the table amount of child support if appropriate. A reduced amount is only ordered or agreed upon when the biological parent is already paying child support.[87] Where the amount of child support is reduced under s. 8, the *with child support* formula range should be calculated using the full table amount rather than the reduced amount.[88]

8.9 A Hybrid Formula for Spousal Support Paid by the Custodial Parent (The *Custodial Payor* Formula)

The basic formula for marriages with dependent children assumes that the higher income spouse pays both child and spousal support to the recipient parent, who also has sole custody or primary care of the children. The spousal support to be paid must then adjust for the payor's child support payments. The shared and split custody situations may change the math, but both still involve the higher income spouse paying both child and spousal support to the recipient.

A different formula is required where the higher income spouse paying spousal support is also the parent with sole custody or primary care of the children. Now spousal support and child support flow in opposite directions. The *without child support* formula does not apply, however, as it assumes

86 *Family Relations Act*, R.S.B.C. 1996, c. 128, s. 1 "parent." Section 1(2) requires that the step-parent be married to the parent or that they lived together in a marriage-like relationship for at least two years.

87 Sometimes a court will order the step-parent to pay less than the full table amount, leaving the custodial parent to take steps to obtain or increase child support from the biological parent.

88 Given the way the formula works, any reduction in the step-parent's child support would otherwise lead to an increase in the range for spousal support, an inappropriate result.

no dependent children. While we could have left this situation as an exception, with no formulaic solution, it is common enough that we constructed a formula to guide outcomes in this situation.

Formula for Spousal Support Paid by Custodial Parent (The *Custodial Payor* Formula)

(1) Reduce the payor spouse's Guidelines income by the **grossed-up notional table amount** for child support (plus a gross-up of any contributions to s. 7 expenses).
(2) If the recipient spouse is paying child support, reduce the recipient's Guidelines income by the **grossed-up amount of child support paid** (table amount plus any s. 7 contributions).
(3) Determine the **adjusted gross income difference** between the spouses and then quantum ranges from 1.5 percent to 2 percent for each year of marriage, up to a maximum of 50.
(4) **Duration** ranges from .5 to 1 year of support for each year of marriage, with the same rules for indefinite (duration not specified) support as under the *without child support* formula.

Either of the two formulas could be used as a starting point and then modified to accommodate custodial payors. We chose to start from the *without child support* formula for custodial payors. In this situation the recipient parent does not have the primary care of children and thus more closely resembles the single recipient in the *without child support* formula. The primary rationale for the payment of spousal support in these cases will be merger over time, rather than parental partnership. That said, a number of lower income recipient spouses in this situation will continue to play an important role in their children's lives and any formula must be able to adjust in such cases. The other advantage of the *without child support* formula is ease of calculation, but the formula will have to be modified to back out child support and to take into account tax implications.

Most of these cases will involve older children and longer marriages, where the husband is the higher-income payor and the parent with primary care. In many of these cases, the non-custodial wife may have a sizeable compensatory claim from her past role in child-rearing, which will be reflected in the range for spousal support, and the location of any amount within that range. In these cases involving older children and longer marriages, the children will cease to be children of the marriage within a few years and the wife will cross-over into the *without child support* formula, as is explained below in Chapter 14 on variation and review. In a subset of custodial payor cases, there will be illness or disability issues for the non-custodial spouses, many of which can be accommodated within the ranges or restructuring, but exceptions will be made in some cases, as discussed below in Chapter 12 below. There is a small minority of custodial payor cases that involve young children, shorter marriages and husbands claiming spousal support from their wives.

In reducing gross incomes by grossed-up amounts for child support, this formula does the same thing conceptually as the basic *with child support* formula—it establishes the spouses' available incomes after their child support obligations are fulfilled. To gross up the child support will require a calculation of the gross value of the non-taxable child support, using the appropriate marginal tax rate for the payor or recipient spouse.

Example 8.6

Matt earns $100,000 gross per year and has custody of two teenage children. Anna earns $30,000 gross per year. The spouses separated after 16 years together. There are no s. 7 expenses.

Assume entitlement to spousal support has been established.

First, Matt's income is reduced by the table amount for two children, $1,404, grossed-up to $2,525 per month or $30,300 annually. Matt's reduced income would thus be $69,700. Anna is required to pay child support at the table amount of $444 per month, grossed-up to $625 monthly or $7,500 annually. Anna's reduced income would be $22,500. After a 16-year marriage, Anna would receive a range of 24 to 32 percent of the adjusted gross income difference of $47,200.

Under the *custodial payor* formula, Matt would pay spousal support in a range from $944 to $1,259 per month, for a duration of 8 to 16 years.

There is one **exception** distinctive to this *custodial payor* formula, discussed in more detail below in Chapter 12. Where the recipient spouse and non-primary parent plays an important role in the child's care and upbringing after separation, yet the marriage is shorter and the child is younger, the ranges for amount and duration applied under this *custodial payor* formula may not allow that spouse to continue to fulfil that parental role. In our view, in such cases, under this **parenting exception**, it should be possible to exceed the upper limits on both amount and duration for that purpose.

8.10 A Hybrid Formula for Adult Children and Section 3(2)(b)

After the release of the Draft Proposal, we added another formula to this family of formulas, another hybrid formula, this time for adult children whose child support is determined under section 3(2)(b) of the *Federal Child Support Guidelines*.

In these cases of children who are the age of majority or over, the table-amount-plus-section-7-expenses approach is considered "inappropriate." Under the case law, these are usually cases where:

(i) the adult child attends a post-secondary institution away from home;
(ii) the adult child makes a sizeable contribution to his or her own education expenses; or
(iii) there are other non-parental resources to defray education expenses, like scholarships or RESP's or grandparent monies.

Under section 3(2)(b), an individual budget is usually prepared for the adult child and, after the child and other contributions are deducted, the remaining deficit is then apportioned between the parents, based upon their incomes or some other arrangement. These child support amounts will differ significantly from any amounts using the table and section 7 expenses, almost invariably lower.

This *adult children* formula will *only* apply where the child support for *all* the remaining children of the marriage is determined under section 3(2)(b) of the *Child Support Guidelines* and there are no children for whom a table amount of child support is being paid under section 3(1) or section 3(2)(a). It should not be used, for example, where there is one older child away at university and another still at home in high school. In that case, the basic *with child support* formula would be used, with any necessary adjustment to the amounts of child support contributed by each parent for the child away at school.

Under this *adult children* formula, like the *custodial payor* formula, the framework of the *without child support* formula is used, but adjusted for the child support amounts paid, another hybrid formula. Once each parent's contribution to the child's budget has been allocated under s. 3(2)(b), those actual child support amounts are grossed up and deducted from each spouse's gross income. Then the *without child support* formula is applied, using the adjusted gross income difference and the length of marriage factor to determine amount and duration. The box above for the *custodial payor* can be used to describe the calculations, with one change: the actual amounts of each parent's contribution to child support will be grossed up, rather than table and section 7 amounts.

Example 8.7

Take Matt and Anna from the previous *Example 8.6* and assume that there is only one child of the marriage, now 20 years old and attending university away from home. Matt earns $100,000 and Anna earns $30,000. Their son's tuition, books and living expenses total $20,000 and, through a mix of summer employment and scholarships, he can contribute $5,000. The parents have agreed to divide the remaining $15,000 between them, $12,000 by Matt ($1,000 per month) and $3,000 by Anna ($250 per month).

Under this formula, Matt's gross income would be reduced by the grossed up amount of the child support, or $21,300, while Anna's grossed up contribution would be $4,100. The adjusted gross income difference would be $78,700 less $25,900, leaving $52,800.

After a 16-year marriage, under this formula, the range for spousal support for Anna is 24 to 32 per cent of $52,800, or $1,056 to $1,408 per month, for whatever duration would remain of the original 8 to 16 years.

Another practical advantage of this formula is that it eases the transition between formulas. Most of these cases are longer marriages and, once the last child ceases to be a "child of the marriage" and child support stops, the spouses will "cross over" to the unadjusted *without child support* formula, described briefly below. In *Example 8.7*, when the son ceases to a "child of the marriage" in a few years, Anna's spousal support would be determined by crossing over to the *without child support* formula, with no adjustment any longer for child support. The range for amount would be 24 to 32 per cent of the gross income difference of $70,000, or $1,400 to $1,867 per month, again for whatever duration would remain of the original 8 to 16 years.

8.11 Crossover to the *With Child Support* Formula

There is one last issue to be flagged here, that of crossover between the two formulas. The most frequent crossover situation will be in cases where child support ceases after a medium-to-long marriage, where the children were older or even university-age at the time of the initial order, as in *Example 8.7* above. At this point, either spouse can apply to vary, to bring spousal support under the *without child support* formula. In most cases, it will be the recipient making the application, to obtain an increase in support under the *without child support* formula, once child support is no longer payable and the payor's ability to pay is improved as a result. Specific examples of crossover are considered in Chapter 14 on variation and review.

Source: Publication: *Spousal Support Advisory Guidelines* prepared by Professor Carol Rogerson, University of Toronto, and Professor Rollie Thompson, Dalhousie Law School, with the support of the Department of Justice Canada, July 2008. http://www.justice.gc.ca/eng/rp-pr/fl-lf/spousal-epoux/spag/pdf/SSAG_eng.pdf.